THE NATIONAL MUSEUM & ARCHIVE OF LESBIAN AND GAY HISTORY

The National Museum & Archive of Lesbian and Gay History catalogues the daily lives and political struggles of lesbians and gay men. One of the largest collections of its kind in the country, the Archive is a repository for the personal papers, correspondence, artifacts, and publications of both individuals and organizations. Taken as a whole, it offers a unique view of the many communities that make up the complex tapestry we recognize as the gay and lesbian community.

THE LESBIAN AND GAY COMMUNITY SERVICES CENTER

Founded in 1983, the Lesbian and Gay Community Services Center has grown to become New York City's largest gay-identified community organization. The Center provides twenty-six services and programs specifically designed for the needs and interests of the gay community, including HIV prevention education; AIDS bereavement services; youth support services; Center Kids, a gay and lesbian family program; and numerous recreational, cultural, and public policy programs. Other Center programs include the Pat Parker/Vito Russo Center Library and the National Museum & Archive of Lesbian and Gay History. In its mission to build community, the Center provides a home for more than 300 lesbian and gay organizations representing every facet of the diverse New York metropolitan community. Each week, 5,000 people come to the Center, which exists through the financial support of members of the lesbian and gay community.

The NYC Lesbian and Gay Community Services Center, founded in 1983, is housed in the former Food and Maritime Trade High School on West 13th Street in Greenwich Village. The building is shown here circa 1927, when it was still a school.

THE GAY ALMANAC

COMPILED BY THE
NATIONAL MUSEUM & ARCHIVE
OF LESBIAN AND GAY HISTORY

*A Program of
the Lesbian and Gay Community Services Center–
New York*

Produced by The Philip Lief Group, Inc.

BERKLEY BOOKS, NEW YORK

THE GAY ALMANAC

A Berkley Book / published by arrangement with
The Philip Lief Group, Inc.

PRINTING HISTORY
Berkley trade paperback edition / June 1996

The Putnam Berkley World Wide Web site address is http://www.berkley.com

ISBN: 0-425-15300-2

BERKLEY®
Berkley Books are published by The Berkley Publishing Group,
200 Madison Avenue, New York, New York 10016.
BERKLEY and the "B" design
are trademarks belonging to Berkley Publishing Corporation.

PRINTED IN THE UNITED STATES OF AMERICA

10 9 8 7 6 5 4 3 2 1

For Steven J. Powsner (1955–1995) and Irving Cooperberg
for their vision, their leadership, and their endless love.
Thank you.

Acknowledgments

Project manager: Paula Martinac

Research/writing team: Terry Boggis, Richard D. Burns, Thom Furr, Stephanie Grant, Katie Hogan, Winnie Hough, Paula Martinac, Gerry Gomez Pearlberg, Penny D. Perkins, and Benjamin Stilp

Thanks to: Jeff Bieganek, Metropolitan Tennis Group; Charlie Carson and Mark Quigley, Team Aquatics New York; Frameline; the Gay and Lesbian Alliance Against Defamation; Robert Giard; Morgan Gwenwald; Donald Huppert; Lambda Legal Defense and Education Fund; The NAMES Project; the NYC Gay and Lesbian Anti-Violence Project; Overlooked Opinions, Inc.; the Pat Parker/Vito Russo Center Library; Rich Wandel; Dr. Barbara Warren; Rhett Wickham; and the entire staff of the NYC Lesbian and Gay Community Services Center.

Thanks also to the many gay news and culture magazines and newspapers that we used in our research, especially *The Advocate, OUT, POZ,* and *The Washington Blade.*

In this almanac, we have attempted to be as up to date as possible, but the gay and lesbian community is constantly changing and growing. If you have information that would help us in updating this book, please write to: *The Gay Almanac,* Lesbian and Gay Community Services Center, 208 West 13th St., New York, NY 10011.

THE GAY ALMANAC

Contents

PART V

We Are (Literally) Everywhere: Statistics on Lesbians
and Gay Men   **99**

PART VI

We Have Lives, Not Lifestyles: Just About Everything
You Wanted to Know About Gay Men   **113**

PART VII

An AIDS Primer   **409**

PART VIII

National Directory of Lesbian and Gay Community Centers   **453**

PART IX

National Directory of Lesbian and Gay Organizations
and Resources   **481**

INDEX   **491**

THE GAY ALMANAC

Introduction

In the mid-1970s, when I was just nineteen, I came out as a gay man. There were no other openly gay men at Hamilton College, and coming out was a lonely process. The gay and lesbian community as we know it today—thriving, visible, and diverse—was something I could hardly imagine.

A few years later, I had the good fortune to find a place for myself on the staff of *Gay Community News* in Boston, which at that time was the only gay and lesbian newsweekly in America. At *GCN* we shared a vision that gay men and lesbians could work together making connections between gay liberation, feminism, and anti-racism. We dreamed of building a community and a better, more just society. I was lucky to find a "home" like *GCN* at a time when there were still so few options for gay men and lesbians to meet as colleagues and friends.

By 1986, when I moved to New York City to become Executive Director of the Lesbian and Gay Community Services Center, the dream we'd believed in at *GCN* was coming true. There were countless gay newspapers and magazines, openly gay elected officials, and a growing body of gay films and literature. The Center, a place where gay men and lesbians could break through their isolation, has been a visible reminder of the great strides we have made in creating a strong, proud community and culture.

This almanac is a celebration of our communities and the distance we've traveled in just a short time. Queerness has always been part of the fabric of American life, but it is only in this century that gay men and lesbians organized around sexual orientation. It is empowering to learn that there is so much gay history before the Stonewall Riots in 1969, which launched the modern gay liberation movement; the first homosexual rights organization in America was actually founded back in the 1920s. "Queer" and "fag"—words of ridicule that many of us have reclaimed—have origins that go back many years. Although gay people have been largely ignored by recorded history, today gay and lesbian historians have made important strides toward unearthing and interpreting the gay past. Our triumphs and our tragedies over the past four hundred years of North American history are at the heart of this almanac.

A pivotal piece of our history has been the formation of grassroots organizations, including the lesbian and gay community centers that are fighting for gay liberation. Our lesbian and gay centers have made it possible for our organizations to grow and prosper, and for us to achieve increased visibility and to seek solace from the pain of isolation and loss from the AIDS epidemic.

This almanac was prepared to enrich our understanding of gay history, culture, and lives and to be a frequently used reference guide. Here you can find out about the expanding network of AIDS-related information available on computer; locate information on gay rights court casts; look up resources on gay fathers and parenting; check to see if the city you're moving to has a gay rights ordinance; or browse through the most up-to-date directory available of lesbian and gay community centers across the United States. Gay trivia and tidbits are here, too; a roster of notable gay men and their accomplishments; a glossary of gay slang; lists of classic gay novels and literature award-winners; spotlights on gay sporting events and athletes; and gay-themed movies by category.

As you wander through the almanac, I hope you will feel proud of all that our diverse gay community has accomplished. I know I do.

—Richard D. Burns
Executive Director
Lesbian and Gay Community Services Center—New York
July 1995

I

Highlights and "Lowlights" of North American Lesbian and Gay History from the Sixteenth Century to the Present

Do you remember when studying history in school meant reading about wealthy white heterosexual men making war with one another? References to the history and lives of women and people of color—when they appeared at all—were relegated to sidebars in our textbooks. Homosexuality was virtually invisible, except as it related to "scandals."

A lot has changed in the last two decades. Social historians influenced by the civil rights and women's movements of the 1960s and the 1970s have been digging into tax records, census reports, court proceedings and criminal records, newspapers, diaries, and church rosters to unearth the history of people who had never been considered important enough to have a history—poor people, women, people of color.

And in the aftermath of the Stonewall riots, fueled by the exciting momentum of their own liberation movement, lesbians and gay men started looking for their history, too. Important grassroots projects like the Lesbian Herstory Archives (founded in 1973) and the San Francisco Lesbian and Gay History Project (1977) used the techniques of the new social history to uncover the past of lesbians and gay men, who had been hidden from history just like so many other marginalized people. As lesbian and gay activists were creating a public presence through organizations, marches, and rallies, lesbian and gay historians—many of whom were self-taught in the techniques of history—began to reclaim our historical presence as well.

Now lesbian and gay archives have sprouted up across the continent, preserving the documents that will make our history more accessible to the next generations. The field of lesbian and gay studies has burgeoned in the last decade, and there

An early gay rights demonstration in Hauppauge, Long Island, 1971. *(Photo by Rich Wandel)*

are now lesbian and gay studies courses and openly lesbian and gay professors in major universities across the United States and Canada. The Center for Lesbian and Gay Studies (CLAGS) at the City University of New York has been a pioneer in advocating the acceptance of lesbian and gay studies as a recognized academic discipline. We used many published histories of lesbians and gay men in compiling this timeline, and they are listed in the bibliography.

Lesbian and gay history has never been easy to research, and some of the pitfalls are obvious ones. To this day, homosexuality is viewed by many as a taboo subject, and in some places, it is still a criminal activity. In early American history, sodomy was a capital offense. A lot of what we have learned about lesbians and gay men has come from criminal records. While people certainly engaged in homosexual relations, their "deviant" sexual behavior was not something they very often divulged. It was not a source of pride. Those who did write letters to lovers may have burned them or written in code. Also, though we may now label a man or woman as gay or lesbian by their sexual activities, he or she may not have done so.

Women and people of color have always been more invisible in the annals of history, and so the history of lesbians and of lesbians and gay men of color is even more difficult to uncover than that of gay white men. Throughout much of American history, women were the property of men and until very recently were discouraged from exploring their sexuality. Most of the early sodomy laws in the American colonies did not even mention the possibility of sex between women.

Poster from the tenth anniversary Stonewall Rebellion commemoration, 1979.
(*Collection of the National Museum & Archive of Lesbian and Gay History*)

African-Americans and Native Americans challenged invisibility and genocide by preserving their histories orally. Sometimes, the whites recorded biased glimpses of their lives. The journals of a number of European explorers, for example, discuss the berdaches among Native Americans. (See the entry for **1804–10**.)

1528–36: Spanish explorer Alvar Nunez Cabeza de Vaca makes the earliest written account of "effeminate" Indians in Florida, who "go about dressed as women, and do women's tasks."

1566: In Florida, Guillermo, a French interpreter accused of being a traitor and "a great Sodomite," is murdered by the Spaniards. Guillermo lived with a local Indian, who was the son of the *cacique* (chief) of the Guale area and reportedly "loved that interpreter very much."

1610: The Virginia Colony passes the earliest American sodomy law, dictating the death penalty for offenders. It does not include women as potential "sodomites."

1613: Francisco de Pareja, a Spanish missionary with the Florida Indians, records in his work *Confessionario (Confessional)* the likelihood of sodomy between native men and of sexual acts between native women.

1624: Though the evidence is slim, Richard Cornish, master of the ship the *Ambrose,* is executed by hanging in the Virginia Colony for alleged "buggery" of one of his indentured servants, the ship's steward, William Cowse.

1629: The Virginia Court records the first incidence of gender ambiguity among the American colonists. A servant, Thomas/Thomasine Hall, is officially proclaimed by the governor to be both "a man and a woman" and ordered to wear articles of each sex's clothing. (It is unclear if Hall was a hermaphrodite or a biological male who dressed in women's clothes.)

• On board the ship Talbot, bound for New England, Rev. Francis Higginson records the discovery of "5 beastly Sodomiticall boyes [sic], which confessed their wickedness not to be named." When the ship lands, Higginson reports the incident to the governor of the Massachusetts Bay Colony, who sends the boys "to be punished in old England as the crime deserved." At that time, English law authorized that males over fourteen could be hanged for sodomy. The fate of the boys is unknown.

1636: In the Massachusetts Bay Colony, Rev. John Cotton proposes the death penalty for sixteen crimes, including sodomy, which he calls "unnatural filthiness" and defines as "carnal fellowship of man with man, or woman with woman." Though Cotton's code was not accepted, Massachusetts adopted a sodomy law five years later (see 1641).

• The codification of the laws of Plymouth Colony include eight offenses punishable by death. Included with treason, murder, and witchcraft are "Sodomy, rapes, buggery." The law does not specify if sodomy pertains only to men, or to men and women equally.

1641: The Massachusetts Bay Colony adopts a body of laws (which remains unprinted until 1648), including sodomy as a capital crime. In this code—unlike John Mather's earlier proposal, which included women as potential offenders—

sodomy is defined as a "man lying with mankind as he lies with a woman." The wording is taken straight from Leviticus 20:13.

1642: Connecticut adopts twelve capital crimes, among which is sodomy, defined as "a man lying with a man."

• In Salem, Massachusetts, a servant, Elizabeth Johnson, receives a whipping for "unseemly practices betwixt her and another maid."

1646: "Jan Creoli, a negro," is executed by choking in New Netherland for sodomy. Manuel Congo, the ten-year-old whom Creoli allegedly sodomized, receives a public flogging.

• In Connecticut, William Plaine, one of the original settlers of the town of Guilford, is accused of committing sodomy twice in England and of corrupting "a great part of the youth of Guilford by masturbations." Plaine is executed at New Haven.

1647: Rhode island passes a law making sodomy between men a capital offense.

1648: A young soldier in Montreal is charged with "the worst of crimes," interpreted to be sodomy. The Jesuits intervene on the youth's behalf, and his sentence to hard labor is commuted on condition that he become New France's first executioner.

1649: In Plymouth, two married women, Sara Norman and Mary Hammon, are charged with "lewd behavior . . . upon a bed." Hammon, who is fifteen, is cleared of the charges; Norman, apparently older (and referred to throughout the record as "the wife of Hugh Norman"), is required to acknowledge publicly her "unchaste behavior" and receives a warning that if there are any subsequent "carriages," her punishment will be "greater."

1656: New Haven passes a law that punishes by death "men lying with men as with women" and women changing "the natural use, into that which is against nature." This law is unique among colonial legislation for its inclusion of women's "unnatural acts."

1660: In New Netherland, Jan Quisthout van der Linde is executed by drowning for sodomy. Hendrick Harmensen, "the boy on whom Quisthout committed by force the above crime," is sentenced to a private whipping.

1665: Conquered by the English in 1664, New Netherland becomes a proprietary colony of the Duke of York. The following year, representatives from several towns enact laws that include the death penalty for sodomy between men over the age of fourteen. The law specifies that if "one party were Forced," he was exempt from capital punishment.

1668: New Jersey makes sodomy between men a capital crime, exempting children under fourteen and victims of force. Plymouth and Connecticut subsequently amends their sodomy laws (in 1671 and 1672, respectively) to include the same exemptions.

1673–77: Father Jacques Marquette makes his first voyage down the Mississippi River and recounts that "some Illinois [Indians], as well as some Nadouessi, while still young, assume the garb of women, and retain it throughout their lives."

1680: New Hampshire passes its first capital laws, including sodomy between men, "unless one party were forced, or were under fourteen years of age."

1682: The Province of Pennsylvania, a Quaker colony, enacts legislation that makes sodomy by "any person" a noncapital offense—the first American colony to show such "leniency." The punishment is limited to whipping, forfeiting one-third of one's estate, and six months at hard labor. This law is amended in 1700 to require life imprisonment and, for married men, castration for the offense.

1712: Mingo, a slave of Wait Winthrop, chief justice of Massachusetts, is executed in Charlestown for "forcible buggery."

• South Carolina legislators include the text of the English "buggery law" of 1533, including its death penalty, in their colonial statutes.

1718: Pennsylvania revises its sodomy law, making it a capital offense.

1719: The Delaware Assembly adopts a sodomy law, reproduced from the 1718 Pennsylvania law.

1721: Jesuit explorer Pierre Francois Xavier de Charlevoix notes in his journal that "effeminacy and lewdness were carried to the greatest excess" by the Iroquois, the Illinois, and other Indian nations of the area that would become Louisiana.

1776: Fleury Mesplet, a friend of Benjamin Franklin and a fellow printer, publishes the play *Jonathas et David, or Le Triomphe de l'amitie*, which becomes the first book ever printed in Montreal. The play is a tragedy in three acts, describing the thinly veiled homoerotic relationship between Jonathan and David in the Old Testament.

1778: In the newly formed Continental Army, Lieutenant Frederick Gotthold Enslin is court-martialed for "attempting to commit sodomy."

1782: Deborah Sampson, a descendent of Governor William Bradford, is excommunicated from the First Baptist Church of Middleborough, Massachusetts, for "dressing in men's clothes" and for behaving "very loose and unchristian like."

1798: Moreau de St. Mery, a French lawyer and politician, writes that women in Philadelphia, where he has lived for several years, "are not at all strangers to being will to seek unnatural pleasures with persons of their own sex."

1804–10: Nicholas Biddle, a member of the Lewis and Clark expeditions, records that "among Minitarees [Indians] if a boy shows any symptoms of effeminacy or girlish inclinations he is put among the girls, dressed in their way, brought up with them, & sometimes married to men. . . . the French called them Birdashes [sic]."

1811: In an account of events at Fort Astoria in the Oregon Territory, Gabriel Franchere makes the first written reference to a female berdache from the Kutenai Indian nation, who dressed as a man and was accompanied by a "wife."

1824–26: A printed broadside by Louis Dwight is the first known document in the United States to discuss homosexuality in the country's prisons.

1839: In Montreal, two boys—Thomas Clotworthy, seventeen, and Henry Cole, eleven—both apprenticed to a local gilder, are discovered in bed together, committing sodomy. They are prosecuted, but nothing is known of their fate. This is the only documented North American civilian case of sodomy prosecution resulting from bed sharing.

1846: Edward McCosker is dismissed from the New York City Police Department for making "indecent" advances to other men while on duty.

1848: The first Women's Rights Convention in Seneca Falls, New York, passes a "Declaration of Sentiments and Resolutions." The forerunner of the modern feminist movement, this convention jettisons several probable lesbian and bisexual women into the national limelight, most notably Susan B. Anthony.

1860: Walt Whitman publishes the homoerotic *Leaves of Grass*, which later inspires numerous gay poets.

1866: Horatio Alger, the author of numerous popular books for boys, is accused by the Unitarian Church of Brewster, Massachusetts, of "practicing" on boys "deeds . . . too revolting to relate." Alger neither denies nor confirms the charges and leaves town immediately after "for parts unknown."

1870: Bayard Taylor's *Joseph and His Friend*, the first U.S. novel to touch on the subject of homosexuality, is published.

1886: A news story in Montreal's *La Presse* features the earliest available documentation of gay nightlife in the city, when it describes the activity in a nocturnal cruising spot, the Champs-de-Mars, and the arrest of a gay man, Clovis Villeneuve, through police entrapment.

1892: In Tennessee, Alice Mitchell is tried for the murder of her lover, Freda Ward, and judged to be insane. The teenage girls were "engaged" and planned to marry, with Alice intending to pass as a man. When the affair was discovered and broken up by Freda's older sister, Alice "could not bear the thought of losing her" and slit Freda's throat in a mad fit of passion.

1896: For the first time on the American stage, two women hug and kiss in a scene of the play *A Florida Enchantment*. Though the play is not lesbian in content, the scene is so controversial that, at intermission, ushers offer ice water to any audience member who feels faint.

1897: Havelock Ellis writes in his famous *Sexual Inversion* of "the great prevalence of sexual inversion in American cities." His book is the first to treat homosexuality impartially, but his observations are limited to men.

1901: Influential New York politician Murray Hall dies and is revealed to have been a passing woman.

1912: At Polly Halliday's restaurant in New York City, Heterodoxy, a feminist luncheon club for "unorthodox women," begins meeting bimonthly. Among its members are many prominent lesbians, including Helen Hull, Katharine Anthony, Dr. Sara Josephine Baker, and Elisabeth Irwin, and bisexual women such as Mabel Dodge Luhan. Heterodoxy meets on a regular basis to discuss politics and social issues until the early 1940s.

1914: In Portland, Oregon, a dictionary of criminal slang is published, in which the first printed use of the word "faggot" to refer to male homosexuals appears.

1916: The Provincetown Playhouse—the first major off-Broadway theater—is founded in New York's Greenwich Village. In its early days, Edna St. Vincent Millay and Djuna Barnes are associated with the theater. In a later incarnation, the theater presents Edward Albee's first play, *The Zoo Story*, and Charles Busch's *Vampire Lesbians of Sodom*.

1917: In Montreal, nineteen-year-old Elsa Gidlow, a budding writer and a lesbian, starts an artists' salon in her parents' home, which welcomes several women writers, a painter, and a gay man named Roswell George Mills, who becomes her mentor. Subsequently, the salon members publish a literary magazine called *Les mouches fantastique*, the informal name of the group. Gidlow later moves to the United States, writes fifteen books, and becomes a mentor to a younger generation of lesbian writers.

1919: Dispatching a squad of young enlisted men to act as decoys, the U.S. Navy, under the orders of Assistant Secretary of the Navy Franklin Roosevelt, initiates a search for "sexual perverts" at the Newport (Rhode Island) Naval Training Station. Based on information the plants gather, twenty sailors and sixteen civilians are arrested on morals charges by naval and municipal authorities.

1920–1935: Referred to as the Harlem Renaissance, this period witnesses an unprecedented flourishing of African-American culture in the United States. Central to this significant time in African-American history are many gay and lesbian writers, artists, and musicians, including Countee Cullen, Claude McKay, Langston Hughes, Bessie Smith, Ma Rainey, Alain Locke, Bruce Nugent, and Ethel Waters.

1923: Sholom Asch's *God of Vengeance*, one of the earliest plays with lesbian con-

Stereotyped cartoon of gay men as "pansies," from a New York tabloid *Broadway Brevities*, 1932.

"Oh, shucks! There goes my hankie again."

tent, opens on Broadway. The play was originally written in Yiddish in 1907 and first produced in Berlin.

1924: Henry Gerber and others found the Society for Human Rights in Illinois, believed to be the first homosexual organization in the United States. Though it lasts only a few months, the society publishes two issues of *Friendship and Freedom,* the first gay liberation magazine in the country.

1926: *The Captive,* another early play with lesbian content, opens on Broadway, starring Helen Menken, then the wife of Humphrey Bogart. As one newspaper critic put it, "Lesbian love walked out onto a New York stage. . . ." The play raises a flurry of public controversy, and William Randolph Hearst, the newspaper magnate, makes it a campaign issue to "wipe out those evil plays now menacing the future of the theater." *The Captive* is raided and shut down, and the following year the Wade "Padlock" Law is enacted, prohibiting Broadway plays

Gay male couples, circa 1930s. (*Collection of the National Museum & Archive of Lesbian and Gay History*)

from depicting "sex perversion." Though only occasionally enforced, the law remains on the books until 1967.

- The journal *Fire!*, a periodical showcasing the work of Harlem Renaissance
writers, publishes its first and only issue. Included is the erotic narrative poem
"Smoke, Lilies and Jade," by Bruce Nugent, which is the first published piece
about homosexuality by an African-American writer.

1927: Written and produced by Mae West, *The Drag*, the first play with gay male
content to be produced in the United States, debuts in Connecticut on its way
to Broadway. It further fuels the controversy started by the Broadway run of *The
Captive* and is closed before it reaches New York.

1929: New York publisher Covici-Friede is convicted of obscenity for publishing
Radclyffe Hall's lesbian novel *The Well of Loneliness*. The conviction is later appealed and overturned.

1930: Hollywood studios enact the Motion Picture Production Code, prohibiting
all references to homosexuality or "sexual perversion" in the movies. Though
initially not enforced, the code is strengthened in 1934 under pressure from the
Catholic-led Legion for Decency and remains in effect until the 1960s.

1934: Despite the Padlock Bill, Lillian Hellman's play *The Children's Hour*—
about two teachers "accused" by a student of being lesbians—opens on Broadway. It may have escaped closing because of its moralistic ending—the one
character who is indeed a lesbian kills herself.

1942: The U.S. military issues further official prohibition against homosexuals in
the armed forces. Because the country is in the middle of World War II, the policy is not stringently enforced until after the war.

- The book *A Generation of Vipers*, by Philip Wylie, is published, coining
the word "Momism" to blame American mothers for overprotecting their sons
and raising "unmasculine" boys unfit for military service.

- In Los Angeles, Jim Kepner begins his private collection of gay-related
books, clippings, photographs, and artifacts, which later becomes the International Gay and Lesbian Archive, the oldest and largest in North America. The
archive opens to the public in 1979.

1947: The pseudonymous Lisa Ben (an anagram for "lesbian") begins publishing
Vice Versa, the first U.S. lesbian magazine, in Los Angeles. From her desk as a
secretary at RKO Studios, Ben types each issue twice using four carbons, then
circulates the ten copies of the publication to lesbian friends, who in turn pass
it on to others.

1948: The Kinsey Institute publishes its groundbreaking study of sexual behavior
in American men. Among its findings are these: 50 percent of those surveyed
admitted erotic responses to other men; 37 percent had had at least one adult
homosexual experience; and 10 percent were exclusively homosexual for at least
three years of their adulthood. The celebrated "Kinsey scale" displays a significant amount of fluctuation in sexual activity, from 1 (exclusively heterosexual) to
6 (exclusively homosexual). Kinsey's findings shake the heterosexual world and
help foster a sense of community and self-acceptance among homosexuals. (See
1953.)

1951: Harry Hay, Chuck Rowland, and others form the Mattachine Society in Los

Angeles, one of the first gay organizations in the United States and forerunner of the current gay liberation movement.

1952: The United States Congress enacts a law banning lesbian and gay foreigners from entering the country. The legislation is on the books until its repeal in 1990.

• George Jorgensen, a former sergeant in the U.S. Army, undergoes his famous sex-change operation in Denmark, becoming Christine Jorgensen.

1953: President Eisenhower signs Executive Order 10450, making "sexual perversion" grounds for exclusion from federal employment.

• The magazine *ONE*, designed to air gay and lesbian opinions and concerns to the public, begins publication in Los Angeles.

• The Kinsey Institute publishes its second historic study on human sexuality, *Sexual Behavior in the Human Female*. Its findings include the following: 28 percent of women surveyed responded erotically to other women; 13 percent had had at least one adult lesbian sexual experience; and between 2 and 6 percent identified their sexual orientation as exclusively lesbian between the ages of twenty and thirty-five.

• Dr. Evelyn Hooker begins her historic study of the male homosexual personality. In the late 1950s, she publishes the findings of her research in a series of monographs, reporting that she can find no signs of maladjustment in homosexual men's personalities. Her study thus disputes the prevailing medical theory that homosexuality is a "sickness."

1954: The Los Angeles postmaster seizes copies of *ONE* magazine and refuses to mail them, on the grounds that they are "obscene, lewd, lascivious and filthy." *ONE* editors challenge the postmaster, but in 1956 and 1957 two courts uphold the postal service's action. Finally, in 1958, the U.S. Supreme Court, in a "legal and publishing landmark," reverses the rulings of the two lower courts, ensuring the distribution of lesbian and gay materials through the mail service.

1955: The Daughters of Bilitis, the first lesbian organization in the United States, is founded in San Francisco by Del Martin and Phyllis Lyon.

1956: *The Ladder,* the official magazine of the Daughters of Bilitis, begins publication.

1957: The American Civil Liberties Union (ACLU) adopts a national policy statement that sustains the constitutionality of state sodomy laws and federal security regulations denying employment to gay men and lesbians. The ACLU finally reverses this policy in 1964.

1960: The first national lesbian conference, a convention of the Daughters of Bilitis, is held in San Francisco.

1961: Illinois becomes the first state to abolish its laws against consensual homosexual sex.

1964: The first homosexual rights demonstration in New York City takes place. Ten participants from the Homosexual League of New York and the League for Sexual Freedom picket the Army Induction Center on Whitehall Street, protesting the army's dishonorable discharges of gay soldiers.

Frank Kameny, an early gay rights activist, was one of the founders of the Washington, D.C. Mattachine Society. (*Photo by Richard C. Wandel*)

- Jane Rule publishes her first lesbian novel, *Desert of the Heart*, which becomes an instant classic and is made into the popular movie *Desert Hearts* in 1985.
- The earliest known homosexual rights button is produced for the Washington, D.C., conference of East Coast Homophile Organizations (ECHO).
- *Two* magazine, whose name was inspired by the U.S. magazine *ONE*, begins publication and continues publishing until 1966. It is the first gay magazine in Canada.
- The Association for Social Knowledge (ASK), the oldest known homophile organization in Canada, is formed in Vancouver.

1965: The Mattachine Society leads a picket in front of the White House, protesting the government's discriminatory employment practices. Seven men and three women participate in the action. The first of its kind ever, the picket receives national TV coverage.

The Oscar Wilde Memorial Bookshop in New York City, the first gay bookstore in the world, founded in 1967. *(Photo by Winnie Hough)*

1966: The National Organization for Women is founded in New York.
- The SIR Center (Society for Individual Rights) opens in San Francisco, the first gay community center in North America.
- ASK Community Center opens in Vancouver, Canada, to "serve the homosexual community." It is the first gay community center in Canada.

The Stonewall Inn, as it appears today. *(Photo by Winnie Hough)*

1967: *The Advocate,* the oldest continuing gay publication in the United States, begins publishing in Los Angeles.

• The Oscar Wilde Memorial Bookshop, the oldest gay bookstore in the United States, opens in New York City, on Mercer Street. In 1973, the store relocates to its current site at the junction of Christopher and Gay Streets.

• John Herbert's play about homosexuality in the Canadian prison system, *Fortune and Men's Eyes,* is published in Toronto.

An early meeting of the Gay Activists Alliance (Jim Owles, Arthur Evans, Arnie Kantrowitz), 1970. *(Photo by Richard C. Wandel)*

- In San Francisco, a group of radical gays form the Circle of Loving Companions and begin publishing a monthly called *Vanguard*.

1968: The Metropolitan Community Church is founded in Los Angeles by Rev. Troy Perry for gay people who want to worship together.

- At Johns Hopkins University, Dr. John Money performs the first complete male-to-female sex-change operation in the United States.

1969: In late June, when plainclothes police raid the Stonewall Inn in New York's Greenwich Village, they meet violent resistance from gay patrons of the bar and people on the street, including transvestites, butch lesbians, and gay teenagers. The weekend of riots is now viewed as the start of the modern gay liberation movement.

- Taking its name from the National Liberation Front in Vietnam, the Gay Liberation Front (GLF) is founded in New York by participants in the Stonewall riots and others in the gay community as an ongoing militant political action group.

- *Time* magazine's "The Homosexual in America" becomes the first cover story on gay rights in a national magazine.

- *Gay Power* becomes the first gay newspaper to appear after the Stonewall Riots.

- Amendments to the Canadian criminal code take effect, legalizing private sexual acts between consenting adults over the age of twenty-one.

- The University of Toronto Homophile Association (UTHA), the first gay liberation organization in Canada, begins meeting.

1970: The first legislative hearings on gay rights in the United States are convened in New York City by three New York State Assembly members.

- The first march to commemorate the Stonewall riots is held in New York. Several thousand participants march up Sixth Avenue to Sheep Meadow in Central Park, where the march is followed by a be-in.

- Catalyst Press, the first gay press in Canada, is launched in Toronto by Ian Young and publishes its first book, *Cool Fire,* by Young and Richard Phelan.

- Radicalesbians, a New York–based group of lesbian-feminists who split from the Gay Liberation Front, publish the manifesto "The Woman-Identified Woman," which defines a lesbian as "the rage of all women condensed to the point of explosion."

- The first lesbian/feminist bookstore in the United States, Amazon Bookstore in Minneapolis, opens for business. Also that year, A Woman's Place bookstore is started in Oakland, California.

- Robin Morgan publishes her compilation *Sisterhood Is Powerful: An Anthology of Writings from the Women's Liberation Movement.*

1971: The Los Angeles Gay and Lesbian Community Services Center is founded.

- The Furies, a lesbian-feminist separatist collective, is founded by lesbian activists fed up with mainstream women's organizations like the National Organization for Women (NOW). Original members include Joan E. Biren, Rita Mae Brown, Charlotte Bunch, and Helaine Harris.

A gay rights march on the state capitol in Albany, New York, 1971. *(Photo by Richard C. Wandel)*

• NOW approves its first resolution supporting lesbian rights. A similar resolution in the previous year had been attacked and defeated by NOW founder Betty Friedan, who labeled lesbians "the Lavender Menace."

• The American Library Association begins awarding an annual Gay Book Award. The first goes to Isabel Miller for her novel *Patience and Sarah*.

• A full ten years after Illinois, Connecticut becomes the second state to repeal its sodomy laws.

• The first francophone gay organization in Canada, Front de liberation homosexuel, is formed in Montreal, sponsoring rap groups and organizing the first gay dances in the city.

• The "We Demand" brief—sponsored by Canadian gay groups and calling for legal reform and changes in public policy relating to homsexuals—is presented to the federal government. The first public gay demonstration in Canada takes place a week later on Parliament Hill in support of the brief.

1972: The United States Senate approves the Equal Rights Amendment (ERA), which would prohibit discrimination on the basis of gender, and sends the bill to the state assemblies for ratification. Phyllis Schlafly and the Eagle Forum lead the fight to block ratification, and after a bitter ten-year fight, the ERA is defeated in 1982.

• A U.S. District Judge rules that the Civil Service Commission cannot discriminate against gay employees unless it can prove that being gay would interfere with their jobs.

• The first gay synagogue in the United States, Beth Chayim Chadashim in Los Angeles, is founded. The following year, the second and now the largest gay synagogue in the world, Congregation Beth Simchat Torah in New York, is formed.

• The first Canadian nonfiction book on homosexuality, *A Not So Gay World: Homosexuality in Canada,* is published.

• East Lansing, Michigan, becomes the first city in the United States to ban antigay bias in city hiring.

• William Johnson becomes the first openly gay man to be ordained as a minister by a major religious denomination, the United Church of Christ, in California.

• The first issue of *The Other Woman,* a predominantly lesbian-feminist publication, is produced in Toronto.

• Toronto Gay Action organizes its first Gay Pride Week, August 19–27.

1973: The Supreme Court of the United States rules in *Roe v. Wade* that constitutional privacy rights include a woman's right to a first-trimester abortion. Twenty years later, Norma McCorvey, a lesbian, reveals herself as "Jane Roe."

• Under the auspices of the YWCA, the first national lesbian conference in Canada is held in Toronto, and Montreal Gay Women is founded as a separatist group the same year. Shortly after, the first lesbian journal in Canada, *Long Time Coming,* begins publication in Montreal.

• The Toronto City Council passes a resolution banning discrimination in municipal hiring on the basis of sexual orientation, the first such legislation in North America.

Publications of
the Mattachine
Society, early
1970s.
*(Collection of the
National
Museum &
Archive of
Lesbian and Gay
History/Photo by
Winnie Hough)*

- The National Gay Task Force (later the National Gay and Lesbian Task Force), a civil rights group, is founded in New York by activists Martin Duberman, Ron Gold, Barbara Gittings, Frank Kameny, Dr. Howard Brown, Bruce Voeller, and Nathalie Rockhill. The Task Force opens an office in Washington in 1986.
- The Canadian Gay Archives is founded by *The Body Politic,* with the newspaper's back files as a foundation.
- *Gay Community News* is founded in Boston and is the only lesbian and gay newsweekly in the United States at that time.
- The first pan-Canadian conference of gay organizations, hosted by Centre humanitaire d'aide et de liberation (CHAL), is held in Quebec City.
- Daughters, Inc., a lesbian-feminist publishing house founded by June Arnold and Parke Bowman, publishes the first edition of Rita Mae Brown's *Rubyfruit Jungle,* which is later sold to Bantam Books as a mass-market paperback.
- Naiad Press is started in Florida by Barbara Grier and Donna McBride. Naiad is now the oldest surviving lesbian book publisher in North America.

The National Gay Task Force (later the National Gay and Lesbian Task Force) contingent in the 1974 Gay Pride March, New York City. *(Photo by Richard C. Wandel)*

- Olivia Records, the leader in women's music, is founded by a lesbian-feminist collective. The company cuts its first single a year later, with Meg Christian on one side and Cris Williamson on the other.
- The American Psychiatric Association decides that homosexuality should no longer be classified as a mental disorder.
- The Lesbian Herstory Archives is started in New York City, housed in the apartment of founders Joan Nestle and Deborah Edel and taking as its mission the preservation of the lives and works of all lesbians.
- The American Bar Association passes a resolution recommending the repeal of all state sodomy laws.
- The Supreme Court of the United States restricts the availability of sexually explicit material in two rulings, *Miller v. California* and *Paris Adult Theater I v. Slaton*. The rulings allow local communities to define obscenity and eliminate a national standard.
- Lambda Legal Defense and Education Fund is founded as a nonprofit gay law firm dedicated to obtaining gay civil rights through the courts.

1974: HR-14752, a bill to prohibit antigay discrimination across the United States—the first of its kind in U.S. history—is introduced into the House of Representatives by Bella Abzug and Edward Koch. The bill seeks to add protections for gays to the 1964 Civil Rights Act.

• Comunidad Orgullo Gay (COG), the first gay and lesbian organization on the island of Puerto Rico, is founded to work for the repeal of the sodomy laws included in the New Penal Code under consideration by the legislature.

• In Milton, Ontario, fundamentalist minister Ken Campbell, outraged by members of a local gay group addressing his daughter's high school class, forms the Halton Renaissance Committee—the forerunner of Renaissance Canada, which would become one of the strongest organizations opposing gay rights in Canada.

• *Lesbian Connection*—now the largest-circulation lesbian periodical in the United States—begins publication in East Lansing, Michigan, by the Ambitions Amazons collective.

• Elaine Noble, elected to the Massachusetts state legislature, becomes the first openly gay elected official in the United States.

1975: Santa Cruz County, California, becomes the first U.S. county to ban antigay discrimination.

• *Consenting Adult,* Laura Z. Hobson's groundbreaking novel about a gay teenage boy, is published.

• In Canada, a joint parliamentary committee on immigration policy recommends that homosexuals no longer be prohibited from entering Canada under the revised Immigration Act.

1976: The lesbian-feminist journal *Conditions* is founded in New York by Elly Bulkin, Jan Clausen, Irena Klepfisz, and Rima Shore. The journal is dedicated to publishing the work of lesbians, particularly working-class lesbians and lesbians of color.

• Montreal police launch a series of raids on gay bars designed to "clean up" the city before the opening of the summer Olympics. The largest gay demonstration to date, organized by Comite homosexuel anti-repression/Gay Coalition against Repression, is held to protest the raids. The group later evolves into the Association pour les droits des gai(e)s du Quebec (ADGQ).

• In *Rose v. Locke,* the U.S. Supreme Court rules that cunnilingus is covered by Tennessee's "crimes against nature" statute, even though it is not expressly mentioned there.

• The first Michigan Womyn's Music Festival, a celebration of lesbian culture, includes musical performances by Holly Near, Linda Tillery, and Maxine Feldman.

• Armistead Maupin begins serializing his famous "Tales of the City" in the *San Francisco Chronicle.*

• The Lesbian Organization of Toronto (LOOT) is founded, with its first priority the establishment of a lesbian center.

1977: Voters in Dade County, Florida, repeal a gay rights law by a two to one margin. The fight to repeal is led by fundamentalist singer, orange juice industry spokesperson, and former Miss America contestant Anita Bryant.

• Toronto police raid the offices of *The Body Politic,* Canada's leading gay newspaper, seizing records, manuscripts, and subscription lists. The news-paper is charged with using the mail service to distribute "indecent" material. After a long and costly legal battle (and another police raid in 1982), the paper is acquitted, but its financial problems force it to cease publication in 1987.

• The Women's Archives is formed in Toronto to preserve and record Canadian women's history.

• The Combahee River Collective, an African-American lesbian-feminist group, publishes "A Black Feminist Statement," a historic manifesto that puts forth a political analysis recognizing the interconnectedness of oppressions based on identity.

• Coop-femmes, the first francophone lesbian group in Canada, is founded in Montreal.

• Senior Action in a Gay Environment (SAGE) is founded in New York to serve the social and political needs of older lesbians and gay men.

• The province of Quebec amends its provincial Charter of Human Rights, adding lesbians and gay men to the list of those protected, thus banning antigay discrimination in employment, housing, and public accommodations. It is the first major city in North America to protect its citizens against discrimination on the basis of sexual orientation.

1978: The U.S. Supreme Court, in *Federal Communications Commission v. Pacifica Foundation*, approves restrictions on broadcast material that is "indecent," but not "obscene." The case will be used to block the broadcast of gay-themed programs.

• San Francisco Supervisor Harvey Milk, an out gay man, and Mayor George Moscone are murdered by Dan White.

• The rainbow flag, which will become one of the most prominent symbols of lesbian and gay pride, is designed by Gilbert Baker in San Francisco and flown in the Gay Freedom Day Parade there.

• An hour-long radio program, "Gay News and Views," begins airing on an Ontario station, the first regularly scheduled gay radio program in Canada.

• *Dancer from the Dance,* by Andrew Holleran, is published and is now considered a classic novel about white gay male life and culture before AIDS.

• Gay and Lesbian Advocates and Defenders (GLAD), New England's non-profit, public-interest gay and lesbian law foundation, is founded in Boston by John Ward, Richard Burns, Cindy Rizzo, and others.

• California voters defeat the Briggs Initiative, which would have barred lesbians and gay men from teaching in the state's public schools.

1979: The first national March on Washington for Gay and Lesbian Civil Rights draws over one hundred thousands marchers.

• Dan White is acquitted of first-degree murder in the deaths of Harvey Milk and George Moscone and convicted of the lesser charge of manslaughter. His lawyer successfully argues that White's mental capacity was diminished by his excessive consumption of Twinkies and other junk food. In 1985, White is released from prison and then kills himself.

• *Conditions* magazine publishes the groundbreaking "Black Women's Issue," later the basis for the anthology *Home Girls*, one of the first titles from Kitchen Table: Women of Color Press (see 1981).

• The first issue of the francophone journal *Le Berdache* is published in Montreal.

- The U.S. Mint issues the Susan B. Anthony dollar, named for the noted feminist and probable lesbian.
- Fundamentalist minister Jerry Falwell founds the Moral Majority in Lynchburg, Virginia. The organization lists as its goals opposition to abortion, feminism, pornography, communism, and gay rights.
- Stephen Lachs becomes the first openly gay judge in the United States, appointed to the Superior Court of Los Angeles.

1980: The Gay Community Appeal of Toronto is incorporated and begins plans to launch the first United Way–type fundraising drive for a gay organization in North America.

- Alyson Publications, the largest gay press in the United States, is founded in Boston by gay activist Sasha Alyson.
- Mel Boozer, an African-American gay man, becomes the first openly gay person to have his name placed in nomination as a candidate at the Democratic National Convention. As a vice-presidential nominee, he addresses the convention.
- The Canadian Union of Postal Workers ratifies a contract that includes a nondiscrimination clause protecting gay people. This is the first time gay employees of a federal government anywhere in the world are awarded such protection.
- The Toronto Board of Education amends its policy to ban discrimination on the basis of sexual orientation, but adds a clause forbidding "proselytizing of homosexuality in the schools."
- The Fifth Canadian Binational Lesbian Conference draws women from across Canada and results in the organization of Canada's first lesbian pride march.

1981: The U.S. Department of Defense revises its policy on lesbians and gays in the military. The new policy bars gay people from serving in the military and requires that questions about sexual orientation be asked of all recruits.

- Toronto police undertake a massive raid on gay bathhouses and arrest over three hundred men. It is the largest mass arrest in Canadian history and the largest mass arrest of gay men in North America. The arrests generate a riot that has been called the Canadian Stonewall.
- The *New York Times* reports the first cases of Kaposi's sarcoma, a rare form of cancer, in forty-one gay men. In addition, the Centers for Disease Control (CDC) make known the growing number of cases of pneumocystis carinii pneumonia (PCP) among gay men.
- A new Kinsey Institute study reports that neither parental nor societal influences have much effect on a person's sexual orientation.
- Governor Jerry Brown of California appoints Mary Morgan to the state supreme court, making her the first openly lesbian judge.
- Kitchen Table: Women of Color Press, the first publishing house in North America devoted to producing works by women of color, is founded in New York by Barbara Smith, Audre Lorde, Cherie Moraga, and a group of other writers and activists.

• The first lesbian pride march in Toronto, "Dykes in the Streets," is sponsored by Lesbians against the Right.

• A group of Los Angeles parents form the support group Parents and Friends of Lesbians and Gay Men (P-FLAG), to help one another and to help combat society's homophobia against gay people.

• Marilyn Barnett files a "galimony" suit against her former employer and lover, tennis champion Billie Jean King. King says she is straight, but doesn't deny the affair.

• The New York City Gay Men's Chorus becomes the first gay musical group to perform at Carnegie Hall. A year later, Meg Christian and Cris Williamson become the first out lesbians to play there.

1982: Wisconsin becomes the first state to enact statewide gay rights legislation.

• A Los Angeles man files a palimony suit against entertainer Liberace, who denies that he is gay.

• The first Gay Games are held in San Francisco, with 1,300 participants from twelve countries.

• Gay Related Immune Disorder (GRID) acquires the new name of Acquired Immune Deficiency Syndrome (AIDS).

• Gay men in New York found Gay Men's Health Crisis (GMHC), a social service and education agency, to deal with growing concern over the spread of AIDS among gay men.

• The first Montreal lesbian publications in French, *Amazones d'hier, Lesbiennes d'aujourd'hui* and *Ca s'attrape,* are circulated.

• Byton High in Philadelphia, the first gay high school in the United States, is started as an alternative to the public school system.

• The province of Quebec passes legislation giving homosexual relationships equal status with heterosexual ones.

1983: Representative Gerry Studds (D-Ma.) declares on the floor of the U.S. House of Representatives that he is gay.

• Howard Cruse's gay comic strip "Wendel" first appears in *The Advocate*. Alison Bechdel's comic strip "Dykes to Watch Out For" is first published in New York's *Womanews*.

• Les Archives gaies du Quebec opens in Montreal with the mission of collecting books, manuscripts, magazines and newspapers, photographs, films, and objects related to gay life in the province.

• A group of lesbian and gay activists acquire a former public high school building from the city of New York, and the Lesbian and Gay Community Services Center is born. The following year, the building is purchased for $1.5 million.

1984: San Francisco Health Department head Mervyn Silverman closes fourteen gay bathhouses after investigators uncover high-risk sexual behavior in them.

• Government officials announce the discovery of the "probable cause" of AIDS, then known as HTLV-III, but soon to be renamed HIV (human immunodeficiency virus).

• Berkeley, California, becomes the first city in the United States to extend domestic partnership benefits to lesbian and gay city employees.

- West Hollywood incorporates as a municipality and elects a largely gay city council and a lesbian mayor.

1985: After repeated denials, movie and television actor Rock Hudson finally issues a public statement that he has AIDS, and dies three months later.

- A test for HIV antibodies is licensed by the U.S. Food and Drug Administration (FDA), allowing for the testing of both individuals and the existing blood supplies.

- The Democratic Party votes to drop official recognition of some caucuses, including the Gay and Lesbian Caucus.

- Canadian customs bans *The Joy of Gay Sex*, one of many such instances of censorship by the Canadian government.

- More than a hundred well-known women—including Lily Tomlin, Yoko Ono, Joanne Woodward, and Joyce Carol Oates—sign a *Ms.* magazine "Petition for Freedom of Sexual Choice," condemning all government attempts to interfere in "the sexual lives of consenting adults."

- Angered by the media's poor coverage of the AIDS epidemic, a group of New York activists found the Gay and Lesbian Alliance Against Defamation (GLAAD) during a meeting at the Lesbian and Gay Community Services Center. GLAAD serves as a watchdog on the presentation of lesbians and gay men in Hollywood and the media.

- The Harvey Milk School, a public high school for lesbian and gay youth, is started in New York City as a collaborative project of the Hetrick-Martin Institute, a social service agency for gay youth, and the city's public school system.

1986: The province of Ontario, Canada, passes a gay rights ordinance.

- In *Bowers v. Hardwick*, the U.S. Supreme Court upholds the constitutionality of Georgia's sodomy law. In Atlanta in 1982, police tried to serve Michael Hardwick at home with a warrant for a traffic violation and found him having sex with another man. Hardwick was arrested for sodomy, and his appeal went all the way to the Supreme Court.

- The U.S. Public Health Service releases the experimental drug AZT to people with PCP.

- The U.S. Justice Department ends its policy of asking prospective federal prosecutors if they are gay.

- Californians reject an initiative that calls for the quarantine of people with AIDS.

1987: Delta Airlines apologizes for arguing in plane crash litigation that it should pay less in compensation for the life of a gay passenger than for a heterosexual one because he may have had AIDS.

- The second national March on Washington for Lesbian and Gay Rights draws approximately a half-million participants. During a weekend of events, two thousand lesbian and gay couples participate in a mass wedding in front of the Internal Revenue Service building. Also, the NAMES Project quilt, which is the size of two football fields, is displayed on the mall in front of the U.S. Capitol.

- President Reagan undergoes testing for HIV when he becomes concerned about the blood transfusions he received when he was shot in 1981. According to a White House spokesperson, he tests negative.
- Massachusetts Representative Barney Frank tells an interviewer in the *Boston Globe* that he is gay.
- Robert Bork, who openly opposes gay rights, is rejected as a candidate for the U.S. Supreme Court.
- Vermont becomes the first state to distribute condoms to prison inmates.
- At a meeting at the New York Lesbian and Gay Community Services Center, activist Larry Kramer and others start the AIDS Coalition to Unleash Power (ACT UP), a direct action group whose purpose is to draw public and government attention to the need for AIDS funding and research.
- The *Lambda Book Report* begins publication, the first journal devoted to reviews of works by lesbian and gay writers.

1988: The first World AIDS Day, organized by the World Health Organization, is held.

- On October 11, the first anniversary of the historic 1987 lesbian and gay march on Washington, National Coming Out Day is first celebrated, set aside as a day when gay people can each make a step toward coming completely out of the closet.
- Citizens of Oregon repeal a ban on antigay job discrimination, paving the way for the antigay initiatives in Oregon in the early 1990s.
- In Canada, sodomy and anal intercourse between consenting adults over eighteen are eliminated as criminal offenses.
- President Reagan's newly founded National AIDS Commission releases a report, with over five hundred recommendations for addressing the epidemic. A presidential advisor reduces the list to ten items.
- *OUT/LOOK*, a national lesbian and gay magazine of politics and culture, begins quarterly publication.
- Democrat Svend Robinson becomes the first member of the Canadian Parliament to come out as gay.

1989: In *Watkins v. United States Army,* a federal court orders the reinstatement of Perry Watkins, who had been dismissed from the service because he was gay.

- The U.S. Supreme Court, in *Price Waterhouse v. Hopkins,* rules that the accounting firm violated sex discrimination laws by dismissing a woman for "masculine behavior."
- The Corcoran Art Gallery in Washington, D.C., cancels a retrospective of Robert Mapplethorpe's photographs after the exhibit is attacked by Senator Jesse Helms and others for its homoerotic content. The director of the gallery resigns, and in the ensuing brouhaha, Mapplethorpe's name becomes a household word, synonymous with artistic censorship.
- The first annual Lambda Literary Awards for excellence in lesbian and gay writing are held at the American Booksellers Association convention in Washington, D.C.

• Mayor Ed Koch dedicates "Stonewall Place" in New York City—the strip of Christopher Street where the Stonewall riots took place—to commemorate the twentieth anniversary of the event.

• The U.S. Post Office issues a lesbian and gay pride postmark, commemorating the twentieth anniversary of the Stonewall riots and featuring the artwork of gay artist Keith Haring.

• San Francisco's Maud's, "the world's oldest lesbian bar," closes after twenty-three years.

• Massachusetts becomes the second state to pass a gay civil rights law.

• Over five thousand ACT UP activists stage a massive protest in front of and inside New York's St. Patrick's Cathedral, rallying against the Catholic Church's negative policies on homosexuality and AIDS.

1990: Cincinnati Museum of Art director Dennis Barrie is charged and acquitted of obscenity for booking a traveling exhibit of homoerotic photographs by Robert Mapplethorpe.

• The Americans with Disabilities Act, which also prohibits AIDS-based discrimination, is signed into law.

• During President Bush's first major address on AIDS, NGLTF Executive Director Urvashi Vaid interrupts his speech and protests his inactivity. She is escorted outside.

• Queer Nation—an in-your-face direct action group with the rallying cry "We're here, we're queer, get used to it!—is founded in New York City at a meeting at the Lesbian and Gay Community Services Center.

A Queer Nation meeting at the NYC Lesbian and Gay Community Services Center. (*Photo by Terry Boggis*)

- The Astraea Foundation (founded in 1977) changes its name to the Astraea National Lesbian Action Foundation, becoming the first national foundation to fund lesbian cultural and social-change projects exclusively.

- During Lesbian and Gay Pride weekend in June, the top of the Empire State Building is lit up in lavender for the first time.

- In an unprecedented move, National Endowment for the Arts Chair John Frohnmayer revokes grants already awarded by a peer panel to four solo theater artists—Karen Finley, John Fleck, Holly Hughes, and Tim Miller. Frohnmayer cites as his rationale "political realities," but the artists (who soon become known as "The NEA Four") cry censorship, and their "defunding" becomes a cause celebre in the lesbian and gay arts community. Three of the four are gay, and all create performance art dealing explicitly with sexuality. The investigation that led to the "defunding" was initiated by none other than Senator Jesse Helms, who says he wants the public to know what filth their tax dollars are funding. The four artists bring a lawsuit against the NEA and in 1993 settle out of court for $252,000.

- Philip Morris—particularly its products Miller Beer and Marlboro cigarettes—becomes the object of a national gay boycott, to protest the company's alleged funding of the campaign of virulently antigay senator Jesse Helms.

1991: The Minnesota Court of Appeals awards guardianship of Sharon Kowalski, a lesbian severely injured in a car crash, to her lover, Karen Thompson, over the objections of Kowalski's parents.

- Patricia Ireland, executive director of the National Organization for Women, admits to having a female lover —in addition to a husband.

- *The Advocate* outs Department of Defense spokesperson Pete Williams.

- Lesbian poet, teacher, and activist Audre Lorde is named Poet Laureate of New York State.

- *Tongues Untied*, Marlon Riggs's documentary about African-American gay men, airs on PBS and draws complaints to the FCC from some homophobic viewers.

- Dr. Simon LeVay releases a controversial study suggesting a biological influence for sexual orientation, widely referred to as "the gay brain."

- The first Black Gay and Lesbian Pride March is held in Washington, D.C.

1992: Aileen Wuornos, the first lesbian serial killer in the United States, is sentenced to death in Florida.

- Canadian country and pop star k.d. lang becomes the first major female recording artist to come out as a lesbian.

- Democratic candidate Bill Clinton, in his acceptance of his nomination for president, mentions gay people in his speech—the first time a presidential candidate has done so at the convention.

- Roberta Achtenberg, a lesbian member of San Francisco's Board of Supervisors, Bob Hattoy, a member of Clinton's campaign staff and a gay man with AIDS, and Elizabeth Glaser, an HIV-positive heterosexual woman, address the Democratic National Convention in New York.

- The Republican National Convention in Miami is a gay-bashing travesty filled with the rhetoric of "family values." However, Mary Fisher, an HIV-positive woman, is permitted to address the convention.

• The first National Lesbian Conference, designed as a strategy-building meeting for lesbian liberation, draws 2,500 participants to Atlanta.

• Lesbian Avengers, International—a direct action group dedicated to fighting lesbian oppression—is launched by activists Anne Christine d'Adesky, Marie Honan, Anne Maguire, Sarah Schulman, Anna Maria Simo, and Maxine Wolfe at a meeting at the Lesbian and Gay Community Services Center in New York. Within two years, the direct action group has grown to thirty-five chapters in North America and Europe.

• The first U.S. governor to do so, William Weld of Massachusetts, signs an executive order granting lesbian and gay state workers the same bereavement and family leave rights as heterosexual workers.

• The Canadian government releases documents that show that the Canadian Mounted Police spied on gay men in Ottawa during the Cold War period, creating files against them and purging hundreds from government jobs.

• Antigay initiatives are introduced in Oregon and Colorado. After bitter fights, the Colorado initiative passes and the more harshly worded Oregon one is rejected. The passage of the Colorado initiative sparks a national boycott of Colorado by gay people and their supporters.

• Canada lifts its ban on lesbians and gays in the military.

• In a decision historic for all of North America, the Canadian immigration service grants immigrant status to an Irish lesbian whose lover is a Canadian citizen.

• The National Gay and Lesbian Task Force announces that almost 1,900 incidents of antigay assaults, murder, vandalism, and threats were reported this year, up 4 percent from 1991.

• The Canadian YMCA board of directors reluctantly extends family membership discounts to lesbian and gay couples.

• New Jersey, Vermont, and California enact statewide bans on antigay discrimination.

• Louisiana governor Edwin Edwards issues an executive order banning antigay discrimination in state agencies, making his the first state in the southeast to do so.

1993: President Bill Clinton directs the secretary of defense to investigate the possibility of drafting an executive order to overturn the 1981 ban on gays in the military. However, encountering fierce opposition from Congress, Clinton settles for a "don't ask, don't tell" compromise, which does not significantly change the earlier ban.

• The March on Washington for Gay, Lesbian, and Bi Equal Rights attracts an estimated 750,000 participants to the capital.

• Organized by the Lesbian Avengers, the first International Dyke March is held the evening before the March on Washington.

• A federally funded survey by the Battelle Human Affairs Research Centers concludes that only 2.3 percent of U.S. men have had sex with other men, and only 1.1 percent consider themselves exclusively homosexual. The Christian

1993 March on Washington for Lesbian, Gay, and Bisexual Rights. *(Photo by Dave LeFave)*

Right jumps on the findings to say that homosexuality is a "behavioral oddity" and that gays do not deserve "protected status."

• For the first time in a Canadian province, the Ontario Human Rights Commission rules that a lesbian, Jan Waterman, was fired from her job because of her sexual orientation. She receives $27,000 in compensation from National Life Assurance and two of its employees.

• Hawaii Supreme Court rules that a lower court improperly dismissed a lawsuit challenging a state policy of denying marriage licenses to gay and lesbian couples. The court rules that the prohibition of same-sex marriages constitutes sex discrimination and is probably unconstitutional. The decision sparks hope that same-sex marriages will eventually be made legal in Hawaii.

• After months of futile negotiations with the Ancient Order of Hibernians, the Irish Lesbian and Gay Organization (ILGO) is once again excluded from New York's annual St. Patrick's Day Parade (their first attempt to participate was in the 1991 parade). In protest, both Mayor David Dinkins and Governor Mario Cuomo stay away from the parade, as do thousands of others, making it the smallest St. Patrick's Day parade in the city's recent history. Over two hundred people, including openly gay city councilman Tom Duane, are arrested when they stage an alternative parade on the same day.

• Voters in Cincinnati, Ohio, Portsmouth, New Hampshire, and Lewiston, Maine, approve antigay ballot measures.

• After a fierce struggle over a proposed multicultural, gay-tolerant curriculum ("The Rainbow Curriculum") for New York City schools, the city Board of Education does not renew the contract of public schools chancellor Joseph Fernandez, who had backed the progressive curriculum.

• After a bitter debate in which Senator Jesse Helms calls her a "damned lesbian," Roberta Achtenberg is approved by the Senate as assistant housing secretary, becoming the highest ranking out lesbian in the U.S. government.

• The commission of Cobb County, Georgia, sets a dangerous precedent by voting unanimously to cease its arts-related funding for fear that it might be subsidizing lesbian and gay art and artists.

• A twenty-nine-cent stamp depicting a red ribbon and the words "AIDS Awareness" is issued by the U.S. Post Office.

• In a nationwide survey, fifty-five percent of all Canadians consider homosexuality "morally acceptable."

• Navy airman Terry Helvey is court-martialed for the brutal murder of a gay shipmate, Allen Schindler.

• After months of criticism from activists, President Clinton appoints the first "AIDS czar," Kristine Gebbie. She is widely criticized by AIDS activists for her low profile and lack of experience and is forced to resign the following year. In her place, Clinton names Patsy Fleming, an African-American woman with a gay son who considers herself an AIDS activist.

An assortment of gay and lesbian rights buttons from the last two decades. *(From the collections of Terry Boggis, Paula Martinac, and the National Museum & Archive of Lesbian and Gay History. Photo by Winnie Hough)*

1994: A bill that would prohibit antigay employment discrimination is introduced into the U.S. House of Representatives.

• The Virginia Court of Appeals overturns a lower court ruling that stripped lesbian Sharon Bottoms of custody of her two-year-old son on the basis of her sexual orientation.

• The first Latina Lesbian Leadership and Self-Empowerment Conference is held in Tucson, Arizona.

• In Boston, organizers of the St. Patrick's Day Parade cancel the event rather than comply with a court order allowing the Irish-American Gay, Lesbian, and Bisexual Group to participate.

• Straight actor Tom Hanks wins an Academy Award for Best Actor for his portrayal of a gay man with AIDS in *Philadelphia*.

• The United Nations revokes the consultative status granted the International Lesbian and Gay Association (ILGA) in 1993, ostensibly because of claims that some of its members are affiliated with pedophile groups, most notably the North American Man-Boy Love Association (NAMBLA).

• Openly gay choreographer Bill T. Jones and openly lesbian poet Adrienne Rich are recipients of MacArthur Foundation "genius" awards.

• Gay Games IV attracts approximately fifteen thousand participants in New York City.

• Stonewall 25 draws 1.1 million marchers in New York City, for the silver anniversary of the Stonewall Riots.

• The Tenth International Conference of AIDS convenes in Yokohama, Japan, attracting fewer activists than in past years.

• In the national midterm elections, Republicans—with major backing from the homophobic Christian right—take over the majority in both houses of the U.S. Congress and win gubernatorial elections in many large states, in a sweep that threatens the future of lesbian and gay civil rights in the United States.

• At the Virginia Slims women's tennis tournament in New York City, Martina Navratilova—nine-time Wimbledon singles champion and arguably the greatest woman tennis player of all time—plays her last professional singles match, and loses to Gabriela Sabatini. A banner with her name on it will be displayed at the Virginia Slims tournament each year at Madison Square Garden. She is the first woman (and out lesbian) to receive the honor.

• The American Medical Association finally adopts a statement removing all references to "sexual orientation related disorders" from its official policy, which has been used for years to justify "therapies" for "treating" homosexuality. In handing down its new decision, the AMA acknowledges that anti-gay health-care professionals need to work on changing their attitudes instead of their clients' sexual orientation.

• The National Association of Lesbian and Gay Community Centers is founded by the centers in New York, Los Angeles, Minneapolis, Denver, and Dallas.

1995: British actor Nigel Hawthorne, star of the film *The Madness of King George,* becomes the first openly gay Best Actor nominee in the history of the Academy Awards.

CONGRESS MEMBERS WHO OPENLY DENOUNCED ARMEY'S SLUR

Reps. John Lewis (D-Ga.) and Nancy Pelosi (D-Calif.) led a press conference of seventeen representatives who denounced Richard Armey's slur against Barney Frank. The members appearing at the press conference included John Baldacci (D-Maine), Rosa DeLauro (D-Conn.), Anna Eshoo (D-Calif.), Elizabeth Furse (D-Ore.), Nita Lowey (D-N.Y.), Jim McDermott (D-Wash.), Cynthia McKinney (D-Ga.), George Miller (D-Calif.), John Olver (D-Mass.), Lynn Rivers (D-Mich.), Tom Sawyer (D-Ohio), Chuck Schumer (D-N.Y.), Jose Serrano (D-N.Y.), Mike Ward (D-Ky.), and Lynn Woolsey (D-Calif.). Jerrold Nadler (D-N.Y.) issued a written statement.

- In what he claims is an honest "slip," Rep. Dick Armey (R-Tex.) publicly refers to openly gay Congressman Barney Frank (D-Mass.) as "Barney Fag." Armey is not reprimanded, denies responsibility, and will not acknowledge that using the epithet "fag" is injurious to gay people.
- Four-time Olympic gold medalist Greg Louganis, considered by many to be the greatest diver of all time, reveals in a television interview with Barbara Walters on *20/20* that he has AIDS. His announcement that he was HIV-positive when he hit his head on the diving board during the 1988 Olympics, drawing blood and requiring stitches, causes a flurry of indignation that he may have put other athletes and the doctor who stitched his wound at risk for HIV. The doctor, however, tests negative, and experts maintain that a few drops of blood in a chlorine-treated pool would not endanger anyone.
- Rhode Island becomes the ninth state to pass a statewide gay rights bill, protecting lesbians and gay men in housing, public employment, credit, and public accommodations.
- Wearing a red ribbon, Cherry Jones becomes the first out lesbian to win a Tony Award for Best Leading Actress in a Play, for her role in *The Heiress*.
- Our timeline scratches the surface of North American lesbian and gay history. The following list of books used to compile our highlights and "lowlights" is suggested for further reading.

UNITED STATES

Berube, Allan. *Coming Out Under Fire: The History of Gay Men and Women in World War II.* Plume, 1991.

Chauncey, George. *Gay New York: Gender, Urban Culture, and the Making of the Gay Male World, 1890–1940.* Basic Books, 1994.

D'Emilio, John. Sexual Politics, *Sexual Communities: The Making of a Homosexual Minority in the United States, 1940–1970.* University of Chicago Press, 1983.

Duberman, Martin B., Martha Vicinus, and George Chauncey, Jr., eds. *Hidden from History: Reclaiming the Lesbian and Gay Past*. New American Library, 1989.

Faderman, Lillian. *Odd Girls and Twilight Lovers: A History of Lesbian Life in Twentieth-Century America*. Columbia University Press, 1991.

Katz, Jonathan Ned. *Gay/Lesbian Almanac*. Carroll & Graf, 1994.

_____. *Gay American History: Lesbians and Gay Men in the U.S.A.* Meridien, 1992.

Kennedy, Elizabeth Lapovsky and Madeline D. Davis. *Boots of Leather, Slippers of Gold: The History of a Lesbian Community*. Routledge, 1993.

Marcus, Eric. *Making History: The Struggle for Gay and Lesbian Equal Rights, 1945–1990, An Oral History*. HarperCollins, 1992.

Miller, Neil. *Out of the Past*. Vintage, 1995.

Rutledge, Leigh. *The Gay Decades*. Plume, 1991.

Schwartz, Judith. *Radical Feminist of Heterodoxy: Greenwich Village, 1912–1940*. New Victoria Publishers, 1986.

Thompson, Mark, ed. *Long Road to Freedom:* The Advocate *History of the Gay and Lesbian Movement.* St. Martin's, 1994.

CANADA:

Adam, Barry. *The Rise of the Gay and Lesbian Movement*. Twain Publishers, 1987.

Body Politic. *Flaunting It: A Decade of Gay Journalism from the Body Politic*. Pink Triangle Books and New Star Books, 1982.

Herman, Didi. *Rights of Passage: The Struggle for Lesbian and Gay Legal Equality*. University of Toronto Press, 1994.

Kinsman, Gary. *The Regulation of Desire*. Black Rose Books, 1987.

Stone, Sharon. *Lesbians in Canada*. Between the Lines, 1990.

For a separate timeline on the AIDS epidemic, see pp. 410–417.

REPOSITORIES OF LESBIAN AND GAY HISTORY

You don't have to be famous to leave your letters, photographs, and other personal documents to an archive to be preserved for posterity. Those letters that document your first love affair, the photos of you and your friends at the March on Washington, your collection of lesbian and gay buttons— all these items are valuable to lesbian and gay history archives. Lesbian and gay lives deserve to be remembered and chronicled! Here are just a few of the places that will welcome the artifacts of your own lesbian or gay history. Write or call first for their donation guidelines or for information on doing research in these collections.

Archives Gaies du Quebec
4067 St-Laurent, Suite 202
Montreal, QC H2W 1Y7
Canada
(514-287-9987

Blanche Baker Memorial Library
  and Archives/ONE, Inc.
3340 Country Club Drive
Los Angeles, CA 90019
213-735-5252

Canadian Gay Archives
P. O. Box 639, Station A
Toronto, Ontario M5W 1G2
Canada
416-921-6310

Dallas Gay and Lesbian Historic
  Archives
2701 Reagan
Dallas, TX 75219
214-528-4233

Douglas County Gay Archives
P.O. Box 942
Dillard, OR 97432-0942
503-679-9913

Gay and Lesbian Archives of
  Washington, D.C.
P. O. Box 4218
Falls Church, VA 22044
703-671-3930

Gay and Lesbian Historical Society
  of Northern California
P.O. Box 424280
San Francisco, CA 94142
415-626-0980

Henry Gerber/Pearl M. Hart
  Library and Archives
Midwest Lesbian/Gay Resource
  Center
3352 N. Paulina St.
Chicago, IL 60657
312-883-3003

Homosexual Information Center
115 Monroe St.
Bossier City, LA 71111
318-742-4709

International Gay and Lesbian
  Archives
P. O. Box 38100
Los Angeles, CA 90038-0100
310-854-0271

June Mazer Lesbian Collection
626 N. Robertson Blvd.
West Hollywood, CA 90069
310-659-2478

Kentucky Collection of Lesbian
  Her-Story
P.O. Box 1701
Louisville, KY 40201

Lesbian and Gay Archives of San
  Diego
P.O. Box 40389
San Diego, CA 92164
619-260-1522

Lesbian Herstory Archives
P.O. Box 1258
New York, NY 10116
718-768-DYKE

National Museum & Archive of
  Lesbian and Gay History
Lesbian and Gay Community
  Services Center
208 West 13th St.
New York, NY 10011
Phone: 212-620-7310
Fax: 212-924-2657

New York Public Library
Division of Humanities, Social
  Sciences, and Special Collections
Fifth Ave. and 42nd St.
New York, NY 10018
212-930-0584

Southeastern Lesbian Archives

Box 5502

Atlanta, GA 30307

Stonewall Library and Archives

330 SW 27th St.

Fort Lauderdale, FL 33315

THE NATIONAL MUSEUM & ARCHIVE OF LESBIAN AND GAY HISTORY

Its name may sound grandiose, but the National Museum & Archive of Lesbian and Gay History, a program of New York City's Lesbian and Gay Community Services Center, simply preserves the history of the daily lives and political struggles of lesbians and gay men.

One of the largest collections of its kind in the United States, the Archive is a repository for the personal papers, correspondence, artifacts, and publications of both individuals and organizations. Among the Archive's current holdings are the papers of activist and singer Michael Callen, who died of AIDS in 1994; the records of the committee that organized the National March on Washington for Lesbian and Gay Rights in 1979; the FBI files on the Mattachine Society, the Gay Liberation Front, and the Gay Activists Alliance; and the records of the Christopher Street Liberation Day Committee from the 1970s.

The Archive offers researchers the chance to piece together the pictures of a community that has been frequently overlooked or misrepresented. The collections of the Archive are accessible on Thursday evenings from 8 to 10 P.M. and by appointment with the archivist, Rich Wandel. The Archive welcomes donations of personal papers and artifacts—here's your chance to be written into history! Call the archivist to find out how to make a donation, whether it's one photograph or a roomful.

The Museum sponsors regular exhibitions of art and history. Its inaugural exhibition in 1988 featured portraits of lesbian and gay writers by photographer Robert Giard. Since then, other displays have included *Keepin' On: Images of African-American Women from the Lesbian Herstory Archives; A Memorial Dew Cloth: Celebrating 500 Years of Native American Survival;* and *Out on the Island: 60 Years of Lesbian and Gay Life on Fire Island.* To celebrate the twenty-fifth anniversary of the Stonewall riots, the Museum presented *Windows on Gay Life,* an art and archival exhibition in shop windows along Christopher Street near where the original Stonewall Inn was located.

The National Museum & Archive of Lesbian and Gay History
The Lesbian and Gay Community Services Center
208 West 13th St.
New York, NY 10011
Phone: 212-620-7310
Fax: 212-924-2657

HOW THE CANADIAN AND UNITED STATES LESBIAN AND GAY LIBERATION MOVEMENTS DIFFER: AN INTERVIEW WITH GENS HELLQUIST

Gens Hellquist has lived in Saskatoon, Saskatchewan, since he was five years old. "I'm the town fag. I stayed here because I believe if we are ever going to win the fight for equality, it will be won in small towns and communities."

Gens is a social worker, the current director of Gay and Lesbian Health Services, and the editor of *Perceptions*, the prairie lesbian and gay news magazine. He has been involved in the gay and lesbian liberation movement since 1971, when the movement "hit the prairies."

In addition to his gay civil rights work, he has also been instrumental in the formation of local AIDS organizations. Gens is particularly concerned with mental illness, suicide, substance abuse, and other serious self-esteem problems. "AIDS rates are going down," he notes, "but not among gay people with self-esteem issues."

In some ways, gays in Canada have made more progress than their sisters and brothers south of the border. The Charter of Rights and Freedoms, enacted in 1982, proclaimed basic human rights for all Canadians and encompassed sexual orientation. Seven of ten Canadian provinces (encompassing 85 percent of the population) have legislative protection for lesbians and gay men; Alberta is the only major province without such protection. The Canadian government has promised since 1987 to pass national gay rights legislation. This legislation will protect gay rights in all nationalized business—in the civil service as well as the transportation and communications industries.

"I don't mean to suggest all is perfect here," Gens says. "We're still in court a lot. We have censorship problems." Canadian customs officials are infamous for confiscating at the border shipments of lesbian and gay material from the United States. Until October of 1994, depictions of anal sex were illegal in Canada. Gens points out the irony of the situation: "We could do it, but we couldn't read about it." Other depictions of lesbian and gay sexuality still continue to be censored. Currently, Little Sisters Bookstore in Vancouver is challenging Canada's censorship laws in court.

"I think the key difference between U.S. and Canadian life is that we're not as persecuted by the religious right here," Gens observes. "In our public opinion polls, people consistently and overwhelmingly favor gay rights, although public support breaks down as soon as children enter the picture."

Although the National Gay and Lesbian Rights Coalition was formed in Canada during the 1970s, the group became regionalized and broke apart. There are currently no national gay organizations in Canada, something that also marks a difference from the United States. "We tend not to work together well," Gens explains. "Quebec is always flirting with separation, a rift that trickles down to gay politics."

II

Don't I Know You from Somewhere?

A Guide to Notable North American Gay and Bisexual Men

Sexuality is a tricky thing. This should not be read as a roster of "perfect 6s" on the Kinsey scale; sexuality is often much more fluid than that. No matter what label we give our identities—gay, bisexual, or straight—many of us have engaged in both homosexual and heterosexual relations over the course of our lives.

And even though we may claim a man as gay by his sexual activity or by his emotional affinity with other men, he may not have done so. In fact, some men on this list are probably turning in their graves at being labeled "gay"! We ask, then, that you view this as a list of men who have, at some time in their lives, loved other men.

There are a lot of celebrities—particularly film and TV stars currently acting in Hollywood—who are either reputed or known to be gay, but who adamantly refuse to come out of the closet. So far, only a few brave souls have ventured out, like Dan Butler, one of the stars of *Frasier,* and singer Elton John. We have not intentionally outed any living celebrities here—but we wish we could add them to the next edition of this almanac!

Ailey, Alvin, 1931–1989: dancer and choreographer; founder of multiracial modern dance ensemble, the Alvin Ailey American Dance Theatre, in 1958.

Albee, Edward, b. 1928: playwright; works include *The Zoo Story, Who's Afraid of Virginia Woolf?*, and the Pulitzer Prize–winning *Three Tall Women.*

Alger, Horatio, 1832–1899: writer; best known for rags-to-riches stories of impoverished boys, such as *Ragged Dick* and *Tattered Tom.*

Araki, Gregg, b. 1962: filmmaker; films include *The Living End, Nowhere, Totally F***ed Up.*

Ardolino, Emile, 1943–1993: film director; films include *Dirty Dancing, Chances Are, Sister Act,* and the made-for-TV *Gypsy,* with Bette Midler.

Arenas, Reinaldo, 1943–1990: Cuban-born writer; works include *Singing from the Well, Hallucinations, El Central,* and *Before Night Falls.*

Larry Kramer (*Copyright © 1989 by Robert Giard*)

Ashman, Howard, 1951–1991: lyricist; wrote lyrics for *Little Shop of Horrors* and
the Disney cartoons *The Little Mermaid, Beauty and the Beast* (the title song
won an Academy Award), and *Aladdin.*

Auden, W. H., 1907–1973: British-born poet; author of *Homage to Clio, City
Without Walls,* and the Pulitzer Prize–winning *Age of Anxiety.*

Baitz, Jon Robin, b. 1961: playwright; plays include *The Substance of Fire, The
End of the Day, Three Hotels.*

Baldwin, James, 1924–1987: writer and civil rights activist; author of novels *Go Tell
It on the Mountain, Giovanni's Room,* and *Another Country,* and essay collections *The Fire Next Time* and *Notes of a Native Son.*

Banneker, Benjamin, 1731–1806: mathematician and astronomer; author of *Banneker's Almanack,* which contributed to the U.S. abolitionist campaign by pop-
ularizing the antislavery cause; served on commission that laid out the plan for
Washington, D.C.

Barber, Samuel, 1910–1981: composer; works include *Adagio for Strings* and the Pulitzer Prize–winning opera *Vanessa*.

Barnett, Allen, 1954–1990: writer; author of the short fiction collection *The Body and Its Dangers*.

Bartel, Paul, b. 1938: film director; films include *Private Parts, Eating Raoul, Cannonball,* and *Scenes from the Class Struggle in Beverly Hills*.

Bauman, Robert, b. 1937: former Republican congressman from Maryland.

Bawer, Bruce: writer; regular contributor to right-wing magazine *The New Criterion* and gay magazine *The Advocate;* author of the staunchly anti-left book *A Place at the Table*.

Beam, Joseph, 1954–1988: writer and editor; edited African-American gay anthology, *In the Life*.

Beaton, Cecil, 1904–1980: British-born costume designer and photographer; film credits include *Gigi* and *My Fair Lady,* for which he won Academy Awards for costume design.

Beecher, Henry Ward, 1813–1887: lecturer, abolitionist, and minister; brother of writer Harriet Beecher Stowe; famous for his eloquent and fiery sermons on human vice.

Bennett, Michael, 1943–1987: Broadway dancer, director, and choreographer; conceived, directed, and choreographed the Pulitzer Prize–winning *A Chorus Line*; choreographed *Promises, Promises, Coco, Company,* and *Follies*.

Bernstein, Leonard, 1918–1990: conductor of the New York Philharmonic Orchestra; composer of music for stage *(West Side Story)* and film *(On the Waterfront)*.

Berube, Allan: historian and writer; author of the pioneering study *Coming Out Under Fire: The History of Gay Men and Women in World War II*.

Boozer, Mel: activist and politician; in 1980 became first openly gay man to run for U.S. vice president.

Boswell, John, 1947–1994: historian; author of *Christianity, Social Tolerance, and Homosexuality* and *Same-Sex Unions in Pre-Modern Europe*.

Bowles, Paul, b. 1910: writer; novels include *The Sheltering Sky, Let It Come Down,* and *Up Above the World*.

Boyd, Malcolm, b. 1923: theologian and activist; author of best-selling book *Are You Running with Me, Jesus?*.

Bridges, James, 1935–1993: film director; films include *The Paper Chase, September 30, 1955, The China Syndrome, Urban Cowboy,* and *Bright Lights, Big City*.

Brown, Dr. Howard, 1925–1975: doctor and activist; his public coming out in 1973 made the front page of the *New York Times*, because he was the former New York City health services administrator and a respected professor at New York University; also one of the founders of the National Gay and Lesbian Task Force.

Buchanan, James, 1791–1868: fifteenth president of the United States.

Burke, Glenn, 1952–1995: athlete; former outfielder for Los Angeles Dodgers and Oakland A's.

George
Chauncey
(*Photo by
David
Martin*)

Burns, John Horne, 1916–1953: writer; novels include *The Gallery, Lucifer with a Book,* and *A Cry of Children.*

Burns, Richard D., b. 1955: activist and lawyer; former editor of *Gay Community News;* currently executive director of the New York Lesbian and Gay Community Services Center.

Burr, Raymond, 1917–1993: actor; best known for TV series *Perry Mason* and *Ironside;* films include *A Place in the Sun, Rear Window, A Cry in the Night,* and *Airplane II.*

Burroughs, Williams S., b. 1914: writer; novels include *Naked Lunch* and *Queer.*

Busch, Charles: actor and playwright; off-Broadway plays include *Vampire Lesbians of Sodom, Psycho Beach Party, The Lady in Question,* and *Red Scare on Sunset.*

Butler, Dan, b. 1955: actor; plays Bulldog Briscoe on the TV sitcom *Frasier;* 1995 one-man, off-Broadway show *The Only Thing Worse You Could Have Told Me.*

Button, Dick, b. 1929: Olympic figure skater and sports commentator.

Buttrick, Merritt, 1960–1989: film actor; best known as Captain Kirk's son in *Star Trek II: The Wrath of Khan* and *Star Trek III: The Search for Spock.*

Cadmus, Paul, b. 1903: artist; career flourished with famous painting *The Fleet's In!*

Cage, John, 1912–1992: composer; works included "Imaginary Landscape 4," "Williams Mix," "Hpschd," "Roaratorio," and "Europera 5"; longtime lover and collaborator of dancer Merce Cunningham.

Callen, Michael, 1954–1993: singer and AIDS activist; founder and member of gay a cappella group, The Flirtations.

Cameron, Peter, b. 1939: writer; author of story collection *One Way or Another* and novels *Leap Year* and *The Weekend*.

Capote, Truman, 1924–1984: writer; works include novels *Other Voices, Other Rooms* and *Breakfast at Tiffany's* and nonfiction *In Cold Blood*.

Casey, Warren, 1935–1988: composer; cowrote the hit musical *Grease*.

Cathcart, Kevin: activist and lawyer; executive director of Lambda Legal Defense and Education Fund.

Chauncey, George: historian and editor; author of the groundbreaking *Gay New York: Gender, Culture, and the Making of the Gay Male World, 1890–1940*; coeditor of *Hidden from History: Reclaiming the Gay and Lesbian Past* (with Martin Duberman and Martha Vicinus).

Cheever, John, 1912–1983: writer; most famous novels include *The Wapshot Chronicle, Falconer,* and *Bullet Park*.

Cheney, Russell, 1881–1945: painter; longtime lover of F. O. Matthiessen.

Claiborne, Craig, b. 1920: author and gourmet chef; longtime food editor of the *New York Times;* author of autobiography *A Feast Made for Laughter*.

Clift, Montgomery, 1920–1966: actor; films include *Suddenly Last Summer, Raintree County, The Misfits,* and *Judgment at Nuremberg*.

Coco, James, 1930–1987: actor; plays include *Next* (his role was written specifically for him by playwright Terrence McNally) and *The Last of the Red Hot Lovers;* films include *Man of La Mancha, Murder by Death, The Cheap Detective, Only When I Laugh,* and *There Must Be a Pony*.

Cohn, Roy, 1927–1986: attorney; former counsel to Senator Joseph McCarthy and assistant prosecutor in the trial of Ethel and Julius Rosenberg.

Cole, Jack, 1911–1974: choreographer; Broadway stage credits include *A Funny Thing Happened on the Way to the Forum* and *Man of La Mancha*.

Cooper, Mario: activist; former manager of the Democratic National Convention; chair of the AIDS Action Council, first African-American to lead a such a national organization.

Copland, Aaron, 1900–1990: composer; works include *Rodeo* and the Pulitzer Prize–winning *Appalachian Spring*.

Corigliano, John, b. 1938: composer; works include *Symphony No. 1* and *The Ghosts of Versailles: Of Rage and Remembrance*.

Coward, Sir Noel, 1899–1973: British-born actor, dramatist, and composer; stage credits include *Design for Living, Blithe Spirits, Private Lives,* and *Cavalcade*.

Cox, Wally, 1924–1973: actor; star of TV series *Mr. Peepers;* films include *State Fair, Spencer's Mountain, The Yellow Rolls Royce,* and *The Barefoot Executive*.

Crane, Hart, 1899–1932: poet; best-known poems are "The Bridge" and "White Buildings."

Crisp, Quentin, b. 1908: British-born writer and humorist; books include *The Naked Civil Servant, Love Made Easy,* and *How to Become a Virgin*.

Crowley, Mart, b. 1935: playwright and screenwriter; most famous work, *The Boys in the Band*.

Cruz, Wilson, b. 1974: actor; regular on TV series *My So-Called Life,* playing a bisexual teenager.

Cukor, George, 1899–1983: film director; credits include *The Philadelphia Story,*

Samuel R. Delany (*Copyright © 1987 by Robert Giard*)

Dinner at Eight, Little Women, Camille, The Women, Gaslight, Adam's Rib, Born Yesterday, Pat and Mike, A Star Is Born, and *My Fair Lady.*

Cullen, Countee, 1903–1946: poet; works include *The Ballad of the Brown Girl, Color,* and *Copper Sun.*

Cunningham, Merce, b. 1922: dancer and choreographer; former soloist with Martha Graham, he founded his own dance company and experimented with multimedia works; works include *Symphony by Chance* and *Square Game;* longtime lover and collaborator of composer John Cage.

Curry, John, 1949–1994: figure skater and gold medal winner at the 1976 Winter Olympics.

Daly, James, 1928–1978: actor; films included *Planet of the Apes* and *The Big Bounce;* regular on TV series *Medical Center.*

Day, F. Holland, 1864–1933: photographer; one of first American proponents of photography as an art form; first American photographer to enjoy an international reputation; known for his male nudes and Greek themes.

Dean, James, 1931–1955: actor; film credits include *Rebel Without a Cause, Giant,* and *East of Eden.*

Melvin Dixon (*Copyright © 1988 by Robert Giard*)

Delaney, Samuel R., b. 1942: writer; author of numerous Nebula Award–winning science fiction novels, including *The Einstein Connection* and *Babel-17*; an autobiography, *The Motion of Light in Water;* and a mystery novel, *Mad Man*.

D'Emilio, John: historian; author of *Sexual Politics, Sexual Communities: The Making of a Homosexual Minority in the United States, 1940–1970* and *Intimate Matters: A History of Sexuality in America* (with Estelle B. Freedman).

Demuth, Charles, 1883–1935: painter; best known for industrial and urban paintings, also painted a series on sexual solicitation in gay bathhouses.

Denneny, Michael: editor; pioneering editor of gay titles at St. Martin's Press (Stonewall Inn editions) and currently at Crown.

dePaola, Tomie, b. 1932: children's book author and illustrator; books include *Strega Nona, Oliver Button Is a Sissy,* and *The Clown of God*.

Divine (Harris Glenn Milstead), 1946–1988: actor and drag queen; most famous movies include *Polyester* and *Hairspray*.

Dixon, Melvin, 1950–1993: writer; author of novels *Trouble the Water* and *Vanishing Rooms.*

Dolan, Terry, 1950–1986: conservative activist; founder of National Conservative Political Action Committee.

Duberman, Martin, b. 1930: historian, editor, activist, and playwright; works include biographies *Charles Francis Adams* (winner of the Bancroft Prize), *Paul Robeson, Stonewall,* and the memoir *Cures;* co-edited *Hidden from History;* one of the founders of the National Gay and Lesbian Task Force; director of the Center for Lesbian and Gay Studies (CLAGS) at the City University of New York.

Duncan, Robert, 1919–1988: poet and essayist; author of groundbreaking 1944 essay, "The Homosexual in Society"; author of *Heavenly City Earthly City* and *Medieval Scenes;* winner of American Book Award for *Ground Work: Before the War.*

Eakins, Thomas, 1844–1916: painter and photographer; leading American realist painter.

Ellis, Perry, 1941–1986: fashion designer; one of the most influential designers of 1970s and 1980s.

Epstein, Rob, b. 1955: documentary filmmaker; films include *The Times of Harvey Milk* and (with lover Jeffrey Friedman) *Common Threads: Stories from the Quilt,* both of which won Academy Awards.

Feinberg, David B., 1957–1994: writer; books include novels *Spontaneous Combustion* and *Eighty-Sixed* and the nonfiction *Queer and Loathing: Rants and Raves of a Raging AIDS Clone.*

Ferro, Robert, 1942–1988: writer; author of novels *Second Son, The Blue Star,* and *The Family of Max Desir.*

Fierstein, Harvey, b. 1954: actor and playwright; plays include *Torch Song Trilogy* and *Safe Sex;* films include *Torch Song Trilogy* and *Mrs. Doubtfire;* currently a regular on TV sitcom *Daddy's Girls.*

Flynn, Errol, 1909–1959: actor; famous Hollywood swashbuckler whose films included *Captain Blood, The Adventures of Robin Hood,* and *Gentleman Jim.*

Forbes, Malcolm, 1919–1990: publisher of *Forbes* magazine.

Foster, Stephen, 1826–1864: composer; compositions include the American standards "Beautiful Dreamer," "[I Dream of] Jeannie with the Light Brown Hair," "O Susannah," "De Camptown Races," and "The Old Folks at Home."

Frank, Barney, b. 1940: Massachusetts member of the U.S. House of Representatives.

Friedman, Jeffrey, b. 1952: documentary filmmaker; films include (with lover Rob Epstein) *Common Threads: Stories from the Quilt,* which won an Academy Award.

Frey, Leonard, 1939–1988: stage and film actor; credits include *The Boys in the Band* and *Fiddler on the Roof.*

Frowick, Roy Halston (better known as "Halston"), 1933–1990: fashion designer.

Gallin, Sandy, b. 1940: talent agent and manager, film and television producer;

Allen
Ginsberg
(*Copyright
Morgan
Gwenwald*)

current manager for such celebrities as Dolly Parton, Michael Jackson, Neil Diamond, and Margaret Cho; previously managed Barbra Streisand, Cher, Joan Rivers, Lily Tomlin, and Whoopi Goldberg.

Gerber, Henry, 1892–1972: gay liberation activist; helped found the Society for Human Rights in 1924, the first homosexual rights group in the United States, and its magazine, *Friendship and Freedom.*

Geer, Will, 1902–1978: actor; best known as Grandpa on the 1970s TV series *The Waltons;* films included *Advise and Consent, In Cold Blood, Pieces of Dreams,* and *Jeremiah Johnson.*

Geffen, David, b. 1943: entertainment industry executive and AIDS activist; produced films *Personal Best, Risky Business,* and *Beetlejuice;* Geffen Records signed artists such as Donna Summer and Elton John.

Gernreich, Rudi, 1922–1985: Austrian-born fashion designer; famous for designing the topless bathing suit in the late 1960s.

Gielgud, John, b. 1904: British-born actor; began career as Shakespearean stage actor in London; films include *Julius Caesar, Becket, The Loved One, Murder on the Orient Express, The Elephant Man, Chariots of Fire, Arthur,* and *The Shooting Party;* in television series *Brideshead Revisited.*

Gill, Tim: businessman; founder of Quark, Inc., which produces the premier computer software for desktop publishing.

Ginsberg, Allen, b. 1926: poet; one of central figures of Beat movement in 1950s; most famous work, *Howl.*

Glaser, Garrett: journalist; television reporter for *Entertainment Tonight.*

Gomes, Rev. Peter: minister of Harvard's Memorial Church; author of *Fighting for the Bible,* a book which made him one of the most highly paid openly gay authors in the United States; delivered benedictions at the inaugurations of both Presidents Reagan and Bush.

Goodman, Paul, 1911–1972: writer, psychologist, and social critic; author of *Growing Up Absurd*; one of the major gurus of the counterculture of the 1960s.

Goulding, Edmund, 1892–1959: British-born film director; films include *The Devil's Holiday, Grand Hotel, Dark Victory,* and *The Old Maid.*

Grant, Cary, 1904–1986: British-born actor; one of the premier comedic actors of his generation; films include *Blonde Venus, She Done Him Wrong, I'm No Angel, Sylvia Scarlet, Topper, Bringing Up Baby, Holiday, His Girl Friday, The Philadelphia Story, Arsenic and Old Lace, Notorious, Houseboat, An Affair to Remember, North by Northwest, Father Goose, That Touch of Mink,* and *Charade.*

Griffes, Charles Tomlinson, 1884–1920: composer; works include *Symphony in Yellow, These Things Shall Be,* and *Salut au Monde.*

Gunderson, Steve, b. 1951: politician; Republican congressman from Wisconsin, attempting to shift his party back more toward the moderate political center.

Haines, William, 1900–1974: actor; silent films include *Three Wise Fools, Tower of Lies, Sally, Irene and Mary, Brown of Harvard, Show People,* and *Tell It to the Marines.*

Haring, Keith, 1959–1990: pop artist; known for his black-and-white and primary-colored faceless stick figures.

Hart, Lorenz, 1895–1943: songwriter and lyricist; with partner Richard Rodgers, cowrote such Broadway musicals as *Pal Joey* and *Babes in Arms;* also such standard songs such as "Isn't It Romantic?," "My Funny Valentine," "The Lady Is a Tramp," and "Where or When."

Hartley, Marsden, 1877–1943: painter; best known for his landscapes of the coast of Maine.

Hay, Harry, b. 1912: gay rights activist; cofounder of the Mattachine Society in 1950 and of the Los Angeles Gay Liberation Front in 1969.

Hayes, Bruce, b. 1964: athlete; 1984 Olympic gold medal for swimming relay.

Haynes, Todd: film director; films include *Superstar: The Karen Carpenter Story, Assassins,* and *Poison.*

Hemphill, Essex; poet; author of *Conditions* and *Ceremonies;* editor of anthology *Brother to Brother.*

Herman, Jerry, b. 1933: composer and lyricist; Broadway plays include *Hello Dolly!, Mame,* and *La Cage aux Folles.*

Hetrick, Emery S., died 1987: activist and educator; with lover Damien Martin, founded the Institute for the Protection of Lesbian and Gay Youth (now called the Hetrick-Martin Institute) in New York City, which includes the Harvey Milk High School.

Higgins, Colin, 1941–1988: screenwriter and film director; film credits included *Harold and Maude, Silver Streak, Foul Play,* and *Nine to Five*

Hockney, David, b. 1937: British-born painter; well-known for "swimming pool" series of paintings; has also designed sets for opera.

Holleran, Andrew, b. 1946: writer; most famous work, *Dancer from the Dance.*

Hoffman, William, b. 1939: playwright; author of *As Is,* first Broadway play about AIDS.

Hoover, J. Edgar, 1895–1972: director of the FBI from 1924 to 1972 who was publicly homophobic and actively kept files on lesbian and gay activists during his tenure.

Horton, Edward Everett, 1886–1970: actor; over eighty film credits, in which he usually played a stereotypically effeminate "pansy," include *The Front Page, The Gay Divorcee*, and *Holiday.*

Hudson, Rock, 1925–1985: actor; films include *Magnificent Obsession, Giant,* and a series of light comedies with Doris Day; star of 1970s TV show *McMillan and Wife.*

Hughes, Langston, 1902–1967: poet and writer; works included *The Weary Blues, The Ways of White Folks, Shakespeare in Harlem,* and *Ask Your Mama.*

Hunter, Tab, b. 1931: actor; films include *Damn Yankees, Battle Cry, Polyester;* later a regular on TV series *Mary Hartman, Mary Hartman.*

Inge, William, 1913–1973: playwright; most famous works include the Pulitzer Prize–winning *Picnic, Splendor in the Grass, Come Back, Little Sheba, Bus Stop,* and *The Dark at the Top of the Stairs.*

Isherwood, Christopher, 1904–1986: British-born writer; works include "Goodbye to Berlin" (which inspired the play *Cabaret*), *Christopher and His Kind,* and *A Single Man.*

Ivory, James, b. 1928: film director; with partner, producer Ismail Merchant (b. 1937), films include *Shakespeare Wallah, The Europeans, Heat and Dust, The Bostonians, A Room with a View, Maurice, Mr. & Mrs. Bridge, Howard's End,* and *The Remains of the Day.*

Jackson-Paris, Bob and Rod: bodybuilders and activists; founders of the Be True to Yourself Foundation for lesbian and gay youth projects; have appeared on the TV talk show circuit (on *Oprah* and *Donahue*); Bob is a former Mr. Universe.

Joffrey, Robert, 1930–1988: dancer and choreographer; founder and artistic director of New York City's Joffrey Ballet company.

John, Elton, b. 1947: rock singer and composer; classic songs include "Goodbye Yellow Brick Road," "Your Song," "Bennie and the Jets," "Candle in the Wind," and "Rocket Man"; albums include *Don't Shoot Me I'm Only the Piano Player, Madman Across the Water,* and *The One.*

Johnson, Philip, b. 1906: architect; designer of the New York State Theater at Lincoln Center and the AT&T Building in New York City; first director of the Department of Architecture and Design at the Museum of Modern Art.

Jones, Bill T., b. 1952: dancer and choreographer; cofounder Bill T. Jones/Arnie Zane Dance Company.

Kaye, Danny, 1913–1987: actor; films include *Hans Christian Andersen, White Christmas, The Secret Life of Walter Mitty, The Court Jester, The Inspector General,* and *Merry Andrew;* star of 1960s TV variety show, *The Danny Kaye Show;* enjoyed a long-term love affair with actor Sir Laurence Olivier.

Keenan, Joe, b. 1958: writer; author of novels *Blue Heaven* and *Putting on the Ritz;* story consultant for television sitcom *Frasier.*

Kenan, Randall: writer; author of novels *A Visitation of Spirits* and *Let the Dead Bury The Dead* and young adult biography of James Baldwin.

Kepner, Jim: archivist and activist; in 1942, he began collecting gay and lesbian literature, information, and memorabilia, which grew into the International Gay and Lesbian Archives, now one of the most extensive in the world.

Kerouac, Jack, 1922–1969: writer; prominent figure of Beat Generation; novels include *The Town and the City, On the Road, The Dharma Bums,* and *Visions of Gerard.*

Kopay, David, b. 1942: former National Football League running back, who played for the San Francisco Forty-Niners, the Detroit Lions, the Washington Redskins, the New Orleans Saints, and the Green Bay Packers.

Kramer, Larry, b. 1935: writer and activist; plays include *The Normal Heart* and *The Destiny of Me;* cofounder of Gay Men's Health Crisis and ACT UP.

Kushner, Tony, b. 1956: playwright; works include *A Bright Room Called Day* and *Angels in America: A Gay Fantasia on National Themes,* winner of a Pulitzer Prize.

LaFosse, Robert, b. 1959: dancer and choreographer; principal dancer with the New York City Ballet since 1986.

Laughton, Charles, 1899–1962: British-born actor; films include *Witness for the Prosecution, Mutiny on the Bounty,* and *The Private Life of Henry VIII.*

Laurents, Arthur, b. 1917: novelist, screenwriter, and playwright; most famous films are *The Snake Pit, The Way We Were,* and *The Turning Point;* plays include *Gypsy, West Side Story,* and *Hallelujah, Baby.*

Leavitt, David, b. 1961: writer; author of story collection *Family Dancing* and novels *The Lost Language of Cranes, Equal Affections,* and *While England Slept.*

LeVay, Simon, b. 1943: British-born neurobiologist whose research on "the gay brain" seeks to prove that homosexuality (in men) is biologically determined.

Leventhal, Stan, 1951–1995: writer; books include novels *Mountain Climbing in Sheridan Square, Skydiving on Christopher Street,* and *Fault Lines;* cofounder of the Pat Parker/Vito Russo Center Library, the first gay/lesbian lending library in the U.S.; cofounder of Amethyst Press.

Leyendecker, J. C., 1874–1951: commercial artist; paintings of American life often appeared on the cover of *Saturday Evening Post.*

Liberace, 1919–1987: entertainer and pianist; albums include *Mr. Showmanship, Liberace Now,* and *Piano Gems.*

Liebman, Marvin, b. 1923: Republican political figure; worked on the campaigns of Barry Goldwater, Ronald Reagan, and many other conservative politicians; author of *Coming Out Conservative.*

Locke, Alain, 1886–1954: writer; first black American Rhodes scholar; professor of philosophy at Howard University; works include *The New Negro* and *The Negro in America.*

Lopez, Temistocles: Venezuelan-born film director; films include *Exquisite Corpses* and *Chain of Desire.*

Louganis, Greg, b. 1960: athlete; four-time Olympic gold-medal and one-time silver-medal winner for diving; holder of forty-seven national diving titles.

Lucas, Craig, b. 1951: playwright and screenwriter; author of *Prelude to a Kiss* and *Longtime Companion.*

Ludlam, Charles, 1943–1987: actor, writer, entertainer; founder of Ridiculous Theatrical Company in New York City.

Lynde, Paul, 1926–1982: actor; films include *Bye Bye Birdie, Send Me No Flowers,* and *The Glass Bottom Boat;* regular on TV sitcom *Bewitched* and game show *Hollywood Squares* ("I'll take Paul Lynde to block").

Lynes, George Platt, 1907–1955: photographer; known for his male nudes and his recording of the work of the American Ballet Theater from 1935 until his death.

McAlmon, Robert, 1896–1956: writer and publisher; husband of British lesbian writer Bryher; author of poetry collections *Explorations, The Portrait of a Generation,* and *Not Alone Lost,* and of memoir *Being Geniuses Together.*

McCauley, Stephen: writer; novels include *The Object of My Affection* and *The Easy Way Out.*

McKay, Claude, 1890–1948: writer; books include *A Long Way from Home, Banana Bottom, Banjo,* and *Home to Harlem.*

McKellan, Ian, b. 1935: British-born actor; began career as Shakespearean actor in London; starred on Broadway in *Amadeus;* films include *Alfred the Great, Priest of Love, Scandal, Last Action Hero, The Ballad of Little Jo, And the Band Played On, Six Degrees of Separation,* and *The Shadow.*

McKinney, Stewart B., 1931–1987: liberal Republican congressman from Connecticut.

McKuen, Rod, b. 1933: poet and songwriter; books include *Stanyan Street and Other Sorrows* and *Listen to the Warm;* wrote scores to movies *The Prime of Miss Jean Brodie* and *A Boy Named Charlie Brown.*

McNally, Terrence, b. 1939: playwright; Broadway and off-Broadway credits in-

Terrence McNally
(From the collection of the Lesbian and Gay Community Services Center– New York)

Eric Marcus
(*From the
collection of the
Community
Services Center–
New York*)

clude *Lips Together, Teeth Apart, Kiss of the Spiderwoman, Love! Valor! Compassion!;* wrote TV drama, *Andre's Mother.*

Mann, Thomas, 1875–1955: German-born writer; fiction includes *Buddenbrooks, The Magic Mountain,* and *Death in Venice.*

Mantello, Joe, b. 1963: stage actor and director; acting credits include *Angels in America;* directing credits include *Love! Valor! Compassion!* and *What's Wrong with This Picture?*

Mapplethorpe, Robert, 1946–1989: filmmaker, sculptor, and photographer; exhibits of his homoerotic photographs in Washington, D.C., and Cleveland sparked a wave of controversy and censorship.

Marcus, Eric: writer; author of *Making History: The Struggle for Gay and Lesbian Equal Rights* and *Is It a Choice? Answers to 300 of the Most Frequently Asked Questions About Gays and Lesbians;* ghostwriter for Greg Louganis's *Breaking the Surface.*

Martin, Damien, died 1991: activist and educator; with lover Emery S. Hetrick, founded the Institute for the Protection of Lesbian and Gay Youth (now called the Hetrick-Martin Institute) in New York City, which includes the Harvey Milk High School.

Mathis, Johnny, b. 1935: singer and entertainer; hit recordings include "Chances Are," "The Twelfth of Never," and "It's Not for Me to Say."

Matlovich, Sgt. Leonard, 1943–1988: gay rights activist and former Air Force

Harvey Milk

sergeant, who was discharged for coming out as gay and subsequently sued the Air Force.

Matthiessen, F. O., 1902–1950: scholar and literary critic; longtime lover of painter; author of the massive *American Renaissance* on the works of writers Emerson, Thoreau, Melville, and Whitman.

Maugham, W. Somerset, 1874–1965: British-born writer; novels include *Of Human Bondage, Cakes and Ale,* and *The Razor's Edge.*

Maupin, Armistead, b. 1944: writer; novels include *Tales of the City* (which started as a serial in the *San Francisco Examiner*), *More Tales of the City, Babycakes, Sure of You,* and *Maybe the Moon.*

Melville, Herman, 1819–1891: writer; works include fiction *Moby Dick* and *Billy Budd,* and travel books *Typee* and *Omoo.*

Meredith, William, b. 1919: poet; works include *Love Letter from an Impossible Land, The Open Sea,* and the Pulitzer Prize–winning *Partial Accounts: New and Selected Poems.*

Paul Monette *(Copyright © 1988 by Robert Giard)*

Merrill, James, 1926–1995: poet; works include *Nights and Days,* and the Pulitzer Prize–winning *Divine Comedies.*

Milk, Harvey, 1930–1978: gay rights activist and member, San Francisco Board of Supervisors, murdered along with mayor George Moscone by Supervisor Dan White.

Miller, Merle, 1919–1986: writer; works include *Plain Speaking, Lyndon: An Oral Biography,* and *On Being Different: What It Means to Be a Homosexual.*

Miller, Neil: writer; author of *In Search of Gay America, Out in the World,* and *Out of the Past.*

Mineo, Sal, 1939–1976: actor; films included *Rebel Without a Cause, Exodus,* and *The Gene Krupa Story.*

Mixner, David: political consultant and unofficial advisor to President Clinton; as a member of Clinton's campaign team, helped raise funds and mobilize the lesbian and gay community for his candidate.

Monette, Paul, 1945–1995: writer; works include the memoirs *Borrowed Time,*

Michael Nava *(Copyright © 1988 by Robert Giard)*

Becoming a Man (which won a National Book Award), and *Last Watch of the Night;* poetry collection *Love Alone: Eighteen Elegies for Rog;* and novels *Taking Care of Mrs. Carroll, Afterlife,* and *Halfway Home.*

Moore, Robert, 1927–1984: actor and director; Broadway plays included *Jenny Kissed Me, The Owl and the Pussycat,* and *Cactus Flower;* directed Broadway plays *The Boys in the Band, Promises, Promises, The Last of the Red Hot Lovers,* and *Deathtrap;* directed films *Tell Me That You Love Me, Junie Moon* (which he also acted in), *Murder by Death, The Cheap Detective,* and *Chapter Two.*

Nava, Michael: writer; author of mystery novels *Goldenboy, The Little Death,* and *How Town;* coauthor (with Robert Dawidoff) of the nonfiction *Created Equal: Why Gay Rights Matter to America.*

Novarro, Ramon, 1899–1968: Mexican-born actor; most famous roles were, in the silent era, *Ben-Hur, Scaramouche,* and *The Arab,* and in the talking era, *Mata Hari, The Cat and the Fiddle,* and *The Big Steal.*

Nugent, Richard Bruce, 1906–1987: writer; his narrative "Smoke, Lilies, and Jade" in the magazine *Fire!* (1926) was the first gay-themed work to be published by an African-American.

Nureyev, Rudolf, 1938–1993: Russian-born ballet dancer; danced as guest artist with most of the world's prominent ballet companies, often with Margot Fonteyn.

Nyswaner, Ron: screenwriter; film credits include *Mrs. Soffel, Swing Shift,* and *Philadelphia.*

O'Hara, Frank, 1926–1966: poet, playwright, and art critic; plays include *Love's Labour, Awake in Spain!,* and *The Houses at Fallen Hanging.*

Olivier, Sir Laurence, 1907–1989: British-born actor; the quintessential Shakespearean actor of his generation; seen in films *Hamlet, Henry V, Othello, King Lear, Richard III;* non-Shakespearean *Wuthering Heights, Rebecca, The Entertainer, Marathon Man,* and *The Boys from Brazil;* and for TV the movie *Love Among the Ruins* and the series *Brideshead Revisited;* enjoyed a long-term love affair with actor Danny Kaye.

Ong, Han, b. 1968: playwright; works include *Reason to Live, Bachelor Rat,* and *Symposium in Manila.*

Perkins, Anthony, 1932–1992: actor; films include *Friendly Persuasion, On the Beach,* and *Murder on the Orient Express;* best known as Norman Bates in the Hitchcock thriller *Psycho;* later made *Psycho II* and *Psycho III.*

Perry, Reverend Troy: minister and author; founder of the Universal Fellowship of Metropolitan Community Churches (MCC), a Protestant denomination primarily for lesbians and gay men; author of the memoir *The Lord Is My Shepherd and He Knows I'm Gay.*

Picano, Felice, b. 1944: writer and publisher; author of *Ambidextrous, Smart as the Devil, Eyes,* and *The Lure;* founder of the Sea Horse Press/Gay Presses of New York.

Plunkett, Walter, 1902–1982: Hollywood costume designer; films include *Gone with the Wind, Adam's Rib, Kiss Me Kate, Lust for Life, How the West Was Won,* and *An American in Paris,* for which he shared an Academy Award with designers Orry-Kelly and Irene Sharaff.

Porter, Cole, 1892–1964: composer and lyricist; most famous songs include "Night and Day," "You're the Top," "I Get a Kick Out of You," "I've Got You Under My Skin," and "Begin the Beguine"; Broadway shows included *Kiss Me, Kate, Anything Goes,* and *The Gay Divorcee.*

Power, Tyrone, 1913–1958: actor; films include *The Razor's Edge, Alexander's Ragtime Band, Blood and Sand, The Mark of Zorro, The Sun Also Rises,* and *Witness for the Prosecution.*

Preston, John, 1945–1993: writer and editor; works include *Personal Dispatches, Hometowns, The Big Gay Book,* and a host of gay male porn novels, including the classic *Mr. Benson;* coedited *Sister and Brother* (with Joan Nestle) just before his death.

Purdy, James, b. 1923: writer; novels include *Garments the Living Wear, Out with the Stars,* and *In a Shallow Grave.*

Rambo, Dack, died 1994: actor; starred on TV's *Dallas* in the 1980s.

Darrell Yates Rist
*(Photo by
Mariette Patty
Allen)*

Reed, Robert, 1933–1992: actor; star of TV show *The Brady Bunch*; TV movie
credits included *Rich Man, Poor Man, Roots,* and *Scruples.*

Reeves, Ken: politician and mayor of Cambridge, Massachusetts; only openly gay
African-American mayor in the United States.

Richardson, Tony, 1928–1991: British-born film director; films include *Look Back
in Anger, The Entertainer, The Loneliness of the Long Distance Runner, Tom
Jones, The Loved One, A Taste of Honey, A Delicate Balance, The Hotel New
Hampshire,* and *Blue Sky.*

Riggs, Marlon, 1957–1994: documentary filmmaker; films include *Tongues Untied, Color Adjustment,* and *Ethnic Notions.*

Rist, Darryl Yates, died 1994: writer and activist; one of cofounders of the Gay and
Lesbian Alliance Against Defamation; author of *Heartlands,* which chronicled a
trip across gay America.

Ritts, Herb, b. 1952: celebrity and fashion photographer; photos have appeared on
the covers of *Vogue, Vanity Fair, Rolling Stone,* and *GQ,* and have spearheaded
the ad campaigns of such companies as Armani, Calvin Klein (remember Marky
Mark in his underwear?), and The Gap; also director of TV commercials for
Levi's, Calvin Klein, and Chanel.

Paul Rudnick
(*Photo by*
Terry Boggis)

Rivera, Rey "Sylvia Lee," b. 1951: drag queen and gay rights activist; one of original participants in the Stonewall riot of 1969.

Robinson, Max, 1939–1988: broadcast journalist; first African-American network news anchorman.

Rodwell, Craig, 1941–1993: gay rights activist; founder and owner of the first gay bookstore in the United States, the Oscar Wilde Memorial Bookshop in New York City.

Rofes, Eric, b. 1954: activist and author of seven books, including "Reviving the Tribe: Regenerating Gay Men's Sexuality and Culture in the Ongoing Epidemic." (Haworth Press, 1996); former executive director of the Los Angeles Gay and Lesbian Community Services Center and of the Shanti Project in San Francisco.

Rorem, Ned, b. 1924: classical composer; won a Pulitzer Prize for *Air Music*.

Rouilard, Richard: journalist and editor; former senior editor at the *Los Angeles*

RuPaul, flanked by the Academy Award–winning costume designers of the movie *The Adventures of Priscilla, Queen of the Desert* (*Copyright Ken Levine, Berliner Studio; Courtesy of Gay and Lesbian Alliance Against Defamation [GLAAD]*)

Herald Examiner and executive editor of *The Advocate;* currently a senior editorial consultant at the *Los Angeles Times.*

Rudnick, Paul, b. 1957: playwright and screenwriter; author of plays *Jeffrey* and *I Hate Hamlet;* screenplay of *Addams Family Values.*

RuPaul, b. 1960: singer, entertainer, and drag queen; recordings include the albums *Supermodel of the World* and *Soul Food;* author of autobiography, *Lettin' It All Hang Out.*

Russo, Vito, 1946–1990: writer and film critic; author of *The Celluloid Closet,* the definitive book on homosexuality in film.

Rustin, Bayard, 1912-1987: civil rights activist; chief organizer of 1963 civil rights march of Washington.

Saint, Assotto, 1958–1994: Haitian-born poet and editor; founder of Galiens Press and Other Countries, an African-American gay male writers' workshop; books

Vito Russo *(From the collection of the Lesbian and Gay Community Services Center–New York)*

include the anthologies *Here to Dare* and *The Road Before Us,* and the poetry collections *Triple Trouble* and *Stations.*

Sandler, Barry, b. 1951: screenwriter; author of *Making Love, Kansas City Bomber,* and *The Mirror Crack'd.*

Santayana, George, 1863–1952: Spanish-born poet and philosopher; famous for the adage "Those who cannot remember the past are doomed to repeat it."

Sargent, Dick, 1933–1994: actor; best known as "the second Darren" in the 1960s TV series *Bewitched.*

Schlesinger, John, b. 1926: British-born film director; films include *Darling, Far from the Madding Crowd, Midnight Cowboy, Sunday, Bloody Sunday, The Day of the Locust, Yanks,* and *Madame Sousatzka.*

Schmaltz, Jeffrey, 1954–1993: journalist; *New York Times* reporter who covered AIDS before succumbing to it himself.

Schuyler, James, 1923–1993: poet; works include *Salute, Alfred and Guinevere, May 24th or So,* and the Pulitzer Prize–winning *The Morning of the Poem.*

Scott, Randolph, 1898–1987: actor; best known as star of westerns such as *Home on the Range, Jesse James, Carson City, Hangman's Knot,* and *Belle Starr.*

Shawn, Ted, 1891–1972: dancer and choreographer; founded Denishawn school, a dance academy, with wife Ruth St. Denis; the Ted Shawn Dance Theater was the first theater designed especially for dance; his farm in Mass-

Assotto Saint
(*Copyright ©
1991 by Morgan
Gwenwald*)

achusetts became the setting for Jacob's Pillow, the annual summer school and festival.

Shilts, Randy, 1951–1994: journalist; first openly gay reporter on a major U.S. newspaper (the *San Francisco Chronicle*); author of *The Mayor of Castro Street, And the Band Played On,* and *Conduct Unbecoming.*

Signorile, Michelangelo, b. 1960: writer and activist; gained notoriety for his regular column in *OutWeek* magazine "outing" celebrities and public figures; author of *Queer in America: Sex, the Media, and the Closets of Power* and *Outing Yourself.*

Sondheim, Stephen, b. 1930: composer, lyricist, writer; Broadway shows include *A Funny Thing Happened on the Way to the Forum, Company, A Little Night Music, Sunday in the Park with George, Sweeney Todd,* and *Follies;* wrote Madonna's show tunes for film *Dick Tracy;* cowrote the screenplay for *The Last of Sheilah* with Anthony Perkins.

Stambolian, George: writer and editor; edited the pioneering series of anthologies of gay male short fiction *Men on Men.*

Strub, Sean: businessman, writer, and publisher; founder of Strubco, a fund-raising and marketing firm that has pioneered in the area of lesbian and gay direct mail; founder and publisher of *Poz,* a magazine dedicated to HIV/AIDS issues; author of *Rating America's Corporate Conscience.*

Studds, Gerry Eastman, b. 1937: Massachusetts member of U.S. House of Representatives.

Sullivan, Andrew, b. 1963: British-born editor of the conservative magazine *The New Republic* since 1991.

Sweeney, Terry: actor and writer; former regular on *Saturday Night Live,* where he developed a memorable impersonation of Nancy Reagan; star of one-man show *It's Still My Turn,* as Nancy Reagan; wrote screenplays for films *Shag* and *Love at Stake.*

Sweeney, Tim: activist and lawyer; former executive director of Lambda Legal Defense and Education Fund and of Gay Men's Health Crisis.

Sylvester, 1946–1988: singer; disco hits included "You Make Me Feel (Mighty Real)" and "Dance (Disco Heat.).

Taylor, Robert, 1911–1969: actor; films included *Magnificent Obsession, Camille, A Yank at Oxford, Billy the Kid, Ivanhoe,* and *Quo Vadis.*

Thomson, Virgil, 1897–1989: composer; cowrote the opera *The Mother of Us All* with Gertrude Stein.

Thurman, Wallace, 1902–1934: writer; author of *Infants of the Spring,* about the Harlem Renaissance.

Tom of Finland, 1919–1991: artist and illustrator; since 1950s was famous for his explicitly sexual drawings of muscular, well-endowed gay men, usually in uniform or leather; an icon in the realm of gay male erotic illustration.

Van Sant, Gus, b. 1952: film director; credits include *Even Cowgirls Get the Blues, Drugstore Cowboy,* and *My Own Private Idaho.*

Van Vechten, Carl, 1880–1940: writer and photographer; best-known works, *Nigger Heaven* and *The Blind Bow-Boy.*

Vidal, Gore, b. 1925: writer; works include the novels *The City and the Pillar, Myra Breckinridge, Lincoln,* and *Live from Golgotha*; and screenplays *The Best Man, Ben-Hur* (uncredited), and *Suddenly Last Summer.*

Villard, Tom, 1953–1994: actor; films include *Heartbreak Ridge* and *My Girl*; regular on TV show *We Got It Made.*

Waddell, Dr. Tom, 1937–1987: Olympic decathlon athlete; physician; founder of Gay Games in 1982.

Warhol, Andy, 1930–1987: pop artist and filmmaker; films included cinema-verité *Chelsea Girls, Trash,* and *Heat;* museum dedicated to his work opened in Pittsburgh in 1994.

Waters, John, b. 1946: film director; films include *Polyester, Mondo Trasho, Cry-Baby, Hairspray,* and *Serial Mom.*

We'wha, 1849–1896: one of the most famous Native American berdaches; member of Zuni nation.

Webb, Clifton, 1891–1966: actor; famous for playing a "deadly sissy" in films such as *Laura* and *The Razor's Edge*; other films include *Cheaper by the Dozen, Stars and Stripes Forever, Three Coins in the Fountain,* and *The Man Who Never Was.*

Whale, James, 1896–1957: film director; famous for horror films such as *Franken-stein, The Invisible Man,* and *The Bride of Frankenstein.*

White, Andrew Dickson, 1832–1918; educator, historian, and diplomat; one of the founders of Cornell University; later ambassador to Germany.

White, Edmund, b. 1940: writer; books include *Genet: A Biography* and novels *A Boy's Own Story* and *The Beautiful Room Is Empty;* cowrote collection of stories *The Darker Proof* with Adam Mars-Jones.

White, Mel, b. 1940: writer, activist, dean of Dallas's Cathedral of Hope congre-gation; formerly a ghostwriter for such noted evangelical homophobes as Jerry Falwell and Pat Robertson.

Whitman, Walt, 1819–1892: poet; most famous collection, *Leaves of Grass.*

Wilder, Thornton, 1897–1976: writer; plays include *Our Town, The Skin of Our Teeth,* (which both won Pulitzer Prizes) and novels include *The Bridge of San Luis Rey.*

Williams, Tennessee, 1911–1983: playwright; works include *The Glass Menagerie; Suddenly Last Summer; The Night of the Iguana;* and *A Streetcar Named De-sire* and *Cat on a Hot Tin Roof,* both of which won Pulitzer Prizes.

Wilson, Billy, 1935–1994: choreographer and director; Broadway credits included *Bubbling Brown Sugar, Guys and Dolls,* and *Stop the World—I Want to Get Off.*

Wilson, Lanford, b. 1937: playwright; works include *Balm in Gilead, Fifth of July, Hot l Baltimore, Burn This,* and the Pulitzer Prize–winning *Talley's Folly.*

Wilson, Phill: activist; current public policy director at AIDS Project Los Angeles; cofounder (with Mandy Carter) of the Black Gay and Lesbian Leadership Forum's Fight the Right program.

Wojnarowicz, David, died 1992: artist and writer; books include *Close to the Knives* and *Memories That Smell Like Gasoline.*

Wolfe, George C., b. 1954: stage director; credits include *Angels in America, The Colored Museum, Jelly's Last Jam,* and *Spunk;* artistic director of the New York Shakespeare Festival/Joseph Papp Public Theater.

Woolley, Monty, 1888–1963: actor; films include *The Man Who Came to Dinner, Young Dr. Kildare, Irish Eyes Are Smiling, Night and Day,* and *Kismet.*

Zane, Arnie, 1948–1988: dancer and choreographer; cofounder of Bill T. Jones/Arnie Zane Dance Company.

Zeffirelli, Franco, b. 1923: Italian-born film director; films include *The Taming of the Shrew, Romeo and Juliet, Brother Sun, Sister Moon, Endless Love,* and *Hamlet* (with Mel Gibson).

III

‸

Say What?

Quotable Quotes by and About Gay Men

‸

I WANT YOUR SEX

A cock's pleasure is like a fist, concentrated; anal pleasure is diffused, an open palm, and the pleasure of an anal orgasm is founded on relaxation. It's hard to understand how a man can write well if he doesn't like to be fucked.

—ROBERT GLUCK, 1982

I want what seems like a complete contradiction. I want society to cease viewing gays as defined solely by our sexuality, and at the same time I want the freedom to be as unabashedly sexual as I wish.

—VITO RUSSO, film critic, 1980

How the hell would I know what the big deal about sex is? I haven't gotten laid in months.

—TONY KUSHNER, playwright, 1994

There's nothing great about sex—never was. What usually comes from it? Sweat, fatigue, and dirty linens. . . .

—QUENTIN CRISP, writer-actor, 1994

When a straight guy meets a gay guy, right away he thinks to himself that the gay guy wants to suck his dick. I say, "Doll, don't flatter yourself!"

—SCOTT VALENTINE, actor, 1992

The best homosexuality is in America, like the best of everything else, and California, where all national tendencies achieve their most hyperbolic expression, is a living beach of writhing male bodies.

—ANTHONY BURGESS, 1979

Every woman's husband, and every man's wife.

> —popular Roman epithet for JULIUS CAESAR

I like opening up. I like all the tensing and relaxing of muscle and meat that fucking demands. I want it—in this case, a cock—inside me, going deep. Getting fucked gives me that feeling of openness, receptivity, and that fantastic sense of pulling something inside myself.

> —THOMAS MEYER, poet

I WANT YOUR LOVE

I am the love that dare not speak its name.

> —LORD ALFRED DOUGLAS, 1894

I think, as gay men, we're attracted to all the bad stuff in men. We want the tough guy—this butch, ideal man. That's terrible. It's the worst kind of relationship. It's like we all want the right to sing Billie Holiday songs or something.

> —HARVEY FIERSTEIN, 1994

Your love was wonderful to me, passing the love of women.

> —DAVID TO JONATHAN, 2 Samuel I:26

How idiotic people are when they are in love. What an age-old devastating disease!

> —NOEL COWARD, playwright

I like homosexuality where the lovers are friends all their lives, and there are many lovers and many friends.

> —ALLEN GINSBERG, poet

I want to love a strong man of the lower classes and be loved by him, and even hurt by him.

> —E. M. FORSTER, writer

PERSONALLY POLITICAL

I'm in bed with this guy and I hear the door to my room open. A little later, I look up, and there's a man standing over us in full police drag. My first thought was, This can't be happening.

> —MICHAEL HARDWICK, twenty-eight-year-old Atlanta man arrested in his own home on charges of sodomy by a policeman who was trying to serve a warrant for a minor traffic violation. Hardwick's case eventually went to the Supreme Court, where the constitutionality of the states' sodomy laws was upheld.

To be overtly homosexual, in a culture that denigrates and hates homosexuals, is to be political.

—MICHAEL BRONSKI, writer, 1984

I speak for the individual. For anyone out there who's ever had a dream and has had to listen to "Honey, you can't do that." "We don't allow blacks here." "We don't allow fags here." "We don't allow women in this bar." I am a giant "Fuck you" to bigotry. Buddha, Krishna, Jesus, and now RuPaul.

—RUPAUL, drag performer, 1994

W. H. Auden wrote, ". . . we must love one another or die." He then changed this to ". . . we must love one another and die." Was the first injunction impossible to achieve? I think it is. I can't love everyone. I don't denigrate love. I've learned to respect the word respect. It is what is most important for daily living, for getting along with others. We must respect one another, no matter what shade, what shape, what orientation. Beyond this, I fail. I cannot tolerate intolerance.

—PAUL CADMUS, painter

Sarah Jane Moore got life for missing Gerald Ford.

—Spectator at Dan White's trial. White, former San Francisco supervisor, shot and killed openly gay city supervisor Harvey Milk and San Francisco mayor George Moscone.

We're fine for show during Gay Pride Week when a little color is needed, or for a quick fuck in the dark, when none of their friends are looking, but middle-class whites don't want to pass along any useful job or investment information or include us in their social circles. They don't hire us to work in their bars and businesses, and after a roll in the hay, they just may not speak the next time they see you.

—Unnamed black gay man quoted in a 1982 article in *The Advocate*

The Air Force pinned a medal on me for killing a man and discharged me for making love to one.

—FORMER AIR FORCE SERGEANT LEONARD MATLOVICH (1943–1988), 1975 military plaintiff

It is better to be hated for what one is than loved for what one is not.

—ANDRE GIDE (1869–1951), French writer

They've lost that wounded look that fags all had ten years ago. . . .

—ALLEN GINSBERG, poet, after the Stonewall Riots, 1969

Would you ask me how I dare to compare the civil rights struggle with the struggle for lesbian and gay rights? I can compare them and I do compare them, because I know what it means to be called a "nigger" and I know what it means to be called a "faggot," and I understand the differences in the marrow of my bones. And I can sum up that difference on one word: none.

—MEL BOOZER, after being nominated for vice president of the United States at the Democratic Convention in New York City in 1980

I came here to let them know I say ptui *to their rejection of the proposal.*

> —PEARL, a bearded man in drag who showed up at an Oklahoma City City Council meeting in October 1993 to protest the council's rejection of a gay rights measure. Pearl, who performs in bars as Pollyanna Peters, carried a sign reading "PTUI."

As much of gay society disgusts me as hetero society. There are as many creepy, clony, Republican, preppy, uptight, materialistic homos struggling to conform as straight ones. It's repulsive, and it shouldn't be. Just being a minority should push people toward the edge.

> —MYKE REILLY, of the band Voice Farm, 1993

I believe the human family is a single unit. Therefore, one has to fight for justice for all. If I do not fight bigotry wherever it is, bigotry is thereby strengthened. And to the degree that it is strengthened, it will, thereby, have the power to turn on me.

> —BAYARD RUSTIN, civil rights activist, organizer of Dr. Martin Luther King's 1963 March on Washington for Civil Rights

At this point people call me a living legend, or, humorously, the world's oldest living homosexual, or the grandfather or the great-grandfather of the gay movement, which is not technically correct.

> —FRANK KAMENY, founder, in 1961, of the Washington, D.C., chapter of the Mattachine Society

I was sworn in [as municipal court judge] eighteen years to the day I was arrested at California Hall [for attending the landmark costume ball of the Council on Religion and the Homosexual, in San Francisco in 1965].

> —JUDGE HERB DONALDSON, on being appointed judge by Governor Jerry Brown.

FAGGOTRY

White people invented black people to give white people identity. . . . Straight cats invented faggots so they can sleep with them without becoming faggots themselves.

> —JAMES BALDWIN AND NIKKI GIOVANNI, 1993

We all know a fag is a homosexual gentleman who has just left the room.

> —TRUMAN CAPOTE

In this town, a faggot is a homosexual gentleman who's had a few flops.

> —ANONYMOUS gay television producer quoted in *TV Guide*

It is a great shock at the age of five or six to find that in a world of Gary Coopers you are the Indian.

—JAMES BALDWIN

They tell me Mr. Hemingway usually kicks people like me in the crotch.

—TENNESSEE WILLIAMS, when critic Kenneth Tynan offered to introduce him to Hemingway, 1959

A patriot put in prison for loving his country loves his country, and a poet in prison for loving boys loves boys. To have altered my life would have been to have admitted that Uranian [homosexual] love is ignoble. I hold it to be noble—more noble than other forms.

—OSCAR WILDE, 1890s

ON THE DEATH OF A LOVER

When he died, I went to pieces. I retreated into a shell. For nine months, I wouldn't speak to a living soul. I just clammed up. I wouldn't answer the telephone and I wouldn't leave the house.

—TENNESSEE WILLIAMS, on the death of his lover Frank Merlo, from lung cancer, in 1963

ART AND SENSIBILITY

The best thing about being a gay artist is you get to meet other gay artists and go hang out.

—GUS VAN SANT, filmmaker

It's not enough to be an artist. If you live in cataclysmic times, if the lightning rod of history hits you, then all art is political, and all art that is not consciously so still partakes of the politics, if only to run away.

—PAUL MONETTE, writer

If I had to assess what I've done up to this point, I'm very proud that I represent the possibility for black gay men to write and create, that the possibility does exist, that you may even be able to do it full-time.

—ESSEX HEMPHILL, writer, 1993

A streetwise kid who figures he can make a lot of money by packaging his slick portraits and S&M photography as art . . . blatantly tailored to appeal to interior decorators with vulgar taste. . . . These images were not born of passion, but of boredom and cynicism. . . .

—*CHRISTOPHER STREET* review on the photography of Robert Mapplethorpe

Oh, I , you know, I mean, of course I like Henry James. I'm just a little frustrated with Henry James.

—DAVID LEAVITT, author

An artist's first responsibility is to tell the truth as he or she sees it. You really get into trouble if you try to please some imaginary committee.

—RON NYSWANER, screenwriter and playwright

My desire is memory, and yet I know it is not enough to just remember. I feel that my job as a writer is to be a documentarian. Record the losses. In a poem, maybe, but also in a rant.

—LUIS ALFARO, writer, performance artist

At one moment with my cock in his arse, the image was, and as I write still is, overpoweringly erotic, and I reflect that whatever the Sunday papers have said about Crimes of Passion *was of little or no importance compared with this.*

—JOE ORTON, regarding the mixed reviews of his play *Crimes of Passion*

They used to say my work was homosexual and therefore had no validity, which is like saying if a Negro prepares food, the food is dirty.

—JAMES PURDY, 1974

Fun and wit are their own justification, but camp fun has other merits too: it's a form of self-defense. Particularly in the past, the fact that gay men could so sharply and brightly make fun of themselves meant that the real awfulness of their situation could be kept at bay. . . . Camp kept, and keeps, a lot of gay men going.

—RICHARD DYER, 1977

I WISH I'D SAID THAT

Remember, the serpent is still living in the Garden of Eden—only the heterosexual couple was expelled.

—EDWARD CARPENTER

I sleep with Mr. Williams.

—FRANK MERLO (1922–1963), secretary and lover to Tennessee Williams, when asked by Hollywood mogul Jack Warner at dinner one night, "And what do *you* do, young man?"

When I'm introduced at functions with Mark, if someone asks me what I do, I like to borrow from the story about Tennessee Williams and Frank Merlo. I tell them, "I sleep with Mr. Thompson."

—MALCOLM BOYD, writer, about his life partner, the writer Mark Thompson

Above All, Audacity.

—HARRY HAY, founder of The Mattachine Society

We're tapping into a very old and venerable tradition. The drag queen as nun—it's one of the classic "types."

> —SISTER MISSIONARY POSITION OF THE SISTERS OF PERPETUAL INDULGENCE, direct action/drag performance group

I would sooner have fifty unnatural vices, than one unnatural virtue. It is unnatural virtue that makes the world, for those who suffer, such a premature Hell.

> —OSCAR WILDE, 1897

I have never penetrated a woman in my life, so it is unlikely to be me.

> —BOY GEORGE, at a court hearing, denying a woman's claims that he is the father of her seven-year-old son, 1993

Hopefully, history will record that I was hell of a nice guy and that the people who have criticized me are a bunch of fools and bimbos.

> —RANDY SHILTS, author of the controversial *And The Band Played On*, 1994

My life is a red ribbon. In fact, sometimes I feel like a big red ribbon with a little Paul Monette pinned to the lapel.

> —PAUL MONETTE, writer, 1993

Well, this should be interesting.

> —DR. TOM WADDELL's final words; Waddell was a former Olympian and founder of the Gay Games

---

AIDS

Before AIDS, going to the baths had an aura almost like smoking. People knew it wasn't too good for them, but it was socially acceptable. Now it has the aura of shooting heroin.

> —MARK CHATAWAY, 1988

The arrival of a fatal, sexually transmissible disease, the perfect image to revive the most ancient and popular hostilities against us and within us, is rearranging the practical details of our lives, the imagery of our lives, our self-perceptions.

> —NEIL BARTLETT, 1988

I've lost over twenty friends [to AIDS]. I've seen a world vanish—a culture that has been oppressed in one generation, liberated in the next, and wiped out in the next.

> —EDMUND WHITE, writer

Sex isn't the enemy. That's what I wish people would understand. The disease is the enemy.

> —HARVEY FIERSTEIN, 1988

A lot of Europeans have no compassion when it comes to AIDS. They see it as a gay disease that's been put on earth by God to punish homosexuals. And the pope, that bitch, doesn't do anything to change those views. Fuck the pope—if it is not already done.

—JEAN PAUL GAULTIER, designer, 1993

What disturbs me is how gay men all over this country can sit around with their friends dying, their lovers dying, their lives threatened, and not get off their asses and be activists again. Do they have a death wish? What's the matter with them?

—VITO RUSSO, film critic

Like some rabid animal, AIDS picked me up by the scruff of my neck, shook me senseless, and spat me out forever changed. I am today a totally different person than I was when the decade and epidemic began. AIDS has been a cosmic kick in the ass, a challenge to finally begin living fully.

—MICHAEL CALLEN, singer, AIDS activist

AIDS is character-building. It's made me see all of the shallow things we cling to, like ego and vanity. Of course, I'd rather have a few more T-cells and a little less character.

—RANDY SHILTS, author of *And the Band Played On*

I'd rather be writing glib novels than going through the holocaust.

—PAUL MONETTE, writer, 1993

Something is wrong with the health-care system when a wealthy man and a friend of the President has to go to Europe for treatment.

—RON NAJMAN, media director for the NGLTF, on Rock Hudson's trips to Paris to receive experimental treatments with HPA-23

I may eventually die as a result of this disease, but I would consider my death an act of murder for the lack of government funding. I would consider it murder by my own government.

—DIEGO RIVERA, AIDS activist

The hardest thing is just knowing that there's so much more stuff to do.

—KEITH HARING, artist, six months before his death from AIDS

IDENTITY: ON BEING TRUE TO OURSELVES

Eventually I not only come to terms with being a gay man, but I came to recognize that I love being one, and want to be no other. That's been, and continues to be, a miraculously wonderful coming of age.

—LARRY KRAMER

I remember members of the Mattachine Society saying that we had to look like heterosexuals—that in order to talk to the press we should look as normal as possible. We young ones yelled back. "Fuck you! We are what we are!" In our own way, we were screaming, "We're here, we're queer, get used to it."

—HARVEY FIERSTEIN

Better than I've ever felt in my life.

—REP. GERRY STUDDS (D-Mass.), after being asked how he felt now that he'd come out

I received no end of letters, kindly meant, but full of warnings and advice—deprecating the idea of a menage without a woman, as a thing unheard of . . . hinting at the risk to my health, to my comfort, at bad cooking, untidy rooms, and an abundance of cobwebs, not to mention the queer look of the thing.

—EDWARD CARPENTER, when he and his lover decided to live together, 1916

I've been discriminated against by gay people. I've been discriminated against by black people. I've been discriminated against by everybody and what it all boils down to is this: You have to learn how to love yourself.

—RUPAUL, drag performer, 1993

Homosexuality is a way of life that I've grown accustomed to. What's the big deal about my sexuality?

—JOHNNY MATHIS, singer/songwriter

How annoyed I am with Society for wasting my time by making homosexuality criminal. The subterfuges, the self-consciousness that might have been avoided.

—E. M. FORSTER, writer

Transsexual dressing is a gay contribution to the realization that we're not a hundred percent masculine or feminine, but a mixture of hormones—and not being afraid of that natural self which the hormones dictate.

—ALLEN GINSBERG, poet, 1987

We had a rabbi perform our wedding. She wore a sleeveless red mini-dress. My Aunt Sadie was much more freaked out about that, than about the fact that we were getting married.

—ROB EPSTEIN, Academy Award–winning filmmaker, about his wedding to Jeffrey Friedman, with whom he won an Oscar for *Common Threads: Stories from the AIDS Quilt*

You do grow weary of "courageous" announcements of Homosexual Studies—of scientists achieving breakthroughs on this "complex condition." Do the scientists have courses in Heterosexual Studies?

—NED ROREM, composer and writer

Hey, I'm not the only one!

　　—DAVID KOPAY, former NFL running back who came out publicly in 1975

God does not despise anything that God has created.

　　　　—JOHN J. MCNEILL, former priest, spiritual leader

I get so tired of these stories about, "Oh, the torture and torment of coming out." There's no torment in coming out. The torment is in being in.

　　　　　　—ARMISTEAD MAUPIN, writer

IN THE NAVY

If there's a place in the Guinness records for the woman kissed most by gay men, I'm it.

　　　　—DOROTHY HAJDYS, mother of slain sailor Allen Schindler, 1993

The men had not been home or had a furlough or leave or anything like that for two or three years. Years, not months. They were under the stress of war, and they were going into combat again where a lot of them were not going to come out. So if they went up under the coco trees and sucked a little cock and jacked off together or something like that, so what? Who was harmed? Nobody. That's the way the armed forces should look at it. The armed forces could not operate without homosexuals. Never could. Never has. And never will.

　　—HAL CALL, executive director of the Mattachine Society since 1953

We don't have ourselves dry-cleaned. We've been taking showers for a long time.

　　—BARNEY FRANK (D-Mass.), deriding straight soldiers' fears about gays in the barracks, 1993

Everyone in my unit called me "Sis" or "Simone," which was my drag name. No one called me by my name and rank.

　　—PERRY WATKINS, openly gay Army sergeant, who served successfully and received an hornorable discharge from the military; Watkins even peformed in drag on base.

In 1993 I lost a flourishing military career because our president cowered to the bigots who would decree that we be stoned to death had they that power. As much as I lost, though, I gained in the love and acceptance of my community. In 1993 I was reborn as a proud gay man. . . .

　　—JOE ZUNIGA, Sixth U.S. Army Soldier of the Year, discharged after coming out

Our biggest mistake was unconditionally believing in them, believing that they were really not lying to us, placing too much power and too much faith in them.

We should never have put our fate in one individual's hands, especially in a non-gay individual's hands.

> —DAVID MIXNER, on Clinton's reversal on lifting the military ban, 1994

The military ban has gone from a "No way" issue to an "Oh shit" issue in Congress.

> —CONGRESSMAN BARNEY FRANK, 1993

FLORIDA SUNSHINE

Why do you think homosexuals are called fruits? It's because they eat the forbidden fruit of the tree of life . . . which is male sperm. . . . There is even a Jockey short called Forbidden Fruit. Very subtle. Did you know that?

> —ANITA BRYANT

As to Anita's fear that she'll be assassinated? The only people who might shoot Anita Bryant are music lovers.

> —GORE VIDAL, 1978

Oh, Squeaky Fromme, where are you when we need you?

> —JOHN WATERS, when asked his opinion of Anita Bryant

THE BAD GUYS: INFAMOUS HOMOPHOBES

The poor homosexuals—they have declared war upon nature, and now nature is exacting an awful retribution.

> —PATRICK BUCHANAN, presidential candidate

I think obviously you can't compare a lime to a lemon in the same exact mold, but they are similar in that they are both citrus fruits.

> —LON MABON, anti-gay Oregon political organizer, explaining why he considers it appropriate to compare gays and lesbians to people who commit sex crimes

It is easier to nauseate than educate.

> —TONY MARCO, cofounder of Colorado for Family Values, on his group's publicity tactics for getting the state's antigay amendment passed

I have always believed that the body of man-made law must be founded upon the higher natural law.

> —FORMER GOVERNOR RONALD REAGAN upon the repeal of California's 103-year-old sodomy laws

I love him as much as any of my sons, but I don't think there's any place for him in the military.

> —MARINE COLONEL FRED PECK, testifying before the Senate Armed Services Committee about his gay son, Scott Peck, who resigned from the military because of his sexual orientation, 1993

I warn you . . . these kissy-poo fag preachers telling you it's OK to play with gerbils and worship the rectum will send you to hell, and Fred Phelps is the best friend you fags have got in this world.

> —FRED PHELPS, in a letter to *The Advocate,* 1993

Mr. Hoover would like to be taken off your mailing list.

> —FBI AGENT JOHN A. O'BEIRNE to Frank Kameny of the Washington, D.C., Mattachine Society, regarding the Mattachine's *Gazette*, which was sent to J. Edgar Hoover, director of the FBI, and other public officials, including the President.

THE GOOD GUYS: FAMOUS FRIENDS

Are you saying child slaughter and homosexuality are the same thing?

> —REP. TED WEISS (D-N.Y.) to Connie Marshner of the National Pro-Family Coalition, who was testifying at a congressional subcommittee hearing on federal gay rights legislation; Marshner responded: "I think they're in a very close category."

If a woman-in-a-man's-body goes after a man, is she attracted to the same or the opposite sex? If a man-in-a-woman's-body wants a woman, is he a lesbian or straight? Prejudice is only cowardice in the face of complexity.

> —JAY LEMKE, anthropologist, on transsexuality

AIDS is not the only issue in the nation tonight. Be concerned about AIDS, but also sickle-cell anemia. . . . Be concerned about the human rights of gays, but also Native Americans trapped on reservations and blacks in ghettos. I would urge you, as I urge black people . . . the bigger you get beyond yourselves, the more you protect yourselves.

> —JESSE JACKSON, addressing a gay fund-raising dinner in New York City

It does not appear that Reverend Hart is an advocate for civil rights as most people understand the term.

> —Senator commenting on the nomination of radio evangelist Sam Hart to fill a vacancy on the U.S. Civil Rights Commission; Hart said, among other things, that "homosexuals can repent like any other sinner. . . ."

We believe that the rights of all people must be protected and guaranteed. We believe that the gay and lesbian community must be supported in their civil rights as well as their right for their own sexual preference.

—CORETTA SCOTT KING

Given a choice between sharing a park with homosexuals or a bunch of white-sheeted, racist, hate-peddling losers, we think we would prefer the homosexuals.

—*ARLINGTON TEXAS DAILY NEWS* editorial denouncing an upcoming anti-gay rally by the Ku Klux Klan in the city's Randol Mill Park

The threat of AIDS should be sufficient to permit a sex education curriculum.... There is no doubt that we need sex education in schools and that it include information on heterosexual and homosexual relationships.... The need is critical and the price of neglect is high.

—SURGEON GENERAL C. EVERETT KOOP

I've learned that God doesn't punish people. I've learned that God doesn't dislike homosexuals, like a lot of Christians think. AIDS isn't their fault, just like it isn't my fault.

—RYAN WHITE, sixteen-year-old PWA

Dan Quayle was asked the other day if he suppports sending military aid to the Straits of Hormuz. "Well, it's all right to send it to the straights," he replied, "but the gays are on their own."

—JOHNNY CARSON, on Dan Quayle

COME OUT, COME OUT WHEREVER YOU ARE

There is no truth to the rumors that Bert and Ernie are married.

—JIM HENSON PRODUCTIONS, in response to rumors surrounding a November 1993 performance in Tupelo, Mississippi

Every gay person must come out. As difficult as it is, you must tell your immediate family, you must tell your relatives, you must tell your friends if indeed they are your friends, you must tell your neighbors, you must tell the people you work with, you must tell the people at the stores you shop in. And once they realize that we are indeed their children, that we are indeed everywhere—every myth, every lie, every innuendo will be destroyed once and for all. And once, once you do, you will feel so much better.

—HARVEY MILK, in a speech following the defeat of Proposition 6, which would have barred homosexuals from teaching in the public schools.

I think outing is wrong and unconscionable.... It makes people more afraid, not less afraid. I think that terrorists like Michelangelo Signorile have not done any

good. I think he's an angry, hostile, jealous guy who has his nose pressed up against the window at the party that he imagines is going on but that he hasn't been asked to.

—DAVID GEFFEN, 1993

BIOLOGY AS DESTINY?

I pride myself on being without question Yale's first (and oldest) woman graduate.

—DR. RENEE RICHARDS, famous MTF transsexual

Female animals can only produce a limited number of offspring, but males can produce almost infinite numbers. So it's a better strategy in evolutionary terms for males to be promiscuous, to try and screw as many females as they can. Females' best strategy is to remain selective and try and make sure that the males that do impregnate are the fittest in some sense. That's true in all mammals, and it's true in humans too. Straight men are basically restricted by the reluctance of women to be promiscuous, and gay men are not. So they tend to have more sex partners.

—SIMON LeVAY, biologist, author of *The Sexual Brain*, 1993

Homosexuality is a genetic means of high importance in preventing . . . disaster to the race . . . by acting to preserve variety and diversity in the range of traits inherited by each generation.

—HARRY HAY, *RFD*, 1975

SOURCES

The Advocate
BLK
Marcus, Eric. *Making History: The Struggle for Gay and Lesbian Equal Rights, 1945–1990.* HarperCollins, 1992.
OUT magazine
Rutledge, Leigh W. *Unnatural Quotations.* Alyson Publications, 1988.
_____. *The Gay Decades, From Stonewall to the Present: The People and Events That Shaped Gay Lives.* Plume, 1992.
Sherman, Phillip, and Samuel Bernstein. *Uncommon Heroes: A Celebration of Heroes and Role Models for Gay and Lesbian Americans.* Fletcher Press, 1994.

IV

I Wonder What *That* Means:

A Glossary of Sayings, Slang, Signs, and Symbols for Gay Men

Gay men have, over time, developed a language all their own—words and phrases that pertain to their culture, experiences, sexual behavior, and history. Some phrases, such as to let one's hair down and "closet," have infiltrated general usage, though with different meanings from the original. The following is a list of terms and sayings that are or have been common in gay lives, though not all of them are exclusive to gay men.

Note: Many slang terms specific to gay men in Quebec are anglicisms—un trick, un-fuck-buddy, etc.—and have been omitted from this list. (For a gay French Canadian glossary see Ghislain Lapointe's *Les mamelles de ma grand-mere; les mamelles de mon grand-frere: petit lexique quebecois incomplet*.)

AC/DC: In the 1960s, an adjective describing a person who had sex with either men or women; bisexual. The term came from the abbreviations for two types of electrical currents, alternating current and direct current.

ACTIVIST: One who actively engages in efforts to change the existing social or political order.

AMYL NITRITE: Drug used medically to revive heart patients, but also used by some gay men as an aphrodisiac to enhance sexual experience. Also called "poppers."

ANDROGYNE: In the early twentieth century, a scientific term for an effeminate gay man.

ANILINGUS: To tongue the anus. See *rim*.

ANONYMOUS SEX: Sex between consenting adults who don't know each other and never exchange full names.

AUNTIE: A derogatory term for an older gay man, especially one who is a gossip.

81

BACHELOR: A man who remains unmarried; in the early twentieth century, a euphemism or code word for homosexual.

BACK ROOM: A dark room designated for sex at the back of a bar or club. During the sexually experimental 1970s, gay men's bars initiated the use of back rooms for anonymous sex. Inspired by gay male sexual openness, lesbian clubs in cities such as New York and San Francisco began to feature back rooms in the early 1990s. In the age of AIDS, back rooms come equipped with safer sex items, such as condoms and latex gloves.

BAITING: The verbal attacking, insulting, taunting, or criticizing of lesbians and gay men on the basis of their sexual orientation.

BALLS: Testicles; also gutsiness or moxie, as in "She really has balls."

BASHING: Physical assault of lesbians and gay men on account of sexual orientation; also commonly called queer bashing, gay bashing, and fag bashing. See *Bias crime.*

BASKET: A man's crotch, particularly the eye-catching bulging of his genitals in tight pants.

BATHS/BATHHOUSE: turkish baths that were popular sites of gay male cruising and anonymous sexual encounters before the AIDS pandemic; also sometimes called "the tubs." Most bathhouses were closed in the mid-1980s out of concern for the spread of HIV.

BATTY-MAN: afro-Caribbean equivalent of "sissy."

B & D: Bondage and discipline; a form of sexual play in which one partner is tied up and the other (or others) "discipline" her or him, verbally and/or physically. See *S/M.*

BEARD: A person of the opposite sex, either heterosexual or homosexual, who knowingly dates or marries a closeted lesbian or gay man to provide that person with a heterosexual "disguise," usually for family or career purposes. "Beard" has been in use since the first half of this century and originally applied only to a straight woman who provided cover for a gay man. In his classic gay novel of 1948, *The City and the Pillar,* Gore Vidal wrote: "A number of women acted as outriders to the beautiful legion, and they were often called upon to be public escorts. They were known as 'beards.'" See also *Front marriage* and *Passing.*

BEAT OFF: see *Jerk off.*

BERDACHE: In approximately 130 American Indian cultures, a man or woman who was unable or unwilling to fit into the role assigned to his/her gender. The word is a French colonialist one (meaning "slave boy"), first used by explorers who observed and wrote about North American Indian "men-women" as early as the seventeenth century. Indian languages had their own words for these gender-benders, who were allowed to occupy a place somewhere between male and female and were often honored as healers and shamans. Male berdaches specialized in traditional women's skills, while female berdaches sometimes became recognized warriors and guides.

BIAS CRIME: A crime perpetrated on a person on account of his/her race or ethnicity, gender, religion, or sexual orientation; also called "hate crime." See also *Bashing.*

BISEXUAL/BI: A person who has sexual and emotional relationships with both women and men, though not necessarily at the same time.

BLACK TRIANGLE: A symbol in the shape of an inverted triangle adopted by lesbian culture in remembrance of the lesbians who were killed by the Nazis in Europe. Between 1933 and 1945, the Nazis rounded up and arrested millions of individuals whom they perceived as threats to their power, and incarcerated them in concentration camps. Each category of prisoner had its own identifying triangle or symbol. Included with Jews, homosexuals, and gypsies were thousands of "prostitutes, anti-socials, and misfits," who were required to wear an inverted black triangle sewn onto their clothing. Though the Nazis had no specific category for lesbians, it is believed that lesbians may have been included in the "anti-social" category. Women who wore the black triangle were often forced to have sex with male camp personnel, which may have been viewed as a way to "cure" lesbians.

BLOW JOB/BLOW: Oral stimulation of the penis; fellatio.

BONER: An erect penis; a hard-on.

BOTTOM: An erotic sex role; the "passive" recipient in sex. See also *Top*.

BRING OUT: To aid and abet the coming-out process, as in "He brought me out"; usually refers to an "experienced" gay man initiating a sexual relationship with a younger man who has never had homosexual sex.

BROWNING: Anal sex; in use since the mid-1900s. Also called brown holing or brown job. Related nouns for one who engages in anal sex include: the Brown family, brown-hatter, brownie, brownie king, and brownie queen.

BUFFET FLAT: An after-hours partying spot in Harlem of the 1920s, usually in someone's apartment, which was a common place for African-American lesbians and gay men to socialize. "Buffet" referred to a smorgasbord of sexual possibilities—straight, gay, group sex, etc.

BUGGERY: An archaic term for sodomy that dates back to the Middle Ages in Europe. The law in Tudor England on which colonial American sodomy laws were based was called "the buggery law."

BUNKER SHY: A young man afraid of being forced into homosexual sex. From an early nineteenth-century prison term.

BUTCH: (1) A lesbian who prefers masculine dress, style, expression, or identity. Though there have been butch lesbians throughout history, the term was probably first used in the United States in the 1940s. "Butch" was formerly a common nickname for a young boy and also the name of a severe men's haircut. (2) A gay man who is traditionally virile or "masculine" in speech, dress, and sexual behavior.

BUTT-RAMMING: Anal sex. Also called "butt fucking."

CAMP: A style of humor or satire based on exaggeration, artifice, and androgyny. Within the lesbian and gay community, the term most often refers to gay men assuming a comically exaggerated feminine manner in order to entertain; but there is also a tradition of lesbian camp. "High camp" is over the top. The word also appears as a verb, as in "to camp it up," and an adjective, "campy." According to Judy Grahn (*Another Mother Tongue*), "camp" comes from the British term "camping," which was the practice of young men wearing women's clothing in a play and which in turn came from the French *campagne*, the outdoor space where medieval minstrels performed.

CAMP NAMES: In camp, the exchange of gay men's names for women's. George, for example, might be called Georgette; Robert, Roberta. There are also standard camp names by which gay men refer to each other, like Mary or, especially among African-American gay men, Miss Thing.

CANNIBAL: See *Man-eater.*

CATAMITE: Originally (since the 1500s), a young boy or man kept by an older man for sexual purposes; now, any male bottom in anal sex. Related terms are bronco and peg boy.

CHERRY GROVE: A summer beach resort community on Fire Island founded in the late nineteenth century. Though originally frequented by middle-class heterosexual families, Cherry Grove became a predominantly gay or "bohemian" community in the1930s and has remained so ever since. Today, it attracts more lesbians and people of color than its sister community, Fire Island Pines, an upscale, mostly white gay male colony founded a mile up the beach from Cherry Grove in the 1950s.

CHICKEN: A young gay boy or man, especially when pursued by an older man, or chicken hawk.

CHICKEN HAWK: An older gay man who pursues young boys or men. See *Chicken.*

CIRCLE JERK: Group masturbation or jerking off.

CLONE: A gay man of a standardized appearance. In the 1970s, when "clone" was first used, the look included very short hair, a mustache, good muscle definition, a flannel shirt, and Levi's. In the late 1980s–early 1990s, an "ACT UP clone" sported very short hair with long sideburns, a clean-shaven face, good muscle definition (some things never change), a white T-shirt, Levi's, and Doc Marten boots.

CLOSET: The confining state of being secretive about one's homosexuality. According to historian George Chauncey, the word "closet" cannot be found in lesbian and gay literature before the 1960s and probably was not used until then.

CLOSET CASE/CLOSETED: One who does not admit her/his homosexuality, and who often actively denies it.

COALITION POLITICS: Type of political analysis and action that recognizes the interconnectedness of oppressions (e.g., racism, sexism, homophobia) and establishes bridges across difference to a common goal of social and political change.

COCK: Penis. This slang term was first used in sixteenth-century England.

COCK RING: A ring made of metal or leather placed around the cock and testicles to increase an erection.

COCKSUCKER: A hostile term for a male homosexual.

COLORS HISTORICALLY ASSOCIATED WITH HOMOSEXUALITY: Green—United States, 1930s to 1950s; red—late nineteenth- and early twentieth-century United States; pink—Nazi Germany; scarlet—Imperial Rome; violet—ancient Greece and Imperial Rome; blue—present-day Russia; lavender—throughout history and in present-day United States; rainbow—present-day United States.

COME/CUM: (v) to achieve orgasm; (n) semen.

COME OUT: To acknowledge one's homosexuality, either to oneself or to others; most often a public declaration of being lesbian or gay.

COMING-OUT STORY: An individual's personal story about one of the following—(1) realizing she/he is gay for the first time; (2) having lesbian or gay sex for the first time; (3) telling family, friends, or colleagues she/he is gay; (4) being discovered involuntarily as gay by family, friends, or colleagues. Most lesbians and gay men have more than one (aren't we *always* having to come out?), and they are usually a mixture of humor and pathos.

COMMITMENT CEREMONY: Any ritual, religious or secular, for honoring the union of lesbian or gay male couples in "marriage." Since same-sex marriages are not legally recognized in the United States or Canada—they are, in fact, legal only in the progressive Scandinavian countries of Denmark and Norway—lesbian and gay couples sometimes hold commitment ceremonies (which came to be called that in the 1980s), usually with friends and families present, to venerate their decision to stay together "for better or for worse."

CONDOM: Latex shield placed over penis or sex toy during penetration.

CORNHOLER: The top in anal sex.

CRIME AGAINST NATURE: Term used especially by religious fundamentalists to describe homosexuality, taken from wording in the Old Testament. Homosexual sex is described as being "against nature" because it does not lead to the procreation of children, the supposed "natural" use of sexual organs.

CROSS-DRESSING: The practice of dressing in clothes traditionally assigned to the opposite gender; also called transvestism or drag.

CRUISE/CRUISING: To look for sexual partners; to flirt, with the intention of finding a sexual partner.

CUT: Circumcised.

DAISY CHAIN: Three or more men engaged in simultaneous anal sex.

DAY WITHOUT ART: December 1 (World AIDS Day), when many cultural institutions, museums, and galleries either close their doors, drape works of art, or offer special programs in memory of those who have died of AIDS. The project started in 1989 in New York City and has since spread around the world.

DICK: Penis; from an old English word for dagger.

DIRECT ACTION: A form of activism in which participants become directly, physically involved in trying to disrupt or change the social or political order. ACT UP, Queer Nation, and Lesbian Avengers are examples of direct-action groups. See also *Zap/zap action.*

DISH: (n) gossip, hearsay, or buzz, often critical ("What's the dish on Bruce?"); (v) to engage in gossip ("We dished for hours").

DO: To perform fellatio; to blow (as in, "I want to do you").

DOMESTIC PARTNERSHIP: An official recognition of partners (either homosexual or heterosexual) who are not legally "married" but who cohabit and share a committed, spousal relationship. In about a dozen U.S. cities and one state, government employees are eligible to receive health benefits for their domestic partners, and a number of private corporations also extend such domestic partnership benefits.

DRAG: Cross-dressing, assuming both the dress and mannerisms of the opposite gender. See *Cross-dressing*.

DRAG BALLS: In Harlem since the early twentieth century, cross-dressing fashion and dance competitions attended by both straight and gay people.

DRAG QUEEN: A male transvestite; a man who dresses in women's clothing and affects women's mannerisms. Drag queens usually assume camp names for their characters.

DRAG SHOW: A performance by one or more female impersonators.

DRAGUER: French Canadian word meaning; in English "to cruise."

DROP BEADS/DROP HAIRPINS: In the early twentieth century, to leave obvious clues as to one's homosexuality.

EARRING: In the 1970s and 1980s among gay men, wearing a stud or post earring in the left ear was code for "gay." The queer movement of the 1990s has adopted the code of an earring in each ear, most commonly a silver ring.

EAT: To perform fellatio.

ECSTASY: Designer hallucinogenic drug.

ESSENTIALISM: The theory that homosexuality is biologically determined and is a permanent, immutable characteristic incapable of being reversed or changed. See, in contrast, *Social constructionism*.

ETRE AUX HOMMES: French Canadian term meaning in English "to be gay."

FAG/FAGGOT: A gay man. Some people believe that the use of the epithet "faggot" for a gay man began as far back as the fourteenth century, with the medieval practice of executing homosexuals by burning them at the stake using bundles of sticks, or "faggots." In the 1500s, the term "faggot" also referred to a disagreeable or outcast woman and may have been extended to include gay men, who were equated with women. Other possible origins of the term include the early twentieth-century British slang for a cigarette, a "fag," since at that time, smoking anything other than a cigar was considered effeminate. British slang also included "fagging," the system in public schools in which older boys were the "masters" of younger boys, exacting menial labor from them and sometimes sexual service as well. To be one of these lackeys was to be a "fag." Whatever its origins, by the early twentieth century, "faggot" was being used in the United States as a hostile term for a gay man. It is one of many such epithets reclaimed by gay men for themselves after the Stonewall rebellion.

FAG BASHING: See *Bashing*. Also called "fag busting."

FAG HAG: A straight woman who actively seeks out friendships with gay men.

FAG JOINT: Since the early 1900s, a meeting place for gay men. Also "fag factory."

FAG MAG: A magazine or publication for gay men featuring nudity.

FAIRE DU CRUISING: French Canadian term meaning in English "to cruise."

FAIRY: Since the early twentieth century, a gay man, especially an effeminate one; derogatory when used by straight people.

FEIGELE: yiddish expression for gay, from the word for bird.

FELLATIO: Oral stimulation of a man's genitals.

FELUETTE: French Canadian for a gay man.

FEMALE IMPERSONATOR: A man who dresses in women's clothing and affects women's mannerisms for the purpose of public entertaining, usually impersonating a celebrity such as Judy Garland, Barbra Streisand, or Bette Davis.

FIF/FIFI: French Canadian for a gay man.

FIRE ISLAND: A barrier island off the coast of Long Island, New York, known for its two gay beach resorts, Cherry Grove and Fire Island Pines.

FIRE ISLAND PINES: An upscale, mostly white gay male summer beach colony, which was founded in the 1950s a mile up the beach from Cherry Grove on Fire Island. Referred to simply as "The Pines."

FIST FUCK: To insert all or most of the hand into the anus or vagina.

FLAMING: Exaggerated, campy behavior that cries out "gay."

FLAVOR: Among African-American gay men, gender expression.

FLOR: Spanish slang for a gay man; in English translation, "flower."

FREEDOM RINGS: Necklace created by David Spada, a New York designer, in 1991, comprised of anodized aluminum rings in the colors of the rainbow flag and worn loose on a chain. Freedom rings, signifying gay pride and unity, have since been incorporated into numerous kinds of gay jewelry, including earrings, rings, and bracelets; sometimes colored aluminum triangles are substituted for circles.

FRONT MARRIAGE: A marriage between a lesbian and a gay man for the purpose of passing, at work and/or with family. See also *Beard.*

FRUIT: Since the early twentieth century, a derogatory term for a gay man, especially an effeminate one. Related terms include fruitcake, fruiter, fruitfly, and fruit plate.

FRUIT-PICKER: In the mid-1900s, a heterosexually identified man who engaged in occasional homosex.

FRUIT-STAND: In the mid-1900s, a gay bar or othering gay gathering place.

FUCK BUDDY: A casual sex partner, usually a friend with whom one has infrequent sex without commitment.

FUDGE-PACKER: The top in anal sex.

GAG REFLEX: A screening test employed by Army doctors during World War II to try to detect homosexual men in the ranks. According to historian Allan Berube, a tongue depressor was inserted deep into a soldier's throat to see if he gagged; if he didn't, it was considered likely that he was accustomed to performing fellatio.

GAY: Homosexual. The term refers to both men and women, though many gay women since the 1970s have preferred to call themselves lesbians. According to historian George Chauncey, it was in the seventeenth century that the word "gay," which had always connoted pleasurable things, began to take on a different meaning, indicating a life of immoral pleasures. Later, when applied to women in the nineteenth century, "gay" meant prostitute. By the early 1900s, homosexuals had appropriated the term as a camp word to refer not only to themselves, but to promiscuity, flamboyance, and lack of restraint. Since the 1940s, "gay" has been the preferred term used by homosexuals to refer to themselves.

GAY AS PINK INK: In the mid-1900s, to be obviously homosexual.

GAY BRAIN: Scientific theory developed by Dr. Simon LeVay in 1992, based on his controversial research on the brains of gay and straight men. LeVay concluded that, since the hypothalamus gland in gay men's brains was larger than that in straight men's, homosexuality might be biologically determined or "caused."

GAYDAR: The uncanny and seemingly innate ability lesbians and gay men have to recognize and detect one another; from "gay" and "radar."

GAY LIBERATION: The goal of radical social change that would permit the free expression of homosexuality without stigma or oppression.

GAY VOTE: In electoral politics, the tendency of lesbians and gays to vote in a particular way, or as a bloc, reflecting their needs and desires as a minority group. Political candidates who recognize this tendency and seek to take advantage of it are said to "court" the gay vote. Lesbians and gay men have been found in local and national elections to vote overwhelmingly for Democratic candidates.

GENDER BENDER: One who blurs gender lines, usually by dressing or acting in a way traditionally assigned to the opposite sex.

GENDER FUCK: Gender bending, with an attitude.

GENDER SNAP: Among African-American gay men, a gender fuck.

GIRL/GIRLFRIEND: In camp, especially among African-American gay men, a fellow gay man who is a friend and confidant but not a lover.

GIVE HEAD: To perform fellatio; to give a blow job.

GLORY HOLE: (1) A hole drilled through the partition between two stalls in a men's public toilet (see *Tearoom*) to permit anonymous sex or voyeurism. (2) The anus.

GO DOWN ON: To perform fellatio.

GOLDEN SHOWER: Urination used for sexual or erotic play; also called "water sports."

GRANDE/GRANDE FOLLE: French Canadian for queen.

GREEN SUIT: In the early twentieth century, wearing a green suit was considered a bold statement of homosexuality, a code by which gay men could identify each other. A "green and yellow fellow" in the mid-1900s meant a gay man.

GUPPIES: Gay yuppies.

HAND JOB: Manual stimulation of a man's genitals.

HERMAPHRODITE: A person born with both male and female sexual organs.

HETEROSEXISM: A bias toward heterosexuality, to the exclusion of homosexuality.

HOMME AUX HOMMES: French Canadian for a gay man.

HOMOEROTIC: An erotic presentation that is suggestively homosexual in nature. For example, commercial ads or billboards that show two men together in a suggestively erotic pose are said to be "homoerotic."

HOMOPHILE: In the early twentieth century, a homosexual. Up until the Stonewall Rebellion, political gay organizations in particular referred to themselves as "homophile."

HOMOPHOBE: One who is actively homophobic.

HOMOPHOBIA: Literally, the fear of homosexuals and homosexuality, sometimes merely implied, but often taken to the point where biased statements are made or biased actions are taken against lesbians and gay men. Homophobia can be both societal, (or external) or internalized.

HOMO: Derogatory term for a homosexual.

HOMOSEXUAL PANIC: Conscious fear of one's own possible homosexuality. Homosexual panic implies that a man will take whatever steps necessary—open denial, heterosexual marriage and fatherhood, etc.—to prove to himself and others that he is not really gay.

HOUSE: In Harlem drag culture, a "family" of transvestites and transsexuals, bonded for support, community, camaraderie, and protection.

HOUSE MOTHER: In the Harlem drag culture of houses, the authority figure or "mother" who heads or oversees the "family."

HUMPY: Adjective for a gay man who is good-looking and sexually desirable.

HUNG/WELL HUNG: Having a particularly large penis.

HUSTLER: A male prostitute.

IDENTITY POLITICS: Identifying and allying for political reasons with a minority group to which one belongs—for example, along lines of ethnicity, race, gender, age, or sexual orientation.

INTERGENERATIONAL SEX: Sexual relations between an older man and a boy or young man who has not reached the age of majority. Also called "man-boy love."

INTERNALIZED HOMOPHOBIA: The unconscious fear and hatred of homosexuality as experienced by lesbians and gay men themselves. Because society is so riddled with blatant homophobia, gay people often turn hatred of homosexuality back against themselves. In one common example, when a gay man does not come out to his parents, stating that it would "hurt" them, he implicitly buys into the notion that being gay is "bad," and his own internalized homophobia shows its face.

IN THE LIFE: In the African-American lesbian and gay community of the 1920s and later, the term commonly used for being gay (as in "so-and-so is 'in the life'").

INVERT: Pseudo-scientific term used by psychologists and doctors from the late nineteenth century until the 1940s for a lesbian or gay man. Homosexuality was referred to as "inversion" or "the inverted sexual instinct," because it was viewed as a reversal of "normal," straight sexuality.

JACK AND JILL PARTY: In the late 1980s, a circle jerk party that welcomed gay men and lesbians, who occasionally had sex with one another.

JACK OFF: See *Jerk off.*

JAM: In the mid-1900s, gay slang for straight people.

JERK OFF: To masturbate by manually stimulating one's own penis.

JISM: Semen. Also spelled "gism."

JOYSTICK: Penis.

KEY WEST: A predominantly gay male resort on an island at the western end of the Florida keys.

KINSEY 6: One whose sexual experience and identification is exclusively homosexual. In the Kinsey Institute's landmark studies of male and female sexuality (1948 and 1953, respectively), researchers set up a simple numerical scale to classify human sexuality. A "1" indicated exclusive heterosexuality, a "6" indicated exclusive homosexuality, with a range of behaviors in between. It was the Kinsey study of male sexuality that first established (to the shock of straight people and the delight of gays) that one man in ten is homosexual, a statistic that has been hotly debated ever since.

LAMBDA: An international symbol of being gay, the lambda is both the eleventh letter of the Greek alphabet and the symbol in physics of kinetic energy. The Gay Activists Alliance first adopted the lambda in 1970 to symbolize the energy of the nascent gay movement.

LAVENDER: Throughout Western history, the color most commonly associated with being gay. Lavender is the mixture of blue with pink (male now, but formerly female; or female now, but formerly male).

LAVENDER LAW: The specialized study or practice of lesbian and gay legal issues and concerns.

LESBIAN: A female homosexual. The term literally means a resident of the Isle of Lesbos, the Greek island where the ancient lyric poet Sappho, whose verse often celebrated love between women, lived.

LESBIAN AND GAY STUDIES: The burgeoning interdisciplinary, academic study of lesbian and gay lives, culture, thought, and history.

LESBIAN INVISIBILITY: (1) The conflation of homosexuality with gay men, to the exclusion of lesbians. (2) The omission of lesbian lives and issues from public discussions and media presentations of homosexuality. (3) The tendency in heterosexual society to obscure the fact that lesbianism exists.

LET ONE'S HAIR DOWN/KEEP ONE'S HAIR UP: In the early twentieth century, to reveal one's homosexuality, and conversely, to remain secretive about one's homosexuality. "Let one's hair down" later passed into general usage, meaning to act freely and without inhibition.

LEVITICUS: The books in the Old Testament from which passages are used by the Christian Right to justify homophobia and antigay discrimination. See p. 347 for the exact wording of the passages.

LICK-BOX: In the early 1900s, a gay man.

LIFESTYLE: Term used primarily by heterosexuals to describe lesbian and gay lives, tending to depreciate homosexuality as a "style" or "fad."

"LOVE THAT DARES NOT SPEAK ITS NAME": Phrase used by poet Lord Alfred Douglas (lover of Oscar Wilde) for homosexual love and desire.

LUBE: Lubricant used for anal sex.

MAN-EATER: One who performs fellatio.

MARGARITA: Spanish slang for a gay man; in English translation, "daisy."

MARICON: Spanish slang for a gay man, roughly equivalent to "faggot."

MARIPOSA: Spanish slang for a gay man; in English translation, "butterfly."

MARY: See *Camp names.*

MEAT: Penis.

MEAT-HOUND: In the mid-1900s, a gay man.

MEAT MARKET: A meeting or gathering place for gay male sexual encounters.

MEAT RACK: An outdoor spot where gay men congregate for casual public sex.

MÉNAGE À TROIS: Sexual encounter involving three partners of any combination of genders.

MERGED MEN'S SYMBOLS: The universal symbol for man is a circle with an arrow angling upward from the top right. Two or more men's symbols joined in different configurations indicate homosexuality, or men together. When two joined men's symbols are linked with two joined women's symbols, it signifies lesbian and gay community or solidarity.

MISS THING: See Camp names.

MOLLY: Oldest known British slang term for a gay man. In London in the early eighteenth century, "mollies" were homosexual men who met in taverns ("molly-houses") and were infamous for raucous partying in women's clothing. Mollies had an elaborate camp culture, which included calling each other by women's names. "Molly" was a common word for prostitute at that time; naming themselves "mollies" started a long tradition of homosexual men identifying with outcast women. (Other such terms include queen and faggot.)

MOUMOUNE: french Canadian for a gay man.

NANCY/NANCE: A gay man, taken from nineteenth-century British slang for buttocks. Also called Nancy-boy.

NATURE OR NURTURE: The debate over whether homosexuality is a result of biology (nature) or socialization (nurture).

NELLIE/NELLY: (adj) outrageously effeminate or silly.

ORCHID-EATER: In the nineteenth century, a gay man, especially one who enjoyed performing fellatio. The orchid is a flower whose name comes from the Greek word for testicles, "orkhis."

OUT: To be out of the closet.

OUTING: The controversial practice of publicly revealing the sexual orientation of a gay celebrity or public figure against her or his wishes. The gay magazine *OutWeek*, and reporter Michelangelo Signorile in particular, introduced the technique in 1989–90 and referred to it as "equalizing." Heterosexuals and homosexuals, Signorile said, were treated by the mainstream media in different ways; notably, homosexuality was seen as a matter of "privacy" that should not be broached. This hands-off approach, Signorile maintained, implied that homosexuality was bad or shameful, and his goal was to "equalize" the way heterosexuality and homosexuality were dealt with by the media. *Time* magazine coined the term "outing" to describe the technique. Recently, outing has taken on a broader meaning, signifying any type of unwanted, unwilling exposure.

PALM SPRINGS: A predominantly gay male resort in southern California, between Los Angeles and San Diego.

PANSY: Since the early twentieth century, a gay man. Many other flowery names have been used for gay men in both English and Spanish, including daisy and buttercup.

PANSYLAND: In the mid-1900s, a gathering place for gay men.

PANSY RAID: An attack against gay men.

PASS/PASSING: The pretense of acting or appearing to be heterosexual, when one is in fact lesbian or gay.

PEDOPHILIA/PEDERASTY: Sexual interest in and pursuit of children who have not reached the age of majority.

PERVERT: In the early twentieth century, a derogatory term used by police and other law enforcement agents for a homosexual. Other police terms included "degenerate" and "homo."

PHONE SEX: Sexual play over the telephone, usually involving mutual masturbation. Phone sex became extremely popular as a form of safer sex early in the AIDS pandemic, and phone services specializing in sex networking sprouted up for gay men and, later, lesbians.

PHYSIQUE: The art of bodybuilding; a program of exercise and weight lifting to build, shape, and define the muscles.

PINK TRIANGLE: A symbol in the shape of an inverted triangle adopted by lesbian and gay culture in remembrance of the homosexuals who were killed by the Nazis in Europe. From 1933 to 1945, the Nazis arrested between twenty and fifty thousand gay men for the "crime" of homosexuality (along with millions of Jews, gypsies, and other "criminals") and placed them in concentration camps. Homosexual men were identified in the camps by an inverted pink triangle sewn onto their clothing—pink to suggest that they were like women. Most of the gay prisoners did not survive the work camps; many died from the barbaric conditions, and thousands were executed. See also *Black triangle*.

POPPERS: See *Amyl nitrite*.

POST-OP: A person who has recently undergone sex reassignment surgery and has changed his/her birth sex. See *Transsexual*.

PRE-CUM: Clear fluid produced by a man's penis before ejaculation.

PRE-OP: A person preparing for sex reassignment surgery by taking hormones and receiving counseling.

PRIDE MARCH: A public procession or parade of lesbians and gay men to proclaim the pride, solidarity, and unity of gay people. The biggest pride march takes place in the last weekend in June in New York City, in commemoration of the Stonewall rebellion, but numerous other cities and towns around the world also celebrate the birth of the modern gay movement with pride marches and festivities.

PROVINCETOWN (P-TOWN): Lesbian and gay resort at the tip of Cape Cod in Massachusetts, with a wealth of gay accommodations, businesses, clubs, and restaurants. Provincetown was the original landing site of the Pilgrims in 1620, and for years functioned primarily as a quiet fishing village. It became became an artists' mecca in the early 1900s, and gradually—given the number of gay people in the arts—evolved into a gay haven.

PUBLIC SEX: Sex in a public setting where others can observe or join in, as in a back room.

ALL THE QUEEN'S MEN

By tacking adjectives in front of the word "queen," we arrive at numerous terms (most meant to be jocular) for gay men with specific preferences in lovers or in sexual acts, or with specific behaviors or characteristics. The following is a selected shopping list of queens:

BANANA QUEEN: Has a curved penis.

BODY QUEEN: Prefers muscular men.

BROWNIE QUEEN: The bottom in anal sex.

BUTTERFLY QUEEN: Likes mutual, simultaneous oral sex.

CHERRY QUEEN: Likes to initiate virgins.

CHICKEN QUEEN: Prefers sex with young boys or men.

CLOSET QUEEN: Keeps his homosexuality a secret.

CONTROL QUEEN: Wants to have a say in everything or to take charge of every situation.

DAIRY QUEEN: Likes to suck tits.

DISH QUEEN: Likes to gossip or spread rumors.

DRAG QUEEN: Dresses in women's clothing and affects women's mannerisms.

FIRE QUEEN: Burns other men for sexual pleasure.

FOOT QUEEN: Kisses or fondles another man's feet.

GREEN QUEEN: Prefers sex out-of-doors.

HEAD QUEEN: Likes to perform fellatio.

JEAN QUEEN: Prefers men in denim jeans.

MAIN QUEEN: The bottom in anal sex.

MEAN QUEEN: Into S/M.

MITTEN QUEEN: Likes to masturbate others.

OPERA QUEEN: An opera devotee.

PEE QUEEN: Into water sports.

PEELED QUEEN: Circumcised.

POUNDCAKE QUEEN: Likes to be defecated on.

QUEEN FOR A DAY: Married man who has occasional gay sex; trade.

SALAD QUEEN: Likes rimming.

SHRIMP QUEEN: Likes to suck toes.

SKIN QUEEN: Uncircumsised.

SIZE QUEEN: Obsessed with penis length and size.

SNOWBALL QUEEN: Likes oral exchange of semen after mutual, simultaneous oral sex.

SUCK QUEEN: Likes to perform fellatio.

TEAROOM QUEEN: Specializes in sex in public rest rooms.

VANILLA QUEEN: Into vanilla sex.

WATCH QUEEN: A voyeur. Also the lookout in a public rest room where gay sex is taking place.

QUEEN: An effeminate gay man; from sixteenth-century British slang for a woman of low morals or prostitute.

QUEER: Since the early twentieth century, a derogatory term for homosexual. "Queer" was reclaimed by radical lesbian, gay, and bisexual activists in the 1980s as a proud name for themselves. ("We're here, we're queer, get used to it!") "Queer" blurs both gender and sexual orientation and is regarded as more inclusive of difference than "lesbian" or "gay."

QUEER STUDIES: An offshoot of lesbian and gay studies that tends to be more theoretical in nature, questioning accepted ideas about "community" and "identity," and more inclusive of different types of people—lesbian, gay, bisexual, transgender, and straight people who somehow don't fit society's "norm."

RAINBOW FLAG: Designed in 1978 in San Francisco by artist Gilbert Baker as a symbol of lesbian and gay pride. The rainbow motif may have been taken from "Over the Rainbow," the famous Judy Garland song. Originally, there were eight colors in the flag: pink for sexuality, red for light, orange for healing, yellow for the sun, green for natural serenity, turquoise for art, indigo for harmony, and violet for spirit. In 1979, the flag was modified to its current six-stripe format (pink was omitted, blue was substituted for turquoise and indigo, and violet became a rich purple), signifying the diversity and unity of the lesbian and gay movement.

RED RIBBON: A loop of ribbon fastened to the lapel or shirt with a small safety pin, indicating AIDS awareness and solidarity against the epidemic. Conceived by artist Frank Moore in 1991, who envisioned it as a symbol of compassion for PWAs (people with AIDS) and their lovers and families, just as yellow ribbons had been used during the Iran hostage crisis. The language of ribbons has been extended to many different colors that indicate various diseases and social problems. For example, a pink ribbon signifies solidarity in the fight against breast cancer; pink and red together indicate both AIDS and breast cancer.

RED NECKTIE: In the early twentieth century, wearing a red necktie was a code by which gay men could identify one another.

RENT/RENTER: In the 1800s to early 1900s, a gay man who charged a fee for sex; a hustler.

RENT PARTIES: In 1920s Harlem, house parties at which guests paid a fee to help their host raise money for the rent. Usually a mix of heterosexuals and homosexuals, rent parties were a safe way for African-American lesbians and gay men to socialize away from the speakeasies.

RIDE THE HERSHEY HIGHWAY: Collegiate term for anal sex.

RIM: To tongue the anus; also called anilingus. The act of rimming is also called a rim job.

RIMADONNA: In the mid-1900s, a gay man who liked to perform or receive anilingus.

RING ON PINKY: Wearing a ring on the little finger of the left hand has for much of the twentieth century been a code for "homosexual."

ROLES: Opposite functions played out by sexual partners, such as top or bottom; also, fantasy characters played by sexual partners in a scene.

ROUGH TRADE: An ostensibly heterosexual man who seeks out sex with gay men, either as the top in anal sex or receiving fellatio, and then becomes violent.

RUBBER: A condom.

RUSSIAN RIVER: An area north of San Francisco that has become a popular lesbian and gay resort spot. The town of Guerneville is at the center of lesbian and gay activity there.

SAFER SEX: An array of sexual practices that may decrease the risk of HIV infection by preventing the transmission of bodily fluids during sex. The standard "tools" of gay male safer sex are condoms and latex gloves; some forms of safer sex are kissing, jerking off, phone sex, and rubbing. See also pp. 436–437.

SCENE: In sexual play, a mutually agreed upon fantasy scenario in which partners assume roles.

SCREAMING: See *Flaming*.

SEAFOOD: In the early twentieth century, gay male slang for a sailor.

SECOND-PARENT ADOPTION: The legal adoption of a child who already has one legal parent, by a second parent of the same gender. Also called co-parent adoption.

SEX REASSIGNMENT: The surgical alteration of a person's birth sex. See *Transsexual*.

SEXUAL ORIENTATION: Sexual identification, commonly defined as homosexual, heterosexual, or bisexual, depending on a person's sexual relationships or affinity. This term is currently favored by many gay people over "sexual preference," because it indicates an identity that cannot be changed or cast aside lightly like a preference.

SHE-MALE: Before the Stonewall rebellion, especially in the 1950s and 1960s, a derogatory term for an effeminate gay man who blurred the boundaries of gender. Sometimes also seen as "she-man."

SHORE DINNER: A gay man viewed by a sailor as a potential oral sex partner, or vice versa.

SIGNIFICANT OTHER: One's chosen romantic partner. Because U.S. society is so weighted toward heterosexual marriage, there is no one term to signify the relationship of partners (homosexual or heterosexual) who are outside the bounds of "legal wedlock." Some popular variants in the gay community are lover, boyfriend, partner, life partner, domestic partner, husband, spouse.

SISSY: A boy or man who acts effeminate or not "masculine." Unlike "tomboy," which is seen as a stage of female development that does not necessarily carry the connotation of "lesbian," "sissy," when used by straight people, has a negative connotation and implies "queer" or "gay."

SISTERS: Gay men who confide in each other as friends but are not lovers.

SIXTY-NINE: Mutual, simultaneous oral sex.

S/M: Sadomasochism. A form of consensual sexual play involving the exploration of power and (sometimes) pain. S/M can include a range of activities—everything from domination and submission fantasies and "scenes" to whipping, spanking, and cutting.

SOCIAL CONSTRUCTIONISM: The theory that homosexuality is not innate but that specific social conditions allow it to occur. See *Essentialism*.

SNAP: An African-American gay signifier; snapping of fingers, used to punctuate.

SNAP DIVA: Among African-American gay men, one who has mastered the art of snap.

SNOWBALL: Oral exchange of semen after mutual, simultaneous oral sex.

SODOMY: Any one of a number of sexual acts: (1) sex between two men, (2) sex between two women, or (3) anal sex between a man and a woman. The name comes from the city of Sodom in the Old Testament, where men supposedly performed unspeakably wicked acts that incurred the wrath of God and brought about the destruction of the city. Modern interpreters of the Bible, however, believe that the only "sin" of the Sodomites alluded to in the story was that of inhospitality. Sodomy—which was punishable by death in many of the American colonies—is still a felony or misdemeanor on the books of half of the United States, though it is no longer illegal in Canada.

STONEWALL REBELLION: The riots that took place on the streets of Greenwich Village in New York City in June of 1969, when patrons of a gay bar called the Stonewall Inn on Christopher Street fought back against a police raid of the bar. "Stonewall" has come to signal the birth of the modern lesbian and gay rights movement.

SUBCULTURE: The culture of any minority group in society other than the white heterosexual majority.

SWEET MAN: African-American and Caribbean equivalent of "sissy."

SWISH: (n) an effeminate gay man; (v) for gay men, to act in a traditionally "feminine" way by swinging one's hips when one walks.

TANTE/TANTOUSE: French Canadian for a gay man, similar to aunt or auntie.

TEAROOM: A public toilet, when it is the scene of anonymous sex between gay men; also called "teahouse."

THIRD SEX: Formerly, homosexuals. The "first sex" meant heterosexual men, the "second sex" indicated heterosexual women, and the "third sex" meant those who fell in between.

TONGUE: To go down on; to use the tongue in any way that gives sexual pleasure.

TOP: An erotic sex role; the "active" participant in sex. See *Bottom.*

TRADE: A heterosexually identified man who seeks out sex with gay men, either as the top in anal sex or receiving fellatio. According to historian Jeffrey Weeks, by the 1870s in England, places where men met for sex with each other were commonly called "markets," and a homosexual encounter (whether or not it involved an exchange of money) was referred to as "trade," meaning sexual barter.

TRANSGENDER: An umbrella term for those "gender outlaws" who blur the lines of "traditional" gender expression. Transgendered people include or have been referred to as transvestites, transsexuals, drag queens and kings, cross-dressers, and berdaches, to name just a few.

TRANSSEXUAL (TS): A person who has undergone or is preparing to undergo sex reassignment surgery. Transsexuals can be either MTF (male-to-female) or FTM (female-to-male), homosexual, heterosexual, or bisexual.

TRANSVESTITE (TV): A person who dresses in the clothes of and assumes the gender expression of the opposite sex.

TRICK: A casual sexual partner; a person with whom one has a brief sexual encounter.

TWINKIE/TWINK: A young gay man who is sexually desirable for his handsome looks and/or build and not for his intellect.

UNCUT: Uncircumcised.

URANIAN: Term for a homosexual coined in the 1860s by homosexual rights advocate Karl Heinrich Ulrichs. He took the term from Plato's *Symposium*, in which homosexual love was said to exist under the protection of the goddess Urania. Also called an "urning."

VANILLA SEX: Conventional sex, with the connotation of "boring," that does not incorporate any S/M fantasy or other sexual play.

VOGUE/VOGUING: A dance form consisting of a series of different stylized poses, like those a model might affect on a fashion runway.

WATER SPORTS: See *Golden shower.*

WINKTE: Lakota (Sioux) Indian name for a gay medicine man.

WOLF AND PUNK: According to historian George Chauncey, an erotic system among men in the early twentieth century in which a "wolf," or an older, more experienced man, protected and financially supported a young man, or "punk," in exchange for sex. "Wolf" later came to mean a predatory heterosexual man, and "punk" is now a term for a destructive young man, roughly equivalent to "hoodlum" and without homosexual connotations.

ZAP/ZAP ACTION: A form of direct action intended to be loud, quick, showy, and media attention–getting.

Please see pp. 432–436 for a separate glossary of AIDS-related terms.

SOURCES

The Alyson Almanac, 1994–95 Edition. Alyson Publications, 1994.

Chauncey, George. *Gay New York: Gender, Urban Culture, and the Making of the Gay Male World, 1890–1940.* BasicBooks, 1994.

Duberman, Martin, Martha Vicinus, and George Chauncey, eds. *Hidden from History: Reclaiming the Gay and Lesbian Past.* New American Library, 1989.

Dynes, Wayne, ed. *The Encyclopedia of Homosexuality.* 2 vols. Garland Publishing, 1990.

Fletcher, Lynne Yamaguchi. *The First Gay Pope and Other Records.* Alyson Publications, 1992.

Grahn, Judy. *Another Mother Tongue: Gay Words, Gay Worlds.* Beacon, 1984, 1990.

Katz, Jonathan Ned. *Gay/Lesbian Almanac: A New Documentary.* Carroll & Graf, 1994.

Rodgers, Bruce. *Gay Talk.* Putnam, 1972.

Spears, Richard. *Slang and Euphemism.* Second revised edition. Signet, 1991.

Stewart, William. *Cassell's Queer Companion.* Cassell, 1995.

V

We Are (Literally) Everywhere:
Statistics on Lesbians and Gay Men

Lesbians and gay men have been largely invisible in mainstream surveys and polls. The portrait of a "typical American," as painted by U.S. Census Bureau stats, does not include a separate category for gay people, even though we work, pay taxes, have children, own homes, and are represented in different ethnic and racial groups. The only time we are counted is in surveys on sex and sexual practices, which (as with heterosexuals) is only one aspect of our identity.

Some gay research firms have begun to do exploratory surveys of lesbians and gay men for marketing purposes, to help clients test print ads, refine product concepts, and assess needs. The surveys turn up interesting, if necessarily sketchy and limited, information about lesbians and gays. Also, gay and lesbian organizations and magazines periodically conduct surveys on various aspects of our lives, from religious beliefs to dating practices to the discriminatory violence we face everyday on account of sexual orientation. The following section highlights some of the existing—and very preliminary—findings in the area of lesbian and gay demographics and statistics.

WHERE WE LIVE

FIFTEEN LARGEST CONCENTRATIONS OF LESBIANS AND GAYS IN THE UNITED STATES

1. Manhattan
2. San Francisco
3. Boston/Cambridge
4. Seattle
5. Oakland/Berkeley
6. Washington, D.C.
7. Chicago/Evanston
8. Atlanta
9. Minneapolis
10. Marin County, California
11. Los Angeles
12. Santa Monica Bay

13. Portland, Oregon   15. Pittsburgh
14. San Diego

SOURCE: Raymond G. McLeod, "Gay Market as a Potential Goldmine," *San Francisco Chronicle*, August 27, 1991. Reprinted by permission.

Gay adults under the age of thirty-five change their place of residence more than once every other year.

SOURCE: Overlooked Opinions, Inc., Chicago, Illinois, 1995

QUALITY OF LIFE ISSUES

Overlooked Opinions, Inc., was formed in 1989 in Chicago as a market research and opinion polling firm specializing in the gay, lesbian, and bisexual market. The following are results of a 1992 survey of queer lives. However, the survey has severe limitations and looks at only one segment of the gay and lesbian population.[1] For more information, contact Overlooked Opinions, 3162 North Broadway, Chicago, IL 60657; phone: 800-473-3405.

[1]Sample size = 7,500 gay men and lesbians. Median age = 37 for men, 35 for women. Race/ethnic background = 84.3 percent white for men, 78.9 percent for women; 9.5 percent Latino for men, 11.7 percent for women; 4 percent African-American for men, 5.8 percent for women; 1.2 percent Asian/Pacific Islander for men, 2 percent for women; 1 percent Native American for men, 1.6 percent for women. Self-identification = 57.5 percent identified as gay men, 4.2 percent as gay women, 78.8 percent as lesbians, 32.2 percent as homosexual men, 5.2 percent as homosexual women, 4.7 percent as bisexual men, 7.8 percent as bisexual women.

EDUCATION

	LESBIANS	GAY MEN
Median years of education	15.7	15.7
High school only	16.4%	16.9%
Some college	18.7%	18.5%
Associate degree	7.3%	6.4%
Undergraduate degree	32.0%	31.5%
Graduate degree	25.6%	26.8%

FAMILY SIZE

Average household size	1.9	1.7
Households with children under 18	10.2%	4.8%
In relationship	71.2%	55.5%
Live with partner	52.0%	37.0%

	LESBIANS	GAY MEN
Of those in relationships are monogamous	81.2%	51.8%
Median years in relationship	3.5	3.7

INCOME

Median annual household income	$36,072	$42,689

OCCUPATION

	LESBIANS	GAY MEN
Management	10.9%	13.4%
Health care	16.0%	10.0%
Education	11.7%	9.9%
Sales/marketing	8.1%	9.2%
Technical	5.6%	8.3%
Clerical	7.3%	5.7%
Financial	4.0%	5.6%
Literature/library science	5.0%	4.3%
The arts	3.1%	4.5%
Law	3.3%	3.9%
Entrepreneur	3.0%	3.6%
Science	3.3%	2.3%
Food service	1.9%	2.7%
Public safety	2.5%	1.4%
Other	14.1%	15.1%

RESIDENCE

	LESBIANS	GAY MEN
Home owners	43.1%	47.7%
Median years at present address	2.4	3.0
Urban dwellers	45.1%	52.7%
Suburban dwellers	33.1%	31.7%
Reside in small town	15.0%	11.6%
Reside in rural area	6.8%	4.0%

Over 45 percent of lesbians and gay men have been promoted at work at least once in the past three years.

Over 8 percent of lesbians and gay men report that they have experienced some sort of employment discrimination—being fired, verbal abuse, denial of promotions—in the past six months.

SOURCE: Overlooked Opinions, Inc., Chicago, Illinois, 1995. Reprinted by permission.

GRAB BAG OF STATS

- Lesbians and gay men bought almost 6 million home computers between 1988 and 1991.
- Lesbians and gay men took more than 162 million trips in 1991, 78 percent of which were for business.
- 63.5 percent of lesbians consider themselves politically active.
- 79.3 percent of lesbians and gay men buy based on gay media advertising.
- 89.3 percent of lesbians and gay men dine out on a regular basis.
- 65.3 percent of lesbians go camping.
- 23.6 percent of gay men do aerobics.
- 15.6 percent of lesbians have four or more pets (cats and dogs).
- 37.8 percent of lesbians and gay men play board games.
- 39.1 percent of lesbians and gay men traveled outside the United States in the last year.

RELIGION AND SPIRITUALITY

The now defunct magazine *OUT/LOOK* did a survey of its readership in late 1991 to examine how important religion and spirituality are in lesbian and gay lives. The results from 648 readers (among whom differences in response by gender were negligible) were as follows:

How important is organized religion in your life?

28%   Very important
24%   Somewhat important
48%   Not important
0.2% No answer

How important is spirituality in your life?

58%   Very important
26%   Somewhat important
16%   Not important
0.8% No answer

How important is spirituality in your life? (by age group)

Age 21–29

50%   Very important
34%   Somewhat important
15%   Not important

Age 30–39

60%   Very important
26%   Somewhat important
13%   Not important

Age 40–49

67%   Very important
19%   Somewhat important
14%   Not important

Age 50+

49%   Very important
18%   Somewhat important
32%   Not important

Do you believe in God, or in some transcendent spiritual form?

66.2%   Yes
20.5%   No
12.5%   Don't know
0.8%   No answer

Do you believe that people can contact spirits?

43%   Yes
27%   No
28%   Don't know
1%   No answer

Do you believe in reincarnation?

29%   Yes
37%   No
33%   Don't know
1%   No answer

Do you believe in astrology?

26%   Yes
50%   No
24%   Don't know
1%   No answer

Do you believe that nature has its own wisdom/consciousness?

57%   Yes
25%   No
18%   Don't know
1%   No answer

Current religious affiliations/identities of respondents (if any)

22%   Protestant/other Christian
14%   Recovery program members

14%   Alternative/other religions
12%   "Gay Christian" (for example, Metropolitan Community Church)
6%   Roman Catholic
6%   Jewish
2%   Buddhist
0.7%   Fundamentalist/evangelical
0.6%   Hindu
0.5%   Muslim

How supportive of homosexuality is your particular religious community?

41%   Extremely supportive
18%   Very supportive
14%   Somewhat supportive
12%   Not very
12%   Not at all

Source: *OUT/LOOK* magazine, Issue 14, Fall 1991

What Straights Think About Lesbians and Gays

In the spring of 1993, at the height of the controversy about lesbians and gays in the military, the mainstream magazine *U.S. News & World Report* did a poll of one thousand registered voters and came up with the following results (margin of error = plus or minus 3.1 percent; where percentages don't add up to 100%, it is because some respondents said "I don't know"):

Familiarity

53%   Personally know someone who is gay and this familiarity makes them think more favorably about equal rights
46%   Do not think they know any gay people and oppose gay rights

Family Life

60%   Oppose recognizing "legal partnerships" for homosexuals
35%   Approve of the idea
70%   Oppose allowing gays and lesbians to adopt
24%   Support the idea

Media Images

56%   Worry that media portrayals of gays have had a negative influence on society
33%   Say media images have had a positive influence

President Clinton's Focus

56% Say Clinton has spent too much time on gay rights issues
29% Say he has spent about the right amount of time

AIDS Crisis

39% Say it has made them less sympathetic to gays
35% Say it has made them more sympathetic. The largest group of those whose sympathy grew was African-Americans.

Sex Education

52% Oppose teaching about gay orientation in sex education classes in public schools. Strong opposition comes from those with school children.
43% Favor it

Anti-Bias Law

50% Say that gays suffer from discrimination
65% Say they want to ensure equal rights for gay people, but
50% Oppose extending civil-rights laws to cover homosexuals

The Root "Cause"

46% Believe that homosexuals choose to be gay or lesbian, and this group tends to oppose civil rights for gays. However,
32% Think that gays are born that way

Opinion Cues

The top-ranking influences on voters' attitudes on homosexuality:
29% Say religious organizations (of those, 79% oppose gay rights)
18% Say gay and lesbian acquaintances (of those, 66% support gay rights)
17% Say the media (of those, 44% oppose gay rights)
15% Say family (of those, 47% oppose gay rights)

Patterns

The voters least likely to know a homosexual:

- South Central U.S. (55% do not know anyone gay or lesbian)
- Homemakers (55%)
- Retirees (67%)
- Those with less than a high school education (63%)
- Those in small towns (54%)
  Those most likely to know a homosexual:
- Mountain states (64%)
- Suburbanites (58%)

- College graduates (63%)
- Those between the ages of 35 and 64 (58%)

SOURCE: *U.S. News & World Report*, July 5, 1993

SEX SURVEYS

Various sex surveys have been conducted over the years that have given some hints as to how many self-identifying lesbians and gay men there are in the United States. The following are the results of the first and the most recent studies, which are also the most famous and controversial.

KINSEY REPORT

In 1948, the Kinsey Institute published a groundbreaking study of sexual behavior in 5,300 American men. The celebrated "Kinsey scale" outlined a significant amount of fluctuation in sexual activity, from 1 (exclusively heterosexual) to 6 (exclusively homosexual). Kinsey's findings shook the heterosexual world and help foster a sense of community and self-acceptance among homosexuals. In 1953, the institute published its findings on sexual behavior among 5,940 American women.

Men

10%   Reported being more or less exclusively homosexual for at least 3 years between the ages of 16 and 55

37%   Had some homosexual experience that resulted in orgasm

50%   Responded erotically to other men

Women

2–6%   Reported being more or less exclusively lesbian between the ages of 20 and 35

13%   Had some lesbian experience that resulted in orgasm

28%   Responded erotically to other women

"SEX IN AMERICA" REPORT

Conducted through the National Opinion Research Center at the University of Chicago, the "Sex in America" survey was originally conceived in 1987 by federal AIDS researchers frustrated with the lack of data about sexual practices. The federal government was to fund the study of 20,000 Americans, both heterosexual and homosexual. But Congress pulled the plug on funding four years later, and the scaled-down survey interviewed only 3,400 Americans. Researchers completed the study in late 1994, drawing some conclusions that impact on lesbians and gay men. The numbers of men and women exhibiting same-gender sexuality are significantly larger than those who actually identify as lesbian or gay; but overall, the numbers are much smaller than when the Kinsey Institute undertook its study.

Men

2.8% *Self-identified* gay or bisexual men in study
10.2% Exhibit same-gender sexuality in desire, behavior, and/or self-identification

Women

1.4% *Self-identified* lesbian or bisexual women in study
8.6% Exhibit same-gender sexuality in desire, behavior, and/or self-identification

---

ANTI-LESBIAN/GAY VIOLENCE

Incidents of anti-lesbian/gay violence rose 2 percent overall around the country in 1994, according to a national report coordinated by the New York City Gay and Lesbian Anti-Violence Project (NYC-AVP). Nationally, anti-lesbian/gay violence is becoming increasingly brutal and is being perpetrated by very young people. NYC-AVP and eight other victim assistance programs around the country released the statistics in early 1995, reflecting complete data for 1993 and 1994 from nine cities—Boston; Chicago; Columbus, Ohio; Denver; Detroit; Minneapolis/St. Paul; New York City; Portland, Oregon; and San Francisco—and data for 1994 from eight other cities and states. Copies of the complete seventy-page report are available for $2 from the New York City Gay and Lesbian Anti-Violence Project, 647 Hudson St., New York, NY 10014. To add your name or organization to their mailing list, call 212-807-6761.

INCIDENTS OF ANTI-LESBIAN/GAY VIOLENCE REPORTED TO VICTIM ASSISTANCE ORGANIZATIONS

BOSTON

	1993	1994
Harassment	143	203
Threats or menacing	44	49
Bomb threats	1	1
Physical assaults/thrown objects	60	61
Police verbal/physical abuse	11	8
Vandalism	9	24
Arson	0	0
Murder	0	0
Sexual assault	2	0
Kidnapping, extortion, other	0	0

	1993	1994
Robbery	0	5
Total offenses	270	351
Total incidents reported	187	234
Offenses per incident	1.44	1.50

CHICAGO

	1993	1994
Harassment	114	136
Threats or menacing	54	37
Bomb threats	1	0
Physical assaults/thrown objects	59	62
Police verbal/physical abuse	29	26
Vandalism	9	19
Arson	1	3
Murder	3	2
Sexual assault	16	18
Kidnapping, extortion, other	0	0
Robbery	5	6
Total offenses	291	309
Total incidents reported	204	177
Offenses per incident	1.43	1.75

COLUMBUS, OHIO

	1993	1994
Harassment	50	41
Threats or menacing	17	20
Bomb threats	0	0
Physical assaults/thrown objects	41	47
Police verbal/physical abuse	6	5
Vandalism	16	27
Arson	0	7
Murder	1	1
Sexual assault	14	12
Kidnapping, extortion, other	0	0
Robbery	0	18
Total offenses	145	178
Total incidents reported	140	149
Offenses per incident	1.04	1.19

DENVER

	1993	1994
Harassment	118	84
Threats or menacing	21	58
Bomb threats	4	0
Physical assaults/thrown objects	35	108
Police verbal/physical abuse	5	18
Vandalism	54	20
Arson	0	0
Murder	2	2
Sexual assault	3	12

	1993	1994
Kidnapping, extortion, other	14	44
Robbery	11	26
Total offenses	267	372
Total incidents reported	211	156
Offenses per incident	1.27	2.38

DETROIT

	1993	1994
Harassment	40	45
Threats or menacing	9	13
Bomb threats	0	0
Physical assaults/thrown objects	11	15
Police verbal/physical abuse	15	9
Vandalism	15	13
Arson	0	0
Murder	3	3
Sexual assault	2	1
Kidnapping, extortion, other	11	9
Robbery	0	0
Total offenses	106	108
Total incidents reported	84	96
Offenses per incident	1.26	1.13

MINNEAPOLIS/ST. PAUL

	1993	1994
Harassment	442	225
Threats or menacing	34	40
Bomb threats	3	3
Physical assaults/thrown objects	30	33
Police verbal/physical abuse	10	23
Vandalism	13	11
Arson	1	1
Murder	5	2
Sexual assault	1	3
Kidnapping, extortion, other	3	4
Robbery	7	1
Total offenses	549	346
Total incidents reported	153	190
Offenses per incident	3.59	1.82

NEW YORK CITY

	1993	1994
Harassment	627	653
Threats or menacing	289	288
Bomb threats	2	3
Physical assaults/thrown objects	227	334
Police verbal/physical abuse	83	129
Vandalism	31	51
Arson	3	1
Murder	15	9

	1993	1994
Sexual assault	5	23
Kidnapping, extortion, other	79	65
Robbery	36	42
Total offenses	1,397	1,598
Total incidents reported	587	632
Offenses per incident	2.38	2.53

PORTLAND, OREGON

	1993	1994
Harassment	99	100
Threats or menacing	66	56
Bomb threats	0	1
Physical assaults/thrown objects	26	21
Police verbal/physical abuse	8	0
Vandalism	18	46
Arson	0	0
Murder	0	0
Sexual assault	0	0
Kidnapping, extortion, other	0	1
Robbery	5	3
Total offenses	222	228
Total incidents reported	99	106
Offenses per incident	2.24	2.15

SAN FRANCISCO

	1993	1994
Harassment	262	376
Threats or menacing	122	73
Bomb threats	3	0
Physical assaults/thrown objects	260	160
Police verbal/physical abuse	23	20
Vandalism	39	25
Arson	1	1
Murder	0	3
Sexual assault	12	12
Kidnapping, extortion, other	0	35
Robbery	2	0
Total offenses	724	705
Total incidents reported	366	324
Offenses per incident	1.98	2.18

NATIONAL VICTIM PROFILE

	1993	1994
• Gender		
Women	624	833
Men	1,578	1,674
Unknown or Institution	113	232
• Race		
African-American	159	171
Asian/Pacific Islander	24	39

	1993	1994
Latina/o	182	180
Native American	13	10
White/European	1,207	1,398
Unknown	382	595
Other	72	70

- Age

	1994
Under 18	51
18–29	592
30–44	759
45–64	146
Unknown	614

NATIONAL OFFENDER PROFILE

	1994
• Race	
African-American	522
Asian/Pacific Islander	40
Latina/o	374
Native American	3
White/European	884
Unknown	1,016
Other	44
• Age	
Under 18	488
18–29	741
30–44	361
45–64	118
Unknown	1,175

VI

We Have Lives, Not Lifestyles:
Just About Everything You Wanted
to Know About Gay Men

I. GAY ACTIVISM

Anita Bryant, the '79 march, the '87 march , the military issue—everything is an
organizing tool. Each time we have to defend ourselves as a community, more
people come out of the closet, take risks, write letters, give money, and perform
acts of courage. I think that when we go through one of these processes, we
emerge stronger because our numbers become greater.

—RICHARD BURNS, Executive Director,
Lesbian and Gay Community
Services Center, New York

You may think that gay activism started with Stonewall, but gay men in the United States have been organizing for their rights since the early twentieth century. The very first homosexual organization in the United States, the Society for Human Rights, was founded in Illinois in 1924 by Henry Gerber and others. Though it lasted only a few months, the society also published two issues of *Friendship and Freedom,* the first gay liberation magazine in the country.

Other pioneers of gay activism included Harry Hay, who with others founded the Mattachine Society in 1951, and Jim Kepner, who started a collection of gay-related books, clippings, photographs, and artifacts that later became the International Gay and Lesbian Archive, the oldest and largest in North America.

But it is in the period since the Stonewall riots of 1969 that gay activism has taken off in full force. In the last quarter century, we've witnessed the founding of

The Gay Activists Alliance Firehouse on Wooster Street in New York City, 1971.
(Photo by Richard C. Wandel)

gay community centers, organizations, newspapers, and publishers, all designed to
unite and strengthen the gay community. The AIDS crisis has further politicized
the gay community into taking action to safeguard our rights and save our lives.

But our activism doesn't always mean being on the front lines of a protest or
starting a new gay organization. Activism can have many faces: writing a letter to
a congressional representative, marching in a gay pride parade, or coming out to
someone on National Coming Out Day. Any action that makes gay people more
visible is a form of activism.

GAY ACTIVISM 101: A BIBLIOGRAPHY

Adam, Barry. *The Rise of a Gay and Lesbian Movement.* Twayne, 1987.

Altman, Dennis. *Homosexual Oppression and Liberation.* Outerbridge & Dienst-
frey, 1971.

Bullough, Vern. *Homosexuality: A History.* Meridian, 1979.

Cant, Bob, and Susan Hemmings, eds. *Radical Records: Thirty Years of Lesbian
and Gay History.* Routledge, 1988.

Come Out: Selections from the Radical Gay Liberations Newspaper. Times
Change Press, 1970.

D'Emilio, John. *Sexual Politics, Sexual Communities: The Making of a Homosex-*

The second annual Christopher Street rally in Central Park, 1971. *(Photo by Richard C. Wandel)*

ual Minority in the United States, 1940–1970. University of Chicago Press, 1983.

Humphreys, Laud. *Out of the Closets: The Sociology of Homosexual Liberation.* Prentice-Hall, 1972.

International Lesbian and Gay Association (ILGA). *Second Pink Book: A Global View of Lesbian and Gay Liberation and Oppression.* ILGA, 1988.

Jay, Karla, and Allen Young, eds. *Out of the Closets: Voices of Gay Liberation.* Harcourt, 1972.

Marcus, Eric. *Making History: The Struggle for Gay and Lesbian Equal Rights, 1945–1990.* HarperCollins, 1992.

Marotta, Toby. *The Politics of Homosexuality: How Lesbians and Gay Men Have Made Themselves a Political and Social Force in Modern America.* Houghton Mifflin, 1981.

Peck, Abe. *Uncovering the Sixties: The Life and Times of the Underground Press.* Pantheon, 1985.

Schulman, Sarah. *My American History: Lesbian and Gay Life During the Reagan/Bush Years.* Routledge, 1994.

Sweet, Roxana Thayer. *Political and Social Action in Homophile Organizations.* Arno, 1975.

Teal, Donn. *The Gay Militants.* Stein and Day, 1971.

Thompson, Mark, ed. *Long Road to Freedom: The Advocate History of the Gay and Lesbian Movement.* St. Martin's Press, 1994.

Tobin, Kay, and Randy Wicker. *The Gay Crusaders.* Arno, 1972.

Vaid, Urvashi. "We Have a Blueprint; Now We Need Tools," *OUT/LOOK*, 5 (Summer 1989), 59–60.

FILE UNDER: KNOW YOUR ENEMIES!

The following is a short list[1] of "family values" hate groups that have declared open season on the rights of lesbians and gay men. Unfortunately, there are many more.

American Family Association

Objects to homosexuality, pornography, profanity, "anti-Christian bigotry," liberal media. Has been influential on National Endowment for the Arts (NEA) funding and public school curricula. 600,000 members in 640 chapters. Donald Wildmon, P.O. Box 2440, Tupelo, MS 38803.

Concerned Women of America

Antigay, anti-abortion, "pro-family." Grassroots organizing and congressional lobbying. Sponsors "prayer chains," i.e., pressures elected officials via local groups. 600,000 members in 800 U.S. chapters. Beverly LaHaye, 370 L'Enfant Promenade SW, #800, Washington, DC 20024.

Eagle Forum

Women's organization powerful in national and Republican party politics. Anti AIDS education, sex education, day care, family leave, abortion, and NEA funding. 80,000 members. Phyllis Schlafly, Box 618, Alton, IL 62002.

Family Research Council

Anti gay/lesbian/bisexual rights, reproductive freedom, government-funded health care, child care and equal protection laws for women in the workplace. Believes allowing gay men in the military will cause drastic increase in AID incidence. Split from Focus on the Family in 1992. Gary Bauer, 700 13th St., N.W., Ste. 500, Washington, DC 20005.

Focus on the Family

1,550 radio stations worldwide, with almost 1,000 employees. Major player in passage of Colorado Amendment 2 to disallow equal rights for lesbians and gay men. National training seminars to involve believers in political process. James Dobson, P.O. Box 35500, Colorado Springs, CO 80935; 719-531-3400. Press contact: Paul Hetric.

---

[1] With thanks to P-FLAG, 1012 14th St., N.W., Ste. 700, Washington, DC 20005.

Traditional Values Coalition

Anti gay rights, reproductive rights, the teaching of evolution, and sex education other than abstinence. Organizes anti-gay ballot initiatives. Helped repeal gay and lesbian rights in California municipalities. Advocates AIDS quarantine. 25,000 churches across the country. Rev. Lou Sheldon, 100 S. Anaheim Blvd., Ste. 320, Anaheim, CA 92805; Washington, DC. Contact: Kelly Mullins, 202-547-8570.

Free Congress Foundation

Research and education organization which created National Empowerment Television (NET) to mobilize the Right. Four television programs, one to college campuses, another addressed to African-American conservatives. Paul Weyrich, 717 Second St., N.W., Washington, DC 20002.

Operation Rescue

Well known for violent disruption of abortion clinics and the harassment, intimidation, and terrorization of women and health-care providers, it added the opposition of gay rights to its agenda when the military ban issue came to prominence. 35,000+ members. Randall Terry, P.O. 1180, Binghamton, NY 13902.

National Association of Christian Educators/Citizens for Excellence in Education

Primarily attacks public school curricula, textbooks, and school board members in order to bring public education under Christian control. 1,250 chapters. Dr. Robert L. Simonds, P.O. Box 3200, Costa Mesa, CA 92628.

Others We Can't Afford to Ignore

Chalcedon—P.O. Box 158, Vallecito, CA 95251, (209) 736-4365. Major think tank; center of the Christian Reconstruction Movement. Establishes Christian legal organizations. Has publications, speakers bureau, sponsors seminars.
Christian Coalition, Chesapeake, VA; 804-424-2630. Contact: Michael Russell.
Oregon and Idaho Citizens Alliances
Colorado for Family Values

RIGHT-WING WATCHDOG GROUPS

The following groups keep track of what the right wing is up to:

People for the American Way, Washington, DC; 202-467-4999.
Institute for First Amendment Studies, Great Barrington, MA. Contact: Skip Portius, 413-274-3786

More Unforgettable Quips from the Right Wing

"Our children will never be safe from militant homosexuals and lesbians. Because as homosexuals die off due to AIDS, the remaining AIDS carriers prey on children to replenish the 'Homosexual Community'."

—Eugene Delgaudio, Public Advocate

"Discrimination against those with homosexual inclinations, like discrimination against the able-bodied who refuse to work, is both necessary for the greater good of society and the individual himself. In fact, such discrimination is an attempt to prevent persons tempted by homosexuality from suffering the pathologies it induces."

—Paul Cameron, Family Research Institute

"The militant homosexuals are making tremendous gains in our public schools— teaching small children how to become homosexuals. I hope and pray that you will stand with me to defend our small children, stand by the word of God, and battle the homosexuals who want to steal the minds and souls of our youth."

—Martin Mawyer, Christian Action Network

"Don't be fooled when homo-propagandists use the word AIDS 'awareness' and 'AIDS education.' These are just code words for programs which: encourage young people to engage in homosexual conduct; spread the lie that an abomination can be rendered acceptable by using certain techniques."

—Howard Phillips, The Conservative Caucus

"I remember that Homosexual March on Washington parade last spring. Those bare breasted women flaunting themselves in the streets in front of the White House. And the homosexual perverts simulating sex on each other in public for innocent children to witness. And the transvestites, and the child molesters, and those who mocked God and spat on the Bible."

—Jerry Falwell, Liberty Alliance

Key Lesbian and Gay Rights Issues

Marriage
Foster parenting and adoption
Child custody and visitation
Second-parent adoption
Housing
Tax equity
Immigration
Public services and accommodations
Sodomy laws
AIDS-related discrimination (employment, testing, privacy rights)

ACTION OPPORTUNITY

According to the Gay and Lesbian Alliance Against Defamation (GLAAD), companies that advertise in gay and lesbian publications frequently fall victim to attacks from the right wing. These courageous advertisers indicated that their advertising support of queer publications will continue as long as there is positive response from the gay market. Pay attention to these advertisers, purchase their products, and write and thank them for their support.

Military ban
Employment and benefits
Freedom of speech/expression
Anti-gay initiatives

A CALL TO ACTION

In light of the court battle for the right of same-sex couples to marry scheduled to take place in Hawaii this fall, conservative legislators in some of the other forty-nine states are taking preemptive actions against recognizing same-sex marriages

Irish Lesbian and Gay Organization (ILG)) at the 1993 Gay Pride March, New York City *(Photo by Harry Stevens)*

Members of We Wah and Bar Chee Ampe, a Native American lesbian and gay
organization, at a 1991 fund-raiser at the New York City Lesbian and Gay
Community Services Center *(Copyright Morgan Gwenwald)*

in their home states. Two states—Utah and South Dakota—have already considered denying recognition of gay marriages, regardless of where they take place.
South Dakota's measure went down to defeat in the Senate after passage in the
House and a month of debate. In Utah, however, the bill sailed through both
houses in less that an hour on March 1, 1995. Similar legislative attempts are predicted all over the country. Said the National Gay and Lesbian Task Force's Fight
the Right Project field organizer, "This isn't just about marriage. This is possibly
the final frontier of gay activism."

ACTIVISM SAVES THE DAY—A CLOSE CALL

On March 22, 1995, a measure was introduced in the Montana legislature that
would require convicted "deviate sexual conduct" lawbreakers to register as violent offenders with law enforcement officials for the rest of their lives. This bill
would have placed gay men and lesbians convicted of homosexual acts in the same
class as murderers and rapists. That same day, Montana activists called the National Gay and Lesbian Task Force for help. The Montana gay community needed
others from around the country to register with Montana Governor Racicot their
strong and outraged objections to this bill.

NGLTF was able to mobilize national public pressure through its network of
human and civil rights groups, major metropolitan newspapers covered the story,

Members of Latino Gay Men of New York meeting at the New York City Lesbian and Gay Community Services Center. *(Photo by Terry Boggis)*

and within hours, there were over a hundred phone calls to Governor Racicot. Twenty-four hours later, the Montana legislature decided to reconsider the bill. According to Montana State Senator Vivian Brooke, "NGLTF's quick mobilization really made a difference."

ARMCHAIR ACTIVISM: ORGANIZING ONLINE

The Internet—the most revolutionary catalyst of gay and lesbian community organizing and communicating since the invention of the gay bar a century ago. . . . Gay liberation is thriving in cyberspace like nowhere else on earth.

—*New York Newsday* columnist GABRIEL ROTELLO

- Lesbian and Gay Community Services Center–New York, is now on the world-wide web, linking activists to information about the programs and work of the Center and providing a path to other gay community organizations around the country. The Center can be accessed at http://www.panix.com/~dhuppert/gay/center/center.html
- Gay and Lesbian Victory Fund, a network of donors who contribute $100 or more to join, and pledge to contribute at least $100 to two or more gay or les-

1992 Gay Pride parade, New York City *(Photo by Harry Stevens)*

bian candidates for public office of the member's choice from Victory Fund's recommended list, and can be accessed on America Online (member: VictoryF); Internet (victoryf@aol.com.); and the Victory Fund BBS. For more information, contact Van Do, 202-842-8679.

- National Gay and Lesbian Task Force (NGLTF) is online in the Gay and Lesbian Community Forum of America Online. NGLTF's Legislative Alert outlines homophobic amendments and describes alternative amendments representatives should be encouraged to support. To be added to the Legislative Alert E-mail Distribution List, send e-mail address to Tanya Domi, NGLTF Legislative Director (tldngltf@aol.com), or Beth Barrett, NGLTF Public Information Assistant (babngltf@aol.com).
- Queer Resources Directory can be accessed at qrd2vector.casti.com
- *GayNet Digest*: You can subscribe by sending e-mail to majordomo2queernet.org; type this message: subscribe gaynet-digest.
- Lesbian and gay action alert e-mail list: To be added to the distribution list, send e-mail to majordomo@vector.casti.com and type this message: subscribe action alert. To send an action alert message, e-mail actionalert@vector.casti.com.
- "Culture Wars" online information clearinghouse on the radical right: For information, contact AlterNet, 77 Federal St., San Francisco, CA 94107. Fax: 415-284-1414. E-mail: 71362,27 CompuServe.
- Digital Queers, San Francisco: digiqueers@aol.com; phone: 415-252-6282. Promotes gay and lesbian workplace rights via the development of a lesbian and gay

high-tech computer infrastructure. Computer-industry queers offer training in use of the computer as an organizing tool.

GREAT WORDS FROM GREAT WARRIORS

"I leave you the will to fight; the desire to live; the right to anger, to love . . . to joy, to transform silence into language and action. I leave you a litany for survival."

—AUDRE LORDE

"By 'toleration' he means 'no hitting'"

    —REP. BARNEY FRANK (D-Mass.), commenting on Newt Gingrich's assertion that he is in favor of toleration of lesbians and gay men

"Feelings alone, directly and powerfully expressed, can change things."

—ACT UP

"Ultimately, this nation is being won over by people who make the decision to come out. It is through that single all-powerful act that stereotypes and prejudice are being stripped away . . . I have come to realize that some of this nation's most important battles are fought not by soldiers but by ordinary citizens working to realize the promise of freedom in the context of everyday life."

    —JOE STEFFAN, who was discharged from the U.S. Naval Academy for admitting he was gay

"I am a 35-year-old who came out at 33. . . . My lover got sick and on December 13, 1993, died of AIDS. . . . Devastated, I went to the bar here, and coming out I was attacked from behind. I received a broken bone in my face, broken teeth, and my right ear lost all of its capability to hear. . . . I filed a charge of assault. . . . The person was picked up and charged and I took him to court. . . . [I was] the first gay man [in Moncton] to take a person to court. He pled guilty, received a $35,000 fine and several days in jail, and he is never to come near me again. . . . A lot of people thanked me, but above it all, the person I did it for was my lover, who I miss. . . . I have been even more outspoken since my own diagnosis. Stand up and be proud of what you are and believe in yourself."

    —LINDSAY PARENT, Moncton, New Brunswick, Canada, in a letter to *Out* magazine, February 1995. Reprinted with permission from *Out* magazine, February 1995. Copyright © 1995 by Out Publishing, Inc. All rights reserved. For subscription information, call 800-876-1199.

"If my work does not stand for the rights of poor and working people, then I do not stand on the side of justice. I am of the poor, and I want more than anything to stand on the side of justice."

—SCOT NAKAGAWA, NGLTF Fight the Right activist

"I became an activist to reconcile myself, to give voice to experiences of oppression, and to resist the slow death of silence and inaction. At the core of my public

At the 1993
March on
Washington for
Lesbian, Gay, and
Bisexual Rights
(*Photo by Dave
LeFave*)

*message and organizing strategies as a lesbian and gay rights activist are three
principles: working to end racism, individual autonomy in human sexuality, and
economic justice.*"

— CARMEN VAZQUEZ, Public Policy Director, Lesbian and Gay Community
   Services Center, New York

"*We should not be ashamed of standing up for the most vulnerable in our community—our youth. . . . This must become a part of the movement, not just for
gay and lesbian kids, but also for the ninety percent who are not gay, who must
learn not to hate.*"

— DAMIEN MARTIN AND EMERY S. HETRICK, Founders of the Hetrick-Martin
   Institute for Lesbian and Gay Youth

"*Every gay person must come out. . . . And once—once you do, you will feel so
much better.*"

— HARVEY MILK, late Member, San Francisco Board of Supervisors

"*All homosexuals have the potential for being gay. Some just haven't found out
how to do it yet.*"

— MORRIS KIGHT, gay rights activist

Doesn't This Make You Mad?

Twenty-three states have laws on their books prohibiting sex acts between consenting adults. Six of those states define "deviate sexual conduct" as only homosexual behavior. This means that in nearly half the states of the union, lesbian and gay people are considered to be criminals.

"I don't fight to live in the lesbian community. I fight to live in the whole world."

—URVASHI VAID, writer, attorney, political analyst, former executive director, NGLTF

"Activists embody the highest standard of values. In the Paul Revere tradition, activists alert the populace about what needs to be changed by going out into the streets and yelling."

—ANN NORTHROP, lesbian activist

"Above All, Audacity."

—HARRY HAY, founder, Mattachine Society

"When the night of the Stonewall riots came along, just everything came together at that one moment. People quite often ask, 'What was special about that night, Friday, June 27, 1969?' There was no one thing that was special about it. It was just everything coming together, one of those moments in history where, if you were there, you just knew that this is IT. This is what we've been waiting for."

—CRAIG RODWELL, early gay rights activist, in *Before Stonewall: The Making of a Gay and Lesbian Community* a film by Andrea Weiss and Greta Schiller

NATIONAL LESBIAN AND GAY DIRECT ACTION AND ADVOCACY ORGANIZATIONS

ACT-UP (AIDS Coalition to Unleash Power)
135 W. 29th St., 10th floor
New York, NY 10001
Phone: 212-564-2437
Fax: 212-989-1797
  A direct action group that works for AIDS funding, research, and visibility.

Queer Nation
c/o Lesbian and Gay Community Services Center
208 W. 13th St.
New York, NY 10011
212-260-6156
  A multicultural, direct action group dedicated to fighting homophobia, queer invisibility, and all forms of oppression.

1993 March on Washington for Lesbian, Gay, and Bisexual Rights *(Copyright 1993 by Morgan Gwenwald)*

Gay and Lesbian Alliance Against Defamation (GLAAD)
    A national organization, founded in 1985, which advocates for fair, accurate, and inclusive portrayals of lesbian, gay, and bisexual lives in all forms of the media.

New York Office
150 W. 26th St., Suite 503
New York, NY 10001
Phone: 212-807-1700
Fax: 212-807-1806

Los Angeles Office
8455 Beverly Blvd., #305
Los Angeles, CA 90048
English hotline: 213 U R GLAAD
Spanish hotline: 213-658-6074
Phone: 213-658-6775
Fax: 213-658-6776

National Field Office, Portland
Donna Red Wing, Director
Phone: 503-224-5285
Fax: 503-224-5480

Atlanta
Phone: 404-876-1398
Fax: 404-876-4051

Chicago
Phone: 312-871-7633
Fax: 312-338-5482

Dallas
Phone: 214-521-5342, ext. 816
Fax: 214-522-4604

Denver
Phone: 303-331-2773
Fax: 303-494-7216

Kansas City
Phone: 816-374-5927
Fax: 816-756-1760

San Diego
Phone: 619-688-0094
Fax: 619-294-4814

San Francisco Bay Area
Phone: 415-861-2244
Fax: 415-861-4893

Washington, DC
Phone: 202-429-9500
Fax: 202-857-0077

Human Rights Campaign
P.O. Box 1396
Washington, DC 20013
or:
1104 14th St., N.W., Suite 200
Washington, DC 20005
202-628-4160

The nation's largest political organization fighting for the rights, health, safety, and dignity of lesbians, gay men, and bisexuals. Established 1980. 80,000 members, staff of 40. Lobbies Congress on issues that affect the lesbian and gay community, fights anti-gay state ballot initiatives, and supports candidates who believe that discrimination based on sexual orientation is wrong. Has political action committee (PAC) supporting candidates who support an end to anti-gay discrimination, more AIDS funding, women's health issues, and choice. HRC's SPEAK OUT program allows gay and lesbian input into congressional decision-making through overnight mail. Sponsors annual National Coming Out Day on October 11.

National Gay and Lesbian Task Force (NGLTF)
2320 17th St., N.W.
Washington, DC 20009
Phone: 202-332-6483
Fax: 202-332-0207
TTY: 202-332-6219
E-mail: ngltf@aol.com

Lobbies, organizes, educates, and advocates for gay and lesbian civil rights and
for responsible AIDS policies. NGLTF's Fight the Right Project provides lobbying, media, fund-raising, computer activism, and other training to local activists.
Long-term, grassroots, multiracial, multicultural movement-building directly in
the field.

Lambda Legal Defense and Education Fund
A national organization committed to achieving full recognition of the civil rights
of lesbians, gay men, and people with HIV/AIDS, through impact litigation, education, and public policy work. Founded in 1973.

National Headquarters
666 Broadway, Suite 1200
New York, NY 10012
Phone: 212-995-8585
Fax: 212-995-2306

Midwest Regional Office
17 E. Monroe, Suite 212
Chicago, IL 60603
Phone: 312-759-8110
Fax: 312-641-1921

Western Regional Office
6030 Wilshire Blvd., Suite 200
Los Angeles, CA 90036
Phone: 213-937-2728
Fax: 213-937-0601

Gay and Lesbian Victory Fund
1012 14th St., NW, #707
Washington, DC 20005
Phone: 202-842-8679
Fax: 202-638-0243

Dedicated to electing openly gay politicians. Founded in 1991 as a political action committee (PAC) assisting only openly gay and lesbian candidates. Helped
elect 14 such municipal and state candidates during the 1994 elections, including
the first openly gay officials elected to the Missouri and Arizona legislatures, the
Washington State Senate and the California State Assembly.

Pride at Work: The National Gay, Lesbian, Bi, and Transgender Labor
   Organization
P.O. Box 9605
North Amherst, MA 01059
Phone: 413-549-5972

Funded by the American Federation of State, County, and Municipal Employees (AFSCME) and 11 other unions, this group, formed during the Stonewall 25 celebration, welcomed more than 300 representatives of unions and gay labor groups at its first conference.

A VERY PERSONAL ACTIVISM: TEN TIPS FOR COMING OUT TO PARENTS

Coming out to anyone is a form of activism, and coming out to parents is one of the hardest things to do. Most of us reach the point where we can no longer hide and we want our families to understand us more fully. But even though you're happy being gay, there's no predicting how your parents will react. Here are some things to keep in mind as you get ready to "break the news" to your parents.

1. Be prepared to be emotional, even if you feel calm beforehand or rarely cry. Many of us have found that the intense relief of coming out has brought on a flood of tears. Breathe deeply and remember that there are millions of gay men in the world—you aren't the only one.
2. Be prepared for your parents to be emotional. Even if your parents suspected what you were going to tell them, they may cry when they actually hear you say the words.
3. It's better to consider what you're going to say before you say it. Although you may be very comfortable with your sexual orientation because you've known about it for years, your parents may have a lot of questions that you don't have responses to on the spur of the moment. Think about your answers to obvious questions, like "How long have you known?" or "But what about that girlfriend you had in college?" or their questions about AIDS and your sero status. Be positive and affirming. Your parents aren't made of glass, and being gay isn't something to hide or be ashamed of.
4. If you plan to come out to them in person, ask a supportive sibling to come with you. If that isn't possible, then:
5. Have a supportive friend, lover, or sibling waiting for you who can help you afterward if your parents have a bad response or who can celebrate with you if their reaction is supportive.
6. If you live with your parents, have a place to go after you tell them—to a friend's or an older sibling's house—to give you and them some time apart to breathe.
7. If you live in another city, consider writing your parents a letter. You can get all your thoughts down clearly and give them time to absorb the announcement before you actually see or talk to them.
8. Don't set up a coming out scenario that leaves no "breathing room" for you or your parents. One young man told his parents at the beginning of a ten-hour car trip from his college back to their home. His parents weren't happy about the announcement, and it made for a very long trip for everyone!
9. Request the pamphlet "Can We Understand?" from your local P-FLAG (Parents and Friends of Lesbians and Gay Men) chapter. The booklet is a guide to

help parents understand and accept their children's sexual orientation by answering some of the most common questions parents have. Read it yourself, then take it to your parents or send it to them after you visit. Give them the address and phone number of the nearest P-FLAG chapter, in case they want help accepting your news.

Parents and Friends of Lesbians and Gay Men
National Office
P.O. Box 27605
Washington, DC 20038
202-638-4200

10. Do something "gay" for yourself in the next day or two after you come out—buy yourself a present at the gay bookstore, go to a gay event. Remember that bringing your "secret" out of the closet is ultimately the best present you could give to yourself. And it is a personal triumph of gay activism.

NEW YORK CITY YOUTH ACTIVISM

Before the Stonewall Riots, Gay Youth of New York was founded to combat the oppression of gay youth. Their slogan was "Youth Organized, Youth Run."

Over the next decade, the organization evolved into Gay and Lesbian Youth of New York (GLYNY). When the Lesbian and Gay Community Services Center was formed in 1983, it welcomed GLYNY, providing the organization with free meeting space and a mailbox.

In 1989, the Center launched its own youth program, Youth Enrichment Services (Y.E.S.), a creative arts–based substance and alcohol abuse prevention and intervention program. The program's third director, Barbara Bickart, founded its theater component, the Alternate Visions Theater Group.

During the 1992–93 year, GLYNY changed its name to Bisexual, Gay and Lesbian Youth of New York (BiGYLNY), and Y.E.S. began providing leadership development training for members of BiGLYNY, creating a formal working relationship between the two youth groups. BiGLYNY, now a multiservice support and social group, holds rap sessions every Saturday. The organization sponsors an outreach program to high schools, and many social events. It is the oldest independent, ongoing gay organization in New York City.

In 1992, Y.E.S. and members of BiGLYNY began production of *OutYouth Newsmagazine,* currently published twice a year and distributed to young lesbians and gay people across the United States and to youth groups abroad.

PROFILE

Harry Hay

Harry Hay was a member of the Industrial Workers of the World (IWW) in his early life, as well as a member of the Communist Party. Beginning with only a half dozen members, Harry formed the Mattachine Society in 1950. Initially, the fledgling organization's intent was to hold discussion groups about the condition of being gay. According to Hay: "We didn't know at that point that there had ever been a gay organization of any sort anywhere in the world before . . . .So [we] felt that we had to be very, very careful in everything that we did." The society's magazine, *The Mattachine Review,* was launched in 1951, and the group's first convention was held in 1953. Harry left Mattachine soon thereafter, when conservative members shifted the group's political leanings to the right. Harry became an anti-war activist, and a counterculture revolutionary in California during the sixties. He continues to be active, mostly as co-founder of Radical Faeries.

2. GAY ART AND DESIGN

"There would be no art in America if it weren't for gays!"

—ELIZABETH TAYLOR

Well, okay, there'd be *some*, but it's hard to imagine the American artistic legacy without the paintings of Paul Cadmus, Charles Demuth, Marsden Hartley, and Andy Warhol; the sculptures of Richmond Barthé; the architecture of Phillip Johnson; the designs of Isaac Mizrahi and Perry Ellis.

Throughout the course of Western history—from ancient Greece statue and vase carvers to Renaissance masters like Leonardo daVinci and Michelangelo—the arts have often been associated with gay men. This is no less true in contemporary art in North America—perhaps it is even more true because of the increased visbility of gay artists and a slackening in cultural taboos surrounding sexuality.

However, as long as there has been "gay art" (or art reflecting a homoerotic sensibility), there has also been censorship against such imagery. Representing the "love that dare not speak its name" visually is in some ways more powerful than speaking about it.

Sadly, we've lost too many of our most innovative visual artists—like Keith Haring and Robert Mapplethorpe—to AIDS. But the AIDS pandemic has also cre-

Inaugural display of 1,920 panels of the NAMES Project AIDS Memorial Quilt, Washington, DC, 1987 *(Photo by Marc Geller)*

ated a wealth of art that attempts to address the losses and the grief of the gay community. AIDS has forever changed the language and landscape of the art world. From the AIDS Memorial Quilt to the annual observation of A Day Without Art on December 1, the effects of AIDS on artists and the arts community is recognized throughout the world.

As we move closer to the twenty-first century, the increased visibility, acceptance, and recognition of openly gay artists and subject matter is sure to proliferate—as are the attempts to censor them. But certain doors have been opened to gay artists and their work, and there are more and more closets that will never be opened again.

SHORT BIOS OF SOME FAMOUS GAY PAINTERS
Washington Allston, 1779–1843

A painter in the romantic classicism style and a tortured closeted homosexual.

Paul Cadmus, b. 1904

A painter of the Magic Realist movement. A WPA surrealist, with an emphasis on Americana in a moralistic tone. In 1934 the Corcoran Gallery in Washington, DC, removed *The Fleet's In!*—a street scene of sailors frolicking with each other and prostitutes—after a protest from the secretary of the Navy. Cadmus was close friends with many prominent gay literary and arts figures of the day, including E. M. Forster.

Paul Cadmus *(Copyright © 1992 by Morgan Gwenwald)*

Charles Demuth, 1883–1935

Among his major work evoking the American scene, he did a series on New York's gay baths, as well as sailors (important gay icons of the period).

Thomas Eakins, 1844–1916

His paintings showed a clear love of the male body, but there is no definitive proof of his orientation.

Marsden Hartley, 1877–1943

Painter, poet, and essayist, made expressionist portraits of his lover, a German lieutenant killed in the first days of WWI. He was close friends with many gay/lesbian artists and writers, including Demuth, Gertrude Stein, Djuna Barnes, and Hart Crane.

Robert Indiana

He painted the famous "LOVE" design in the 1960s (which the postal service designated as the first "Love" stamp in 1973).

Andy Warhol, 1930–1987 (see also profile p. 149)

The first "queer" artist. While his homosexual contemporaries painted in coded and veiled ways, Warhol created images about what it was like to be queer in the 1950s; he was the presiding muse over New York's chic art scene for the 1960s and 1970s

OTHER GAY OR BISEXUAL VISUAL ARTISTS

Richmond Barthé	Larry Johnson
Darrel Ellis	Cary S. Leibowitz/Candyass
Robert Giard	Robert Mapplethorpe
Keith Haring	Donald Moffett
Lyle Ashton Harris	Peter Nagy
David Hockney	Richard Bruce Nugent
Edward Hopper	Tom of Finland
Peter Hujar	David Wojnarowicz
Jasper Johns	

SOME OF THE SEVENTEEN OPENLY GAY AND LESBIAN ARTISTS IN THE 1995 WHITNEY BIENNIAL

This very gay, very postmodern, very political show was assembled by the Whitney's openly gay curator, Klaus Kertess.

Keith Haring mural in the second-floor men's room of the New York City Lesbian and Gay Community Services Center *(Photo by Morgan Gwenwald)*

David Armstrong
Nicole Eisenman
Lyle Ashton Harris
Nan Goldin
David McDermott

Peter McGough
Frances Negron-Mutaner
Katherine Opie
Jack Pierson
Lari Pittman

SOME MAJOR MUSEUM RETROSPECTIVES OF GAY ARTISTS

Marsden Hartley, 1980 at the Whitney Museum of American Art, NYC
David Hockney, late 1980s at the Metropolitan Museum of Art, NYC
Andy Warhol, 1989 at the Museum of Modern Art, NYC
Bruce Weber, retrospective at the 1987 Whitney Biennial, Whitney Museum of American Art, NYC

OTHER MAJOR EXHIBITIONS OF GAY ARTISTS

Ross Bleckner at the Guggenheim Museum, NYC, 1995
Felix Gonzalez-Torres at the Guggenheim Museum, NYC, 1995
(both are openly gay artists whose primary subject matter is AIDS)

GAY PHOTOGRAPHERS OF THE PAST

Sir Cecil Beaton, 1906–1980

A campy gay photographer and costume designer famous for his portraits of society and theatre figures.

F. Holland Day, 1864–1933

America's first advocate of photography as an art form. Well known at the turn of the century, he photographed a staged crucifixion with an undraped Christ (a self-portrait that showed full frontal nudity). His studio and most photographs were destroyed in a fire in 1904. He ran a school, called the New School of American Photography, and made important series of "Grecian" nude boys and men.

George Platt Lynes, 1907–1955

He explored the eroticism of the male body, exhibited nudes influenced by surrealism, and pursued a career in both mainstream and gay publications/media.

Minor White, 1908–1976

He also was interested in a "closely observed" male body in his art.

Robert Mapplethorpe, 1947–1989

He reexamined studio techniques of the 1930s and 1940s, often with a homoerotic or sadomasochistic twist. A retrospective in 1989 made Mapplethorpe the center of a debate on censorship; well-received at the Whitney Museum of American Art in NYC, a show was canceled by the Corcoran in Washington, DC, after an outcry from Senator Jesse Helms.

SOME GAY PHOTOGRAPHERS AND THEIR FAMOUS HOMOEROTIC
PHOTOS, ACCORDING TO ALLEN ELLENZWEIG

F. Holland Day, *Study for the Crucifixion*, 1898 (self-portrait as Christ on the cross, although the cross is barely visible and Day is shown in full frontal nudity, arms upraised, head thrown back, hips tilted and knees bent).
Robert Mapplethorpe, *Dennis Walsh, New York*, 1976 (portrait of Dennis in a white tank T-shirt, arms behind head, and all surroundings fading into black).
Duane Michals, *Certain Words Must Be Said*, 1976 (photograph of two women in

a bedroom, one looking out the window, with hand written text that indicates they are breaking up).

Frank M. Sutcliffe, *Natives*, 1980 (three young nude boys leaning against a beached fishing boat in imitation of a classic pose).

Arthur Tress, *Teenage Runners*, 1979 (one teenage boy track member peeling a Band-Aid off the other's thigh).

SOURCE: *OUT/LOOK*, No. 7, Winter 1990

CONTEMPORARY GAY ARTISTS FEATURED IN *ART IN AMERICA* FOR THE TWENTY-FIFTH ANNIVERSARY OF STONEWALL

Ross Bleckner (b. 1949)
Cary S. Leibowitz/Candyass (b. 1963)
Lyle Ashton Harris (b. 1965)

Donald Moffett
Frank Moore (b. 1953)
Hugh Steers (b. 1962)

GALLERIES WHERE GAY ARTISTS HAVE HAD SOLO SHOWS

The Drawing Center, New York, various artists
Jack Tilton Gallery, New York (Lyle Ashton Harris, 1994)
Mary Boone Gallery, New York (Ross Bleckner, 1994)
Midtown Payson Gallery, New York (Hugh Steers, 1989; Paul Cadmus, 1992)
Richard Anderson Fine Arts, New York (Hugh Steers, 1994)
Sperone Westwater, New York (Frank Moore, 1993)
Texas Gallery, Houston, TX (Donald Moffett, 1991)
Tom Cuglinani Gallery, New York (John Lindell, 1992)
Trial Balloon Gallery, New York, various artists

THE NEW STANDARD FOR LESBIAN/GAY ART EXHIBITIONS

In a Different Light, University Art Museum, at the University of California at Berkeley, January 11–April 9, 1995, was an extensive exhibition unprecedented in its theoretical concerns and in the sheer volume of material presented. With more than two-hundred cataloged pieces, the show was presented in nine groupings: "Void," "Self," "Drag," "Other," "Couple," "Family," "Orgy," "World," and "Utopia." For those who were unable to attend, be sure to pick up the catalog for the exhibition *In a Different Light* copublished by City Lights Books and the University Art Museum/Pacific Film Archive, and edited by Nayland Blake, Lawrence Rinder, and Amy Scholder.

A few of the gay artists and works represented include:

Peter Hujar, *Candy Darling*, 1974. Gelatin silver print.

Andy Warhol, *Jackie*, 1964. Acrylic on canvas.

David Wojnarowicz, *Fever*, 1988–89. Three gelatin silver prints.

OTHER ART EXHIBITIONS WITH GAY THEMES

Liquid Eyeliner, a group show by drag artists and gender-benders at the Art Commission Gallery in San Francisco, June, 1990.

Key West International Gay Arts Festival, June 17–24, 1995, an annual gathering of accomplished gay and lesbian artists from around the world. For more info, 1-800-429-9759.

Homo Video: Where We Are in the 1980s (December 1986–February 1987) at the New Museum of Contemporary Art.

The Long Road to Freedom: The Advocate *History of the Gay and Lesbian Movement*, June 16–30, 1994, at the Seagram Building, New York (also available as a book with the same title from St. Martin's Press).

SOME AIDS ART EXHIBITS

Art Against AIDS, a fund-raising drive for AIDS research, that included benefit exhibitions at more than seventy New York galleries in 1987.

From Media to Metaphor: Art About AIDS, Grey Art Gallery, University of New York, NYC.

Witnesses: Against Our Vanishing, an AIDS-inspired show in NYC, early 1990s.

Beyond Loss: Art in the Era of AIDS, April 23–May 30, 1993, at the Washington

Opening reception of "Out on the Island: Sixty Years of Lesbian and Gay Life on Fire Island," an exhibit of the National Museum & Archive of Lesbian and Gay History, 1993.

Projects for the Arts (cosponsored by the Whitman-Walker Clinic, in honor of the 1993 March on Washington). Exhibition featured visual artists whose works have been informed by the AIDS crisis.

The AIDS Quilt, unfolded in Washington, DC, for the second time in its two-year history, with ten thousand panels, October 1989.

THE NAMES PROJECT

In the late 1980s the NAMES Project in San Francisco began commemorating the thousands who have died of AIDS by encouraging people to make quilt panels for departed loved ones. The images of the individual panels (three feet by six feet) were chosen and sewn by surviving friends and relatives. The quilt has been exhibited all over the world, several times in Washington, and most recently during the 1994 March on Washington.

The NAMES Project
P.O. Box 14573
San Francisco, CA 94114
415-863-5511

For further reading, see Cindy Ruskin's *The Quilt: Stories from the Names Project*, Pocket Books, 1988.

ART EXHIBITIONS AT THE NATIONAL MUSEUM & ARCHIVE OF LESBIAN AND GAY HISTORY, A PROGRAM OF THE NEW YORK CITY LESBIAN AND GAY COMMUNITY SERVICES CENTER

Founded in the winter of 1988, the Center's National Museum and Archive of Lesbian and Gay History preserves lesbian and gay heritage and makes it accessible through regular exhibits, publications, and scholarly research activities. The Center's Museum and Archive is one of the country's major collections of lesbian and gay history; its goal is to gain a clearer understanding of our community's past and present, as well as insight into our future, through the work of our artists and historians.

The first exhibition of the museum was in the fall of 1988. Since then, the museum has presented several exhibitions each year and has coordinated the Center's observances of A Day Without Art, held on December first of each year to commemorate World AIDS Day.

In 1994, in honor of the twenty-fifth anniversary of the Stonewall rebellion, the museum produced *Windows on Gay Life*, a site-specific exhibit in the storefront windows of more than thirty businesses along and adjacent to Christopher Street. Curated by Joe E. Jeffreys, the exhibit emphasized both the history of the gay liberation movement and the culture of the community, while recognizing the significance of the Christopher Street neighborhood in lesbian and gay life. *Windows on Gay Life* used photographs, objects, artifacts, and text to cover topics such as erotica, night and street life, business, performance, activism, families, AIDS, and homophobia.

Other exhibits in 1994 included *OUT Houses*, an exhibit of works from Big Dicks Make Me Sweat Productions, a militant dadaist gay men's art collective, and Fierce Pussy, a lesbian activist public art collective. The works were installed in the Center's newly renovated ground-floor bathroom from February through March.

Still on view throughout the Center are most of the site specific installations created by more than fifty artists for *The Center Show* in June 1989, in celebration of the twentieth anniversary of Stonewall. Among the many highlights of this exhibition is the mural created by Keith Haring in the second-floor men's room.

CENTER MUSEUM EXHIBITS THROUGH 1995

Portraits of Gay and Lesbian Writers: An Exhibition of Photographs by Robert Giard, 1988

For Love and For Life: Photo-Documentary Exhibit by Marilyn Humphries, 1989

The Center Show, Rick Barnett and Barbara Sahlman, curators, 1989

A Hundred Legends, Don Ruddy, curator, 1989

Imagining Stonewall, Mark Johnson, curator, 1989

Mariette Allen Transformations: Cross-Dressers and Those Who Love Them, 1989

The Cartoon Show, Jennifer Camper, Burton Clarke, Howard Cruse, Mark Johnson, curators, 1990

Prejudice and Pride, 1990

Where Are the Women? Cheryl Gross, curator, 1990

Images from the Front: Photography Challenging AIDS, Morgan Gwenwald, Mark Johnson, Tracey Litt, Robert Mignott, Robert Vazquez, jury, 1990–91. Artists included: John Lesnick, Y. Nagasaki, Henry Baker, Tom McKitterick, Tom McGovern, Michael Transue, Joe Ziolkowski, among others.

Works by Lesbian Artists, Lesbians About Visual Arts (LAVA), curators, 1990. This show coincided with the Women's Caucus for Art Conference which was also held at the Center.

Keepin' On: Images of Afro-American Women from the Lesbian Herstory Archives, Lesbian Herstory Archives, curator (Morgan Gwenwald, Georgia Brooks, and Paula Grant), 1991

Lasting Impressions: Women with Tatoos, Cheryl Gross, curator, 1991

New York in June: A History of the Lesbian and Gay Pride March, 1991

Graphic Facts: AIDS Posters from Around the World, Joe E. Jeffries, curator, 1991–92

Coming of Age: BiGLYNY, 1969–1992, Steven Cohen, producer, 1992

Body Parts: Visions from the Inside, Seth Gurvitz, producer; Barbara Bickart, Bridget Hughes, Lisa Jacobsen, curators, 1992

Out and Exposed: Young Lesbian and Gay Artists, New Work, 1992

A Memorial Dew Cloth: Celebrating 500 Years of Native American Survival, Rich Wandel, producer; We Wah and Bar Chee Ampee Native Two Spirits in New York City, curator, 1992

Center Kids and AIDS: How Our Children See AIDS, Center Kids, curator, 1992

Marked Men: Photographs of Seth Gurvitz, Joe E. Jeffries, producer, 1993

Out on the Island: Gay and Lesbian Life on Fire Island, Steve Cohen, producer; Esther Newton, Steve Weinstein, curators, 1993

OUT Houses, Seth Gurvitz, curator, 1994

Windows on Gay Life, Joe E. Jeffries, curator, 1994

Nuestras Vida, Nusetras Familias, Nuestras Comunidad, Las Buenas Amigas, curator, 1995

CENTER COOPERATIVE ART EXHIBITS WITH THE 24 HOURS FOR LIFE GALLERY

Eclipse del Alma by Javier Cintron, December 7, 1993

Santo Nino Incarnate by Paul Pfeiffer, March 3, 1994

Pride in Our Diversity: A Group Photo Exhibition, June 14, 1994

GAY/LESBIAN ART AND CENSORSHIP

"Art hath an enemy called Ignorance."

—BEN JOHNSON

In the late 1980s and early 1990s a great debate about art and censorship arose in the United States. There were primarily three "scandals" that brought this topic to national prominence: Senator Jesse Helms's (R-North Carolina) outcry about a Robert Mapplethorpe retrospective (which included homoerotic and S/M photographs); NEA funding of an exhibition that included Andres Serrano's work *Piss Christ* (a large photograph of a crucifix submerged in a yellow liquid identified as urine); and the funding (followed by the de- funding and later court-ordered refunding) of the so-called "NEA Four," four performance artists whose work became "controversial" after right-wing Christians began a smear campaign against them. Three of these artists (John Fleck, Holly Hughes, and Tim Miller) were openly gay and included lesbian and gay material in their work.

Christina Orr-Cahall was director of the Corcoran Gallery in Washington, DC, who canceled the Robert Mapplethorpe retrospective scheduled there in 1989 after uproar from Jesse Helms. She canceled the show in order to avoid controversy—a few of the photographs depicted homoerotic and S/M activity—but instead drew the ire of the art and gay communities. She resigned a few months afterward.

Mapplethorpe's work was the center of another controversy, this time in Cincinnati in 1990 when the local sherif arrested Dennis Barrie, director of the Cincinnati Contemporary Arts Center, on obscenity charges. Barrie was acquitted, but the five photographs in question, of homoerotic sex or of children's genitals, became the focus of a nationwide debate on art and obscenity.

ARTISTIC FREEDOM UNDER ATTACK

The People for the American Way—a 300,000-member nonpartisan constitutional liberties organization—published *Artistic Freedom Under Attack*, Volume 2, in 1994. According to the introduction, this publication provides "a nationwide snapshot of challenges to artistic free expression in America during 1992 and 1993." Not surprisingly, the study found lesbian and gay issues behind a significant portion of the art attacked: "The types of objections raised about art reflected deep divisions in American society around hot-button issues of sexuality, religion, race, sexual orientation, and gender. The most common type of objections to artistic works (with some statistical overlap) include: nudity and/or sexual material (50%); alleged anti-religious content (16%); homosexuality (13%); content alleged to be sexually harassing (6%)."

The study noted the censorship of community productions of two plays that touched on gay themes—John Guare's *Six Degrees of Separation* and Terrence McNally's *Lips Together, Teeth Apart*. The latter production in Cobb County, Georgia, sparked such controversy that the County Commission approved a general anti-gay resolution and voted to end the county's public arts funding.

In a section called "Battles Over Art Reflect Cultural and Social Tensions" the study has this to say: "The increased visibility of [lesbians and gay men], and gay artists, in American society is leading to a rash of attacks on artistic freedom that reflects the culture's lingering discomfort with homosexuality. Parents in Duluth, Minnesota, attacked a dance performance by an all-male troupe, which was scheduled to perform for local schoolchildren, because of unfounded fears concerning homosexual content. And in Danville, Virginia, administrators at Averett College canceled a planned screening of the film *Henry and June* because the film's homosexual content allegedly conflicted with the religious college's 'Christian heritage and values.'"

The study contains hundreds of documented cases of art censorship and their outcomes. It is available from the organization at: People for the American Way, 2000 M Street, N.W., Suite 400, Washington, DC 20036.

A SELECTED HISTORY OF ANTI-GAY CENSORSHIP

Comstock censorship: Self-proclaimed morals crusader Anthony Comstock (1844–1915) was the head of the New York Society for the Suppression of Vice and was responsible for the destruction of 160 tons of literature and pictures. Since homosexual activity and images were practically synonymous with "vice," it does not take much of a stretch of imagination to deduce that a substantial portion of this censorship was aimed at eradicating such images and written depictions. Comstock also spearheaded the push for strong censorship legislation.

Postal censorship: Restrictions on the mailing of "obscenities" were particularly detrimental to published materials dealing with homosexuality. This was not amended until 1954 when the gay publication *ONE* won a Supreme Court decision to be distributed through the mail.

Broadway censorship: In the early part of the century, entire casts of "scandalous" dramas were arrested, including those of the lesbian-themed *The Captive* in 1926. In 1927 the New York State Wade "Padlock" Law went into effect, preventing Broadway plays from overtly portraying lesbians and gay men. The statute was removed from the books only in 1967.

Hollywood censorship: From 1930 until 1956 the movie industry committed self-censorship under the Motion Picture Production Code, also known as the "Hays Code." In addition to adding a "morals" code into actors' contracts, the Code also mandated that lesbians and gay men either not be included in films or be shown in a negative light on the rare occasions they were allowed to be included.

GAY POSTMARKS

In 1989, the U.S. Postal Service issued the first ever gay/lesbian postmark, with an imprint celebrating the Stonewall riots. With art drawn by gay pop artist Keith Haring, of lesbian and gay couples, the imprint read "Stonewall Sta., 20 Years 1969–1989, Lesbian & Gay Pride."

ONLY GAY ARTIST TO HAVE HIS OWN MERCHANDISING SHOP

Keith Haring's Pop Shop
292 Lafayette St.
New York, NY 10012
212-219-2784
For information about Keith Haring, see *Keith Haring: The Authorized Biography*, by John Gruen, Simon & Schuster, 1991.

ARTISTS AND DESIGNERS WHO HAVE DIED OF AIDS

Dan Eicholtz, cartoonist
Perry Ellis, fashion designer
Keith Haring, pop artist
Antonio Lopez, illustrator
Robert Mapplethorpe, photographer
Willi Smith, fashion designer
Hugh Steers, figurative painter
David Wojnarowicz, painter, photographer, writer, filmmaker

SOME OF DAVID WOJNAROWICZ'S PAINTINGS

Queerbasher/Icarus Falling, 1986. Spray paint/acrylic on masonite.
Fire, 1987. Acrylic and mixed media on wood.
Anatomy & Architecture of Desire, 1988–89. Mixed media on wood.
The Weight of the Earth Part 2, late 1980s, photo collage.
Biography of Peter Hujar (7 miles a second), n.d. Acrylic, spray paint, collage on canvas.
Wind (for Peter Hujar), n.d. Acrylic on canvas.
Sex Series (train), 1988–89. Black-and-white photograph.
I Feel a Vague Nausea 1990. Acrylic and photograph on board.

GRAPHIC ART RESPONSES TO AIDS

AIDS Demo Graphics, by Douglas Crimp and Adam Rolston (Bay Press, 1990), describes the work of ACT UP—the AIDS Coalition to Unleash Power—and the graphics it has used to help end the AIDS crisis and increase public awareness of AIDS and the politics of it.

From the introduction: "The simple graphic emblem—SILENCE=DEATH printed in white Gill sans serif type underneath a pink triangle on a black background—has come to signify AIDS activism to an entire community of people confronting the epidemic.... Although identified with ACT UP,... [SILENCE=DEATH] was created by six gay men calling themselves the SILENCE=DEATH Project.... [They] were present at the formation of ACT UP, and they lent their graphic design for placards at ACT UP's second demonstration—at New York City's main post office on April 15, 1987."

COLLECTIVIST ART GROUPS AGAINST AIDS

The SILENCE=DEATH Project
Gran Fury
Little Elvis
Testing the Limits (video production)
DIVA TV (Damned Interferring Video Activists Television)
LAPIT (Lesbian Activists Producing Interesting Television, a lesbian task group
  within DIVA TV)

HELP FOR ARTISTS WITH AIDS

Four times a year Visual Aid gives grants for $250 or less in the form of vouchers redeemable at art stores.

Visual Aid: Artists for AIDS Relief
530 Bush St., Suite 403
San Francisco, CA 94108
415-391-9663

Some gay artists who have received funding from Visual Aid:

Richard Davenport, *Self-Portrait with Headset*, 1983, 22" x 30". Watercolor
  and gouache.
Earl Corse, *Are there Faeries in Your Garden?*, 1985, 14" x 32". Collage
  glued to panel, surrounded by strips of album covers.
Sam Allen, *Two Diners*, 1985, 21" x 30". Cut paper.
Ed Aulerich-Sugai, *Battle Between Karsu Tengu and Shoki*, 1989, 27" x 12".
  Watercolor, gouache, and acrylic on paper.
Mark Paron, *Rubber Rug*, 1989, 43" x 93". Rubber cord woven into metal
  mesh backing.
John Davis, *Boy with Sewing Machine*, 1990, 6" x 9". Tinted photograph.
David Cannon Dashiell, *The Pantocrator*, 1990, 36" diameter. Acrylic on
  Plexiglas security mirror.

SOME GAY DESIGNERS AND ARCHITECTS

Matthew Batanian, fashion designer
Cecil Beaton, Hollywood costume designer
Leo Blackman, lamp and furniture designer, architect
Perry Ellis, fashion designer
Rudi Gernreich, fashion designer
Halston, fashion designer
Phillip Johnson, architect
Orry-Kelly, Hollywood costume designer
Isaac Mizrahi, fashion designer
Todd Oldham, fashion designer
Walter Plunkett, Hollywood costume designer
Emilio Pucci, wallet designer
Willi Smith, fashion designer
David Spada, jewelry designer (designed freedom rings)
Jheri Williams, fashion designer

DESIGNER SPECIAL MENTION

Erté (a.k.a., Romain de Tirtoff), 1893–1990. Although Russian born, this acclaimed international designer created dresses for everyone from Mata Hari to the dancers and actors of the Ziegfeld Follies. His designs of extenuated women with long, flowing gowns were on the cover of hundreds of *Harper's Bazaar* magazines throughout the mid-century.

WHO IS THAT MAN IN THE ARROW SHIRT?

J. C. Leyendecker, 1874–1951, one of the leading U.S. commercial artists of his day, used his lover (of more than fifty years), Charles Beach, for his model of the original Arrow collar man, a pervasive symbol of masculinity in the first part of the century.

FIRST MAKEUP ARTIST TO BE HONORED WITH AN AWARD OF EXCELLENCE FROM THE COUNCIL OF FASHION DESIGNERS OF AMERICA

In 1995, openly gay Kevyn Aucoin, author of the best-selling *The Art of Makeup* (HarperCollins).

DESIGNERS FIGHTING AIDS

DIFFA—Design Industries Foundation Fighting AIDS—mobilizes the immense talents and resources of the design and related industries to fight HIV disease and AIDS. Their national office is

DIFFA
150 West 26th St., Suite 602
New York, NY 10001
Phone: 212-727-3100
Fax: 212-727-2574

"Fashion is an important aspect of my AIDS activist work because I use it as an asset to reach young gay communities—which comprise much of the fashion world—and to bring attention to people of color."
    —model and ACT UP member Blane Mosely. As an example of his double life, one week Mosely was in the papers for bolting himself inside the office of Burroughs Wellcome, protesting the cost of AZT; the next week his photo was in People *magazine, vogueing at Suzanne Bartsch's Love Ball.*

DESIGN CONFERENCES

Queer by Design, a working conference for lesbian and gay graphic designers, art directors, photographers, illustrators, and other communication professionals, was held in 1991 in San Francisco.

Design Pride '94, held June 1994 at Cooper Union in New York City and sponsored by the Organization of Lesbian and Gay Architects and Designers, was the first ever international conference for lesbian and gay architects, interior designers, landscape architects, and product designers. Participants met to talk about the history of lesbian and gay design and to discuss issues in the workplace.

LESBIAN AND GAY COMIC STRIPS AND CARTOON CHARACTERS

The first comic strips as we know them in modern times appeared in the Sunday supplements of Hearst newspapers in 1897 as a circulation-boosting tactic. The first commercial pulp book appeared during the Depression, in 1934. These works generally avoided all explicit indications of sex or alternative culture.

• Of note is the *Batman* and *Wonder Woman* books, which were early mainstream series interpreted by gay men and lesbians to suggest their desires and power.

• The earliest predecessor to actual gay comics is the illustrated stories of *Blade* (Carlyle Kneeland Bate, 1917–1989) in the late 1940s. In animated cartoons of the forties, Bugs Bunny often dressed in drag to "catch" his man, Elmer Fudd.

• The social revolutions taking place in the 1960s, in conjunction with dismantled censorship laws, allowed the first exploration of once taboo subjects.

• One of the first explicitly gay comic characters ran in 1964 in *Drum*, a Philadelphia gay monthly newspaper: *Harry Chess*, drawn by Al Shapiro, a.k.a. A. Jay.

- In the 1970s more sexually explicit characters were drawn by such artists as Bill Ward, Sean, and Stephen. *The Advocate* ran a regular one-panel series by Joe Johnson called *Miss Thing*. *Christopher Street* also published a series of cartoons.
- In the early 1980s, Howard Cruse began *Gay Comix*, a series of pulp books, which included comics by both men and women.
- Also in the early 1980s, Alison Bechdel began to run a series of plates called *Dykes to Watch Out For* in the New York City newspaper *Womanews*. Later, she began expanding the idea in a regular cartoon strip, which is now syndicated in lesbian and gay newspapers and magazines across the country.
- Today there are several lesbian and gay cartoons that run regularly in the lesbian and gay media. There are also lesbian and gay characters in strips drawn by straight artists and syndicated in mainstream venues. Below is a selected survey of both types:
- Northstar, gay comic book hero in straight comic
- Shadow Hawk was a mainstream super hero with AIDS (who died in Issue #18).
- Andy Lippincott, a *Doonesbury* character, drawn by Gary Trudeau, came out on February 10, 1976.
- Akbar & Jeff, from *Life in Hell* drawn by Matt Groening
- Homer Simpsons's male secretary, from the animated TV show *The Simpsons*, also created by Matt Groening. The voice was provided by Harvey Fierstein.
- Captain Maggie Sawyer, comic book hero from *Metropolis S.C.U.*, from DC Comics
- Maggie and Hopie, from *Love and Rockets*, by Jaime Hernandez
- *Hothead Paisan: Homocidal Lesbian Terrorist*, comic book cult classic, by Diane Dimassa
- Lawrence Poirier, from strip *For Better or For Worse*, drawn by Lynn Johnston (gay teenager who came out and was thrown out of his home by his parents), 1993
- *Outland*, a comic strip by Berke Breathed
- Bert and Ernie on *Sesame Street*. (In June 1994, fundamentalists outed the muppet couple, saying that they "live together in a one-bedroom house, never do anything without each other and exhibit feminine characteristics." In a press release the Children's Television Workshop, which produces the show, flatly denied that Bert and Earnie were a gay couple. You can make up your own mind, regardless of the political context.)

For more information, see *Gay Comics*, by Robert Triptow, New American Library, 1989.

THE (BRIEF) HISTORY OF ANDY LIPPINCOTT IN *DOONESBURY*

1976: Andy comes out, but is gone from the strip by the end of the year.

Mid-1980s: Andy surfaces again briefly as an organizer of the "Bay Area Gay Alliance" but is quickly offstage again.

1989: Andy is introduced for a third and final time as dying with AIDS. Andy is dead by the end of the year, never being seen outside the context of a hospital bed.

GRAN FURY ART COLLECTIVE

Gran Fury was a collective art group formed in 1988 for a window installation entitled *Let the Record Show* at the New Museum of Contemporary Art in New York. (New Museum curator Bill Olander, a person with AIDS and member of ACT UP, had offered the window space for a work about AIDS.) Members of Gran Fury were from ACT UP, and wanted to do political action through art and agitprop.

According to the book *AIDS Demo Graphics*, after finishing *Let the Record Show*, the artists "resolved to continue as an autonomous collective—a 'band of individuals united in anger and dedicated to exploiting the power of art to end the AIDS crisis.' Calling themselves Gran Fury, after the Plymouth model used by the New York City police as undercover cars, they became for a time ACT UP's unofficial propaganda ministry and guerrilla graphic designers."

One of their more famous posters/graphics was a sign seen on the sides of buses and in subways showing three couples kissing (an interracial male/female couple, an interracial male/male couple, and a black lesbian couple) with this headline: "Kissing Doesn't Kill: Greed and Indifference Do."

Another one of their signature pieces included this text "Corporate Greed, Government Inaction, and Public Indifference Make AIDS a Political Crisis" and "ALL PEOPLE WITH AIDS ARE INNOCENT" (1988).

ANDY WARHOL

Andy Warhol was born Andrew Warhola, Jr. around 1930, to a working-class family of Eastern European origin in Forest City, Pennsylvania. He attended the Carnegie Institute of Technology in Pittsburgh, studying art, and afterward moved to New York City, where he quickly became prominent in commerical art. He met two other gay artists, Jasper Johns and Robert Rauschenberg, who were also seminal in the new popular art movement of Pop Art. Warhol's signature Campbell soup cans and Brillo boxes were at first iconoclastic pieces. He soon became as famous for the company he kept as for his work.

With money he had made as a commericial artist he bought a large warehouse that became known as the Factory, where assistants and associates made art under his direction. With the money he made from his paintings and lithographs he began making art films, which, like everything he had done, helped expand and break stereotypes of people and art forms. (For instance, *Blow Job* is a film of a man's face while—off screen—he is getting a blow job from another man; and *Empire* is a nine-hour movie of nothing but the top of the Empire State Building.)

In 1968 Warhol was shot and seriously wounded by former factory actress Valerie Solanas. He never quite got over this attack and gravitated toward a wealthier, more socialite crowd. In the 1970s he established *Interview* magazine, which charted the lifestyle of his new circle. Warhol's fame continued to spread, especially after he died in 1987 of complications from routine surgery. His place as a great twentieth-century voice was cemented when the Museum of Modern Art held a retrospective of his work in 1989. The Andy Warhol Museum opened in Pittsburgh in 1995.

Gay Art Films by Warhol

Blow Job (1963)   *Vinyl* (1965) (S/M film)
My Hustler (1965)   *Chelsea Girls* (1966)

3. GAY BUSINESS AND INDUSTRY

"I now recognize the countless ways I was told—formally and informally, in word and in deed—that I was unwelcome in this organization [an ad agency]. Like the company's other lesbian and gay employees, I sensed the moral judgment implicit in social invitations for 'you and a girlfriend,' in the occasional joke about who was or wasn't a queer, and in the seductive advertisements, depicting heterosexual romance and love, that I [was] helping to create."

—JAMES D. WOODS, *The Corporate Closet: The Professional Lives of Gay Men in America* Free Press, 1993.

Some of us are fortunate enough to work in gay organizations or to be in business for ourselves. But like James Woods, many gay men have faced homophobia in the business world and found it difficult—or impossible—to come out in the one area where they spend most of their waking hours. Having to hide in the closet at work can sap both our energy and our creativity. How many times have we avoided divulging anything about our personal lives, when everyone around us was talking about "the wife and kids"?

Fortunately, gay and lesbian employee associations and union groups are sprouting up across corporate America, lobbying for gay employees' rights and domestic partner benefits. Many major companies have already instituted progressive policies for their gay employees. The following is a guide to some of the groundbreaking work that is being done to make more workplaces "gay friendly."

How to Come Out in the Workplace

Coming out on the job can be an awkward experience, but it doesn't have to be, especially if you heed the following suggestions for dispelling co-workers' confusion and easing any misgivings of your own:

- *Come out to workplace friends first.* Building a support system of trusted co-workers who respect you and your sexual identity is an important first step toward fully coming out.
- *Make coming out to the boss your next priority.* Choose an environment in which you feel comfortable. The occasion need not be formal or the statement overt; casually mentioning the name of a partner or boyfriend while sharing a cab to a meeting or over a drink after work should be sufficient notification.
- *Initiate gay and lesbian awareness in the workplace.* Start or support existing programs that are homo-friendly. Something as simple as asking co-workers to sponsor you in a fundraising event with a gay theme can boost employee consciousness and possibly alert other gay employees to your identity.
- Visibility in the workplace is important; it can foster heightened sensitivity among employees who are not gay and help other gays and lesbians feel more relaxed about coming out.

QUEER LABOR NOTES FROM HERE AND THERE

- The first regional chapter of the U.S. Department of Agriculture's Gay, Lesbian, and Bisexual Employee's Organization (USDA GLOBE) was formed in Northern California in May 1995. USDA GLOBE was informally organized in December 1993 and was officially recognized by USDA on March 25, 1994. It has 118 members stationed around the nation.
- In mid-1994, the Service Employees International Union (SEIU) added two gay groups to its shop roster: the Human Rights Campaign Fund (HRCF) and the San Francisco AIDS Foundation.
- In March of 1995, gay, lesbian, and unmarried heterosexual municipal employees in Denver won a victory in gaining permission to take sick leave to care for their domestic partners under a policy change approved 4–1 by the city personnel board.
- The first ever gay newspaper to unionize was the *San Francisco Bay Times*, whose five full-time employees became affiliated with the Northern California Newspaper Guild in March of 1995.
- In 1994, Capital Cities/ABC Inc., which has about twenty thousand employees, became the only one of the four major television networks to extend spousal benefits to the domestic partners of gay and lesbian employees.

SOURCES: Washington Blade, May 26, 1995; *The Advocate,* May 31, 1994; October 10, 1994, and April 18, 1995.

LABOR HIGHS AND LOWS IN THE NATION'S CAPITAL

The phrase "Lavender Hill Mob" took on new meaning in May 1994, when the Lesbian and Gay Congressional Staff Association became an officially registered staff organization on Capitol Hill. The group's cofounder, Mark Agrast, senior legislative assistant to openly gay representative Gerry Studds (D-Mass.), explained the purpose of the group by observing that "the working environment on Capitol Hill varies sharply from one office to the next. Our goal is to improve the quality of life for lesbian and gay congressional employees."

GAY EMPLOYEE ORGANIZING

The National Gay and Lesbian Task Force Workplace Initiative Project publishes a four-page pamphlet called "Organizing a Gay, Lesbian, and Bisexual Employee Association," which is available for $1 from NGLTF. The pamphlet discusses the logistics of forming an employee group, including such issues as getting the word out, confidentiality, diversity, and member dues.

NGLTF also publishes tips on gay union organizing and domestic partnership lobbying. For a complete publications list or to order the pamphlet mentioned write to NGLTF/Publications, 2320 17th Street, NW, Washington, DC 20009.

But nothing is ever so simple and straightforward in Washington. As of mid-1995, activities of this kind by federal employees have come under direct attack from two bills introduced by—who else?—Senator Jesse Helms (R-North Carolina). One bill would ban the use of federal funds to carry out pro-gay programs for federal employees—initiatives just like the Lesbian and Gay Congressional Staff Association. The bill could prevent gay employee groups from meeting in federal offices, posting notices on bulletin boards, or using interoffice mail for communications. The second bill would give special exemption from workplace nondiscrimination policies to government employees who voice prejudice against lesbian and gay coworkers.

SOURCES: *Washington Blade,* May 26, 1995; *The Advocate,* April 18, 1995.

GROUNDBREAKING UNIONS

- The first union involvement in gay and lesbian issues came in 1973, when the leadership of the American Federation of Labor and Congress of Industrial Organizations responded to firings of gay members of the American Federation of Teachers by publicly stating its support for gay rights.
- In 1982, the gay and lesbian union caucus at *The Village Voice* was the first ever to win domestic-partnership benefits.
- In the mid-1980s the Service Employees International Union (SEIU) (which has thousands of members in over twenty lavender caucuses) and the American Federation of State, County, and Municipal Employees (AFSCME) negotiated full domestic partnership benefits in Seattle and other cities, years ahead of gay-friendly corporate America.
- The Stonewall 25 celebration in New York City saw the formation of Pride at Work: The National Gay, Lesbian, Bi, and Transgender Labor Organization. Funded by AFSCME and eleven other unions, the organization's founding conference brought together more than three hundred representatives of twenty-five unions and local and regional gay and lesbian union groups.

BUSINESS-RELATED QUOTATIONS

"WE NEED A LISTING OF ALL THE GAY PEOPLE IN SAN FRANCISCO."

—one of the entries in *San Francisco Business's* compilation of the zaniest questions and requests received by the city's Chambers of Commerce in 1993

"In American life, business and politics are two sides of the same coin—and that's a good reason for gays and lesbians to keep an eye on the business world.... Whether we function as consumers, activists, or entrepreneurs, one thing is certain: Taking care of business is a great way to make changes."

— *Special Report on Gay Money/Gay Power* (quoted in *The Advocate,* April 18, 1995)

"Many single gay and lesbian employees—as well as those with domestic partners—now see [domestic partner benefits] as a simple matter of equal pay for

equal work. Extensions of equal benefits has become a tangible symbol that their employer pays and values them as much as it does their heterosexual colleagues."

—C. ARTHUR BAIN, "How Do I Find a Gay-Friendly Employer?" *The Advocate*, October 4, 1994.

"So how do you get [domestic partnership benefits]? My standard motto is, 'Don't ask, don't get.'"

—ED MIKENS, *The Advocate*, February 22, 1994

STATES THAT FORBID ANTIGAY DISCRIMINATION IN EMPLOYMENT (AS OF MAY 1995)

California
Connecticut
Hawaii
Massachusetts
Minnesota

New Jersey
Rhode Island
Vermont
Wisconsin

BUSINESS QUICK FACTS

- Half of the Fortune 1000 companies have nondiscrimination policies protecting their gay and lesbian employees.[1]
- More than twenty federal agencies currently have nondiscrimination policies that include sexual orientation.[2]
- More than sixty American companies have lesbian, gay and bisexual employee groups—many officially recognized and funded by the company—and new groups are forming all the time.[3]
- When Vermont became the first state to provide domestic partner health benefits to its state employees, in August of 1994, of the 136 unmarried couples claiming the benefit, 119 were heterosexual, while only 17 same-sex couples applied. This ratio is typical for companies offering these benefits throughout the nation.[4]
- Multinational corporations often do not require their foreign subsidiaries to apply the same nondiscrimination policies that their U.S. offices follow.[5]
- It is estimated that gay men and lesbians spend as much as $500 billion annually in the United States.[6]

[1]SOURCE: Elizabeth Birch, executive director of the Human Rights Campaign Fund, as quoted in *The Advocate*, April 18, 1995, p. 40.

[2]SOURCE: *The Advocate*, "Federal Employees Under Siege," April 18, 1995, p. 40.

[3]SOURCE: *The Advocate*, "How Do I Find a Gay-Friendly Employer?" by C. Arthur Bain, October 4, 1994, p. 49.

[4]SOURCE: *The Advocate*, "Straight Couples Come Out" October 4, 1994, p. 49.

[5]SOURCE: *The Advocate*, "How Do I Find a Gay-Friendly Employer?" by C. Arthur Bain, October 4, 1994.

[6]SOURCE: *The Advocate*, "Ikea's Gay Gamble," by John Gallagher, May 3, 1994, p. 25.

The Impact of HIV on Business

A study published in the Spring 1994 issue of *Inquiry*, a journal put out by Blue Cross and Blue Shield, revealed the following cost impact of HIV on business in the United States: a maximum of $32,000 over five years per HIV-infected employee and an average of $17,000 total. The added costs examined included health care, disability, hiring and training, and pensions. These figures reflect the better health and changing treatment costs for people with HIV, and show that much of the widely accepted $85,000–$100,000 lifetime cost of AIDS care is borne by society, not business.

SOURCE: *The Advocate*, June 14, 1994

HIV-Related Business

The entrepreneurial spirit has found a home pretty much everywhere in America, and the "world of AIDS" is no exception. The horrendous fact of the growing HIV/AIDS epidemic here and worldwide has given rise to a plethora of businesses and profit-generating services geared toward persons living with HIV/AIDS. These businesses run the gamut from shamefully exploitative to genuinely beneficial. Viatical settlement companies will purchase your life insurance policy in exchange for cash in hand. AIDS jewelry, from eighteen-karat-gold "AIDS bracelets" to condom earrings, can be found on the pages of mail-order catalogs and department store shelves alike. Nightsweats & T-Cells, a company owned and operated by HIV-positive persons, sells T-shirts and other items delivering "in your face" messages and benefiting people with AIDS. And then there's *Poz* magazine. . . . In short, there is something for just about everyone in the HIV/AIDS "marketplace" today.

Some Major (Recent) Queer Moments in "Pushing Product"

- RuPaul recently became the featured "covergirl" for M.A.C. Cosmetics' "Who's That M.A.C. girl?" ad campaign, which included posters throughout New York City.
- In 1995 Nike began airing a television commercial featuring Ric Muñoz, a media darling of last year's Gay Games IV, with captions reading: "80 miles every week—10 marathons every year—HIV Positive—Just Do It." (William Burroughs, *Naked Lunch* author, cyber/queer literary forefather, and famed heroin addict, was also featured on a Nike TV ad which aired in 1994.)
- In the public service arena, Melissa Etheridge posed nude with her (also nude) girlfriend on behalf of People for the Ethical Treatment of Animals.
- Minneapolis-based Dayton Hudson Corporations, one of the nation's largest retailers, began test-marketing gay-themed greeting cards at two of its Marshall Field's department stores in Chicago and a Dayton's department store in Minneapolis. The cards are created and distributed by Cardthartic, a Chicago firm that describes itself as "Hallmark-like."
- A recent addition to the ongoing, oh-so-Britishly acerbic ad series for Tanqueray gin featured the regularly appearing Mr. Jenkins character alongside the fol-

lowing copy: "Mr. Jenkins hopes to see you riding in front of him in the California AIDS Ride 2 as the view from behind Mr. Jenkins may not be too flattering." In addition to selling gin, the ad promoted the annual May California AIDS Ride. Tanqueray also underwrote and promoted the 1995 Boston–New York AIDS Ride.

SOURCES: *OUT*, May 1995; *The Advocate*, April 5, 1994

MARKETING TO THE "GAY NICHE"

One of the sexiest and most dramatic homoerotic ads to hit the print media in 1995 was brought to us by Diesel Jeans and Workwear. The ad features a beautiful black-and-white photograph by David LaChapelle of "superhunks" Bob and Rod Jackson-Paris in sailor garb engaged in a deep embrace and even deeper kiss amid a boisterous retro-looking V-Day celebration—a flurry of American flags wave and "Victory," "Peace At Last," and "Welcome Home Boys" signs populate the background of their ecstatic embrace. The "small print" on the corner of the ad tells us that this image is "Number 35 in a series of Diesel "How To . . ." guides to successful living for people interested in general health and mental power."

According to Diana Loguzzo, who does advertising and PR for Diesel Jeans and Workwear, the company has received "Nothing but positive feedback about the ad. We get an average of forty to fifty calls a day from people who love it." What's more, the New York Historical Society has plans to place it in its permanent collection. The ad, which ran nationally, is, according to Loguzzo, "about tolerance, respect, love and many other things."

IKEA

Advertising history was made on March 30, 1994, when the nationwide home furnishings chain IKEA premiered a thirty-second television spot featuring a gay male couple shopping for a dining room table. The spot was shown on local TV stations in Philadelphia, New York City, and Washington, DC. It is believed to be the first mainstream TV commercial built around a self-identified same-sex couple to be shown in the U.S. (In 1991, Toyota of Australia aired a now famous—in Australia, anyway—"family car" ad featuring a male couple and their dogs.)

The ad was one of several IKEA commercials depicting a diversity of Americans and American lives. A recently divorced woman and a family adopting a child were among the other scenarios presented in the series. The following is a transcript of IKEA's gay male "dining room spot":

STEVE: Well, you know, we went to IKEA 'cause we thought it was time for a serious dining room table and—
MITCH: We have slightly different tastes. I mean, Steve's more into country. It frightens me, but at the same time I have compassion.
STEVE: We've been together about three years.
MITCH: I met Steve at my sister's—

BOTH: Wedding.

MITCH: I was really impressed with how, just, well-designed the IKEA furniture was.

STEVE: He's really into craftsmanship.

MITCH: These chairs are really sturdy.

STEVE: This table included a leaf.

MITCH: A leaf means—

STEVE: Commitment.

MITCH: Staying together, commitment. We've got another leaf waiting when we really start getting along.

SOURCES: "Ikea's Gay Gamble," by John Gallagher, *The Advocate,* May 3, 1994 and *The Village Voice* Official Program Guide for the 1995 2d National Gay and Lesbian Business and Consumer Expo, April 1995.

GAY BUSINESS TRAVEL

A recent special advertising section in *The Advocate* featured a "how-to" guide for the queer business traveler. Although most of us associate "gay travel" with "vacation," the fact is that most gay people—like most Americans—do much of their traveling for business purposes. Surveys assessing the amount of all travel done by gay men and lesbians—a volume estimated to be as high at $17 billion annually—find that a large percentage of this travel is business-related. A number of mainstream travel companies are now seeking to attract this substantial gay and lesbian consumer base through gay-focused marketing and policy changes that address the needs and concerns of gay business travelers. Herewith is a brief listing of travel companies rated by *The Advocate* (using information culled from *Out & About,* the gay and lesbian travel newsletter) as "exceptional," "gay-friendly," or "antigay."

Exceptional Policies or Practices

American Airlines   National Care Rental
Northwest Airlines   Hyatt Hotels
Virgin Airlines   American Express Credit Card
Avis Car Rental

Gay-Friendly Businesses

Continental Airlines   Lufthansa Airlines
Kiwi Airlines   Alamo Car Rental

Anti-Gay Policies or Practices

TWA Airlines   Hertz Car Rental

THE BEST AND THE WORST COMPANIES FOR GAYS AND LESBIANS

Cracking the Corporate Closet, a gay and lesbian guidebook on the "best" and "worst" companies to work for, buy from, and invest in, uses three major criteria for assessing how "gay-positive" or "gay-friendly" a given company is. The first is fundamental: Is sexual orientation included in the company's anti-discrimination policy? Any company lacking such a policy automatically received a low ranking. Here are a few of the "winners" and "losers" on the anti-discrimination policy "litmus test":

Twenty "Losers"—A Sampling of Companies That Do Not Include Sexual Orientation in Their Anti-Discrimination Policies[1]

American Home Products	Burger King
Corning	Hill and Knowlton
Hilton	Hoffman–La Roche
Home Depot	J.C. Penney
Lands' End	Lockheed
Marriott	Mobil
Motorola	PBS
Pepsico	Phillips
Reynolds Metal	Rite Aid
The Gap	Toys 'R' Us

[1]As of July 1994.

Twenty "Winners"—A Sampling of Companies That Do Include Sexual Orientation in Their Anti-Discrimination Policies

Allstate	Apple Computers
AT&T	Bankers Trust
Ben & Jerry's	Burroughs Wellcome
CBS	Citicorp
Disney	Eastman Kodak
General Motors	Harley-Davidson
Hewlett-Packard	McGraw-Hill
Procter & Gamble	RJR Nabisco
Seagram	Sprint
Tambrands	Xerox

The second criterion is whether the company goes beyond basic anti-discrimination protections and extends domestic partnership benefits to its employees. This is important, since according to the U.S. Chamber of Commerce, nearly 40 percent of the average American worker's earnings are received in benefits. Since extending domestic partner benefits costs the company money, the number of corporations extending such benefits to their lesbian and gay employees is signficantly smaller than those providing basic anti-discrimination protections. Here's a list of ten companies that do extend such benefits:

Apple Computer	Ben & Jerry's
Boston Globe	Charles Schwab
Fannie Mae	Levi Strauss & Co.
Lotus	MCA (Universal)
Microsoft	Quark
Viacom	Village Voice

Interestingly, according to a study by *Human Resources Focus* (January 1994), the four top reasons cited by companies that do not offer domestic partnership benefits are the following: fear of rising benefits expenditures; too few employee requests; lack of senior management support; and anxiety over moving into uncharted waters.

The third method used in *Cracking the Corporate Closet* for making overall determinations of how well corporations did by their gay and lesbian employees was conducting interviews with present and former employees of the companies under consideration and searching through press reports of "corporate behavior" on relevant issues. Based on these three criteria, the guidebook provides the following rankings on the "best" and "worst" American companies for gay male and lesbian employees.

The Twelve Best Companies for Gay and Lesbian Employees

1. Apple Computer
2. Ben & Jerry's
3. Boston Globe
4. Charles Schwab
5. Fannie Mae
6. Levi Strauss & Co.
7. Lotus
8. MCA (Universal)
9. Pacific Gas and Electric
10. Quark
11. Viacom
12. Ziff-Davis

The 13 Worst Companies for Gay and Lesbian Employees

1. Abbott Laboratories
2. American Home Products Corp.
3. Circle K Corporation
4. Coastal Corporation
5. Cracker Barrel Old Country Store
6. Delta
7. First Interstate Bank
8. General Electric
9. Great Republic Insurance Co.
10. Guardian Life Insurance Corp.
11. H & H Music Company
12. HealthAmerica Corp.
13. Milliken & Company

GAY AND LESBIAN EMPLOYEE GROUPS

In conducting extensive research on the level of "gay-friendliness" in America's corporate world, the authors of *Cracking the Corporate Closet* (from which the selected listing below is taken) found that "active, vocal lesbian and gay employee groups are a key factor in effecting change within a corporation." They point out that very few corporations have adopted domestic partnership benefits, anti-gay discrimination clauses, and related policies without pressure from such groups.

Often beginning as informal social networks, these employee groups eventually took the step of announcing their existence publicly, soliciting new members, and advocating for an improved work environment for lesbians and gay men.

AT&T
LEAGUE—Lesbian, Bisexual, and
  Gay United Employees at AT&T
4 Campus Drive
Parsippany, NJ 07054
Contact: Ms. Kathleen Dermody,
  908-658-6013

Coors
LAGER—Lesbian and Gay Employee
  Resource
Mail Stop #NH420
Coors Brewing Co.
Golden, CO 80401
Contact: Mr. Earl Nissen,
  303-277-5309

The Walt Disney Co.
LEAGUE
500 South Buena Vista St.
Burbank, CA 91521-5209
Contact: Mr. Garrett Hicks,
  818-560-1000

Hewlett-Packard
GLEN—Gay, Lesbian and Bisexual
  Employee Network
P.O. Box 700542
San Jose, CA 95170
Contact: Mr. Kim Harris,
  415-857-7771 or
Mr. Greg Gloss 415-447-6123

Johnson & Johnson
RWJPRI
700 Route 200
Raritan, NJ 08869
Contact: Ms. Cheryl Vitow,
  908-704-5607

Levi Strauss & Co.
Lesbian and Gay Employee
  Association
1155 Battery St.
San Francisco, CA 94111

Contact: Ms. Michele Dryden,
  415-544-7103

Lockheed Missiles and Space
GLOBAL—Gay, Lesbian, or Bisexual
  at Lockheed
LMSC Management Assn.—Bay Area
  Chapter
Dept. 27-62, Building 599
P.O. Box 3504
Sunnyvale, CA 95088-3504
Contact: Mr. Frederick Parsons,
  408-255-4936, or Mr. Patrick Miller,
  408-369-1713

Microsoft
GLEAM—Gay, Lesbian & Bisexual
  Employees at Microsoft
1 Microsoft Way
Redmond, WA 98052
Contact: Mr. Jeff Howard,
  206-936-5581

New York Times Co.
Gay & Lesbian Caucus
229 W. 43rd St.
New York, NY 10036
Contact: Mr. David Dunlap,
  212-556-7082

Polaroid
Polaroid Gay, Lesbian and Bisexual
  Association
585 Technology Square-4
Cambridge, MA 02139

Prudential
EAGLES—Employee Association of
  Gay Men and Lesbians
P.O. Box 1566
Minneapolis, MN 55440-1566
Contact: Ms. Cathy Perkins,
  612-557-7918

United Airlines
GLUE Coalition—Gay & Lesbian
   United Employees
2261 Market St., #293
San Francisco, CA 94114
Contact: Mr. Tom Cross,
   800-999-3448

The Village Voice
Lesbian & Gay Caucus
36 Cooper Square
New York, NY 10003
Contact: Mr. Richard Goldstein,
   212-475-3300

Wells Fargo
Mail Stop #MAC 0188-133
111 Sutter St., 13th Fl.
San Francisco, CA 94104
Contact: Ms. Barbara Zoloth,
   415-396-2767

Xerox
GALAXE—Gays and Lesbians at
   Xerox
P.O. Box 25382
Rochester, NY 14625
Contact: Mr. David Frishkorn,
   716-423-5090

OTHER RESOURCES

Newsletters/Magazines

Gay/Lesbian/Bisexual Corporate Letter
Art Bain
P.O. Box 602
Murray Hill Station
New York, NY 10156-0601
212-447-7328
Internet address: corpletter@aol.com
$20 for four quarterly issues
   Aimed at gay, lesbian, and bisexual employees, corporate human resources de-
partments, and others concerned with gay issues in the workplace.

Working It Out: The Newsletter for Gay and Lesbian Employment Issues
Ed Mickens
P.O. Box 2079
New York, NY 10108
212-769-2384
Fax: 212-721-2680
$60 for four quarterly issues

Victory!
"Written by, for, and about gays and lesbians working for themselves."
1500 W. El Camino Ave.
Suite 526
Sacramento, CA 95833
916-444-6894
   Aimed at corporate human resource departments, management, and others con-
cerned with gay issues in the workplace.

Workplace-Related—Legal

These groups can provide information regarding domestic-partner benefits and discuss the work-related laws that pertain to sexual orientation, AIDS, transgenderism, and other issues.

American Civil Liberties Union (ACLU)
National Gay and Lesbian Rights Project
132 West 43rd St.
New York, NY 10036
212-944-9800 (ext. 545)

Gay and Lesbian Advocates and Defenders (GLAD)
P.O. Box 218
Boston, MA 02112
617-426-1350

Lambda Legal Defense and Education Fund
666 Broadway
New York, NY 10012
212-995-8585

National Lesbian and Gay Law Association
Box 77130
National Capital Station
Washington, DC 20014
202-389-0161

Workplace-Related—Political

These organizations coordinate national civil-rights efforts or are specifically devoted to work-related issues. They can provide information about what other corporations are doing, provide model nondiscrimination policies, information on legislation, and other resources.

Hollywood Supports
6430 Sunset Blvd., Suite 102
Los Angeles, CA 90028
213-962-3023

Human Rights Campaign
1012 14th St. NW
Washington, DC 20005
202-628-4160

Interfaith Center on Corporate Responsibility
475 Riverside Dr., Rm 566
New York, NY 10115
212-870-2296

National Gay and Lesbian Task Force (NGLTF)
1734 14th St. NW
Washington, DC 20009-4309
202-332-6483

The NGLTF has a network of grassroots organizing teams which includes workplace issues among its areas of focus. NGLTF also publishes a variety of pamphlets on workplace issues for minimal cost (see box p. 128).

Wall Street Project/Community Lesbian and Gay Rights Institute
217 E. 85 St.
Suite 162
New York, NY 10028

Workplace-Related—Unions

Pride at Work: The National Gay, Lesbian, Bi, and Transgender Labor
  Organization
P.O. Box 9605
North Amherst, MA 01059-9605
413-549-5972

AIDS-Related Resources

Many national and local AIDS service organizations provide some form of workplace training and education on HIV/AIDS issues. The National AIDS Clearinghouse sells a $25 manager's kit entitled "Business Responds to AIDS." NAIC is located at P.O. Box 6003, Rockville, MD 20849-6003; 800-458-5231.

A source of general information on the impact of AIDS in the workplace is the National Leadership Coalition on AIDS, 1730 M Street, NW, Washington, DC 20036; 202-429-0930.

Books

Baker, Dan, and Sean Strub. Cracking the Corporate Closet. *HarperCollins, 1995.*
Beer, Chris, et al. *Gay Workers: Trade Unions and the Law*, State Mutual Books, 1983.
Frank, Miriam, and Desma Holcomb. *Pride at Work: Organizing for Lesbian and Gay Rights in Unions*. Lesbian and Gay Labor Network, P.O. Box 1159, Peter Stuyvesant Station, New York, NY 10009.
Harbeck, Karen M., ed. *Coming Out of the Classroom Closet: Gay and Lesbian Students, Teachers, and Curricula*. Harrington Park Press, 1992.
Hunter, Nan, Sherryl Michaelson, and Thomas Stoddard. *The Rights of Lesbians and Gay Men: The Basic ACLU Guide to a Gay Person's Rights*. Southern University Press.
McNaught, Brian. *Gay Issues in the Workplace*. St. Martin's Press, 1993.

Mickens, Ed. *The 100 Best Companies for Gay Men and Lesbians*. Pocket Books, 1994.

Stone, Susan Carol, and Anthony Patrick Carnevale. *Our Diverse Work Force: A Survey of Issues and a Practical Guide*. U.S. Dept. of Labor and the American Society of Training and Development, 1993.

Woods, James D., and Jay H. Lucas. *The Corporate Closet: The Professional Lives of Gay Men in America*. The Free Press, 1993.

Videos

Gay Issues in the Workplace: Gay, Lesbian and Bisexual Employees Speak for Themselves with Brian McNaught, (TRB Productions, P.O. Box 2362, Boston, MA 02107, 1993).

Brokering Resources

The "Gales Investment Letter" is an investment advisory newsletter devoted to gay-friendly growth stocks. Wesley Hicks is the publisher and can be reached at 800-226-9245.

Howard Tharsing, an independent broker, is also the director of Progressive Asset Management's Lavender Screen Project, which uses a five-point scale in evaluating companies on their level of gay-friendliness. A leading participant in NGLTF workplace activities, Tharsing provides competitively priced brokerage services and can be reached in Oakland, California, at 800-786-2998.

4. GAY CULTURE

*"I speak for the individual. For anyone out there who's ever had a dream and has
had to listen to 'Honey, you can't do that.' 'We don't allow blacks here.' 'We don't
allow fags here.' 'We don't allow women in this bar.' I am a giant 'Fuck you' to
bigotry. Buddha, Krishna, Jesus, and now RuPaul. I'm about the politics of the
soul. I transcend the gay community. I speak to everyone with pain in their heart.
I am here for all of them. But now the challenge for me is to project that message
when I'm not in drag."*

—RuPAUL, as quoted in *The Advocate*, August 23, 1994

FEMALE IMPERSONATION WAY BACK WHEN

Varius Avitus

A beautiful boy-priest of the ancient Roman Empire. Probably the greatest female
impersonator of his time, who gave lavish dance performances. Those audience
members who didn't appreciate the dances might be put to death.

Julius Caesar, Nero, and Commodus

Roman emperors who enjoyed dressing as women. They wore makeup, perfume,
jewelry, and rich silks. Occasionally impersonated mythological heroines in public
performances.

Shakespearean Boy-Actors

Boys played female roles on stage, because the Catholic Church declared it "immoral" for women to act on stage. Female impersonation thus became an important ingredient of Elizabethan and Jacobean theater. The word "drag" for female
impersonation is believed to have its origins at this time, possibly referring to the
way the boy-actors' gowns would drag behind them.

SOURCE: *What A Drag: Men as Women and Women as Men in the Movies,* by Homer Dickens
(Quill/William Morrow, 1982).

CAMP—SOME DEFINITIVE DEFINITIONS

*"Camp was at once a cultural style and a cultural strategy, for it helped gay men
make sense of, respond to, and undermine the social categories of gender and sexuality that served to marginalize them. . . . The drag queen . . . epitomized camp."*

—GEORGE CHAUNCEY, *Gay New York*, Basic Books, 1994

*"The essence of camp is the unspoken amusement derived from knowing some-
thing is camp without having to explain why. Nobody asked Carmen Miranda*

The Imperial Court of New York (*Courtesy of the Lesbian and Gay Community Services Center–New York*)

why she wore ten-inch heels and danced around with a dozen bananas on her head. Carmen Miranda was just 'too much.'"

—VITO RUSSO, *The Advocate*, 1976

"[Camp is] to speak, act, or in any way attract or attempt to attract attention especially if noisily, flamboyantly, bizarrely, or in any other way calculated to announce, express, or burlesque one's own homosexuality or that of any other person."

—JONATHAN NED KATZ, *Gay/Lesbian Almanac*, HarperCollins, 1983

"A continuous theater of multiple identities, where irony is constant."

—FRANK BROWNING, *The Culture of Desire: Paradox and Perversity in Gay Lives Today*

From Yale
Collection of
American
Literature,
Beinecke Rare
Books and
Manuscripts
Library, Yale
University.
"Certificate" was
circulated by gay
men in the
1930s.

Frank Browning,
author of the
nonfiction book,
*The Culture of
Desire*

BORED MALE: *"I think I'll call Percy and we'll make a party of it.*

From the New York tabloid *Broadway Brevities*, 1932.

A FEW "NOM DE DRAGS" BACK WHEN

Queen Mary	Salome
Cinderella	Violet
Blossom	Edna May
Big Tess	Dixie
Chuckles	Theda Bara
Greta Garbo	Mae West
Daisy	

SOURCE: George Chauncey, *Gay New York*, Basic Books, 1994

A FEW "NOM DE DRAGS" TODAY

Pussy Tourette	Divine
Lady Bunny	Lipsynka
Misstress Formica	Ebony Jett
Endive	Brie
Afrodite	Miss Guy
Midnight Lasagna	Mona Foot
Glamamore	RuPaul

GOOD NEWS

At last, Paducah, Kentucky, is safe for transvestites. As part of a project to revise its city ordinances and to remove ones that are outdated, the burg dropped a law that made it illegal for people older than fourteen to cross-dress. But remaining on the books—at least so far—is a statute prohibiting "use of any derogatory words relating to the privates of a male, female, or hermaphrodite."

"That night [of the Stonewall riots, 1969] I was wearing this fabulous woman's suit I had made at home. It was light beige—very summery. Bell bottoms were in style then. I had my hair out. Lots of makeup and lots of hair. I was wearing boots. I don't know why I was wearing boots."

—REY "SYLVIA LEE" RIVERA, quoted in Eric Marcus, *Making History: The Struggle for Gay and Lesbian Equal Rights, 1945–1990*, HarperCollins, 1993

SOURCE: *The Advocate*, December 13, 1994

FEMALE CELEBRITIES MOST OFTEN IMPERSONATED BY DRAG PERFORMERS

Carol Channing
Barbra Streisand
Marilyn Monroe
Bette Midler
Madonna
Celia Cruz
Tina Turner
Joan Collins (as Alexis Carrington)
Iris Chacon
Whitney Houston
Tammy Faye Bakker
Twiggy
Diana Ross & The Supremes
Gloria Swanson
Mae West
Elvira
Patsy and Edina from *Absolutely Fabulous*

Bette Davis
Judy Garland
Liza Minnelli
Donna Summer
Gloria Gaynor
Liz Taylor
Ethel Merman

Dolly Parton
Gloria Estefan
Nancy Reagan
Grace Jones
Cher

Joan Crawford
Marge Simpson

SOME GAY ICONS—AND WHY WE LOVE 'EM

Bette Davis: She was feisty, intelligent, savvy, and tough—and she got to say some of the greatest lines in movie history, starting with "I'd love to kiss ya, but I just washed my hair!" and continuing right on down to "Fasten your seat belts, it's

At the 1993 gay
Pride March,
New York City
*(Photo by Harry
Stevens)*

going to be a bumpy night." In her heyday, her films included *Cabin in the Cotton, Of Human Bondage, The Petrified Forest, Marked Woman, Jezebel, Dark Victory, The Little Foxes, Now, Voyager, Mr. Skeffington,* and *All About Eve.* In middle age, she was unforgettably sinister in *Whatever Happened to Baby Jane?* and *Hush . . . Hush, Sweet Charlotte.*

Judy Garland: The relentless pain Judy experienced in her life—an early, unwanted push into show biz, five beleaguered marriages, drug dependence, chronic dieting, insomnia, and suicidal tendencies—seemed to strike a romantic chord with a generation of gay men. Also, both her father and her second husband Vincente Minnelli were rumored to be gay. In films such as *The Wizard of Oz, For Me and My Gal, Meet Me in St. Louis, Easter Parade,* and *A Star Is Born,* her heart-rending performances of songs she made classics continue to haunt us.

Marilyn Monroe: Like Judy Garland, Marilyn was ill-treated and misunderstood by the Hollwood establishment that created her image. Throughout her career, she, too, suffered from depression, drug dependence, and suicidal tendencies, and she died at a young age. Her exaggerated, almost campy, sensual manner made her a natural character for female impersonators. Among her most popular movies were *Niagara, Gentlemen Prefer Blondes, The Seven Year Itch, Bus Stop,* and *Some Like It Hot.*

Barbra Streisand: An ambitious, feisty performer who got her start at a singing contest in a gay bar in New York, Barbra grew up feeling like an ugly outsider and yearning to be a glamorous movie star. She rose to the top of her profession through talent and hard work and a firm belief in herself. In recent years, she has proven an outspoken proponent of lesbian and gay rights. Her films include *Funny Girl, Funny Lady, Hello, Dolly!, The Way We Were, Yentl,* and *The Prince of Tides.*

Bette Midler: Like Barbra Streisand, Bette Midler got her start singing in a gay venue—at the Continental Baths in New York, accompanied on the piano by Barry Manilow. Known for her boisterous, bawdy image, the Divine Miss M's performances have always been high camp. Her film appearances have run the gamut from the melodramatic *The Rose, Beaches,* and *Stella,* to a string of entertaining comedies, including *Ruthless People, Outrageous Fortune, Big Business,* and *Scenes from a Mall.*

Madonna: Flamboyantly sexual in an anything-goes way, Madonna has enjoyed a wide following among both gay men and lesbians. Her brother is openly gay, and she has been gay-friendly for years—even flirting with bisexual romances, most notably with actor-comedian Sandra Bernhard. Her films include *Desperately Seeking Susan, Dick Tracy, Truth or Dare, A League of Their Own,* and *Body of Evidence.*

SOURCE: *Images in the Dark: An Encyclopedia of Gay and Lesbian Film and Video,* by Raymond Murray, TLA Video Management, Inc. 1994

MOST NOTABLE FEMALE IMPERSONATION FEAT IN THE ANIMAL KINGDOM

The male Collie Pal and his male descendants, who successfully impersonated the female Lassie to a generation of moviegoers.

SOURCES: *What a Drag: Men as Women and Women as Men in the Movies,* by Homer Dickens (Quill/Wlliam Morrow, 1982)

THE UNDERPINNING OF DRAG CULTURE

If drag queens belong on pedestals, the whole of modern drag culture can be said to rest on a "pedestal" of sequins. While the origins of the sequin are somewhat sketchy, we do know that the word comes from the Italian *zecchino,* meaning a Venetian gold coin. Originally made of metal (for the bulletproof drag queen ala Divine), sequins are now made of plastic. The first mention of the word "sequin" is documented by the *Oxford English Dictionary* as having appeared in 1882.

THE START OF THE NEW YORK DRAG BALLS

1890s: Gay men began organizing drag balls, which were their subcultural response to established institutions in mainstream culture, such as masquerade balls. Walhalla Hall on New York's Lower East Side was a popular site for drag balls at this time.

1910s–1920s: Other drag balls were held at Webster Hall and the Little Beethoven Assembly Room, also on the Lower East Side.

1920s: The Hamilton Lodge Ball became the largest annual gathering of gay people in Harlem, organized by Hamilton Lodge No. 710 of the Grand United

NIGHT NO. 10
in FAIRY-LAND

Our Tireless Picket Tracks the Restless Androgyne to
CHILDS on Fifth Avenue and to LOUIS' on
49th Street.

From the New York tabloid *Broadway Brevities*, 1924.

Order of Odd Fellows. The official name was the Masquerade and Civic Ball, but it was popularly called the "Faggots' Ball." The ball included a costume contest with judges and prizes. Lavish costumes including plumes, jewelry, and feathers were common. Most of the guests were black, though some whites attended, too. A majority of the drag queens were young working-class men. About eight hundred guests attended in 1925, and the number soared to fifteen hundred a year later.

Late 1920s: Six or seven enormous drag balls were held each year at mainstream venues, including Madison Square Garden, the Astor Hotel, and the Savoy Ballroom in Harlem.

1930s: Drag balls reached a peak. In 1934, over four thousand spectators gathered at the Hamilton Lodge Ball to "gawk" at the costumed guests.

SOURCE: George Chauncey, *Gay New York*, Basic Books, 1994

HOT SPOTS

Below is a selected listing of clubs, bars, saloons, speakeasies, brothels, hotels, baths, and other gathering places frequented by gay men in New York City at various points in time between 1890 and 1940:

the Barrel House	the Hobby Horse
the Black Rabbit	the Hot Cha
Club Abbey	the Jungle
Club Calais	the Left Bank
Cock Suckers Hall (Sharon Hotel)	Paul and Joe's
Cyril's Cafe	the Pink Elephant
the Daisy Chain (a.k.a. 101 Ranch)	the Red Mask
the Dishpan	the Slide
the Flower Pot	Tillie's Kitchen
the Golden Rule Pleasure Club	Trilby's

Source: George Chauncey, *Gay New York*, Basic Books, 1994

CLONING

"In gay ghettos, the Clone look took hold by the mid-'70s. It was a way for men to recognize each other and meet on the streets, in the subway, at the library, in the park, at the movies. It provided an identity to scores of gay men who had none. Most worked in the system, usually getting nothing in return. As Clones they could, at least part of the time, be something and belong to a group they called their own, instead of living as the flat, gray heterosexuals they were forced to imitate at work."

—MICHELANGELO SIGNORILE

Invitation to "Drag Ball" at Manhattan Casino in Harlem. From Yale Collection of American Literature, Beinecke Rare Books and Manuscripts Library, Yale University

THE "OLD" CLONE LOOK (CIRCA 1975)

Hair: Midwestern cut, over to the side, heavily barbered. Mustache, thick and well-manicured.

Clothes: White cotton tank top; plaid flannel shirt (L.L. Bean); Champion gray cotton zip-up sweatshirt with hood; Levi's blue denim jacket; Levi's button-fly jeans; Redwing tan construction boots.

Accoutrements: Dark or mirrored aviator sunglasses; red cotton hanky (placement in right or left back pockets and various colors may signify various sexual proclivities—see "Remember When . . . ? Hanky Codes").

THE "NEW" CLONE LOOK (CIRCA 1990)

Hair: Close-cropped sides and top with small bangs in front (option: buzzed or shaved head).

Clothes: "Read My Lips" T-shirt; leather motorcycle jacket; cut-off gray Levi's 501 jeans (optional color: black; optional length: full, rolled up just above boots); white sweat socks; standard black Doc Martens (optional: calf-length Docs, U.S. Army combat boots).

Accoutrements: Small drop earrings; hoop earrings; tattoos of crosses, daggers, hearts, pink triangles, or eagles; Gay and Lesbian Anti-Violence Project silver

Dancing at a New York City Lesbian and Gay Community Services Center dance *(Copyright © 1993 by Micha Kwiatkowska)*

whistle; silver chain necklaces; Mardi Gras beads; school rings; crosses; crystals; leather cord; leather wristband; silver, pewter, or rubber bangle bracelets; leather rope bracelets; silver chains bracelets; wide black leather belt.

Source: Michelangelo Signorile, "Clone Wars," *Outweek*, November 26, 1990

Richard D.
Burns,
Esq.,
Executive
Director,
The
Lesbian
and Gay
Community
Services
Center–
New York
(*Photo by
David
Morgon*)

REMEMBER WHEN . . . ?—HANKY CODES

In the 1970s, for gay men and lesbians who could "read" the signs, handkerchief coding utilized both color and location to indicate sexual interests and identify potential sex partners on the basis on visual cues.

LEFT SIDE	COLOR	RIGHT SIDE
Fist fucker	Red	Fist fuckee
Anal sex, top	Dark blue	Anal sex, bottom
Oral sex, top	Light blue	Oral sex, bottom
Light S/M, top	Robin's egg blue	Light S/M, bottom
Food fetish, top	Mustard	Food fetish, bottom
Anything Goes, top	Orange	Anything Goes, bottom
Gives Golden Showers	Yellow	Wants golden showers
Hustler, selling	Green	Hustler, buying
Uniforms/military, top	Olive drab	Uniforms/military, bottom

Likes novices, chickenhawk	White	Novice (or virgin)
Victorian scenes, top	White lace	Victorian scenes, bottom
Does bondage	Gray	Wants to be put in bondage
Shit scenes, top	Brown	Shit scenes, bottom
Heavy S/M and whipping, top	Black	Heavy S/M & whipping, bottom
Piercer	Purple	Piercee
Group sex, top	Lavender	Group sex, bottom
Breast fondler	Pink	Breast fondlee

SOURCES: *Coming to Power: Writings and Graphics on Lesbian S-M (Alyson, 1982)* and *Gay Semiotics: A Photographic Study of Visual Coding Among Homosexual Men*

A FEW FABULOUS GAY PARTIES

Hotlanta

The Hotlanta River Expo is billed as the biggest gay party in the world. Started in 1979, it was originally a raft party on the Chattahoochee River, filled with water fights, rowing, and lots of carousing. By the early 1990s, the number of men in attendance topped fourteen thousand. Every year, Hotlanta takes place the first weekend in August, starting on Thursday night, and includes a drag contest, a dance party, and a "Mr. Hotlanta" contest that attracts gay bodybuilders from everywhere.

Mardi Gras

The quintessential drag party. In New Orleans, Mardi Gras "season" starts January 6, but the height of the festivities happens on Shrove Tuesday, the day before Ash Wednesday, the start of Christian Lent. Costume competitions and parades take place all over the city, and gay groups such as the Lords of Leather sponsor special contest and balls.

Morning Party

Held in Fire Island Pines each August, the Morning Party is a fundraiser for Gay Men's Health Crisis that takes place at the height of the summer season on a roped-off and platformed section of the beach. When things get going, though, the festivities tend to spill over into the rest of the gay resort. Thousands of hunks dance the day away for a good cause.

Hollywood Boy Party

In Palm Springs, California, a Hollywood Boy Party takes place every Easter and Labor Day. Thousands of West Hollywooders drive to the Springs for poolside tanning and partying, though others come from as far away as New York. Very glitzy, posh affairs.

Sources: Frank Browning, *The Culture of Desire,*(Vintage, 1993) and John Preston, *The Big Gay Book* (Plume, 1991)

SOURCES FOR FURTHER READING

Browning, Frank. *The Culture of Desire: Paradox and Perversity in Gay Lives Today*. Vintage, 1993.

Chauncey, George. *Gay New York: Gender, Urban Culture, and the Making of the Gay Male World 1890–1940*. Basic Books, 1994.

Dickens, Homer.*What A Drag: Men as Women and Women as Men in the Movies*. Quill/William Morrow and Co., 1982.

Duberman, Martin, Martha Vicinus, and George Chauncey, eds. *Hidden from History: Reclaiming the Gay and Lesbian Past*. New American Library, 1989.

Haggerty, George E., and Bonnie Zimmerman. *Professions of Desire: Lesbian and Gay Studies*. Modern Language Association of America, 1995.

Newton, Esther. *Mother Camp: Female Impersonators in America*. University of Chicago Press, 1972, 1979.

Preston, John. The Big Gay Book. Plume, 1991.

Stewart, William. *Cassell's Queer Companion*. Cassell, 1995.

Thanks to Joseph Cavalieri and Stephen Wilder for various drag culture tidbits.

Peninsula
GAY PRIDE WEEK CONFERENCE
at Stanford University June 24-29

Don't tread on me

June 24: RELIGION AND GAY PEOPLE — Stanford Memorial Church, 8 p.m. - Rev. Bill Johnson, speaker

June 25: CIVIL RIGHTS AND GAY PEOPLE — Cubberley Auditorium, 8 p.m. - Sheriff Richard Hongisto

June 26: WOMEN'S MOVEMENT AND GAY WOMEN — Stanford Women's Center, 8 p.m. - Gay Women's Collective

June 27: ALTERNATIVES FOR GAY MEN — Prometheus Growth Center, 401 Florence, Palo Alto, 8 p.m.

June 28: HEALTH CONCERNS AND GAY PEOPLE — Old Firehouse, Stanford, 2 p.m. - Dr. Jim Paulsen

June 28: OPEN HOUSE AND ENTERTAINMENT — Cubberley Auditorium, 8 p.m. - The Angels of Light

JUNE 29, Saturday: SPIRIT OF '76, a GAY CIVIL RIGHTS EVENT-- Registration begins at 8:30 a.m. $3 students, $4 nonstudents

FULL DAY CONFERENCE with DR. HOWARD BROWN, National Gay Task Force; BARBARA GITTINGS; DAVID GOLDSTEIN. Dance at 9 p.m.

CONFERENCE WORKSHOPS at 1:30 and 3 p.m.   Free at Last ● The Civil Rights Quest for Gay People ● Transvestism and Transsexualism

Gay Women's Concerns ● Gay Scholarship and Research, and the Need for Both ● Homophobia and What to Do About It ● Being a Gay Parent

Starting and Running a Gay Students Organization ● Working Together to Form a Gay Community ● Gays and the Arts ● Religion and Gays

Gay Publications and Straight Media ● Starting and Running Lavender University ● Public Sex ● Affirmative Action Programs for Gay People

Being a Gay Street Person ● Setting Parents Straight about Growing Up Gay ● Gay Teachers Coalitions ● Growth through Gay Encounter

Physical and Mental Health Care Services for Gay People ● Gays, Prisons, and the Law ● Coming Out Yourself: A Visit with Howard Brown

Accepting One's Own Gayness and Making Friends ● A Humanistic Approach to Gay Politics ● Alternative Gay Lifestyles ● Gay Marriage

Intimacy and Promiscuity ● Sex Roles: What Else Besides Butch and Femme? ● Gay Liberation and Writing

FOR INFORMATION CALL THE GAY PEOPLE'S UNION AT STANFORD: Phone 497-1323

This Conference is sponsored by the Gay People's Union at Stanford and the Whitman Radclyffe Foundation, with assistance by the U.S. Office of Education

Poster for the Gay Pride Week Conference at Stanford University, 1974. (*Collection of the National Museum & Archive of Lesbian and Gay History*)

5. GAY EDUCATION

"You do not have to explain about sex for children to understand that two people can love each other. Young children understand mothers' and fathers' love for each other without knowing about heterosexual sex. Yes, two men or two women can love each other and want to live together. They also sometimes raise children together."

—Children of the Rainbow activist, as quoted in "Sexuality, Multicultural Education, and the New York City Public Schools," *Radical Teacher,* No. 45, Winter 1994, p. 15

The institution of education offers both hope and disappointment for gay students and teachers. At the college and university level, great strides have been made. Lesbian and gay studies courses have been appearing in college catalogs, and the first lesbian and gay studies conference took place at Yale University in 1989. Subsequent conferences have been held at Harvard, Rutgers/Princeton, and the University of Iowa. In both classes and at conferences, discussion is no longer dominated by coming out, but has evolved into a truly interdisciplinary dialogue.

University presses such as Minnesota, Duke, NYU, Columbia, and Temple now publish a variety of lesbian and gay scholarly titles. The Center for Lesbian and Gay Studies (CLAGS) at the City University of New York, the first institution of its kind in the country, awards research grants to both affiliated and independent scholars.

Still, compared to other academic fields, there is very little funding for students and professors working in the area of lesbian and gay studies. There is also evidence that some funding agencies are biased against lesbian and gay research proposals. Although there have been more job openings in the academy recently for queer scholars, they have mostly been in the areas of English and women's studies, departments that are already glutted with qualified candidates, and rarely are positions advertised in history or the social sciences.

At the grade school and high school level, lesbian and gay studies are virtually nonexistent. Conservative school districts—see the story of New York's Rainbow Curriculum below—stifle efforts to integrate lesbian and gay experience into the curriculum. Add to that the fact that it is even harder for lesbian and gay teachers to come out in many schools, for fear of losing their jobs. The prevailing cultural belief that homosexuality is a perversion convinces misinformed parents that gay teachers might sexually abuse their children or "recruit" them to their "lifestyle."

To fill in the gaps, lesbians and gay men have created such institutions as the Harvey Milk High School for lesbian and gay high school students and professional organizations such as the Lesbian and Gay Teachers Association (LGTA) in New York. Unfortunately, though LGTA estimates that there are probably five thousand lesbian and gay teachers in the city, the organization's current membership is only two hundred teachers.

TIMELINE OF "FIRSTS"

1956: ONE Institute in Los Angeles is founded as an educational institute. In 1981, it became the first gay graduate school when it was recognized as such by the state of California. It offers a Ph.D. in homophile studies and has so far awarded two, as well as four master's degrees and four honorary doctorates.

1966: The Student Homophile League at Columbia University is founded by a bisexual undergraduate, Robert A. Martin, making it the first (and eventually the oldest) gay campus organization. Its first formal program is held on October 28, 1966. The group was then officially recognized as a campus organization on April 19, 1967. Martin, now known as Stephen Donaldson, went on to help establish chapters at New York University (chaired by Rita Mae Brown) and Cornell (chaired by Gerald Moldenhauer). The Columbia group, though having gone through many name changes, is still going.

1969: The first college-level homosexual dance is the "First NYC All-College Gay Mixer," sponsored by the New York University and Columbia University chapters of the Student Homophile League. The dance is held in the parish hall of the Church of the Holy Apostles and draws several hundred people.

> • The Supreme Court of California rules in the case of *Morrison* v. *State Board of Education* that the state cannot revoke the teaching license of a homosexual teacher unless it can demonstrate "unfitness to teach" with factual evidence rather than with a presumption of "immorality."

1970: The first gay studies course is taught, at the University of Nebraska. It is an interdisciplinary course through the anthropology, sociology, and English departments, and is taught by Louis Compton. The course focuses on the civil rights of homosexuals and includes a critique of the "sickness theory."

1972: The District of Columbia school board, at the urging of the local Gay Activists Alliance, enacts a resolution prohibiting discrimination in any aspect of the DC school system's hiring practices and thus becomes the first school board to ban anti-gay discrimination.

1973: George Washington High School in Manhattan and the Bronx High School of Science become the first high schools to officially recognize gay student groups. Both groups were formed after representatives from the Gay Activists Alliance's Agitprop Committee spoke at classes and assemblies at each school.

1974: Lavender U: A University for Gay Women and Gay Men, offers its first classes, in San Francisco. Classes are taught out of private homes or public facilities, and have titles like Gay Greek Literature I and II, The Bath Experience, Opera Appreciation, and A Rose Is a Rose Is a Rose. Founded by seven gay men and two lesbians, Lavender U is considered the first gay university and had an enrollment of about two hundred people from its first catalog.

> • The National Education Association, the nation's largest organization of public school employees, adds "sexual orientation" to its resolution on nondiscriminatory personnel policies and practices that it urges its members' employers to follow.

1977: Santa Barbara, California, becomes the first school district to ban discrimination against gay students. The board of education votes to broaden its policy of nondiscrimination against teachers and other gay school employees to include gay students while also establishing a grievance procedure for handling cases of discrimination against employees or students.

1982: Bryton High in Philadelphia is founded as the first gay high school. The school was started for gay teens as an alternative to the public high school system. The class of 1983, its first graduates, consisted of three male students and one female.

1988: Lambda Delta Lambda wins official recognition from the University of California, Los Angeles, making it the first lesbian sorority.

1990: The first college ban on ROTC in protest of the military's anti-gay policies is approved at Pitzer College in Claremont, California .

1991: The Center for Lesbian and Gay Studies (CLAGS)—under the direction of historian Martin Duberman—at the City University of New York becomes the first university-affiliated research center in the United States devoted exclusively to the study of gay and lesbian subjects.

Martin Duberman (left), executive director of the Center for Lesbian and Gay Studies, and historian Jonathan Ned Katz *(Copyright © 1993 by Micha Kwiatkowska)*

FACTS AND STATISTICS

- A survey of Americans in 1993 found that 52 percent were opposed to teaching about lesbian and gay orientation in sex education classes in public schools.
- Since 1982, more than sixteen hundred school districts have adopted sex education curricula that present sexual abstinence and monogamy within heterosexual marriage as the only sexual choices available to teenagers.
- In a psychological test that predicts the success of teachers in the classroom, administered to seventy-four gay and lesbian and sixty-six heterosexual teachers in 1990, there were no differences in scores between the two groups.
- Eight out of ten prospective teachers and nearly two-thirds of guidance counselors expressed negative feelings about homosexuality and about lesbians and gay men, said a study conducted by the South Carolina Guidance Counselors' Association in 1987.
- Citizens for Excellence in Education, a right-wing group based in Costa Mesa, California, says that more than two thousand of its members have been elected to school boards across the United States.
- 45 percent of gay males and 20 percent of lesbians experience physical or verbal assault in high school. 28 percent of these young people feel forced to drop out of school due to harassment problems based on sexual orientation.
- In 1988 there were no gay/straight school alliances in private high schools. By 1993, at least sixteen independent schools had such alliances, and seventeen had at least one openly gay teacher.
- As of 1993, there were more than one hundred lesbian and gay support groups in high schools across the nation.
- As of January 1992, 15 U.S. colleges and universities had lesbian/ gay/bisexual task forces or offices, 248 had nondiscrimination policies that included sexual orientation, and at least 43 offered some sort of lesbian, gay, and bisexual courses.

GAY EDUCATION BIBLIOGRAPHY

Bull, Chris. "Why Johnny Can't Learn About Condoms: How the Religious Right Censors Sex Education across the U.S.," *The Advocate*, December 15, 1992.

Dorning, Mike. "Schools' Support Groups Helping Gay Teens to Cope," *Chicago Tribune*, November 30, 1993.

"Factfile: Lesbian, Gay, and Bisexual Youth," Hetrick-Martin Insitute, 1992 and 1993.

Haggerty, George, and Bonnie Zimmerman, eds. *Professions of Desire*. The Modern Language Association of America, 1990.

Harbeck, Karen M., ed. *Coming Out of the Classroom Closet: Gay and Lesbian Students, Teachers and Curricula*. Harrington Park, 1992.

hooks, bell. *Teaching to Transgress*. Routledge, 1994.

Jennings, Kevin, ed. *Becoming Visible: A Reader in Lesbian and Gay History for High School and College Students*. Alyson, 1994.

Lesbian/Gay/Queer Studies issue, *Radical Teacher,* No. 45, Winter 1994.

Levine, David, and Robert Lowe. *Rethinking Schools : An Agenda for Change.* The New Press, 1995.

Malinowitz, Harriet. *Textual Orientations: Lesbian and Gay Students and the Making of Discourse Communities.* Boynton/Cook, 1995.

Martin, M. "Gay, Lesbian, and Heterosexual Teachers: Acceptance of Self Acceptance of Others," unpublished report, 1990.

McConnell-Celi, Sue. *Twenty-First Century Challenge: Lesbians and Gays in Education—Bridging the Gap.* Lavender Crystal Press, 1993.

McLaughlin, Daniel, and William G. Tierney, eds. *Naming the Silenced Lives: Personal Narratives and the Process of Educational Change.* Routledge, 1992.

Shapiro, Joseph, et al. "Straight Talk about Gays," *U.S. News and World Report,* July 5, 1993.

Singer, Bennet L., and David Deschamps, eds. *Gay and Lesbian Stats.* The New Press, 1994.

Woog, Dan. *School's Out: The Impact of Gay and Lesbian Issues on America's Schools.* Alyson, 1995.

Yamaguchi Fletcher, Lynne. *The First Gay Pope and Other Records.* Alyson, 1992.

GRANTS AVAILABLE TO GAY STUDENTS

NEW YORK CITY LESBIAN AND GAY COMMUNITY SERVICES CENTER

Paul Rapoport Memorial Scholarship

The scholarship honors the memory of Paul Rapoport, a founder of the Lesbian and Gay Community Services Center, NYC. His commitment to educational achievement and his efforts to encourage lesbian and gay youth to obtain a higher education is acknowledged in the awarding of these scholarships every year during Lesbian and Gay Pride Month.

Paul Rapoport received his education at Cornell University, (AB, LLB) and New York University, (LLM-Taxation). The students of these institutions are especially encouraged to apply.

The scholarship —funded by the Paul Rapoport Foundation—is awarded at the Center's annual Garden Party in June, enabling lesbian and gay students to begin or continue their college and graduate school studies.

For more information call the New York Lesbian and Gay Community Services Center, 212-620-7310 or write The Lesbian and Gay Community Services Center, re: Paul Rapoport Memorial Scholarship, 208 West 13th St., New York, New York 10011.

Application deadline is April 21.

CENTER FOR LESBIAN AND GAY STUDIES (CLAGS)

Rockefeller Residency Fellowship in the Humanities

First Annual Lesbian, Gay, and Bisexual History Month Essay and Visual Arts Competitions

Sponsored by the Gay, Lesbian, and Straight Teachers Network (GLSTN), the first Lesbian, Gay, and Bisexual History Month Essay and Visual Arts Competitions were held in Spring 1995, to focus young people's attention on the contributions of lesbians, gay men, and bisexuals to the development of the United States. Open to youth age twenty-two and under, the essay competition asked participants to address—in 750 words or less—the subject "Why it's important to know lesbian, gay, and bisexual history." The visual arts competition for the same age group requested entries of logos for Lesbian, Gay, and Bisexual History Month, suitable for use on T-shirts and posters. The winner in each category received a $250 prize.

For information on the 1996 competition, write to Lesbian, Gay, and Bisexual History Month Competition, c/o Gay, Lesbian, and Straight Teachers Network, Box 390526, Cambridge, MA 02139-0006. Or send e-mail requests to GLSTN@aol.com.

Amount: Fellows will receive $35,000, plus a $2,000 travel and relocation stipend for residency from September 1 to June 1.

Eligibility: Open to all academic scholars in the humanities and related areas who have shown a genuine commitment to lesbian and gay studies. Activists, junior faculty, and independent scholars are especially encouraged to apply. *Dissertation proposals will not be considered.*

Deadline: February 15

1993–94 Winners: Carra Leah Hood and Charles I. Nero

1994–95 Winners: Allan Berube and Janice Irvine

Ken Dawson Award

Amount: $5,000

Eligibility: Anyone working in the field of gay and lesbian history. Preference will be given to proposals in the media of print. No university affiliation is required.

Deadline: March 15

1994 Winner: Jonathan Ned Katz

Constance Jordan Award

Amount: One $4,000 award per year for each of the academic years 1995–96, 1996–97, and 1997–98. The winner of the first year may reapply once.

Eligibility: CUNY doctoral students working on a topic in gay and lesbian literary studies with historical content.

Deadline: May 1

CUNY Student Paper Awards

Amount: First Prize $250; Second Prize $150

Eligibility: CUNY graduate students on masters or doctoral levels with papers on a topic related to lesbian and gay studies in any academic discipline or professional program.

Deadline: May 15

1994 Winners: Ira Elliott and Tracy Morgan

Scholarly Grants-in-Aid

CUNY graduate students may apply to CLAGS for up to $500 to assist in their work in lesbian and gay studies. The fund may be used to cover travel to libraries, conferences, or professional society meetings, costs of translations or photocopying, and so on.

Deadline: October 15 for fall semester; March 1 for spring semester. Emergency situations will be considered between the two dates.

An application consists of (1) purpose of request; (2) time, date, and place; (3) an itemized budget; (4) a statement of how this request relates to the individual's academic/career plans.

For more information on any of these grants or for application forms, call the CLAGS office at 212-642-2924 or write Center for Lesbian and Gay Studies, The Graduate School and University Center of the City of New York, 33 West 42nd Street, Room 404N, New York, New York 10036-8099.

PROFILE

Center for Lesbian and Gay Studies

(reprinted with permission from the preface of CLAGS's *Directory of Lesbian and Gay Studies*)

The Center for Lesbian and Gay Studies (CLAGS) was formally established in April 1991, after five years of planning, at the Graduate School of the City University of New York. The first university-affiliated research center in the United States devoted exclusively to the study of gay and lesbian subjects, CLAGS from the start has operated under the principles of gender parity, ethnic and racial diversity, and the participation of unaffiliated scholars.

CLAGS, its staff, scholars, and students gather, disseminate, and encourage research on the lives of gay men and lesbians from multicultural, multiracial, and feminist perspectives.

CLAGS also serves as a national clearinghouse for scholarly research through the publication of a biannual newsletter and through a nationwide Directory of Lesbian and Gay Scholars.

CLAGS offers financial support for research and awards for outstanding work in the field, including the first Rockefeller Humanities Fellowships ever given to a gay or lesbian institution, and the David R. Kessler endowed lectureship for a noteworthy contribution to gay and lesbian life.

CLAGS has begun to examine curriculum reform at all grade levels, and is preparing pilot studies syllabi for those seekng help in offering gay and lesbian courses. Assistance has been given in response to inquiries from all over the U.S., as well as from China, New Zealand, Europe, and Latin America.

CLAGS offers symposia, conferences, and regular public programs on issues of scholarly and general interest, like "AIDS and Public Policy"; "The Brain and Homosexuality"; "Latin American Perspectives on Homosexuality"; "Homa/Economics: Market and Community in Lesbian and Gay Life"; "Sissies and Tomboys"; and "Black Nations/Queer Nations?"

CLAGS is under the direction of Distinguished Professor of History Martin Duberman.

PROFILE

The Rainbow Curriculum

In New York City in 1989, a plan to introduce non-European, women's, and gay and lesbian history and culture into every stage of education, from kindergarten through high school, was mandated by the central Board of Education. This multicultural curriculum, specifically the first-grade portion, "Children of the Rainbow," caused an uproar with local school board conservatives and made New York the first city with a nonwhite majority targeted by the religious right. The organizers against the Rainbow Curriculum used "the empowerment of parents of color" as a goal that could only be reached by disempowering gays and lesbians throughout the school system. This battle hit its peak in spring of 1993, just before the school board elections.

"Through old-fashioned, grassroots organizing and savvy media work, they [the religious right] made homophobia more socially acceptable in the city where the contemporary gay and lesbian movement began," wrote Donna Minkowitz in her *Nation* article "Wrong Side of the Rainbow."

Mary Cummins, president of the Queens School Board 24, said, "I will not demean our legitimate minorities, such as blacks, Hispanics, and Asians, by lumping them together with homosexuals in that curriculum." She was responsible for kicking off the fight against the multicultural curriculum, by refusing to have it taught in her school district.

According to Minkowitz, "Many in the media have portrayed the anti-Rainbow movement as a spontaneous outpouring of parental outrage. In reality, it was anything but spontaneous. For over a year, conservative evangelicals and Catholics organized in Latino, white, and a few African-American neighborhoods, telling parents that the gay-inclusive curriculum was a plot by a 'Manhattan elite' of gays and lesbians to gain control of schools so they could 'recruit' and 'brainwash' children into becoming gay (as anti-Rainbow organizer Dolores Ayling put it)."

Religious right organizers tried to tie together race and sexuality in order to pit one against the other. Leaflets said things like "The Rainbow program is not a program against racial discrimination, it has nothing to do with color, it has to do with homosexuals and lesbians." But the Rainbow Curriculum had plenty to do with race. The majority of the first-grade plan teaches children about the different holidays, art forms, and histories of people of various ethnic backgrounds. In a curriculum that totals over four hundred pages, references to gay and lesbian families appear on only three pages. The children's books *Heather Has Two Mommies* and *Daddy's Roommate*, which were widely criticized, appeared only on a suggested reading list for teachers and were not part of the mandated curriculum.

Some activists suspected that the Right's obsessive focus on those three pages and on the books stemmed from a desire to derail the entire multicultural curriculum, said Minkowitz. Opponents of the Rainbow Curriculum implied that lessons depicting lesbian and gay families are inherently dirty and corrupting. While local school boards, especially District 24, were working hard to dismantle the Rainbow Curriculum, they were neglecting some fundamental problems within their own districts. The Right needed people of color to defeat the multicultural plan, so they picked "battlegrounds," or school districts where large populations of working-class and poor people of color coexisted with mostly white communities of lesbians and gay men and other progressives. This backfired somewhat on the religious right, and there is evidence to show that lesbians and gay men in the three "battleground" districts voted in higher numbers and greater unity in this 1993 school board election than they have in any previous New York election.

In numerical terms, the election proved to be a win for gays and progressives, with openly lesbian and gay candidates being the leading vote-getters in the most heavily contested districts. But for the Rainbow Curriculum it was another story. Recently the curriculum was finally dismantled, all references to homosexuality removed.

The information from this section was taken primarily from Donna Minkowitz's article "Wrong Side of the Rainbow: The Religious Right Hits N.Y.C.," in the June 28, 1993, issue of *The Nation,* and has been quoted at length with her permission.

PROFILE

Ronald Madson

An old red schoolhouse from the late 1800s is the most appropriate home one could imagine for a man like Ronald Madson. Not only does he rest his head at night in a building that once hummed with students, he has spent the past twenty-nine years of his life teaching at Public School 20, in Brooklyn, New York. For twenty-three of those years, Ronald has been the art teacher for kindergarten through sixth grade.

Ronald, forty-eight, grew up in Ridgewood, Queens, with his two older sisters and one younger brother, "all whom are straight with children."

"I enjoy being a teacher," he says. "I wouldn't have stayed at it this long if I didn't enjoy it, but it has its ups and downs." He has been out publicly for eight

Ronald Madson (right) and his lover, Richard Dietz (*Collection of the National Museum & Archive of Lesbian and Gay History*)

years and has a very good reputation as a teacher, and the parental support to back that reputation.

"I never was really in the closet as far as faculty was concerned, or at least that's what I thought. Since Richard and I have been together almost the length of my career, I would talk about my friend Richard, my partner, in the faculty room. I would talk about what we did on the weekends, the same way other faculty would." Ronald and his lover Richard Dietz are excited to be celebrating their twenty-fifth anniversary. They met in 1970, when they were both twenty-three, and have been together ever since. "But in terms of the kids," says Ronald, "I was not always out to the kids."

In 1987, Ronald and Richard joined the case against the Board of Education in New York City to sue for domestic partnership benefits, and came out publicly in the newspaper. Since then, Ronald has been out to the kids, too. Depending on the situation, and taking into account the age of the students, he handles being out in different ways.

"Some of the students are very accepting and some of them aren't so much, but if they like me that's fine, if they don't like me, that's also fine. I'm not going to campaign for understanding. I'm the example of the gay person in front of them at that moment and they can take me for what they want."

Certain parent organizations in the school have issues with Ronald being out. "A couple of years ago when Children of the Rainbow came up, the PTA wrote what I thought was a very negative article about gay people in general and about the Children of the Rainbow, with no real knowledge of the planned curriculum. Obviously they had not seen it. So I answered their letter publicly in a letter to the staff, because I had no access to the parents." The PTA became upset about his response and invited Ronald to a meeting. His union advised him to leave the matter in the hands of the principal, so he didn't attend the meeting. Ronald later found out that the meeting had been a "planned lynching." The superintendent supported Ronald and warned the PTA that Ronald could sue them for violating his right of free speech.

Ronald began actively attending meetings of the Lesbian and Gay Teachers Association (LGTA) in 1987. At the first meeting he attended, it was announced that Lambda Legal Defense was looking for a couple who was willing to be named in a suit to sue for medical benefits for their partners from the Board of Education in NYC. "Richard and I had been together at that time for seventeen years. We had often talked about how unfair it was that we had been together all these years and could get no benefits. So I came home and said to him, 'I think our time has come.'"

The other reason Ronald and Richard entered the case was in memory of their best friend Gene. "In 1984, our best friend got AIDS and we cared for him for two years. After we had helped him live his life through that period, we had decided that there was nothing that anybody could do short of physically harming us that we hadn't already been through. Gene was really an inspiration to us because we had no experience with anything like this. It was very early on in terms of the disease, and we had no other friends who had AIDS up until that point. Since we were his primary caretakers, we had seen a lot of shit and had a lot of dealings with public officials and agencies. I remember saying to one of my friends at the time, 'I will never be afraid about being gay again.'"

According to Richard, they were the perfect "boring" couple. "We had no children or ex-marriages in our background. We had been together a long time and we would probably be together through the case." And though Lambda warned them that the case could take a long time, six years was much longer than anyone anticipated. "The day we won the case, I remember standing here crying, saying, 'We finally did something for Gene because we owed him.'"

The case was kept out of court for two mayoral administrations. A settlement was reached only three days before the last mayoral election. Since then, domestic partners in the field of New York public education have been able to have most of the same medical benefits as their married counterparts. There have been a few knots to work out, and the case has only been really settled in the last month due to the complicated way that medical benefits in the city work. Ronald was very satisfied with the settlement that was reached. "However, I have to say this—domestic partnership is a very poor second to marriage in terms of what you get as 'benefits.' I really am a strong advocate for [legalized gay] marriage."

Since the domestic partnership case, there have been other issues that Ronald has worked on through LGTA. All teachers in the school system are required to take a human relations course. LGTA, and later the Educational Coalition on Lesbian and Gay Youth (ECOLAGY), had worked for many years with the Board of Ed. to have sexual orientation included in those courses. "Though we already had a nondiscriminatory policy that included sexual orientation, these classes addressed every other issue in that policy except ours." Because of the work of LGTA and ECOLAGY, sexual orientation must now be discussed in the human relations courses. Ronald himself speaks to teacher groups in these courses, but LGTA still doesn't get invited to as many courses as are given, and has no idea how the topic is handled by the other teachers.

"LGTA is basically a small organization with a loud voice," Ronald says. It was started as a support group when Mark Rubin and Merill Friedman put a notice in *The Village Voice*, attracting almost forty people to their first meeting. Presently, there are approximately two hundred members, a figure that bespeaks how closeted teachers still are. LGTA estimates that there are a minimum of at least five thousand lesbian and gay teachers in New York City alone. It wasn't long before the group became active with the teachers unions and the Board of Ed. to get their causes heard. The union has always been supportive around lesbians and gay men as teachers, but in terms of issues with curriculum, union backing has not been so strong.

ECOLAGY, the other group Ronald is actively involved in, is a coalition of educationally oriented community activists. It was formed to be the main voice at the Board of Ed. during the development of the Rainbow Curriculum. Dr. Marjorie Hill, who was then liaison with the mayor's office, called together as many community groups that were active at the board as possible. ACT-UP, P-FLAG, LGTA, and others came together and formed the group that has now been active for the past six years.

One area they have been working on is getting guidance counselors trained to be sensitive to gay issues. Ronald said that it took four years to actually stop training supervisors of guidance counselors and train the counselors that actually deal with kids. "We were able to do that last year because of the Gay Games. We said, 'You are going to have almost a million gay and lesbian people coming into this city, and the prime gay bashers are older teens and young adults. These are kids in your schools, and we need to do something about it.'" Sixty people were then trained. ECOLAGY is also working to get into schools Project 10, a program that was started in San Francisco. The plan is to have in each school a resource person that is sensitive to lesbian and gay issues, for kids, parents, administration, and teachers to be able to talk to.

Ronald's future plan is to teach until he is fifty-five, then retire. He wants to devote more time to doing community work around education. He is also an artist, and he hopes to have time one day again to pursue that. Becoming involved with LGTA was a milestone for Ronald, and, as he says when he gives speeches, "I found my voice and they haven't been able to shut me up."

PROFILE

Harvey Milk School

(Reprinted with permission from "The Harvey Milk School: A Program of the HMI and the New York City Board of Ed.")

The Harvey Milk School is an alternative public high school established in 1985 in a unique collaboration between the Hetrick-Martin Institute (HMI) and the

New York City Public Schools. The school was founded because the staff of HMI, a social service agency for lesbian, gay, and bisexual youth, recognized that these young people often meet with violence and intolerance in school, and that many drop out. Some, under the immense pressure of hiding their real identities, leave both school and home. In addition, the children of gay or lesbian parents also suffer painful harassment.

The Hetrick-Martin Institute was founded in 1979 in response to the difficulties that lesbian, gay, and bisexual youth experience as they are growing up. After just serving a handful of people in the beginning, HMI now serves at least fifteen hundred clients. When the Institute's social workers first determined that many of their clients were not going to school, they sought to bring these disaffected young people back into the school system. Working with the New York City Public Schools, they employed a school system policy that provides for a teacher to be assigned to any social agency with at least twenty-two clients who are not attending school. Today the Harvey Milk School reopens the door to school for lesbian and gay youth, and offers them an education in an environment that is safe and supportive. Whenever possible, Harvey Milk School students are mainstreamed back into their community high schools.

The Harvey Milk School enrolls a maximum of thirty youths per year and is one of twenty-five alternative city high school programs. The students range in age from age fourteen to twenty-one. Currently 80 percent of the students are African-American and Latino.

Young people enter the school with varying backgrounds. Individualized programs are developed to enable students to meet graduation requirements and to take the New York State Regents examination.

Group classes such as Literature, Math for Living, Art, Law, and Health take place two periods per day, and for other subjects, students study independently and at their own pace, with the assistance of their teachers.

Because of the stigma they face, lesbian, gay, and bisexual youth confront many complicated issues that make adolescence a particularly difficult time. Students of the Harvey Milk School have access to the Institute's extensive counseling services to help them address emotional concerns as well as academic issues. Students are also encouraged to participate in several other programs at the Institute.

HMI's after-school Drop-In Center is a safe place for lesbian, gay, and bisexual youth to socialize and participate in arts and educational activities. Through their mentoring program, the Institute helps youths reach their academic and career goals in a place where they can be open about who they are. HIV/AIDS prevention education is provided in all of the Institute's programs.

Through direct service, education, and advocacy, the Hetrick-Martin Institute is committed to creating a world where lesbian, gay, and bisexual youth can grow successfully into adulthood and find understanding and respect from the larger society.

For more information on the Hetrick-Martin Institute and the Harvey Milk School, call 212-674-2400, TTY 212-674-8695, or write Hetrick-Martin Institute, 2 Astor Place, New York, New York 10003-6998

Profile

Thom Furr

Thom Furr was born and raised in Rochester, New York. At twenty-two, he recently graduated from Sarah Lawrence College in Bronxville, New York. He has been a member of the information, reception, and referral staff in the New York Lesbian and Gay Community Services Center for the past two years.

When Thom started school, he had a loose idea of what he wanted to do: writing, poetry writing. But he was soon to discover a new passion. "My freshman year, I compared AIDS with the Black Death for a Renaissance class that I was taking. When we were studying the Black Death, during the waning of the Middle Ages, it just struck me how much responses and attitudes to disease are the same transhistorically.

"I also did a paper on homosexuality in the Renaissance. That was my first experience with lesbian and gay issues in relation to my academic work. It was very, very exciting to me. I never had thought of queer issues in that context, and my professor had a lot of knowledge and background, especially on the historical side, so it just sort of snowballed from there."

Thom also took a class called Twentieth-Century Politics and Society, and his conference work was on AIDS. His paper for the course, "AIDS, Knowledge, and Resistance," was Thom's focus for his last semester. "It has a broader scope than I wanted it to; it is quite abstract. It locates the most damaging aspects of the AIDS *crisis*, as opposed to the AIDS virus. That is a distinction that I make. The AIDS virus is something empirical and real, that causes biological deterioration and suffering of people. The AIDS crisis on the other hand, is an epistemological formation, specifically modern, that designates people with AIDS as ultimate others, therefore eliminating the possibility for empathic response, not to mention any sort of action toward engagement with, confrontation with, and ending the crisis. In other words, HIV is indifferent, but AIDS is not."

There are very few lesbian and gay studies courses offered at Sarah Lawrence. "The only ostensibly lesbian and gay studies course I took was Sexuality and Representation with Douglas Crimp. His course was a survey class that covered historical perspectives, film and video, literature, general queer theory, women's studies issues, AIDS, and more." Thom wishes there were more courses available that were specifically queer/lesbian and gay studies, and says that Sarah Lawrence is in the process of trying to get more.

"There has now been a lesbian and gay studies steering committee established and they are trying to get more faculty members hired specifically for that. Currently we only have one member of the faculty that is designated to be there for lesbian and gay studies. When Douglas was there he was only a guest professor. Right now as it is, you can only do lesbian and gay studies issues mostly through conference; there are very few classes that specifically focus on it."

As a lesbian and gay studies student, Thom is very familiar with the question of how to differentiate between lesbian and gay studies and queer studies. "It is quite complicated. It is something that would come down to taxonomy more than any-thing else and depends on the associations that people make with those specific la-bels. 'Lesbian and gay,' some people would say is reductive. 'Queer' on the other hand is supposed to, presumably, encompass different identities and different people: Transgendered people, bisexual people, straight people could even be queer. 'Queer' is more of a perspective, where 'gay and lesbian' is more of an iden-tity.

"Nothing can be predicted about lesbian and gay studies. Right now it is in the middle of growing exponentially, and I don't think any of us can anticipate what exactly is going to become of it. We really shouldn't anticipate. We should always question it as it is happening and not allow it to turn into something fixed and de-fined."

Now that Thom is moving on from Sarah Lawrence, questions of what the fu-ture holds are imminent. He does not want to limit himself to the academic realm. "Although teaching is something I would enjoy doing, I don't want to be trapped in the university system. That is something that working at the Center has con-firmed for me.

"I'm thinking of going to law school, but I'm taking at least a year off between then and now to allow myself time to change my mind. I'm pretty sure that what-ever I end up doing it will be within the lesbian and gay community, I'm just not sure what. If I get a law degree, I might work for an organization like the Anti-Vi-olence Project, or Lambda; some sort of public advocacy position is what I would like to have. I see a law degree as being something that is very useful. My main de-sire is to be a useful part of the movement. . . . Working at the Center has just shown me that . . . the day to day issues of living are important. . . . You really get to see that community means something different to everybody.

"Though there are more things to divide us than to keep us together, the one thing we have in common is our sexuality and a shared history of oppression be-cause of that. It is a philosophical issue, and people have tried to solve it and no one really has. The thing that relates us is intangible, but when we need to or if we need to, we can harness that into some sort of collective identity to resist the things that we need to, to further our goals and our aims and ourselves, as gay people, however tenuous that category is."

A Short Reading Course

When lesbian and gay studies first emerged, works in and pertaining to the field could have been contained in a rather brief bibliography. Today, however, it would be impossible to concisely list the texts and essays available to anyone interested in the field. An unprecedented outpouring of new work has coincided with the in-creasing acceptance of lesbian and gay studies. Listed below are a few popular texts under traditional liberal arts headings. There are, of course, many other rel-evant works; the bibliographies in those mentioned here should be useful for fur-ther suggestions. Also, the specific areas of study are not absolute, as the field itself tends to be interdisciplinary. In addition, the canon is not by any means fixed, nor should it be, for new and exciting work is appearing all the time.

General Anthologies

Abelove, Henry, Michele Aina Barale, and David Halperin, eds. *The Lesbian and Gay Studies Reader.* Routledge, 1993.

Fuss, Diana. *Inside/Out.* Routledge, 1991.

Moraga, Cherrie, and Gloria Anzaldua, eds. *This Bridge Called My Back: Writings by Radical Women of Color.* Persephone Press, 1981. (reprinted by Kitchen Table: Women of Color Press)

History

Duberman, Martin, Martha Vicinus, and George Chaney, eds. *Hidden from History.* Meridian, 1989.

Faderman, Lillian. *Odd Girls and Twilight Lovers: A History of Lesbian Life in Twentieth-Century America.* Columbia University Press, 1991.

Katz, Jonathan Ned. *Gay American History.* Thomas Y. Crowell, 1976; revised, 1992.

Literature

Dollimore, Jonathan. *Sexual Dissidence.* Clarendon Press, 1991.

Haggerty, George, and Bonnie Zimmerman, eds. *Professions of Desire.* MLA, 1995.

McKinley, Catherine E., and L. Joyce Delaney, eds. *Afrekete: An Anthology of Black Lesbian Writing.* Anchor, 1995.

Sedgwick, Eve Kosofsky. *Epistemology of the Closet.* University of California Press, 1990.

Politics/Culture

Beam, Joseph. *In the Life.* Alyson, 1986.

Browning, Frank. *The Culture of Desire: Paradox and Perversity in Gay Lives Today.* Crown, 1993.

Jay, Karla, and Allen Young, eds. *Out of the Closets: Voices of Gay Liberation.* New York University Press, 1972; revised, 1992.

Nestle, Joan, The Persistent Desire: A Femme-Butch Reader. Alyson, 1992.

AIDS

Stoller, Nancy, and Beth Schneider, eds. *Women Resisting AIDS: Feminist Strategies of Empowerment.* Temple University Press, 1995.

Patton, Cindy. *Inventing AIDS.* Routledge, 1990.

Crimp, Douglas, ed. *AIDS: Cultural Analysis/Cultural Activism.* MIT Press, 1988.

Watney, Simon. *Policing Desire.* University of Minnesota Press, 1987.

Queer Theory

Foucault, Michel. *History of Sexuality, Vol.1*. Vintage Books, 1978.
Laurentis, Teresa de. *The Practice of Love: Lesbian Sexuality and Perverse Desire*. University of Indiana Press, 1994.
Weeks, Jeffrey. *Sexuality and Its Discontents*. Routledge, 1985.

Other

Film: Gever, Martha, John Greyson, and Pratibha Parmar, eds. *Queer Looks*. Routledge, 1993.
Cross-Dressing: Garber, Marjorie. *Vested Interests*. Routledge, 1992.
Music: Koestenbaum, Wayne. *The Queen's Throat*. Vintage Books, 1993.
Brett, Philip, Elizabeth Wood, and Gary C. Thomas, Eds. *Queering the Pitch: The New Gay and Lesbian Musicology*. Thomas. Routledge, 1994.

RESOURCE GUIDE FOR QUEER STUDENTS

There is an important and interesting book that all lesbians and gay men considering college should take a look at. Though surveyed from a somewhat narrow perspective, *The Gay, Lesbian, and Bisexual Students' Guide to Colleges, Universities, and Graduate Schools*, by Jan-Mitchell Sherrill and Craig A. Hardesty (NYU Press, 1994), gives *students'* perspectives about how homo-friendly their schools are. Everything from actual school policy to homophobia on campus, to what types (if any) of lesbian and gay studies courses are available. The students tell whether they would recommend their school to another lesbian or gay student. Almost two hundred colleges are listed, making the book a good starting point of reference.

QUEER MLA

The following were calls for papers for the 1995 Modern Language Association Convention in Chicago:

GJM Seeks Lesbian and Gay Studies Work on 17th- and 18th-Century English, French, American (Other European?) Literature. Turn-ons: eggheads with communications skills. Turnoffs: theoryheads into big words (verbal size queens), reflex social constructionism.

Buying "Out": Consumer Culture and Queer Identity in Literature and Mass Media. This interdisciplinary panel will address both appropriation of "the homosexual" within consumer culture and representations of gay men and lesbian women as particular kinds of consumers.

Lesbianism and Orality. Orality as a determining trope in figurations of lesbianism. Orality and narrative, speech and writing, oral erotics and notions of the "pre" (presexual, preoedipal, precultural). Deconstructive and psychoanalytic perspectives especially welcome.

Queer Autobiography. Possible topics: representing the queer body; queering gender or genre difference; outlaw subjects; figuring queer space (borderlands, home, the closet); questions of passing and reading.

Queering the Sixties. Any lesbian, gay, bisexual, transsexual, transvestite, or otherwise queer aspect of British, American, or other anglophone literary, artistic, or cultural production during the 1960s.

Queer Montaigne. Topics might include the (homo)erotics of melancholia or of influence and citation; friendship, freedom, and voluntary servitude; sex, heterosex, and impotence; Montaigne in/and translation; Montaigne and a homosexual literary tradition.

Queer Primitivism(s). How have fantasies of the "primitive" influenced the imagining of queer identities? Does the "primitive" continue to exert a pull on the queer imagination?

Tutti Frutti: Gender Studies on Outrageous Performers Who Have Become Cultural Icons of the Modern Era (Liberace, Carmen Miranda, etc.)

SOURCE: Reprinted by permission of the Modern Language Association from *MLA Newsletter,* Vol. 27, No. 1, Spring 1995

INQUEERY, INTHEORY, INDEED

InQueery, InTheory, InDeed, the sixth annual North American Lesbian, Gay, Bisexual Studies conference, was held at the University of Iowa in November 1994, and attended by over one thousand students, faculty, and activists. Topics for papers ranged from the serious to the sublime. The following are a list of presentations and panels recorded in the conference program.

"Beyond Binary: Queer Family Values and the Primal Cream." (Keynote address by Lani Ka'ahumanu)
"Your Blues Ain't Like Mine: Black Demogogues and the Politics of Homophobia"
"The Dialectics of Dominance and Submission: Emmanuel Levinas as Butch/Top"
"Is There Heterosexuality in the Bible?"
"Bisexuality in a Gender Container: The Tupperware Theory"
Panel: "Butch Rage: Daggers, Dykes, and Daddies"
"Harder, Pussycat, More, More!"
"Teutonic Sexuality"
"Buckling Down or Knockling Under: Discipline or Punish in Lesbian and Gay Studies"
Workshop: "The Erect Penis: Can We Top It? A Visual and Theoretical Interrogation of Imagery for Active Female Desire"
"Unspecified Details: Banishing the Specter of Female Homoeroticism in 19th-Century Anti-Masturbatory Writing"

Panel: "Clits in Court: Lesbians and the Law"

"Moving the Pink Agenda into the Ivory Tower"

"Trans(homo)sexuality?: Double Inversion, Psychiatric Confusion, and Hetero-Hegemony"

Panel: "Anals of History"

Panel: Sex Between Men in the Hebrew Bible and Rabbinical Culture I and II

"Rectal Foreign Bodies: A Review of the Medical Literature"

"G.I. Joes in Barbie Land: Recontextualizing the Meaning of Butch in Lesbian Culture"

"The Sexism-Homophobia Connection: A Model"

"Fruitcakes at Christmas"

Presentation: "Save Our Children: Queer Activism and the Youth Public Sphere"

Presentation: "Lesbian, Gay, and Bisexual Curriculum Inclusion Advocacy at the K-12 Level"

6. GAY MEN IN FILM, TELEVISION AND VIDEO

The Sergeant *is not about homosexuality, it's about loneliness.*

—ROD STEIGER, 1968

Windows *is not about homosexuality, it's about insanity.*

—GORDON WILLIS, 1979

Staircase *is not about homosexuality, it's about loneliness.*

—REX HARRISON, 1971

Sunday, Bloody Sunday *is not about the sexuality of these people, it's about human loneliness.*

—JOHN SCHLESINGER, 1972

Gay men have always been hungry for images of themselves. But a strict Hollywood censorship code, in effect from 1930 until 1968, made gay people virtually invisible on the big screen. When they appeared as characters in movies at all, gay men have been stereotyped as everything from sissies to psychotic cross-dressing killers to pathetic suicides.

Network television's record has been even worse. Until very recently, gay men have rarely surfaced, except as the brunt of bad sitcom jokes. When two gay men were written into the script of *thirtysomething* in 1989, in a scene where they simply sat in bed together, network sponsors raised such a fury that the episode was only allowed to air after midnight, with a warning for "adult" audiences, and not in its regular 10 P.M. time slot.

It was mainly through the activist efforts of the Gay and Lesbian Alliance Against Defamation (GLAAD)—a watchdog organization founded in 1985 to make mainstream media and Hollywood aware of and receptive to lesbian and gay concerns—that Hollywood film and television studios began to attempt more accurate depictions of gay lives. GLAAD turned the heat up on the Hollywood studios for two vicious portrayals of gay people, in the films *Silence of the Lambs* and *Basic Instinct*, and in fact, director Jonathan Demme's next movie after *Silence of the Lambs* was the big-budget, gay-positive *Philadelphia*.

A host of AIDS-themed films—including the feature-length *Longtime Companion*, and the TV dramas *An Early Frost* and *Andre's Mother*—appeared in the late 1980s and presented moving portrayals of gay lives, though they didn't attract large audiences. But when major film star Tom Hanks won an Academy Award for playing a gay man with AIDS in Demme's *Philadelphia*, gay men (and AIDS) on the big screen were suddenly marketable.

Though not all gay men were happy with the way Hollywood chose to depict them in *Philadelphia*, some doors on gay lives in film and television definitely opened. A handful of projects about gay men have been produced in Hollywood, including a film version of Paul Rudnick's hit play *Jeffrey*, which opened in August 1995.

Ron Nyswaner,
screenwriter for
Philadelphia
(*Photo by Terry
Boggis*)

TV actor Roseanne (who has a gay brother and a lesbian sister) has probably done more than anyone else to boost the appearance of lesbians and gay men on television. Besides featuring two regular gay characters on her popular weekly show, in a spring 1994 episode her character Roseanne Connor was kissed by a woman at a gay bar and the world didn't stop spinning. The same season, *Northern Exposure* dared present a gay male commitment ceremony. Since then, television has witnessed an explosion of lesbian and gay characters and themes on other major sitcoms and dramas, including *Frasier, Daddy's Girls, Friends, Sisters,* and *Melrose Place.* In the fall of 1994, *Roseanne* took us to a gay Halloween party, where many of the men, including the gay character Leon, were in full drag.

Unfortunately, gay men have never had any out movie stars to call their own, though the question of who's gay in Hollywood has been a topic of lesbian and gay gossip for decades. Rock Hudson's sexual orientation only became a matter of public knowledge when he was dying of AIDS, and other respected actors never felt free enough to reveal their sexual orientation. Today, gay male movie and television actors still dodge the question of sexuality in interviews. Dan Butler of *Frasier,* along with Brad Davis (*Midnight Express*), Dack Rambo of *Dallas,* and Dick Sargent of *Bewitched* fame (all three now deceased), are notable for publicly acknowledging being gay and taking pride in it, as is British stage and film actor Sir Ian McKellan. Coming out may be easier to do from the other side of the camera, and openly gay directors such as Gus Van Sant, John Schlesinger, and John Waters have been very successful. If Hollywood retains its interest in gay male topics, maybe more actors will find a safe atmosphere for coming out of the closet.

SOURCES FOR FURTHER READING:

"Hollywood Power: The Industry Comes Out." *Out* magazine special issue, November 1994.

Murray, Raymond. *Images in the Dark: An Encyclopedia of Gay and Lesbian Film and Video.* TLA Publications, 1994.

Russo, Vito. *The Celluloid Closet.* Harper & Row, 1987, 1981.

Weiss, Andrea. *Vampires and Violets: Lesbians in Film.* Penguin Books, 1994.

EXCERPTS FROM MOVIE PRODUCTION CODE OF 1930

"No picture shall be produced which will lower the standards of those who see it. Hence the sympathy of the audience should never be thrown to crime, wrong-doing, evil or sin."

"Sex perversion or any inference to it is forbidden."

"The sanctity of the institution of marriage and the home shall be upheld. Pictures shall not infer that low forms of sex relationships are the accepted or common thing."

GUIDELINES FROM THE GAY ACTIVISTS ALLIANCE, IN COOPERATION WITH THE NATIONAL GAY TASK FORCE, 1973

Some general principles for motion picture and television treatment of homosexuality:

1. Homosexuality isn't funny. Sometimes anything can be a source of humor, but the lives of twenty million Americans are not a joke.
2. Fag, faggot, dyke, queer, lezzie, homo, fairy, mary, pansy, sissy, etc., are terms of abuse. If you don't want to insult, the words are gay, lesbian, and homosexual. That doesn't mean nobody on film can use a dirty word, but if you have rules about kike, wop, spic, nigger, etc., use them [the rules] for fag and dyke.
3. Use the same rules you have for other minorities. If bigots don't get away with it if they hate Catholics, they can't get away with it if they hate gays. Put another way, the rights and dignity of homosexuals are not a controversial issue.
4. Stereotypical people do exist. But if such a minority of any group receives exclusive media exposure, that's bigotry. Until a broad spectrum of the gay community is expressed on film and the stereotypes are put into perspective, their use is damaging.
5. Homosexuality is a natural variant of human sexuality. It is not an illness, nor is it a problem for the majority of gays, who are happy to be what they are. If

all blacks or Jews or Irish or Chicanos were portrayed as anguished, oddball, or insane, they'd be angry, too. Gays are angry.

6. If you are doing a drama or a comedy or a talk show about homosexuality, you have an obligation to do your homework and free yourself from the myths.

7. There is a wide variety of available themes concerning the place of homosexuality in contemporary society and the range of gay relationships and lifestyles. Many of these can provide entertainment for a broad, general public. Gays do not want to return to media invisibility.

8. A permanent board of consultants consisting of gay men and women is available to the industry. But there are gay people all around you in your jobs. It is up to you to provide a climate in which they feel free to speak out openly.

SOME FAMOUS MAINSTREAM GAY OR BISEXUAL FILM DIRECTORS

Ardolino, Emile, 1943–1993: films include *Dirty Dancing, Chances Are, Sister Act*, and the made-for-TV *Gypsy*, with Bette Midler

Bartel, Paul, b. 1938: films include *Private Parts, Eating Raoul, Cannonball*, and *Scenes from the Class Struggle in Beverly Hills*

Bridges, James, 1935–1993: films include *The Paper Chase, September 30, 1955, The China Syndrome, Urban Cowboy*, and *Bright Lights, Big City*

Cukor, George, 1899–1983: films include *The Philadelphia Story, Dinner at Eight, Little Women, Camille, The Women, Gaslight, Adam's Rib, Born Yesterday, Pat and Mike, A Star Is Born*, and *My Fair Lady*

Goulding, Edmund, 1892–1959: films include *The Devil's Holiday, Grand Hotel, Dark Victory*, and *The Old Maid*.

Higgins, Colin, 1941–1988: films included *Harold and Maude, Silver Streak, Foul Play*, and *Nine to Five*.

Ivory, James, b. 1928: with partner, producer Ismail Merchant (b. 1937), films include *Shakespeare Wallah, The Europeans, Heat and Dust, The Bostonians, A Room with a View, Maurice, Mr. and Mrs. Bridge, Howard's End*, and *The Remains of the Day*.

Lopez, Temistocles: films include *Exquisite Corpses* and *Chain of Desire*.

Moore, Robert, 1927–1984: films include *Tell Me That You Love Me, Junie Moon* (which he also acted in), *Murder by Death, The Cheap Detective*, and *Chapter Two*.

Richardson, Tony, 1928–1991: films include *Look Back in Anger, The Entertainer, The Loneliness of the Long Distance Runner, Tom Jones, The Loved One, A Taste of Honey, A Delicate Balance, The Hotel New Hampshire*, and *Blue Sky*.

Schlesinger, John, b. 1926: films include *Darling, Far from the Madding Crowd, Midnight Cowboy, Sunday, Bloody Sunday, The Day of the Locust, Yanks*, and *Madame Sousatzka*.

Van Sant, Gus, b. 1952: films include *Even Cowgirls Get the Blues, Drugstore Cowboy*, and *My Own Private Idaho*.

Waters, John, b. 1946: films include *Polyester, Mondo Trasho, Cry-Baby, Hairspray*, and *Serial Mom*.

Whale, James, 1896–1957: famous for horror films such as *Frankenstein, The Invisible Man,* and *The Bride of Frankenstein.*

Zefferelli, Franco, b. 1923: films include *The Taming of the Shrew, Romeo and Juliet, Brother Sun, Sister Moon, Endless Love,* and *Hamlet* (with Mel Gibson).

IMAGES OF GAY MEN IN MAINSTREAM FILMS— THE SILENT ERA TO THE PRESENT

SCREEN SISSIES

The Soilers (1923): a sissie cowboy in this Laurel and Hardy comedy.

Irene (1926): George K. Arthur as the dressmaker Madame Lucy.

The Broadway Melody (1929): yet another nellie costume designer.

Lady of the Pavements (1929): Franklin Pangborn, a career sissy, flounces about.

The Front Page (1931): Edward Everett Horton, who made a career of playing sissies, as the poet reporter Lewis Milestone.

Movie Crazy (1932): Grady Sutton jumps on top of a table at the sight of a mouse.

Professional Sweetheart and *Only Yesterday* (1933): Franklin Pangborn as a duo of sissies.

Sailor's Luck (1933): James Dunn plays a lisping bathhouse attendant.

The Warrior's Husband (1933): Ernest Truex plays Sapiens, a member of Queen Hippolyta's court who curls his beard while the women make all the decisions.

The Gay Divorcee (1934): Edward Everett Horton again, this time as Egbert Fitzgerald.

It's Love I'm After (1937): Eric Blore as Leslie Howard's dresser, Diggs.

The Wizard of Oz (1939): Bert Lahr as the most famous sissy of all, the Cowardly Lion.

Laura (1944): Clifton Webb as Waldo Lydecker, the bitchy gossip columnist.

The Razor's Edge (1946): Clifton Webb as Elliot Templeton, the aging male spinster.

Adam's Rib (1949): David Wayne plays Kip, Katherine Hepburn's "girlfriend."

CROSS-DRESSERS

The Leading Lady (1911): John Bunny was one of the first men to appear on film in drag.

A Florida Enchantment (1914): Sidney Drew took magic seeds that turned him into a woman.

Miss Fatty's Seaside Lovers (1915): Fatty Arbuckle plays the daughter of a rich man on a beach and reprises the role in *Fatty in Coney Island* (1917).

Spit-Ball Sadie (1915): Harold Lloyd plays a female pitcher on an all-woman baseball team.

A Woman (1915): Charlie Chaplin in the title role.

1914–1916: Wallace Beery portrays a coy Swedish maid named "Sweedie" in a series of films.

Bumping into Broadway (1919): Gus Leonard played Ma Simpson, the vigilant landlady of a theatrical boardinghouse.

Yankee Doodle in Berlin (1919): Bothwell Browne plays a femme fatale trying to obtain secret information from the Kaiser.

I Was a Male War Bride (1949): Cary Grant poses as a female nurse to get into the United States with WAC wife Ann Sheridan.

Glen or Glenda? (1953): Ed Wood's cult classic of a young man who loves to wear women's clothing.

Some Like It Hot (1959): Jack Lemmon and Tony Curtis as musicians in an all-girl band.

The Further Perils of Laurel and Hardy (1968): Stan Laurel played drag to his partner Oliver Hardy.

Pink Flamingos (1972): Divine as zaftig Babs Johnson.

La Cage aux Folles (1978): Michel Serrault as the female impersonater, Albin. Plus two sequels, *La Cage aux Folles II* (1980) and *La Cage aux Folles III: The Wedding* (1986).

Polyester (1981): Divine is divine as Baltimore housewife Francine Fishpaw.

Tootsie (1987): Dustin Hoffman as an out-of-work actor who dresses as a woman to land a plum role.

Torch Song Trilogy (1988): Harvey Fierstein as female impersonator Arnold Beckoff.

Mrs. Doubtfire (1993): estranged from his wife, Robin Williams becomes Mrs. Doubtfire, so he can be nanny to his children.

The Adventures of Priscilla, Queen of the Desert (1994): two drag queens and a MTF transsexual on a bus trip across Australia.

To Wong Foo, Thanks for Everything, Julie Newmar (1995): Wesley Snipes and Patrick Swayze in a drag queen road trip movie.

HOMICIDAL TRANSVESTITES

Murder (1930): Esme Percy plays a murderous transvestite trapeze artist.

Psycho (1960): the infamous Norman Bates, played by Anthony Perkins.

Caprice (1967): Ray Walston plays a transvestite cosmetician who commits murder.

Freebie and the Bean (1974): the killer transvestite and blackmailer played by Christopher Morley.

Silence of the Lambs (1992): transvestite Jamie Gumb murders and skins women and then fashions a coat for himself.

HOMOCIDAL HOMOSEXUALS

Rope (1948): Farley Granger and John Dall are pretentious lovers who murder a former classmate on a whim. Based on the Leopold and Loeb story, which was retold in *Compulsion* (1959) and *Swoon* (1992).

Strangers on a Train (1951): Robert Walker's queer Bruno Anthony tricks unsuspecting Farley Granger into exchanging murders.

The Detective (1968): William Windom as a homocidal detective who is "more ashamed of being a homosexual than a murderer."

Diamonds Are Forever (1971): Vicious killer lovers Mr. Wint and Mr. Kidd.

The Laughing Policeman (1973): San Francisco cops Walter Matthau and Bruce Dern uncover a mass murderer in a closeted gay man (Albert Paulsen).

Drum (1976): John Colicos plays an evil white slaver who rapes and castrates black men.

Cruising (1980): a repressed homosexual kills his tricks.

Deathtrap (1982): Michael Caine and Christopher Reeve are lovers who kill Caine's troublesome wife, Dyan Cannon.

Partners (1982): a gay serial killer is hunted by two cops, straight pretty boy Ryan O'Neal and closeted gay John Hurt.

Manhunter (1986): a serial killer who murders entire families but only molests his male victims.

No Way Out (1987): Will Patton would kill to protect his boss, Secretary of Defense Gene Hackman.

Confessions of a Serial Killer (1992): homosexuality as just another facet of a serial killer's deranged behavior.

ACHINGLY REPRESSED HOMOSEXUALS

Billy Budd (1962): Robert Ryan and Peter Ustinov drool over beautiful Billy (Terence Stamp).

The Leather Boys (1963): chum Pete (Dudley Sutton) is probably the reason Reggie (Colin Campbell) isn't interested in his wife.

Becket (1964): Henry II (Peter O'Toole) is lovesick for Thomas Becket (Richard Burton).

Reflections in a Golden Eye (1967): Marlon Brando is a latent homosexual army officer with an unsatisfied wife (Elizabeth Taylor).

The Sergeant (1968): Master Sergeant Rod Steiger commits suicide after his kisses a young private.

Women in Love (1969): Gerald (Oliver Reed) and Rupert (Alan Bates) engage in a homoerotically charged nude wrestling match. From the novel by D. H. Lawrence, with a screenplay by Larry Kramer.

Midnight Cowboy (1969): the tender relationship between Joe Buck (Jon Voigt) and Ratso Rizzo (Dustin Hoffman) is left undeveloped.

Death in Venice (1971): Thomas Mann's classic tale of an older man (Dirk Bogarde) obsessed with an unattainable young man.

A Separate Peace (1972): Gene (Parker Stevenson) develops an unspoken love for his school chum, Finny.

Brideshead Revisited (1980): Charles Ryder (Jeremy Irons) is infatuated with his Oxford friend Sebastian Flyte (Anthony Andrews).

The Hitcher (1986): a twisted homoerotic relationship between crazed killer Rutger Hauer and boyishly naive C. Thomas Howell.

Apartment Zero (1989): sexual tension in Buenos Aires between Adrian LeDuc (Colin Firth) and his American boarder (Hart Bochner).

Europa, Europa (1991): though he fails to seduce him, German Robert protects Jewish Solomon during World War II.

The Hours and the Times (1991): What might have happened between John Lennon and his manager, Brian Epstein, a gay man, on a holiday together in Spain?

My Own Private Idaho (1991): River Phoenix breaks our hearts as he professes his love for Keanu Reeves.

Backbeat (1994): a repressed John Lennon again, this time experiencing homosexual tension with pal Stu Sutcliffe ("the Fifth Beatle").

CLASSIC ANIMATED QUEERS

Pinocchio (1940): Honest John, the fox, and Gideon, a cat, are best buddies who procure lost boys for sale to an evil coachman who takes them to Pleasure Island.

Cinderella (1950): mice pals Jock and Gus-Gus volunteer to help finish Cinderella's dress in time for the ball.

Water, Water Every Hare; Slick Hare; Knighty Knight Bugs; What's Opera, Doc?; The Rabbit of Seville (1930s–1950s): Swishy Bugs Bunny did not think twice about cross-dressing or dancing with, kissing, or marrying a man (more often than not Elmer Fudd) to get out of trouble.

TRANSGENDERED OR TRANSSEXUAL

Boy! What a Girl (1945): Tim Moore stars as a butch drag queen pursued by three men with marriage on their minds in this all-black musical.

The Christine Jorgensen Story (1970): based on the biography of the first transsexual to undergo sex reassignment surgery.

Come Back to the Five and Dime, Jimmy Dean, Jimmy Dean (1982): Karen Black as an MTF transsexual, who, the last time her friends saw her, twenty years before, was gay Joe.

Second Serve (1986): made-for-TV movie about MFT transsexual tennis player Renee Richards, played by Vanessa Redgrave.

Paris Is Burning (1990): lesbian director Jennie Livingston's portrait of Harlem's drag ball culture.

The Crying Game (1992): Jaye Davidson makes his screen debut, fooling Stephen Rea and most of America.

Lip Gloss (1993): Montreal's bustling world of drag queens, transvestites, and female impersonators.

M. Butterfly (1993): Jeremy Irons as a French diplomat who falls in love with a Chinese woman, who is in fact a man (John Lone).

Le Sexe des Etoiles (1993): Canadian melodrama about a young girl trying to accept her transsexual father.

The Adventures of Priscilla, Queen of the Desert (1994): Transsexual Terence Stamp teams up with drag queens Guy Pearce and Hugo Weaving on a cross-country trip through the Australian outback.

SCREEN SUICIDES

Victim (1961): Peter McEnery kills himself rather than let his pillar-of-society and happily married heartthrob Dirk Bogarde get blackmailed.

Advise and Consent (1962): after being blackmailed by his political opponents, Senator Brig Anderson, played by Don Murray, slits his throat with a straight razor.

This Special Friendship (1964): a schoolboy jumps in front of speeding train, not because he is homosexual, but because school priests have told him that his friend no longer loves him.

The Detective (1968): closeted murdered William Windom commits suicide after killing a wealthy gay man.

The Sergent (1968): Rod Steiger blows his brains out after kissing a fellow soldier.

Fortune and Men's Eyes (1971): prison inmate Rocky slits his throat with a razor when forced to be a bottom instead of a top.

Play It As It Lays (1972): Anthony Perkins plays a chronically unhappy gay producer who overdoses on pills.

Ode to Billy Joe (1976): Bobbie Gentrie's hit song inspired this movie, which posits that Billy Joe jumped off the Tallahatchee Bridge because he was ashamed of having had homosex.

The Betsy (1978): closeted queer Paul Rudd poisons himself after finding his wife in bed with his father.

And Justice for All (1980): a transvestite hangs himself.

The Name of the Rose (1986): Brother Adelmo hurls himself down an embankment after Brother Berringer makes advances to him.

No Way Out (1987): Will Patton blows his brains out when he realizes that his love for his boss, Gene Hackman, is unrequited.

HOMOS KILLED OFF BY THE END OF THE MOVIE

Suddenly Last Summer (1959): poet Sebastian Venable is eaten by cannabilistic Spanish street youths; the lurking Venable, who is "famished for the dark ones," never appears on screen. *Suddenly Last Summer* ties *Theatre of Blood* for the award for the most creative homosexual death on film.

Caprice (1967): Ray Walston, the evil transvestite Dr. Clancy, is pushed from a balcony by Doris Day.

The Detective (1968): gay beach bum Tony Musante is wrongly executed for the bludgeoning death of wealthy queer James Inman, who was actually murdered by the self-hating homo William Windom, who kills himself at the end of the movie.

The Damned (1969): every one of the entire homosexual-infiltrated SA Brown Shirts is slaughtered by rival SS troops, on what is known as the "Night of the Long Knives."

Justine (1969): Cliff Gorman plays The Homosexual, who gets murdered.

Diamonds Are Forever (1971): evil fags Mr. Wint and Mr. Kidd are set aflame by James Bond.

The Day of the Jackal (1973): a nameless homosexual is shot to death.

Theatre of Blood (1973): gay theater critic Robert Morley dies when he is forced to eat his two poodles, baked into a pie.

Freebie and the Bean (1974): transvestite Christopher Morley gets his just desserts (read: is killed in the end) from James Caan.

The Eiger Sanction (1975): villainous Jack Cassidy is left to die in the desert, though his pooch, named Faggot, is saved at the end.

Swashbuckler (1976): Peter Boyle plays gay villain Lord Durant, who gets his in the end.

The Choirboys (1977) : a gay high school student, played by Michael Wills, is shot to death.

The Long Good Friday (1979): the lieutenant of an underworld boss, played by Paul Freeman, is murdered while cruising a public bathhouse.

Cruising (1980): not one, not two, but *three* gay men are murdered.

The Fan (1981): Michael Beihn knifes the gay man who gives him a blowjob, then sets him on fire.

Road Warrior (1982): the Golden Youth, boyfriend to a leather-clad motorcycle villain, is killed with steel boomerang.

Streamers (1983): the gay soldier Richie, played by Mitchell Lichtenstein, is murdered.

The Boys Next Door (1984): Charlie Sheen and Maxwell Caulfield as teenagers who pick up a gay man in a bar and kill him.

Mike's Murder (1984): Debra Winger investigates boyfriend Mike's (Mark Keyloun) murder, only to find he was involved with a man.

Braveheart (1995): the gay character Gaviston is hurled out a window by Edward (Mel Gibson)

AND NOW FOR THE *POSITIVE* GAY CHARACTERS

Making Love (1982): a soap opera of coming out for Michael Ontkean, a doctor who leaves his wife for Harry Hamlin.

Another Country (1984): Rupert Everett (himself gay) portrays real-life traitor-defector Guy Burgess in his public school days, when he had a gay affair, with Cary Elwes as his lover.

My Beautiful Laundrette (1986): the love affair between a young English-born Pakistani and his punk lover, played by Daniel Day-Lewis.

Maurice (1987): from partners James Ivory and Ismail Merchant, the classic coming-out story by E. M. Forster, with James Wilby as Maurice and Rupert Graves as Alec, the working-class man who becomes his lover.

Longtime Companion (1990): a group of gay friends confronts the AIDS crisis, in a screenplay written by Craig Lucas. Bruce Davison received an Academy Award nomination for his moving portrayal of a man who watches his lover's slow, painful decline, then dies himself.

My Own Private Idaho (1991): gay director Gus Van Sant's touching portrayal of young male hustlers on the streets of Portland, Oregon, with River Phoenix and Keanu Reeves

The Crying Game (1992): Stephen Rea, a former IRA revolutionary, finds love with genderbending Jaye Davidson.

Philadelphia (1993): Tom Hanks won an Oscar for his role as a gay lawyer with

AIDS who wins a discrimination suit against his firm when he is fired; Antonio
Banderas portrays his sexy lover.

The Wedding Banquet (1993): Wai Tung (Winston Chao) arranges a marriage of
convenience for himself so his parents will leave him alone to enjoy his gay life
in peace.

The Adventures of Priscilla, Queen of the Desert (1994): two gay drag queens and
a transsexual on a trek across the Australian outback, with graphic portrayals of
homophobia and a touching treatment of a boy's love for his gay father (Hugo
Weaving).

Four Weddings and a Funeral (1994): Simon Callow and John Hannah play a gay
couple whose true bonds of love and "marriage" are only allowed to surface
after one of them dies.

Naked in New York (1994): Ralph Macchio in a supporting role as a young gay man
pining after his best friend from college, a straight man played by Eric Stoltz.

Priest (1995): sexually active Catholic priests, one of whom is a gay man who dons
a leather jacket at night to go out cruising.

SIGNIFICANT GAY-THEMED FILMS

The Boys in the Band (1970): from Mart Crowley's classic play about eight gay
friends who get together for a birthday party. The movie is significant for its gay
content, but the overwhelming message is that being gay means being lonely
and unhappy.

Sunday, Bloody Sunday (1971): features a historic kiss between lovers Peter Finch
and Murray Head.

Dog Day Afternoon (1975): Al Pacino as a gay thief, who turns to robbing banks to
pay for the sex-change operation of his lover, Chris Sarandon. Both were nominated for Oscars.

Taxi Zum Klo (Taxi to the Toilet) (1980): gay infidelity and intimacy in pre-AIDS
Germany.

Kiss of the Spiderwoman (1985): William Hurt portrays a romantic and politically
naive gay man sharing a prison cell with the hard-boiled revolutionary Raul
Julia, in an unnamed South American country.

Prick Up Your Ears (1987): the life and brutal death of British playwright Joe Orton
(played by Gary Oldman), focusing on his abusive relationship with his lover-
murderer, Kenneth Halliwell (Alfred Molina), rather than on his important career.

Edward II (1991): Derek Jarman's graphically violent reworking of Christopher
Marlowe's play about the tragic King Edward and his lover, Gaviston.

For a Lost Soldier (1992): a controversial story of man-boy love in the Netherlands
during World War II.

Six Degrees of Separation (1993): Will Smith stars as a young gay man who pre-
tends to be the son of Sidney Poitier in order to ingratiate himself to a number
of upper-middle-class white families.

Wittgenstein (1993): Derek Jarman's biographical film about the Austrian-born
philosopher.

Farewell My Concubine (1993): the fifty-year relationship between two male opera stars in China, which won the top prize at the Cannes Film Festival.

Fall Time (1995): Stephen Baldwin and Mickey Rourke play lovers and partners in crime.

NOTABLE GAY INDEPENDENT FEATURE FILMS AND THEIR DIRECTORS

Buddies (1985): directed by Arthur Bressan; first dramatic feature about AIDS, about a volunteer who visits and helps a PWA.

Parting Glances (1986): directed by Bill Sherwood; considered one of the best gay films of the 1980s, about a young gay couple, played by Richard Ganoung and John Bolger, who are about to separate when one is transferred overseas.

Fun Down There (1989): directed by Roger Stigliano; a gay neophyte from upstate New York moves to the big city to explore his sexuality.

Exquisite Corpses (1989): directed by Temistocles Lopez; a gay casting agent transforms a young hick into a sexy cabaret performer.

Poison (1991): directed by Todd Haynes; three unconnected stories about a young boy killing his abusive father, a scientist who isolates the human sex drive in liquid form, and unrequited love in prison.

Young Soul Rebels (1991): directed by Isaac Julien; a late 1970s period piece about two African-British DJs, one gay, one straight.

The Living End (1992): directed by Gregg Araki; black comedy about two HIV-positive gay men on a lawless road trip.

Rock Hudson's Home Movies (1992): directed by Mark Rappaport; a gay revisionist look at Rock Hudson's movie career.

Swoon (1992): directed by Tom Kalin; a new queer cinema retelling of the Leopold and Loeb murder scandal of the 1920s.

Zero Patience (1993): directed by John Greyson; satiric musical-comedy about Gaetan Dugas, a French-Canadian flight attendent known as "Patient Zero," reported by health officials (and gay writer Randy Shilts) to have brought AIDS to North America.

*Totally F***ed Up* (1994): directed by Gregg Araki; the subculture of queer teens in Los Angeles.

"I don't think the right wing realizes this, but the more you tell artists not to do something, the more they want to do it. That's where a lot of the new gay and lesbian filmmaking is coming from."

—GREGG ARAKI, 1992

SOME IMPORTANT GAY DOCUMENTARIES

Gay USA (1977): directed by Arthur Bressan; lesbian and gay pride marches intercut with on-the-street interviews with gay people.

The Times of Harvey Milk (1984): directed by lovers Robert Epstein and Jeffrey Friedman; Academy Award–winning look at activist Harvey Milk's life and the aftermath of his murder.

Before Stonewall (1985): directed by Greta Schiller and Robbie Rosenberg; the evolution of the lesbian/gay rights movement, from the 1920s until the Stonewall rebellion.

Common Threads: Stories from the Quilt (1989): directed by Epstein and Friedman; Academy Award–winning interviews with surviving relatives and friends of five people who died of AIDS.

Looking for Langston (1989): directed by Isaac Julien; a meditation on the life and work of queer poet Langston Hughes.

Tongues Untied (1989): directed by Marlon Riggs; through poetry and personal testimony, a look at the homophobia and racism that confronts black gay men.

Absolutely Positive (1991): interviews with out gay men living with HIV and AIDS

Urinal (1991): directed by John Greyson; homosexual repression in Canada, specifically the entrapment of gay men by homophobic police in Ontario.

No Regrets (Non, Je Ne Regrette Rien) (1992): directed by Marlon Riggs; five black HIV-positive gay men talk about their lives and their illness, interspersed with music and song.

Sex Is . . . (1992): directed by Mark Huestis; interviews with gay men about their sexual lives before and since AIDS.

Silverlake Life: The View from Here (1993): a disturbing video diary made by two lovers (Tom Joslin and Peter Friedman) as they slowly succumb to AIDS.

Coming Out Under Fire (1994): directed by Arthur Dong; profiles of nine women and men discharged from the service for homosexuality, based on Allan Berube's prize-winning look at lesbians and gays in the U.S. military during World War II.

MADE-FOR-TELEVISION MOVIE QUEERS

That Certain Summer (1972): landmark broadcast about a son who visits his divorced father and his new lover for the summer. Seven Emmy nominations; one award.

Sergeant Matlovich vs. the U.S. Air Force (1978): dramatization of the life of gay soldier ousted from the military.

Fifth of July (1984): Adaptation of Lanford Wilson's play, starring most of the original Broadway cast, including Richard Thomas (who replaced Christopher Reeve on Broadway) as a disabled gay veteran and Jeff Daniels as his supportive lover.

Consenting Adult (1985): Parents Marlo Thomas and Martin Sheen are tortured by their son's coming out and try to find a cure for his "illness."

An Early Frost (1985): landmark TV-movie about a gay man (Aidan Quinn) who must tell his family that he is gay and that he has AIDS. Thirteen Emmy nominations; three awards.

Tidy Endings (1988): Stockard Channing and Harvey Fierstein lose the same man to AIDS—her ex-husband and his lover.

Andre's Mother (1989): The battle between the mother of a man who has died of AIDS and his surviving partner. One Emmy award.

Our Sons (1991): Julie Andrews and Ann-Margret as the mothers respectively of lovers Hugh Grant and Zeljko Ivanek, the latter of whom has AIDS and has been rejected by his mother.

The Lost Language of Cranes (1992): from David Leavitt's novel, a British production about a father who faces his own homosexuality after his son comes out.

Citizen Cohn (1992): the career and death from AIDS of closeted conservative lawyer Roy Cohn, played by James Woods.

And the Band Played On (1993): a dramatization of Randy Shilts's chronicle of the start of the AIDS pandemic, starring Ian McKellan, who received an Emmy nomination.

Tales of the City (1994): Armistead Maupin's novel brought to the small screen.

Roommates (1994): in an AIDS hospice, Eric Stoltz is a gay man paired with a homophobic roommate, Randy Quaid.

My Brother's Keeper (1995): John Lithgow as identical twin gay brothers, both teachers, who come out of the closet when one tests positive for HIV.

FAVORITE GAY OR BISEXUAL TV STARS

Burr, Raymond, 1917–1993: star of *Perry Mason* and *Ironside*.

Butler, Dan, b. 1955: sportscaster Bulldog on *Frasier*.

Cox, Wally, 1924–1973: star of *Mr. Peepers*.

Cruz, Wilson, b. 1974: regular on *My So-Called Life*, playing a gay teenager.

Daly, James, 1928–1978: regular on *Medical Center*.

Fierstein, Harvey, b. 1954: regular on *Daddy's Girls*.

Geer, Will, 1902–1978: Grandpa on *The Waltons*.

Hudson, Rock, 1925–1985: star of *McMillan and Wife* and featured character on *Dynasty*.

Hunter, Tab, b. 1931: regular on *Mary Hartman, Mary Hartman*.

Kaye, Danny, 1913–1987: star of variety hour, *The Danny Kaye Show*.

Liberace, 1919–1987: star of variety hour, *The Liberace Show*.

Lynde, Paul, 1926–1982: Uncle Arthur on *Bewitched* and the middle "square" of *Hollywood Squares* ("I'll take Paul Lynde to block"); also starred in short-lived *The Paul Lynde Show*.

Rambo, Dack, died 1994: regular on *Dallas*.

Reed, Robert, 1933–1992: star of *The Brady Bunch*.

Sargent, Dick, died 1994: "the second Darren" on *Bewitched*.

Sweeney, Terry b.: regular on *Saturday Night Live*, where he developed a memorable impersonation of Nancy Reagan.

GAY CHARACTERS ON TELEVISION SERIES 1971–1995

All in the Family: in a 1971 episode, "Judging Books by Covers," possibly the first explicitly gay-themed show to air on TV, Archie Bunker discovers that a football-player pal is gay.

Sound Bytes from Paul Lynde on "Hollywood Squares"

Peter Marshall: Paul, why do motorcycle riders wear leather?
Paul Lynde: Because chiffon wrinkles.

Peter Marshall: Paul, at what age does a person understand the meaning of a spanking?
Paul Lynde: The true meaning?—Twenty-three.

Peter Marshall: Kate Smith was once quoted as saying, "That's the most disgusting thing I could ever imagine." What was she talking about?
Paul Lynde: Showering with Orson Welles.

An American Family (1973): a twelve-part documentary series on PBS about the "average" American Loud family; during the series, son Lance Loud came out on national TV.

Cagney & Lacey: featured a gay neighbor.

Daddy's Girls: costarred Harvey Fierstein as a gay fashion designer; the series was canceled after a few episodes.

Doctor, Doctor: featured a gay college professor.

Dynasty: Al Corley played the sometimes-gay, sometimes-straight Steven Carrington.

Hooperman: costarred Joseph Gian as a gay cop, Officer Rick Silardi.

Hope & Gloria: the butch hair stylist, Isaac, is allowed to have real feelings when a relationship ends on account of his lover's internalized homophobia.

Hot L Baltimore: first recurring gay character on a series; canceled after one season.

Love Sidney: Tony Randall went from a gay man to a "confirmed bachelor" in this sitcom. Explicit references to Sidney's homosexuality were in the pilot, but not in any of the forty-four episodes that followed.

Melrose Place: features a gay social worker, Matt Fielding.

My So-Called Life: co-stars Wilson Cruz as Rickie Vasquez, a gay Puerto Rican teenager.

Northern Exposure: has two recurring gay male characters, Ron and Erick, who moved into town, started a bed-and-breakfast inn, and eventually had a commitment ceremony on screen.

NYPD Blue: has recurring character who is an out administrative assistant with a closeted gay cop lover; one episode focused on them being gay bashed by cops in the lover's precinct.

Roc: featured Richard Roundtree as a gay relative who announced his upcoming wedding.

Roseanne: her business partner is a gay man, Leon, played by Martin Mull.

Sara: featured a gay lawyer.

Soap: Jodie, played by Billy Crystal.

thirtysomething: had a recurring gay character, who caused a controversy when he was shown sitting up in bed talking to his lover.

Three's Company: John Ritter played a straight man masquerading as a gay man in order to live with two women.

The Tracey Ullman Show: offered two gay men parenting a teenage daughter.

ADDRESSES OF THE MAJOR AND MINOR TV NETWORKS

If you see something on TV that you like or dislike, you can make your opinion heard by writing to the powers-that-be at the various networks:

ABC, Audience Information, 77 W. 66th St., New York, NY 10023-6298
CBS, Audience Services, 51 W. 52nd St., New York, NY 10019
FOX, P.O. Box 900, Beverly Hills, CA 90213
NBC, Audience Services, 30 Rockefeller Plaza, New York, NY 10112
PBS, 1320 Braddock Place, Alexandria, VA 22314-1698

AMC (American Movie Classics),
150 Crossways Park West, Woodbury, NY 11797

A&E (Arts & Entertainment Network),
235 East 45th St., New York, NY 10017

BET (Black Entertainment Television)
1232 31st St., N.W., Washington, DC 20007

CNN (Cable News Network) and TBS, TNT (Turner Network Television)
One CNN Center, Box 105366, Atlanta, GA 30348-5366

CBN ("Family Channel")
100 Centerville Turnpike, Virginia Beach, VA 23463

MAX (Cinemax)
200 Avenue of the Americas, New York, NY 10036

C-SPAN
400 North Capitol Street, N.W., Suite 412, Washington, DC 20001

TDC (The Discovery Channel)
7700 Wisconsin Avenue, Bethesda, MD 20814-3522

DIS (The Disney Channel)
3800 W. Alameda Ave., Burbank, CA 91505

E! (Entertainment Television)
1800 N. Vine St., 3rd Floor, Hollywood, CA 90028

ENC (Encore)
4643 South Ulster St., Suite 300, Denver, CA 80237

ESPN (Entertainment and Sports Programming Network)
ESPN Plaza, Bristol, CT 06010

Galavision
2121 Avenue of the Stars, Suite 2300, Los Angeles, CA 90067

HBO (Home Box Office)
1100 Avenue of the Americas, New York, NY 10036

LIFE (Lifetime)
36-12 35th Ave., Astoria, NY 11106

TMC (The Movie Channel)
1633 Broadway, New York, NY 10019

MTV (Music Television)
1515 Broadway, New York, NY 10036

TNN (The Nashville Network)
2806 Opryland Drive, Nashville, TN 37214

NICK (Nickelodeon)
1515 Broadway, New York, NY 10036

SHOW (Showtime)
1633 Broadway, New York, NY 10019

USA (USA Network)
1230 Avenue of the Americas, New York, NY 10177

PROFILE

Queer TV Celebrities

On National Coming Out Day, October 11, 1994, talk show host Marilu Henner (*Marilu*, CBS) welcomed four openly gay celebrities to her show to discuss coming out personally and on the job. The four guests were actor Amanda Bearse, who plays neighbor Marcy D'Arcy on *Married . . . with Children*; Dan Butler, the macho sportscaster Bulldog on *Frasier*; stand-up comedian Suzanne Westenhoefer, who recently starred in her own HBO special; and *Entertainment Tonight* reporter Garrett Glaser. The following are excerpts from their discussion of coming out in the entertainment business:

AMANDA BEARSE: I came out professionally a little over a year ago. And that was a decision that I knew was inevitable, given the amount of success that I was reaching in my career. It was a decision that I gave a lot of thought to. It wasn't a difficult decision, it was just an important one. . . . Being in someone's home every week or every day, now that *Married . . . with Children*'s in syndication . . . it gives it [coming out] more power. It makes a more powerful statement to say, "You're used to me, you've known me for many, many years, now you know this about me."

DAN BUTLER: I never really hid it [being gay], because it was just a part of me, it was natural. This year I professionally came out. I'm doing a one-man show that I've written called *The Only Thing Worse You Could Have Told Me*, which comes from a conversation I had with my dad when talking about it. But it was a natural step. You know, people ask me, "Well, did you go through a lot of trauma or thought?" . . . I didn't think about it that much. . . . It was just something I was clear I wanted to do.

SUZANNE WESTENHOEFER: I came out four years ago on stage. . . . You know, comedy is about honesty. Most people you see who are comics are telling you all these personal stories about their lives. I didn't want to be standing up there going, "And then my g-g-boy-girl-boyfriend. . . ."

GARRETT GLASER: I think . . . people are becoming used to hearing about gay people, and the more of us who say, "Yeah, I'm gay," "I'm lesbian," the more it becomes a non-issue.

AMANDA BEARSE: Everybody that takes that step to come out, it's a baby step for our community. And you're not going to get giant steps without those baby steps. And so everybody who makes the decision to do that fights the discrimination.

Reprinted by permission of Group W Productions, Inc.

PROFILE

FRAMELINE

Based in San Francisco, Frameline is the only national distributor solely dedicated to the promotion, distribution, and exhibition of lesbian and gay films and videotapes. Frameline was established in 1980 in conjunction with the San Francisco International Lesbian and Gay Film Festival and has over one hundred forty titles for rental. Films and videos span a variety of genres, from features and documentaries to experimental and short works.

A few of their gay titles for distribution, and their directors, include the following:

Absolutely Positive (Peter Adair)
Affirmations (Marlon Riggs)
Before Stonewall (Greta Schiller and Robbie Rosenberg)
Boys Shorts: The New Queer Cinema (Marlon Riggs, Mark Christopher, and others)
Fear of Disclosure (Phil Zwickler)
Homoteens (Joan Jubela; see box)
Mala Noche (Gus Van Sant)
No Regrets (Non, Je Ne Regrette Rien) (Marlon Riggs)
Sis: The Perry Watkins Story (Chiqui Cartegena)
Stop the Church (Robert Hilferty)
The Terence Davies Trilogy (Terence Davies)

Marlon Riggs (left) *(Courtesy Frameline)*

This Is Not an AIDS Advertisement (Isaac Julien)
Tongues Untied (Marlon Riggs)
Urinal (John Greyson)
Voguing: The Message (David Bronstein, Dorothy Low, and Jack Walworth)

For more information, contact Frameline, 346 Ninth Street, San Francisco, CA 94103; phone: 415-703-8654; fax: 415-861-1404.

Homoteens (1993, directed by Joan Jubela)
Two young lesbians and three teenage gays in New York City produced their own unique videotapes with the help of filmmaker Joan Jubela. Monique talks about her girlfriends and about being a Latina dyke. Peter tapes the story of his long-distance relationship with his closeted boyfriend, Richard. An anonymous fifteen-year-old discusses being harassed at school and shows off his scrapbooks of African-American history. Seventeen-year-old community organizer Henry Diaz looks at Youth Force, the organization that helped him come out. And Nicky, an African-Caribbean-American lesbian, tells us about her girlfriend and about being institutionalized for being queer.
Winner, Best Video, San Francisco Lesbian and Gay Film Festival, 1993.

Homoteens
(*Courtesy
Frameline*)

Profile

GAY AND LESBIAN ALLIANCE AGAINST DEFAMATION

The Gay and Lesbian Alliance Against Defamation (GLAAD) advocates for fair, accurate, and inclusive representations of lesbian and gay lives in the media. Founded in 1985 in New York City, GLAAD currently boasts chapters in Atlanta, Dallas, Denver, Kansas City, Los Angeles, San Diego, San Francisco, and Washington, DC. GLAAD fulfills its mission by aggressively challenging defamation whenever it occurs and through special projects and initiatives that foster increased awareness and understanding of gay and lesbian lives and culture.

GLAAD accomplishments include the following:

1986 *Naming Names*, a weekly three-to-four minute radio broadcast is made available to six hundred public radio stations nationwide.
1987 *The New York Times* agrees to change its editorial policy to use the word "gay" instead of "homosexual."

1988 Bob Hope produces PSA condemning anti-gay violence after using the word "fag" on *The Tonight Show.*

1989 *Daily Variety* reverses policy against listing survivors of same-sex couples in obituaries.

• NYNEX Yellow Pages agrees to include a new "Gay & Lesbian Organizations" section.

• U.S. Postal Service issues commemorative Stonewall cancellation for the month of June, on the occasion of the twentieth anniversary of the Stonewall rebellion.

1989 Wendy's Restaurants apologizes to the gay and lesbian community after making a negative statement about sponsoring an *LA Law* episode featuring a positive gay character.

1990 CBS suspends and reprimands Andy Rooney because of the homophobic remarks he made on *60 Minutes.*

• GLAAD publishes full-page ads in *Daily Variety* and *Hollywood Reporter* about gay bashing in movies and the absence of lesbian and gay characters on television.

1991 GLAAD protests homophobic Hollywood films *Silence of the Lambs* and Basic Instinct.

Roseanne accepting an award at the GLAAD Media Awards. (*Copyright Ken Levine, Berliner Studio. Courtesy Gay and Lesbian Alliance Against Defamation*)

- GLAAD calls for an end to PBS censorship and exclusion after the network cancels the airing of two films that address homophobia and AIDS.
- GLAAD and Gay Men of African Descent protest the homophobic segment "Men on Film" on FOX's *In Living Color*.

1992 *Entertainment Weekly* names GLAAD as one of Hollywood's 100 most powerful entities.

1993 GLAAD and Hollywood Supports initiate "Sexual Orientation in the Workplace" seminars for the entertainment industry.

- GLAAD participates in the publicity for the movie *Philadelphia* and appears on *Nightline*.

1994 GLAAD launches campaign to ensure the episode of *Roseanne* featuring a lesbian kiss airs as scheduled.

- GLAAD works with the coproducers of *Beverly Hills 90210* to present screenings of the "Blind Spot" episode to youth organizations; the episode deals with outing on a college campus.

For more information about the work of GLAAD, write GLAAD/NY, 150 West 26th St., 5th floor, New York, NY 10001 or GLAAD/LA, P.O. Box 931763, Los Angeles, CA 90093-1763.

PROFILE

Wilson Cruz

Twenty-year-old Wilson Cruz portrays Puerto Rican gay teenager Rickie Vasquez on the critically acclaimed hour-long television drama *My So-Called Life*. In Wilson's case, art does imitate life: gay himself, he was thrown out of his home, as was the character Rickie, when he told his father he was gay.

"My father pulled me aside and asked me if I was gay," Wilson told *Entertainment Tonight* a year after the incident with his father occurred. "I said yes, and he asked me to leave. I had no money, but I had friends." Wilson says he felt passionate about the *My So-Called Life* episode of Rickie's coming out and rejection by his father, because it so much resembled his own experience. He has since reconciled with his father.

My So-Called Life was Wilson's big break, after years as a young performer in theater and at Disney World. Now he has become a role model for gay teens, who are at greater risk for depression, suicide, and substance abuse than straight teens. One gay teenager recently wrote to Wilson, thanking him for his portrayal of Rickie and confessing that he had considered suicide. There were dried tears on the page. "I'm just glad he had someone to write to," Wilson says.

Wilson Cruz
*(Photo by Athena
Gassoumis)*

7. GAY HEALTH

In the last century, we've come a long way in the medical establishment's treatment of homosexuality. Gay men were once subjected to medical "cures" ranging from hypnosis to castration to lobotomy. Neither the American Psychiatric Association nor the American Medical Association consider homosexuality an illness anymore, but gay men may still face bias in their health care simply because they are homosexual.

Often in the age of AIDS, we forget that gay men face a variety of health-care concerns, such as other sexually transmitted diseases, substance abuse, finding affordable health insurance, and mental health concerns. The following material provides some guidelines and resources for dealing with the general health concerns of gay men.

Please note: This section is meant only to offer suggestions and guidance about where to go if you have a health or medical problem. Please consult a doctor or health care professional with questions and concerns about your health.

(For information on gay men and AIDS, see pp. 409–451.)

PRESCRIBED MEDICAL "CURES" FOR HOMOSEXUALITY OVER THE YEARS

Until 1973, the American Psychiatric Association viewed homosexuality as a mental disorder to be "cured." And not until late 1994 did the American Medical Association remove all references to "sexual orientation related disorders" from its official policy, which was used for years to justify "therapies" for "treating" homosexuality. Since the late 1800s, gay men have been subjected to everything from lobotomies to shock therapy as the medical establishment attempted to find a "cure" for homosexuality.

The following are some of the "cures" prescribed for gay men over the years:

1. Castration (1890s)
2. Vasectomy (1890s)
3. Hypnosis (1890s to 1960s)
4. Lobotomy (early 1900s to 1950s)
5. Analysis (1920s to 1970s)
6. Institutionalization or hospitalization (1920s to 1970s)
7. Aversion therapy, inducing nausea through drugs or electroshock (to the 1970s)
8. Abstinence (1890s to present; still advocated by some organized religions)

AN EXAMPLE: THE "WISDOM" OF DR. LOUIS W. MAX, 1935

New York University's Dr. Max reported at the 1935 American Psychological Association meeting on his experiments in the use of electric shock to "treat" homosexuality. This was the first documented use of aversion therapy on a gay man.

A homosexual neurosis in a young man was found upon analysis to be partially fetishistic, the homosexual behavior usually following upon the fetishistic stimulus. An attempt was made to disconnect the emotional aura from this stimulus by means of electric shock, applied in conjunction with the presentation of the stimulus under laboratory conditions. Low shock intensities had little effect but intensities higher than those usually employed on human subjects in other studies, definitely diminished the emotional value of the stimulus for days after each experimental period. Though the subject reported some backsliding, the "desensitizing" effect over a three-month period was cumulative. Four months after cessation of the experiment he wrote, "That terrible neurosis has lost its battle, not completely but 95 percent of the way." Advantages and limitations of this technique are discussed. . . .

SOURCES: Jonathan Ned Katz, *Gay American History: Lesbians and Gay Men in the U.S.A.* Revised edition, 1992.

FINDING A GAY PHYSICIAN

How many times have you been stung by a doctor's homophobia or sexism? Not gotten the care you need because you're afraid to come out to your doctor? The Gay and Lesbian Medical Association can refer you to one of sixteen hundred practicing lesbian and gay doctors across North America. For names of the doctors nearest you, write to GLMA, 273 Church St., San Francisco, CA 94114, or call 415-255-4547.

FINDING A GAY THERAPIST

The Committee on Gay and Lesbian Concerns of the American Psychological Association publishes a therapist roster, listing the names, addresses, specialties, and interests of individual therapists across the United States. Write to: Committee on Gay and Lesbian Concerns, American Psychological Association, 1200 17th Street NW, Washington, DC 20036 or call the APA at 202-336-5500.

For referrals, you can also contact the Association of Lesbian and Gay Psychiatrists, 1439 Pineville Road, New Hope, PA 18938.

INTERVIEWING A PROSPECTIVE THERAPIST

Before choosing a therapist, think about the following questions:

1. Would you feel most comfortable talking to a man or a woman?
2. Would you feel most comfortable talking to someone your own age, or someone older or younger than you?
3. Is it important that you know if your therapist is gay?

There are different types of therapists, and the following list may help you sort out the array of practitioners available:

Clinical or counseling psychologist: has completed postgraduate study in psychology with a degree of Ph.D., Psy.D., or Ed.D. Training includes psychological testing and psychotherapy.

Psychiatrist: a medical doctor who specializes in psychiatry, or the prevention, causes, and diagnosis/treatment of mental, emotional, and behavioral disorders. Can prescribe medication.

Social worker: has completed a graduate degree in social work (M.S.W.) and has received specialized training in individual, group, or community work. Some insurance companies will not reimburse for this type of therapy unless the social worker has passed a state certification process and achieved the rank of C.S.W.

Pastoral counselor: a theological counselor with graduate study in a related field, possessing experience in both pastoral counseling and ministry.

You can also get referrals from your medical doctor, from friends in the medical field, or from the therapists of friends. It's a good idea to "interview" several therapists before choosing one you feel you can work with. In the interview (it's best to do it face-to-face, to test your comfort level), you can ask the following questions to help you make your decision:

1. What is the therapist's training? Is the therapist licensed? Does he or she fall into a particular school of thought (e.g., Jungian, Freudian)? How many years of experience does the therapist have?
2. Has the therapist counseled people with issues similar to yours (e.g., HIV/AIDS, couples, sexual abuse, work-related issues, substance abuse, family issues, bereavement)?
3. Does the therapist feel comfortable counseling gay men? Has he or she counseled other gay men or lesbians? (If you feel you only want to work with a gay therapist, you should make that clear.)
4. What type of treatment approaches does the therapist use (e.g., behavior modification, hypnosis, group therapy, medication, psychoanalysis)? Does he or she work primarily in short-term or long-term counseling? How does the therapist feel about medications?
5. What are the therapist's fees? Are they insurance reimbursable? What method of payment does the therapist accept? Does the therapist charge for missed appointments?
6. Where will the appointments be held and how often? How long will they last?
7. Is the therapist available for emergencies between sessions? What is the therapist's policy about receiving calls from clients outside of scheduled appointments?

Remember: You don't have to be in crisis to start therapy. Most people wait until they are in pain, but therapy can aid in preventing crises, as well as in achieving self-knowledge, self-esteem, and personal growth.

Thanks to Dr. Barbara Warren for her help in compiling this section.

Resources for Gay Men's Health—Organizations and Newsletters

(For sources on HIV/AIDS, see pp. 438–442.)

General

National Lesbian and Gay Health Association, 1407 S St. NW, Washington, DC 20009. Phone: 202-939-7880. Fax: 202-797-3504.

Recovery

International Advisory Council for Homosexual Men and Women in AA, P.O. Box 90, Washington, DC 20044-0090.
Pride Institute, 14400 Martin Drive, Eden Prairie, MN 55344, 800-54-PRIDE.
Project Connect, Lesbian and Gay Community Services Center, 208 West 13th St., New York, NY 10011, 212-620-7310.
Spencer Recovery Center, 343 West Foothill Blvd., Monrovia, CA 91016, 800-232-5484 or 818-358-3662.

Gay-Friendly Health Care Clinics (by state or province)

(See also pp. 438–441 for a listing of community centers and the services provided—some of the larger ones offer health care.)

Canada

Hassle-Free Clinic, 556 Church St., 2nd floor, Toronto, Ontario M4Y 2E3, 613-922-0603 (men)

United States

Beach Area Community Health Center, 3705 Mission Blvd., San Diego, CA 92109, 619-488-0644.
Hartford Gay and Lesbian Health Collective, P.O. Box 2094, Hartford, CT 06145-2094, 203-236-1959.
Whitman Walker Clinic, 1407 S St., NW, Washington, DC 20009. Phone: 202-797-3500.
Howard Brown Memorial Clinic, 945 West George St., Chicago, IL 60657, 312-871-5777.
Chase-Brexton Clinic, 101 West Read St. #211, Baltimore, MD 21201, 410-837-2050.
Fenway Community Health Center, 7 Haviland St., Boston, MA 02115, 617-267-0900.
Community Health Project, Lesbian and Gay Community Services Center, 208 West 13th St., New York, NY 10011. Phone: 212-675-3559. TTY: 800-662-1220.

DOMESTIC PARTNER HEALTH BENEFITS

The National Lesbian and Gay Journalists Association has just produced an eight-page booklet called "News Media Executive's Guide to Domestic Partner Benefits." The booklet is aimed at the news industry, but could be given to any employer to show that offering health insurance to the domestic partners of employees is affordable, feasible, and fair. For a copy, send a $2 check (tax-deductible) made out to NLGJA to: NLGJA, 874 Gravenstein Highway South, Suite 4, Sebastopol, CA 95472. Phone: 707-823-2193. Fax: 707-823-4176. NLGJA also publishes a list (constantly updated) of U.S. employers offering domestic partner benefits, available at the same address for $2.70.

Companies with Domestic Partner Health Benefits

Apple Computers
Ben & Jerry's Ice Cream
Borland International
The Boston Globe
Capital Cities/ABC
Adolph Coors Co.
FNMA (Fannie Mae)
Frame Technology
International Data Group
KQED TV and Radio (San Francisco)
Levi Strauss & Co.
Lotus Development Corp.
MCA/Universal Studios
Microsoft Corp.
Minnesota Communications Group/MN Public Radio
Montefiore Medical Center (New York City)
National Public Radio
Charles Schwab
The Seattle Times
Silicon Graphics
Starbucks Coffee
Sun Microsystems
Time-Warner Inc. (including many of its divisions: HBO, Time Inc., Warner Brothers Pictures, and Atlantic Pictures)
Viacom
The Village Voice
WGBH-TV (Boston)
Ziff-Davis Publications

Insurance Companies That Have Provided (or Are Willing to Provide) Domestic Partner Health Benefits

Aetna
Blue Cross
Bridgeway
Cigna
Consumers United
Fireman's Insurance Co.
Foundation Health Plan
George Washington University HMO
Great West Life
Group Health Cooperative of Puget Sound
Group Health Insurance of New York
Harvard Community Health Plan
Kaiser Permanente
Liberty Mutual
Mass Mutual
Pacific Care
Pacific Health
Prudential
Qualmed
Vision Service Plan

SOURCES: "Domestic Partner Benefits: At What Cost?" National Lesbian and Gay Journalists Association, 1994.

MAKING SENSE OF HEALTH INSURANCE

If you're self-employed, your employer doesn't provide medical benefits, or your workplace makes available a number of health care options, it's often a challenge to determine which health care plan would work best for you. There are basically three types of health insurance available:

Health Maintenance Organizations (HMO's): Health maintenance organizations represent "prepaid" insurance plans in which individuals or their employers pay a fixed monthly fee for services, instead of a separate charge for each visit or service. The monthly fees remain the same, regardless of the types or levels of services provided. Services are provided by physicians who are employed by, or under contract with, the HMO. HMOs vary in design. Depending on the type of HMO, services may be provided in a central facility, or in a physician's own office. *Independent Practice Associations (IPAs)* are similar to HMOs, except that individuals receive care in a physician's own office, rather than in an HMO facility.

In general, HMOs are designed for people in good health, who need only basic preventive care coverage and who don't have any specific or chronic health concerns. They are also not available in some areas of the country.

Indemnity Health Plan: Indemnity health insurance plans are also called "fee-for-service." These are the types of plans that primarily existed before the rise of HMOs, IPAs, and PPOs. With indemnity plans, the individual pays a predetermined percentage of the cost of health care services, and the insurance company (or self-insured employer) pays the other percentage. For example, an individual might pay 20 percent for services and the insurance company pays 80 percent. The fees for services are defined by the providers and vary from physician to physician. Indemnity health plans offer individuals the freedom to choose their health care professionals.

Preferred Provider Organization (PPO): With PPOs, you or your employer receive discounted rates if you use doctors from a preselected group. If you use a physician outside the PPO plan, you must pay more for the medical care. PPOs differ from HMOs because the physicians are only affiliated with the PPO, not employed by it.

The following questions may help you decide among the three types of plans:

1. What services does the plan cover?
2. What, if any, are the deductibles? Are they one-time or yearly?
3. What preventive health services are covered? How many preventive visits are covered?
4. What is the maximum lifetime dollar limit that the policy will pay? What are the limits for chronic conditions? (especially important where HIV/AIDS is an issue)
5. What is the maximum out-of-pocket expense you are likely to incur in a given year?
6. Are mental health services included? Alternative forms of health care, such as chiropractic and acupuncture? What are the limits of coverage on these services?
7. Are treatments for substance abuse covered?
8. What are the policy's restrictions on pre-existing conditions?
9. What is the average turnaround time on claims?
10. What are the restrictions on inpatient and outpatient care?
11. Will the policy cover medical emergencies when you travel?
12. Do you have the freedom to choose a physician? If it is an HMO, can you change physicians within the health care facility? Must you choose a physician from among those specified? Can you see a list of physicians before making your choice? Can you find out which, if any, have dealt with your particular health concerns? Are the physicians board-certified? How can you change physicians if you choose one you don't like? Are there physicians within your geographic area?
13. Can you choose the hospital of preference if you require inpatient care?

Myths and Facts About the Disabled

Myth: Gay disabled people are not sexual.
Fact: Disabled people have the same sexual and emotional needs as everyone else. We are sexual, we can give and receive love and establish relationships. Many disabled gays and lesbians are in loving, adult relationships.

Myth: The disabled are deformed and unattractive
Fact: Many of us do not have visible signs of disability and not all visible disabilities are unattractive. Beauty is in the eye of the beholder.

Myth: There are no disabled gay men or women.
Fact: Ten percent of the population is gay and lesbian. Therefore it is common sense to assume a percentage is physically disabled.

Myth: Disabled lesbians and gays isolate themselves by choice.
Fact: Isolation is rarely a matter of choice. Physical barriers and society's prejudices can cause isolation and withdrawal.

Myth: The disabled are unable to make their own choices or decisions.
Fact: Disabled individuals are often not asked what they want; it is assumed their dependencies are across the board. Just because someone cannot do what they want does not mean they don't know what they want.

Myth: The disabled are an embarrassment.
Fact: The public response to the disabled is often one of embarrassment and discomfort. We are an embarrassment of riches and have the same variety of skills and talents as everyone else. Disabled does not mean un-abled!

Myth: The disabled have nothing to offer and cannot be helpful.
Fact: Many disabled people hold valuable positions in all walks of life regardless of our balance and posture.

Sources: EDGE (Education in a Disabled Gay Environment).

Quick Facts about Gay Health

- A study of 1,009 physicians in San Diego in 1986 found that 40 percent felt uncomfortable treating lesbians and gay men; 30 percent opposed admitting lesbians and gay men into medical school; and 40 percent would not refer patients to a lesbian or gay health care provider
- In three studies conducted between 1986 and 1989, it was determined that between 9 and 19 percent of all gay men and lesbians in the United States are alcoholics, while about one-tenth of the general population is alcoholic.
- A 1994 survey of members of the Gay and Lesbian Medical Association (GLMA) indicated that more than half of the GLMA physicians observed their heterosexual colleagues providing substandard care to gay and lesbian clients.

- Domestic violence is the third largest health problem facing gay men, after substance abuse and AIDS. Between 350,000 and 650,000 gay men in the United States are victims of domestic violence.
- The number of people seeking anonymous HIV antibody tests at the Los Angeles Gay and Lesbian Community Services Center increased 41 percent in the two weeks after diver Greg Louganis announced he had AIDS.

SOURCES: *The Advocate; Queer State: The Facts About Gays and Lesbians* edited by Bennet L. Singer and David Deschamps (New Press, 1994).

PROFILE

Project Connect

The New York City Lesbian and Gay Community Services Center is home to an award-winning addiction prevention and intervention program called Project Connect. Established in 1987, it has become a model for similar drug and alcohol programs across the country. Project Connect provides information, counseling, support groups, and referrals to gay-affirmative treatment to all those interested in pursuing recovery from substance abuse, and to family members, friends, and lovers of problem drinkers and drug users. Under the guidance of Dr. Barbara Warren, the Center's director of mental health and social services, Project Connect has served more than three thousand lesbians and gay men throughout the five boroughs of New York.

Project Connect is the only gay- and lesbian-identified program of its kind on the East Coast and is the winner of numerous awards, including the Outstanding Community Health Promotion Program Award from the U.S. Secretary of Health and Human Services.

Essential to Project Connect's mission of serving gay and lesbian substance abusers is its commitment to training and educating mainstream treatment facilities about the needs of their lesbian and gay clients. Project Connect has provided more than 250 diversity trainings, which make the linkages, for client and staff alike, between the recovery process and issues surrounding lesbian and gay identity and between the recovery process and issues surrounding race and gender.

In 1993, a contract under the Ryan White Emergency Care Act enabled Project Connect to offer more enhanced services, including relapse prevention counseling on individual and group bases and recovery readiness programming for HIV-positive men and women.

Project Connect, Lesbian and Gay Community Services Center, 208 West 13th St., New York, NY 10011. Phone: 212-620-7310. Fax: 212-924-2657.

Profile

National Lesbian and Gay Health Association

In June 1994, eleven lesbian and gay community health centers from around the United States joined together with a network of twenty thousand lesbian and gay health care providers to form the National Lesbian and Gay Health Association. NLGHA is now the only national lesbian and gay organization headquartered in the nation's capital that focuses solely on improving our community's health.

NLGHA resulted from the merger of the National Alliance of Lesbian and Gay Health Clinics and the National Lesbian and Gay Health Foundation. The National Alliance of Lesbian and Gay Health Clinics was founded in 1992 to facilitate communication among clinics and to foster a national lesbian and gay health care agenda. The National Lesbian and Gay Health Foundation, started in 1978, sponsored an annual conference for sixteen years, which was the first conference to feature an international forum on HIV/AIDS.

Currently, NLGHA has two full-time staffers and a twenty-plus member board of directors. The association is dedicated to enhancing the quality of health care for lesbians and gay men through education, policy development, advocacy, and the facilitation of health care delivery.

The association holds a contract with the U.S Public Health Service to provide technical assistance, training materials, and educational initiatives to health care institutions, organizations, and providers. The particular emphasis is on sensitizing health care professionals to lesbian and gay health needs.

Other projects of the association include establishing a national research institute on lesbian and gay health; setting up a resource center on lesbian and gay health issues; undertaking the annual publication of a white paper on lesbian and gay health; and linking current lesbian and gay health organizations, centers, and providers for information sharing and networking. There are also numerous projects currently being handled by undergraduate and graduate interns and volunteers, including compiling a press list, developing a newsletter, creating an electronic network, and tracking legislation related to lesbian and gay health concerns.

National Lesbian and Gay Health Association, 1407 S St. NW, Washington, DC 20009. Phone: 202-939-7880. Fax: 202-797-3504.

8. GAY HOMES AND FAMILIES

"Good parents are good parents—regardless of their sexual orientation. It's clear that the sexual orientation of parents has nothing to do with the sexual orientation or outlook of their children."

—former U.S. Surgeon General Joycelyn Elders

We're here, we're queer, we're redefining the term "family."

In a 1992 study of the United States, 55 percent of gay men and 71 percent of lesbians were in what they considered to be "committed," or steady, relationships. But as of this writing, both the United States and Canada continue to deny les-

Father and
daughter at the
1993 Gay Pride
March, New York
City *(Photo by
Harry Stevens)*

bians and gay men the right to marry and the legal benefits that a marriage certificate brings, though an important court case pending in the state of Hawaii may
soon change that by setting a legal precedent for same-sex marriage. Until then,
lesbians and gay men continue to create their own weddings and commitment ceremonies, the largest of which was the three-thousand-couple mass wedding that
took place during the third March on Washington for Lesbian, Gay, and Bisexual
Rights in April, 1993.

In the last decade, some inroads have been made for domestic partners (couples who live together in relationships without being legally married). In thirteen
U.S. cities and one state (Vermont), for example, government employees have
been afforded health care benefits for their same-sex domestic partners. And several dozen private-sector companies and organizations have also begun to recognize same-sex relationships in their employee benefits programs.

A 1993 study indicated that in the United States there were between 3 and 8
million lesbian and gay parents, raising between 6 and 14 million children. Most
of these children live with parents who were formerly in heterosexual marriages or
relationships and then came out as lesbian or gay. But a growing number of lesbians and gay men in the last decade have opted to become parents.

The term "lesbian baby boom" refers to the sudden sharp increase in the number of lesbians who, since the mid-1980s, have been choosing to have children—
sometimes on their own but usually with a lesbian partner; occasionally with a gay
male friend as sperm donor, but more often using the services of sperm banks.
And gay men have enjoyed a parenting boom all their own, relying on adoptions
and surrogacy arrangements to create their new families.

In a few areas of the United States, particularly California, coparent adoption—
the legal adoption of a child, who already has one legal parent, by a second parent
of the same gender—has been possible for dozens of these lesbian parents.

To respond to the growing need, advocacy organizations and groups have
sprung up for lesbian and gay parents and their children. Programs such as Center Kids at New York's Lesbian and Gay Community Services Center provide support not only for parents and children, but for those gay people contemplating
parenthood.

Despite the myth that lesbians and gay men do not make "fit" parents, and that
children must be "protected" from gay people, psychologists' studies continue to
show that the children of lesbian and gay parents are neither emotionally nor psy-
chologically disadvantaged simply by having same-sex parents. Nor do they necessarily grow up to be gay themselves.

It is young lesbians and gays, often stigmatized by their peers and rejected by
their families, who continue to be the ones in jeopardy. Gay teens are among those
at highest risk for alcoholism, drug abuse, suicide, and HIV infection and are in
desperate need of positive role models and risk-prevention programs that will help
them make it to adulthood.

Some of us are lucky—our parents accept us, even if they don't always under-
stand us. Supportive parents formed their own organization in the early 1980s—
Parents and Friends of Lesbians and Gays (P-FLAG)—which is still going strong.
Their mission is not only to support one another and their children, but to spread

the word to those who are misinformed that gay people are healthy human beings who are part of families everywhere.

SOME STATISTICS

- There were between 3 and 8 million gay and lesbian parents in the United States in 1993, raising between 6 and 14 million children.
- A 1988 newspaper article reported one thousand surrogacy births in the prior ten years. Other experts believe two thousand to be a more accurate number.
- Two states, Florida and New Hampshire, expressly forbid gay and lesbian adoption. As of 1993, more than two hundred second parent adoptions had been granted in eight jurisdictions: Alabama, California, Minnesota, New York, Oregon, Vermont, Washington, and Washington, DC.
- In New York and California, laws exist protecting gay men and lesbians from discrimination in adoption and foster care. In Ohio, the state supreme court recently allowed a gay man to adopt a child.

FROM THE MOUTHS OF ACADEMIC RESEARCHERS

"All the studies agree that when lesbian couples choose to become parents together, they most often strive for, and often achieve, a near 50/50 sharing of all aspects of family life: decision-making, child care, household tasks.

"Our study was also consistent with the others in showing that, in most couples, both partners had not only a strong measurable involvement in parenting, but also a profound subjective sense of themselves as parents.

"On the basis of our data, we suggested that planned lesbian families present a viable model of an effectively functioning family in contemporary America."

—DRS. VALORY MITCHELL AND DIANE WILSON, Institute for the Psychology of Women, California School of Professional Psychology, Alameda, California, in an ongoing study of planned lesbian families.

A TIMELINE OF GAY AND LESBIAN FAMILY ISSUES

1953: *ONE* magazine begins publication, the first openly gay magazine to achieve wide circulation. The U.S. Post Office claims articles about homosexuality are obscene, specifically an article on gay marriages.

1962: A study by Dr. Irving Bieber concludes that homosexuality is largely caused by seductive mothers and hostile fathers.

1970: Jack Baker, student at University of Minnesota, unsuccessfully applies for a marriage license with his lover, Jim McConnell. They do, however, manage to file joint tax returns in 1972 and 1973.

1972: Camille Mitchell is the first open lesbian to be awarded custody of her chil-

dren in a divorce case. The judge restricts the arrangement by precluding Ms.
Mitchell's lover from moving in with her and the children.

   • A made-for-TV film about a fourteen-year-old boy who discovers his father is gay, *That Certain Summer*, airs on ABC. This is one of the first TV dramas to portray homosexual issues in a relatively non-homophobic way, and is
generally well reviewed.

1973: Controversial gay minister Rev. Ray Broshears marries three WAC couples
in San Francisco, generating much publicity in the process. Two of the women,
Gail Bates and Valerie Randolph, were discharged from the military.

1977: Two lesbians win custody cases. In Michigan, Jacqueline Stamper won joint
custody rights for her two children in spite of her ex-husband's charge that she
was "morally unfit" because she was a lesbian. In Denver, Donna Levy won custody of her deceased former lover's daughter, against opposition by the child's
aunt and uncle.

1979: Seventeen-year-old Randy Rohl of Sioux Falls, South Dakota, takes a male
date to the prom. A year later, Rhode Island high school student Aaron Fricke
takes a gay date to his prom, following a court order forcing school administrators to relax their refusal.

1981: New Kinsey study reports neither parental nor societal influences have
much effect on sexual orientation.

   • Parents and Friends of Lesbians and Gays form in Los Angeles.

1983: Karen Thompson's eight-year struggle for legal guardianship of her lover,
Sharon Kowalski, begins when a drunk driver collides with Sharon's vehicle,
placing her in a coma for several months and leaving her quadriplegic and severely brain-damaged. Despite Sharon's wishes to be cared for by Karen,
Sharon's parents refused Karen full access or input into her care. Karen Thompson became a key spokesperson for lesbian and gay couples' rights. Karen's case
was won in 1991.

1984: Gay, lesbian, and unmarried heterosexual couples can receive the same
benefits as married couples in areas such as health care and bereavement leave
in Berkeley, California, the first U.S. city to pass a "domestic partners" law for
municipal employees.

1985: Following the loss of a highly publicized lawsuit filed by two gay men who
had been evicted from Disneyland for dancing together, the amusement park
announces that it will allow same-sex couples to dance together, stating the rule
was changed to accommodate teenage girls who came without dates and wanted
to dance.

1987: Approximately two thousand same-sex couples are "married" in a mass wedding on the steps of the Internal Revenue Service in Washington, DC, on October 10. The ceremony is part of the 1987 March on Washington activities,
dramatizing the tax benefits for married people that lesbian and gay couples are
denied.

1989: A New York State court rules that a gay couple could be considered family
for purposes of rent controlled apartments. The California Bar Association
urges that lesbian and gay marriage be legally recognized, and in Seattle, San

Francisco, and other cities, "partners" regulations extending certain protections and rights to unmarried couples—straight and gay—are adopted.

• The New York State Court of Appeals declares that a lesbian or gay couple living together for at least ten years can be considered a family for purposes of rent control protection, the first time a state's highest court rules that a gay couple can be called a family. On the same day in July, a recent ordinance giving limited protections to same-sex couples in San Francisco is suspended after opponents gather enough signatures on petitions to place the issue on the November ballot. The ordinance lost that vote by only a 1 percent margin.

• Center Kids, the family project of the Lesbian and Gay Community Services Center, founded in New York to provide support and networking opportunities for lesbian and gay parents and their children.

1990: For the first time, the U.S. Census includes a question that more or less identifies gay couples. It finds 88,200 gay male couples, with an average household income of $56,863, and 69,200 lesbian couples, with an average household income of $44,793.

1991: *Pediatrics* magazine reports nearly half of the lesbian and gay teenagers interviewed for a study say they have attempted suicide.

1992: Domestic partners of employees of Levi Strauss & Co. are granted full medical benefits.

• The province of Ontario, Canada, extends spousal benefits to same-sex partners of government workers.

• William Weld, governor of Massachusetts, signs an executive order granting lesbian and gay state workers the same bereavement and family leave rights as heterosexual workers.

• A proposed multicultural curriculum for first graders that includes references to lesbian and gay parents results in heated debate, demonstrations, threats of violence toward gay parents, the forced resignation of the New York City School chancellor, and the largest turnout for a school board election in the city's history. The curriculum is revised to delete virtually all mention of lesbian and gay families.

1993: Hawaii Supreme Court rules that a lower court improperly dismissed a lawsuit challenging a state policy of denying marriage licenses to gay and lesbian couples. The court rules that the prohibition of same-sex marriages constitutes sex discrimination and is probably unconstitutional.

• Lesbian mother Roberta Achtenberg is confirmed by the U.S. Senate to become the assistant secretary for fair housing and equal opportunity at the Department of Housing and Urban Development, the first time an openly gay person had been confirmed by the Senate for a high-level government position.

1994: The Virginia Court of Appeals overturns a lower court ruling, which, based on her sexual orientation, stripped lesbian mother Sharon Bottoms of custody of her son.

• A resolution is passed at the convention of the Oregon PTA that reads: "Resolved that the Oregon PTA rejects prejudice, harassment, discrimination or intolerance directed against students, parents, teachers or staff members as a result of their sexual orientation; and be it further resolved that the Oregon PTA opposes all legislative attempts to suppress discussion of family diversity and sexual orientation."

• Portland, Oregon, allows nonmarried city employees' domestic partners to be eligible for full spousal benefits.

• On July 9, what would have been the most comprehensive domestic partner law in North America, equalizing seventy-nine statutes that use the word "spouse," to include lesbian and gay couples, was defeated by the Ontario Parliament due to a stalemate on the ever-controversial issue of gay and lesbian adoption. Following the vote, five thousand lesbians and gay men marched on Parliament chanting "Equal Taxes, Equal Rights!"

BIBLIOGRAPHY

Gay and Lesbian Parenting

Barret, Robert L., and Bryan E. Robinson. *Gay Fathers.* Lexington Books, 1990.
Bozett, Frederick W., ed. *Gay and Lesbian Parents.* Praeger, 1987.
Burke, Phyllis. *Family Values: Two Moms and Their Son.* Random House, 1993.
Corley, Rip. *The Final Closet: The Gay Parents' Guide for Coming Out to Their Children.* Editech Press, 1990.
Curry, Hayden, and Denis Clifford. *A Legal Guide for Lesbians and Gay Couples.* Nolo Press, 1991.
MacPike, Loralee, ed. *There's Something I've Been Meaning to Tell You: An Anthology About Lesbians and Gay Men Coming Out to Their Children.* Naiad Press, 1989.
Martin, April. *Lesbian and Gay Parenting Handbook: Creating and Raising Our Families.* HarperCollins, 1993.
Pies, Cheri. *Considering Parenthood: A Workbook for Lesbians.* Spinsters Ink/Aunt Lute, 1985.
Rizzo, Cindy, et al., eds. *All the Way Home: Parenting and Children in the Lesbian and Gay Community—A Collection of Short Fiction.* New Victoria Publishers, 1995.
Schulenberg, Joy. *Gay Parenting: A Complete Guide for Gay Men and Lesbians with Children.* Doubleday/Anchor, 1985.

Gay and Lesbian Parenting Newsletters

The Family Next Door, Next Door Publishing, Ltd., P.O. Box 21580, Oakland, CA 94620, 510-482-5778. Provides lesbian and gay parents, their families, and friends with a forum for communication and support. Published six times a year.
Gay Fathers of Los Angeles, GFLA, 7985 Santa Monica Blvd., Suite 90046, 213-654-0307. 213-654-0307.
Love Makes A Family, P.O. Box 11694, Portland, OR 97211, 503-228-3892.
News Updates, Gay Fathers of Toronto, GFT Box 187, Station F. Toronto, Ontario M4Y 2L5 416-975-1680, 1-800-663-5016.

Triangles and Hearts, Houston Gay and Lesbian Parents, HGLP, P.O. Box 35709-0262, Houston, TX 77235-5709; Glenda Redworth, editor, 713-666-8256.

Children of Gay Parents

'Homosexuality is now the number-one topic for censorship, especially if the books are for children."

—Ros Udow, National Coalition Against Censorship

Bosche, Susanne. *Jenny Lives with Eric and Martin.* Gay Men's Press, 1983. Ages 4–7. Photo narrative of young Danish girl's life with her two dads.

Brown, Forman. *The Generous Jefferson Bartleby Jones.* Alyson Publications, 1991. Ages 5–8. Since Jefferson B. Jones is fortunate enough to have two dads, he's always willing to lend one to friends.

Heron, Ann, and Meridith Maran. *How Would You Feel If Your Dad Was Gay?* Alyson Publications, 1991. Ages 6–12. Three kids with gay and lesbian parents discuss their concerns. Major characters are African-American.

Homes, A. M. *Jack.* Macmillan, 1989. Young adult child of divorced parents; dad comes out.

Nelson, Theresa. *Earthshine.* Orchard Books, 1994. Ages 11–14. Slim McGranahan lives with her dad and his lover, and her father is dying of AIDS.

Valentine, Johnny. *The Daddy Machine.* Alyson Publications, 1992. Ages 3–8. Two kids with lesbian moms fantasize about what it would be like to have a father. They make themselves a Daddy Machine, and forget to include an "off" switch.

———. *One Dad, Two Dads, Brown Dad, Blue Dads.* Alyson Publications, 1994. Ages 2–6. Two children compare notes on their families.

———. *The Duke Who Outlawed Jellybeans.* Alyson Publications, 1993. Ages 5–10. Five original and enchanting fairy tales.

———. *The Day They Put a Tax on Rainbows.* Alyson Publications, 1992. Ages 5–10. Adventures of kids who happen to have lesbian and gay parents.

Willhoite, Michael. *Families: A Coloring Book.* Alyson Publications, 1991. Ages 2–6. Many kinds of families.

———. *Daddy's Roommate,* Alyson Publications, 1990. Ages 2–7. A boy describes his weekend with his dad and his dad's lover. Upbeat and positive.

———. *Uncle What-Is-It Is Coming to Visit.* Alyson Publications, 1993. Ages 2–6. A brother and sister don't know what to expect when their gay uncle comes for a visit.

Parents of Gay and Lesbian Children

Dew, Robb Forman. *The Family Heart: A Memoir of When Our Son Came Out.* Addison-Wesley, 1994.

Fairchild, Betty, and Nancy Howard. *Now That You Know: What Every Parent Should Know About Homosexuality.* Harcourt-Brace Jovanovich, 1978.

Griffin, Carolyn, Marian Wirth, and Arthur Wirth. *Beyond Acceptance: Parents of*

Lesbians and Gays Talk About Their Experiences. St. Martin's Press, New York, 1986.

Gay and Lesbian Youth

Alyson, Sasha, ed. *Young, Gay and Proud*. Alyson Publications, 1991.

Fricke, Aaron. *Reflections of a Rock Lobster: A Story About Growing Up Gay*. Alyson Publications, 1981.

Grima, Tony. *Not the Only One: Lesbian and Gay Fiction for Teens*. Alyson Publications, 1995.

Heron, Ann, ed. *Two Teenagers in Twenty: Writings About Gay and Lesbian Youth*. Alyson Publications, 1994.

Rench, Janice E. *Understanding Sexual Identity: A Book for Gay Teens and Their Friends*. Lerner, 1990.

Gay and Lesbian Couples

Ayers, Tess, and Paul Brown. *The Essential Guide to Gay and Lesbian Weddings*. HarperSanFrancisco, 1994.

Berzon, Betty. *Permanent Partners: Building Gay and Lesbian Relationships*. New American Library, 1990.

Curry, Hayden, Dennis Clifford, and Robin Leonard. *A Legal Guide for Lesbian and Gay Couples*. 8th edition. Nolo Press, 1992.

Marcus, Eric. *The Male Couple's Guide: Finding a Man, Making a Home, Building a Life*. HarperPerennial, 1989.

Mendola, Mary. *The Mendola Report: A New Look at Gay Couples*. Crown Publishers, 1980

Videotapes

Both of My Moms' Names Are Judy: Children of Lesbians and Gays Speak Out, produced by Camomile Bortman, Lisa Rudman, Dwayne Schanz, and Diane Livia. Handouts accompanying the video include a pamphlet of myths and realities about lesbian and gay parents, articles by young people with gay friends or family members, suggestions for how to handle harrassment and ways to include the issue in the classroom, a bibliography and resource list. Available from: Lesbian/Gay Parents Association (LGPA), 6705 California St., Apt. 1, San Francisco, CA 94121.

Not All Parents Are Straight, by Kevin White, 1987, 16mm or video, 58 minutes. Family profiles of lesbian and gay parents and their children. Available from: Cinema Guild, Suite 802, 1697 Broadway, New York, NY 10019, 212-246-5522.

We Are Family, by Amee Sands and Dasal Banks, 1987, 3/4" video. Legal and social implications of gay and lesbian parenting explored through three families. Available from: WGBH-TV, 125 Western Ave., Alston, MA 02134, 617-492-2777.

SOME FAMOUS NORTH AMERICAN GAY/LESBIAN/BISEXUAL PARENTS

Roberta Achtenberg

Dorothy Allison

Joan Baez

Josephine Baker

Ann Bannon

Amanda Bearse

Leonard Bernstein

Susie Bright

Margarethe Cammermeyer

John Cheever

Aaron Copeland

Samuel Delaney

Lilian Faderman

Malcolm Forbes

Stephen Foster

Paul Goodman

Harry Hay

James Hormel

Audre Lorde

JoAnn Loulan

Thomas Mann

Del Martin and Phyllis Lyon

Rod McKuen

Herman Melville

Robin Morgan

Rev. Troy Perry

Minnie Bruce Pratt

Adrienne Rich

Mariana Romo-Carmona

Eleanor Roosevelt

Dr. Tom Waddell

JURISDICTIONS WHERE SECOND-PARENT ADOPTIONS HAVE BEEN GRANTED

Alaska

California

District of Columbia

Illinois

Massachusetts (statewide)

Michigan

Minnesota

New Jersey

New York

Ohio

Oregon

Pennsylvania

Rhode Island

Texas

Vermont (statewide)

Washington

SOURCES: GLPCI Network, Summer 1994

RESOURCES

General:

Lambda Legal Defense and Education Fund, 666 Broadway, 12th fl., New York, NY 10012, 212-995-8585. One of the oldest (1973) and largest gay legal organizations. Advocates for the rights of lesbian and gay people.

Parents of gay men and lesbians

Federation of Parents and Friends of Lesbians and Gays, Inc., 1012 14th St., N.W., #700, Washington, DC 20005, or Box 27605, Washington, DC, 20038; 202-638-0243; 202-638-4200. To help parents and friends of gay men and lesbians understand homosexuality through education and support, to educate the larger community on the issue, and to advocate for lesbian and gay civil rights.

Gay moms of gay son, 1993 Gay Pride March, New York City *(Photo by Harry Stevens)*

National Federation of Parents and Friends of Gays, 8020 Eastern Avenue, N.W., Washington, DC 20012; 202-726-3223. Provides educational materials to anyone searching for understanding of human sexuality issues.

Parents and Friends of Integrity, Box 19561, Washington, DC 20036. For relatives and friends of gay people, with ties to the Episcopal Church.

Lesbian and gay parents (national)

Gay and Lesbian Parents Coalition International (GLPCI), P.O. Box 50360, Washington, DC 20091, 202-583-8029. Coalition of gay parenting groups across the country. Sponsors annual national conference of lesbian and gay parents and their children. Newsletter, bibliographies.

Gay Fathers Coalition, P.O. Box 19891, Washington, DC 20036; 202-583-8029. A coalition of local support groups for gay fathers.

Lavender Families (formerly Lesbian Mothers National Defense Fund), P.O. Box 21567, Seattle, WA 98111, 206-325-2643. Attorney referrals, legal information, personal support for lesbians and gay men involved in custody disputes.

Local lesbian and gay parenting organizations (by state)

Gay and Lesbian Parent Support Network, P.O. Box 66823, Phoenix, AZ 85082-6823, 602-256-9173

Gay and Lesbian Parents of Los Angeles, Suite 109-346, 7985 Santa Monica, West Hollywood, CA 90046, 213-654-0307

Gay Fathers of Long Beach, c/o The Center, 2017 E. Fourth St., Long Beach, CA 90814

Outreach for Couples, 405 W. Washington St., #86, San Diego, CA 92103

Gay and Lesbian Parents—Denver, P.O. Box Drawer E, Denver, CO 80218, 303-937-3625

Gay Fathers of Greater Boston, P.O. Box 1373, Boston, MA 02205

GLPCI Central Florida Chapter, P.O. Box 561-504, Orlando, FL 32856-1504, attn: Chris Alexander, 407-420-2191

Evansville GLPC, P.O. Box 8341, Evansville, IN 47716

Gay and Lesbian Parents—Indiana, P.O. Box 831, Indianapolis, IN 46206, 317-926-9741 (Craig or Terry)

Gay and Lesbian Parenting Coalition of Metropolitan Washington, 14908 Piney Grove Ct., North Potomac, MD 20878, 301-762-4828

Lesbian/Gay Family and Parenting Services, Fenway Community Health Center, 7 Haviland St., Boston, MA 02115, 617-267-0900, ext. 282

Gay and Lesbian Parents Association—Detroit, P.O. Box 2694, Southfield, MI 48037-2694, 313-891-7292 or 313-790-2440

New Hampshire Gay Parents, P.O. Box 5981, Manchester, NH 03108, 603-527-1082

Center Kids, the family project of the Lesbian and Gay Community Services Center, 208 W. 13th St., New York, NY 10011, 212/620-7310, 212/924-2657 (fax).

Gay Fathers Coalition of Buffalo, Westside Station, P.O. Box 404, Buffalo, NY 14213, 716-633-2692

Gay Fathers Forum of Greater New York, Midtown Station, P.O. Box 1321, New York, NY 10018-0725, 212-721-4216

Gay Fathers N.Y., Church St. Station, P.O. Box 2553, New York, NY 10008-7727

Gay Fathers Group, P.O. Box 25525, Rochester, NY 14625

Gay Fathers of Long Island, P.O. Box 2483, Patchogue, NY 11772-0879

GLP/Queen City—Charlotte, 4417-F Sharon Chase Dr., Charlotte, NC 28215

Gay and Lesbian Parenting Group of Central Ohio, P.O. Box 16235, Columbus, OH 43216

Gay Fathers of Austin, c/o Robert H. Havican, P.O. Box 16181, Austin, TX 78761-6181

Gay Fathers/Fathers First of Houston, P.O. Box 981053, Houston, TX 77098-1053, 713-782-5414

Houston Gay and Lesbian Parents Support, 1301 Richmond, #T10, Houston, TX 77006, 713-522-6766

SAGL Parents, P.O. Box 15094, San Antonio, TX 78212, contact: Rob O. Blanch, 512-828-4092

Gay and Lesbian League of Parents (GALLOP), PO Box 64736, Burlington, VT 05406. National network providing variety of resources relevant to lesbian and gay parents.

Gay Fathers Coalition of Washington, D.C., P.O. Box 19891, Washington, DC 20036, 202-583-8029

Gay and Lesbian Parents Coalition of Milwaukee, P.O. Box 93503, Milwaukee, WI 53203

Canada *(by province)*

Gay Fathers of Winnipeg, Box 2221, Winnipeg, Manitoba R3C 3R5
Gay Fathers of Toronto, P.O. Box 187, Station F, Toronto, Ontario M4Y 2L5

Adoptive parents organizations (by state)

AASK America (Aid to Adoption of Special Kids), 450 Sansome St., Suite 210, San Francisco, CA 94111, 415-781-4112. Chapters and cooperative agencies throughout the country. Places children with disabilities; sibling groups, children of color and racially mixed children, those born with drug dependencies, and babies with HIV/AIDS. The national board has an explicit non-discrimination policy on the basis of sexual orientation.

Chain of Life, PO Box 8081, Berkeley, CA 94707, Janine Baer, ed. Gay/lesbian/feminist adoption newsletter.

Gay and Lesbian Adolescent Social Services (GLASS), 89012 Melrose Ave., Suite 202, Los Angeles, CA 90069-5605, 213-653-3496. Primarily services to adolescents, but has placed lesbian and gay youth in foster homes and in families for adoption.

The Triangle Project, 1296 North Fairfax Ave., West Hollywood, CA 90046, 213-656-5005. Lesbian and gay social service agency for gay youth, actively recruits prospective foster parents.

International Concerns Committee for Children, Report on Foreign Adoption, 911 Cypress Drive, Boulder, CO 80303, 303/494-8333. Publishes annual listing of U.S. agencies handling international placements.

American Adoption Congress, Suite 9, 1000 Connecticut Ave., N.W., Washington, DC 20035. Umbrella organization for hundreds of local search and support organizations in U.S. Most are searching adult adoptees and birth parents.

National Adoption Information Clearinghouse, Suite 600, 1400 I St., N.W., Washington, DC 20005, 202-842-1919. Information and referrals. Directory of adoption agencies and support groups.

Americans for African Adoptions, Inc., 8910 Timberwood Dr., Indianapolis, IN 46234, Sheryl Carter Shotts, Managing Director, 317-271-4567. Will accept applications from singles. Has openly sought lesbian and gay families.

Committee for Single Adoptive Parents, P.O. Box 15084, Chevy Chase, MD 20815. For U.S. and Canadian singles; domestic and foreign adoptions.

National Adoption Information Clearinghouse, 11426 Rockville Pike, Suite 410, Rockville, MD 20852, 301-231-6512. Provides information about adoption nationwide. Maintains active search of resources and information. Can do computer searches on topics, e.g., lesbian and gay adoption.

Resolve, Inc., 5 Water St., Arlington, MA 02174, 617/643-2424. Education and support for infertility; adoption information.

Adoptive Families of America, Inc., *Ours* magazine, Suite 203, 2207 Highway 100 North, Minneapolis, MN 55422, 612/535-4829. National support, advocacy, and education for adoptive and preadoptive parents.

North American Council on Adoptable Children (NACAC), 970 Raymond Ave.,

Suite 106, St. Paul, MN 55114-1149; 612-644-3036. National advocacy organization. Nationwide resources/referrals.

North American Council on Adoptable Children, Suite S-275, 1821 University Avenue, St. Paul, MN 55104, 612-644-3036. Focuses on needs of waiting U.S. and Canadian children.

Family Focus Adoption Services, 54-40 Little Neck Parkway, Suite 3, Little Neck, NY 11362, 718-224-1919. Handles hard-to-place children; gives referrals to social workers for home studies for private adoptions. Has international adoption resources. Comfortable with lesbians and gay men.

Family Service of Westchester, Inc., One Summit Ave., White Plains, NY 10606, 914-948-8004. Works with pre- and post-adoptions families as well as pregnant women. Adoption counseling, home study, placements. Willing to work with lesbian and gay families.

Little Flower Children's Services, 186 Remsen St., Brooklyn, NY 11201, 718-260-8840. Full service agency offering public adoptions. Has made placements in gay and lesbian homes.

Lutheran Community Services, Inc., 27 Park Place, New York, NY 10007, 212-406-9110. Full service adoption agency offering public adoptions. Has made placements in gay and lesbian homes.

New Life Adoption Agency, Inc., 117 South State St., Syracuse, NY 13202-1103; 315-422-7300. New York State authorized and approved private adoption agency; social, legal, and medical professionals. Foster care, adoption. Can assist with international adoptions from China and Eastern Europe. Have nondiscrimination policy as part of their mission statement.

Adoption Information Services, 901-B E. Willow Grove Ave., Lyndmoor, PA 19118, 215-233-1380. Counseling and education on adoption, with specific help for gay men and lesbians.

Three Rivers Adoption Council, 307 Fourth Ave., Suite 710, Pittsburgh, PA 15222, 412-471-8722. Counseling, support services and parent education, referral to agencies, resource publications, and an adoption exchange. Contacts in western Pennsylvania, eastern Ohio, and West Virginia. Maintains lists of waiting families and waiting children of special needs adoptions. Very willing to work with lesbian and gay families.

Friends in Adoption, Box 7270, Buxton Ave., Middletown Springs, VT, 05757, 802-235-2312. Works with those interested in adopting and with those considering placing their children. Open to lesbians and gay men.

Surrogacy

The following are surrogate mother matching services, all of which have worked successfully with gay clients.

Center for Reproductive Alternatives—Southern California, Kathryn Wyckoff, 727 Via Otono, San Clemente, CA 92672, 714-492-2161.

Infertility Center of America (three locations): Noel Keane, J.D., Suite 309, 14 E. 60th St, New York, NY 10022, 212-371-0811; 2601 Fortune Circle East, Suite

102 B, Indianapolis, IN 46241, 317-243-8793; 101 Larkspur Landing Circle, Suite 318, Larkspur, CA 94939, 415-925-9020.

Surrogate Mothers, Inc., Steven Litz, J.D., P.O. Box 216, Monrovia, IN 46157, 317-996-2000.

Children of lesbian and gay parents

Children of Lesbians and Gays Everywhere (COLAGE), 2300 Market St., #165, San Francisco, CA 94114, 415-206-1930; Box 187, Station F, Toronto, ON M4Y 2L5. Outgrowth of Gay and Lesbian Parents Coalition International, run by and for children of gay parents. Publishes *Just for Us*, a monthly newsletter, has pen pal connection service, holds annual two-day conference for people age thirteen and up.

Lesbian and gay young people

Bisexual, Gay and Lesbian Youth of New York (BiGLYNY), c/o The Center, 208 W. 13th St., New York, NY 10011, 212-620-7310. Peer-run social and support network open to anyone twenty-two years and under.

Hetrick Martin Institute for Lesbian and Gay Youth, 2 Astor Place, New York, NY 10003, phone: 212-674-2400; fax: 212-674-8650. Social service, education, and advocacy organization for lesbian, gay, and bisexual adolescents, homeless/run-

BiGLYN contingent at the 1992 Gay Pride March, New York City (*Photo by Harry Stevens*)

away youth, and youth with HIV. Home of Harvey Milk High School, an alternative public school for gay and lesbian students.

The Neutral Zone, 162 Christopher St., New York, NY 10014, 212-924-3294. Substance violence-free center open late for lesbian, gay, and bisexual teens.

Youth Enrichment Services (Y.E.S.), the youth program of the Lesbian and Gay Community Services Center, 208 W. 13th St., New York, NY 10011, 212-620-7310. Creative arts-based youth empowerment, substance and alcohol abuse prevention, and HIV prevention program for lesbian, gay, and bisexual youth ages thirteen to twenty-two.

Lesbian and gay seniors

Senior Action in a Gay Environment (SAGE), 208 W. 13th St., New York, NY 10011, 212-741-2247. Homebound program, support groups, counseling, drop-in center, women's events, AIDS and seniors programs, education, community outreach.

Lesbian and gay couples

Partners, P.O. Box 9685, Seattle, WA. 98109, 206-784-1519. Information, support, and advocacy for same-sex couples, asserting that gay and lesbian couples are families. Newsletter.

Members of Senior Action in a Gay Environment (SAGE)

The Census Bureau reported in 1991 that only 26 percent of U.S. households fit the conventional definition of a family: a married couple with at least one child. That misses the essence of the American family, which is a unit joined by love and support. Homophobia, not homosexuality, constitutes a threat to this family.

According to a National Gay and Lesbian Task Force study, gay and lesbian youth are two to three times more likely to attempt suicide than their heterosexual peers. Twenty-six percent of gay and lesbian youth are forced to leave home due to family complications over their sexual orientation.

When such conditions cease, and when lesbian and gay parents are no longer denied custody or access to their own children, the American family will be a lot stronger. In a period when the strife and violence in our world are reflected within many families, it is important to recognize that a supportive home in which children are truly wanted is a valuable contribution to society, and more crucial than the sexual orientation or marital status of the parents.

What some people forget is that all lesbians and gay men were once children who suffered from thinking that no one they knew or admired was like them. As adults, we affirm our right to let children know that their homosexual feelings are part of what it means to be human, and that a healthy set of values includes respect for one's own uniqueness.

SOURCES: Gay and Lesbian Alliance Against Defamation–New York (GLAAD/NY)

PROFILE

Tim Fisher

Tim Fisher and his lover, Scott Davenport, met in the University of Pennsylvania glee club during Tim's first week of college (Scott was a sophomore) in 1976. A year later, they were in love.

"We always talked about having kids," Tim said. "In fact, it came up when I first came out to my parents. I said something like, 'I'm not willing to give up having kids.' Reaching thirty was a turning point, and our New Year's resolution in 1989 prompted us to place a classified ad in the *Washington Blade*, seeking contact with anyone who knew anything about adoption and surrogacy. We got one letter in reply, from a woman interested in a surrogacy arrangement. She got pregnant on the first try, and our Kati was born in March of 1990. Our son, Fritz, followed two years later."

Scott, a management consultant, is the breadwinner for the Montclair, New Jersey, family. Tim, who had been actively involved with the Gay and Lesbian Parents Coalition International (GLPCI) since Kati's infancy, is a stay-at-home dad with an additional responsibility. He became GLPCI's unpaid National Executive Director in October of 1993.

At the first march on Washington for lesbian and gay rights in 1979, representatives from different regional gay fathers' groups got together and discussed how helpful it would be if there was a way these far-flung support groups could organize and create a forum for support of gay dads on a national level. From this meeting, the Gay Fathers Coalition was formed, sponsoring an annual conference that allowed gay fathers from around the country to come together, get acquainted, and create a national network.

In the early 1980s, Canada joined the coalition, which then changed its name to Gay Fathers Coalition International. It was finally named Gay and Lesbian Parents Coalition International (GLPCI) in the mid-eighties, when the lesbian parents participating insisted on inclusion in the name. In 1987, the children of the gay and lesbian parents attending the annual conferences began holding their own concurrent, separate, parallel conference, giving rise to the organization now known as Children of Lesbians and Gays Everywhere (COLAGE).

Today, there are 2,600 member families and 88 chapters in GLPCI, spread across eight countries (with Argentina and Australia expected to join soon). The organization provides advocacy, education, and support services for gay and lesbian parents and prospective parents.

More information on GLPCI and its activities can be obtained by writing: Gay and Lesbian Parents Coalition International, P.O. Box 50360, Washington, DC 20091.

PROFILE

Stefan Lynch

Stefan Lynch is the twenty-three-year-old cochair of Children of Lesbians and Gays Everywhere (COLAGE), a program for children with gay parents that evolved out of, and is still affiliated with, the Gay and Lesbian Parents Coalition International (GLPCI). COLAGE provides support for children of lesbian and gay parents, and advocates for lesbian and gay family rights.

"Once we realized that our problems were not caused by our gay and lesbian parents but by a society that is hostile to gay and lesbian people, we decided that the best thing we could do to support kids like ourselves was to focus on changing that society. We realized that support for each other was not enough. We were angry. So in 1993 Just for Us became COLAGE, and we started to be aggressively out, to be incredibly visible. We felt that was one thing we could do that would make a difference.

"Increasingly, we are looking at the way the courts affect kids' lives. For example, in cooperation with the National Center for Lesbian Rights, we gathered testimony from thirty kids with lesbian and gay parents in southern states in support of Sharon Bottoms (a lesbian mother in Virginia who lost custody of her young son).

"I was born in Toronto, and my dad came out when I was one year old. My parents stayed friends through the separation. My father was very involved in the gay and lesbian community in Toronto as a writer/activist/academic. He was one of the original collective members of *Body Politic*, the gay magazine. In fact, he started about half of the lesbian and gay groups in Toronto—the gay academic association at the University of Toronto, Gay Fathers of Toronto, the Toronto Center for Lesbian and Gay Studies, the AIDS Committee of Toronto. He wrote one of the first articles on AIDS to appear in *Body Politic*, in 1982.

"When I was seven, my dad organized a benefit for *Body Politic*, and brought in the actress Pat Bond from the States to provide the entertainment. My mom and Pat Bond fell in love on the spot, so my mom came out, too. I don't remember feeling any shock or surprise about it—I just remember thinking it was so cool that my mom was moving to California. Within the year, I was spending half my time with my gay dad in Toronto, and half with my lesbian mom in San Francisco.

"In 1987, when I was fifteen, my father's former longtime lover, a man who had been in my life in a major way from the time I was five, died within three weeks of receiving an AIDS diagnosis. That same summer, my father was diagnosed HIV positive. I was very freaked, very miserable. Although everyone in Toronto knew, I didn't tell anyone in California for a long time. Just before I left school, I did an AIDS education report and talked about my dad and my life. Reactions were mixed, but I was supported by a couple of really popular kids—I was totally surprised. Years later, I discovered the reason was that their parents were gay, and they felt unable to tell anyone.

"I nearly flunked out of school. Fortunately, I was able to find a college that would take me early, and after my sophomore year in high school I went off to Simons Rock College in Great Barrington, Massachusetts, with three hundred other liberal students. It was a major lifesaver. My first day there, I overheard my resident advisor dishing new students. Here he was, this completely out black gay man—I was so happy. All my life I'd known gay people, but they were all my parents' age. This was the first time I'd met gay people who were my peers.

"My father had seen a lot of guys die horrible hospital deaths, and he made me promise him, when I was fifteen, that I wouldn't send him to the hospital. So, when I was nineteen and he became really ill, I left school to take care of him for what turned out to be the last eight months of his life.

"I had a lot of help. He had so many friends. We set up a caregivers support team of about forty people, so he was never alone. He died in 1991.

"I'm straight, but a big part of me would prefer to be gay—it would be easier for me in many ways. It would give me greater access to a group of people with the values, humor, and historical references I love, the ones I grew up with, the culture I grew up in and totally accepted. But now that I'm twenty-three, not with my parents, and erotically straight even though I'm culturally queer, I find I'm sort of considered a gray area, someone sometimes seen as one who gets the benefits of the culture without having to pay the price.

"Sometimes I feel self-righteous about this. I've been coming out my whole life—longer than most of the gay people I meet! I was an AIDS activist at fifteen; I've been distributing leaflets for lesbian and gay organizers since I was a child. My girlfriend is a lesbian-identified bisexual woman who sells sex toys to dykes at Good Vibrations, and my lover before had been a lesbian separatist for ten years before we got together. Some of my best memories as a kid are of going to drag parties as Tallulah Bankhead and Bette Midler, and still somehow these doors are not completely open to me.

"I look forward to ten or fifteen years from now, when the kids born into gay homes are old enough to make noise, and make a difference. I'm more active in the movement than many of my peers who grew up with gay parents because I was accepted into my parents' lives, and was comfortable there. Many kids my age were not—their parents may have acknowledged their sexuality to their kids, but they kept their social lives separate from their lives with their children.

"I don't see that kind of separation so much in the lesbian and gay households being formed today. Those kids can learn that they are a part of the movement, a part of something larger than themselves and their own individual families, and I think they'll be a bridge between the mainstream and gay cultures."

PROFILE

Center Kids

Children raised in lesbian and gay households are the youngest members of the lesbian and gay community. Center Kids, the family project of New York's Lesbian and Gay Community Services Center, provides children from gay homes in the New York area with frequent play opportunities with children from families like their own. Children in Center Kids have ongoing opportunities to befriend dozens of others who come from same-sex parents, while their parents have a chance to meet and socialize for support.

Founded in 1988 by a small group of new gay parents who gathered in Central Park to share their stories and garner support, Center Kids now has a mailing list of 1,800 lesbian and gay households.

Those contemplating parenthood may choose from Center Kids support groups on adoption, alternative insemination and other options for biological parenthood. A support group exists for parents separated from their children by gay "divorce." Center Kids sponsors forums and panels throughout the year on topics such as legal concerns for lesbian and gay families, child development issues in single-sex households, and how to explain bigotry and prejudice to children. In addition, discussion groups are held throughout the year, covering subjects ranging from "Dealing with Family Occasions" to "Answering Kids' Difficult Questions" to "Known vs. Unknown Donors."

Kids' Talk, the Center Kids monthly newsletter, contains a calendar of family-related events and information on gay and lesbian family issues, and is available to the 1,600 households on the program's mailing list.

The Center Kids contingent in the Lesbian and Gay Pride March is reliably one of the largest and, with young and old alike in cherry-red Center Kids T-shirts and

"Center Kids"
with Urvashi
Vaid, former
executive
director of the
National Gay
and Lesbian
Task Force
(*Photo by
Morgan
Gwenwald*)

balloons festooning strollers, one of the most colorful and engaging. It is a symbol of the profound joy of lesbian and gay parents, who come by their families through long consideration, effort, and an abiding belief in their often disputed right and ability to raise healthy, happy children.

For more information on lesbian and gay parenting issues, and on Center Kids' advocacy, education, and social support efforts, contact: Center Kids, the Lesbian and Gay Community Services Center, 208 W. 13th St., New York, NY 10011, 212-620-7310, or fax the program at 212-924-2657.

PROFILE

Jeanne Manford

"In 1972, when my son Morty came out to me and to my husband, we didn't really understand about homosexuality, but my first words were, 'I love you. You are the same person today as you were yesterday,'" says Jeanne Manford, the "founding mother" of Parents and Friends of Lesbians and Gays.

But Jeanne herself was not ever to be the same. When Morty and other gay activists were beaten in a public forum, she wrote an outraged letter to the *New York Post* complaining that her gay son was attacked while the police looked on and did nothing. "People were flabbergasted that I would admit that I had a gay son in the newspaper," she says. The letter led to a guest spot on New York radio talk show host Barry Farber's program, and a television appearance in Boston. When Morty asked her to march with him in the Lesbian and Gay Pride March the same year, she did so with a sign proclaiming her love and support for her gay son—"Parents of gays unite in support of our children," it read. "This created quite a stir," Jeanne recollects quietly. "People ran up to kiss me, and they asked me to speak to their parents on their behalf. And Morty himself felt so angry that so many of his friends couldn't tell their parents. So Morty put up fliers in bars and other places, announcing our first parents support meeting. That was in 1973. There were about twenty of us there." And Parents, Families and Friends of Lesbians and Gays (Parents-FLAG, or P-FLAG) was born.

Today, P-FLAG has more than thirty thousand member households in chapters throughout the United States and around the world, including England, Holland, Canada, and Israel. The group members advocate and educate on behalf of their lesbian and gay loved ones, and offer one another support.

Although Morty died of AIDS in 1993, and she lost her husband in 1982, Jeanne's work on behalf of lesbian and gay children continues. She recently spearheaded the formation of a Queens, New York, chapter of P-FLAG. And this July, she'll become a great-grandmother.

"Looking back, everyone kept saying how brave I was, and it seems to me as if I did nothing. I loved my son, and supported him. That's all." To the gay and lesbian children of straight parents, that's everything.

9. GAY LEGAL ISSUES

Note: The legal issues section of this almanac was prepared almost exclusively from *The Lambda Update,* a triannual newsletter, and *The Lambda 1994 Annual Report,* which are publications of Lambda Legal Defense and Education Fund. For information on Lambda, see p. 265.

ANTI-GAY INITIATIVE CAMPAIGNS

The radical right's hostility toward lesbians and gay men is expressed most clearly in anti-gay ballot initiatives. These referenda attempt to write gay and lesbian people out of state and local constitutions by preventing the passage of legislation protecting our rights, by curtailing our ability to petition our government for civil rights, and by diminishing our political clout as a community.

Anti-gay initiatives invite the general public to vote on whether lesbians and gay men are entitled to the same civil rights as other Americans. These referenda, which mimic a rash of ballot measures targeted at African-American civil rights in the 1960s and 1970s, threaten all communities not in the majority.

Legal organizations fighting the radical right work through preemptive legal challenges to prevent anti-gay initiatives from reaching the ballot. When preventive efforts fail, activists work to educate the public about the anti-democratic nature of anti-gay initiatives. If anti-gay initiatives are ultimately approved by a majority of voters (as they have been in Colorado and Cincinnati, Ohio, for example) legal activists pursue litigation to invalidate anti-gay initiatives on the grounds that they are unconstitutional.

So far, a broad coalition of community organizations, legal activists, and political organizers have come together to defeat in the courts the voter-approved initiatives of Colorado and Cincinnati. Similar coalitions have also been effective in thwarting other initiatives in a variety of ways:

Arizona: radical right does not gather enough signatures to place anti-gay initiative on the ballot, November 1994.

Florida: state-wide anti-gay measure struck from the ballot, March 1994.

Idaho: anti-gay measure voted down by informed electorate, November 1994.

Michigan: radical right does not gather enough signatures to place anti-gay initiative on the ballot, November 1994.

Missouri: radical right does not gather enough signatures to place anti-gay initiative on the ballot, November 1994.

Nevada: radical right does not gather enough signatures to place anti-gay initiative on the ballot, November 1994.

Ohio: radical right promises a statewide anti-gay initiative campaign, but does not follow through, 1994.

Oregon: anti-gay measure voted down by informed electorate, November 1994.

Washington: radical right does not gather enough signatures to place anti-gay initiative on the ballot, November 1994.

CASE HISTORY: *EVANS ET AL. V. ROMER AND NORTON*

On October 11, 1994, the Colorado Supreme Court upheld the district court's ruling that the anti-gay initiative known as Amendment 2 violates the United States Constitution. The court soundly rejected each of the six justifications offered by the state for Amendment 2. The ruling followed the Colorado Supreme Court's previous ruling in this case, in July 1993, when it found that the measure infringed on the fundamental constitutional rights of lesbians, gay men, and bisexuals, and upheld the preliminary injunction against the measure's enforcement.

Amendment 2 would prohibit all branches of state government in Colorado (including cities, school districts, and courts) from passing legislation or adopting policies to protect lesbians, gay men, and bisexuals from discrimination based on their sexual orientation. Although approved by Colorado voters in 1992, Amendment 2 has never taken effect, thanks to the preliminary injunction.

Just over a month after the Colorado high court issued its ruling, the state filed a petition for review with the United States Supreme Court. The Supreme Court heard oral argument in October 1995. Counsel for Evans et al. urged the court to uphold the Colorado Supreme Court's ruling that the amendment violates the U.S. Constitution. The challenge was brought by Lambda Legal Defense, the ACLU, and attorneys from the Colorado Legal Initiatives Project.

The Colorado Supreme Court's invalidation of the amendment was based on a review of evidence introduced at a two-week trial in Denver in October 1993, at which the court heard testimony about a range of issues affecting lesbians and gay

Colorado contingent, 1993 March on Washington for Lesbian, Gay, and Bisexual Rights *(Photo by Paula Martinac)*

COLORADO'S PERNICIOUS AMENDMENT 2

Neither the state of Colorado, through any of its branches or departments, nor any of its agencies, political subdivisions, municipalities, or school districts, shall enact, adopt, or enforce any statute, regulation, ordinance, or policy whereby homosexual, lesbian, or bisexual orientation, conduct, practices, or relationships shall constitute or otherwise be the basis of, or entitle any person or class of persons to have or claim any minority status, quota preferences, protected status, or claim of discrimination.

men, including discrimination and bias-motivated violence. This ruling is the first state supreme court decision to declare unconstitutional an anti-gay initiative passed by voters. The influence of this victory continues to be felt as others around the country work to block passage of similar amendments in their own communities.

SODOMY LAW REFORM

Sodomy laws are used to make second-class citizens of gay people, to stigmatize sexual identity, and to justify many forms of discrimination against lesbians, gay men, and bisexuals. Since the U.S. Supreme Court's disappointing 1986 decision in *Bowers* v. *Hardwick* (in which the constitutionality of state sodomy laws was upheld) lesbian and gay legal organizations have sought to challenge the sodomy statutes in state constitutions to secure the protection of private sexual intimacy for all people regardless of sexual orientation.

CASE HISTORY: *BOWERS V. HARDWICK*

In 1982 in Atlanta, twenty-eight-year-old Michael Hardwick was arrested and convicted of sodomy after police officers who were trying to serve a warrant for a minor traffic violation found him at home in his bed having mutual consensual oral sex with another man. Hardwick argued that the state sodomy law violated his right to privacy. The federal Court of Appeals agreed with him, ruling that Georgia's sodomy law was unconstitutional and that the right to privacy includes choices that are "intimate and personal" and "central to personal dignity and autonomy." The State of Georgia then appealed to the Supreme Court. "It is the very act of homosexual sodomy that epitomizes moral delinquency," wrote Michael Bowers, the state attorney general, in his brief to the Court.

In a 5–4 decision, the Supreme Court reversed the lower appellate court, rejecting that court's expansive view of the right to privacy. In his opinion, Justice Byron White concluded that the right to privacy does not extend to homosexuals, and for proof he invoked the Bible, stating, "Proscriptions against *that conduct* [emphasis added] have ancient roots." In a concurring opinion, Chief Justice Warren Burger wrote that "condemnation of *those practices* [emphasis added] is firmly rooted in Judeo-Christian moral and ethical standards."

> *"The cop stood there for like . . . thirty-five seconds while I was engaged in*
> *mutual oral sex. When I looked up and realized he was standing there, he*
> *then identified himself. He said I was under arrest for sodomy. I said,*
> *'What are you doing in my bedroom?'"*
>
> —MICHAEL HARDWICK

In a dissenting opinion, Justice Harry Blackmun wrote, "I can only hope that . . . the Court will reconsider its analysis and conclude that depriving individuals of the right to choose for themselves how to conduct their intimate relationships poses a far greater threat to the values most deeply rooted in our Nation's history than tolerance of nonconformity could ever do. Because I think the Court betrays those values, I dissent."

CASE HISTORY: *ENGLAND V. CITY OF DALLAS*

In 1993, an intermediate appellate court upheld the lower court victory of Mica England, who was denied employment as a police officer because she is a lesbian and thus in violation of the state sodomy law. The court affirmed the trial court's ruling that the Texas sodomy law, which singles out "homosexual conduct," violates the state constitution, and struck it down. The court retained the judges' order that the police department not rely on the statute as a pretext for anti-gay discrimination.

In September 1994, the case was finally settled when the City of Dallas agreed

STATES WITH SODOMY LAWS

The following twenty-one states still have statutes on their books that outlaw consensual homosexual sex (termed "sodomy" regardless of what variety of homosexual activity it is):

Alabama	Mississippi
Arizona	Missouri
Arkansas	Montana
Florida	North Carolina
Georgia	Oklahoma
Idaho	Rhode Island
Kansas	South Carolina
Louisiana	Texas
Maryland	Utah
Massachusetts	Virginia
Minnesota	

Source: *OUT* magazine, June 1995

THE LITTLE BLACK BOOK

Lambda Legal Defense's "Little Black Book"—what to do if you're arrested, entrapped, or abused by police

Lambda Legal Defense and Education Fund (LLDEF) publishes a free pamphlet called *The Little Black Book: This One Can Keep You Out of Trouble,* which is the definitive guide on entrapment and what to do about it, written in non-legalese. The pamphlet describes the connection between the prejudices caused by the sodomy laws and entrapment operations and how that affects homophobic court decisions, like *Bowers* v. *Hardwick.* Underwritten by a grant from the Henry van Ameringen Foundation, the booklet is available free from LLDEF, 666 Broadway, 12th floor, New York, NY 10012, 212-995-8585.

to pay England $75,000 in damages. The Texas sodomy law remains off the books under the appellate court ruling despite the Texas Supreme Court's refusal in another case (*Morales*) to strike down the sodomy law itself.

EMPLOYMENT DISCRIMINATION

United States laws provide few protections for lesbian and gay workers. Only eight statewide laws prohibit discrimination based on sexual orientation. None exist at the federal level. In fact, discrimination against lesbians and gay men by some federal employers—like the military—is official policy.

The discrimination experienced by lesbian and gay people in the workplace can be subtle or overt, motivated by private prejudice or sanctioned by company policy. Not limited to losing one's job or not being hired because one is gay, employment discrimination also takes the form of harassment, impeded advancement, and unequal benefits. The "closet" is arguably the most ubiquitous and debilitating side effect of anti-gay employment discrimination, and a form of discrimination itself.

CASE HISTORY: *DEMUTH V. MILLER*

Daniel Miller is a certified public accountant whose former employer fired him pursuant to a provision in his contract that said homosexuality would be "cause" for firing. The employer also sued Miller under the clause that provided that, if fired "for cause," Miller might have to pay hefty penalties for any clients who chose to take their business to Miller.

Miller sought representation from Lambda Legal Defense and Education Fund after a trial in which the jury entered a verdict against him. The Superior Court of Pennsylvania upheld the $110,000 verdict in January 1995, although the three-judge panel disagreed sharply over whether the judgment amounted to state-sanctioned discrimination, with one judge in dissent, advocating for full employment rights for lesbian and gay men. Miller has filed a petition for review by the United States Supreme Court.

HOUSING DISCRIMINATION

Lesbians and gay men are frequently targets of sexual orientation discrimination by landlords, homeowners, or realtors who don't want to rent or sell to us. Fewer than ten states have laws prohibiting housing discrimination based on sexual orientation and there is no federal prohibition.

In the last ten years, combatting housing discrimination has taken on a new urgency because of the AIDS epidemic. Surviving partners of people who die of AIDS are often discriminated against by landlords, co-op boards, homeowner's associations, and city and county taxing authorities whose rules protect only heterosexual spouses from displacement after the death of a life partner.

Lesbian and gay legal advocates pursue litigation to prevent housing discrimination against surviving lesbian or gay life partners and to assure that, at their time of greatest loss, gay people will not have to face the anxiety of total dislocation.

Lesbians and gay men do not all share the same burdens in terms of discrimination. Some of us are immediately identifiable as gay men or lesbians and therefore face quick and overt hostility; others of us do not. Many face additional forms of discrimination based on our race or our class, our health status or our age. Litigation on our behalf must take into account all of the burdens faced by members of our community.

CASE HISTORY: IN RE *JORDAN-COATES*

Bradley Jordan-Coates successfully appealed a reassessment of the property tax on his home which was imposed after the death of his life partner, Kevin Jordan-Coates. San Diego County reassesses all residential property upon a transfer of ownership, but to protect widows and widowers there is a spousal exemption in the reassessment requirement. Even though Kevin and Bradley owned their home jointly, as most married couples do, the county reassessed the value of Jordan-Coates's property. The property taxes multiplied exponentially and Bradley faced the likelihood of having to move and sell his home because of the exorbitant increase.

The Assessment Appeals Board in San Diego agreed that the spousal exemption should apply to Bradley. The county has appealed, however, and Bradley will be represented by Lambda Legal Defense and Education Fund in superior court should the court decide to review the case.

EQUAL MARRIAGE LAWS

In January 1995, after years of laying the groundwork for winning and keeping the right to marry, Lambda Legal Defense and Education Fund announced the formation of its Marriage Project.

The Marriage Project is litigating Lambda's pioneering Hawaii case, *Baehr* v. *Lewin*, indisputably the most promising challenge to unequal marriage laws in the country, a suit brought by two lesbian couples and one gay male couple. The Project also works to mobilize the lesbian and gay movement and our allies to secure this most basic civil right.

To ensure that other states and the federal government recognize marriages validly contracted in Hawaii, Lambda's Marriage Project is preparing for the federal and state-by-state litigation that will follow a victory in *Baehr* v. *Lewin*. The Project is developing a network of volunteer attorneys, law professors, and law students to research the legal arguments available against backlash and in favor of recognition. Working with other organizations, the Marriage Project will serve as a national coordinator and clearinghouse for the analysis and materials developed.

To help promote the recognition of equal marriage rights and to build a national coalition, the Project has developed the Marriage Resolution and is asking community members, organizations and allies to adopt and promote the resolution:

Because marriage is a fundamental right under our Constitution, and because the Constitution guarantees equal protection under the law,

RESOLVED, the State should permit gay and lesbian couples to marry and share fully and equally in the rights and responsibilities of marriage.

Joseph Melillo and Patrick Lagon, plaintiffs in the Hawaii marriage suit, *Baehr* v.
Lewin (Courtesy Lambda Legal Defense and Education Fund)

CASE HISTORY: *BAEHR V. LEWIN*

On May 5, 1993, the Hawaii Supreme Court took a giant step toward allowing lesbians and gay men to marry. The court's ruling in *Baehr* v. *Lewin* held that the refusal to issue marriage licenses to same-sex couples appeared to violate the state
constitutional right to equal protection, and ordered a trial in which the state
would either have to present "compelling" reasons for continuing to discriminate
against gay and lesbian couples who want to marry, or stop discriminating.

Since the ruling, there has been significant political and legislative ferment in
Hawaii around the issue, with momentum building toward acceptance of equal
marriage rights in the face of a heavy right-wing attack. Both of the state's largest
newspapers have editorialized in support of equal marriage laws, and the new governor campaigned in favor of equality, while the legislature has passed a law reaf-
firming its desire to discriminate on the basis of gender in precisely the manner
the court held unconstitutional.

POLITICAL ASYLUM AND IMMIGRATION

Gay men, lesbians, and people with HIV are seeking safe haven in the United
States. In many countries, members of our community are singled out for govern-
ment-sanctioned persecution in varying degrees of severity. In one country, the
penalty for consensual same-sex relations is death.

On June 19, 1994, Attorney General Janet Reno designated as precedent a

Board of Immigration Appeals decision finding that gay men or lesbians who are persecuted by their governments may be eligible for relief from deportation. Since then, advocacy efforts have been aimed toward strengthening this policy and pressing for reasonable standards by which lesbian and gay people can demonstrate their fear of persecution, especially in countries where there is scant documentation of anti-gay violence.

WHAT A POTENTIAL IMMIGRANT NEEDS TO KNOW:

Currently, there are three ways to immigrate legally to the United States: (1) family sponsorship; (2) sponsorship through employment or profession; and (3) asylum. One should consult with an immigration lawyer or specialist before attempting any of the three avenues.

- It is not yet possible for U.S. citizens to sponsor their gay or lesbian lovers; the INS does not currently recognize the validity of such unions. This is true even if the ceremony was held in one of the few countries that recognize gay and lesbian marriage (Denmark, Sweden). The Lesbian and Gay Immigration Rights Task Force advocates for changes in the INS's discriminatory policies with regard to lesbians, gay men, and people with HIV.
- Gay men and lesbians are no longer excludable or deportable from the United States based solely on sexual orientation, although INS officers often harass people perceived as gay or lesbian.
- Despite national efforts to have the restriction removed, infection with HIV currently remains a ground for exclusion. Some people may qualify for a waiver of the exclusion. Never assume that HIV infection will irretrievably doom an immigration application.
- Immigration procedures and forms can be misleading—especially those related to family sponsorship. Many people run afoul of the INS because they make innocent errors on the documents. In preparing to immigrate, any applicant should consult an immigration lawyer or specialist.
- Arrests, prior immigration difficulties, receipt of public assistance of any kind, and certain health conditions are serious complications. If a potential immigrant has ever had any of these problems, he or she should not attempt to process a case without legal assistance.
- Applicants should never argue with, insult, or visibly lose their temper with an INS officer. If problems arise, applicants should note the officer's badge number, and pursue options after leaving the officer's presence.
- Asylum cases are politically sensitive and extremely complex. Anyone attempting to claim asylum in the United States should seek a qualified immigration law practitioner to handle the case.

CASE HISTORY: IN RE: *A.T.*

An Iranian gay man who fears that if he returns to his home country, he will be persecuted or put to death, has filed an application seeking political asylum. For a first offense in engaging in same-sex sexual activity, A.T. could be subject to one

Openly gay judge Richard Failla, who died of AIDS in 1993 (*From the collection of the Lesbian and Gay Community Services Center–New York*)

hundred lashes. A third offense is punishable by execution. A.T. has had a formal interview with an asylum officer and is awaiting the INS's decision.

AIDS

Legal advocates working in the AIDS arena must address the broad spectrum of public policy issues raised by the HIV pandemic. Generally speaking, AIDS-related cases fall into two categories: discrimination and access to health care. Thus far, precedent-setting cases have challenged discrimination in employment, housing, public accommodations, medical treatment, and provision of benefits. But because medical intervention can prolong the lives of people with HIV, the fight for access to basic health care, as well as access to essential treatments refused by insurers as "experimental," has become paramount. Legal advocates challenge discrimination and deficiencies in the health care system, as it affects both providers and consumers, and work toward winning access to sound treatment for people with HIV.

At the same time, activists and lawyers continue to identify areas of unmet need and to advocate vigorously for members of our community whose voices have been denied or ignored: victims of HIV-related bias crimes, the incarcerated, individuals caught in—or kept out of—the foster care and adoption systems, and others whose survival often hinges on the cooperation of hostile bureaucracies.

CASE HISTORY: *S.P. V. SULLIVAN*

In 1993, the Centers for Disease Control (CDC) announced new regulations governing disability benefits for people with HIV infection. These changes addressed virtually all of the concerns raised by a lawsuit challenging the Social Security Administration's (SSA) reliance on a grossly inadequate definition of AIDS from the CDC for awarding Social Security benefits. The new regulations add the predominant manifestations of HIV in women, drug users, and low income people as criteria by which HIV-infected individuals can qualify for disability.

Previously, the SSA regulations required people suffering from aggressive and recurrent infections such as pneumonia, sepsis, endocarditis, and meningitis to meet extremely stringent functional tests while persons suffering from disease contained in the CDC's definition of AIDS could qualify on the basis of medical evidence alone. Additionally, the new regulations list disabling conditions common in women, such as pelvic inflammatory disease, which did not appear at all in the earlier standards.

CASE HISTORY: *STATE OF MISSISSIPPI V. MARVIN McCLENDON*

On October 8, 1994, two unarmed gay men, Robert Walters and Joseph Shoe-maker, were shot to death in Laurel, Mississippi. A local teenager, Marvin Mc-Clendon, was arrested and confessed to the murders. McClendon alleged that the victims had tried to sexually assault him and he acted in self-defense.

Lambda Legal Defense and Education Fund became involved in the case when the defendant's attorney moved that the victim's blood be tested for HIV, arguing that had the victims been HIV-positive, McClendon would have been justified in killing them.

Lambda submitted a brief which the local district attorney used in its entirety to support his motion to block the use of HIV serostatus as evidence. The brief argued that the HIV status of the two victims was irrelevant to the case and that disclosure would violate Mississippi law, and would serve to encourage and justify attacks on people with HIV or other disabilities.

Ultimately, the judge allowed the HIV serostatus to be entered as evidence. Despite the defense attorney's attempt to stoke prejudice and fear, and despite the trial judge's apparent collusion, the jury found McClendon guilty of two counts of murder.

CASE HISTORY: *SCOLES V. MERCY HEALTH CORPORATION OF SOUTH-EASTERN PENNSYLVANIA*

Dr. Paul Scoles, an orthopedic surgeon, was denied admitting privileges at Mercy Health Corporation of Southeastern Pennsylvania after he disclosed his HIV status. Mercy Health officials sent 1,050 letters informing former patients about Scoles's HIV status, removed his name from a list of orthopedic consultants, and suspended his surgical privileges. The hospital later modified its policy and decided to allow Dr. Scoles to continue performing surgery, but only under the condition that he inform all patients of his HIV status.

Scoles's lawsuit successfully argued that Mercy Heath's actions violated both the Rehabilitation Act of 1973, and the provisions of the Americans with Disabilities Act, which prohibit discrimination against employees with HIV unless there is a "direct threat to the health or safety of other individuals in the workplace."

Scoles and Mercy Health reached a satisfactory settlement in February 1995.

FAMILY LAW

For those accustomed to legal recognition of their families, it is often hard to imagine the difficulties presented by living in a family configuration not sanctioned by the state.

Lesbian and gay couples have long struggled with the indignities and inequities of such a limitation, from being denied insurance coverage as spouses or family members, to being denied access to the hospital room of a dying partner, to being refused the promise of burial in a family plot. When our families include children, this lack of legal recognition has even more sinister implications.

Legal advocates are working to gain fair treatment for lesbian and gay couples in many contexts, to protect the rights of all gay and lesbian parents, to insure the adoption and foster parent privileges of gay men and lesbians, and to expand marriage law to recognize same-sex unions.

Like other marginalized communities, the gay and lesbian community has a long history of creating family configurations—both with and without children—that support and nurture its members. And like others not in the majority, our family forms often have been met with fear and hostility from the mainstream.

Family law advocates work not only to assure the rights of lesbian and gay couples and families, but to expand our country's notion of family itself—from single mothers to coparents to extended networks of parents, partners, and caregivers—so that the ideal more accurately reflects the complex reality of American lives.

CASE HISTORY: IN THE MATTER OF *THE ADOPTION OF A CHILD WHOSE FIRST NAME IS BYRON,* AND IN THE MATTER OF *THE ADOPTION OF A CHILD WHOSE FIRST NAME IS WOLFGANG*

The Albany Family Court denied the adoption petition of C.F., who had been raising Byron and Wolfgang as a foster parent with his partner K.L., because the petition was by a single man. The judge acknowledged that the previously troubled boys were flourishing in their new two-parent home with C.F. and K.L., but nevertheless denied C.F.'s petition because he was "single." The New York Appellate Division reversed the decision in June 1994. Wolfgang, Byron, and Dads continue to flourish in what they call their "forever family."

MILITARY

For information about important legal cases affecting gays in the military, see pp. 306–308.

SUPREME COURT DECISIONS THAT HAVE AFFECTED LESBIANS AND GAYS

1958: In *ONE Inc. v. Olesen* the Supreme Court overturns a California district court that banned the mailing of *ONE* magazine, one of the first gay publications.

1967: In *Boutilier* v. *Immigration and Naturalization Service,* the Supreme Court votes 6–3 that the INS can prevent homosexuals from entering the United States.

1976: In *Doe* v. *Commonwealth's Attorney* the Court upholds a Virginia court's ruling that there is no constitutional right to engage in private homosexual acts.
In *Enslin* v. *North Carolina*, the Court upholds the conviction of a man sentenced to one year in jail for having consensual oral sex with a man in his own home.
1986: In *Bowers* v. *Hardwick*, the Court votes 5–4 to uphold Georgia's sodomy law.
1995: The Court will determine whether or not Colorado's Amendment 2 is unconstitutional. (*See* "Anti-Gay Initiative Campaigns" above.)

SOURCE: Leigh Rutledge, *The Gay Fireside Companion.* Alyson Publications, 1989.

PROFILE

GLAD: Gay and Lesbian Advocates and Defenders

In 1978, Boston's gay community found itself under siege. During a reelection bid, Suffolk County District Attorney Garret Byrne inflamed anti-gay hysteria by setting up an anonymous hotline to gather "tips" on gay men having sex with minors, in the midst of what was called the "Revere Sex Ring Scandal." Plainclothes Boston police officers entrapped and arrested more than one hundred individuals for acts of "public lewdness" in the Boston Public Library.

Feeling vulnerable and unprotected, the gay community called for a local organization to help people facing anti-gay harassment or discrimination and to advocate for advances in gay/lesbian rights. Led by attorney John Ward, activists met at the Old West Church to organize such a group, and Gay and Lesbian Advocates and Defenders was born. Ward became the first executive director and Richard Burns became the first president of the board of directors.

For the last fifteen years, GLAD has litigated or participated in thousands of cases. At the forefront of virtually every area of lesbian and gay legal rights in New England, GLAD has pursued both local issues, such as securing the right of the Irish-American Gay, Lesbian, and Bisexual Group of Boston (GLIB) to march in Boston's St. Patrick's Day Parade (a decision overturned by the U.S. Supreme Court in June 1995), and test-case litigation with a national implications, including the landmark second-parent adoption case *Adoption of Tammy* (see family law case history above).

GLAD's list of organizational alumni reads like a virtual Who's Who of lesbian and gay activism:

Richard Burns, GLAD's first board president 1978–1986, is now executive director of the Lesbian and Gay Community Services Center of New York.
Kevin Cathcart, executive director, 1984–1992, is now executive director of Lambda Legal Defense and Education Fund.
Linda Giles, former litigation committee member, became the first openly lesbian judge in Massachusetts in 1992, also serving on the Boston Municipal Court.
Emily Hewitt, former board member, was named by President Clinton as general counsel to the General Services Administration in 1993.
Tim McFeeley, former board member and development committee chair, went on

to become the executive director of the Human Rights Campaign Fund in Washington, DC.

Denise McWilliams, former AIDS Law Project director, is now director of legal programs for JRI Health in Boston.

Dermot Meagher, former board member, became the first openly gay judge in Massachusetts in 1989, and still serves on the Boston Municipal Court.

Neil Miller, former board member, is now the author of *In Search of Gay America, Out in the World,* and *Out of the Past.*

Cindy Rizzo, former board president, is now associate director of development for Fenway Community Health Center in Boston.

Urvashi Vaid, GLAD's first legal intern, served as executive director of the National Gay and Lesbian Task Force in Washington, DC, from 1989 to 1992.

PROFILE

Lambda Legal Defense and Education Fund

Lambda Legal Defense and Education Fund is a national organization committed to achieving full recognition of the civil rights of lesbians, gay men, and people with HIV, through impact litigation, education, and public policy work.

Founded in 1973, Lambda challenges discrimination in employment, in housing, in public services and accommodations, and in the military; Lambda advocates for parenting rights, for domestic partner benefits, and for equal marriage rights; and Lambda works to protect privacy, equal protection, and first amendment rights.

History

In 1972, a New York court denied Lambda's application for incorporation on the grounds that Lambda's "stated purposes are on their face neither benevolent nor charitable, nor, in any event, is there a demonstrated need for this corporation."

New York's highest court overturned the ruling in 1973, and Lambda was born. In its early years, Lambda was an *entirely* volunteer organization, with legal work provided by William Thom—who had filed the initial suit—and a network of supporting attorneys. In 1977, Lambda began to change from a volunteer organization into one with a governing board of directors and a paid executive director. Lambda opened its first offices, housed at the New York Civil Liberties office, in 1979. By 1982, its offices had doubled in size and its board of directors was transforming from a local board to a national one, with almost half of its members from outside of New York City.

Lambda fought and won the nation's first AIDS discrimination lawsuit in 1983. Lambda and cooperating attorney Bill Hibsher represented Dr. Joseph Sonnabend, whose coop board tried to evict him and his medical practice because he was treating patients with AIDS. Since then, Lambda has become the nation's premier legal organization advocating for the rights of people with HIV/AIDS.

In 1987, Lambda moved its offices to its present site at 666 Broadway. Now in its twenty-first year, Lambda Legal Defense and Education Fund is the country's oldest and largest legal organization working to advance the civil rights of lesbians, gay men, and people with HIV. With offices in New York, Los Angeles, and Chicago, Lambda's impact is felt nationwide: Its staff attorneys work in cooperation with a network of more than four hundred volunteer attorneys across the country; its legal services are provided without charge to clients.

LEGAL RESOURCES

United States

Calm, Inc. (Custody Action of Lesbian Mothers), P.O. Box 281, Narberth, PA 19702, 215-667-7508.

Gay and Lesbian Advocates and Defenders (GLAD), P.O. Box 218, Boston, MA 02112, 617-426-1350.

Lambda Legal Defense and Education Fund, National Headquarters, 666 Broadway, 12th Floor, New York, NY 10012, 212-995-8585. Test case litigation only.

LeGAL: Lesbian and Gay Legal Association (formerly the Bar Association for Human Rights), P.O. Box 1899, Grand Central Station, New York, NY 10163. Lawyer referral, 24-hour answering service (next-day callback): 212-459-4873. Pro bono committee: 212-459-4754. Other business: 212-302-5100.

National Lesbian and Gay Law Association, Box 77130, National Capital Station, Washington, DC 20014, 202-389-0161.

Canada

EGALE (Equality for Gays and Lesbians Everywhere), P.O. Box 2891, Station D, Ottawa, ON K1P 5W9, 613-230-4391.

10. GAY LITERATURE

ALL NEW YORK IS TALKING

All New York is talking about and reading an unusual novel which has been called "the finest handling of this important theme yet attempted . . . better than *The Wall of Loneliness.*" The talented Andre Tellier, who wrote it, has achieved "a beautiful handling of a delicate subject." The title of the book is

TWILIGHT MEN

It is on sale at $2.50 at all bookstores. Published by GREENBERG, 160 Fifth Ave., New York

ALREADY IN ITS 3RD LARGE PRINTING

From Yale Collection of American Literature, Beinecke Rare Books and Manuscripts Library, Yale University. Unknown New York Newspaper, 1931–1955.

"Or if you will, thrusting me beneath your clothing,
Where I may feel the throbs of your heart or rest upon your hip,
Carry me when you go forth over land or sea;
For thus merely touching you is enough, is best,
And thus touching you would I silently sleep and be carried eternally."

—Walt Whitman

Before 1969, gay men appeared in literature, but they looked very different from today. During the nineteenth century in the United States, even slight allusions to homosexuality were rare. We can find ourselves in the homoeroticism of Herman Melville or Walt Whitman, but for more explicit portrayals of gay men, we have to look to the late 1800s and early 1900s, when an explosion of scientific and medical writings on homosexuality began to appear and to make their influence felt in literature.

The first mention of explicit homosexuality in North American literature came in Chester Alan Dale's novel *A Marriage Below Zero,* published in 1889. But this and other early works mimicked the medical establishment's portrait of homosexuals as "inverts." The first positive portrayal of homosexual behavior in a novel came in Xavier Mayne's *Imre: A Memorandum* (1906).

The sexual openness of the 1920s was reflected in literature by a new acceptability of the discussion of homosexuality, and the Harlem Renaissance of that decade was overwhelmingly a queer movement, with writers such as Langston Hughes, Countee Cullen, and Wallace Thurman achieving renown. By the 1930s, major white authors like F. Scott Fitzgerald, Thomas Wolfe, and John Dos Passos included minor gay characters in their writings. But most of these characters were effeminate stereotypes and many came to violent ends or to a realization that they would be lonely and unhappy all their lives.

The years right after World War II saw a lot of literature about homoeroticism in the military. They also witnessed the first works by what would become major gay voices—Gore Vidal's *The City and the Pillar* (1948), Truman Capote's *Other Voices, Other Rooms* (1948), and Paul Goodman's *Parents' Day* (1951). This brief flowering, however, came to an abrupt end with the repressive fifties. From the early fifties until Stonewall, most literature that included gay characters viewed them from the psychoanalytic stance of the day—that homosexuality was a pathology that led to unhappiness and premature death.

With the gay liberation movement, an outgrowth of other civil rights movements of the 1960s, gay literature took an about-face. The female-identified characters, the pathetic suicides and vicious murders, began disappearing, replaced by more accurate descriptions of gay lives and loves. Some gay literature took on a tone of political rights advocacy. And gay writers stopped speculating on the *causes* of homosexuality, because it was no longer dealt with as a disease.

Though there had been many prominent poets and playwrights who were gay-identified before Stonewall, few wrote openly about love between men. They chose "safer" topics, or codes with which to hide their sexuality. The gay liberation movement opened the doors to a new generation of out gay poets and playwrights, writing proudly about their feelings and their lives.

By the 1980s, when AIDS began ravaging the gay community, death and illness found their way into gay literature as constant themes. Though at first many gay novelists set their novels in pre-AIDS times, almost as if to deny the power of the disease, by the middle of the decade, an outpouring of literature on AIDS had appeared, creating its own genre of illness and loss. The number of writers our community has lost to the pandemic is staggering, and the voices of Paul Monette, Melvin Dixon, David Feinberg, Robert Ferro, Allen Barnett, Assotto Saint, Craig G. Harris, Donald Woods, and Stan Leventhal, to name only a few, can never be replaced.

A Selection of Novels with Gay Content Published Before Stonewall

Baldwin, James. *Giovanni's Room.* (1956)
Barr, James. *Quatrefoil.* (1950)
Bruce, Kenilworth. *Goldie.* (1933)
Burns, John Horne. *The Gallery.* (1947)
Capote, Truman. *Other Voices, Other Rooms.* (1948)
Dale, Chester Alan. *A Marriage Below Zero.* (1889)
Ford, Charles Henri and Parker Tyler. *The Young and Evil.* (1933)
Goodman, Paul. *Parent's Day.* (1951)
Isherwood, Christopher. *A Single Man.* (1964)
Mayne, Xavier. *Imre: A Memorandum.* (1906)
Meeker, Richard. *Better Angel.* (1933)

Niles, Blair. *Strange Brother.* (1949)

Rechy, John. *City of Night.* (1963)

Renault, Mary. *The Charioteer.* (1959)

Stoddard, Charles Warren. *For the Pleasure of His Company: An Affair of the Misty City.* (1903)

Taylor, Bayard. *Joseph and His Friend.* (1870)

Thomas, Ward. *Stranger in the Land.* (1949)

Thurman, Wallace. *Home to Harlem.* (1927)

Vidal, Gore. *The City and the Pillar.* (1948)

PULITZER PRIZE–WINNER GAY MALE WRITERS

1948 Tennessee Williams, drama, *A Streetcar Named Desire*

1948 W. H. Auden, poetry, *The Age of Anxiety*

1953 William Inge, drama, *Picnic*

1955 Tennessee Williams, drama, *Cat on a Hot Tin Roof*

1967 Edward Albee, drama, *A Delicate Balance*

1970 Richard Howard, poetry, *Untitled Subjects*

1975 Edward Albee, drama, *Seascape*

1976 Michael Bennett, with James Kirkwood and Nicholas Dante, drama, *A Chorus Line*

1977 James Merrill, poetry, *Divine Comedies*

1979 John Cheever, fiction,, *The Stories of John Cheever*

1980 Lanford Wilson, drama, *Talley's Folly*

1981 James Schuyler, poetry, *The Morning of the Poem*

1988 William Meredith, poetry, *Partial Accounts: New and Selected Poems*

1993 Tony Kushner, drama, *Angels in America: Millennium Approaches*

1994 Edward Albee, drama, *Three Tall Women*

GAY MALE WINNERS OF THE AMERICAN ACADEMY AND INSTITUTE OF ARTS AND LETTERS AWARD FOR LITERATURE

1944 Tennessee Williams	1964 Thom Gunn
1946 Langston Hughes	1970 Richard Howard
1950 Paul Bowles	1971 Reynolds Price
1951 Fredrick Newton Arvin	1973 Lanford Wilson
1953 Paul Goodman	1975 William S. Burroughs
1956 James Baldwin	1977 James Schuyler
1958 William Meredith	1983 Alfred Corn
1959 Truman Capote	1983 Edmund White

GAY MALE WINNERS OF THE NOBEL PRIZE FOR LITERATURE

1909 Selma Lagerlof (Swedish novelist)

1922 Jacinto Benavente (Spanish dramatist)

1929 Thomas Mann (German novelist)
1947 Andre Gide (French novelist)
1973 Patrick White (Australian novelist)
1977 Vincente Alexandre (Spanish poet)

GAY MALE NATIONAL BOOK AWARD WINNERS

Frederick Newton Arvin, 1951, for *Herman Melville*
W. H. Auden, 1956, for *The Shield of Achilles*
John Boswell, 1981, for *Christianity, Social Tolerance and Homosexuality*
Allen Ginsberg, 1974, for *The Fall of America: Poems of These States 1965–1971*
Richard Howard, 1983, for translating *Les Fleurs du Mal*, by Baudelaire
James Merrill, 1979, for *Mirabell: Books of Number*, and 1967, for *Nights and Days*
Paul Monette, 1992, for *Becoming a Man: Half a Life Story*
Frank O'Hara, 1972, for *The Collected Poems*

AMERICAN LIBRARY ASSOCIATION GAY/LESBIAN BOOK AWARD

Since 1971, the Gay/Lesbian Book Award of the American Library Association (ALA) has been given annually to English-language books of exceptional merit relating to the gay/lesbian experience. Awards are in two categories: literature and nonfiction. Nominations are accepted from the general public, librarians, members of the Gay/Lesbian Task Force of the AMA and the Gay/Lesbian Book Awards Committee of the AMA. Winners are chosen by the Book Awards Committee.

Gay Winners

1972 Peter Fisher, *The Gay Mystique*
1975 Jonathan Katz, *Homosexuality: Lesbians and Gay Men in Society, History, and Literature*
1977 Howard Brown, *Familiar Faces, Hidden Lives*
1980 Winston Lelyand, *Now the Volcano: An Anthology of Latin American Gay Literature*
1981 John Boswell, *Christianity, Social Tolerance, and Homosexuality: Gay People in Western Europe from the Beginning of the Christian Era to the Fourteenth Century*
1982 Vito Russo, *The Celluloid Closet*
1984 John D'Emilio, *Sexual Politics/Sexual Communities: The Making of a Homosexual Minority in the United States, 1940–1970*
1987 Walter Williams, *The Spirit and the Flesh: Sexual Diversity in American Indian Culture*
1988 Randy Shilts, *And the Band Played On: Politics, People, and the AIDS Epidemic*
1989 Alan Hollinghurst, *The Swimming-Pool Library*

1990 David B. Feinberg, *Eighty-Sixed*
1990 Neil Miller, *In Search of Gay America: Women and Men in a Time of Change*
1991 Wayne Dynes, ed., *Encyclopedia of Homosexuality*
1992 Paul Monette, *Halfway Home*

LAMBDA LITERARY AWARDS

The Lambda Literary Awards are held each year on the eve of the American Booksellers Association's annual convention, cosponsored by the Publishing Triangle and Lambda Rising Bookstore. Since 1988, the "Lammy" has recognized excellence in gay and lesbian writing and publishing. Current categories include fiction, poetry, lesbian studies, gay men's studies, mystery, biography/autobiography, anthologies/fiction, anthologies/nonfiction, humor, science fiction/fantasy, drama, children's/young adult books, and lesbian and gay small press books. Nominations can be made by the general public. Winners are chosen by a panel of seventy-five judges representing a broad cross-section of the lesbian and gay literary community.

Gay Winners: 1994

Alan Hollinghurst, *The Folding Star,* fiction
Thom Gunn, *Collected Poems,* poetry
George Chauncey, *Gay New York,* gay men's studies
Tony Kushner, *Angels in America: Perestroika,* drama
Abraham Verghese, *My Own Country,* biography/autobiography
Joan Nestle and John Preston, eds., *Sister and Brother,* anthologies/nonfiction
John Berendt, *Midnight in the Garden of Good and Evil,* mystery

Lambda Literary Awards in Gay Fiction Since 1988

1988 Edmund White, *The Beautiful Room is Empty*
1989 David Feinberg, *Eighty-Sixed*
1990 Allen Barnett, *The Body and Its Dangers*
1991 Harlan Greene, *What the Dead Remember*
1992 Randall Keenan, *Let the Dead Bury Their Dead*
1993 Joseph Hansen, *Living Upstairs*

Lambda Literary Awards in Gay Poetry Since 1988

1988 Carl Morse and Joan Larkin, eds., *Gay and Lesbian Poetry in Our Time*
1989 Michael Klein, ed., *Poets For Life*
1990 Michael Lassell, *Decade Dance*
1991 Assotto Saint, *The Road Before Us: 100 Gay Black Poets*
1992 Edward Field, *Counting Myself Lucky*
1993 James Schuyler, *Collected Poems,* and Michael Klein, *1990* (tie)

Assotto Saint, writer and publisher *(Copyright © 1987 by Robert Giard)*

The Literature of AIDS

For a listing of novels, poetry volumes, memoirs, anthologies, and essay collections of the subject of HIV/AIDS, see pp. 446–450.

Lesbian/Gay Lending Libraries

Blanche Baker Memorial Library and Archives (ONE, Inc.)
3340 Country Club Drive
Los Angeles, CA 90019
213-735-5252

Gerber/Hart Library and Archives
3352 N. Paulina Street
Chicago, IL 60657
312-883-3003

Pat Parker/Vito Russo Center Library
Lesbian and Gay Community Services Center
208 West 13th St.
New York, NY 10011
212-620-7310

Quatrefoil Library
1619 Dayton Ave., #105-107
St. Paul, MN 55104
612-641-0969

Stonewall Library and Archives
330 SW 27th St.
Fort Lauderdale, FL 33315

ANNUAL LESBIAN/GAY WRITING CONFERENCE

OutWrite, the lesbian, gay, bisexual, and transgendered writers' conference, is produced annually in Boston the first weekend in March by the Bromfield Street Educational Foundation, publisher of *Gay Community News*. Over two thousand writers, readers, booksellers, agents, and editors take part in sessions, workshops, readings, and roundtables. The 1995 conference featured keynote speakers Tony Kushner, Pulitzer-Prize-winning playwright, and Linda Villarosa, executive editor of *Essence* magazine. Cherrie Moraga delivered the Audre Lorde Memorial Lecture. For information on future conferences contact: OutWrite, 29 Stanhope Street, Boston, MA 02116.

LESBIAN/GAY WRITING AWARDS GIVEN BY THE PUBLISHING TRIANGLE

The Publishing Triangle is a dues-paying membership organization dedicated to the furtherance of lesbian and gay writing and publishing. In addition to organizing regular forums on writing and publishing and cosponsoring the Lambda Literary Awards, PT also presents the following three prestigious annual awards to lesbian and gay writers:

Robert Chesley Playwrighting Award: named for the first playwright to produce a full-length play on AIDS, Robert Chesley, who died of the disease. This award acknowledges playwriting that adds to lesbian and gay mythology. Cash prize of $1,000, one each to a lesbian and a gay man. By internal nomination.

Ferro-Grumley Award: named for novelists/lovers Robert Ferro and Michael Grumley, who both died of AIDS. This award recognizes excellence in lesbian and gay-themed writing. Cash prize of $1,000, one each to a lesbian and a gay man. By internal nomination.

Bill Whitehead Prize: named for the pioneering gay editor Bill Whitehead, who died of AIDS. This prize honors lifetime achievement for a body of work with significant lesbian or gay content. Cash prize of $1,000, given in alternate years to a lesbian and a gay man. By internal nomination.

For more information about The Publishing Triangle, write to them at P.O. Box 114, Prince Street Station, New York, NY 10012. A one-year membership, which includes a newsletter subscription, is $30.

FUNDING AND ASSISTANCE FOR WRITERS WITH AIDS

PEN American Center's Fund for Writers and Editors with AIDS offers small grants and interest-free loans under $1,000 to individuals facing unanticipated financial emergencies. Applications are accepted year-round and reviewed every six weeks. Decisions are confidential. For application forms and guidelines, contact Karen Hwa, Writers Fund, PEN American Center, 568 Broadway, New York, NY 10012, 212-334-1660.

Safe House, a project of the Publishing Triangle, preserves the manuscripts and papers of writers with AIDS. When a writer donates his or her work and its copyright to Safe House, the organization ensures that the writings are available for publication. If a publisher becomes interested in a writer's work posthumously, Safe House acts as a literary agent and represents the writer's best interest. This can be especially helpful if the writer's literary executor knows little about the publishing industry or might suppress writing about AIDS or homosexuality. For more information write: Publishing Triangle, P.O. Box 114, Prince Street Station, New York, NY 10012.

For free legal help with a will, HIV-positive writers can contact Volunteer Lawyers for the Arts, a national network of attorneys who provide pro bono assistance to low-income writers. For more information write to: Volunteer Lawyers for the Arts, 1 East 53rd St., New York, NY 10022 or call 212-319-2787.

SOURCE: *Poets and Writers Magazine*, January/February 1993.

PROFILE

Norman Wong

Norman Wong was born in Honolulu, Hawaii, in 1963. The son of Chinese immigrants, he grew up speaking Cantonese. Wong attended the Iolani School, and then later the University of Chicago, where he studied English literature. In 1989, he received his Masters in Creative Writing from Johns Hopkins University. Wong accepted his first teaching job in New York City at a drug rehab center. He continues to teach, at the prestigious Writer's Voice at the 63rd Street YMCA.

Growing up, Wong worked at the family-owned Chinese restaurant in Honolulu and some of this experience is reflected in his fiction. In New York, he has worked for several gay community institutions, including Gay Men's Health Crisis, American Foundation for AIDS Research, and Lambda Legal Defense and Education Fund, where he currently works in the development department and rubs elbows with another notable gay author, Peter Cameron (*One Way or Another, Leap Year, Far Flung, The Weekend*).

Norman Wong (*Photo by Jim Marks*)

Wong's stories have been published in many magazines and literary journals, including *Men's Style Magazine, Bakunin, The Asian Pacific American Journal, The Kenyon Review, The Threepenny Review,* and *The Little Magazine.* His first book, *Cultural Revolution,* was published by Persea Books in 1994.

Cultural Revolution is a collection of linked short stories about the Laus, an immigrant Chinese family living in Honolulu, Hawaii. The stories focus especially on Michael, the "number one son" who comes of age with the secret that he is homosexual.

Wong is currently at work on a novel, entitled *Children Warriors.*

PROFILE

Other Countries

For close to ten years, Other Countries has nurtured and promoted the literary voices of African-American gay men. Started as a writing workshop by Daniel Gar-

Members of Other Countries, a black gay men's writing workshop. *From left:* Kevin McGruder, Bert Hunter, Robert Penn, Eddie Nash, and Allen Wright. *(Photo by Candace Boyce)*

rett in June 1986, Other Countries has grown into a community institution that provides an ongoing workshop, creates regular performance opportunities, produces a quarterly newsletter, publishes literary journals, and offers an outreach and educational program to young African-American gay men, and others whose voices are frequently marginalized in the dominant gay culture.

Arguably New York City's longest-running gay workshop, Other Countries Workshop has met at 5 P.M. every Saturday night at the Lesbian and Gay Community Services Center since its first meeting in 1986. The workshop has provided critical peer review for a generation of nascent Black gay writers, as well as a safe environment in which to explore the complexities of a Black gay identity.

In the spring of 1988, Other Countries published its first literary journal, *Other Countries: Black Gay Voices*. This collection includes essays, poetry, plays, short fiction, and graphics of "love and eros . . . humor and pathos . . . alienation and brotherhood . . . politics and too seldom told histories." *Black Gay Voices* also features an interview with openly gay civil rights leader and organizer of the 1963 March on Washington Bayard Rustin.

Other Countries' second publication, *Sojourner: Black Gay Voices in the Age of AIDS*, appeared in the summer of 1993 and won the Lambda Literary Award that year for Lesbian and Gay Small Press Books. *Sojourner*, in the words of managing editor B. Michael Hunter, is a collective search "for ways to face the day after the wakes, the funerals, the memorials of yet another friend-lover-family member. This is a journal about those who are HIV positive, have AIDS, are Black, Gay, HIV negative, surviving or any combination of these and other identities—those we claim and those we don't."

The lists of Other Countries' participants and alumni reads like a literal Who's Who of Black gay men's writing. Contributors to the journals over the years include Melvin Dixon, Donald Woods, Craig G. Harris, Assotto Saint, David Warren Frechette, Roy Gonsalves, Cary Alan Johnson, Guy Mark Foster, B. Michael Hunter, Colin Robinson, Bil Wright, and Allen Wright. Prominent visual artists Lyle Ashton Harris and Mike Lee, as well as Emmy Award–winning filmmaker Marlon T. Riggs, have also contributed.

In the context of the ravaging AIDS epidemic, Other Countries' journals serve more than a literary function. *Black Gay Voices* and *Sojourner* are valuable historical documents that chronicle the life of a vibrant community under siege and forever memorialize the work of writers—established and emerging—who may not have had access to other venues for publication in their lifetimes.

The Other Countries collective has read and performed at the New York City Lesbian and Gay Community Services Center, the Studio Museum of Harlem, the Schomberg Center for Research in Black Culture, the NYC Public Library in Harlem, the Nuyorican Poets Cafe, B. Dalton, Tracks Disco, as well as at several universities. Its outreach and education program has performed and conducted workshops at City-As-School, the Harvey Milk High School, and the Hetrick-Martin Drop-In Center, and has participated in various African-American community cable television programs. Several members of Other Countries are featured in the films *Tongues Untied* and *Non, Je Ne Regrette Rien (No Regrets)*, by the acclaimed director Marlon T. Riggs.

PROFILE

Alyson Publications

In 1977, Sasha Alyson founded Alyson Publications in a room in his home in Boston. Alyson's goal was to distribute books and magazines from small progressive, feminist, and gay publishers. A short year later he realized that acting solely as a distributor for other publishers was too limiting; he had no control over the quality and appearance of the books, the pricing, or whether a brisk-selling book stayed in print. He decided to publish an occasional book under the Alyson imprint.

In September 1979, Alyson released its first publication: *Energy, Jobs and the Economy*. Six months later, in March of 1980, Alyson's second book and its first gay title reached the bookstores: *Young, Gay and Proud!*, a work which remains in print and continues to sell steadily. Three more titles were released that year, including *The Men with the Pink Triangle*, also still in print and one of Alyson's most enduring works.

In 1981, Alyson decided to specialize in titles with gay and lesbian themes. Since then, Alyson has been part of a small core of exclusively lesbian and gay publishers, providing a venue for many authors who otherwise might never have seen their words in print. In the last several years, as lesbian and gay writers have been accepted more and more by the mainstream, Alyson has concentrated on publishing work from underrepresented communities within the lesbian and gay community: bisexual men and women, African-American and South-Asian queers, lesbian and gay teachers, and the deaf queer community.

Like other lesbian and gay presses and like many lesbian and gay bookstores, Alyson Publications has served its community in more ways than one. In 1983, Sasha Alyson founded and began publishing *Bay Windows*, a news and arts-oriented weekly for Boston's growing lesbian and gay community. When publishing fifteen to twenty titles a year, distributing other publishers' books, and publishing a weekly newspaper grew to be too much too handle, Alyson sold *Bay Windows*. Now more than a decade old, the paper continues to provide excellent news and arts coverage and enjoys a wide readership in the Boston area.

Alyson has a long history of serving lesbian and gay teens. *Young, Gay and Proud!* was followed quickly by *Reflections of a Rock Lobster*, the story of Aaron Fricke, the nation's first gay teen to take his boyfriend to the high school prom. In 1983, editor Ann Heron's groundbreaking *One Teenager in Ten* appeared. A notice on the back of the book announced a free pen pal service for gay youth, the Alsyon Teen Letter Exchange. Through this service, gay, lesbian, and bisexual people under the age of twenty-one write to one another confidentially, sharing experiences, fears, knowledge. Still in operation, the Alyson Teen Letter Exchange has served close to ten thousand teens in its dozen years.

In 1987, Sasha Alyson grew impatient with the publishing industry's lack of response to the AIDS epidemic. For the next year, Alyson coordinated the publication of *You CAN Do Something About AIDS*, a can-do, accessible guide for people who want to respond to the AIDS crisis but don't know what to do. More than a million copies of the book, which contains suggestions from some fifty contributors, from local AIDS activists to national celebrities, have been distributed since 1988. *You CAN Do Something about AIDS* is still in print.

The 1990s saw two new Alyson imprints: Alyson Wonderland, which features books for the children of lesbian and gay parents, and Alycat, which features low-priced editions of popular titles. Under the leadership of the new director, Helen Eisenbach, and with the continued involvement of founder Sasha Alyson, Alyson Publications will continue to shed the light of the printed word on all aspects of lesbian and gay culture and community.

PROFILE

Jaime Manrique

Born in the coastal city of Barranquilla, Colombia, Jaime Manrique grew up loving books and movies better than reality. In his early teens he wrote poems and short stories that he tried to publish in Bogotá's newspaper. It was a great time for Colombian literature: Gabriel García Márquez had begun publishing his early novels; the elegant and eloquent controvertist Marta Traba dominated Colombian literary affairs; and the Nadaístas (a tropical version of the French existentialists) scandalized Colombian society by dressing entirely in black, and writing about drug addicts, homosexuals, and other outcasts. Manrique knew immediately that he wanted to join this company of authors.

When he was in the tenth grade, Manrique scored his first success as a writer. His play *In Whose Hands?*, a bleak existentialist drama, was performed in Barranquilla's Teatro de Bellas Artes. The performance was a scandal; it was written about and praised in the local press. The author was hooked.

In 1975, Manrique published a volume of poems, *Los adoradores de la luna*, which received Colombia's National Poetry Award. These poems, influenced by Sylvia Plath, Anne Sexton, and John Berryman, were written after Manrique's first, and catastrophic, love affair with a man. Next he published a novella, *El cadáver de papá*, which he wrote "to get even with his father" and which he describes as an attempt to do in fiction what Plath did in her famous "Daddy" poem.

Next came a collection of essays about the movies, *Confessiones de un crítico amateur*. In 1983, Manrique moved to Manhattan, where he published, in English translation, *Colombian Gold*, a political thriller about Colombian society. After the novel was published, it became unsafe for him to return to Colombia. Since then, he has considered the United States his home.

In the 1980s, Manrique began writing in English, although the next book, *Scarecrow*, a poetry chapbook, was published in a bilingual edition, with translations by Edith Grossman and Eugene Richie. In 1992 he published his first novel in English, *Latin Moon in Manhattan*. Since then, he has finished a young adult biography of Federico García Lorca, which is forthcoming from Chelsea House, and completed a collection of short stories and a novella, tentatively titled *To Love in Madrid*.

11. GAY MEDIA

Reporter Andy Humm interviews former New York Governor Mario Cuomo *(Photo by Roberta Raeburn)*

> *"Homosexuals, more than ever before, are out to win their legal rights, to end the injustices against them, to experience their share of happiness in their own way. If* The Advocate *can help in achieving these goals, all the time, sweat, and money that goes into it will be well spent."*
>
> —from the first editorial of *The Los Angeles Advocate,* 1967 (later *The Advocate,* now the largest gay magazine in the country)

The lesbian and gay press has shaped and reflected the rise of gay and lesbian liberation. The proliferation of gay and lesbian newspapers, newsletters, and magazines in the United States has allowed us to weave a well-informed network of previously isolated individuals and communities, empowering and unifying gay and lesbian people.

In 1924, Chicago's Society for Human Rights published two issues of the journal *Friendship and Freedom* before organizers were arrested on obscenity charges. Sadly, no copies of this first U.S. gay publication are known to exist in any collection, but several earlier European gay and lesbian periodicals have survived. Lisa Ben's *Vice Versa* appeared in 1947 as a typewritten, carbon-copied, and retyped newsletter passed hand to hand—the first lesbian periodical in the United States.

In the 1950s, homophile groups—the Daughters of Bilitis, the Mattachine Society, and ONE—built themselves into national organizations by defying U.S. law that prohibited homosexual publications from being distributed by mail. Although the Comstock Act was changed with *ONE*, Inc. vs. *Olesen* in 1958, many gay and lesbian publications, especially those dealing directly with gay/lesbian sexuality, have continued to face censorship and harassment from the U.S. Postal Service, U.S. Customs, local government, and religious and political groups.

As a national gay and lesbian community became united, a gay liberation movement emerged, symbolized most often today by the New York City Stonewall riots in June 1969. The *Los Angeles Advocate* (not *The Advocate*), *Gay Community News*, and *Fag Rag* all date from these days of gay liberation. In the 1970s and 1980s, feminist publications began addressing lesbian concerns. During the 1980s and into the 1990s, gay and lesbian activism restructured to address the AIDS epidemic. Armed with a bold, life-affirming, sex-positive analysis, gay and lesbian publications promoted safer sex practices for "queers," countering homophobic mainstream admonitions to celibacy, blame, and self-loathing. With the rise of groups like ACT UP, a brazen sensibility ascended that changed the face of the gay/lesbian press, and also impacted the mainstream press as never before. The practice of "outing" homophobic public figures who are themselves gay or lesbian began with an article exposing entrepreneur Malcolm Forbes in New York's *Out-Week* magazine (which published from 1989 to 1991), prompting intense coverage in the mainstream media.

Another phenomenon in late 1980s/early 1990s gay/lesbian publishing is the fanzine craze. 'Zines, as they are popularly known, are homemade, some desktop published, comics-like productions that are uniformly creative, irreverent, outrageous, and usually sexually explicit. Underground 'zine favorites, sold in bookstores and by subscription, include *Thing*, My *Comrade/Sister*, *Lana's World*, *BimBox, Pansy Beat, Homocore, JDs, and Taste of Latex*.

Recent years have also seen the proliferation of newsletters and journals from gay and lesbian people of color within the United States, especially African-Americans and Asian-Americans. The airing of these voices of the previously silenced makes sure that the debate over gay and lesbian rights or liberation is no longer limited to whites.

Despite the growth of the computerized indexing industry, the gay and lesbian press is still routinely excluded from mainstream periodical indexes. While articles about outing from *Newsweek, The Village Voice*, and the *National Review* can be found online, on disc, and with paper indexes, the original *OutWeek* article is not included in any periodical index. Similarly, critiques of HIV drugs and treatment programs in community-based gay/lesbian publications are ignored entirely by indexers, despite their undeniable value to doctors, researchers, students, and pharmaceutical industry, and HIV-positive people. Only one current periodical index, the *Alternative Press Index*, regularly includes a significant number of gay/lesbian titles. Under pressure from the American Library Association's Gay and Lesbian Task Force, however, Gale Research and Information Access Company began in

1991 to include five previously unindexed gay periodicals. Sadly, other publishers have refused to correct the bias in their indexing.

—POLLY THISTLETHWAITE AND DANIEL C. TSAN

Source: Reprinted with permission of R. R. Bowker, a Reed Reference Publishing Company, from "Magazines for Libraries," 7th Edition, © 1992, Reed Elsevier Inc. (Pages 680 and 681).

HISTORIC GAY/LESBIAN PUBLICATIONS

Photos from physique magazines, circa 1960s.

Friendship and Freedom

Published by the Chicago Society for Human Rights, which only produced two issues in 1924 before closed down by the police; produced by Henry Gerber.

Chanticleer

A mimeographed newsletter, started in 1934, again by Henry Gerber and Jacob Houser.

Vice Versa

The first American publication by and for lesbians, by Lisa Ben (an anagram of "lesbian"). In 1947–48, Lisa Ben typed the magazine in her spare time at work, making four carbon copies each of two originals, for a total of ten copies of each issue.

These were circulated among friends and friends of friends. She published a total of nine issues, which included poetry, short stories, editorials, reviews of plays, books, and films, and an annotated bibliography of novels of interest to lesbians.

ONE Magazine: The Homosexual Viewpoint

Founded in 1952, it was the first gay magazine in the U.S. to reach a wide audience (5,000 readers at its peak). The U.S. Postal Service did not want to allow mailings of it, and in 1958 ONE won a decision from the U.S. Supreme Court to be allowed through the mails, thus opening a venue for all gay/lesbian magazines. It ended publication in 1972.

The Mattachine Review

More restrained in its gay activism than ONE and somewhat more scholarly. Started in 1955, it folded in the mid-1960s when newer publications more accurately reflected an increasingly militant community.

The Ladder

Started in 1956, a monthly publication of the Daughters of Bilitis, the first American organization for lesbians; purposely kept nonpolitical, it aimed at "the lonely isolated lesbians away from big cities." It was the oldest continuously published gay periodical in the U.S. until it folded in 1972.

Vector

The magazine of the Society for Individual Rights, the leading gay advocacy group on the West Coast at the time. Started in 1964.

The Los Angeles Advocate (now known as The Advocate)

Founded in 1966 by Dick Michaels in response to being at a gay bar during a routine police raid. It quickly became and still is the country's most prominent gay publication.

POST STONEWALL STANDARDS, LATE 1960S, EARLY 1970S

Come Out! (NYC)
Body Politic (Toronto)
Gay (NYC)
Gay Community News (Boston)
Gay Sunshine (Berkeley)

The 1970s saw the rise of magazines and newsletters for more specialized or specific gay and lesbian audiences, e.g., religion, politics, or professions.

Also in this period was the rise of erotic publications and classified ads, for instance in *The Advocate* or in *Blueboy*. During this same period there was also the rise of scholarly publications, such as *Gay Books Bulletin* (1979–85) and the *Journal of Homosexuality* (1974–present).

The Gay and Lesbian Press Association was established in the late 1970s, and the National Lesbian and Gay Journalists Association was established in the late 1980s. (To reach the NLGJA in New York, call 212-629-2045.)

In the late 1970s and increasingly in the 1980s and '90s, there was a surge in "culture" magazines. For example, one of the first was published in 1976, *Christopher Street*, which had intentions of being the "gay *New Yorker*;" You can contact *Christopher Street* at P.O. Box 1475, Church Street Station, New York, NY 10008, 212-627-2120.

Today, in the mid-1990s, lesbian, gay, bisexual, and transgender/transsexual magazines, newspapers, and newsletters continue to proliferate both in North America and around the world at an unprecedented rate. As an example, the 1987 edition of the *International Directory of Gay and Lesbian Periodicals* listed 609 gay periodicals and 626 lesbian periodicals (please note that there is a great overlap between the two categories). Since that time, hundreds of new publications—from newsletters to 'zines to national glossies—have brought their lesbian, gay, bisexual, and transgendered perspective to the world.

FIRST PUBLISHED ESSAY ON HOMOSEXUALITY BY AN AFRICAN-AMERICAN

"Smoke, Lilies, and Jade" by Richard Bruce Nugent in *Fire!* in 1926. This was the first and only issue of a little magazine published by the self-named "Niggerati Manor," a small rooming house on 137th Street in Harlem, which was a center of creativity during the Harlem Renaissance and was home to gay/bisexual artists Langston Hughes, Wallace Thurman, and Bruce Nugent, among others. The magazine was meant to shock the public and Nugent's fiercely erotic tale of homosexual self-discovery was included to ensure that response.

AVANT-GARDE MAGAZINE PUBLISHED IN THE 1970S BY A GAY MAN

Interview, produced by Andy Warhol (now edited by lesbian Ingrid Sischy); 575 Broadway, New York, NY 10012, 212-941-2900

SOME CURRENT PUBLICATIONS BY AND FOR PEOPLE OF COLOR

Asians & Friends/New York, P.O. Box 6628, New York, NY 10163, 212-674-5064; monthly magazine for Asian and Pacific Islander gay men.
BG (New York)
Blackleather in Color (New York City)
BLK (Los Angeles)
Black/Out (published by the National Coalition of Black Lesbians and Gays)
COLORLife! (New York City)

Other Countries (New York); literary/arts journal for black gay men.
Paz Y Liberacion, P.O. Box 66450, Houston, TX 77266; quarterly newsletter featuring lesbian and gay news about Latin America, Asia, Africa, and Middle East.
Thing (Chicago)

THE FIRST LESBIAN/GAY NEWSPAPER TO APPEAR IN NEW YORK AFTER THE STONEWALL REBELLION

Come Out! (associated with the Gay Liberation Front) in 1969.

FIRST LESBIAN/GAY NEWS WEEKLY TO RUN A COPY OF THE FIRST COVER OF *COME OUT!* ON ITS FIRST COVER

OutWeek: New York's Lesbian and Gay News Magazine. A weekly magazine that began in June 26, 1989, published by Gabriel Rotello.

BISEXUAL MAGAZINES

Anything That Moves: Beyond the Myth of Bisexuality, a quarterly magazine (published by the Bay Area Bisexual Network); 2404 California St. #24, San Francisco, CA 94115, 415-564-2226.
Bisexuality: The North American Journal.
Bisexuality, P.O. Box 20917, Long Beach, CA 90801, 310-597-2799; bimonthly newsletter.

HOW HAS JOURNALISTIC LANGUAGE CHANGED OVER TIME IN TALKING ABOUT HOMOSEXUALITY?

One of the major successes of the gay movement in the 1960s was the breakthrough into mainstream publications. Although hardly flattering, the stories at least began to break the silence and invisibility surrounding gay and lesbian lives. Here is a selected timeline of homosexuality in the mainstream media:

1892: The word "lesbian" is first used in a newspaper article. It is in *The New York Times*, and the article is entitled "Lesbian Love and Murder," about Alice Mitchell's murder of Freda Ward. (Mitchell and Ward were teenagers who had exchanged rings, and when their parents discovered their relationship, they barred them from seeing each other. Mitchell claimed in court that the young lovers had made a pact to kill each other if they couldn't be together.)
1924: *The New York Times* first uses the word "homosexual." It is in a review of the book *The Doctor Looks at Love and Life*, by Dr. Joseph Collins, which included a substantial chapter on homosexuality.

1948: *Life* magazine publishes an article entitled "Test By Portraits: Pictures of Pathological Types Help Diagnosis of Mental Illness." Of course, two (of the sixteen) photographs are that of "homosexuals." The pictures included two types of each of the "major kinds of mental disturbances: the sadist, the homosexual, the hysteric, the depressive, the manic, the epileptic, the catatonic, and the paranoid." Oh, such company we keep!

The 1950s: *The New York Times* routinely uses the word "perverts" to describe homosexuals. Actual headlines include "Federal Vigilance On Perverts Asked," "126 Perverts Discharged: State Department Reports Total Ousted Since Jan. 1, 1951," and "Perverts Called Government Peril."

1955: *People Today*, a national magazine, provides sympathetic coverage of a gay organization. This was the first instance of positive reporting about gay issues by a mainstream news source. It was an article on the group that published *ONE* magazine, entitled "Third Sex Comes Out of Hiding."

1963: *The New York Times* publishes a large feature entitled "Growth of Overt Homosexuality Provokes Wide Concern: Condition Can Be Prevented or Cured, Many Experts Say; Conflicting Points of View Spur Discussion of Inverts." Although we're getting more "airplay," the notion of respect still has a long way to go.

1964: *Life* magazine publishes an unprecedented look at gay life, entitled "Homosexuality in America." Although mostly negative in its take, it did try to explain the homosexual underground to the mainstream society.

1969: The *Los Angeles Times* is boycotted for refusing to allow the word "homosexual" to appear in any advertising. Today, the paper has many openly gay reporters and editors, as well as a gay caucus that meets weekly.

1970: On the first Gay Pride Parade in New York City after Stonewall, *The Daily News* reports the following, on August 31, in an article entitled, "Cops Will Go 2 by 2 In the Dark of the City" (where Police Commissioner Howard Leary directed that policemen would no longer walk city streets alone after dark): ". . . more than 100 policemen were battling an unruly Greenwich Village crowd that included hundreds of homosexuals, hippies, and young militants. Seven policemen were hurt, including one who was knifed, and 18 persons were arrested. . . . The Greenwich Village ruckus followed a peaceful parade of some 350 homosexuals, members of the Gay Activists Alliance and the Gay Liberation Front, from Times Square to the Village."

1977: Harvey Milk is endorsed by the San Francisco *Chronicle*, a mainstream paper.

1978: *Time* magazine publishes a homophobic caricature of "Gay Bob," the world's first gay doll, showing him with false eyelashes, lipstick, rouge, and a limp wrist. They later apologized for reinforcing stereotypes.

1981: The first story to bring AIDS (though still unnamed as such) to the general public appears July 3 in *The New York Times*. It is entitled "Rare Cancer Seen in 41 Homosexuals."

1984: The *Wall Street Journal* begins using the word "gay" as an adjective.

1987: *The New York Times* begins using the word "gay" as an adjective.

1989: *The San Francisco Examiner* runs an unprecedented sixteen-day report entitled "Gay in America" detailing what it is like "to live as a gay or lesbian person in America 20 years after the Stonewall Riots knocked down the closet doors and forced the nation to confront its most virulently disliked minority." The *Examiner* interviewed thousands of people in the Bay Area and across the country to study gay and lesbian Americans, American society, and the often uneasy intersection between them.

1990: *The San Francisco Examiner* runs a long feature in its Style section on gay and lesbian dance clubs, featuring The Box, which it reported "attracts a dance-mad collection of blacks, whites, straights, gays, Asians, Hispanics, and more."

1992: Publisher of *The New York Times*, Arthur Ochs Sulzberger, Jr., announces that diversity will be a priority at the paper of record. By the end of the year, *The Times* has become a leader on reporting gay and lesbian issues, which has significant influence on other media.

• *Newsweek* runs a cover story entitled "Is This Child Gay? Born or Bred: The Origins of Homosexuality" discussing recent studies on the possible biological origin of homosexuality (e.g., Dr. Simon LeVay and his study of hypothalamus sizes, and the Bailey-Pillard study on gay male twins).

1993: *Newsweek* and *New York* magazine finally discover lesbians, each running a cover story on so-called "lesbian chic."

THAT SPECIAL SEASON

In January 1993, the inauguration of Bill Clinton and the quickly ensuing controversy over lifting the ban on gays in the military brought media attention on lesbian and gay issues to a new height. For a few weeks (if not months) we and some of our issues were on the lips of practically every newscaster, spin doctor, and dinner table expounder in the country.

In April 1993, again the media response to a gay and lesbian event was overwhelming—this time it was the 1993 March on Washington for Lesbian, Gay, and Bi Equal Rights and Liberation. One of the largest civil rights marches in history got the coverage it deserved with more than one hundred mainstream papers featuring it on their covers the next day.

UNDERGROUND 'ZINE FAVORITES

Thing
Lana's World
BimBox
Pansy Beat

Homocore
Taste of Latex
JDs (Juvenile Delinquents)

SOME PROMINENT GAY JOURNALISTS

Garrett Glaser, *Entertainment Tonight* reporter.
Edward Gomez, former senior editor of *Metropolitan Home;* has also written for *Time.*

Peter McQuaid, *Us* magazine senior editor; *OUT* magazine editorial board editor.

Adam Moss, *New York Times* editor.

Michael Musto, *Village Voice* columnist, "La Dolce Musto."

Max Robinson, broadcast journalist; first African-American network news anchorman; died of AIDS 1988.

Gabriel Rotello, former editor in chief of *OutWeek*; columnist for *New York Newsday*

Richard Rouilard, former senior editor at the *Los Angeles Herald Examiner* and executive editor of *The Advocate;* currently a senior editorial consultant at the *Los Angeles Times.*

Jeffery Schmaltz, a respected editor for *The New York Times;* covered the AIDS "beat"; died of AIDS 1994.

Randy Shilts, first openly gay reporter on a major U.S. newspaper (the *San Francisco Chronicle*); died of AIDS 1994.

Kevin Sessums, feature writer for *Vanity Fair.*

Michelangelo Signorile, columnist, *The Advocate, OutWeek,* and *OUT.*

Andrew Sullivan, editor of *The New Republic.*

Mark Thompson, former editor at *The Advocate*

Jeff Yarbrough, current editor-in-chief of *The Advocate.*

New Republic editor Andrew Sullivan (*photo by Ellen Neipris*)

The National Lesbian and Gay Journalists Association

Founded by Leroy F. Aarons, a former editor at the *Washington Post* and vice president of the Oakland *Tribune*, the NLGJA largely consists of lesbian and gay men who work in the straight media, although a growing number of members are from the gay and lesbian press. They hold regular conferences, publish a variety of informative pamphlets, and recently produced an employee guide to securing domestic partnership benefits at work. You can reach them at: National Lesbian Gay Journalists Association, 874 Gravenstein Highway South, Suite 4, Sebastopol, CA 95472. Phone: 707-823-2193. Fax: 707-823-4176.

Censorship in the Classifieds

For many years, many daily newspapers, including major papers such as the *Los Angeles Times* and the *Washington Post*, refused to run ads that contained the word "homosexual" or, later, "lesbian and gay." Today, the situation is better, but there are still battles around the country away from the major cities.

In 1970, ads for the movie *The Boys in the Band* were rejected from major daily papers in Chicago, San Francisco, and Boston. Ads were initially rejected by the *Los Angeles Times* and the *New York Daily News* but later ran.

In 1987, the *Seattle Times* barred PFLAG from publishing a meeting announcement unless it changed "lesbians and gay" to "homosexuals."

In 1988, a Dallas newspaper refused to run a Coming Out Day ad. Finally, the *Dallas Morning News* ran the ad, after Coming Out Day was over, but blacked out all the names—for fear that someone with a similar name would sue for libel.

In 1990, the *Wisconsin Green Bay Press-Gazette* refused to run ads for "gay and lesbian resources" and "hand-painted sweatshirts for lesbians." The case was taken to court by Lambda Legal Defense and Education Fund but was lost on appeal.

Gay and Lesbian Newspapers in the Twenty-Five Largest U.S. Cities

Atlanta, GA: *Etcetera, Southern Voice*
Baltimore, MD: *Baltimore Gay Paper, The Alternative, Woman's Express*
Boston, MA: *Bay Windows, The Guide, Sojourner, Gay Community News*
Chicago, IL: *Windy City Times, Outlines, Gay Chicago Magazine*
Cleveland, OH: *Gay People's Chronicle, Now Cleveland, What She Wants*
Columbus, OH: *Stonewall Union, Gaybeat*

Dallas, TX: *Dallas Voice, This Week in Texas*
Denver, CO: *Quest, Outfront*
Detroit, MI: *Metro* magazine, *Cruise*
Houston, TX: *The New Voice*
Indianapolis, IN: *Heartland, New Works News*
Kansas City, MO: *Alternative News*
Los Angeles, CA: *Lesbian News, Frontiers, Edge*
Miami, FL: *The Weekly News*
Milwaukee, WI: *The Wisconsin Light*
Minneapolis, MN: *Twin Cities Gaze, Equal Time, GLC Voice*
New York, NY: *Sappho's Isle, HX (HomoExtra), Parlee Plus* (Long Island), *LGNY, New York Native, Next*
Norfolk, VA: *Our Own Community Press, Out in Virginia*
Philadelphia, PA: *Philadelphia Gay News, Au Courant*
Sacramento, CA: *Mom, Guess What!*
St. Louis, MO: *St. Louis Lesbian and Gay News Telegraph*
San Diego, CA: *San Diego Update, San Diego Gay Times, Bravo, The Lesbian Press*
San Francisco, CA: *Bay Area Reporter, San Francisco Sentinel, Bay Times*
Seattle, WA: *Seattle Gay News, LRC Community News*
Washington, DC: *The Washington Blade*

CURRENT NATIONAL GAY/LESBIAN NATIONAL NEWS AND CULTURE MAGAZINES

The Advocate, 6922 Hollywood Blvd., 10th Floor, Los Angeles, CA 90028, 213-871-1225. Circulation: 200,000. First issue: 1967.

OUT, 110 Greene St., Suite 800, New York, NY 10012, 212-334-9119. Circulation: 100,000+. First issue: Summer 1992.

Ten Percent, 54 Mint St., Suite 200, San Francisco, CA 94103, 415-905-8590. Circulation: 83,000. First issue: Winter 1992.

Genre Magazine, 8033 Sunset Blvd., #261, Los Angeles, CA 90046, 800-576-9933 (subscription), 213/467-8300 (editorial). Circulation: 75,000. First issue: 1991.

A LANDMARK IN MAINSTREAM TV JOURNALISM

Mike Wallace's CBS Report, "The Homosexuals" aired nationwide on March 7, 1967.

HIGHLIGHTS IN MEDIA ADVOCACY

In 1974, in response to outrageous stereotyping, the National Gay Task Force got the Television Review Board of the National Association of Broadcasters to mandate that the Television Code's injunction that "material with sexual connotations shall not be treated exploitatively or irresponsibly" applied to homosexuals.

In the 1970s, there was Newton Deiter's Gay Media Task Force, which monitored television scripts for the networks.

In 1987, the Gay and Lesbian Alliance Against Defamation was created. It still organizes successful campaigns against stereotyping.

SELECTED LESBIANS AND GAYS WHO CAME OUT IN MAINSTREAM NEWSPAPERS

In 1973, Dr. Howard J. Brown, a former New York City health commissioner, on a front page article in *The New York Times*.

In 1975, Dave Kopay became the first professional athlete to come out; he did so in an interview for a series on gays in sports in the *Washington Star*.

In 1981, Martina Navratilova came out in an interview with the *New York Daily News*, making her the first big-time athlete to come out while still competing.

In 1982, Dan Bradley, the highest-ranking government official to date to do so, former head of the Legal Services Corporation, a federally funded agency, came out in an interview in the *New York Times*.

In 1987, U.S. Congressman Barney Frank came out in an interview in the *Boston Globe*, making him the first publicly elected person to a national office to come out voluntarily.

PROFILE

COLORLife!

COLORLife!: The Lesbian, Gay, Two Spirit and Bisexual People of Color Magazine published its premiere issue in October 1992, featuring on its cover a profile of activist, mother, and visionary Sandy Lowe, and an activist response to the Quincentennial of the arrival of Columbus, "500 Years of Occupation."

COLORLife! is produced by a collective of people of color who came together in March 1992. Some members of the collective were also members of the Lesbian and Gay People of Color Steering Committee (LGPOCSC), a New York City–based coalition of lesbian and gay people of color and anti-racist, progressive organizations. It quickly became apparent that a large majority of the LGPOCSC groups (between twenty-five and thirty) had their own newsletters and spent considerable resources in putting out their publications. Mariana Romo-Carmona, one of the founders of *COLORLife!* who was at the meeting, states, "We saw that there were many different smaller publications in the community because there really wasn't a central publication that met a broad range of people's needs. We decided our efforts would be more useful in producing one comprehensive newsletter or publication."

This was the birth of the Cairos Project, which is the name of the collective that produces *COLORLife!* Mariana explains the origin of the name, "*Karos* is a Greek word which means 'a decisive moment in time,' and we were convinced as a group that this was certainly a decisive moment in time for people of color communities."

One of the primary reasons for creating a publication like *COLORLife!* was a fierce commitment that each contributor's work was going to be looked at with respect and consideration. "A lot of journalists of color do not receive a minimum standard of respect at mainstream gay publications, which have predominately white staffs," Mariana noted. "In these venues, traditionally there has been no real development or support of individual writers of color, nor has there been a building or progression surrounding our issues in terms of journalism. We started *COLORLife!* with the philosophy that journalists of color were going to get an equal ground. That is, writers of color were not only going to be nurtured, but editors were also not going to question what they were saying."

As part of this "equal ground" philosophy, *COLORLife!* presents a series of regular sections, in each issue, including the following:

"Speaking for Ourselves," a listing of all people of color organizations in the metropolitan tristate area, with descriptions written by those organizations, including an uncensored expansion or focus on a few groups in each issue.

"Role Model," a personal feature that recognizes an individual's contribution to the community, from the well-known role models such as Audre Lorde to the perhaps lesser-known ones, such as activist attorney Angie Martell.

"International News," a feature greatly appreciated by the diverse readership, since in the various communities served by *COLORLife!* readers have identities that encompass many different geopolitical borders.

"Identity Politics," where well-known and emerging writers alike (such as Beth Brant and Mona Oikawa) speak their minds on the politics of being a person of color, particularly regarding the intersection of sexual orientation and race.

"Commentary," a series of critical articles analyzing political issues and situations of local, national, and international interest.

In addition to these regular sections (and letters and editorials), there are also art features and reviews of film, literature, dance, and music, as well as original poetry and fiction. In fact, *COLORLife!* has received and featured previously unpublished work by artists of stature such as Audre Lorde and Sapphire.

For a magazine that is "officially" based in New York City, *COLORLife!* has an exceptionally broad readership and support—drawing a national and international audience. Mariana notes, "We don't always have a consistent distribution internationally, but we know that it does get out there." For instance, during the 1994 Gay Games IV, people from all over the world were asking for copies of the publication at the people of color information booth. She adds, "The reason *COLORLife!* has a lot of international news, politics, and literature is that as lesbian and gay people of color we have something to say about the whole. And if one of our constituents says a subject is relevant to our communities, then we assume that it is." That's why, for instance, in the initial October 1992 issue, the collective ran a whole section on the five hundred years of occupation, otherwise known as the Quincentennial; that is also why the magazine provides a forum for the progressive deeds of nongay activists.

Future plans for the magazine include expanding the length and further increasing the production values. For instance, the first issues of *COLORLife!* were printed on newsprint; it is now printed on a better quality paper which lasts longer and thus will ensure a longer archival life. However, the collective is committed to ensuring that the quality of the content is everything it can be before they "go glossy." In the meantime, *COLORLife!* remains a quarterly publication, and one that is completely self-supporting (primarily through subscription and reader donations). Moreover, the collective has made a commitment not to accept advertising from tobacco and alcohol companies, since these products have ravaged so many lives in our various communities.

Another hallmark of *COLORLife!* is its production by a collective process. There is a commitment to gender parity in the collective, and Lidell Jackson and Mariana Romo-Carmona are the co–managing editors. The current editorial staff includes Vondora Corzen, Manny Torrijos, Adele Choo, Dale Ogaswara, and Lazerne. Art production is handled by Myrna Morales, and the production is handled by June Chan. "We are always open for people in the community to participate," states Mariana. "Anyone who wants to get involved is always welcome to come in and help."

For more information about getting involved with this publication, or for subscriptions, which are $15.00/year, write: *COLORLife!*, 301 Cathedral Parkway, Suite 287, Annex Building, New York, NY 10026.

To view all the issues of *COLORLife!*, you can check out your local university library (many around the country subscribe), or make appointments at the Lesbian Herstory Archives (in Brooklyn) or the Schomburg Center (in Harlem). The New York Public Library also subscribes to and catalogues *COLORLife!*

PROFILE

Les Simpson

A favorite in the underground 'zine world, whose influence can also be seen in such "upperground" gay publications as *OutWeek*, *OUT*, and *The Advocate*, *My Comrade/Sister* was the brainchild and one-man-band showpiece of downtown man-about-town (and part-time dragster) Les Simpson.

The first issue, proclaiming "Gay Lib" on the cover, came out in early 1988. It was a wild Xeroxed compendium of gay news, articles, humor, sex, drag queens, advice columns, recipes, centerfolds, and "photo novellas." The typefaces and cut-out photos were kitschy, campy, and catchy, and the 'zine's star quickly rose. In the fall of 1988, Les took lesbians into the fold and added *Sister* to the pages of *My Comrade* (in a very clever logistical move, *Sister* is the cover on one side of the magazine and *My Comrade* is the cover—upside-down—on the other). The dual 'zine proliferated throughout the late eighties and early nineties, and (sadly) published its last issue in the winter of 1994.

Here is Les's commentary on his experience publishing *My Comrade/Sister*, in an interview with lesbian culture vulture and 'zine fan Penny Perkins:

PP: What prompted all this *My Comrade* activity in the first place?
LS: I got into it initially simply because there was a need. Most of the mainstream gay journalism at the time was very dull and stagnate, and even worse, they were constantly emphasizing the negative. The gay press was just so *lugubri-*

Linda Simpson (Les Simpson) *(Photo by Michael Wakefield)*

ous, you know? In a sense, it was understandable, for it was a difficult atmosphere at the time—the AIDS backlash was at full force, and with the so-called Christian forces taking up the banner, gay people were being vilified left and right-wing, so to speak. But I felt there needed to be a vehicle that provided a more inspirational and more life-affirming forum for our community—especially a community in the midst of a health and civil rights crisis. And to get that inspirational, *joi de New Age* "feel" for *My Comrade*, I just played into the whole downtown, campy atmosphere.

PP: It seemed to have really struck a nerve.

LS: Yes, and what was surprising to me, it struck a nerve even for people who weren't involved with the whole drag queen, Wigstock, Alphabet City scene at that time.

PP: I guess you could say it was a *seminal* publication.

LS: Yeah, you go. But because *My Comrade/Sister* was born and bred in New York, it did get into a lot of influential hands. And I think it's even safe to say that it helped liven up gay journalism, in general.

PP: It did seem to be riding—or even spearheading—a new wave of gay journalism. *OutWeek* was definitely influenced by your publication, especially in its attempts to infuse humor in its pages.

LS: And now with the handful of glossy national magazines, especially *OUT* and *The Advocate*, there clearly is an influence of the 'zine style being exhibited in their design and photo spreads and various chatty, campy, bitchy, sexy tidbits.

PP: And their appropriation even goes so far as to recycle former 'zine publishers as special columnists, correct?

LS: To be sure. [Editor's note: Les now writes a column in *OUT* as his drag alter ego, "Star Chat with Linda."]

PP: So what were *your* influences in creating *My Comrade*?

LS: The biggest inspiration was the 'zine *R.O.M.E.*—chic, scandalous, seductive *R.O.M.E.* It was a one-man show of social commentary produced by journalist George Wayne, who writes for *Vanity Fair*. I was very intrigued with the idea of one person publishing their own magazine and it inspired me to try my hand at it.

PP: And were there other 'zine influences, too?

LS: Yes, there eventually was a loose, informal network of us. Some of my favorites were *J.D.s*, a Toronto-based fanzine for gay punks; *Thing*, from Chicago; *Bimbox*, also from Toronto; and *Fertile Latoya* and *Vaginal Cream Davis*.

PP: Well, with such underground stardom, such influence, and such marvelous company, why did it all end?

LS: *My Comrade/Sister* ended because eventually I became more involved with other things. And with the constant lack of money and manpower, it just became more and more difficult to get the issues out. You have to understand, it was completely a labor of love (and maybe a little lust)—I didn't have a computer, everything was hand-typed and hand-pasted, and plus I worked full-time to make a living. Frankly, I got burned out.

PP: Well, at least you didn't overstay your welcome on the pop culture radar screen—you left us still wanting more.

LS: Yes, for better or worse *My Comrade/Sister* was a cult magazine. It came out whenever it came out—it didn't have a "production schedule," it was more like a "debt schedule"—but that was part of its charm. But to run an operation like that—off the cuff, whenever the resources appear—year after year is difficult.

PP: What were some of the other things you got involved with?

LS: For one, in late 1993, I was approached by Michael Goff to do a column for *OUT* magazine, written by my alter ego—Linda Simpson.

PP: Did you have any anxiety dreams about "selling out," gay style?

LS: Not as many as you might think. A lot of the attitudes and style behind the whole 'zine culture have become much more a part of the gay mainstream print media. You know, you can paddle water on the edges forever or you can sink or swim in the mainstream; it's America, and we're programmed to seek mainstream approval, to get bigger and better. So when the time came, I didn't have much trouble making the leap.

PP: Are you implying that Linda and Les have found fame and fortune in new venues?

LS: Please. I'm still working full-time in offices—mostly freelancing in the art departments of magazines—and I'm also working at nightclubs to pick up extra change.

PP: And what were the origins of your alter ego, Linda?

LS: Linda was really developed on the stage at the Pyramid [in New York City]. Linda's persona expanded when I started Channel 69—a gay drag cabaret that was seminal (to use your word) in the drag world. I'm still working the club scene, but certainly not as much.

PP: Besides "Star Chat With Linda" in *OUT*, what else have you been working on?

LS: Currently, I'm very involved with *Party Talk*, a gay and lesbian entertainment show that appears on cable in New York, Los Angeles, San Francisco, Atlanta, and Miami. I'm one of the cohosts. In general, most of my extracurricular energy has been going into the *OUT* column and *Party Talk*.

PP: And what does the future hold for Linda/Les?

LS: Well, I'd like to concentrate on writing, but I've also been moving in the direction of television. I've been on *Donahue* and some other talk shows; so that's an interesting and new avenue to explore. In some ways, my aspirations are to become a UBMP—a Ubiquitous Bold Media Personality—and not to just acquire fame and feel fabulous about myself, but to break some barriers and stereotypes. The real reason to acquire fame in this culture is for the power that goes along with it —because when you are in that position, when you are in the public spotlight, you can advocate beliefs that are not in the mainstream.

PP: In that case, the ideas and philosophy that inspired *My Comrade/Sister* could live on in a more widely accessible forum?

LS: Exactly. And, in the meantime, I'm still doing temp work and working nights at the Palladium.

PP: As a UBWS?

LS: Yes, a Ubiquitous Bold Working Stiff.

PROFILE

Gabriel Rotello

Gabriel Rotello, a former music industry professional, founded *OutWeek* magazine in June of 1989, and was editor in chief for its two-year existence.

"I had joined ACT UP," he explains about the birth of the magazine, "and watched as it unfolded into this whole new wave of activism. It was very exciting, but sadly ACT UP's work was not being represented in the New York gay press (which at that time was only *The Native*). It was ironic and scandalous that ACT UP's actions were covered in the mainstream press but not New York's only gay paper. *The Native* actually had a blackout policy on ACT UP."

Pondering this situation, it occurred to Gabriel one day while walking on Eighth Street, that a new publication was needed which would actively reflect what was going on in the world of gay activism and culture. He soon found entrepreneur Kendall Morrison as a backer. Morrison owned Dial New York and Dial Boston, gay male phone sex lines, and was looking for an advertising outlet. After procuring additional investors, the operation was up and running, with the first issue hitting the streets during Gay Pride weekend 1989.

OutWeek published for exactly two years, folding on Gay Pride weekend in 1991. During its brief but influential life span, the magazine managed to incite just about every human emotion possible from its vociferous and tenacious supporters and detractors—and spawned the practice which became known as "outing" to boot.

Gabriel actually left the magazine about a month and a half before it folded—a demise that was quick and rather ignominiously played out in a series of very public feuds and falling outs. After leaving *OutWeek*, Gabriel began writing for other publications, including *The Village Voice*, but primarily *New York Newsday*. At first, he wrote articles and occasional columns, but he was later hired to write a regular column. Gabriel's op-ed column, called "City Scape," generally focuses on lesbian and gay and AIDS issues, although not exclusively. For example, recently he penned a column about the Oklahoma City bombing. His column, which is generally political, appears every Thursday, and is distributed nationally on the Los Angeles and Washington Post network wire services.

In addition to "City Scape," Gabriel has also written stories on the AIDS crisis for *OUT* magazine, and within the last six months has been writing for *The Advocate*'s "Last Word" column, an activity he shares with three other columnists. Other publications that have sought out his commentary include *The Nation* and *New York* magazine.

Currently, Gabriel's main project is his forthcoming book, tentatively titled *Sexual Ecology: The Birth of AIDS and the Destiny of Gay Men*. The book charts how the AIDS epidemic spread within a gay male context, focusing on the epidemiology of the crisis. Characterizing the AIDS epidemic for gay men as an epidemic of large-scale multipartnerism, the book will review what Rotello believes are mistakes activists made in responding to the crisis and will make suggestions about how to fix past errors and get the AIDS epidemic under control. The book will be published by Dutton sometime in mid-1996.

Before embarking on his career as a journalist, Gabriel had been in the entertainment industry in a variety of capacities including keyboard player, jingles writer, and producer and director of various musical projects. He was also an impresario on the New York nightclub scene, producing and promoting club nights at places such as the Limelight, the Tunnel, and the Palladium in their heyday.

12. GAYS AND THE MILITARY

"If elected, I would reverse the ban on gays and lesbians serving in the United States Armed Forces. Every patriotic American should be allowed to serve their country, regardless of sexual orientation."

—presidential candidate BILL CLINTON, 1992

Clinton had the right idea, but unfortunately he bowed to pressure from both the Pentagon and the U.S. Congress. His compromise measure—popularly referred to as "don't ask, don't tell"—was nothing more than a continuation of the half-century–old ban against gays and lesbians in the military, with two new stipulations: commanding officers could not ask subordinates or recruits questions about their sexual orientation, and service members should not come out of the closet.

Gay men and lesbians have always served in the military of the United States and other countries, and served with distinction and honor. The military has provided an avenue by which less privileged Americans could gain access to the education and job training often unavailable to them in the civilian sector.

Lesbians have been the most vulnerable to discharge, experiencing investigation and discharge three times more often than men. The armed forces remain the bastion of "manhood," and women who want to serve can be immediately suspect.

The question is, shouldn't all service members—regardless of their sexual orientation—be allowed to serve *openly*, without fear of discharge based on status rather than on conduct?

TIMELINE OF GAYS IN THE U.S. MILITARY

1778: Baron Frederich von Steuben, one of Europe's greatest military minds and a homosexual man, is engaged to train and discipline the disparate armies of the thirteen rebellious American colonies.

  • After being discovered in bed with a private, Lieutenant Gotthold Frederick Enslin becomes the first known soldier to be dismissed from the U.S. military for homosexuality.

1916: Punishment of homosexual soldiers is first codified in American military law. The Articles of War, which take effect the following year, include "assault with the intent to commit sodomy" as a capital crime.

1919: A revision of the Articles of War of 1916 includes the act of sodomy itself as a felony.

  • Dispatching a squad of young enlisted men to act as decoys, the U.S. Navy initiates a search for "sexual perverts" at the Newport (Rhode Island) Naval Training Station. Based on information the plants gather, twenty sailors and sixteen civilians are arrested on morals charges by naval and municipal authorities. This is the first known attempt to purge homosexuals from the military.

1920s–1930s: Homosexuality continues to be treated as a criminal act, and thousands of gay soldiers and sailors are imprisoned. The military's move to transform homosexuality from a crime to an illness does not take place until the massive mobilization of World War II.

1941–1945: Nearly ten thousand enlisted people receive dishonorable "blue discharges" for homosexuality from the armed forces, so-called because they are typed on blue paper.

1942: The Armed Forces release the first regulations instructing military psychiatrists to discriminate between homosexual and "normal" service members. Those who "habitually or occasionally engaged in homosexual or other perverse sexual practices" are deemed "unsuitable for military service."

1943: Final regulations are issued banning homosexuals from all branches of military service. These have remained in effect for the last fifty years, with only slight modifications.

1950: The U.S. Congress establishes the Uniform Code of Military Justice (UCMJ), which sets down the basic policies, discharge procedures, and appeal channels for the disposition of homosexual service members.

UNIFORM CODE OF MILITARY JUSTICE

Subchapter X, Section 925, Article 125(a): "Any person subject to this chapter who engages in unnatural carnal copulation with another person of the same or opposite sex or with an animal is guilty of sodomy. Penetration, however slight, is sufficient to complete the offense."

1957: A 639-page Navy report—called the Crittenden Report for the captain who headed the committee—concludes that there is "no sound basis" for the charge that homosexuals in the military pose a security risk. The Pentagon denies the existence of this report for nearly twenty years.

• Federal courts rule that military personnel may appeal military court decisions to civil courts. This allows lesbians and gay men discharged for homosexuality to appeal to civil courts.

1966: Gay groups stage the first demonstrations protesting the treatment of lesbians and gays in the military.

1975: After being dismissed for homosexuality, Sgt. Leonard Matlovich sues the Air Force to be reinstated. Matlovich is thrust into national attention when he is featured on the cover of *Time* magazine with the headline "'I Am a Homosexual': The Gay Drive for Acceptance." NBC subsequently makes a TV movie of his story. His suit drags on until 1980, when a federal judge orders Matlovich reinstated. Instead of re-entering the Air Force, Matlovich accepts a settlement of $160,000. Matlovich becomes a gay rights activist and dies of AIDS in 1988.

VIETNAM

Gay Anti-War Slogans, ca. 1969

SOLDIERS—MAKE EACH OTHER, NOT WAR
SUCK COCK TO BEAT THE DRAFT

Advice from a Draft Resistance Manual, ca. 1968
   The draft resistor movement of the Vietnam War era spawned many "gay poseurs"—heterosexual men who sought exemption from the draft by pretending to be gay, usually by employing blatantly stereotyped behavior. The following appeared in a draft resistance manual of the time, as a tactic to use during a draft board interview:

   Dress very conservatively. Act like a man under tight control. Deny you're a fag, deny it again quickly, then stop, as if you're buttoning your lip. But find an excuse to bring it back into a conversation again and again, and each time deny it and quickly change the subject. And maybe twice, no more than three times over a half-hour interview, just the slightest little flick of the wrist.

SOURCE: Randy Shilts, *Conduct Unbecoming*, St. Martin's, 1992.

1981: During the last week of the Carter administration, Deputy Secretary of Defense Graham Claytor issues a revision in his department's policy to state for the first time that "homosexuality is incompatible with military service." Though Claytor notes that this is not officially a change in policy, the revision is designed to make clear that homosexuality is grounds for discharge. The revision is implemented by the Reagan administration.

1986: Discharged lesbian drill sergeant Miriam Ben-Shalom wins a ten-year battle with the U.S. Army Reserves when a court orders her reinstatement.

1987: U.S. Naval Academy Midshipman Joseph Steffan, at the top of his class, is discharged six weeks prior to graduation because, when asked if he was gay, he answered honestly. Though a three-judge panel of the DC Circuit Court of Appeals rules in Steffan's favor in 1994 and orders his reinstatement, the government appeals the decision to a full panel of judges. In a major setback in early 1995, the full Court of Appeals upholds Steffan's dismissal.

1989: Members of Congress who support lifting the military ban release draft copies of two internal Pentagon reports that find homosexuals in the military pose no security risk and, in many cases, make better soldiers than heterosexuals.

1990: Sgt. Perry Watkins wins a ten-year court battle against the Army, which discharged him in 1981 for homosexuality. The courts find that the Army inducted Watkins and allowed him to re-enlist three times, knowing he was gay. Watkins eventually agrees to forgo re-entry in return for $135,000 in back pay, an hon-

CLAYTOR'S LEGACY

The following three sentences constitute Deputy Defense Secretary Claytor's 1981 revision of the military policy on homosexuality:

"Homosexuality is incompatible with military service. The presence in the military environment of persons who engage in homosexual conduct or who, by their statements, demonstrate a propensity to engage in homosexual conduct, seriously impairs the accomplishment of military missions. The presence of such members adversely affects the ability of the armed forces to maintain discipline, good order and morale; to foster mutual trust and confidence among service members; to insure the integrity of the system of rank and command; to facilitate assignment and worldwide deployment of servce members who frequently must live and work in close conditions affording minimal privacy; to recruit and retain members of the armed forces; to maintain the public acceptability of military service; and to prevent breaches of security."

orable discharge, and full retirement benefits. In the intervening years, Watkins has become an outspoken gay rights activist.

• ROTC cadet James Holobaugh is discharged from the corps on the grounds of homosexuality and ordered to repay his $25,000 scholarship.

1992: The General Accounting Office reports that almost seventeen thousand service men and women were discharged for homosexuality between 1981 and 1990, at a cost of $493,195,968 to replace them. GAO estimates that it would cost about $27 million to recruit and train replacements for the one thousand discharged in 1990 alone. In addition, the GAO finds that women were twice as likely as men to be investigated and dismissed.

• Presidential candidate Bill Clinton promises, if elected, to repeal the military's ban on gay and lesbian service members, because there is no legitimate justification for the exclusionary policy.

• The Navy Reserve Officers' Training Corps (ROTC) program creates a policy requiring midshipmen to sign an affidavit stating that they agree with the military's ban on homosexuals and will refund scholarship money if they are found to be gay.

1993

• *January*: President Clinton issues a Presidential Memorandum instructing Defense Secretary Les Aspin to develop by July of that year an "Executive Order ending discrimination on the basis of sexual orientation in determining who will serve in the Armed Forces." At the same time, Clinton issues an interim policy that preserves all existing restrictions on homosexuals in the military but ends the practice of questioning recruits about their sexual orientation.

- *April:* Secretary Aspin asks the Rand Corporation, a nonprofit research organization, to provide "information and analysis that would be useful in helping formulate the required draft executive order." Aspin also forms a fifty-member Defense Department Military Working Group to study the issue. Three weeks after its first meeting, the group recommends continuing the ban, with the sole change of instructing commanders not to ask soldiers or recruits about their sexual orientation.
- *March–July*: The Senate Armed Forces Committee, headed by Senator Sam Nunn (D-Ga.), holds public hearings to consider the ban.
- *May–July*: The House Armed Services Committee also conducts hearings. At both House and Senate hearings, the overwhelming majority of those testifying are service members opposed to lifting the ban.
- *July*: Secretary Aspin signs a directive adopting the April recommendation of the Military Working Group. One week later, the Senate and House Committees issue their "findings." Both recommend codifying Aspin's directive.
- *August*: The Rand Corporation releases its independent report, stating that "there is ample reason to believe that heterosexual and homosexual military personnel can work together effectively." The government buries the study.

RAND CORPORATION REPORT

In April of 1993, Defense Secretary Aspin commissioned the Rand Corporation, an independent nonprofit research organization, to study the issue of gays in the military. Though the Rand Corporation could find no justification for discrimination against homosexuals in the military, the Pentagon suppressed the report. The printed study, *Sexual Orientation and U.S. Military Policy: Options and Assessment,* is now available for $16.00, plus shipping and handling. Prepayment is required by check or money order. For more ordering information, contact Rand Corporation, Customer Service, 1700 Main Street, P.O. Box 2138, Santa Monica, CA 90407-2138, 310-451-7002.

- *September:* The House and Senate both pass legislation discouraging homosexual enlistment in the military, the language of which is tougher than Clinton's "don't ask, don't tell." The legislation would allow a future defense secretary to reinstate questioning of recruits about their sexual orientation. Within days, Clinton signs the measure with no fanfare and little public notice.

1994
- *March:* Lambda Legal Defense and Education Fund and the American Civil Liberties Union bring a lawsuit in federal court (*Able et al.* v. *USA*) on behalf of six lesbian and gay service members, the first direct constitutional challenge to the military's policy. The government immediately seeks discharge proceedings against some of the plaintiffs.

- *April:* Federal District Judge Eugene Nickerson grants the plaintiffs' preliminary injunction, preventing the military from initiating discharge proceedings while the case is active.

- *June:* U.S. District Court Judge Thomas S. Zilly orders the Army to reinstate Colonel Margarethe Cammermeyer to the National Guard. In his ruling, Zilly holds unconstitutional the old version of the military ban barring service by lesbians and gay men. Colonel Cammermeyer, a twenty-seven-year veteran of the Army and National Guard, and chief nurse of the Washington State National Guard, was discharged from the military in June 1992 after she disclosed her sexual orientation during an interview for top security clearance.

1995: "Don't ask, don't tell" is challenged in a number of appeals courts, with some victories and some losses for gays in the military, including:

- *January:* A three-judge panel of the U.S. Court of Appeals upholds the preliminary injunction and directs the trial court to issue its ruling on *Able v. USA* by March 31, 1995.

- *March:* On March 13, the trial begins for *Able v. USA*. On March 30, Judge Nickerson declares the military's "don't ask, don't tell" policy unconstitutional; the government promises to appeal.

- *June:* A federal appeals court declines to block the discharge of Navy Lieutenant Paul Thomasson, who declared his homosexuality the day after the Clinton administration's "don't ask, don't tell" policy went into effect. The court cites that Thomasson refuses "to rebut the presumption that he would . . . engage in homosexual conduct."

Thanks to Lambda Legal Defense and Education Fund for assistance with the timeline.

Sources for Further Reading

Berube, Allan, *Coming Out Under Fire: The History of Gay Men and Women in World War II.* The Free Press, 1990.

Berube, Allan, and John D'Emilio. "The Military and Lesbians During the McCarthy Years." *Signs: Journal of Women in Culture and Society.* Summer 1984.

Cammermeyer, Margarethe, with Chris Fisher. *Serving in Silence.* Viking Press, 1994.

Dyer, Kate. *Gays in Uniform: The Pentagon's Secret Reports.* Alyson Publications, 1990.

Hippler, Mike. *Matlovich: The Good Soldier.* Alyson Publications, 1989.

Humphrey, Mary Ann. *My Country, My Right to Serve: Experiences of Gay Men and Women in the Military, World War II to the Present.* HarperCollins, 1990.

Murphy, Lawrence R. *Perverts by Official Order: The Campaign Against Homosexuals by the United States Navy.* The Haworth Press, 1988.

Shilts, Randy. *Conduct Unbecoming: Gays and Lesbians in the U.S. Military.* St Martin's Press, 1993.

Steffan, Joseph. *Honor Bound: A Gay American Fights for the Right to Serve His Country.* Random House, 1992.

How to Survive a Witch Hunt

If you're a service member being investigated for homosexuality, facing discharge, being threatened, or considering coming out, you aren't alone. There is confidential legal help available from the Servicemembers Legal Defense Network (SLDN). SLDN has issued the following guidelines for surviving a "witch hunt" if you are targeted by military investigators:

1. **Say nothing**, except to ask to speak to an attorney. Even if you want out of the service, saying the wrong thing could affect your discharge. Giving names of other servicemembers will not help you, no matter what military investigators tell you. Military investigators may say they are your friends, but they aren't.
2. **Sign nothing**. Even initialing something can waive your legal rights. Inform the investigators that you will show any papers they give you to your attorney, who can explain them to you.
3. **Get legal help**. SLDN (202-328-FAIR or SLDN1@aol.com) can assist you confidentially. A military defense attorney may also be able to help, but check to make sure if your conversations are covered by attorney-client privilege and if the attorney will keep what you say confidential. The Military Law Task Force in San Diego may also be able to assist you and can be reached at 619-233-1701.

Very important: There is no confidentiality with doctors and psychologists; they have been instructed to turn in gay service-members. Chaplains are supposed to keep secrets, but often do not. What you tell doctors, psychologists, chaplains, family members and friends can be used against you if they reveal your conversation with them. Don't trust anyone but your defense attorney. E-mail and online communications are not secure and can be used against you.

Source: Servicemembers Legal Defense Network. Reprinted with permission.

Webber, Winni S. *Lesbians in the Military Speak Out*. Madwoman Press, 1993.

Weinberg, Martin S. and Colin J. Williams. *Homosexuals and the Military: A Study of the Less Than Honorable Discharge*. Harper & Row, 1971.

Zeeland, Steven. *Barrack Buddies and Soldier Lovers: Dialogues with Gay Young Men in the U.S. Military*. Harrington Park Press, 1993.

The Vote on the Gay Military Ban in Congress, September 1993

Passed in Senate, 63 to 33.

	FOR BAN	AGAINST BAN
Democrats	25	30
Republicans	38	3

Passed in House, 301 to 135.

	FOR BAN	AGAINST BAN
Democrats	140	121
Republicans	161	13
Independent		1

TEXT OF CONGRESS'S MILITARY BAN

(1) Section 8 of Article I of the Constitution of the United States commits exclusively to the Congress the powers to raise and support armies, provide and maintain a navy, and make rules for the government and regulation of the land and naval forces.

(2) There is no constitutional right to serve in the armed forces.

(3) Pursuant to the powers conferred by Section 8 of Article I of the Constitution of the United States, it lies within the discretion of the Congress to establish qualifications for and conditions of service in the armed forces.

(4) The primary purpose of the armed forces is to prepare for and to prevail in combat should the need arise.

(5) The conduct of military operations requires members of the armed forces to make extraordinary sacrifices, including the ultimate sacrifice, in order to provide for the common defense.

(6) Success in combat requires military units that are characterized by high morale, good order and discipline, and unit cohesion.

(7) One of the most crucial elements in combat capability is unit cohesion, that is, the bonds of trust among individual service members that make the combat effectiveness of a military unit greater than the sum of the combat effectiveness of the unit members.

(8) Military life is fundamentally different from civilian life in that—

(a) The extraordinary responsibilities of the armed forces, the unique conditions of military service, and the critical role of unit cohesion, require that the military community, while subject to civilian control, exist as a specialized society; and

(b) The military society is characterized by its own laws, rules, customs, and traditions, including numerous restrictions on personal behavior, that would not be acceptable in civilian society.

(9) The standards of conduct for members of the armed forces regulate a member's life for 24 hours each day beginning at the moment the member enters military status and not ending until that person is discharged or otherwise separated from the armed forces.

(10) Those standards of conduct, including the Uniform Code of Military Justice, apply to a member of the armed forces at all times that the member has a military status, whether the member is on base or off base, and whether the member is on duty or off duty.

(11) The pervasive application of the standards of conduct is necessary because members of the armed forces must be ready at all times for worldwide deployment to a combat environment.

(12) The worldwide deployment of United States military forces, the international

responsibilities of the United States, and the potential for involvement of the armed forces in actual combat routinely make it necessary for members of the armed forces involuntarily to accept living conditions and working conditions that are often spartan, primitive, and characterized by forced intimacy with little or no privacy.

(13) The prohibition against homosexual conduct is a longstanding element of military law that continues to be necessary in the unique circumstances of military service.

(14) The armed forces must maintain personnel policies that exclude persons whose presence in the armed forces would create an unacceptable risk to the armed forces' high standards of morale, good order and discipline, and unit cohesion that are the essence of military capability.

(15) The presence in the armed forces of persons who demonstrate a propensity or intent to engage in homosexual acts would create an unacceptable risk to the high standards of morale, good order and discipline, and unit cohesion that are the essence of military capability.

QUICK FACTS ABOUT GAYS IN THE MILITARY

- Since 1943, approximately 100,000 gay men and lesbians have been discharged from the U.S. military.
- In the past decade, at least one joint chief of staff was gay, and gay people have served as generals in every branch of the armed forces.
- Gay discharges increased dramatically during the Carter administration.
- From 1980 to 1990, white women accounted for 6 percent of all military personnel and 20 percent of all those discharged for homosexuality.
- There were more discharges for homosexuality in 1980 than at any other time since the McCarthy era.
- Canada lifted its ban on gays in the military in 1992, with no lowered morale or impaired unit cohesiveness.
- Of the sixteen members of NATO, only the United States and Great Britain ban lesbians and gay men from military service.

SOURCE: *Gay and Lesbian Stats*, ed. by Bennett I. Singer and David Deschamps. Copyright © 1994 Bennett I. Singer and David Deschamps. Reprinted by permission of The New Press.

IMPORTANT LEGAL CASES AFFECTING GAYS IN THE MILITARY

The United States military is the single largest employer in the country; it provides many people with the opportunity for jobs, education, and other benefits. For individuals from poor communities, the military offers one of the few doors to a better future. By closing that door to a select class of individuals, thereby excluding

Plaintiffs in *Able* v. *U.S.A.* (*Photo by Denny Lee*)

them from the many opportunities the military provides, the ban against lesbians and gay men in the military violates our country's most basic democratic principles, as well as our Constitution.

Despite efforts to package the latest version of the ban as a change in policy, "don't ask, don't tell" does not allow lesbians and gay men to serve openly or honestly in the military. In order to serve, lesbians and gay men must continue to deny their true identities, and, when found out, face expulsion.

The following case studies are excerpted with permission from the *Lambda Update*, the triannual publication of Lambda Legal Defense and Education Fund.

CASE HISTORY: *STEFFAN* V. *ASPIN*

In early 1995, the D.C. Circuit Court of Appeals issued a ruling in sharp disagreement with a 1994 decision by a three-judge panel which had articulated so beautifully the constitutional flaws of the military's ban on service by lesbians and gay men. The full court's ruling upholds the determination to deny Joseph Steffan his diploma and his commission as an officer because, six weeks before he was due to graduate from the Naval Academy, he answered honestly when asked whether he was gay.

The lengthy opinion, with which seven of the court's judges agreed and from which three dissented, employs the definitional twists and contortions that the government uses to justify a ban on service by lesbians and gay men. In this manner, a case which is actually about a young midshipman who was asked about his sexual orientation is transformed by the court to be one about the military's right and ability to regulate the "conduct" of its soldiers. Because this case concerns the old version of the military ban, the decision will not be appealed. The battle against the government's discrimination against lesbians and gay men in the military will continue in the case known as *Able* v. *U.S.A.* in New York Federal Court.

CASE HISTORY: *CAMMERMEYER* V. *U.S. ARMY*

On June 1, 1994, U.S. District Court Judge Thomas S. Zilly ordered the Army to reinstate Colonel Margarethe Cammermeyer to the National Guard. In his ruling, Zilly held unconstitutional the old version of the military ban barring service by lesbians and gay men.

Colonel Cammermeyer, a twenty-seven-year veteran of the Army and National Guard, and chief nurse of the Washington State National Guard, had been discharged from the military in June 1992 because she was a lesbian. Cammermeyer disclosed her sexual orientation during an interview for top secret security clearance.

An administrative board composed of fellow colonels concluded it was their "sad duty" to recommend her discharge based on the Army's regulation, despite her outstanding record. Among many other honors, Cammermeyer received a Bronze Star for her service in Vietnam and was selected as the 1985 Veterans Administration Nurse of the Year.

The Army immediately appealed Judge Zilly's June 1994 decision and petitioned the Ninth Circuit Court of Appeals to stay Colonel Cammermeyer's reinstatement pending the results of the appeal. The Army's request for a stay was defeated and Cammermeyer has returned to work.

Cammermeyer's story is told in the book, *Serving in Silence,* cowritten by Cammermeyer and Chris Fisher, and published by Viking Press. Her successful struggle against the military ban was featured in a television movie produced by Barbra Streisand and starring Glenn Close as Cammermeyer and Judy Davis as Cammermeyer's lover, Diane.

COUNTERING MYTHS ABOUT GAY AND LESBIAN SERVICE MEMBERS

We've all heard them: the rumors, myths, and lies about the effect lifting the military ban against gay people would have on the armed forces. Here are some sample responses, which you can use to talk back to bigots.

Myth: Integration based on sexual orientation is not similar to integration based on race because race is a nonbehavioral characteristic while sexual orientation indicates a changeable behavior.
Answer: Whether or not sexual orientation is a biological or behavioral characteristic is a constant issue of scientific study, with several recent studies indicat-

ing that there may be a biological link. Regardless of the cause of sexual orientation, many of the arguments used in 1948 during the debate about integration by race were actually based on the ideas that African-Americans engaged in different behaviors than white Americans and that those behaviors would be disruptive to the effectiveness and morale of the military. The stereotypes invoked in 1948 were proven false and integration based on race was implemented. The stereotypes invoked this year are similarly false.

Myth: Military readiness would be hurt by allowing gays in the military.
Answer: Gay men and lesbians are already in the military—tens of thousands of them. They serve at all levels of the armed forces, including in the Pentagon. No one argues that they don't. They served bravely in Operation Desert Storm and are serving in Somalia. The military ban prevents them from serving their country openly.

Myth: Given the special environment of the military, the presence of openly gay and lesbian service members invades the privacy rights of heterosexuals in the foxholes, showers, and sleeping quarters.
Answer: These comments are based on the stereotype that gay people cannot control their sexuality. Gay and lesbian service members are in all those places today, and are behaving themselves appropriately. The penalties for inappropriate sexual behavior, whether by gays or heterosexuals, are the same and are already in effect. Repealing the ban does not alter these regulations. The most similar civilian situation is that of fire and police departments which must often sleep, live, and work in close quarters. The GAO study from June 1992 indicates that those agencies that have ended previous employment bans on gay officers "have not experienced any degradation of mission associated with these policies. Most department officials did not identify major problems related to retaining homosexuals in a work force."

Myth: Straight service members would have to fear sexual harassment and sexual overtures by openly gay and lesbian troops.
Answer: Sexual harassment is already prohibited through military codes of conduct. In recent years, we have seen that heterosexual servicemen have sexually harassed military women and violated many codes of conduct. The Tailhook incident shows that military leaders have often been slow to discipline troops who violate those codes. Instead of fearing the unsupported potential of sexual harassment and misbehavior from openly gay and lesbian troops, military leaders should enforce the current policies fairly, regardless of the sexual orientation of the perpetrators or the victims.

Myth: The presence of gay service members will increase AIDS in the military and make blood transfusions in combat highly risky.
Answer: AIDS is permeating all sectors of American society, and HIV does not discriminate. The spread of HIV among recruiting-age American men and women is growing rapidly, as a result of failure to educate about the risks and self-protection measures involved with HIV. The Department of Defense al-

ready has a strict HIV testing and screening policy and bars new recruits with HIV. The number of service members with HIV has remained fairly level from year to year at about five hundred.

Regarding blood transfusions, the reliance on battlefield transfusions has been historically very low. Instead, the military relies on blood that has been previously stored. Service members with HIV are not placed in deployable units.

Myth: Recent incidents indicate that violence against gay men and lesbians will increase in the military if the ban is lifted and they serve openly.
Answer: The Joint Chiefs of Staff and senior military leaders are responsible for the discipline and conduct of the troops. It should concern the U.S. public if military leaders cannot control the actions of their well-armed troops. If heterosexual service members act out their bigotry through violence against gay fellow service members, military leaders must swiftly discipline the offenders. The Joint Chiefs of Staff plus other senior military leadership must speak out as loudly against anti-gay violence by bigoted troops.

Myth: The military is no place for a "social experiment," and we should respect heterosexual military members who don't want to serve with gays.
Answer: This is not a social experiment. In fact, gay men and lesbians already work, live, and even, in school and sport situations, shower side by side with heterosexuals throughout society. And gay men and lesbians are in the military. Discrimination is wrong and the anti-gay policy should be repealed. The military is no place for bigoted service members who cannot cooperate and work with fellow Americans, gay or straight, who wish to serve their country.

Myth: The sexual practices of gay men and lesbians should not be permitted in the military.
Answer: Current military regulations prohibit many private sexual activities that heterosexuals engage in as frequently as gay men and lesbians. Those codes of conduct must be either revised to reflect the reality of individual sexual behavior, or must be enforced across the board regardless of sexual orientation.

Myth: If the ban were lifted, men would dance with men in officers clubs and women would hold hands with other women on bases.
Answer: The military already has regulations prohibiting open displays of affection while in uniform. This policy would not change if the ban were repealed, and gay and lesbian service members would be required to follow the same policies as heterosexuals. However, gay and lesbian service members would have the right to engage in behavior permissible for heterosexuals. Repealing the ban would end discrimination and allow gay and lesbian service members to serve their country openly and with honor.

Myth: Many other countries prohibit homosexuals from serving in the military.
Answer: Among NATO allies of the United States, only Great Britain has an explicit policy barring gay and lesbian service members, as in the United States.

In 1992, both Canada and Australia successfully lifted their anti-gay bans. The world-renowned Israeli military doesn't ban gay and lesbian service members.

Myth: Even if the ban were lifted, gay and lesbian service members should be segregated from straight service members.
Answer: Segregated forces are unacceptable and unnecessary. Gay and lesbian service members already do serve side by side with heterosexual troops. Enforcing current codes of conduct and instilling a sense of respect for fellow service members, regardless of sexual orientation, is what is necessary to maintain good order and discipline in the troops.

This list was adapted from information provided by the National Gay and Lesbian Task Force. The Military Freedom Initiative of NGLTF challenges the anti-gay discriminatory policy of the U.S. Department of Defense. For further information, contact the Military Freedom Initiative at 202-332-6483.

"It is time to shift the focus from status to misconduct. There are thousands of cases of sexual misconduct that have gone unresolved, while our military has spent nearly half a billion dollars separating sixteen thousand lesbians and gay men."

—SENATOR EDWARD KENNEDY (D-Mass.), 1993

NATIONAL ORGANIZATIONS DEALING WITH LESBIAN/GAY MILITARY ISSUES

American Federation of Veterans, Suite 811, Veterans Hall, 346 Broadway, New York, NY 10013, 212-349-3455.
Gay and Lesbian Military Freedom Project/National Gay and Lesbian Task Force, 1734 14th St., Washington, DC 20009, 202-332-6483.
Gay, Lesbian, and Bisexual Veterans Association of America, 1350 North 37th Place, Milwaukee, WI 53208. Phone: 414-342-6543. Fax: 414-933-6233.
Lambda Legal Defense and Education Fund, 666 Broadway, 12th floor, New York, NY 10012, 212-995-8585.
Pallas Athena Network, P.O. Box 1171, New Market, VA 22844, 703-740-3966.
Servicemembers Legal Defense Network, P.O. Box 53013, Washington DC 20009, 202-328-3244.

VETERANS' HIV NEWSLETTER

If you're a veteran or service member, you can receive a free subscription to "Positive Forces Newsletter," which deals with HIV issues. Send your name and address via e-mail to Kpollanen@aol.com.

13. GAY PERFORMING ARTS

Musical group,
Y'All *(Photo by
Dave LeFave)*

*"Test out a dangerous idea, a theme that threatens to destroy one's whole value
system. Treat the material in a madly farcical manner without losing the serious-
ness of the theme. Show how paradoxes arrest the mind. Scare yourself a bit along
the way."*

—from "Manifesto," axioms to a theater for ridicule, by Charles Ludlam

It is no secret that gay men have always found a home in theater and performance, though in the past few spoke openly of their sexual orientation. Perhaps
our draw to the performing arts comes from years of "acting" straight in a society
that discourages a true performance of self. The Who's Who of the performing arts
has always been a roster of who's queer in America.

But in the last few decades, there has been a mini-explosion of openly gay performers who use gay material. From drag shows to HBO comedy specials, from
disco to modern dance, from cabaret to classical compositions, gay performance

DID YOU GET THE PHONE NUMBER OF THAT SEX ALIEN?

"In many ways, the lesbian and gay fascination with science fiction and alien life is related to the desire for a third gender, neither male nor female. For much of his career, for example, David Bowie presented himself as just such a dually sexed alien, an identification that allowed him to play queer whether or not he was playing gay."

—from the program notes for In A Different Light, *an art exhibition at the University Art Museum at the University of California at Berkeley. David Bowie's album cover* Aladdin Sane (1973) *was included in the exhibition.*

From Yale Collection of American literature, Beinecke Rare Books and Manuscripts Library, Yale University. Unknown Newspaper, 1931–1993.

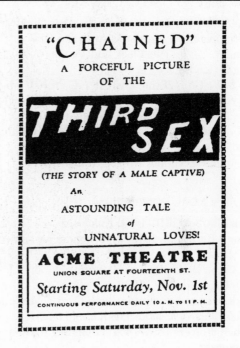

"CHAINED"

A FORCEFUL PICTURE OF THE

THIRD SEX

(THE STORY OF A MALE CAPTIVE)

An

ASTOUNDING TALE

of

UNNATURAL LOVES!

ACME THEATRE

UNION SQUARE AT FOURTEENTH ST.

Starting Saturday, Nov. 1st

CONTINUOUS PERFORMANCE DAILY 10 A. M. TO 11 P. M.

continues to reach new audiences and achieve mainstream acceptance never dreamed of by the Liberaces of the past.

GAY/BISEXUAL SINGERS/MUSICIANS

David Bowie, singer/actor
Boy George, pop singer
John Ellingham Brooks, gay pianist and briefly married to lesbian artist Romaine Brooks
Michael Feinstein, cabaret piano singer

Frankie Goes to Hollywood, pop group
Elton John, singer/songwriter
Leland Pettit, organist at Grace Church in NYC
Jim Morrissey (formerly of the Smiths), pop/rock singer
Jose Sarria, active in 1960s, "The Nightingale of Montgomery Street."
Jimmy Sommerville
Sylvester

MAINSTREAM CROSSOVER THAT WAS AHEAD OF ITS TIME

The Village People singing "YMCA" and "In the Navy." Their hit album Village People came out (so to speak) in 1977.

SOME BEST-SELLING GAY CDs IN SPRING 1995

Sensual Classics, Too, St. Paul Chamber Orchestra (Teldec/Warner)
Gay Happening 2, Eartha Kitty, et al. (ZYX)
Lavender Light, The Black and People of All Colors Lesbian and Gay Gospel
    Choir (LavLight)
Glad to Be Gay, Divine, Sylvester, Culture Club, et al. (Spy)
Glad to Be Gay 2, Pet Shop Boys, Bronski Beat, et. al. (Spy)
Deflowered, Pansy Division (Lookout)
Out in the Country, Doug Stevens and the Outband (Longhorn Productions)
All My Misery, Pussy Tourette (Feather Boa)
Gay Anthems, Various Artists (Almighty)

GAY/BISEXUAL COMPOSERS

Samuel Barber, 1910–1981, composer
Leonard Bernstein, 1918–1990, conductor and composer
Marc Blitzstein, 1905–1968, composer
John Cage, 1912–1992, avant-garde composer, lovers with Merce Cunningham
Aaron Copland, 1900–1990, composer, one of America's greatest composers
David Diamond, composer (both Carson McCullers and her gay husband Reeves
    McCullers were in love with him)
Stephen Foster, 1826–1864, composer, most popular pre–Civil War American
    composer
Jerry Herman, b. 1933, Broadway composer and lyricist
Ned Rorem, b. 1923, one of the greatest living composers of art songs
Stephen Sondheim, b. 1930, prominent Broadway composer
Virgil Thompson, 1897–1989, composer who collaborated with Gertrude Stein on
    the opera *Four Saints in Three Acts*, based on the life of Susan B. Anthony

GAY/BISEXUAL DANCERS/CHOREOGRAPHERS, PAST AND PRESENT

Jack Cole, 1911–1974, choreographer (*A Funny Thing Happened on the Way to
    the Forum, Man of La Mancha*); lived with John David Gray for more than
    thirty years

Merce Cunningham, b. 1922, avant-garde dancer/choreographer, lovers with John Cage

Bill T. Jones, b. 1952, dancer/choreographer

Robert La Fosse, b. 1959, dancer/choreographer

Mark Morris, dancer/choreographer

Harry Otis, 1890-?, dancer

Vaslav Nijinsky, 1890–1950, ballet dancer

Rudolf Nureyev, 1938–1993, ballet master

Jerome Robbins, b. 1918, Broadway choreographer

Ted Shawn, 1891–1972, "the father of American dance," formed the Denishawn company with his wife Ruth St. Denis; had a fifteen-year relationship with dancer Barton Mumaw

Tommy Tune, b. 1939, dancer/choreographer

SOME GAY/BISEXUAL PERFORMERS WHO DIED OF AIDS

Michael Bennett, 1943–1987, director/choreographer, cocreator of *A Chorus Line*

Michael Callen, 1955–1993, singer, well-known tenor in the gay *a cappella* singing group the Flirtations

Wayland Flowers, comedian

Liberace (born Wladziu Valentino), 1919–1987, entertainer with piano

Charles Ludlam, 1943–1987, entertainer, founder of the Ridiculous Theatrical Company, renowned for its operatic camp and all-male performances

The Flirtations

Freddie Mercury, singer
Klaus Nomi, performance artist
Ron Richardson, 1952–1995, Broadway singer and actor
Sylvester (born Sylvester James Hurd), 1948–1988, singer
Ricky Wilson, guitarist with the B-52s

GAY MALE PERFORMERS IN THE HARLEM RENAISSANCE

The Harlem Renaissance, which took place from approximately 1917–1937, was a period of profound artistic, literary, and intellectual activity in the black community of Harlem in upper Manhattan. Many of the leaders of this movement were gay or bisexual, including the following:

Phil Black, female impersonator   Frankie "Half Pint" Jaxon, entertainer
Porter Grainger, popular composer   Hall Johnson, choir leader
George Hannah, singer

SOURCE: "A Spectacle in Color: The Lesbian and Gay Subculture of Jazz Age Harlem," by Eric Garber, in *Hidden from History: Reclaiming the Gay and Lesbian Past*, eds. Martin Duberman, Martha Vicinus, and George Chauncey (NAL Dutton, 1990).

GEORGE HANNAH

During the Harlem Renaissance, George Hannah, a black gay man, sang the lesbian-themed song, "The Boy in the Boat," which included the lyrics, "When you see two women walking hand in hand / just shake your head and try to understand." He also recorded "Freakish Blues" in 1931, about pansexuality.

FIRST GAY CHORUS

San Francisco Gay Men's Chorus, which formed in 1979.

76 TROMBONES? 69 TROMBONES? 13 TROMBONERS? BEST PERFORMANCE GROUP WITH A PUN IN THEIR NAME

You heard it here first: The Big Apple Corps, a gay marching band in New York City.

GAY CHORUS/BANDS THAT PERFORMED AT THE 1993 MARCH ON WASHINGTON

The Windy City Gay Men's Chorus (Chicago)
Atlanta Feminist Chorus

The Lavender Light Gospel Choir *(Copyright Morgan Gwenwald)*

Gay and Lesbian Bands of America
Lavendar Light Gospel Choir

ONE OF THE FIRST BROADWAY PLAYS TO DEAL OPENLY AND HONESTLY WITH HOMOSEXUALITY
The Enclave, by Arthur Laurents

OTHER PLAYS BY ARTHUR LAURENTS

Home of the Brave	Broadway musicals:
A Clearing in the Woods	*La Cage aux Folles* (director)
Invitation to a March	*West Side Story* (book writer)
The Time of the Cuckoo	*Gypsy* (book writer)
Jolson Sings Again	
The Radical Mystique	
My Good Name	

THE MUSICAL DIRECTOR WHO DISCOVERED BARBRA
You guessed it: Arthur Laurents. It was during the first musical he directed, *I Can Get It for You Wholesale*, and the nineteen-year-old girl from Brooklyn played the part of a fifty-year-old spinster.

Gay Playwrights and Some of Their Most Famous Plays

Edward Albee, *Who's Afraid of Virginia Woolf?*, *The Zoo Story*
Harvey Fierstein, *Safe Sex*, *Torch Song Trilogy*
William Inge, *Picnic*, *Come Back, Little Sheba*
Tony Kushner, *Angels in America*, *A Bright Room Called Day*
Craig Lucas, *Prelude to a Kiss*
Terrance McNally, *Lips Together, Teeth Apart*; *Love! Valour! Compassion! Kiss of the Spiderwoman*
Paul Rudnick, *Jeffrey*, *I Hate Hamlet*
Tennessee Williams, *A Streetcar Named Desire*, *The Glass Menagerie*, *Cat on a Hot Tin Roof*
Lanford Wilson, *Fifth of July*, *The Redwood Curtain*
For further reading, see *Gay and Lesbian American Plays: An Annotated Bibliography*, by Ken Furtado and Nancy Hellner, The Scarecrow Press, 1993. Gives plot synopses to nearly seven hundred plays.

Other Gay Play Tidbits

Martin Sherman's play *Bent*, about the lives of a gay male couple in Germany and a concentration camp, was threatened with being closed in Frederick, Maryland, by city officials because of a brief nude scene.

A Durham, North Carolina, high school production of Charles Busch's *Psycho Beach Party* was canceled by the principal because of the drag and gay themes.

Gay Theater Leaders

Bloolips, an English group which often performs in the States
Charles Busch, playwright and drag star, creator of *Vampire Lesbians of Sodom*
Cafe Cino, an early gay theater in New York City (1950s)
Ethyl Eichelberger, drag star
John Epperson, a.k.a. Lypsinka
Harvey Fierstein, author and star of *Torch Song Trilogy*
The Glines, an early gay theater in New York City (1970s) founded by John Glines, still in business
Charles Ludlam, founder of the Ridiculous Theatrical Company
Everett Quinton, heir of the Ridiculous after his lover and colleague Ludlam died
Doric Wilson, author of *Street Theatre*, the acclaimed play about the Stonewall riots

Selected Gay-Themed Plays

Angels in America, by Tony Kushner
As Is, by William M. Hoffman
Bent, by Martin Sherman
The Boys in the Band, by Mart Crowley

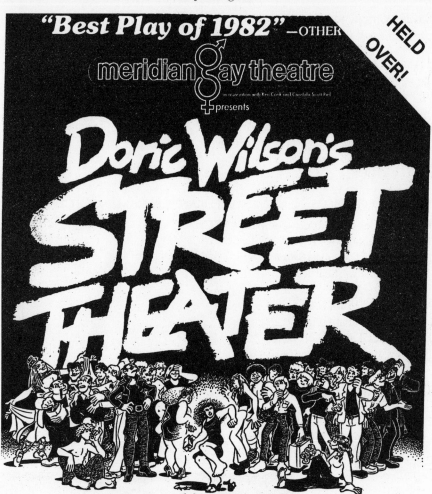

Coming Out, by Jonathan Ned Katz
Falsettos, by William Finn
Jeffrey, by Paul Rudnick
Jerker, by Robert Chesley
A Language of Their Own, by Chay Yew
The Night Larry Kramer Kissed Me, by David Drake
The Normal Heart, by Larry Kramer
Street Theatre, by Doric Wilson
The Sum of Us, by David Stevens
Torch Song Trilogy, by Harvey Fierstein

SELECTED HOTBEDS OF GAY AND LESBIAN PERFORMANCE THEATER

The Ridiculous Theatrical Company (NYC)
Theatre Rhinoceros (SF)
Highways Performance Space (LA)
Alice B. Theatre (Seattle)
WOW Cafe (NYC)
Mark Taper Forum (LA)
Celebration Theatre (LA)
Perry Street Theatre (NYC)
Rainbow Repertory Theatre (NYC)

NEWS ABOUT AMERICA'S PREEMINENT CROSS-DRESSER

RuPaul is reclaiming his public eye spotlight with the release of a new album and an autobiography in 1995. The autobiography is called *Lettin' It All Hang Out*, and

Stand-up comic
Jaffe Cohen (*Photo
by Morgan
Gwenwald*)

Ten Percent describes it as "a bittersweet pop memoir that engagingly traces the rise of this quintessential New York performer from a broken San Diego home—where his sister taught him to 'work the runway'—to international popularity."

The ultimate testimony to the RuPaul manifesto (from, *Lettin' It All Hang Out*: "Learn how to love yourself, 'cause if you don't love yourself, how in the hell are you gonna love somebody else?")

A FEW DRAG PERFORMERS

Holly Woodlawn
Mink Stole
International Chrysis
Zou, 1970s glamour drag performer at the Blue Angel in NYC
Sylvester, disco king/queen, had his stage debut in 1970 as a performer with the
    infamous drag group the Cockettes

Brian Freeman of
Pomo Afro Homos
*(Photo by Dave
LeFave)*

Hot Peaches
RuPaul
Pussy Tourette, lesbian-identified drag queen and singer
United Fruit Company
Justin Bond
Lady Bunny
Hapi Phace
Angie Xtravaganza
Dorian Corey

DRAG PERFORMER WHO ALSO RAN FOR PRESIDENT

Joan Jett Black, in the 1992 campaign.

GAY COMEDIANS AND CARBARETS ACTS

Adult Children of Heterosexuals
Rick Burd
Frank DeCaro
Brian Freeman and Pomo Afro Homos
Funny Gay Males: Jaffe Cohen, Bob Smith, and Danny McWilliams
Frank Maya
The Nelly Olesons

For more on gay/lesbian comedians, see *Out, Loud, and Laughing*, a 1995 collection of monologues, sketches, and stories by lesbian and gay comedians.

PERFORMER RESOURCE

"Booking Yourself," a comprehensive, step-by-step guide for artists and performers to book themselves, including a starter list of three hundred names and contact numbers, is available in book form for $25, or on Mac (Microsoft Word) disk for $40. Contact: Sandy Ayala, 3929 Rhoda Ave., Oakland, CA 94602

SOURCE: America Online, Gay and Lesbian Community Forum

PROFILE

Liberace

Liberace was not always as popular with the critics as he was with his many adoring fans (the majority of which were middle-aged women). To one of his critical detractors he said, "What you said hurt me very much. I cried all the way to the bank."

Liberace—born Wladziu Valentino in 1919—became one of the highest paid entertainers of all time. He grew up in Wisconsin, going to high school in West Milwaukee, where there was some hint at his predilection for theatricality.

He began his career playing background music in fancy restaurants in Wisconsin, with his specialty being syrupy versions of piano classics. However, it was the two-dimensional medium of television where this showman found his ideal home and things began to happen professionally.

After his career as the ultimate "flamboyant" showman took off, two magazines (the London *Daily Mirror* and the American tabloid *Confidential*) both hinted at his homosexuality. Liberace sued them both for libel and, surprisingly, won.

The tables were turned, however, in 1982 when the flamboyant ivory tickler was accused of tickling other organs. Liberace was sued in a "palimony" suit by former lover Scott Thorson, who went on to publish *Behind the Candelabra: My Life with Liberace* with Dutton in 1988.

Liberace died of AIDS in 1987, a condition which he repeatedly denied he had while he was alive. An autopsy, however, confirmed the cause of death.

Mini-Profiles

Chay Yew

Chay Yew, an internationally known and award-winning playwright, is just getting some much-deserved exposure in the United States. His new play, *A Language of Their Own*, opened in April 1995 at the Joseph Papp Public Theatre in New York City. Starring B. D. Wong (of *M. Butterfly* fame), the play features four gay male characters, three of whom are Asian-American.

Born and raised in Singapore, Yew is now a U.S. resident. He won the London version of an Obie for best play in 1993 for *Porcelain*, about an interracial gay relationship. Another one of his plays was once banned in Singapore for "promoting homosexuality."

After its New York performance run, *A Language of Their Own* will tour the country.

Larry Kramer

Larry Kramer, as well known for his activism as for his art, is an Obie Award–winning playwright and the author of the best-selling gay novel *Faggots*.

For many years a film executive at Columbia and United Artists, Kramer wrote the screenplay adaptation and produced the film version of D. H. Lawrence's *Women in Love*, which received four Academy Award nominations, including Best Screenplay, and won Glenda Jackson her first Oscar.

Kramer is the cofounder of two important political groups of our time, the Gay

Men's Health Crisis (GMHC) and the AIDS Coalition to Unleash Power (ACT UP). He is also the author of the nonfiction book *Reports from the Holocaust: The Making of an AIDS Activist*.

Kramer's plays include *Just Say No*; *The Normal Heart*, one of the first plays about AIDS, now being made into a film by Barbra Streisand; and its sequel, *The Destiny of Me*. *The Destiny of Me* earned several distinctions, which include winning an Obie Award, the Hull-Warriner Award of the Dramatists Guild, the Lucille Lortel Award for best play of the year, and being a runner-up for the Pulitzer Prize in drama.

14. GAY POLITICS

"I'm running purely for queer visibility. We're puttin' the camp *back in campaign—and takin' out the* pain. *I'm the only candidate who can successfully skirt all the issues."*

—Queer Nation presidential candidate Joan Jett Black, 1992

1992 may have been one of the most exciting times in the history of electoral politics for gay men and lesbians in the United States. Mainstream politicians courted the "gay vote," and Democratic presidential candidate Bill Clinton included gay people in his speech accepting his party's nomination and counted among his advisers an openly gay man, David Mixner. On the other hand, at the Republican Convention, candidate Patrick Buchanan exhibited such venomous public hatred of gay people that it alienated much of the electorate. To many, it looked like the dawn of a brighter era for gay citizens.

Though Clinton backed down from some of his promises to gay supporters once he was elected, the "gay vote" remains a force to be reckoned with, especially in areas with large gay populations. And the 1994 midterm elections saw openly gay and lesbian candidates running for more offices than ever. Some challengers won, like feminist attorney Sheila Kuehl, who became the first openly gay member of the California Assembly. Even more importantly, all openly gay and lesbian incumbents, from the national to the local level, retained their offices. Now organizations like the Gay and Lesbian Victory Fund help train gay people who are interested in running for political office.

How important is electoral politics? Do our votes and our letters really count? The radical right has become expert at working the electoral system, helping the Republican Party take over the majority in both houses of Congress in 1994. The Right actively registers people to vote and maintains an elaborate network of voters who write letters and make phone calls against such issues as gay rights.

Mainstream politics is one means of working for gay rights. If we don't make our voices and opinions heard, we have no one to blame but ourselves.

OUT GAY AND LESBIAN OFFICIALS IN THE CLINTON ADMINISTRATION

Roberta Achtenberg, Assistant Secretary for Fair Housing and Opportunity, Department of Housing and Urban Development—highest ranking lesbian in the administration (resigned April 1995 to run for mayor of San Francisco)

Daniel Burkhardt, Special Assistant and Counsel to the Director, Office of Correspondence

Bob Chapman, Special Assistant to the Deputy Secretary for Drug Policy, Department of Defense

Bernie Delia, Counsel to the Executive Office for U.S. Attorneys, Department of Justice

Former New York
City Mayor David
Dinkins hands
proclamation of
Lesbian and Gay
Pride Month,
1991, to his liaison
to the gay
community, Dr.
Majorie Hill.
*(Photo by Joan
Vitale Strong)*

Romy Diaz, Deputy Assistant Secretary for International Affairs, Department of
   Energy
Bob Hattoy, Special Assistant to the Deputy Secretary, Department of the Interior
Thomas Hehir, Director, Office of Special Education Programs, Department of
   Education
Mark Hunker, Special Assistant to Assistant Secretary for Administration and
   Management, Department of Labor
Nan Hunter, Deputy General Counsel, Department of Health and Human Ser-
   vices
Bruce Lehman, Assistant Secretary of Commerce and Commissioner of Patents
   and Trademarks
David Martin, Assistant to the Assistant Secretary, Office of Legislative and Inter-
   governmental Affairs, Department of Commerce
Zoon Nguyen, Special Assistant to the Assistant Secretary for Fair Housing and
   Opportunity, Department of Housing and Urban Development (resigned April
   1995 to work on Roberta Achtenberg's campaign)

Patrick Nolan, Special Assistant to the Undersecretary, International Trade Administration, Department of Commerce

David Peterson, Confidential Assistant, Office of the General Counsel, Department of Commerce

Julian Potter, Special Assistant to the Assistant Secretary for Community Planning and Development, Department of Housing and Urban Development

R. Paul Richard, Executive Assistant to Commissioner Paul Steven Miller, Equal Employment Opportunity Commission

Martin Rouse, Special Assistant to the Assistant Secretary, Office of Fair Housing and Equal Opportunity, Department of Housing and Urban Development

Douglas S. Sheorn, Office of Presidential Personnel

Stephanie Smith, Special Assistant to Secretary Cisneros, Department of Housing and Urban Development

Richard Socarides, White House Liaison, Department of Labor

Jay Stowsky, Senior Economist, Council of Economic Advisors

Stan Strickland, Special Assistant, Office of Legislative Affairs, Department of Justice

Brian C. Thompson, White House Liaison, National Archives

David Tseng, Special Assistant to the Assistant Secretary, Pension and Welfare Benefits Administration, Department of Labor

Jesse White, Chair, Appalachian Commission

Victor Zonana, Deputy Assistant Secretary for Public Affairs, Department of Health and Human Services

SOURCE: *OUT* magazine, March 1995. Reprinted with permission.

OPENLY GAY CANDIDATES IN THE 1994 ELECTIONS (* INDICATES CANDIDATE WON RACE)

CHALLENGERS

Statewide office

Karen Burstein (N.Y. Attorney General)
Tony Miller (Calif. Secretary of State)
Joseph Schreiner (Ill. Secretary of State)

State office:

*Cal Anderson (D-Wash.)
Derek Belt (D-Mass.)
Chuck Carpenter (R-Ore.)
*Ken Cheuvront (D-Ariz.)
Scott Evertz (R-Wis.)
Brendan Hadash (D-Vt.)
James Harrison (R-Md.)
Denise Heap (D-Ariz.)

Jerry Keene (R-Ore.)
*Sheila Kuehl (D-Calif.)
Greg Nance (R-Utah)
Mike Pisaturo (D-R.I.)
Bruce Reeves (D-Tex.)
Mark Valverde (Libertarian-Calif.)
*Tim Van Zandt (D-Mo.)

Local office

*Tom Ammiano (San Francisco Board of Supervisors)
Mark Brazil (San Luis Obispo, Calif., City Council)
*Tom Chiola (Cook County, Ill., circuit judge)
Sam Ciraulo (Robla, Calif., school board)
*Bonnie Dumanis (San Diego, Municipal Court)
John Fanning (D.C. school board)
Royce Gibson (D.C. school board)
Ron Gunzberger (Broward County, Fla., judge)
Arthur Jackson (San Francisco Board of Supervisors)
*Marcy Kahn (New York State Supreme Court)
*Leslie Katz (San Francisco Community College Board)
Vicky Kolakowski (AC Transit Board of Directors)
Kearse McGill (Sacramento Utility District)
*Teri Schwartz (Los Angeles Superior Court)
*Lawrence Wong (San Francisco Community College Board of Trustees)

INCUMBENTS

Federal office

*Rep. Barney Frank (D-Mass.)
*Rep. Steve Gunderson (R-Wis.)
*Rep. Gerry Studds (D-Mass.)

GAY CANDIDATES

The Gay and Lesbian Victory Fund endorses openly gay candidates for office and sponsors an annual training weekend for aspiring political candidates. For more information, contact the Victory Fund, 1012 14th St. NW, #707, Washington, DC 20005, 202-842-8679.

The National Gay and Lesbian Task Force (NGLTF) offers a number of publications and several software packages via America OnLine, which are useful in planning a political campaign, including congressional report cards (tracking how congress members voted on issues of concern to gays) and a software program called Precinct Walker, which helps manage a local campaign. Contact NGLTF at 1734 14th St. NW, Washington, DC 20009, 202-332-6483.

The International Network of Lesbian and Gay Officials (INLGO) is a nonprofit organization incorporated in Minnesota, which supports and encourages full participation in all aspects of society by openly gay men and lesbians. Its focus is on openly gay and lesbian elected and appointed officials. INLGO has held conferences annually since 1985, maintains mailing lists and a newsletter, and is working on a system of electronic networking. For more information, contact INLGO at 3801 26th St. East, Minneapolis, MN 55406-1857, or via e-mail at INLGO@aol.com. (See profile p. 338.)

State office

*Rep. Tammy Baldwin (D-Wis.)
*Rep. Kate Brown (D-Ore.)
*Rep. Karen Clark (D-Minn.)
*Rep. George Eighmey (D-Ore.)
*Sen. Will Fitzpatrick (D-R.I.)
*Assemblymember Deborah Glick (D-N.Y.)

*Rep. Bill Lippert ((D-Vt.)
*Rep. Glen Maxey (D-Tex.)
*Sen. Dale McCormick (D-Maine)
*Rep. Gail Shibley (D-Ore.)
*Rep. Cynthia Wooten (D-Ore.)

Local office

°Susan Leal (San Francisco Board of Supervisors)
°Carol Migden (San Francisco Board of Supervisors)

SOURCE: *The Washington Blade*, November 11, 1994. © 1995 The Washington Blade.

STATES, CITIES, AND COUNTIES WHOSE CIVIL RIGHTS LAWS, ORDINANCES, AND POLICIES BAR DISCRIMINATION BASED ON SEXUAL ORIENTATION (AS OF MAY 1995)

SUMMARY OF CIVIL RIGHTS LAWS THAT INCLUDE SEXUAL ORIENTATION

Nine states in the U.S. have civil rights laws passed by the legislature and signed by the governor:

California—1992
Connecticut—1991
Hawaii—1991
Massachusetts—1989
Minnesota—1993

New Jersey—1992
Rhode Island—1995
Vermont—1992
Wisconsin—1982

At least eighteen states in the United States have executive orders.

At least eighty-seven cities or counties in the United States have civil rights ordinances.

At least thirty-nine cities/counties in the United States have council or mayoral proclamations banning discrimination in public employment.

Key to areas of protection from discrimination based on sexual orientation:

1 = Public Employment
2 = Public Accommodations
3 = Private Employment
4 = Education
5 = Housing
6 = Credit
7 = Union Practices
Population figures are from the 1990 United States census.

STATE/CITY	AREAS OF PROTECTION	POPULATION
Alaska		
Anchorage	1	226,338
Arizona		
Phoenix	1	983,403
Tucson	1	405,390
California	1–4	29,760,021
Berkeley	1, 3–7	102,724
Cathedral City	1	30,085
Cupertino	1	39,967
Davis	1–3, 5–7	46,322
Hayward	1, 3–5	111,498
Laguna Beach	1–7	23,170
Long Beach	1, 3	423,433
Los Angeles	1–7	3,485,398
Mountain View	1	67,460
Oakland	1–7	372,242
Palo Alto	4	55,900
Riverside	1	226,505
Sacramento	1–7	369,365
San Diego	1–7	1,110,549
San Francisco	1–7	723,959
San Jose	1	782,248
Santa Barbara	1, 4	85,571
Santa Cruz	1	49,711
Santa Monica	1–7	86,905
West Hollywood	1–7	36,118
Alameda County		1,276,702
San Mateo County	1, 3, 5	649,623
Santa Barbara County	1	369,608
Santa Cruz County	1	229,734
Colorado		
Aspen	1–3, 5	5,049
Boulder	1–3	83,312
Denver	1–5, 7	467,610
Telluride	1–3, 5	
Boulder County	1	225,339
Morgan County	1	21,939
Connecticut	1	3,287,116
Hartford	1–7	139,739
New Haven	1–7	130,474
Stamford	1–7	108,056

STATE/CITY	AREAS OF PROTECTION	POPULATION
District of Columbia		
Washington	1–7	606,900
Florida		
Key West	1–3, 5–7	24,832
Miami Beach	1–3, 5	92,639
West Palm Beach	1	67,643
Alachua County	1–3, 5	181,596
Hillsborough County	2, 5	834,054
Palm Beach County	1–2, 5	863,518
Georgia		
Atlanta	1	394,017
Hawaii	1, 3	1,108,229
Honolulu	1	365,272
Illinois		
Champaign	1–3, 5–7	63,502
Chicago	1–4, 6	2,783,726
Evanston	1, 6	73,233
Oak Park	2, 5	53,648
Urbana	1–3, 4–5	36,344
Cook County	1–4, 6	5,105,067
Indiana		
Bloomington	1–5	60,633
Lafayette	1–5	43,764
West Lafayette	1–5	23,138
Iowa		
Ames	1–7	47,198
Iowa City	1–3, 6, 7	59,738
Louisiana		
New Orleans	1–3, 5	496,938
Maine		
Portland	1–3, 4, 5	64,358
Maryland		
Baltimore	1–5	736,014
Gaithersburg	1, 3, 5–7	39,542
Rockville	1–7	44,835
Howard County	1–7	187,328
Montgomery County	1, 3, 5–7	757,027

STATE/CITY	AREAS OF PROTECTION	POPULATION
Massachusetts	1–7	6,016,425
Amherst	1–7	35,228
Boston	1–4, 6, 7	574,283
Cambridge	1–7	95,802
Malden	1–6	53,884
Worcester	1–6	169,759
Michigan		
Ann Arbor	1–3, 5–7	109,392
Birmingham	5, 6	19,997
Detroit	1–7	1,027,974
East Lansing	1–3, 5–7	50,677
Flint	1–5, 7	140,762
Saginaw	4, 5	69,512
Ingham County	1	282,912
Minnesota	1–6	4,375,099
Marshall	1–3, 4, 5	12,023
Minneapolis	1–7	368,383
St. Paul	1–7	272,235
Hennepin County	1	1,032,431
Missouri		
Kansas City	1, 3, 5, 7	435,146
St. Louis	1–6	396,685
New Jersey	1–3, 4, 5	7,730,188
Essex County	1	778,204
New York		
Albany	1–3, 4, 5	101,082
Brighton	1	34,455
Buffalo	1	328,123
East Hampton	1–3	16,132
Ithaca	1–7	29,541
New York	1–5, 7	7,322,564
Rochester	1	231,636
Syracuse	1–5	163,860
Troy	1	54,269
Watertown	1–6	29,429
Suffolk County	1	1,321,264
Tompkins County	1–7	94,097
North Carolina		
Chapel Hill	1	38,711
Durham	1	136,611
Raleigh	1	207,952

STATE/CITY	AREAS OF PROTECTION	POPULATION
Ohio		
Columbus	1–6	632,910
Dayton	1	182,044
Yellow Springs	1–3, 5–7	3,973
Cayahoga County	1	1,412,140
Oregon		
Portland	1–3, 5	437,319
Pennsylvania		
Harrisburg	1–7	52,376
Lancaster	1–7	55,551
Philadelphia	1–3, 5–7	1,585,577
Pittsburgh	1–3, 5–7	369,879
York	1–3, 5	42,192
State College	5	40,949
Northampton County	1	247,305
Rhode Island	1, 2, 5, 6	947,154
South Carolina		
Columbia	1	98,052
South Dakota		
Minnehaha County	1	123,509
Texas		
Austin	1–3, 5–7	465,622
Dallas	1	1,852,810
Houston	1	1,630,553
Utah		
Salt Lake County	1	159,936
Vermont	1–7	562,758
Burlington	1, 3	39,127
Virginia		
Alexandria	1–6	111,283
Arlington County	1	170,936
Washington		
Olympia	1	33,840
Pullman	1, 5, 6	23,478
Seattle	1, 3, 5–7	516,259
Clallam County	1	56,210
King County	5, 6	1,507,319

STATE/CITY	AREAS OF PROTECTION	POPULATION
Wisconsin	1–7	4,891,769
Madison	1–3, 5–7	191,262
Milwaukee	1	628,088
Dane County	1	367,085

This information is based upon newspaper articles and information sent by activists to the National Gay and Lesbian Task Force. Therefore it is likely that there are cities and counties that have ordinances or proclamations that are not included in this chart. If you know of additions or corrections to this chart, please contact: Karen Bullock-Jordan, Public Information and Fight the Right Associate, NGLTF, 1734 14th St. NW, Washington, DC 20009. Phone: 202-332-6483, ext 3206. Fax: 202-332-0207. E-mail: kbjngltf@aol.com.

SAMPLE GAY RIGHTS ORDINANCE LANGUAGE

Washington, DC

"Every individual shall have an equal opportunity to participate fully in the economic, cultural, and intellectual life of the District and to have an equal opportunity to participate in all aspects of life, including, but not limited to, in employment, in places of public accommodation, resort, or amusement, in educational institutions, in public service, and in housing and commercial space accommodations. . . .

"It shall be an unlawful discriminatory practice to do any of the following acts, wholly or partially for a discriminatory reason based upon race, color, religion, national origin, sex, age, marital status, personal appearance, sexual orientation, family responsibilities, physical handicap, matriculation, or political affiliation, of any individual: . . . to refuse to hire, or to discharge . . . [to] fail to initiate or conduct any transaction in real property . . . to deny, directly or indirectly, any person the full and equal enjoyment of the goods, services, facilities, privileges, advantages, and accommodations of any place or public accommodation; . . . to deny . . . access to, any of [an educational institution's] facilities and services. . . ."

Dallas, Texas

"That the proposed ordinance amending Chapter 34 of the Dallas City Code be amended by renumbering current Sections 21 through 28 as Sections 22 through 29 and adding a new Section 21 to read as follows:

"SECTION 21. That Subsection (b) of Section 34-35, "Fair Employment Practices," of Article V, "Rules of Conduct," of CHAPTER 34, "PERSONNEL RULES," of the Dallas City Code, as amended, is amended to read as follows:

". . . (b) Management Responsibilities

"(1) In keeping with the respect due each employee, city management is committed to:

(A) provide effective and efficient delivery of services;

(B) compensate employees fairly for work done;

(C) provide safe, healthy work conditions in accordance with provisions of all applicable law;

The following governmental agencies have employment policies that bar discrimination based on sexual orientation:

The Federal Bureau of Investigation
The Department of Housing and Urban Development
The Department of the Interior
The Department of Transportation
The Justice Department
The Office of Personnel Management
The White House
The State Department

(D) adequately instruct and train employees in their duties;

(E) supply necessary tools and equipment (except those customarily provided by employees);

(F) provide reasonable opportunities for developmental experience and competitive advancement; and

(G) actively engage in equal opportunity activities.

"(2) City management may not discharge an individual, fail or refuse to hire an individual, or otherwise discriminate against an individual with respect to compensation, terms, conditions, or privileges of employment because of the individual's race, color, age, religion, sex, marital status, sexual orientation, national origin, disability, political opinions, or affiliations. Nothing in this paragraph extends any employee benefits, including but not limited to paid or unpaid leave, medical benefits, or pension benefits, to any individual who is ineligible for those benefits under any other provision of this chapter, the city's master health plan, the employees' retirement fund program, or the police and fire pension system or under any other city ordinance or resolution or state or federal law.

"(3) City management may not limit, segregate, or classify employees or applicants for employment in a way that would deprive or tend to deprive an individual of employment opportunities or otherwise adversely affect an employee's status because of the individual's race, color, age, religion, sex, marital status, sexual orientation, national origin, disability, political opinions, or affiliations."

JESSE HELMS'S HATE BILLS

Senator Jesse Helms (R-N. Carolina) introduced the following two bills into the 104th session of Congress during its first month, pursuing the anti-gay obsession on which he has focused for the last few years.

S.315 104th CONGRESS 1st Session

To protect the first amendment rights of employees of the Federal Government.

IN THE SENATE OF THE UNITED STATES

February 1 (legislative day, January 30), 1995

Mr. Helms introduced the following bill, which was read twice and referred to the Committee on Governmental Affairs

A BILL

to protect the first amendment rights of employees of the Federal Government.

Be it enacted by the Senate and House of Representatives of the United States of America in Congress assembled,

Section. 1. Notwithstanding any other provision of law, no employee of the Federal Government shall be peremptorily removed without public hearings from his or her position because of remarks made during personal time in opposition to the Federal Government's policies, or proposed policies regarding homosexuals, and any such individual so removed prior to date of enactment of this Act shall be reinstated to his or her previous position.

S.317 104th CONGRESS 1st Session

To stop the waste of taxpayer funds on activities by Government agencies to encourage its employees or officials to accept homosexuality as a legitimate or normal lifestyle.

IN THE SENATE OF THE UNITED STATES

February 1 (legislative day, January 30), 1995

Mr. Helms introduced the following bill, which was read twice and referred to the Committee on Governmental Affairs

A BILL

to stop the waste of taxpayer funds on activities by Government agencies to encourage its employees or officials to accept homosexuality as a legitimate or normal lifestyle.

Be it enacted by the Senate and House of Representatives of the United States of America in Congress assembled,

SECTION 1. LIMITATION ON USE OF APPROPRIATED FUNDS.

No funds appropriated out of the Treasury of the United States may be used by any entity to fund, promote, or carry out any seminar or program for employees of the Government, or to fund any position in the Government, the purpose of which is to compel, instruct, encourage, urge, or persuade employees or officials to—

(1) recruit, on the basis of sexual orientation, homosexuals for employment with the Government; or

(2) embrace, accept, condone, or celebrate homosexuality as a legitimate or normal lifestyle.

REGISTERING TO VOTE

By registering to vote and then casting votes on election day, lesbians and gay men make their voices heard and protect their interests and civil rights. Do you know which Congress members support a national gay rights bill and vote for increased AIDS funding? Or which local school board candidates advocate for a tolerant, multicultural curriculum? We're the losers when we remain apathetic about voting; an informed lesbian and gay electorate is a powerful tool toward attaining civil rights. To find out more about the voting record of your congressperson, you can send for the "Congressional Report Card," which is available from the National Gay and Lesbian Task Force, 1734 14th St. NW, Washington, DC 20009, 202-332-6483.

To find out how to register to vote in your city or town or how to apply for an absentee ballot, contact your local board of elections. They're in the blue pages section of the phone book, along with other offices of city goverment.

If your city has a gay and lesbian community center, check to see if the center registers voters. The New York City Lesbian and Gay Community Services Center (208 West 13th St., New York City), for example, has a voter registration project, and visitors to the building can register to vote on the spot at the lobby information desk.

GAY VOTERS

In a 1992 survey of 7,500 lesbians and gay men, Overlooked Opinions, Inc., a gay/lesbian marketing research firm in Chicago, found the following results:

	GAY MEN	NATIONAL
Registered to vote (of those eligible)	92.9%	68.2%
Voted in the 1988 presidential election	87.9%	61.3%
Democrat	62.0%	48.7%*
Independent	19.5%	13.3%*
Republican	13.1%	33.8%*
Socialist	2.3%	NA
Libertarian	2.6%	NA
Other party affiliations	2.4%	4.2%*

*Based on data compiled in the thirty states that tabulate voters' party affiliations.

SOURCE: Overlooked Opinions, Inc., Chicago, and the Bureau of the Census, Washington, DC. Reprinted with permission.

WRITING LETTERS

Writing a letter to a Congress member is a good way to make your voice heard. You may think your letter will get lost in the shuffle, but the number of responses for or against a particular policy or measure is tabulated. And you will often get a letter in response, even if you are against a policy or bill. The radical right has an effective letter writing campaign that floods Congress against issues such as abortion and gay rights. Let them hear from the other side!

To write to your Congress member, always use your name and address and type the letter if possible. Be direct and to the point; make your opinion clear. Avoid threats and demands. Show how you *as a voter* are affected by the policy or bill in question. If you're responding to a particular bill, refer to it by number or name. Letters can be addressed as follows:

Senator (fill in)
Senate Office Building
Washington, DC 20510

Representative (fill in)
House of Representatives Office Building
Washington, DC 20515

PROFILE

International Network of Lesbian and Gay Officials

Founded in 1985 by thirteen openly lesbian and gay political officials, INLGO is a network of elected and appointed officials, their partners, activists, and others interested in electoral politics. The nonprofit organization asserts in its mission statement: "We have a unique opportunity and responsibility to serve as teachers both within the institutions of government and to the larger community."

To that end, INLGO supports local, state, and national legislation in the following areas affecting the lives of lesbians and gay men: the outlawing of discrimination based on sexual orientation, race, religion, sex, marital status, disability status, national or ethnic origin, and age; the overturning of laws that prohibit consensual sexual activity between adults; domestic partnership; child custody, foster care, and adoption; protecting against AIDS and HIV-related discrimination; and increased services for people with AIDS and HIV and funding for research and education.

Each year in November, INLGO sponsors a conference that provides officials with a planning and support network of openly gay officials around the world. The conference is a springboard for ideas on political and social issues. Some topics of discussion include understanding polls, conflict resolution skills, national and local organizing, family issues, building bridges, and balancing public and private life.

Limited grants and scholarships are available to those who need assistance with conference costs. Following each annual conference, participants are hooked up with more seasoned officials to provide a mentor relationship.

Schedule of Conferences since 1985

1985	West Hollywood, California
1986	Washington, DC
1987	Minneapolis, Minnesota
1988	San Diego, California
1989	Madison, Wisconsin
1990	Boston, Massachusetts
1991	Houston, Texas
1992	Chapel Hill, North Carolina
1993	Chicago, Illinois
1994	Seattle, Washington
1995	Toronto, Ontario
1996	West Hollywood, California

Founders of INLGO, 1985

Harry Britt, Supervisor, San Francisco, California
Karen Clark, State Representative, Minnesota
Brian Coyle, City Council Member, Minneapolis, Minnesota
Robert Ebersole, Town Clerk, Tax Collector and Treasurer, Lunenburg, Massachusetts
Robert Gentry, City Council Member, Laguna Beach, California
John Heilman, Mayor, West Hollywood, California
John Laird, City Council Member, Santa Cruz, California
Kathleen Nichols, Supervisor, Dane County, Wisconsin
Steve Schulte, City Council Member, West Hollywood, California
David Scondras, City Council Member, Boston, Massachusetts
Allan Spear, State Senator, Minnesota
Valerie Terrigno, City Council Member, West Hollywood, California
Richard Wagner, Supervisor, Dane County, Wisconsin

Steering Committee, 1994–95

Co-Chairs:	Deborah Glick, New York, NY
	Kyle Rae, Toronto, ON
Secretary:	Kevin Vaughan, Philadelphia, PA
Treasurer:	Tim Cole, Minneapolis, MN
Elected Officials:	Tom Duane, New York, NY
	Will Fitzpatrick, Cranston, RI
	Deborah Glick, New York, NY
	Jill Harris, Brooklyn, NY
	Kyle Rae, Toronto, ON

Openly gay New York City council-member, Tom Duane *(center)*. *(Collection of the Lesbian and Gay Community Services Center–New York)*

Appointed Officials: Tim Cole, Minneapolis, MN
                                Carlie Steen, Detroit, MI
                                Kevin Vaughan, Philadelphia, PA
At Large: Dennis Amick, Laguna Beach, CA
                                Tanya Gulliver, Whitby, ON
                                John Heilman, West Hollywood, CA
Ex Officio: Cal Anderson, Seattle, WA

International Network of Lesbian and Gay Officials, 3801 26th Street East, Minneapolis, MN 55406-1857. E-mail: INLGO@aol.com.

15. GAY RELIGION AND SPIRITUALITY

At the 1991 Gay
Pride March, New
York City (*Photo
by Harry Stevens*)

'This is a society that does tragic things, obscene things; yet it is only the physical
relations between human beings—the sexual relations—that we seem to term obscene."

—MALCOLM BOYD

Across North America, gay people are asserting their need and right to be spiritual—to take part in organized Eastern and Western religions; to establish their
own churches; to create their own forms of spirituality, sometimes through eroticism; to revere pagan traditions; to honor the Two Spirit traditions of Native
Americans; or to invoke the help of a Higher Power in twelve-step groups. In pursuing their spirituality, gay men find the strength and pride they need to live and
love in a homophobic society, in a community that has been devastated by loss.

Gay Religion Timeline

Before the Twentieth Century

Third millennium B.C.: The first joint homosexual burial takes place. The Tomb of Two Brothers at Thebes is an Egyptian sepulcher that contains the remains of two men, Niankhnum and Khnumhotep, who are believed to have been lovers. The walls of the tombs have bas reliefs that show the two men embracing.

1900 B.C.: According to the Book of Genesis, the cities of Sodom and Gomorrah are destroyed with fire and brimstone. This is interpreted by Philo of Alexandria centuries later, and then by religious writers, to have been a wrathful God's punishment for the homosexuality of the inhabitants. That interpretation, although common, hinges on an unlikely translation of the ambiguous Hebrew word meaning "to know." The term is used 943 times in the Old Testament: only 15 of those times is it a euphemism for sexual activity. According to many modern-day scholars, it is likely that the story of Sodom and Gomorrah did not involve homosexuality at all.

A.D. 60: Saint Paul writes certain biblical passages, particularly Romans 1:26–27 and I Corinthians: 6–9, which are often used to prohibit/protest homosexuality. As twentieth-century scholar John Boswell indicates, this interpretation does not necessarily reflect Saint Paul's original meaning, which has been changed through translations.

533: Homosexuality and blasphemy are proclaimed to be equally to blame for earthquakes, famines, and pestilences by Byzantine emperor Justinian I when he combines Roman law and Christian ethics. Castration is ordered for any lawbreaker.

650: Priests are issued The Cummean Penitential, a manual that spells out repentance for different levels of homosexual sin. The age of the offender, and the nature of the offense, are taken into consideration. "Simple kissing" by two males under the age of twenty calls for six special fasts; kissing "with emission or embrace" calls for ten special fasts. Mutual masturbation by men over twenty makes the offenders liable to twenty days penance; for anal intercourse, the period of time increased to seven years.

1252: St. Thomas Aquinas begins his theological teaching. Aquinas pronounced that God created genitalia for no purpose other than reproduction and decreed that homosexual acts were "unnatural" and heretical. Though he did not originate these ideas, he had powerful influence with the church and the narrow-mindedness he espoused continues today.

1310: All French members of the Order of Templars (a religious military order founded at Jerusalem by the Crusaders) are arrested and charged with sodomy, heresy, and being in league with the Moslems; many are tortured and executed. King Phillip the Fair of France, who ordered this action, is said to have benefited enormously from property confiscated as part of the arrests. The accuracy of the allegations is still debated by present-day scholars.

1450–53: The Spanish Inquisition is empowered by Pope Nicholas to investigate and punish homosexuality.

1583: A pronouncement of Christianity by the Third Provincial Council of Peru tells the native Indians of Lima that "sodomy, whether with another man, or with a boy, or a beast . . . carries the death penalty, . . . and the reason God has allowed that you, the Indians, should be so afflicted and vexed by other nations is because of this vice that your ancestors had, and many of you still have."

1620–1725: Approximately 350 persons are accused of witchcraft in colonial New England, of whom 78 percent are women and a number of those thought to have been lesbians. In total, 35 people are executed, 28 of whom are women. More than half of the accusations, trials, and executions took place in the town of Salem, Massachusetts, from 1692–1693.

1641–42: The Massachusetts Bay Colony becomes the first of several New England colonies to incorporate into its laws the language of Leviticus 20:13 : "if a man lyeth with mankinde, as he lyeth with a woman, both of them have committed abomination, they both shall surely be put to death."

The Twentieth Century

1916: The first gay church, an Anglican-derived Liberal Catholic Church, is founded in Sydney, Australia, by Charles Webster Leadbeater.

1946: George Hyde, a youth minister in the independent Catholic Movement, forms a church in Atlanta which is thought to have been the first American church organized primarily for homosexuals.

1956: The first documented gay church, The Church of ONE Brotherhood, is founded in Los Angeles by Chuck Rowland. It lasts only a year.

1957: The Catholic Church, while emphasizing that it believes homosexuality to be a sin, recommends its decriminalization by endorsing the Wolfden Report. This report, published by the British government, recommended the legalization of homosexual acts between consenting adults. Three years later, after much debate nationwide, a proposal to adopt these recommendations was defeated by a two-to-one margin in the House of Commons.

1964: The Council on Religion and the Homosexual is founded in San Francisco by the Reverend Ted McIlvenna and other clergy members "to promote continuing dialogue between the church and the homosexual."

1967: The Glide Methodist Church and the Glide Foundation of San Francisco launchs one of the first economic boycotts on behalf of gay rights by not only stating that they will not buy goods and services from companies that discriminate against homosexuals, but encouraging others to follow their lead.

1968: Rev. Troy Perry, a gay Pentecostal minister, conducts a service for twelve people gathered at a house in Huntington Park, California. This was the first meeting of what was to become the United Fellowship of Metropolitan Community Churches, a nondenominational church for the gay community. Only two years later, MCC had over five hundred members.

1969: The Church of Christ's Council on Christian Social Action adopts one of the first position statements on homosexuality, in which it calls for the decriminalization of homosexual activities between consenting adults.

• The first denominational religious organization for homosexuals begins as a rap group for gay and lesbian Catholics in San Diego. After moving to Los Angeles, the first chapter of Dignity is founded in 1970.

1971–85: Eighteen MCC churches experience arson.

1972: Following a rap session at the Los Angeles Metropolitan Community Church, two gay men and two lesbians discover they are all Jewish and decide to form their own temple. Beth Chayim Chadishm holds its first service in July of 1972 and are chartered on July 19,1974, by the Union of American Hebrew Congregations, making it not only the first gay and lesbian synagogue, but also the first gay religious organization of any kind to be officially recognized by a national body. In 1977 the congregation acquired its own building, dedicated in 1981.

• The United Church of Christ in San Carlos, California, ordains William Johnson, making it the first Christian denomination to ordain an openly gay candidate. Johnson came out in 1970 while studying at the Pacific School of Religion in Berkeley, California.

1973: The first bisexual religious organization, the Committee of Friends on Bisexuality, is founded by Stephen Donaldson (a.k.a. Robert Martin) in Ithaca, New York. They issue the "Ithaca Statement on Bisexuality," during their first gathering in June 1972, which is thought to be the first statement on bisexuality—as well as pro-bisexuality—by any religious body. The committee ended in 1977.

• The Unitarian Universalists become the first denomination to establish a lesbian and gay office. Three years earlier, a resolution was passed by the general assembly banning discrimination against gays in the church.

1978: Rabbi Allen Bennet allows himself to be outed in the *San Francisco Examiner*, making him the first openly gay rabbi. After becoming a rabbi in 1974, Bennet moved to San Francisco to continue his postgraduate studies and joined a gay synagogue, Congregation Sha'ar Zahav, where he then became the rabbi in 1979.

• Witchcraft and the Gay Counter Culture, by Arthur Evans, a historical view of heresy, gayness, and the witch hunts of Europe and England, is published.

1979: The Radical Faeries are established when Harry Hay, a pioneer of gay liberation, organizes a first gathering of approximately two hundred men in the Arizona desert. The Faeries are a national organization of free spirits and flower children known for their pagan-influenced celebration of what's different and special about gay men

1984: The Unitarian Universalists become the first modern Christian denomination to perform gay and lesbian union ceremonies.

1986: A fourteen-page letter issued by Pope John Paul II calls gay people "intrinsically disordered" and states that homosexuality can never be reconciled with church doctrine. From 1986 to 1991, fifty Dignity chapters nationwide were expelled from Roman Catholic Church Property and had to find new places to meet when church officials complied with the order to withdraw all support from gay organizations.

1988: Mary Elizabeth Clark takes vows of poverty, chastity, and obedience at an Episcopal church in San Clemente, California, making her the first transsexual nun, though the religious community she founded, Sisters of St. Elizabeth of Hungary, remains unsanctioned by the bishop of the Episcopal Church. A man named Michael Clark until 1974, Sister Mary Elizabeth is also the only person to serve in the military as both a male and a female.

1989: A survey of 101 gay Catholic priests includes these findings:
- Two-thirds of the sample estimated that 40 to 60 percent of the Catholic clergy are gay.
- "Leading a celibate life" was reported by 63 percent as a frequent source of problems
- 36.6 percent had been occasionally sexually active with another person.
- 36.6 percent had been frequently sexually active with another person.
- 82.2 percent said they would "probably" or "definitely" stay in the priesthood.

1989: Surrounded by controversy, Robert Williams is ordained as an openly gay Episcopalian priest. One month later he publicly comments that "monogamy is as unnatural as celibacy," followed by the remark that Mother Teresa would be better off "if she got laid." In 1991, Williams resigned his priesthood.

1992: MCC's application for observer status within the National Council of Churches of Christ (NCC) is voted to not be acted upon. The debate regarding MCC's status causes some NCC member churches to side with MCC, including the United Church of Christ, the United Methodist Church, and the Swedenborgian Church. Several other groups indicate that they will pull out of the group if MCC's request is granted, particularly orthodox and predominantly black denominations.

- A four-page letter from the Vatican entitled "Some Considerations Concerning the Catholic Response to Legislative Proposals on the Non-Discrimination of Homosexual Persons" is issued to the U.S. Bishops. Basically the letter states the Vatican's opposition to such legislation and urges bishops to actively oppose gay civil rights laws. Bishops in Seattle, Honolulu, and other places make the surprising move of publicly dissenting.

OTHER STATISTICS AND FACTS

- There are words in Greek for same-sex sexual activities, yet they never appear in the original text of the New Testament.
- "Joining a religious community from about 500 [A.D.] to about 1300[A.D.] was probably the surest way of meeting other gay people [in Europe]."
  —John Boswell, "Homosexuality and Religious Life: A Historical Approach," in *Homosexuality, the Priesthood and the Religious Life,* ed. Jeannine Gromick, Crossroad, 1989.
- The word "homosexual" did not appear in any translation of the Christian Bible until 1946.
- Widely known in the Catholic world from the fifth century on, gay clerics are said to have taken part in homosexual marriage ceremonies.

- There are approximately 1 billion adherents of Christianity in the world and 142 million in the United States, including 79 million Protestants and 52 million Roman Catholics—equivalent to 60 percent of the United States population. According to a public opinion survey in 1983, roughly 22 percent of the U.S. population ages eighteen and older were Evangelical Christians. Of these, 88.7 percent expressed strong opposition to homosexuality.
- Buddhism is notable among world religions in that it does not condemn homosexuality.
- The world's fastest growing religion, Islam, has more than 6 million followers in the United States. Islamic law punishes men and women found guilty of "public" homosexual behavior that is witnessed by four adult males, though the Koran does not condemn homosexuality per se.
- Pat Robertson's Christian Coalition, among whose primary objectives are to oppose homosexuality and restrict gay and lesbian rights, has over 250,000 members in forty-nine states.
- Père-Lachaise Cemetery, in Paris, has been called "the world's gayest cemetery," with many notable lesbians, gays, and bisexuals buried there. The list includes Oscar Wilde, Gertrude Stein, Alice B. Toklas, Sarah Bernhardt, Marcel Proust, Isadora Duncan, Jane Avril, Colette, and Anna de Noailles (the "French Sappho"). Rosa Bonheur, Natalie Micus, and Anna Klumpke are all buried together on the Micus family plot. Two nineteenth-century balloonists, Croce-Spinelli and Sivel, were buried together here after they were killed in 1875 in a ballooning accident in India. Their much talked about monument shows them lying naked under a sculpted sheet that covers them from the waist down, holding flowers and hand in hand.
- The Cathedral of Hope Metropolitan Community Church in Dallas, Texas, is the world's largest lesbian and gay congregation, with 892 active members and 2,100 constituent members.
- There are currently 23,561 Roman Catholic churches, 200 Scientology churches, and 230 Metropolitan Community Churches in the United States. Worldwide, MCC has 42,000 voting members and nonvoting adherents in almost 300 churches in sixteen countries, with their congregations growing at a rate of approximately 10 percent a year.
- MCC's income of over $10 million in contributions annually, and property holdings worth $50 million, makes it the largest nonprofit group serving lesbians and gay men.
- New York City's MCC passes out 1,500 bags of groceries to families every week and has six beds for the homeless.
- Dignity, an organization of Catholic lesbians and gay men, has over 6,000 dues-paying members and as many as 18,000 participating in its services and activities.
- Congregation Beth Simchat Torah is the largest gay and lesbian synagogue in the world. With more than 1,000 members, it is also one of the largest synagogues in New York.
- During the High Holidays of Rosh Hashanah and Yom Kippur, Congregation Beth Simchat Torah (CBST) hosts some 2,500 people at a special service at New York City's Jacob Javits Convention Center.

- A conservative estimate of the percentage of homosexual men and women in the Catholic priesthood and religious life is around 30 percent, with approximately the same number in the rabbinate and the Protestant ministry.

THE MOST OFTEN QUOTED REFERENCES TO HOMOSEXUALITY IN THE BIBLE (KING JAMES VERSION)

Leviticus 18:22

"Thou shalt not lie with mankind, as with womankind: it is an abomination."

Leviticus 20:13

"If a man also lie with mankind, as he lieth with a woman, both of them have committed an abomination: they shall surely be put to death; their blood shall be upon them."

Romans 1:26–27

"For this cause God gave them up unto vile affections: for even their women did change the natural use into that which is against nature: And likewise also the men, leaving the natural use of the woman, burned in their lust towards one another; men with men working that which is unseemly, and receiving in themselves that recompense of the error which was met."

Corinthians 6:9–10

"Know ye not that the unrighteous shall not inherit the kingdom of God? Be not deceived: neither fornicators, nor idolaters, nor adulterers, nor effeminate, nor abusers of themselves with mankind, nor thieves, nor covetous, nor drunkards, nor revilers, nor extortioners shall inherit the kingdom of God."

Some responses:

"This crucial issue of homophobia has to be addressed. The six allusions in the Old Testament and the three in the New, are often used as an attempt to justify hatred or even murder and killing of gay brothers and lesbian sisters. The fact that Jesus himself never mentions it (homosexuality), means that it was not as significant to him as it is seemingly to a whole host of other Christians. . . . What is going on is an attempt to use or mobilize the Bible as an authority to reinforce a certain sense of what it means to be Black in the latter part of the twentieth century. What it means to be Black is primarily: Imposing certain controls and regulations over women, over gays, over lesbians, and policing these regulations."

—CORNELL WEST

"If we are going to take the Levitical law, we are going to have to take the whole law. That means: to combine fabrics is against the Levitical law, to tattoo one's skin is against the Levitical law, to eat certain kinds of seafood, such as shrimp is against the Levitical law. And so our challenge to the mainstream church is: How much of this law are you going to exclude, and choose to include, in order to oppress people—specifically lesbian and gay people?"

—REV. ZACHARY JONES, Pastor of Unity Fellowship Church, Brooklyn, NY

IS HOMOSEXUALITY A "SIN"? WHERE RELIGIOUS LEADERS HAVE STOOD

(Excerpted from "Can We Understand? A Guide for Parents," prepared by New York City Parents and Friends of Lesbians and Gays, 1983. Reprinted with permission.)

This is one of the most difficult questions for religious people. Many religions teach that homosexuality is condemned. But *nowhere* in the Bible is there mention of those who's true nature is homosexual. Neither the Ten Commandments nor the Gospels mention homosexuality. Bible scholars tell us that the oft-quoted (out of context) proscriptions in Leviticus 18:22 and 20:13 and St. Paul's Epistles Rom. 1:26–27, refer to male prostitution in temples: sexual practices by *heterosexuals*.

Catholic

"Because of the diverse conditions of humans, it happens that some acts are virtuous to some people, as appropriate and suitable to them, while the same are immoral for others, as inappropriate to them."

—SAINT THOMAS AQUINAS, *Summa Theologiea*

"Homosexuality has nothing necessarily to do with sin, sickness or failure. It is a different way of fulfilling God's plan. . . . Supposedly, the sin for which God destroyed Sodom was homosexuality. That's the great myth. I discovered through scholarly research that it was not true. The sin of Sodom and Gomorrah was inhospitality to a stranger. . . . In Matthew, Jesus says to his disciples: 'Go out and preach the Gospel if you come to any town and they don't receive you well, if they're inhospitable, shake the sand from your sandals and it will be worse for that town than it was for Sodom.' . . .The four Gospels are totally silent on the issue of homosexuality."

—JOHN J. MCNEILL, S.J., in an interview with Charles Ortleb in *Christopher Street*, October 1976

Protestant

"Do I believe that homosexuality is a sin? . . . Homosexuality, quite like heterosexuality, is neither a virtue nor an accomplishment. Homosexual orientation is a mysterious gift of God's grace. . . . Homosexuality is a gift, neither a virtue or a sin. What they do (how about "one does"?) with their ("one's" or "his/her"?) ho-

mosexuality, however, is definitely their (one's) personal, moral and spiritual responsibility. Their *behavior as homosexuals may be very sinful—brutal, exploitative, selfish, promiscuous, superficial. Their behavior as homosexuals, on the other
hand, may be beautiful—tender, considerate, loyal, other-centered, profound.*

"With this interpretation of the mystery that must be attributed to both heterosexual and homosexual orientations, I clearly do not believe that homosexuality is a sin."

—BISHOP MELVIN E. WHEATLY, Jr., Methodist, retired, November 20, 1981

Jewish

*"Above all else, Judaism has always stressed the importance and sanctity of the in-
dividual. The ancient rabbis likened each human life to the entire world. 'Why did
God create each human being different, not stamping us out like so many coins?'
asked the rabbis. 'To show us that each person is unique,' they answered. Judaism
has always gloried in the individuality of human life, and it has always cherished
freedom as the vehicle through which each unique individual can develop his or
her own potential.*

*"It is for this reason, and because we Jews have learned firsthand how stifling
and destructive oppression is, that the Reform Jewish movement in all its
branches has called for gay rights legislation and for loving acceptance of gay people. While all branches of Judaism do not agree, liberal Judaism recognizes that
religious strictures against homosexuality were a product of their time and place,
an ancient age in which existence itself depended upon each member of society
having children to populate the frontier and the army. That was a long time ago,
before modern science and psychiatry brought us new understanding of human
nature. We Jews have always incorporated the latest knowledge in our Judaism—
this adaptability is why we have survived, and why so many other Biblical pro-
hibitions are disregarded. Thinking Jews today, indeed all thinking people, will
refuse to invoke homophobic rules from these long-forgotten laws. After all, even
the most Orthodox no longer stone disobedient children to death and fundamentalist Christians do not call for us to keep kosher, only two of the rules found in
the Bible.*

*"If we Jews, always being victimized for being different, are not accepting, who
in God's name will be?"*

—RABBI CHARLES D. LIPPMAN, 1985

INCREDIBLE STATEMENTS BY RELIGIOUS HOMOPHOBES

"If homosexuality were the normal way, God would have made Adam and Bruce."

—ANITA BRYANT

*"There's a lot of talk these days about homosexuals coming out of the closet. I didn't
know they'd been in the closet. I do know they've always been in the gutter."*

—REV. JERRY FALWELL

"Sweating is good for a boy and will help him avoid homosexual tendencies."

—Baptist minister JACK HYLES

"Homosexuals or lesbians cannot produce a baby, a family or a society.... There are no sexual preferences. The assumption that there are is in itself a defiance of nature, creation and God."

—American Council of Christian Churches

"... Those who behave in a homosexual fashion ... shall not enter the kingdom of God."

—POPE JOHN PAUL II

"They [homosexuals] should be killed through government means."

—Baptist minister DANIEL LOVELY

"Homosexuality makes God vomit."

—fundamentalist JAY GRIMSTEAD

"God made no one homosexual.... God makes everyone heterosexual."

—WILLIAM CONSIGLIO

"This is a socialist, antifamily political movement that encourages women to leave their husbands, kill their children, practice witchcraft, destroy capitalism, and become lesbians."

—PAT ROBERTSON

WHERE SOME MAJOR RELIGIONS STAND ON HOMOSEXUALITY

Question: In your opinion, does God regard homosexuality as a sin?

Dr. Stayton (Baptist): "Absolutely not! There is nothing in the Bible or in my own theology that would lead me to believe that God regards homosexuality as sin. God is interested in our relationships with ourselves, others, the things in our lives, and with God."

Bishop Spong (Episcopalian): "Our prejudice rejects people or things outside our understanding. But the God of creation speaks and declares, 'I have looked out on everything I have made and behold it (is) very good.' (Gen 1.31.) The word of God in Christ says that we are loved, valued, redeemed and counted as precious no matter how we might be valued by a prejudiced world."

Bishop Olson (Lutheran): "Of course not. God could (not) care less about humanly devised categories that label and demean those who do not somehow fit into the norm of those in control. God made all of us and did not make all of us alike. Diversity is beautiful in creation. How we live our lives, in either affirming or destructive ways, is God's concern, but being either homosexually oriented or heterosexually oriented is neither a divine plus or minus."

Rabbi Marder (Judaism-Reform): "The God I worship endorses loving, committed, monogamous relationships, regardless of the gender of those involved."

Rabbi Dr. Teutsch (Judaism-Reconstructionist): "Homosexuality—as is true of heterosexuality—is a naturally occurring sexual orientation that can be expressed in more ethical and less ethical ways. In itself homosexual lovemaking is not sinful."

Dr. McGrath (Former Mormon): "I believe that the Creator of our natural erotic attractions, whether they are of opposite or same-sex persons, views our eroticism as an intrinsic and beautiful part of who God intended us to be. God did not intend that there would be one way of being sexual. Even among heterosexual people, there is no one 'right' way to be sexual. . . . I believe God is pleased when we respond to our unique form of sexuality in ways that are lifegiving. I believe that it is life-giving when sexual relationships reflect a high degree of mutuality, love and justice."

Rev. Holfelder (Presbyterian): "No, I do not think that God regards homosexuality as a sin, I believe that one's sexual preference is first and foremost a matter of biology (creation) and only secondarily a matter of choice (responsibility). Since I also believe that all God creates is good, I conclude that human sexuality (not a matter of choice of anyone) is good, whether that sexual expression be heterosexual or homosexual."

Sister Gramick (Roman Catholic): "God has created peole with romantic and physical attractions to the same sex, as well as those with attractions to the opposite sex. Many, if not most, people, we are now discovering, have both kinds of attractions in varying degrees. All of these feelings are natural and are considered good and blessed by God. These feelings and attractions are not sinful."

Dr. Nelson (United Church of Christ): "I am convinced that our sexuality and our sexual orientations, whatever they may be, are a gift from God. Sexual sin does not reside in our orientations, but rather in expressing our sexuality in ways that harm, oppress, or use others for our own selfish gratification. When we express ourselves sexually in ways that are loving and just, faithful and responsible, then I am convinced that God celebrates our sexuality, whatever our orientation may be."

Dr. Cobb (United Methodist): "Surely being attracted to persons of the same sex is not, as such, a sin. But of course how we act in our attractions, towards whichever sex, is often sinful. The ideal is to be responsible and faithful rather than self-indulgent. Unfortunately, society does not encourage responsible and faithful relations with persons of the same sex. That makes the situation of the homosexual very difficult."

Question: In your opinion, do the Scriptures object to homosexuality?

Dr. Stayton (Baptist): "There is *nothing* in the Bible regarding homosexual orientation. . . . I lead Bible study programs on this subject and am convinced that the Bible does not address the issue of a person's sexual orientation."

Rabbi Marder (Judaism-Reform): "I believe that the Hebrew Bible strongly condemns homosexuality. While it is part of my tradition, I do not regard all Biblical laws as binding on me. The Biblical condemnation of homosexuality is based on human ignorance, suspicion of those who are different, and an overwhelming concern for ensuring the survival of the people."

Rabbi Dr. Teutsch (Judaism-Reconstructionist): "The Scriptural references to homosexuality make no comment on lesbianism. They object to male homosexuality on three grounds: cultic prostitution, unnaturalness, and 'spilling seed' or Onanism. Gay men today are not involved in cultic acts. And the spilling of the seed through heterosexual, homosexual, or masturbatory acts is not an issue for me. Thus I take this prohibition no more seriously than many others, such as that against lending money at interest, that do not make sense in this time and place."

Bishop Olson (Lutheran): "Biblical scholars are busy restudying the few verses which have often been regarded as anti-homosexual. One thing is clear, these few verses do not refer to homosexuality as we understand and use that term today. . . . Here is a partial list of verses that has every right in being equally addressed to homosexual or heterosexual Christians: John 3:16, Galatians 3:27, Ephesians 2:8,9, Romans 3:21-24, Acts 10."

Sister Gramick (Roman Catholic): "When read at face value, the Scriptures have nothing positive to say about homogenital behavior. However, most Christians do not interpret the Bible literally; they try to understand the Scriptures in their historical and cultural context and see what meaning the Scriptures have for us today. . . . It is unfair of us to expect or impose a twentieth century mentality and understanding about equality of genders, races, and sexual orientations on the Biblical writers. We must be able to distinguish the eternal truths the Bible is meant to convey from the cultural forms and attitudes expressed there."

Dr. Schulz (Unitarian Universalist): "Most of the Old Testament is surely not an appropriate resource from which to obtain guidance regarding contemporary ethics! Turning to the New Testament, we discover that Jesus has nothing whatsoever to say regarding homosexuality. Inasmuch as he frequently condemned others of whose behavior he disapproved, it is significant that he makes no reference to homosexuals or their practices."

Question: *In your opinion, does God approve of two gay or lesbian individuals pledging their love to each other in a religious ceremony and raising children who may be born to them or adopted by them?*

Dr. Stayton (Baptist): "Absolutely. God's concern must be that we are good and loving parents, whether gay or straight, and that we bring our children up to be independent of us, loving individuals with a value system that strives to accept, understand, and love all that is good."

Bishop Wood (Episcopalian): "Yes. The image of relationships God seeks for us is clear: self-giving, caring, faithful."

Rabbi Dr. Teutsch (Judaism-Reconstructionist): "Yes. The ideal religious way is one of long-term mutual commitment in a family setting. Those who have not obtained it deserve no condemnation; those who create permanent relationships and/or are raising children deserve our fullest support."

Bishop Olson (Lutheran): "Religious leaders are asked to invoke God's blessings on farms, homes, cemeteries, and people's pets. . . . What is so strange then about blessing the covenant of fidelity of two committed and loving parents who are gay or lesbian? If the home and family they seek to create is a place of love, sacrifice, fidelity and mutual respect it is surely a fit place for the raising of children."

Dr. McGrath (Former Mormon): "God approves of all relationships that are life-giving. . . . My experience with gay couples and lesbian couples who have pledged their love to each other has taught me that they are no less capable than heterosexual couples in creating life-giving relationships into which children can be nurtured and loved."

Rev. Nugent (Roman Catholic): ". . . A religious ceremony would say clearly that the couple took that relationship with God seriously and would also [bear] witness to the social impact of their relationship on others of the faith community. Caring for children born of prior heterosexual unions, adopted or foster children by a same-gender couple would not only be 'approved' by God, but would be a serious religious obligation coming from one's belief in and commitment to God."

Dr. Nelson (United Church): "Yes, I believe God deeply approves of loving, committed, same-sex covenants, and the parenting for such children as may come to them. I rejoice in those churches and synagogues that now celebrate such unions, and I pray for the day when many more will do so."

Dr. Cobb (United Methodists): "I believe this pattern would be the one most pleasing to God of all the options available to gays and lesbians. Of course, the raising of children is not essential to a healthy relationship."

SOURCE: From *"Is Homosexuality a Sin?"* (1992), reprinted with permission of Parents, Families and Friends of Lesbians and Gays.

SOURCES FOR FURTHER READING

Books and Articles

Blumenfeld, Warren J., and Diane Raymond. *Looking at Gay and Lesbian Life.* Alyson, 1993.

Boswell, John. *Christianity, Social Tolerance, and Homosexuality.* University of Chicago Press, 1980.

Boswell, John. "Homosexuality and Religious Life: A Historical Approach," in *Ho-*

mosexuality, the Priesthood and the Religious Life, edited by Jeannine Gramick. Crossroad, 1989.

Boswell, John. *Same-Sex Unions in Pre-Modern Europe.* Villard, 1994.

Boyd, Malcolm, and Nancy Wilson, eds. *Amazing Grace, Stories of Lesbian and Gay Faith.* Crossing Press, 1991.

Brant, Beth. *Writing as Witness: Essay and Talk.* The Women's Press, 1994.

The Catholic Church, Homosexuality and Social Justice: The Report by the Task Force on Gay and Lesbian Issues. Commission on Social Justice, Archdiocese of San Francisco, 1982.

Comstock, Gary David. *Violence Against Lesbians and Gay Men.* Columbia University Press, 1991.

D'Antonio, Michael. *Heaven on Earth: Dispatches from Americas Spritual Frontier.* Crown, 1992.

Dean, Amy. *Proud to Be: Daily Meditations for Lesbians and Gay Men.* Dutton, 1994.

Dynes, Wayne R., ed. *Encyclopedia of Homosexuality.* Garland, 1990.

Dynes, Wayne R., and Stephen Donaldson, eds. *Homosexuality and Religion and Philosophy.* Garland, 1992.

Evans, Arthur. *Witchcraft and the Gay Counter Culture.* Fag Rag Books, 1978.

Gallagher, John. "Is God Gay?," *The Advocate,* December 13, 1994.

Harding, Rick. "Minneapolis Panel: Catholic Officials Violated Bias Law," *The Advocate,* January 1, 1991.

Hasbany, Richard, ed. *Homosexuality and Religion.* Harrington Park, 1989.

Helminiak, Daniel, Ph.D. *What the Bible Really Says About Homosexuality.* Alamo Square Press, 1994.

Hunter, James Davison. *American Evangelicalism.* Rutgers University Press, 1983.

McNeill, John J. *The Church and the Homosexual.* Farrar, Straus, and Giroux, 1994.

Melton, J. Gordon. *The Churches Speak on: Homosexuality.* Gale Research, 1991.

O'Neill, Craig, and Kathleen Ritter, *Coming Out Within: Stories of Spiritual Awakening for Lesbians and Gay Men.* Harper, 1992.

O'Neill, John J. *Freedom, Glorious Freedom: The Spiritual Journey to the Fullness of Life for Gays, Lesbians, and Everybody Else.* Beacon, 1994.

"Rise of the Religious Right," *The New Leader,* September 21, 1992.

Robinson, David J. "Troy Perry: Gay Advocate," in *Gay Speak: Gay Male and Lesbian Communication,* James W. Chesebro, ed. Pilgrim Press, 1981.

Roscoe, Will. *Living the Spirit: A Gay American Indian Anthology.* St. Martin's, 1988.

Singer, Bennet L., and David Deschamps, eds. *Gay and Lesbian Stats: A Pocket Guide of Facts and Figures.* New Press, 1994.

Stuart, Dr. Elizabeth. *Daring to Speak Love's Name: A Gay and Lesbian Prayer Book.* Hamish Hamilton/Penguin Group, 1992.

Thompson, Mark. *Gay Spirit: Myth And Meaning.* St.Martin's Press, 1987.

"The Universal Fellowship of Metropolitan Community Churches Fact Sheet," Universal Fellowship of Metropolitan Community Churches, 1993.

Walker, Mitch. *Visionary Love: A Spirit Book of Gay Mythology.* Treeroot Press, 1980.

Williams, Reverend Robert. *Just As I Am: A Practical Guide to Being Out, Proud, and Christian.* Crown, 1992.

Wolf, James G. *Gay Priests.* Harper & Row, 1989.

Yamaguchi Fletcher, Lynne. *The First Gay Pope and Other Records.* Alyson, 1992.

Newsletters

Living Streams, P.O. Box 178, Concord, CA 94522. "Evangelical/Charismatic publication providing a forum for Christian gays & lesbians."

Malchus, 6036 Richmond Highway #301, Alexandria, VA 22303, 703-329-7896.

Marilyn Medusa Gay-Pagan Journal, 8701 NW 35th St., Coral Springs, FL 33605

New Direction, 1608 N. Cahuenga Blvd. #B-440, Los Angeles, CA 90028. "Publication for gay and lesbian Mormons, relatives, and friends."

Open Hands, 3801 N Keeler Ave., Chicago, IL 60641. Phone: 312-736-5526. Fax: 312-736-5475. "Resources for ministries affirming the diversity of human sexuality."

The Second Stone, P.O. Box 8340, New Orleans, LA 70182, 504-891-7555. "Religious news, information, features."

Solitary, P.O. Box 6091, Madison, WI 53716, 608-244-0072. "Quarterly journal for those practicing spiritual traditions alone while seeking dialogue with those who share a similar solitary pagan path."

PROFILE

Dana Rose

Some would call Dana Rose determined, some would say he is unrealistic. But to most who know his story, he is a man of true conviction and generosity, one whose beliefs will not easily be sacrificed no matter what barriers he encounters on his way. Over the past sixteen years, Dana has been through three states, four dioceses, and an unmeasurable amount of discrimination in his quest to become an ordained minister in the Episcopal Church.

Born in Baltimore, Maryland, Dana moved with his family to Los Angeles when he was sixteen. Dana was raised a nonfundamentalist Baptist, a faith that he eventually rejected altogether. "I used spirituality in the church as a crutch, and I recognized that. So, I went in an opposite direction which sometimes had me wavering." What Dana was looking for in religion was something that "had to speak to me in another way that was very powerful. It had to speak to me in a way that both raised up my spirits and spoke politically as well." He felt he had found this within the Episcopal Church.

"I am very much into sacrament and ritual, so I wanted the kind of thing that would speak to me inwardly so that I could do things outwardly. When I take a wafer at church—to some people that may seem very simple—but once I take that wafer, I think that I am charged to be committed not just to church people, but to the world. And that means the lesbian and gay community. Some people don't see how I connect the two, but I am gay and I just don't see any way of separating my sexual orientation from my spirituality."

Dana's search to define his spirituality soon began to take shape. What influenced him most in college was reading feminist works and works by Black authors who were writing in a stream-of-consciousness fashion. "I remember one day I walked up on A Different Light [the gay bookstore]. I was so happy to see it because I had not known that it had existed. I went in and read a book: *Home Girls* by Barbara Smith. It became, for a while, kind of a bible for me." By mixing the ideas he discovered in these writings with what he believed about spirituality, Dana discovered a solid faith.

"It really calls me to be more effective in the world, to be well with myself and balanced—really demand justice and respect for all people regardless of what color they are, what sex they are, what there sexual orientation is, or their religion (or lack of it). The issue is: Human beings are human beings and I need to be in the forefront of fighting for them. I wished to do it—I later realized—as a priest."

While Dana has been out to himself for most of his life, he had to struggle with the issue of whether or not to come out to the church. "I remember lying about it in the beginning because I *really* wanted to be a priest and I didn't want to get turned down in the first go-round." The Episcopal Church has varying opinions about the ordination of lesbians and gays, and though there are several openly lesbian and gay priests within the church, most have come out after they were ordained. Lesbian and gay people are welcomed in some congregations, but according to Dana, they are warned against seeking ordination.

While at seminary from 1981 to 1984, Dana was part of a lesbian and gay caucus. "No one was supposed to know, other than the people in the group. We knew that wasn't the case. People knew all along and people were being blackballed because of that."

Then, in a burst of honesty, Dana's not-so-secret sexuality came even further out of the closet. "One time a professor showed the film *Word Is Out* in the auditorium. I went to see it, and I came out there, but I didn't realize what I was doing. To come out like that about it was a big thing, and word got back to the bishops. I was blackballed."

The first time Dana felt the repercussions of his coming out was in the diocese of Los Angeles. "There are three levels of the process: Postulancy, Candidacy, and Deaconate. I had completed them all and I was ready for ordination." But he was not allowed to reach the fourth level: Priesthood. "I knew what had happened, I knew why I was not ordained—I was told different reasons, but the real reason was my sexual orientation."

After he recovered from being turned down, Dana left the Episcopal Church in Los Angeles and went to New York to try once again, within the diocese of New York. In each diocese, one must begin the process from the bottom up: In the New York diocese Dana didn't even get a chance. But his faith was far from failing him and he went directly to the diocese of Long Island, which also includes Queens and Brooklyn. "The bishop there was Black and also new. He had vowed publicly to ordain lesbians and gays who were open." Dana went to this priest and was very honest and up front and told him what had been going on. Dana was asked to participate in a parish in Brooklyn and report back in a year.

The year passed, and it became time to pick the candidates for the ordination process. He was interviewed and asked why he wasn't ordained in Los Angeles. Dana gave all the possible technical reasons why he might not have been ordained, but did not mention what he felt was the real reason. He was then shocked when the interviewer asked if it had anything to do with his being gay. Dana was then told that people had been talking behind his back, saying that he "was too swishy and faggoty to be a priest. . . . I was devastated that people were talking about me like that, but I would not deny who I was. I said (to the interviewer) 'Dammit! Yes, I am gay. I'm proud of it and I've done a lot of work on myself to be healthy around that. I don't have to deny it and I'm not ashamed of who I am. I belong to enough organizations to do what I need to do for myself to take care of myself and I resent that people feel they have the right to say these things. I think that I would make a fine priest.'" The interviewer agreed, but even with her backing and that of the bishop who had pledged to ordain gays, Dana was once again denied the process. This time he challenged the decision and was granted postulancy.

After spending two years as a postulant—when the term is supposed to last for only six months to a year—Dana had to face the reality that there was never any real intention of letting him go further. "When I started to instigate the moving process, you never would have heard so much deceit, shame, and fear. The bishop would not support me in any way, and he succumbed to the pressures of a white racist church on Long Island." The bishop wouldn't take the risk of standing up to advisory committees and saying that he believed in Dana. The disappointment Dana felt nearly shattered him.

While he was going through this, people in the lesbian and gay community would often ask: "Why do you put yourself through such a thing?" His response: "I have to stay because there are people there who are like me—who are living in shame but want the freedom of liberation."

Dana's frustration with the church really resides with the upper levels of clergy. "At the parish level, wherever I've worked in this church in this country, I have never had any problems. I have come out to parishes and they have seen my work, they know my sincerity, they know my spirit."

And now, it has been sixteen years since Dana set out to achieve his goal of being a priest in the Episcopal Church. "I have not given up, I refuse to give up. I have now gone to the diocese of Newark, New Jersey." He jokingly says, "I feel like I'm on 'The Diocese Ride' at Disneyland — from diocese to diocese, bishop to bishop. I have seen more dioceses than anybody else in the country."

Along with friends and a life full of community activities, the one thing that Dana says has really kept him grounded has been his past three and one-half years at New York City's Lesbian and Gay Community Services Center. Here he is a part of the Mental Health and Social Services staff, where he heads a bereavement program called "Centerbridge." "Coming here and working at the Center, while I don't do any proselytizing or discussions of religion, I do work around spirituality all the time. This has been a rewarding thing. The Center certainly has been a place where I can fulfill some of my stuff that I need to do: from being able to sit and counsel people right on down to doing rituals and rites of passage with people. So until the time when I am finally ordained, I certainly can do a lot of what I feel called to do here.

"In fact," says Dana enthusiastically, "if I am ordained a priest, I don't want to leave the Center. I would rather work at the Center as a secular priest—that is working outside of the church, but maybe doing a stand-in job on Sundays around different dioceses. To be able to be that presence here in the community is very important."

So where exactly is Dana in the process of seeking ordination in Newark right now? "I am with a parish that is considering sponsoring me. I do some preaching in the parish and work with some of the groups there." If the parish decides to recommend him to the bishop, the whole process would begin again. Since he graduated from seminary ten years ago, he would like to take some refresher courses or possibly get a doctoral degree in spirituality and bereavement.

PROFILE

Rich Wandel

Rich Wandel is archivist of the National Lesbian and Gay Archive housed at the New York City Lesbian and Gay Community Services Center. But he is also a high priest in a Wiccan coven named Polyhymnia. "I am out of the broom closet, so to speak."

Rich was raised a Roman Catholic, and attended Catholic grammar school and high school. He wanted to become a priest, so after high school, he entered a monastic seminary, and became a monk for six years. It wasn't very long after Rich left the monastery when he came out to himself as gay. "Within months after I came out to myself, around 1970, I was on local television, and involved with gay liberation."

He went through a period of time not being a "practicing Catholic" and was interested in Native American spirituality and the writings of Carlos Casteneda. "I had moved away from the church and was very angry for all of the obvious reasons any gay person would be. I even played around with titles like 'agnostic' and 'atheist.' For a very brief time I was even a member of the Gay Atheist League, but that didn't work for me either." He never felt that Dignity or any other gay Catholic organizations were what he was looking for.

"I was looking for the ongoing adventure that any decent spirituality will provide—and there are lots of 'decent' spiritualities— certainly not only Wicca; we are not the one true religion, by any means. I decided that I really had to find something not only spiritual, but religious, that would work for me. Religion is not for all people, but it is for me. For some people it is a blockage to spirituality; for me it is a help."

It was just around this time in early 1984, "as the gods would have it," Rich picked up a weekly newspaper in Queens, and there was an ad in the back advertising Kathexis coven. Kathexis is run by Michael Thorne, who is also very publicly out as both gay and a Witch. Rich started to go and found it was really what he was looking for, especially because of its lack of authoritarianism and dogma.

For Rich, it was more than just the liberality that made him like Wicca, it was also the ritual and liturgy that was reminiscent of the rich liturgy of Catholicism he was raised to appreciate. "It is also speaking to the divine within me, within everyone, and honoring and recognizing the feminine both in terms of women and in terms of the feminine within me as well." Rich was a part of Kathexis for eight years until it was time for him to "hive off" and form a coven of his own with others. Polyhymnia was then founded by Rich and the woman who now serves as high priestess for Polyhymnia, Sonia Ivette Roman.

"There are covens, fine covens, that are all women. There are fine covens that are all men, or all gay men for that matter. But for myself, it is very important for me to be working with a high priestess in general and with Sonia in particular, because gender is a central theme of our time—certainly if you are a gay man or lesbian. For me, I want to jump into that theme as opposed to what would admittedly often be easier, avoiding it by just doing Wicca myself, or with people who are all men or who were raised the same way I was.

"Polyhymnia is a member of the Covenant of the Goddess (CoG), the national organization of covens and solitary and individual witches. It is a church and is recognized as such under tax laws and things of that nature but again there is no authority here, there is no dogma. We help each other, support each other, we work at dispelling false images of the craft, and we work at helping to protect each other when the government or others try to shut us down on the grounds of our religion. Things like this have been happening recently in Florida." It is a Gardnerian coven, a tradition that passes down the knowledge of the craft of Wicca through its elders, or high priests and priestesses. Training takes place before one reaches this status, and ultimately leads to initiation. "In most traditions, witches are initiated. In the Christian tradition, the initiation is called baptism."

"The whole idea of Wicca in general, not just in our tradition, is that we are empowering people to do for themselves, to have their own personal contact with the divine, especially the Goddess. It is not the one true religion, nor are we a coven with the expectation that the high priest and priestess always do for them." The priestess or priest isn't the only one with power. Everyone has the ability to create magic in his or her life, one just needs to know the things that can help achieve it.

"With the magic comes a responsibility," warns Rich. "When someone comes to me and tells me that their fundamentalist Christian parents are praying for their conversion, I consider that black magic. They are doing magic—prayer is magic—to force the will of another person. That is a large, large no-no in the Wiccan community. That is totally unethical." When one knows that magic works, then one must know that doing certain things is harmful. The group generally talks a lot about magic before they do it.

Out of the eight high holidays that are celebrated, Rich does have a couple that he feels extra connected with. "My favorites are easy. I like Samhain, which is Halloween, for it is a time of connection to those who have gone before us and will return again. It is my favorite ritual, and is one we never let the students lead. We do it ourselves, because it is important, particularly in terms of the many friends that all of us in our communities have lost.

"My other favorite is Beltane. The tradition of Beltane is that you have the ritual and then you go 'a-Maying,' that is, you run off into the woods or wherever, with whomever (singular or plural), and fuck all night. I kinda like that. It is a time of physical creativity, birth, and bringing forth."

One of the important things about Wicca is that the goddess and god are felt to be always around: in the sky, in wood, in music. "We are used to religion keeping the lid on the kettle, but we take the lid off the cauldron, and good things bubble there. Now all life is not sweetness and light, but we are changing things. All acts of love and pleasure are Her rituals. To have a good time, when you add that consciousness of Her presence, is a ritual. Being conscious of the deity is a releasing thing for me. I don't get out dancing very often, but when I do the first dance is usually to the God, and I just go with it!"

If you are interested in more information about Polyhymnia, write a brief letter to :

Polyhymnia, P.O. Box 6208, Long Island City, NY 11106.

FEATURE

Native American Berdaches

Native American gay men and lesbians are often referred to as "berdaches," a French term. Colonial French explorers were the first to use the word berdache to describe a male Indian who specialized in the work of women and formed emotional and sexual relationships with other men. Many tribes had female berdaches, too—women who took on men's work and married other women. The Native words for such people varied within different tribal languages.

Most Native American tribes had no set laws to prescribe the path that a young man had to take; he was to make up his own mind and follow his "puberty vision." But tribal mores pushed a young man toward a hunter-warrior career, and if he chose not to take this path he had to sacrifice his right to masculine privilege. In all reports of the berdache, anthropologists and doctors failed to discuss the homosexuality of the berdaches' non-cross-dressing sexual partners. Observers repeatedly use the word "hermaphrodite," without having any physical basis, to refer to an individual who would today be identified as a homosexual transvestite.

The "effeminate" homosexual in Native societies is often described as husky, strong, big, a fast runner, and a fighter. Several reports suggest that homosexuals often performed religious and ceremonial functions among their people, and before Christianity, they generally occupied an institutionalized, important, and respected position within many Native groups. The berdache was often the tribe or band's doctor, medicine man, leading scalp dancer, matchmaker, or storyteller. In some tribes, the berdache was educated as a medicine man (holy man) due to that particular tribe's taboos that forbade the high priest to marry women and father children.

In many tribes berdaches specialized in crafts, such as basketry, rather than religious roles. As well as these documented reports of homosexuality, many of the Native myths contain references to homosexuality, both male and female, as well as figures with a dual-sexual nature.

Many documents suggest that Native societies were very divided along sexual lines—a strict sexual division of labor, something that is said to be a key to understanding the character of homosexuality among Native Americans.

Some prominent male berdaches are described below.

Tolowa: Thirty-four California tribes have been reported to have berdaches. The Tolowa was a tribe on the coast of northern California, with about eight villages near Crescent City where they hunted, fished, and gathered wild foods. The Tolowa had little contact with whites until about 1820. According to an anthropologist, the shamans of that tribe were usually women or transvestite men. Shamans cured both physical and spiritual ills. They danced and entered trances, and then sucked out of the patient and vomited up the foreign object believed to be the cause of the illness. In California tribes, berdaches were not always shamans. Among the Mono and Yokuts tribes, berdaches prepared the dead for burial.

We'wha (Zuni): We'Wha (1849–1896), a Zuni berdache (or lhamana), was one of the most prominent and important members of the Zuni tribe. He lived his life as a woman in woman's dress, but was still powerful in his pueblo's councils and participated in male religious activities. He has been described as the tallest person in the Zuni, and also the strongest both mentally and physically. He managed a large household of adopted family and became one of the first Zunis to earn money, by washing clothes for whites or selling his weaving and pottery. He was also well versed in sacred and secular lore.

We'wha became friends of Matilda Coxe Stevenson, an anthropologist who published a long report on the Zunis in 1904. For years, Stevenson had no idea that We'wha was a transvestite. Even after she realized, Stevenson insisted on using the pronoun "she" when speaking of We'wha, as was the tribal custom.

In 1886, We'wah spent six months in Washington, DC as Stevenson's guest. There he met with President Cleveland and Speaker of the House John Carlisle. He participated in a theatrical charity event sponsored by society women and demonstrated weaving at the Smithsonian Museum. He was well accepted in Washington society as a Zuni "maiden," "priestess," and "princess," his true sex known to no one. We'wha also learned to speak English within the six months, enough to be able to carry on conversations.

Stevenson was with We'wha and his family when he passed away from valvular heart disease in 1896. He was buried in the traditional manner to symbolize his berdache status: dressed in the finest of women's clothing, with a pair of pants slipped on underneath.

Hastiin Klah (Navajo): Hastiin Klah (1876–1937), a berdache or nadle, is known as one of the most famous Navajo artists and medicine men in history. Early in his life, Klah was trained in Navajo ceremonial practice. Since he was a nadle, he also learned the women's work of weaving. He demonstrated Navajo arts at two world's fairs in Chicago in 1893 and 1933. Klah also met Franklin D. Roosevelt. He became close friends with two wealthy women who were interested in Navajo culture, and they encouraged him to weave religious sandpainting designs. Klah became one of the first Navajos to do this type of weaving, and his tapestries were enthusiastically bought by art collectors in the 1920s and '30s.

Today Navajo weaving is considered a fine art, thanks to the craftsmanship and talent of Klah and weavers like him. He worked with specialists to record his thorough knowledge of Navajo religion in order to have it preserved. Many of Klah's weavings, ceremonial artifacts, and transcribed myths, songs, and ceremonies became the core collection in the Wheelwright Museum of the American Indian, founded in Santa Fe in 1937.

16. GAY SEX AND SEXUALITY

A kiss is just a kiss. *(Collection of the Lesbian and Gay Community Services Center–New York)*

> *"If the most common experience among men in the youth-obsessed baths [of the 1970s] was cold, public rejection, the more common gesture in the clubs [of the 1990s] is the affectionate caress that may or may not go further. The style of competitive prowess seems to have been supplanted by an ethic of shared adventure."*
>
> —Frank Browning, *The Culture of Desire* (Vintage, 1993)

From time immemorial, the desire of men for men has had a powerful influence on society. But the actual term "homosexual" did not even exist until the late 1800s, when a medicalization of sex and sexual behavior created the category of the modern homosexual—an identity based exclusively on sexuality.

Gay or gay-friendly sex researchers were instrumental in beginning to turn the tide of "sickness" associated with the new medical term of homosexual. German researchers such as Karl Heinrich Ulrichs and Magnus Hirschfeld were brave pioneers in this effort.

In the twentieth century in America, the most significant events in liberating gay male sexuality, according to historian Allan Berube, were the two world wars, which threw vast numbers of men together far from home. After World War II especially, returning gay soldiers and sailors congregated in port cities and created the subculture and community identity that would eventually lead to the gay lib-

Keith Haring mural in the second-floor men's room of the NYC Lesbian and Gay Community Services Center *(Photo by Morgan Gwenwald)*

eration movement of the late 1960s. And in 1948, Alfred Kinsey documented that homosexual behavior was far more common than anyone had suspected, which helped many gay men realize that they weren't alone in their desires.

After the sexual experimentation of the sixties and the glory days of sex in the seventies, the unfolding and flowering of gay sexuality ran into the stark realities of a life-threatening sexually transmitted disease. With the decimating effects of AIDS on our community, gay sex in the 1980s went through stunning changes— from tearoom sex to safer sex, from bathhouses to j.o. parties, from silence about gay sex to media hysteria. In the 1990s, gay men are challenged with creating new ways to stay safe, sexy, horny, and alive.

Even in the age of AIDS, when gay sex is often burdened by the specter of illness, gay men have found ways to express their sexuality that are safe and erotic, from jack-off clubs and parties to pornographic magazines and videos.

SEX RESEARCH PIONEERS

Havelock Ellis: published *Studies in the Psychology of Sex* (several editions from 1896–1928); wrote *Sexual Inversion* with John Addington Symonds in 1897, one of the first English-language books to argue for increased acceptance of homosexuality.

Alfred Kinsey: author of *Sexual Behavior in the Human Male* (1948) and *Sexual Behavior in the Human Female* (1953), and namesake of the Kinsey scale (1–6 spectrum of gayness).

Evelyn Hooker: psychologist, UCLA. In 1957 sex researcher Evelyn Hooker issued the first of several reports disputing the belief that homosexual men and women are likely to have psychological problems.

Magnus Hirschfeld: famous sexologist and gay rights advocate, a German refugee whose Institute for Sexual Science was burned by the Nazis.

INTERNATIONAL LIST OF SEX RESEARCHERS

Arnold Aletrino

Iwan Block

Sir Richard Burton

Edward Carpenter

Vladimir Fiodorovich

Havelock Ellis

Sigmund Freud

Benedict Friedlaender

Rene Guyon

Magnus Hirschfeld

Heinrich Hoessli

Alfred Kinsey

Richard von Krafft-Ebing

Cesare Lombroso

Albert Moll

L.S.A. M. von Romer

Karl Heinrich Ulrichs

THE KINSEY REPORT

Although widely quoted as the source for the ever-popular figure that 10 percent of the American population is lesbian/gay, Kinsey's famous reports from the late 1940s and early 1950s never stated that. In fact, Kinsey's reports documented a far more complex world of sexual behavior than is even imagined by most people today.

Sexual Behavior in the Human Male, published in 1948, refuted the myth that homosexuals were rare. Alfred Kinsey found that 37 percent of adult men had had a homosexual experience in their adult lives, and that 4 percent were exclusively homosexual as adults.

In 1953 Kinsey followed up with a report on female sexuality, *Sexual Behavior in the Human Female*, finding that 2 percent of adult females were exclusively homosexual and 13 percent had had a homosexual experience as adults.

Kinsey used a continuous spectrum to measure sexual orientation, on a scale of 0 to 6, with 0 representing an exclusively heterosexual orientation/experience and 6 representing an exclusively homosexual orientation/experience. Almost all of the population fell in between the extremes—in other words, Kinsey found a continuous spectrum of sexuality, not a mutually exclusive polarity of homo—or heterosexual.

SEX AND THE LAW

In 1909, since there was no law on the books against oral sex, a Kentucky judge released two black men accused of the deed. Afterward many states specifically outlawed oral sex.

PERSONAL ADS

In the early part of the century, mainstream newspapers in France and Germany ran pieces by homosexuals in the personal columns that were "seeking friendship." In the 1920s the nascent gay press in Germany began to run more sexually explicit notices, but the rise of the Nazis soon stamped this out. Nothing similar appeared in the United States until the 1960s, when alternative and counterculture press began to print sexually explicit descriptions in news stories. These papers subsequently sought to increase revenue by running personal ads specifically soliciting sexual partners. The post-Stonewall gay press followed this practice, and the modern gay personal ad was born.

Heavy on abbreviations, short on beating around the bush, the culture of personal ads has evolved over the last three decades.

For further research, see *Classified Affairs: A Gay Man's Guide to the Personal Ads*, by John Preston and Frederick Brandt: Alyson, 1984.

A SAMPLING OF PERSONAL ADS OVER THE YEARS

From the Village Voice

"Across an Englishman's knee, all inhibitions set free, exciting, revealing & wild, like a man not a child. Across an Englishman's knee, somewhere you long to be. So if wish to risk it all, 'C'mon, luv, make the call.'" (1995)

Selection of headlines from Outweek, 1989:

"Real Batman Seeks Real Robin: Holy partner! Let's ditch Gotham City and concentrate on each other! "

"Need a spanking?"

"Low mileage"

"Complicated guy wants simple life"

"Mildly kinky"

"After-the-office"

"Out As Hell Seeks Closet Case"

And this one complete from Caldwell, NJ

"Old-fashioned, safe, sensuous & erotic 'daddy-enemas,' ass-play & more given with TLC. I cater to shy guys & beginners. Also want to share your childhood experiences."

You might also want to check out the classifieds under the following headings: "photography" (especially "fantasy photography"), "massage," and "model/escorts."

A FEW MASSAGE ADS

"Nude, attractive masseur! Gives deliciously erotic hot oil massage in sensually exotic atmosphere + release! In or Out."

"Body Rub by Guy. Have your body rub the French-Canadian way. Also body clipping."

"Hot Blond Jock. Body-rub by young stud 24 hrs."

"Hot Muscular Stud. Rubdown by Handsome Young Athlete."

A SAMPLE OF MODELS/ESCORT ADS

"Hot California Jock. 22, blond, blue eyes, juicy & big, 3-somes too!"

"HOT SOUTHERN STUD-ATHLETIC, SEXY, VERY HANDSOME, VERSATILE W/BIG TOOL, FR/GR, F/F TOP, 6'2", 30 YEARS OLD. VERY FRIENDLY."

"Rock Hard Muscular Blond Stud. Rugged, Handsome, Ex-Marine, Digs Service."

"Juice Extractor. Gives complete satisfaction. Vito."

THE FIRST BEST-SELLER AMONG MODERN LEATHERMEN

Mister Benson, by John Preston. When it was serialized in *Drummer* magazine, leathermen waited in line at newsstands to get the latest installment. The book depicts the relationship between a "real top" and a "real bottom." According to a review by Pat Califia in *OUT/LOOK*, "Aristotle Benson is not merely sexually dominant and sadistic, he is also wealthy, educated, and older than Jamie. Mr. Benson's power as a master flows seamlessly from his status in the real world. Jamie is younger, malleable, has no real goals, and lives (without benefit of a job or rights to use the furniture) in Mr. Benson's world."

GAY "PHYSIQUE" MAGAZINES—PUBLISHERS AND MODELS

In 1937, the first (of only nine issues) of *Bachelor* magazine appeared on newsstands. With male movie stars attired in swimsuits and gym shorts, it was clear what kind of bachelor this magazine targeted. It folded within a year, probably a little ahead of its time.

In 1945, Bob Mizer founded the Athletic Model Guild in Los Angeles and spawned the leading source of male erotic photography posing as "physique" and "physical culture" magazines.

Other physique studios included Anthony Guyther's Capital Studio in NYC and Bruce Bellas, a.k.a. "Bruce of Los Angeles." Some magazines of the period:

Adonis, 1951
Body Beautiful, early 1950s
Vim, 1954
Trim, 1957
The Young Physique, 1958 (which was the combination of *Adonis* and *Body Beautiful*)
Champ, 1960
Go Guys, 1963

SOME CONTEMPORARY GAY MALE SEX MAGAZINES (THE DESCENDENTS OF THE PHYSIQUE MAGAZINES)

Blueboy
Drummer: America's Mag for the Macho Male
Honcho: The Magazine for the Macho Male
Stroke
Hirsute Club Newsletter: The Club for Hairy Men and Men Who Love Hairy Men
Straight to Hell
First Hand: Experiences for Loving Men
Friction
Man 2 Man
F.Q. (Foreskin Quarterly)
Bound & Gagged, bimonthly magazine featuring true accounts of male bondage
  plus hot personals
Advocate Men
Ad Venture!: Your Passport to Erotic Pleasure
Chiron Pages: The Manhunt Magazine
Skin: The Hardon Magazine
Uncut: The Magazine of the Natural Man

. . . AND FOR THOSE WHO WANT FICTION AS WELL AS FRICTION

In Touch for Men, monthly erotic magazine with news, features, fiction, poetry. 13122 Saticoy St., North Hollywood, CA 91605, 818-764-2288.

A QUARTERLY SEX JOURNAL FOR MEN

"I believe sex and porn are basically good for society." Scott O'Hare, former porn star and editor of *Steam*, published by PDA Press, P.O. Box 460292, San Francisco, CA 94146. *Steam* is full of articles on outdoor and public sex venues.

FOR LEATHER ENTHUSIASTS

The Leather Journal, formerly a gay men's only publication now has a column "For Women, By Women."

BISEXUAL SEX MAGAZINE

Slippery When Wet, their motto, "Don't sweat the petty things, pet the sweaty things." From Productions, P.O. Box 3101, Berkeley, CA 94703.

GAY-FRIENDLY CHAIN SEX SHOP

The Pleasure Chest (specialists in erotica). Stores in New York, Philadelphia, Miami, Washington, DC, Chicago, and Los Angeles.

A BOOK YOU MAY OR MAY NOT NEED

The (New) Joy of Gay Sex, by Dr. Charles Silverstein and Felice Picano, with a preface by Edmund White, HarperPerennial, 1992.

At the 1993 Gay pride March *(Photo by Harry Stevens)*

SEX AND CLOTHING

Havelock Ellis in his 1915 book, *Sexual Inversion*, reports that a red tie was almost synonymous for homosexuality in major American cities
Other clothing styles from past and present:

- Cowboy—work shirt, Levi jeans, boots
- Colored rear-pocket bandanna, 1970s
- Key ring in back pocket to indicate S/M, left or right indicated position preferred
- Leather garments—project sexual power
- Nylon and spandex lingerie—seduction
- Police or military uniforms—project authority
- Athletic clothing, jockstrap—imaginary ideal locker room
- White cotton briefs—innocence and youth

SEX AND CLOTHING, PART II: *GAY SEMIOTICS* FROM 1977

In 1977, Hal Fisher published *Gay Semiotics: A Photographic Study of Visual Coding Among Homosexual Men* (San Francisco: NFS Press) and produced a historical document of the "hankie color coding."

For your information:

- Earrings, keys, and hankies worn on the left side of the body indicated the wearer liked the aggressive role.
- Earrings, keys, and hankies worn on the right side indicated the passive role.
- Handkerchiefs were assigned meaning by color:

  Blue stood for anal intercourse; worn in the left hip pocket meant the wearer would assume the dominate role; worn in the right hip pocket meant the wearer would play the passive role.

  Red = anal/hand insertion.

  Black = S/M activities.

  Yellow = water sports (i.e., play with urine).

LIFE (AND SEX AND CLOTHING) WERE EASIER THEN

Hal Fisher has been asked many times to update his classic historical document, but says that is impossible. Talking to a reporter from *OUT/LOOK* magazine in 1991, he said, "The coding systems and uniforms of the 1970s are still elemental to segments of the gay community, but the vocabulary of forms today is far bigger, taking in everything from nerd eyeglasses to pierced anything. The variations are a lot more subtle —the club look, for example, versus the ACT UP look, versus the Queer Nation look.

"I'm thirteen years older now and I'm no longer directly involved with the nuances of contemporary style articulated by people in their twenties. I'm getting older. Life was easier and less expensive when two pairs of 501s, a couple of flannel shirts, a leather jacket, and a zippered sweatshirt pretty much got gay men in San Francisco through a season in paradise."

SEX AND CLOTHING, PART III: SEXY FABRICS FOR THE 1994–95 SEASON

- Cotton-satin jackets and trousers
- Wraparound sunglasses (not technically a fabric, but you get the drift)
- Lime-green leather
- Red patent leather
- Pink stretch nylon
- Sheer nylon sleeveless shirts
- Linen
- White leather belt
- Silk-shantung suits in Technicolor colors

THE *OUT/LOOK* SEX SURVEY
(FROM ISSUE NO. 8, SPRING 1990)

More than three hundred responses to a survey asking about the nature of friendships, the quality of relationships with best friends, and the dynamics between friendship and lover relationships were analyzed by Claremont College (CA) sociologists Peter Nardi and Drury Sherrod. These were their general findings:

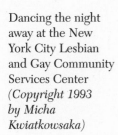

Dancing the night away at the New York City Lesbian and Gay Community Services Center *(Copyright 1993 by Micha Kwiatkowsaka)*

"Gay men appear to have more sex with their casual and close friends than lesbians do. Lesbians, however, are more likely to be best friends with their ex-lovers than gay men are. They also were more likely to have been sexually attracted to their best friend in the past than gay men were.

"Over time, it seems that sexual attractiveness, sexual activity, and romantic love with best friends fade. About 40 percent of the respondents have had some sexual experience with their same-sex gay or lesbian best friend in the past, but less than 5 percent currently do."

Some statistics: For 34 percent of the women who responded, their current best friend is a former lover; for men the percentage was 11. For women, 38 percent had been in love with their current best friend in the past and 27 percent had been sexually involved. For men, 37 percent had been in love with their best friend in the past, and 24 percent had been sexually involved.

THE *OUT/LOOK* SEX SURVEY REDUX (FROM ISSUE 12, SPRING 1991)

Respondents were asked to rank the frequency with which they had achieved orgasm over the past twelve months by using various sexual techniques. Masturbation was the leading way orgasm was achieved for both men and women. It beat out oral-genital contact and "homosexual intercourse," which were close seconds.

The "We Should Have Stated This Earlier" Department

Before you can have sex with a man, you've got to find one first. Perhaps, then, the first step in buddy-fucking is buddy-finding. Some popular meeting places to meet lovers include:

- Lesbian and gay community centers
- The armed forces
- Events—dances, readings, lectures
- ACT/UP and other direct action groups
- Leather conferences
- Activist conferences
- Writers/artist conferences
- Gay pride marches and related events
- Gay Games and other sporting events
- Museums and galleries ("Don't you just adore Paul Cadmus?")

Hit cable show of the 1980s

The Gay Dating Game, with your bachelor host Tommie Saeli, which aired on Fridays, 7:30 P.M. on Channel J on Manhattan Cable

Second runner-up: *The Robin Byrd Show,* "talk" show done in the nude, lots of drag, homoerotic, and just plain gay guys dancing and chatting.

Organizations in the Leather S/M Contingent in the 1989 NYC Gay Pride Parade

Gay male S/M Activists
Hot Ash
Lesbian Sex Mafia
Eulenspiegel Society
The New York Eagle
The Spike
and out of town groups

Gay magazine with the largest classifieds section in the world

Quarterly Interchange, an interracial gay magazine, Thom Bean publisher and editor. Includes the largest international, interracial classifieds in the world. *QI,* P.O. Box 42502, San Francisco, CA 94101.

Popular workshop/consciousness-raising session held by the New York City chapter of Men of All Colors Together

"Cock Size and Penis Power: How I Feel About My Own and Others," co-chaired by Lidell Jackson and John Klauder, held several times in 1989.

Mural by Martin
Wong, NYC
Lesbian and Gay
Community
Services Center
*(Photo by Roberta
Raeburn)*

This is from the C-R session's description:

Let's face it. As men, we're conditioned to be quite—for some of us, maybe even totally—aware of our dicks (we're getting graphic here, because this subject needs a "real deal" approach to get into it). We're always aware of cock size—our own and others—and we must admit they're few men among us who don't judge other men by the size of their cocks. Not only that, but that same judgment sometimes leads to relinquishing power to a dick that's bigger, or to assuming power over one that's smaller—whether it's done consciously or not.

Now maybe this isn't an issue for you. Maybe you feel fine about your cock, whatever size it is, and about the power you get from it. But can you admit that perhaps you *do* get power from it? Not only because of its size, or look, or whatever . . . but because it's there. Because perhaps it makes you feel superior over those who don't have cocks? Let's talk the assumption of power, here.

And let's talk about size. Or maybe it's all relative. (Yeah, right!)

Gay S/M demonstration *(Photo by Dave LeFave)*

Please! Few are the men who can say that the size of a man's dick doesn't matter to them. And we're not just talking gay male life either. How often have you stood at a urinal (or better yet, at a trough) next to a heterosexual man who couldn't help staring at yours, and vice versa? Yes, men are obsessed with each other's cocks . . . and the power, real or symbolic, they carry with them.

Sex Activists and Clubs

Gay Men's Health Crisis, 212-807-6655, distributes condoms and safer sex information in addition to providing services to people with HIV and AIDS; conducts many workshops and produces videos about safer sex, including "Eroticizing Safer Sex," "Keep It Up!" and "Men Meeting Men."

Gay Male S/M Activists (NYC). Dedicated to safe and responsible S/M since 1981. Open meetings with programs on S/M techniques, lifestyle issues, safety and responsibility, and political and social concerns. GMSMA, Dept. O, 496A Hudson St., Suite D23, NYC 10014

New York City chapter of *Uncircumcised Society of America* (NYC-USA), for foreskin lovers (men with or without foreskin), 212-777-4208.

National Association of Black and White Men Together (a.k.a., Men of All Colors Together MACT, or People of All Colors Together, PACT). Begun in 1980 with

Harold Robinson of Gay Men of African Descent helps distribute safer sex materials at the NYC Lesbian and Gay Community Services center. (*Copyright Morgan Gwenwald*)

a small classified in *The Advocate*. People of all colors, genders, and sexual preferences are welcome in all chapters.

The Sisters of Perpetual Indulgence, Inc., drag and safe sex activists (see profile below). San Francisco Order, 584 Castro, Suite 392, San Francisco, CA 94114-2588. 415-864-6722.

THE NUMBER ONE LUBRICANT IN EUROPE, AUSTRALIA, SOUTH AMERICA, CANADA, AND THE UNITED STATES

Wet Personal Lubricant (with nonoxynol-9).

TIPS FROM JOHN WAGENHAUSER ON HOW TO ORGANIZE A J.O. CLUB

- Rent or borrow someone's loft, apartment, or theater space
- Buy beer and soda (in six-ounce cans since attendees have a habit of leaving them around unfinished).

- Stock up on lubricant and paper towels, artfully scattered around the room in convenient locations.
- Agonize over the tapes for the stereo.
- Trade free admission and tips for half an evening's service on clothes check, bartending, and clean-up.
- Right inside the door give everyone a hanger, and position chairs there so no one has to hobble around taking off their pants
- Don't check shoes. The floor gets sticky.

SEX DOCUMENTARY

Sex Is . . . a film by Marc Huestis and Lawrence Helman, had its American premiere at the Biograph Theatre in Washington, DC, on April 23, 1993. The full title of this documentary is *Sex Is . . . A Film Exploring the Meaning of Sex and Sexuality in the Lives of Gay Men.* The film explores the attitudes of a diverse group of gay men toward sex and sexuality in the age of AIDS and HIV.

A VERY SPECIAL THING TO LICK: A PORNOGRAPHIC STAMP?

The following letter was written from Panama City, FL, to the editor of *The American Philatelist*, America's largest stamp collecting journal, in January, 1991:

After I purchased the new American stamp showing the Grand Canyon I was surprised to see in the rock formation the view of a penis and scrotum. This was so obvious that the designer, project manager, art director, and typographer of the U.S. Postal Service should have seen it and had the stamp corrected [castrated?]. This stamp will give a bad impression of the United States and its postal service throughout the world. . . .

According to the *Lambda Philatelic Journal*, Mark Hess of Katonah, New York, was the designer of the 1990 America stamps. And perhaps the subliminal image was included to put the "service" back in postal service.

Copyright © 1991, The American Philatelic Society, Inc.

HANDY ADVICE FOR MAILING A LOVE LETTER, FROM THE GAY/LESBIAN HISTORY STAMP CLUB

Have your love letters canceled from a post office in a town with a romantic name. An article by Michael Greene lists places you can get a "love" postmark by sending your letter inside a larger envelope addressed to "Postmaster" of the town, with a note inside explaining that you would like the enclosed letter postmarked from that post office:

Valentine, Texas 79854   Loveland, Ohio 45140
Valentines, Virginia 23887   Heart Butte, Montana 59448

Lovejoy, Illinois 62059
Loving, New Mexico 88256
Lovelady, Texas 75851

Kissing Bridge, New York
Darling Lake, North Dakota

Taken from the Lambda Philatelic Journal, Volume 9, Issue 4, Winter 1990.

YOU KNOW IT'S TIME TO LEAVE YOUR BOYFRIEND WHEN . . .

- You don't know if fag drama refers to gay theater or your relationship.
- He'd rather sleep with his pet dog than you.
- He'd rather sleep with his best lesbian friend than you.
- He'd rather sleep with his ex-boyfriend than you.
- You'd rather sleep with his ex-boyfriend than him.
- You'd rather he sleep with his ex-boyfriend than you.

HAVE A QUESTION NOT ANSWERED HERE?

You can always try the San Francisco Sex Information (SFSI) line, for free information and referral services. (M–F 3:00 P.M.–9:00 P.M. 415-621-7300) or the Sex Information and Educational Council of the U.S. (SIECUS), 130 W. 42nd St., Suite 2500, New York, NY 10012, 212-819-9770

WHERE YOU CAN GET BOOKS AND VIDEOS ON GAY SEX AND SEXUALITY

In addition to stores mentioned above, A Different Light bookstores are in New York (151 W. 19th St.), San Francisco (489 Castro St.), and West Hollywood, CA (8853 Santa Monica Blvd.). They have mail order available to all areas of the country; call daily between 10:00 A.M. and midnight: 1-800-343-4002. Or mail to: A Different Light Mail Order, 153 West 19th St., New York, NY 10011.

MINI-PROFILES

Lidell Jackson and Jacks of Color

Lidell Jackson—writer, activist, and self-proclaimed sexual being who likes to get his rocks off—is the founder of Jacks of Color, New York City's preeminent safe sex club for men of color, and occasionally their friends.

Jacks of Color is a jackoff and safe sex club for Black, Caribbean, Latino, Asian, Pacific Islander, South Asian, Native American, East Indian, Arab, and other men of color. Started in February 1990 by Jackson and some friends with monthly First Saturday jackoff parties, Jacks of Color has expanded to monthly safer sex parties (i.e., sucking and fucking with condoms). Every other month is now "Men of Color and Their Friends," which include those white men and men of color who feel comfortable in a multiracial crowd. With weekday parties, theme parties, and other improvements in the works or planned, Jacks of Color joins other jackoff and safer sex clubs and spaces in heralding the advent of the "second sexual revolution," where even in the midst of a health crisis, freedom of the sexual expression of gay men is re-emerging.

You can reach the Jacks of Color message line at 212-827-5302.

Barry Douglas

Barry Douglas is a former chair of Gay Male S/M Activists (GMSMA) and has been on the board of directors of that group. He was a member of the National Steering Committee of the 1987 March on Washington, was one of the organizers of the S/M Leather contingent, and was a key coordinator for the same contingent for the 1993 March on Washington for Lesbian, Gay, and Bi Equal Rights and Liberation. Barry was also active with Stonewall 25, the anniversary of the Stonewall riots, held in New York in 1994. He was named the *Leather Journal* Man of the Year in 1988 and was the Eastern Regional winner in 1993.

PROFILE

The Sisters of Perpetual Indulgence

Question: What group published one of the world's first safe sex education pamphlets?

Answer: The Sisters of Perpetual Indulgence, in their innovative *Play Fair!* pamphlet in the early 1980s, when AIDS was still mis-named GRID.

According to their newsletter, *The NUN Issue*, the Sisters of Perpetual Indulgence is a controversial order of gay, bisexual, and transgender "nuns" of various religious backgrounds founded in Iowa in the mid-1970s. The order migrated to San Francisco, where it formally settled on Easter Sunday 1979. In 1987, the order incorporated as a nonprofit, public benefit charitable corporation in California. The Sisters are social and spiritual educators who use the art of theater to educate and enlighten on subjects like freedom of thought and expression, gender polarity and identification, the politics of gender and oppression, AIDS and safe sex responsibility, violence, death and dying, homophobia, dragphobia, AIDSphobia, and bigotry. The Sisters are also preeminent fund-raisers in the lesbian and gay community, having raised hundreds of thousands of dollars for a myriad of AIDS care and other community organizations over the last sixteen years. The Sisters have been on the front lines of the AIDS war since it began. Not only did they publish an early safer sex pamphlet, they also produced the first AIDS fund-raiser in the world, a dog show on Castro Street which eventually drew Shirley MacLaine as Mistress of Ceremonies.

A Sister also created and painted the banner for an early AIDS protest march, "Fighting for Our Lives." And one of the first PWAs in the world to go public was Bobby Campbell, the AIDS Poster Boy and Sister Florence Nightmare, R.N. When *Time* magazine put his picture on the cover, it was the first time the world had seen the face of a person with AIDS.

The Sisters are now an international order with convents in Australia, New Zealand, Germany, France, Great Britain, South Africa, Ireland, and Norway, and new orders are still forming. San Francisco remains the Mother House of the Order, overseeing the international convents and those established in Denver and Seattle, and missions established in Los Angeles, New Orleans, and Short Mountain (Tennessee). The Sisters also tour internationally with their acclaimed safer sex show, *Indulgence Sunday*, featuring their provocative "Condom Savior Mass." Current major projects include: "I Took the Vow," a safe sex and condom distribution program; "Stop the Violence," a neighborhood safety program; "Whistle for Safety," a whistle distribution program; and the annual Castro Halloween fund-raiser.

The names of some Sisters: Cardinal Sin of the Carnal Craving, Father "PAN" PanDeMonium, Sister Hellina Handbasket, Sister Lilly White Superior Posterior, and Sister X-tacy Marie Collettel.

The Sisters of Perpetual Indulgence, Inc., drag and safer sex activists

San Francisco Order	Hollywood Order
584 Castro, Suite 392	1429 N. Curson Ave., #304
San Francisco, CA 94114-2588	Hollywood, CA 90046
415-864-6722	213-851-1873

The Condom Savior Vow

We have gathered today to consecrate and receive the Holy Communion Condom. As I take it onto myself, so shall I keep its ritual sacred. The condom is part of my life—part of my responsibility, now. If I desire to live, and let my sex partners live, I must sanctify my vow to hold the condom savior eternal. My seed is under siege by a horrific virus—Let me not become horrific as well with careless disregard for my life and the lives of those with whom I share the divine gift of love. My life is to promulgate universal joy and expiate myself from stigmatic guilt. In HIS likeness, I am alive and I must protect his handiwork.

I VOW TO LOOK INTO MY HEART AND FURTHER INTO MY SOUL, WHERE I KNOW THAT MY HUMANITY AND SALVATION DEPEND ON HOW SACRED I HOLD THE CONDOM VOW.

LATEX=LUST   LATEX=LIFE   LATEX=LOVE

PROFILE

John Preston

The complaint is often made that both the gay and mainstream press tend to neglect "sexual outlaws" to the detriment of the lesbian and gay community. John Preston—a pre-Stonewall gay activist from Minneapolis, where he founded the gay and lesbian community center, Gay House, Inc.—is someone who made a career out of visualizing and promoting this very same sexual outlaw.

As a pornographer, he told the "Censorship" audience at Outwrite 1993, "Censorship has been a recurring theme in my life. I've had public television specials do profiles on me, I have been profiled on the front pages of all the major newspapers, and they never talk about the erotica." That would be like talking about the Grand Canyon and not talking about the hole, because John Preston was perhaps the most well-known gay male erotica writer in this country.

Specifically, Preston was the author, editor, or coeditor of more than forty books—including *Mr. Benson*, the first best-seller among leathermen, and several seminal nonfiction books and anthologies—and was published in virtually every gay and lesbian periodical in the country, as well as mainstream publications such as *Harper's* and *Interview*. He was also a former editor of *The Advocate* and wrote a regular column for *Lambda Book Report*.

Perhaps as a response to the censorship of his erotica writings, in November of 1993 Preston published the memoir/autobiography/political analysis entitled *My Life as a Pornographer and Other Indecent Acts*.

In his introduction to *A Member of the Family: Gay Men Write About Their Families* (which he edited in 1992), he recalled, "When I was asked why I worked so hard at gay liberation, I said I did it so there would be more healthy men to love, and I meant it. The ghosts of those lost lives and lost careers that had haunted me after college were being exorcised by the new communities that were being built and the relationships that were developing within them."

Preston conducted the end of his remarkable career from Portland, Maine, where he lived the last several years of his life. He died in 1994 of an AIDS-related illness, at the age of forty-nine. The last of Preston's anthologies came out after his death in 1995–*Sister and Brother*, writings by lesbians and gay men about their relationships with each other, coedited with Joan Nestle, and *Friends and Lovers*, a strong collection of many different voices, both familiar and emerging.

For a full listing of the forty-plus books John Preston wrote, edited, or coedited in his twenty-five-year writing career (as well as insight into his life and work), see the anthology *Looking for Mr. Preston: Interviews, Essays, and Personal Reminiscences of John Preston*, edited by Laura Antoniou and published in 1995 by Masquerade Books in New York.

Selected Bibliography

The "Alex Kane" series, including *Deadly Lies*, *Golden Years*, *Secret Dangers*, *Stolen Moments*, *Sweat Dreams*, *Lethal Silence*. (Masquerade Books)

Classified Affairs: A Gay Man's Guide to the Personal Ads. John Preston and Frederick Brandt. Alyson, 1984.

The Flesh and the Word series, anthologies of gay male erotic fiction edited by John Preston. New American Library.

Friends and Lovers, (Dutton, 1995). John Preston.

Hometowns: Gay Men Write About Where They Belong. John Preston, *Personal Dispatches: Personal Dispatches: Writers Confront AIDS*, John Preston.

The "Master" Series, including *The Love of a Master, In Search of a Master*, and several others. (Alyson Publications).

A Member of the Family: Gay Men Write About Their Families. Edited and with an introduction by John Preston. Dutton, 1992.

Mr. Benson. Masquerade Books (reissued in 1992).

Sister and Brother: Lesbians and Gay Men Write About Their Lives Together. Joan Nestle and John Preston eds. HarperSan Francisco, 1994.

Even in the age of AIDS, when gay sex is often burdened by the specter of illness, gay men have found ways to express their sexuality that are safe and erotic. From jack-off clubs and parties to pornographic magazines and videos.

17. GAY SPORTS

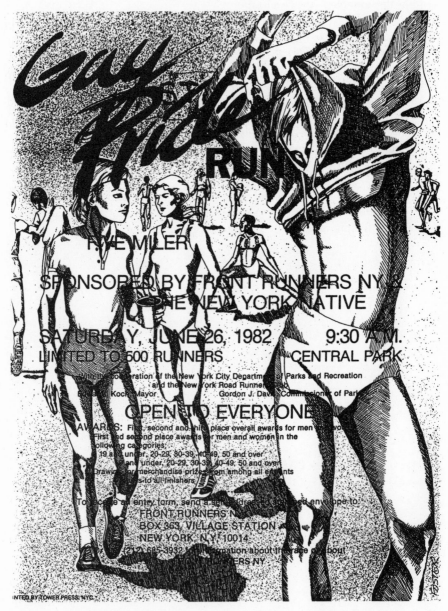

Collection of the National Museum & Archive of Lesbian and Gay History

"To say that gay men simply aren't welcome in the world of big league sports is an enormous understatement."

—DEGEN PENER, former *New York Times* columnist

Sports have been such a symbol of heterosexuality—for men, an initiation into traditional "manhood"—that many gay men have felt alienated from them. Charles Busch, the drag star, speaks for many gay men when he notes that he always associated sports with a certain world (read: straight) that he didn't want to be a part of.

When they have participated in organized professional sports, gay men have often found that they needed to remain closeted because of prejudice that could cost them their jobs or valuable endorsements. Gay athletes such as Glenn Burke, a major league baseball outfielder, and Dave Pallone, an umpire, both lost their jobs when they were suspected of being gay. Olympic diver Greg Louganis's recent coming out as gay and as a person with AIDS has been a much needed step toward blowing the lid off homophobia and AIDS-phobia in the world of sports.

Outside of organized sports, gay men have been making sports their own. In the last decade, gay community sports leagues have grown across the country—everything from gay bowling leagues to gay skydiving clubs to gay rodeos, across the United States and Canada.

The Gay Games have also provided an outlet for gay male athletics. Founded in 1982 by Dr. Tom Waddell, the Games occur every four years and feature everything from bodybuilding and billiards to swimming and track. In 1994, fifteen thousand lesbian and gay athletes descended on New York City to participate in the largest Gay Games ever. The Gay Games have grown from an idea in Tom Waddell's head to the most inclusive event in the world.

SOURCES:

Bull, Chris. "Disclosure." *The Advocate*, March 21, 1995.

Kopay, David, with Perry Deane Young. *The David Kopay Story: An Extraordinary Self-Revelation* (Donald I. Fine, Inc., 1977).

Louganis, Greg, with Eric Marcus. *Breaking the Surface.* Random House, 1995

Pallone, Dave, with Alan Steinberg. *Behind the Mask.* Nal Dutton, 1991.

Pronger, Brian. *Arena of Masculinity: Sports, Homosexuality, and the Meaning of Sex*. St. Martin's Press, 1990.

Reed, Susan. "Unlevel Playing Fields." *OUT* magazine, June 1994.

Young, Perry Deane. *Gays and Lesbians and Sports*. Chelsea House, 1995.

SPORTS TIMELINE

776 B.C.: The first Olympics are held in ancient Greece. Women are excluded, and they compete in their own Heraea Games every four years.

A.D. 393: The end of the Greek Olympics, when the Christian Roman emperor Theodosius the Great bans the games and orders all of the buildings at Olympia destroyed.

1636: A Jesuit missionary in North America observes Huron Indians playing a game with a hide-covered ball hurled from a curved stick with a pouch at the end. The Indians call the game "bagataway," but the French dub it "la crosse" ("the cross"), because the stick resembles a cross.

From medieval times to the 1800s: Tennis is first played in monastic courtyards, but around the reign of Henry VIII becomes a "royal" sport played on the "courts" of Europe. It is exported to the United States in the nineteenth century, when the first official tennis court is built in Boston in 1876.

1823: Since American colonial days, men have been kicking around a pigskin. But in 1823, a new kind of "football"—called rugby after the British school where it is started—allows players not just to kick the ball but to pick it up and run with it. In the United States, this new version of the sport is quickly adopted and transformed into its more violent modern counterpart.

1837: Although people have been swimming for at least two thousand years, this year the first swimming competitions, using the breaststroke, are conducted in London.

1839: According to the Baseball Hall of Fame in Cooperstown, New York, baseball is invented there by Abner Doubleday. (Other versions of the "stickball" game have existed throughout the country and in Europe.)

1844: North American Indians win a 100-yard (91.4 meter) swimming contest in London, using an overarm stroke.

1845: The rules of baseball are formalized and the now familiar diamond-shaped field is used at the New York Knickerbocker Club. Play ball.

1855: The first organized game of ice hockey is played in Kingston, Ontario.

Late 1800s: Swedish and German gymnasts begin performing acrobatic and tumbling routines in swimming areas, developing the sport of diving.

  • The game of soccer, which evolves from centuries of different ball games where participants are not allowed to use their hands, develops formal rules of play.

1880: The first diving competitions are held in England, as a result of arguments among swimming clubs that claim to have the best divers.

1881: The first American national tennis championships are held.

1886: The New York Athletic Club holds the first track and field meet in the United States.

1887: A great moment in lesbian and gay sports history: The softball is invented in November at Chicago's Farragut Boat Club by tying a boxing mitt tightly with twine into a ball. Within a few years, it spreads across the country. Because the ball is "softer" and the bases are shorter, softball becomes one of the few acceptable physical exertions for women.

1891: Basketball is invented by James Naismith of the YMCA in Springfield, Massachusetts, as an indoor sport to play between football and baseball seasons. Women are encouraged to play.

1896: The modern Olympics games are revived, brought about by a Frenchman, Pierre de Coubertin. The first games were held in a restored stadium in Athens. They have been held every four years since, except during World Wars I and II, when they were suspended. Women were banned from participation until 1928.

1972: The Education Act of 1972 is passed, which contains Title IX, prohibiting gender discrimination in educational institutions that receive federal funds. For the first time, any institution receiving federal funds must equally allocate its resources to boys and girls.

1975: The Education Act of 1972 is applied to sports.

• Reporter Lynn Rosellini writes a groundbreaking series of articles on homosexual athletes, "Gays in Sports," in the *Washington Star*. She can find no athlete who will talk openly about his or her sexuality, until former NFL running back Dave Kopay agrees to speak and come out.

Late 1970s: Ed Gallagher, a closeted gay man, is a star lineman for the University of Pittsburgh football team. He goes on to training camp for the New York Giants but is cut after just two weeks under suspicion of being gay.

1977: Glenn Burke, a young outfielder with the Los Angeles Dodgers projected to be "the next Willie Mays" (and at that time a closeted gay man), invents the "high five" during a game with the Houston Astros.

1979: Glenn Burke is "released" from his contract with the Los Angeles Dodgers under suspicion of homosexuality.

1982: Dr. Tom Waddell, a former Olympic decathlete, founds the Gay Games, a version of the Olympics for lesbian and gay athletes. He is prevented by the Supreme Court from calling them "Olympic" games.

1983: Bob Paris wins Mr. Universe and Mr. America titles. He later "marries" Rod Jackson and becomes Bob Jackson-Paris.

1984: Bruce Hayes, a gay man, wins a gold medal for the 800-meter freestyle relay at the Olympic Games. Hayes later comes out and becomes a star of the Gay Games. Greg Louganis wins two gold medals in diving competitions.

1987: Jerry Smith, former NFL tight end and lover of Dave Kopay, dies of AIDS, denying his homosexuality right up until the end.

1988: Diver Greg Louganis wins two gold medals at the Olympics, after testing positive for HIV six months prior.

• Major league umpire Dave Pallone is fired for alleged involvement in a sex ring with teenage boys. Pallone brings a suit against major league baseball and is cleared of all charges, though he does later acknowledge in his autobiography that he is gay.

1993: Barry Meisel writes a series of newspaper articles on gay athletes for the *New York Daily News*, which is widely syndicated and published in papers throughout the country. He finds that attitudes have changed very little since the time of Lynn Rosellini's investigation.

1994: Gay Games IV are held in New York City, coinciding with the twenty-fifth anniversary of the Stonewall riots. More than 15,000 athletes participate and 500,000 spectators watch—the biggest Games ever.

• Olympic figure skater John Curry dies of AIDS.

• Olympic diver Greg Louganis comes out as gay at Gay Games IV.

1995: In a television interview on *20/20*, Greg Louganis tells Barbara Walters that he has AIDS.

Bob Drake and Bob Machado, members of the NYC Metropolitan Tennis Group, wearing their Gay Games IV medals, June 1994 *(Photo by Jeff Bieganek)*

SOME FAMOUS GAY ATHLETES

Glenn Burke, an outfielder for the Los Angeles Dodgers and Oakland A's from 1976 to 1979 (the only major league baseball player ever to come out)

John Menlove Edwards, mountaineering

Ed Gallagher, college football star, founder of Alive to Thrive after a failed suicide attempt because of being gay

Bruce Hayes, 1984 Olympic gold medalist in the 800-meter swimming freestyle relay

Bob Jackson-Paris, bodybuilder and former Mr. America and Mr. Universe; "married" to bodybuilder Rod Jackson-Paris

David Kopay former NFL running back, came out in 1975

Greg Louganis, 1984 and 1988 Olympic gold medal diver

Dave Pallone, former major league baseball umpire

David Slattery, general manager of the Washington Redskins in the 1970s; came out publicly in 1993

Jerry Smith, all-pro tight end with the Washington Redskins (and Dave Kopay's first love)

Tom Waddell, Olympic decathlete and Gay Games founder; died of AIDS in 1987

NUMBER OF PLAYERS WHO HAVE COMPETED AS OPENLY GAY MEN IN THE NATIONAL FOOTBALL LEAGUE, THE NATIONAL BASKETBALL ASSOCIATION, THE NATIONAL HOCKEY LEAGUE, AND BASEBALL'S MAJOR LEAGUES

None

ATHLETES WHO HAVE COMPETED AT AN OLYMPICS AS OPENLY GAY OR LESBIAN

None

FIRST PROFESSIONAL OR NATIONALLY RANKED ATHLETE TO COME OUT WHILE STILL ACTIVE IN HIS/HER SPORT

Canadian Matthew Hall, a twenty-four-year-old figure skater on the Canadian national team, came out in 1992.

THE FIRST PROFESSIONAL ATHLETE IN ANY SPORT TO COME OUT PUBLICLY AND VOLUNTARILY

David Kopay, football pro, b. 1942, came out in an interview in the *Washington Star* in 1975, after his football career. Kopay was a pro running back for ten years, who played for the San Francisco Forty-Niners, the Detroit Lions, the Washington Redskins, the New Orleans Saints, and the Green Bay Packers.

Although David Kopay was the first professional athlete to come out voluntarily, there were of course other gay athletes before him.

SEX RESEARCH ON GAY ATHLETES

After David Kopay came out (circa 1976) there was much speculation about how many gay men there were in professional sports. Researchers from the California State University anonymously interviewed less than a hundred athletes from the NCAA. If you include mutual masturbation, 40 percent of those interviewed had had an orgasm with another man within the past two years. If you don't include it, the number was still impressive at 33 percent. However, keep in mind this was college sports, not professionals, and the sample size was extremely small.

A Gay Games Retrospective

> *"The Gay Games define us as a coherent, diverse population, asserting our right to celebrate ourselves—not ask for someone else's approval. It is the ultimate manifestation of self-esteem."*

> —Ann Northrop, AIDS and lesbian activist, and board member of Gay Games IV and Cultural Festival

Gay Games I

Opening Day: August 28, 1982
San Francisco, California
Attendance: 1,700–1,800 athletes; 10,000 spectators
Masters of Ceremony: Rita Mae Brown and Armistead Maupin
Festivities and events: art exhibitions, music and comedy performances

The opening ceremonies included two former U.S. Olympic team members carrying a torch that had been carried across country from the Stonewall Inn in New York City, site of the Stonewall Riots in 1969—Susan McGrievy, on the 1956 U.S. Olympic swimming team and George Frenn, on the 1972 U.S. Olympic track team.

Gay Games II

August 9–17, 1986
San Francisco, California
Attendance: 3,500 athletes; 10,000–15,000 spectators
Official Slogan: "Something Wonderful Will Happen . . . For the Second Time"
Master of Ceremonies: Rita Mae Brown
Festivities and events:

Sports (17 events): basketball, bowling, boxing, cycling, golf marathon, physique, powerlifting, pool (billiards), racquetball, soccer, softball, swimming and diving, tennis, track and field, triathlon, volleyball, and men's wrestling

Gay Games III

August 4–11, 1990
Vancouver, British Columbia
Attendance: 7,000 athletes; 20,000 spectators
Money the Games brought to the host city: $30 million

Alfonso Ramirez and Rian Smolik, members of the NYC Metropolitan Tennis Group, with Regina Dorian (left), tennis tournament director at Gay Games IV, June 1994 *(Photo by Jeff Biaganek)*

On the blocks for the 200-meter mixed freestyle relay at Gay Games IV, June 1994 *(Photo by Charles Carson)*

Team New York Aquatics members were proud hosts at Gay Games IV, June 1994
(*Photo by Charles Carson*)

Festivities and events:

Cultural festival: readings, exhibits, and workshops
Sports (28 events): basketball, powerlifting, volleyball, racquetball, swimming,
water polo, equestrian, golf, billiards, cycling, tennis, softball, race walking, croquet, martial arts, physique, soccer, bowling, squash, diving, badminton, touch/flag
football, triathlon, marathon, wrestling, track and field, curling, and ice hockey

Gay Games IV

June 18–25, 1994
New York, New York
Attendance: 15,000 athletes; 500,000 spectators
Official Slogan: "Games Can Change the World"
Money the Games brought to the host city: $100 million
Festivities and events:
Cultural festival: 130 different exhibits/performances, including readings, a
Carnegie Hall gay choir performance, a Madison Square Garden gay and lesbian
band performance, a comedy extravaganza at Town Hall, opening ceremonies at
Columbia University's Wien Stadium, and closing ceremonies at Shea Stadium
Sports (31 events): basketball, powerlifting, volleyball, racquetball, swimming,
water polo, equestrian, golf, billiards, cycling, tennis, softball, race walking, croquet,

---

A FEW STARS OF GAY GAMES IV (PROFILED IN *OUT* MAGAZINE, JUNE 1994)

- *Jim Dorrian,* forty-year-old former golf fanatic, a former New York City police officer; his father played on the American soccer team in the 1956 Olympics and his grandfather owned two gay bars in NYC in the 1950s.
- *Brent Nicholson Earl,* track and field, a forty-four-year-old New Yorker, carried the Games' rainbow flag from San Francisco to Vancouver in his 1990 Rainbow Run for the End of AIDS. An HIV-positive athlete, he also completed the American Run for the End of AIDS, a twenty-month solo run from 1986 to 1987, the first person to run the nation's perimeter.
- *Matthew Hall,* twenty-four-year-old top ranked Canadian figure skater; first person in North America to compete as an openly gay person while still active in the sport.
- *James Hollander,* organized the flag football games for Gay Game IV, comes from a family of five brothers who played college sports.

---

martial arts, physique, soccer, bowling, squash, diving, badminton, touch/flag football, triathlon, marathon, wrestling, track and field, curling, ice hockey, and figure skating

Gay Games V (1998)

Scheduled to be held in Amsterdam, the Netherlands.

WORLD RECORDS SET AT GAY GAMES

So far, just one: the 100-meter butterfly, for age group 50–54, by Michael Mealiffe in 1990.

POLITICS AND SPORTS

The U.S. Olympic Committee took the Gay Games to court in order to prevent the games from being called the "Gay Olympics." In 1987 the U.S. Supreme Court

---

SPORTS ONLINE

America Online has a category for the Gay Games under "Leisure Interests" in the Gay and Lesbian Community Forum. There are also numerous folders for different sporting activities, everything from bowling to softball to rodeo to kayaking.

Rich Quigley and Kile Ozier have produced a forty-five-minute video of the opening and closing ceremonies of Gay Games IV. It is available for $8.00 plus $2.90 for mailing. You can order by e-mail at KileO@aol.com.

ruled in a 5–4 vote to forbid the use of the term the "Gay Olympics." However, according to the book *Lavender Lists*, there are thirteen other events that have been allowed the use of the word "Olympic" in their titles: the Special Olympics, Special Olympics, Bridge Olympics, International Police Olympics, Rat Olympics, Armenian Olympics, K-9 Olympics, Senior Olympics, Wheelchair Olympics, Eskimo Olympics, Junior Olympics, Crab Cooking Olympics, Explorer Scout Olympics, and Armchair Olympics.

Excerpt from *Lavender Lists*, by Lynne Yamaguchi Fletcher and Adrian Saks, © 1990 by Alyson Publications. Used by permission of the Publisher.

INTERNATIONAL GAY RODEO ASSOCIATION (IGRA)

In his book *Lesbians and Gays and Sports*, Perry Deane Young states, "Surely the most unexpected and most successful of the gay alternatives to straight sporting events is the most macho of all American activities of any sort, the rodeo. The first gay rodeo was staged in Reno, Nevada, in 1975. From fairly small beginnings, the International Gay Rodeo Association has now expanded to include rodeos in six different cities every year. The 1993 schedule took the show to the East Coast for its first rodeo in the nation's capital, Washington, DC." Also, unlike the straight rodeos, all events and competitions in the gay rodeos are open to women.

IGRA currently has twenty member associations representing twenty-five states, the District of Columbia, and two Canadian provinces. A full season of regional rodeos concludes with international finals in Denver. For more information about IGRA or upcoming rodeo seasons, contact IGRA Executive Office, 900 East Colfax Ave., Denver, CO 80218, 303-832-IGRA.

1995 RODEO EVENTS

Jan.	Road Runner Regional Rodeo, Phoenix, Arizona
March	Saguaro Regional Rodeo, Tucson, Arizona
April	Greater Los Angeles Rodeo, Los Angeles, California
April	Great Plains Regional Rodeo, Little Rock, Arkansas
April	Dixieland Rodeo, Atlanta, Georgia
May	Great Plains Regional Rodeo, Oklahoma City, Oklahoma
June	Bay Area Regional Rodeo, San Francisco, California
July	Rocky Mountain Regional Rodeo, Denver, Colorado
July	North Star Regional Rodeo, Minneapolis, Minnesota
July	IGRA Convention, Chicago, Illinois
Aug.	Greater Motown International Rodeo, Detroit, Michigan
Aug.	Great Plains Regional Rodeo, Wichita, Kansas
Aug.	Greater Northwest International Rodeo, Seattle, Washington
Aug.	Windy City Regional Gay Rodeo, Chicago, Illinois
Sept.	Zia Regional Rodeo, Albuquerque, New Mexico
Sept.	Great Plains Regional Rodeo, Kansas City, Missouri
Sept.	Greater San Diego Rodeo, San Diego, California

Sept.	Pikes Peak United Rodeo, Colorado Springs, Colorado
Sept.–Oct.	Atlantic Stampede, Bethesda, Maryland
Oct.	International Finals Rodeo, Denver, Colorado

OTHER GAY COWBOYS

The Atlanta Gay Rodeo was held in Atlanta this year, April 28–30, and included such spectacles as the Wild Drag Race, the Goat Dressing, and the Calf Scramble, in addition to the more traditional bull riding, bareback bronco riding, and others. The event was sponsored by SEGRA (South East Gay Rodeo Association).

ALL-AROUND CHAMPION COWBOY FOR THREE YEARS IN A ROW

Greg Olson

A SAMPLING OF GAY SPORTS CLUBS

International Gay and Lesbian Outdoor Organization
Houston Outdoors Group (hiking and camping)
Front Runners (NYC running club for men and women)
Metropolitan Tennis Group (NYC lesbian and gay tennis club)
Knights Wrestling Club (NYC)
Metro Gay Wrestling Alliance (NYC)
Ramblers Soccer Club (NYC)
Scrabble Players Club (NYC)
Out Riders (Boston cycling group)
Lavender Winds Kite Club (Vancouver group for kite flying)
Out and Out (Toronto parachuting group)
Gay and Lesbian Tennis Camp (Palm Springs, CA)
Sundance Outdoor Adventure Society (New York hiking, camping, horseback riding, etc.)
Unusual Attitudes (Southern California pilots group)
Gotham Volley (gay and lesbian league in Manhattan founded in 1975)
Finny Dippers (San Diego scuba diving group)
Village Dive Club (New York scuba diving group)
Sea Snakes (San Francisco scuba diving group)
Tarheel Outdoor Sports Fellowship (North Carolina canoeing group)
Denver Gay Ski Club, a.k.a. Colorado Outdoor and Ski Association (COSA)

THE FIRST ANNUAL BOSTON–NEW YORK AIDS RIDE

From September 15 to 17, 1995, the first annual Boston-New York AIDS Ride took place. Underwritten by Tanqueray, the three-day, noncompetitive bicycle ride from Boston to New York City registered nearly three thousand riders, who tackled the 250 miles as a fund-raiser against AIDS. Each rider was asked to raise

$1,200, which went to three beneficiaries who provide services to people with HIV and AIDS: the Fenway Community Health Project in Boston, the Community Health Project in New York, and the New York City Lesbian and Gay Community Services Center. This was an event of community participation, with the riders being ordinary people from all walks of life who felt they wanted to make a personal commitment to do something about AIDS. The ride itself was accompanied by opening ceremonies in Boston and closing festivities in New York. For information about future AIDS rides, contact the NYC Lesbian and Gay Community Services Center, 208 West 13th St., New York, NY 10011, 212-620-7310.

SPORTS, BEING GAY, AND SUICIDE

Ed Gallagher is the director and cofounder of Alive to Thrive, along with two other people who are spinal-cord injured.

Ed was an offensive lineman at the University of Pittsburgh in the late 1970s, where he was constantly at odds with himself about being gay. He couldn't integrate the concepts of being gay and being a jock. At the age of twenty-seven, after his first sexual experience with a man, he tried to commit suicide by jumping off a bridge. He survived, but became a quadriplegic.

Alive to Thrive speaks to students about substance abuse prevention, suicide prevention, disability awareness, and self-esteem enhancement.

THE CONNECTION BETWEEN SPORTS, SEX, AND A NEW JERSEY TURNPIKE REST AREA

Vince Lombardi was one of the most famous and successful coaches in the history of football. As one of the honors of this legacy, the New Jersey Turnpike Authority named one of their rest areas after him. In the late 1980s and early 1990s, the Vince Lombardi Rest Area was infamous as an entrapment place where state troopers enticed gay men into sexual acts and then arrested them.

INTERNATIONAL ASSOCIATION OF GAY AND LESBIAN MARTIAL ARTISTS (IAGLMA)

A voting member of the Federation of Gay Games, and founded in 1990 after the Vancouver Games, IAGLMA helps martial artists of all styles network within the lesbian and gay community. A $20 membership fee to this nonprofit gets you a quarterly newsletter and information about upcoming events, seminars, and competitions. For more information, e-mail at IAGLMA@aol.com, write IAGLMA, P.O. Box 590601, San Francisco, CA 94159, or phone Allen Wood at 415-563-1655.

THE LARGEST GAY/LESBIAN SPORTS GROUP

The International Gay Bowling Organization

What was the scandal in the 13th Gay Softball World Series (held in Atlanta in 1989)?

A "heterosexual" scandal—straight players invaded the gay locker rooms. Atlanta's Bulldog Lushpuppies, who lost to the New York Break Falcons 17–1, complained to the North American Gay Amateur Athletic Association (NAGAAA) that the Falcons had a nongay player. The NAGAAA ruled in Atlanta's favor and New York was forced to forfeit the game.

Profile

Dr. Tom Waddell

Dr. Thomas Waddell was the founder and spirit of the Gay Games. He began planning an Olympic-style games for lesbians and gay men in 1980, and found thousands of athletes eager for such an event. He tried to call the event the Gay Olympics, but the U.S. Olympic Committee sued, and spent millions of dollars to keep the name "Olympics" out of it, eventually winning in the U.S. Supreme Court. Waddell's sports events continued as the Gay Games and the first opened in San Francisco in 1982.

Waddell's philosophy for the Games was refreshing and long overdue. His vision was extraordinarily inclusive. Nobody—including heterosexuals, the disabled, the slow, the unathletic, the sissies, the tomboys—would be excluded. The Games were about competition against oneself, not others. Waddell stated, "Doing one's personal best should be the paramount goal in any athletic endeavor."

"If we're going to be an exemplary community," Perry Dean Young quotes Waddell as saying, "if we're going to teach the society at large, we need to confront issues of racism, ageism, and sexism that still plague us. The primary purpose of sport should be self-fulfillment, but athletics can also be a powerful medium for social change."

Tom Waddell was someone who contradicted all the stereotypes of an athlete and a homosexual. Not only was he an Olympic athlete—he made the U.S. Olympic team when he was thirty years old and finished sixth in the 1968 Olympic decathlon in Mexico City —but he was also a physician, a husband and father, an artist, painter, photographer, and dancer. Even as an athlete he was outstanding in many sports—a college football star, a gymnast, a track and field star—as well as an Olympian.

He was born in 1937 in Paterson, New Jersey, to a poor working-class German Catholic family. His parents separated when he was a teenager and Tom was taken in by another couple who cared for him and legally adopted him when he was twenty-one. He took their last name, Waddell.

He was a high school track star and won a scholarship to Springfield College in Massachusetts. There Tom thought of being a track coach until a tragedy changed his life. He saw his best friend and co-captain of the gymnastics team die in front of him after falling from the high rings. His friend had wanted to be a doctor and

Tom, grief-stricken and heartbroken, took on his friend's ambition. He continued his athletic career, too, and was a star in football, but especially track and field.

Tom knew throughout this time that he was gay, although he had few sexual encounters in college. His first real emotional experience came the summer after college, when the twenty-one-year-old Tom fell in love with a sixty-three-year-old socialist who ran a summer camp for adults, Friedrich Engels Menaker.

In 1960, Tom tried out for the U.S. Olympic decathlon team but didn't make the cut. He then concentrated on his other goal of becoming a doctor and received his M.D. in 1965. He was drafted into the Army the next year (during the Vietnam escalation) and stationed in Washington, DC, as part of an international medical program. There he began training again for his Olympic dream and at age thirty made the 1968 U.S. Olympic decathlon team. He came in at sixth place in Mexico City.

After the Olympics Tom traveled on track and field exhibition tours in South America and Africa. After leaving the Army, he went around the world in his capacity as a doctor. He also continued training for the decathlon for the next Olympics, but a sports injury to his kneecap brought his competitive career to an end in 1973.

Throughout this time, Tom was also becoming more and more involved in lesbian and gay activism, and in 1976 he and his lover were featured in *People* magazine's "Couples" section—the first time gay people were included there.

According to Perry Deane Young, Tom believed that many athletes were driven into athletics not in spite of their homosexuality, but because of it. He quotes Waddell as saying, "Many athletes use sports as a smokescreen. They're doing things that will make them the most masculine—the big jock." By creating one of the gay community's most visible and largest events, Tom has ensured that the conflict between being gay and being an athlete need never haunt our community so severely again.

Another one of the many dreams Tom was able to realize was that of having a child. Someone who shared this dream was his good friend lesbian athlete Sara Lewinstein, who had worked with him on the first Gay Games. They married, and their daughter Jessica was born in 1983.

Tom discovered he was HIV positive a few years after the first Gay Games, and after he married Lewinstein. He died on July 11, 1987, of AIDS. His life has been chronicled in many major media outlets including *20/20*, *Sports Illustrated*, *The Advocate*, and an autobiography, *Gay Olympian: The Life and Death of Dr. Thomas Waddell*, by sports commentator Dick Schaap.

PROFILE

Greg Louganis

Widely regarded as the "best ever" in his event, Greg Louganis, thirty-five, won medals for diving in the 1976, 1984, and 1988 Olympics.

On Friday, February 24, 1995, in an interview with Barbara Walters on ABC's *20/20*, Greg Louganis announced to the world, "I have AIDS." Louganis had already come out publicly as a gay man at the opening ceremonies of the 1994 Gay Games IV. He followed up both disclosures with the release of his autobiography, *Breaking the Surface*, written with Eric Marcus and published in the spring of 1995 by Random House.

Born in 1965, the champion swimmer and diver had a troubled time as a child and as a young athlete. Although he came out to some of his diving friends when he was sixteen, his sexuality was a problem for him, and he was often called names by teammates. In addition to having dyslexia, he also fought depression and attempted suicide several times.

Despite these emotional setbacks, Louganis thrived as an athlete. He won a silver medal for diving in the 1976 Olympics (when he was only sixteen) and gold medals in diving in 1984 and 1988. In fact, he is the only diver to have won double gold medals at consecutive Olympics. But his prowess as an athlete did not protect him from the anti-gay bias of his fellow teammates and competitors.

Louganis learned he was HIV positive six months before he was to travel to Seoul, South Korea, for the 1988 Olympics. He almost didn't compete, but his cousin and doctor convinced him to go. Louganis went on to win two gold medals in Seoul for diving. During the course of the competition, however, he hit his head on a diving board, cutting it so that it required stitches.

When Louganis made his announcement in February that he was HIV positive, there was a firestorm in the media—not regarding his courageousness in coming out as gay and HIV positive, not about his triumph in spite of a homophobia-filled athletic career, or his triumph over and recovery from personal trauma he suffered from low self-esteem and abusive relationships. Instead, the fury was because he cut his head and bled into the pool, and didn't tell the physician who stitched him up that he was HIV positive.

What was virtually ignored by the mainstream media was Louganis's isolation from his teammates because of his sexuality, his ill treatment by them (when he was sixteen and competing in the 1976 Olympics, no one would room with "the fag"), and his abusive six-year relationship with former lover Jim Babbitt, who died of AIDS in 1990.

According to Peter Galvin, writing in *The Advocate*, April 4, 1995:

> Louganis has had to contend with a series of daunting obstacles that would have thwarted a lesser person: the knowledge that he was adopted and perhaps unwanted by his real parents; an adoptive father who initially ignored him and watched from the sidelines as his son was beaten for being a "sissy"; the condition of dyslexia, which left him with the lasting impression that he was a "dummy" and a "retard"; a lover who abused him, raped him, and, acting as his manager, misappropriated his funds; and finally, an HIV-positive diagnosis that came at the apogee of his career.

Both in that interview and in his autobiography, Louganis does state that it was irresponsible not to tell the doctor of his HIV status.

With his announcement of being gay and being HIV positive, Louganis joined a short list of some incredibly courageous people—openly gay professional athletes, including former pro running back Dave Kopay, former Oakland A Glenn Burke (who died of AIDS in spring 1995) and retired tennis superstar Martina Navratilova.

Today, at book signings, at interviews, in appearances, and speeches, Louganis speaks with pride, self-assurance, and strength. After overcoming a painful childhood—one that too many lesbian and gay youths have—he was able to achieve his lifelong dream in sports and be honest with the public and himself about his sexuality and medical condition. Today, Louganis says he is happier than he has ever been and enjoys the freedom of being himself—with no secrets, and no shame.

For more information on this legendary athlete, see his recent autobiography, *Breaking the Surface*, which he wrote with Eric Marcus (Random House, 1995).

18. GAY TRAVEL

Stereotyped image of a "pansy" traveler, from the New York tabloid *Broadway Brevities,* 1931.

"But this is exclusively a woman's hotel"
"Well!"

According to the gay marketing research firm Overlooked Opinions, traveling is one of the foremost activities for gay men. Two-fifths of the respondents to a 1992 poll reported vacationing outside the United States in the prior year, and 80 percent reported traveling on weekend trips during the past year. (See "Demographics and Statistics," p. 99, for the specifics of the poll.)

While this chapter isn't meant to be a definitive gay travel guide (there are dozens of those already out there), it's designed as a guidepost to finding the resources and information you'll need to plan that much needed time away with your sweetie or your friends. Have a great vacation—and send us a postcard!

GAY TRAVEL RESOURCES
Books and Magazines

The resources listed below are available at most gay-friendly bookstores or newsstands, in addition to the direct numbers provided. Also, the International Gay Travel Association (800-448-8550) provides contact information for its member travel agencies, guest houses, and tour operators.

Damron Guides are now in their thirtieth year of publication and the *Damron Address Book* has been called the Bible of gay travel. Originally only focusing on the sexual opportunities available in its listed travel locations, the *Damron Address Book* now includes more information on accommodations, restaurants, gyms, and stores. Its sibling publication, the *Damron Road Atlas*, is quite useful for gay businesspeople with rental cars. Damron publications are available by calling 800-462-6654.

Detour's Guides are written for the more mainstream guppie contingent, with information for the traveler who has a fairly healthy budget. The general tourist listings—accommodations, bars, etc.—are peppered with historical and neighborhood information. Their guides are currently available for New York, New England, Miami, Southern California, Washington, DC, Amsterdam, London, and Paris. To purchase a guide, call 800-888-2052, ext. 62.

Ferrari Guides. Marianne Ferrari has branched out with a book for men and two general gay travel books that contain a unique local perspective on gay-specific destinations. The guides also include comprehensive cruise and tour listings. Another Ferrari guidebook, *Inn Places,* is a source of both lesbian and gay and lesbian/gay-friendly accommodations worldwide. The book consists entirely of paid advertisements, yet as a reference for anyone considering alternative accommodations, it is a must. To order a Ferrari publication, call 602-863-2408.

Our World was started in 1986 and is the first gay travel magazine. It is known for being one of the first gay publications to not accept sexually oriented advertising. Its listings, editorials, and photos can be helpful planning tools for your vacation, just be aware of all the advertising and reprinted press releases. To subscribe to *Our World*, call 904-441-5367.

Out & About has only been in existence for two years, but is a favorite among gay travelers. It describes itself as "a privately published newsletter providing travel information free from advertising bias for lesbian and gay travelers and their travel agents." It is full of information and locations, ranging from traditional to "hold onto your hat" adventures. Monthly issues contain articles on travel from a gay perspective, up-to-date city information, tour and cruise announcements, and bed and breakfast reviews. If you can't find it at your newsstand, write to: Out & About Inc., 8 West 19th St., Suite 401, New York, NY 10011, or call 1-800-929-2268.

Betty and Pansy's Severe Queer Review of New York / San Francisco / Washington D.C. Published by Bedpan Productions, 584 Castro St., Suite 410, San Francisco, CA 94114-2588.

COLUMBIA FUNMAPS: MAPPING THE GAY AND LESBIAN WORLD

These are free travel guides you can pick up at your local gay bookstore, community center, or bar. They are published for different cities (including Toronto, Provincetown, New York, Key West, Montreal, and others) and serve as handy pocket guides to gay bars, lodgings, shops, businesses, restaurants, and services. A map shows you how to get around in your vacation spot. If you can't find the FunMaps in your town, write to Columbia FunMaps, 118 East 28th St., New York, NY 10016.

SELECTED TRAVEL LITERATURE BOOKS

Barnes, Djuna. *New York* (Sun and Moon Press1989 reprint).

Hersey, John. *Key West Tales* (Alfred A. Knopf, Inc. 1993).

Keith, June. *Postcards from Paradise: Romancing Key West* (1995).

Lane, Michael, and Jim Crotty. *Mad Monks on the Road: A 47,000 Hour Dashboard Adventure—From Paradise, California, to Royal, Arkansas, and Up the New Jersey Turnpike* (1993).

Also available: *Monk Magazine* by the same authors. You can be sure it is filled with just as much wacky travel stuff as the book, with articles like "Portland Kicks Butt," etc. Write: 175 5th Ave., Suite 2322, New York, NY 10010 or call 212-465-3231.

Miller, John, ed. *San Francisco Street* (1990).

Newton, Esther. *Cherry Grove, Fire Island: Sixty Years in America's First Gay and Lesbian Town* (1993).

Trebay, Guy, with photographs by Sylvia Plachy. *In the Place to Be: Guy Trebay's New York* (1994).

Van Gelder, Linsey, and Pamela Brandt. *Are You Two . . .Together?* (1991). A guide to western Europe, part travel literature, part travel information.

Gay Travel Organizations

Gay Hospitality Exchange International, P.O. Box 612, Station C, Montreal, QC H2L 4K5

Gayroute: Tour Gay Canada, Box 314-G, Station de Lorimier, Montreal, QC H2H 2N7

International Gay Travel Association, P.O. Box 4974, Key West, FL 33041, 800-448-8550

Traveling Abroad

PASSPORTS

U.S. passports are valid for ten years when issued to travelers eighteen years or older. The initial application must be made in person; renewals (within twelve years of issuance) can be done by mail. To apply you need:

- Proof of citizenship (birth certificate or expired passport); naturalized citizens must present proof of legal entry into the country.
- A completed application (available at most post offices) and two 2" x 2" photographs taken within the last six months (color or b/w)
- Proof of identity (a driver's license will do)
- Fee of $65 for a new passport, payable in check or money order to Passport Services

Passport offices are generally located in federal office buildings. Check your local phone directory's blue pages for the location nearest you.

Note: For travel from the United States to Canada or Mexico, you are now required to have a passport or birth certificate as proof of citizenship. In the past, a driver's license would suffice, but the regulations have been tightened in the last few years.

VISAS

Many countries around the world require visas in addition to passports for U.S. citizens traveling as tourists. Unlike passports, visas are obtained directly from the embassies of the countries to be visited, which are located in major cities such as Chicago, New York, San Francisco, and Washington, DC. The addresses of foreign consular offices in the United States may be obtained from the *Congressional Directory,* which is available in most libraries.

Your travel agent can also assist you in obtaining visas. There are also several visa information services, such as: World Wide Visas (800-527-1861) and International Visa Service (800-843-0050).

CUSTOMS

When you re-enter the United States, you must declare all items that you purchased while traveling abroad, stating their actual purchase price or their market value. You will have to fill out a declaration form before arriving at U.S. Customs.

If you were out of the country for more than two days, you will not have to pay duty on the first $400 worth of purchases. Generally, purchases over that amount are subject to 10 percent duty tax.

There are customs restrictions on plants, animals, medications, and food. You can get a list of restricted items from the U.S. Department of Agriculture, Washington, DC 20205. Further information about customs and duty is available from your travel agent or from the U.S. Customs Service at 202-566-8195.

SOURCE: *New York Times Desk Reference* (1989)

TRAVEL ONLINE

A new guide and resource, called "The Gay Traveler: An Online Lesbian and Gay Travel Resource," opened in May 1995 on America Online under the Gay and Lesbian Community Forum. The new service includes such information as lists of lesbian and gay tour operators and cruise companies; libraries of travel brochures and booklets that you can download; a calendar of lesbian and gay travel events; a directory of people and places; profiles of popular lesbian and gay resorts, such as Provincetown, Palm Springs, and Key West; and travel tips for every part of the globe, from North America to the Pacific Rim.

"The Gay Traveler" also features a "Friday Letter" every week, chock full of interesting travel information, and a "Travel Conference" live every Wednesday night from 9 to 10 P.M. EST in the GLCF Community Conference Room.

Don't miss this information-packed resource guide that's waiting for you on your computer!

NATIONAL CAR RENTAL: THEY DEFINITELY TRY HARDER

Renting a car anywhere in the United States? In late 1994, National Car Rental became the first major car rental agency to recognize domestic partners when accepting additional drivers on car rental contracts. All other companies charge unmarried couples an additional $5 per day when they add a second driver, while legally married couples can add another driver at no cost, a policy which clearly discriminates against lesbians and gays. National has also pledged to donate to lesbian and gay charities 5 percent of the gross receipts of cars reserved through travel agents affiliated with the International Gay Travel Association (IGTA).

Lesbian and gay travelers interested in reserving National rental cars should contact their local IGTA travel agent or call National directly at 800-328-4567.

SOURCE: "The Gay Traveler Friday Letter," America Online, May 26, 1995. Reprinted with permission.

INTERNATIONAL GAY TRAVEL ASSOCIATION

The International Gay Travel Association, an association of travel professionals who work in the lesbian and gay market, met in May 1995 in the "Emerald City" of Seattle, Washington, for their twelfth annual convention. The 220 members who gathered at the Seattle Westin Hotel reflected IGTA's international diversity. In addition to the United States and Canada, delegates came from Australia, Germany, France, England, Mexico, Virgin Islands, and the Netherlands.

From May 11 to 14 the convention delegates spent their time networking, tending to association business (including the election of board members and officers), learning about gay and lesbian travel opportunities, and socializing. Plenary sessions discussed changes in the airline industry commission structure and association requirements and fees. There were breakout caucuses for travel agents, tour operators, and hotel managers. Seminars covered topics such as stress management, the internet, and commission caps.

Officers elected for 1995–1996 are President Tracy Michaels, Skylink Travel, Santa Monica, CA; Vice President Jim Boin, Yankee Clipper Travel, Los Gatos, CA; Secretary Paul Moreno, Five Star Travel Services, Boston, MA; and Treasurer Richard Gray, Royal Palms Hotel, Ft. Lauderdale, FL. Kevin Kailey of Above and Beyond Tours, San Francisco, CA, outgoing president, and David Alport, *Out & About*, New York, NY, outgoing vice president, presided over the conference.

Three members were inducted to the IGTA Hall of Fame: Marianne Ferrari, Ferrari Guides, Phoenix, AZ; Dan Delbex, Tara Country Retreat, Berry, New South Wales, Australia, founder of the Australian Gay and Lesbian Travel Association; and, posthumously, Rod Stringer, founder of the Damron Company, San Francisco, CA.

Six IGGY awards were presented for outstanding marketing or advertising campaigns—two each to Atlantis Events, Inc., Los Angeles, CA; Royal Palms Hotel, Ft. Lauderdale, FL; and Five Star Travel, Boston, MA. The Hall of Fame induction and the IGGY awards were presented at the annual gala dinner held Saturday night, May 13, after which conference guests were hosted by Virgin Atlantic Airways at Seattle's "The Prom . . . you never went to!" presented by the Lavender Valley High Prom Committee and The Detention Hall Honor Society as a fund-raiser for Seattle charities.

More than any other year, the convention attracted the attention of national, mainstream travel institutions, including American Airlines, the Canadian Consulate General's Office, Carey International, Hyatt Regency Hotels, Lufthansa German Airlines, Martinair Holland, National Car Rental, the Netherlands Board of Tourism, New York State Department of Parks and Recreation, Northwest Airlines, Outrigger Hotels of Hawaii, the Philadelphia Convention Bureau, Quantis Airways, Ramada Hotels, *Travel Weekly* Magazine, and Virgin Atlantic Airways.

The 1996 convention will be in Sydney, Australia. Philadelphia has made a bid to host the convention in 1997 during the annual Philadelphia Pride Fest. Travel professionals interested in joining the IGTA may obtain membership information by writing the organization at P.O. Box 4974, Key West, FL, 33041, by phoning 305-292-0217, by voice mail at 800-448-8550, or by fax at 305-296-6633.

SOURCE: "The Gay Traveler's Friday Letter," America Online, May 19, 1995.

GAY PRIDE AROUND THE GLOBE, 1995

Many cities all over the world have gay pride festivities, and they are not always the last weekend in June, when the Stonewall riots actually occurred. The following select list of gay pride events for 1995 can help you plan your future travels to coordinate with the "gayest" times in various cities.

Atlanta: Sunday, June 25
Baltimore: Saturday, June 10
Berlin: Saturday, July 1
Boston: Saturday, June 10
Chicago: Sunday, June 25
Cleveland: Saturday, June 17
Colorado Springs: Sunday, June 18
Columbus, Ohio: Sunday, June 25
Dallas: Sunday, September 24
Denver: Sunday, June 25
Detroit: Sunday, June 4
Edmonton, Alberta: Saturday, June 24
Ft. Lauderdale: Saturday, June 24
Houston: Sunday, June 25
Laguna Beach, Calif.: May 5–7
London: Saturday, June 24
Long Beach, Calif.: Sunday, May 21
Los Angeles: Sunday, June 25
Miami: Saturday, June 24
Minneapolis: Saturday, June 24

Montreal: Sunday, August 6
New York City: Sunday, June 25
Palm Springs: Sunday, October 8
Paris: Saturday, June 24
Philadelphia: Sunday, May 7
Phoenix: Friday, June 2
Pittsburgh: Saturday, June 24
Portland, Oregon: Saturday, June 17
Reykjavik, Iceland: Saturday, June 24
Rio de Janeiro: Gay Pride Carnival, June 18-25
San Diego: Saturday, July 15
San Francisco: Sunday, June 18
Santa Cruz, Calif.: Saturday, June 4
St. Louis: Sunday, September 24
Seattle: Sunday, June 25
Torino, Italy: Wednesday, June 28
Toronto: Sunday, July 2
Vancouver: Monday, August 7
Washington, DC: Sunday, June 18

PROFILE

Provincetown

As the heat of summer settles over the cities of the northeastern United States, the thoughts of lesbians and gay men turn to the gay resort at the tip of Cape Cod, affectionately known as P'town.

For many years a quiet fishing village, Provincetown was the site where the first British settlers landed in the early 1600s. It is now "the definitive gay resort," according to the lesbian and gay travel magazine *Out & About*, with accommodations, businesses, bars, and restaurants catering to lesbian and gay clientele.

Memorial Day weekend marks the beginning of the ten-week season for this New England resort town. Traditional summer holidays like Memorial Day, July 4th, and Labor Day mean big crowds and a tight market for accommodations. The Carnival held each August is another time when the town fills to overflowing. But with nearly fifty hotels and guest houses, Provincetown almost always has room for a couple more.

On the other hand, it's best not to just drop in to Provincetown in the summer without reservations. During the season, most of the better resorts have a five-day minimum stay. While there may always be room at the inn, it may not be exactly the inn you envisioned on those hot sweltering days at home. Early planning pays off in P'town. The town has a wide variety of hotels, b&b's, and quaint inns, some predominently gay male, some mixed lesbians and gay men. You can also rent cottages and condos, if you're planning a longer stay.

No cars are necessary in Provincetown—in fact, make sure your inn has free parking, or a car can be a bit of a hindrance. Everything you need—from restaurants to shops to dancing—is accessible by foot along Provincetown's main thoroughfare, Commercial Street.

Summer is chock full of entertainment, and the local clubs book many nationally known lesbian and gay performers. You can catch comedian Kate Clinton's act or run into her shopping on Commercial Street—she's a year-long resident of P'town.

Handy numbers for planning your P'town vacation
In Town Reservation: 800-67P'TOWN (accommodations)
Provincetown Reservations System: 800-648-0364 (accommodations)
Provincetown Business Guild: 800-637-8696 (offers a free guide to the town)

E-mail addresses for planning your P'town vacation
P Banner1@aol.com: *Provincetown Banner* (local newspaper)
Idilu@aol.com: timeshare information
AKHalles@aol.com: apartment and cottage rental
CrazyCJ@aol.com: a P'town specialist offering info on the best resorts, clubs, etc., by mail. Make sure you include your mailing address.

SOURCE: "The Gay Traveler," Gay and Lesbian Community Forum, America Online

PROFILE:

Cherry Grove, Fire Island

> "If San Francisco was America's gay capital in terms of political clout, the Grove was its summer capital, the pleasure island of gay imagination. The resort's lack of formal power was no indication of what its rumored existence represented in hope and possibility."
>
> —ESTHER NEWTON

Geographically, Fire Island is a barrier island that buffers the southern edge of Long Island, New York, from the Atlantic Ocean. Until the 1850s, according to legend, the beach was considered dangerous to visit because of pirates, ghosts, and "murdering Indians." Cherry Grove, created in 1869 and getting its name from the

Postcards from Fire Island. Collection of the National Museum & Archive of Lesbian and Gay History *(Photo by Winnie Hough)*

wild black cherry trees that cover the area, is the oldest and continuously inhabited resort on Fire Island.

Gay people started coming to Cherry Grove from New York City in the 1920s and 1930s, most of them affiliated with the theater in some way. "Gay theater people's migration to Cherry Grove is one of the clearest proofs we have that sexual preference was becoming the basis for a complete social identity," says Esther Newton in her history of Cherry Grove. Then, after the area was devastated by a hurricane in 1938, gay men and some lesbians found a place they could afford, and began buying property that no one else would.

Cherry Grove was the first, and for years the only, gay-controlled area in the United States. Many gay vacation spots like Provincetown, Massachusetts, Key West, Florida, and Cherry Grove were (and to a large degree, still are) the *only* public resort places lesbians and gay men could gather and be social without being subjected to the same level of pressure and hostility they would receive from straight society in other cities. "Of these resorts," says Newton, "the Grove was the only one with such a substantial gay majority, and so it was the safest."

It is important to recognize that the place where lesbians and gays were first able to be openly together was a resort. Cherry Grove was considered a "private sphere" as opposed to the "public sphere" of the city. So, though gay people could be open about their sexuality while "on the island" this was clearly a case of keeping all sexuality in the private sphere. Cherry Grove was the proverbial bedroom in which gay people were to keep their sexual business.

Gay people in Cherry Grove eventually became very visible not only to one another, but to the outside world. This visibility has created what Newton describes
as "the false idea that gay is synonymous with young, white, male, promiscuous, ar-
tistically inclined, and middle class." An important part of the Grove history has
been other gay people that do not fit these stereotypes, fighting to be recognized,
both on the island and off.

One must realize that Cherry Grove was not a fantasy island that gay people
necessarily chose because they wanted to, but instead a place where they retreated
due to the lack of tolerance and choices available within a straight society. It was
a matter of settling for certain possibilities.

Cherry Grove has historically had more gay male visitors and residents than lesbian, though the resort is now more mixed than Fire Island Pines, founded in the
1950s, which is predominently white, middle-class, and male. When AIDS hit
hard during the 1980s, male predominance in the Grove weakened. This fact, accompanied by an increase in some women's discretionary income and a softening
of the lesbian separatist ideas of the 1970s, brought during the mid-1980s the
largest influx of women to the Grove since its inception.

SOURCE: Esther Newton, *Cherry Grove, Fire Island: Sixty Years in America's First Gay and Lesbian
Town* (Beacon Press, 1993).

HOW TO GET THERE

*Cherry Grove is accessible via the Long Island Railroad (for schedules, phone:
718-217-5477) from Penn Station, New York, to Sayville (fare: $17.50 roundtrip
peak, $12 roundtrip off peak; you'll transfer at either Babylon or Jamaica). When
you exit at Sayville, shuttle buses (fare: $2 each way) will be waiting to take you
to the ferry (for departure times, phone: 516-589-0810; fare: $10 roundtrip). The
entire trip will take approximately two hours.*

VII

An AIDS Primer

Displaying 20,064 panels of the NAMES Project AIDS Memorial Quilt, Washington, DC, 1992. (*Photo by Jeff Tinsley*)

INTRODUCTION: GAY MEN AND HIV/AIDS

Since 1981, when it first began ravaging the gay community, this four-letter acronym for Acquired Immunodeficiency Syndrome has consumed our thoughts and lives. AIDS has played an important role in our health concerns, political organizing, community building, and culture. We've constructed health and treatment networks, clinics, and national organizations to care for our own. We've taken to the streets of Washington and our state capitals for needed funding. We've sponsored bereavement programs to deal with the realities of grief and multiple loss. We've created films, art, music, and literature on the political and personal faces of the pandemic, trying to make sense out of our pain.

In this section, we'll briefly outline the AIDS pandemic, define some of its most frequently used terms, and look at the responses our community has had to the health crisis within it and without.

A TIMELINE OF THE AIDS PANDEMIC

1959: A twenty-five-year-old British man dies of a mysterious disease in Manchester. His doctor stores samples of his tissues for future research, and since 1990, many scientists have believed that he was the first recorded person to die of AIDS.

1977: A Danish woman surgeon in Zaire dies of Pneumocystis carinii (PCP) at the age of forty-seven.

1981: An article headlined "Rare Cancer Seen in 41 Homosexuals" appears on a back page of *The New York Times* on July 3. The cancer is Kaposi's sarcoma (KS), and this is the first major reporting on what would later become known as AIDS.

• A Canadian nun who spent thirty years in Haiti rehabilitating prostitutes dies of PCP. She is reported to have had one male sexual partner while in Haiti and no other known risk factors.

• The Centers for Disease Control (CDC) release information about the growing number of cases of Pneumocystis carinii pneumonia (PCP) among gay men. Researchers try to make a connection between the mysterious disease and the use of the drug amyl nitrite (poppers) among gay men.

• Researchers begin to link the outbreaks of KS and PCP among gay men. In an inaccurate and stigmatizing choice of names, a scientist dubs the new disease Gay-Related Immune Disorder (GRID).

• By the end of the year, the disease has begun to show up among intravenous drug users.

1982: At the beginning of the year, the CDC reports that two hundred and fifty Americans have developed GRID, and ninety-nine of them have died.

• Writers Larry Kramer and Edmund White and four other men found the Gay Men's Health Crisis (GMHC), a nonprofit organization based in New York City to confront "gay cancer" by raising money for research. GMHC also trains volunteers to staff a hotline for the community's questions and concerns about the disease.

• The *Miami Herald* reports that the "gay plague" has begun to show up among heterosexual Haitian refugees, in the form of PCP and toxoplasmosis, a brain infection.

• Lab tests on gay men at St. Luke's-Roosevelt Hospital in New York City show a connection with cytomegalovirus (CMV) and GRID and also indicate a serious depletion of the T-4 (helper) cells in the men's blood, suggesting a breakdown of their immune systems.

• The first reported cases of GRID among hemophiliacs appear.

• Because GRID has continued to show up in heterosexuals, researchers search for other more accurate acronyms for the disease. Among those suggested are ACIDS (Acquired Community Immune Deficiency Syndrome) and CAIDS (Community Acquired Immune Deficiency Syndrome). Finally, they settle on the new name of AIDS (Acquired Immune Deficiency Syndrome), which is sexually neutral.

• *CBS Nightly News* with Dan Rather broadcasts one of the first network news pieces about AIDS.

• One of the first links between AIDS and blood transfusions is made at Bellevue Hospital in New York City, where a heterosexual Latino, who has not used IV drugs but has had massive blood transfusions, comes down with PCP.

• The American Red Cross advises lesbians not to give blood, as gay men have also been urged not to do.

• The Centers for Disease Control (CDC) report cases of immunodeficiency and opportunistic infection in infants born to mothers at risk in New York, New Jersey, and California.

• The CDC reports that 6 percent of the total AIDS cases are women.

1983: In January, the *Morbidity and Mortality Weekly Report* (*MMWR*) on AIDS establishes the last major risk group for the disease: female sexual partners of male persons with AIDS (PWAs).

• Two years into the epidemic, *The New York Times* does its first cover story on AIDS.

• U.S. scientists start to look for the beginnings of AIDS, and their findings take them back to Africa, where a Danish woman surgeon living in Zaire died of PCP in the early 1970s.

• The phrase "innocent victims" begins to be applied to children and blood transfusion recipients, while other PWAs are stigmatized by "aberrant" sexual and drug-use behavior.

• In New York's gay newspaper, *The Native,* a March 7 cover story by Larry Kramer, "1,112 and Counting," not only indicts the CDC, *The New York Times*, and the New York City health commissioner for lack of response to the AIDS crisis, it also lashes out at apathetic gay men who continue to have "careless sex" in the middle of an epidemic.

• Reverend Jerry Falwell, founder of the Moral Majority, tells his followers in Lynchburg, Virginia, that AIDS is "the judgment of God."

• A news release of the American Medical Association reports findings (later discredited) that AIDS can be transmitted through casual contact, causing a rash of AIDS hysteria stories in the press.

- The CDC reports immunodeficiency among female sexual partners of men with AIDS.

- *Ms.* is the first women's magazine to mention AIDS in an article by lesbian writer Linsey Van Gelder, though the article does not specifically mention the risk to women.

- The CDC reports that almost 7 percent of all AIDS cases are women.

- Dr. Mervyn Silverman, San Francisco's public health director, orders the city's gay bathhouses to display warning posters against promiscuous sex and recreational drug use. He threatens to close any bathhouses that do not comply.

- By Gay Pride weekend in 1983, seventeen hundred people have been diagnosed with AIDS in the United States, and seven hundred and fifty of those have died.

- The CDC defines a new phenomenon called AIDS-related complex (ARC), in which people show clinical conditions that seem to precede AIDS.

- In Geneva, Switzerland, AIDS experts from around the world convene at the World Health Organization headquarters for the first meeting on the international implications of the epidemic. The disease has thus far been reported in thirty-three countries on five continents.

- CDC researchers determine that the incubation period for AIDS is somewhere between five and eleven years.

1984: Dr. Robert Gallo, a National Cancer Institute researcher, informs the director of the National Health Institutes that he has isolated the virus that causes AIDS, a variant of the human T-cell leukemia virus (HTLV) family that he discovered in 1980. He calls it HTLV-III. Days later, researchers at the Pasteur Institute in Paris show proof that they have discovered the AIDS virus, which they call LAV (lymphadenopathy-associated virus). In subsequent tests, it becomes clear that both Gallo and the French have isolated the same microbe.

- The Shanti Project, a community clinic in San Francisco since 1974, turns its focus exclusively to AIDS and HIV treatment.

- By early 1984, thirty-five hundred people in the United States have been diagnosed with AIDS, of whom fifteen hundred have died.

- The San Francisco AIDS Foundation receives a grant from the State Department of Health to develop a pilot program on women and AIDS, the first such study to focus on women.

- *Mademoiselle* publishes one of the first articles addressing women's risk of AIDS.

- With the announcement of the isolation of the AIDS virus, researchers push to develop a blood test and begin talk about an AIDS vaccine.

- After repeated reports about unsafe sexual practices in San Francisco bathhouses, Dr. Mervyn Silverman orders their closing. "These fourteen establishments," he announces, "are not fostering gay liberation. They are fostering disease and death." Only months later, Silverman resigns his position as public health commissioner.

1985: The Food and Drug Administration (FDA) approves the first HTLV blood test, which tests for the presence of antibodies to the AIDS virus in the bloodstream.

• Blood banks begin testing their blood supplies for the presence of antibodies to HTLV.

• By mid-1985, the CDC reports that eleven thousand Americans had contracted AIDS and of those, fifty-four hundred have died.

• After repeated denials, movie and television actor Rock Hudson issues a public statement that he has AIDS, and dies three months later.

• Following San Francisco's lead, public health officials in New York City and Los Angeles close gay bathhouses in their cities. The New York City Health Department also closes the Mineshaft, a famous gay bar, after undercover inspectors report on the sexual acts taking place there.

1986: Amid competition between the National Cancer Institute and the Pasteur Institute over which could claim discovery of the AIDS virus, an international committee renames it the human immunodeficiency virus, or HIV.

• U.S. Surgeon General C. Everett Koop cites the growing threat of AIDS as the reason for much needed sex education in secondary schools on both heterosexual and homosexual relationships.

1987: President Reagan undergoes testing for HIV when he becomes concerned about the blood transfusions he received when he was shot in 1981. According to a White House spokesperson, he tests negative.

• The AIDS Coalition to Unleash Power (ACT UP) is founded by writer Larry Kramer and others at a public forum at New York's Lesbian and Gay Community Services Center. The direct action group stages its first protest in the financial district of the city, demanding that the Reagan administration stop dragging its feet on the approval of new drugs to help people with AIDS.

• Mandatory testing of pregnant women and marriage applicants is put in place in some states.

• The *Journal of the American Medical Association* publishes one of the first medical accounts of women and AIDS.

• President Reagan gives his first speech on AIDS, in which he calls for more HIV testing. By this time, thirty-six thousand Americans have been diagnosed with AIDS and almost twenty-one thousand have died.

• U.S. Attorney General Edwin Meese announces two new administration policies on AIDS: that all federal prisoners will receive mandatory HIV testing; and that immigrants and refugees known to be HIV-positive will be denied entry to the country.

• AZT (zidovudine) becomes the first FDA-licensed antiviral in the fight against AIDS. AZT slows down the replication of HIV within healthy cells and helps prevent the onset of opportunistic infections, but it often has negative side effects, ranging from nausea to serious liver problems.

• The NAMES Project AIDS Memorial Quilt is displayed for the first time, on the mall in front of the U.S. Capitol during the Second March on Washington for Lesbian and Gay Rights.

• San Francisco reporter Randy Shilts's book *And the Band Played On,* which chronicles and criticizes the Reagan administration's blatant disregard of the AIDS pandemic, is published.

1988: The World Health Organization (WHO) decrees the first World AIDS Day.

• Delegates to the Southern Baptist Convention pass a resolution blaming gay men for AIDS and condemning homosexuality as "an abomination."

• Studies report that antigay violence is on a rise, with AIDS-phobia a factor in many reported instances.

• President Reagan's newly founded National AIDS Commission releases a report, with over five hundred recommendations for addressing the epidemic. A presidential advisor reduces the list to ten items.

• AIDS is the fifteenth leading cause of death among Americans, according to the National Center for Health Statistics.

1989: The first Advanced Immune Discoveries Symposium is held, centering on holistic and natural therapies for combatting AIDS.

• The FDA approves the antiviral ddI (dideoxyinosine), which slows down the replication of HIV in healthy cells. Like AZT, though, ddI is shown to have side effects, ranging from neuropathy to diarrhea to pancreatitis.

• Over five thousand activists stage a massive protest in front of New York's St. Patrick's Cathedral, rallying against the Catholic Church's negative policies on homosexuality and AIDS. A half dozen of the protestors chain themselves to pews inside the cathedral and are arrested. This is the largest AIDS demonstration in the United States to date.

• A report from the National Association of State Boards of Education reveals that only twenty-four states in the United States require HIV/AIDS education in public schools, and of those, only three direct teachers to discuss condom use.

1990: The third antiviral for the treatment of HIV/AIDS, dideoxycytidine (ddC), becomes available.

• The movie *Longtime Companion,* the first major Hollywood film about AIDS, opens in theaters.

• According to the CDC, the number of deaths from AIDS in the United States has topped one hundred thousand. There are approximately 1,100 AIDS deaths every week.

1991: ACT UP leads a massive demonstration at the Centers for Disease Control in Atlanta, to protest the agency's underestimating of the number of women with AIDS.

• The first clinical trials for the Salk immunogen vaccine, designed by polio vaccine pioneer Dr. Jonas Salk, take place in Philadelphia. The Salk vaccine is for those already infected with HIV, to stop the erosion of their immune systems.

• A number of alarming studies across the United States shows that unprotected anal intercourse is on the rise among gay and bisexual men, resulting in a new wave of HIV infections.

• After protest demonstrations by lesbian health activists, Gay Men's Health Crisis adds lesbians to their mission statement. The following year, GMHC's

Lesbian AIDS Project is founded, and Amber Hollibaugh becomes its first coordinator.

• Professional basketball star Earvin "Magic" Johnson publicly announces that he has tested positive for HIV. As when Rock Hudson revealed he had AIDS in 1985, the media rushes to cover AIDS issues that had held little interest for them before. Johnson is promptly appointed by President Bush to the National Commission on AIDS.

1992: For the first time at both the Democratic and Republican national conventions, HIV-positive speakers present the concerns and needs of people with AIDS—the "human face" of AIDS. At the Democratic convention, Bob Hattoy, an adviser to Bill Clinton, and Elizabeth Glaser, a pediatric AIDS activist, take the podium, while at the Republican convention, Mary Fisher, the daughter of a prominent Republican fund-raiser, addresses the delegates.

• The National Commission on AIDS, established late in the Reagan administration, says, "President Bush and the Department of Health and Human Services have failed to meet fully their responsibility in leading the national response" to the epidemic. Magic Johnson, a highly visible member of the commission, resigns to protest the President's inaction.

• The Centers for Disease Control initiates Business Responds to AIDS, an HIV prevention program encouraging businesses to take an active role in providing HIV/AIDS education to their employees.

1993: The Centers for Disease Control once again expands their definition of "full-blown AIDS," increasing the number of indicator diseases that spell the onset of immunosuppression to include more of the opportunistic infections that attack women with AIDS. This far-reaching move nearly doubles the number of people with AIDS across the country and is the most dramatic change in the CDC definition since the start of the pandemic.

• William Roper, head of the CDC and an opponent of sexually explicit content in federally funded AIDS education programs, is dismissed. The Clinton administration maintains that AIDS prevention programs must address sexual behavior as well as IV drug use.

• At the Ninth International Conference on AIDS in Berlin, scientists report that the way in which HIV destroys the immune system are far more complex than previously thought, thus dimming the hope for a vaccine or "magic bullet" drug.

• President Clinton appoints Kristine Gebbie, the former Washington state health department director, to be his first "AIDS czar." AIDS activists view this as a weak and disappointing choice, since Gebbie has shown no commitment to the AIDS fight or experience in AIDS issues.

• AIDS becomes the leading killer of American men between the ages of twenty-five and forty-four and the fourth leading killer of women in the same age group.

• The U.S. Congress boosts spending for AIDS research in fiscal 1994 to the highest it has ever been—a full 27 percent over fiscal 1993.

• Tuberculosis begins to spread at an alarming rate across the United States, posing a new threat to PWAs.

At the 1993 Gay Pride March, New York City (*Photo by Harry Stevens*)

1994: The CDC reports that in 1993 heterosexually acquired cases of AIDS rose
130 percent over the previous year, while cases attributed to homosexual sex
rose 87 percent.

• The first HIV Prevention Summit is held in Dallas, Texas, in an attempt to
address the problem of the breakdown of safer sex and the resulting rise of new
HIV infections—the "second wave" of HIV.

• The Concorde Project, a British-French study of AZT, concludes that the
antiviral does not delay the onset of AIDS symptoms in those who are HIV positive, though it may prolong life in people with AIDS.

• Canada begins a two-year inquiry into charges that health officials allowed
HIV-infected blood products to be distributed there after the HIV antibody test
had been developed.

• AIDS czar Kristine Gebbie, widely criticized by AIDS activists for her low
profile, lack of experience, and ineffectiveness, resigns from office. In her place,
Clinton names Patsy Fleming, an African-American woman with a gay son who
considers herself an AIDS activist.

• Recognizing that the search for traditional drug and vaccine therapies for
AIDS has been ineffectual, the National Institute of Allergy and Infectious Diseases awards a $25 million grant for research in alternative treatments for AIDS.

1995: New findings on the replication and mutation of HIV show that the immune system wages a fierce battle against the virus from the very beginning of

Former AIDS czar,
Kristine Gebbie *(Photo
by Terry Boggis)*

infection, losing just a little ground each day until the virus eventually wins and
immunosuppression sets in. Research, scientists conclude, should focus on finding ways to boost the immune system's powers so it does not lose the battle.

• Olympic gold medalist Greg Louganis, considered by many to be the greatest diver of all time, announces in a television interview on *20/20* with Barbara
Walters that he has AIDS. His announcement that he was HIV positive when
he hit his head on the diving board during the 1988 Olympics, drawing blood
and requiring stitches, causes a flurry of indignation that he may have put other
athletes and the doctor who stitched his wound at risk. The doctor, however,
tests negative, and experts maintain that a few drops of blood in a chlorine-
treated pool would not endanger anyone.

• The Centers for Disease Control report that 50 percent of all new HIV infections are among women, with the disease being transmitted fastest among
black and Latina women. In 1994, the number of AIDS cases increase 151 percent for women, compared with 105 percent for men.

• Congressman Robert Dornan (R-Calif.) introduces a measure into the
House of Representatives that would discharge all HIV-positive people from
the U.S. Armed Forces. Although HIV-positive people are not allowed to enlist
in the military, Pentagon officials say there is no reason to dismiss those who become HIV positive during their service, as long as their health remains good.

SOURCE: *The Advocate; And the Band Played On*, (Viking Penguin, 1993) by Randy Shilts; and *Invisible Epidemic*, (HarperCollins, 1992) by Gena Corea

"Rare Cancer Seen in 41 Homosexuals

Outbreak Occurs Among Men in New York and California— 8 Died Inside 2 Years"

by Lawrence K. Altman

Doctors in New York and California have diagnosed among homosexual men 41 cases of a rare and often rapidly fatal form of cancer. Eight of the victims died less than 24 months after the diagnosis was made.

The cause of the outbreak is yet unknown, and there is as yet no evidence of contagion. But the doctors who have made the diagnoses, mostly in New York City and the San Francisco Bay area, are alerting other physicians who treat large numbers of homosexual men to the problem in an effort to help identify more cases and to reduce the delay in offering chemotherapy treatment.

The sudden appearance of the cancer, called Kaposi's Sarcoma, has prompted a medical investigation that experts say could have as much scientific as public health importance because of what it may teach about determining the causes of more common types of cancer.

"If KS [Kaposi's sarcoma] were a new form of cancer attacking straight people, it would be receiving constant media attention, the pressure from every side would be so great upon the cancer-funding institutions that research would be proceeding with great intensity."

—Larry Kramer, 1981

"[Kaposi's sarcoma] afflicts members of one of the nation's most stigmatized and discriminated against minorities. . . . Legionnaire's Disease affected fewer people and proved less likely to be fatal. What society judged was not the severity of the disease but the social acceptability of the individuals affected with it."

—Congressman Henry Waxman (D-Calif.), 1982

"The poor homosexuals — they have declared war upon nature, and now nature is exacting an awful retribution."

—Patrick Buchanan, May 1983

"1,112 AND COUNTING"

by Larry Kramer

If this article doesn't scare the shit out of you we're in real trouble. If this article doesn't rouse you to anger, fury, rage and action, gay men may have no future on this earth. . . . Unless we fight for our lives we shall die. In all the history of homosexuality we have never been so close to death and extinction before. Many of us are dying or dead already.

. . . I am sick of guys who moan that giving up careless sex until this thing blows over is worse than death. How can they value life so little and cocks and asses so much?

Excerpted from the *New York Native*, March 7, 1983. Full text reprinted in *Reports from the Holocaust*, by Larry Kramer, New York, 1995.

"AIDS DISEASE COULD ENDANGER GENERAL POPULATION"

CHICAGO (AP)—A study showing children may catch the deadly immune deficiency disease AIDS from their families could mean the general population is at greater risk from the illness than previously believed, a medical journal reported today.

If "routine" personal contact among family members in a household is enough to spread the illness, "then AIDS takes on an entirely new dimension," said Dr. Anthony Fauci of the National Institutes of Health in Bethesda, Maryland.

SOURCE: Associated Press, May 6, 1983. Reprinted with permission.

"Tragically, funding levels for AIDS investigations have been dictated by political considerations rather than by the professional judgments of scientists and public health officials who are waging the battle against the epidemic. The inadequacy of funding, coupled with inexcusable delays in research activity, leads me to question the Federal Government's preparedness for national health emergencies, as well as this administration's commitment to an urgent resolution to the AIDS crisis."

—CONGRESSMAN TED WEISS (D-N.Y.), 1984

"We must conquer AIDS before it affects the heterosexual population."

—U.S. Secretary of Health and Human Services MARGARET HECKLER, April 1985

HOLLYWOOD (UPI)—Actor Rock Hudson, last of the traditional square-jawed, romantic leading men, known recently for his roles on "McMillan and Wife" and "Dynasty," is suffering from inoperable liver cancer possibly linked to AIDS, it was disclosed Tuesday.

SOURCE: United Press International, July 23, 1985

"You get the feeling you're in Beirut or on the front lines of a war."

—DR. DANIEL WILLIAM, a Manhattan physician specializing in the treatment of AIDS, 1985

"Everyone detected with AIDS should be tattooed in the upper forearm, to protect common-needle users, and on the buttocks, to prevent the victimization of other homosexuals."

—WILLIAM F. BUCKLEY, JR., 1986

"AIDS is spreading and killing in every corner of the world. . . . It is an equal-opportunity merchant of death. . . . Ultimately, we must protect those who do not have the disease."

—Vice President and presidential candidate GEORGE BUSH, 1987

"History will deal harshly with the Reagan administration for its failure to face up to the unprecedented threat of the AIDS pandemic. Not since Hoover has a president done less when he should have known better."

—Tennesee Senator and presidential candidate AL GORE, 1987

"It simply became an overwhelming experience. You saw that quilt go down, and it was at dawn, and people were reading the names, and the names of all those people that have died. And all the talent gone, and the lives lost. And it simply became an overwhelming experience. It became a lot more than just my son."

—SUE CAVES, who sewed a panel in memory of her son, 1987

Working on the NYC Lesbian and Gay Community Services Center Quilt Project, 1988 *(Copyright Roberta Raeburn)*

Part of the NYC Lesbian and Gay Community Services Center Quilt *(Copyright Roberta Raeburn.)*

"*Lesbians are not an isolated community: There are lesbians who shoot drugs and share needles, there are lesbians who have been married, who have babies, who are in prisons, who have sex for money, who get raped. When examining the AIDS epidemic, it becomes obvious that stereotypes are useless: it's not who you are that puts you at risk, it's what you do.*"

—ZOE LEONARD, artist, filmmaker, activist, 1990

"*It is an excess of free speech . . . to resort to some of the tactics these people [ACT UP activists] use.*"

—PRESIDENT GEORGE BUSH, 1991

"*I was very closeted about [having AIDS] at first. I didn't want the news to get out before the book did. I spent four years on Conduct Unbecoming; it is my definitive statement on homophobia, and I didn't want all of the press to be about me having AIDS. I don't want to be a professional AIDS patient.*"

—RANDY SHILTS, author of *And the Band Played On*, 1993

"*I am the face of the HIV virus. You see me every day, you pass me on the street, you work next to me, yet you don't know my secret. We are invisible. . . . Women are an invisible component of this disease for several reasons: fear of losing custody of children, fear of losing jobs or insurance, and fear of negative judgment.*"

—an anonymous lesbian mother, 1993, quoted in *Until the Cure: Caring for Women with HIV*, edited by Ann Kurth (Yale University Press, 1993).

"*We would not be able to have the Year of the Queer, the decade of the nineties, if it were not for the last decade of the AIDS epidemic. . . . It has created such unstoppable, ferocious determination in all of us. It has telescoped what would have been decades of change.*"

—TORIE OSBORN, former director of the National Gay and Lesbian Task Force, 1993

"Gebbie was perfect for the position as it was defined: She wasn't good and she wasn't effective. But there was no way the office could be effective. It never had any real power."

—ACT UP activist STEVE MICHAEL on Kristine Gebbie's resignation as AIDS czar, 1994

"Too many of us have been in denial for far too long, whether about how we have been engaging in unsafe sex, or how we promote an often oppressive sexual culture that enables — and sometimes even encourages—others to do so."

—MICHELANGELO SIGNORILE, 1994

"Why are we spending so much on AIDS?"

—REP. BOB LIVINGSTON (R-La.), 1995, to Donna Shalala, Health and Human Services Secretary

"I just held my head in the hopes . . . I [didn't] know if I was cut or not. But I wanted to keep the blood in or just not let anybody touch it. Dealing with HIV was really difficult for me because I felt like, God, the U.S. Olympic Committee needs to know this. But I didn't anticipate hitting my head on the board. That's where I became paralyzed with fear."

—Olympic diver GREG LOUGANIS, 1995, on ABC's 20/20

"Women's access to health care is intrinsically linked to sexism, poverty, and racism. Remember that 75 percent of women with AIDS are women of color, many of whom are poor. So it's no surprise that research, treatment, and outreach efforts directed to this discounted group of women fall far short of meeting their needs."

—MARION D. BANZHAF, Executive Director, New Jersey Women and AIDS Network, 1995

HIV/AIDS STATISTICS

The following tables are reprinted from Centers for Disease Control and Prevention, *HIV/AIDS Surveillance Report,* 1994, Vol. 6, No. 2: pp. 11, 12, 20, 25, 35. Copies of the complete report are available free from the CDC National AIDS Clearinghouse, P.O. Box 6003, Rockville, MD 20849-6003, 800-458-5231.

MALE ADULT/ADOLESCENT AIDS CASES BY EXPOSURE CATEGORY AND RACE/ETHNICITY, REPORTED IN 1994, AND CUMULATIVE TOTALS, THROUGH DECEMBER 1994, UNITED STATES

EXPOSURE CATEGORY	White, Not Hispanic				Black, Not Hispanic				Hispanic			
	1994		CUMULATIVE TOTAL		1994		CUMULATIVE TOTAL		1994		CUMULATIVE TOTAL	
	NO.	(%)	NO.	(%)	NO.	(%)	NO.	(%)	NO.	(%)	NO.	(%)
Men who have sex with men	21,536	(72)	153,150	(77)	7,959	(35)	44,597	(40)	4,945	(41)	28,232	(45)
Injecting drug use	3,224	(11)	16,632	(8)	8,290	(36)	40,580	(37)	4,385	(36)	23,911	(38)
Men who have sex with men and inject drugs	1,990	(7)	15,503	(8)	1,251	(5)	8,479	(8)	559	(5)	4,275	(7)
Hemophilia/coagulation disorder	353	(1)	2,848	(1)	68	(0)	338	(0)	48	(0)	285	(0)
Heterosexual contact:	584	(2)	2,374	(1)	1,651	(7)	5,876	(5)	689	(6)	2,320	(4)
Sex with injecting drug user	192		1,069		529		2,789		193		839	
Sex with person with hemophilia	1		14		2		4		—		6	
Sex with transfusion recipient with HIV infection	23		95		17		79		19		60	
Sex with HIV-infected person, risk not specified	368		1,196		1,103		3,004		477		1,415	
Receipt of blood transfusion, blood components, or tissue	220	(1)	2,711	(1)	137	(1)	790	(1)	59	(0)	443	(1)
Risk not reported or identified	2,003	(7)	5,604	(3)	3,482	(15)	10,298	(9)	1,331	(11)	3,468	(6)
Total	29,910	(100)	198,822	(100)	22,838	(100)	110,958	(100)	12,016	(100)	62,934	(100)

	Asian/Pacific Islander				American Indian/Alaska Native				Cumulative totals*			
	1994		CUMULATIVE TOTAL		1994		CUMULATIVE TOTAL		1994		CUMULATIVE TOTAL	
EXPOSURE CATEGORY	NO.	(%)	NO.	(%)	NO.	(%)	NO.	(%)	NO.	(%)	NO.	(%)
Men who have sex with men	377	(73)	2,085	(78)	94	(51)	544	(61)	34,974	(53)	228,954	(61)
Injecting drug use	22	(4)	120	(4)	32	(17)	110	(12)	15,968	(24)	81,491	(22)
Men who have sex with men and inject drugs	18	(3)	84	(3)	31	(17)	155	(17)	3,853	(6)	28,521	(8)
Hemophilia/coagulation disorder	5	(1)	41	(2)	6	(3)	24	(3)	483	(1)	3,545	(1)
Heterosexual contact:	19	(4)	49	(2)	2	(1)	12	(1)	2,946	(4)	10,641	(3)
Sex with injecting drug user	6		17		—		4		920		4,719	
Sex with person with hemophilia	—		—		—		—		3		24	
Sex with transfusion recipient with HIV infection	1		3		1		1		61		239	
Sex with HIV-infected person, risk not specified	12		29		1		7		1,962		5,659	
Receipt of blood transfusion, blood components, or tissue	11	(2)	84	(3)	2	(1)	7	(1)	432	(1)	4,047	(1)
Risk not reported or identified	66	(13)	204	(8)	17	(9)	36	(4)	6,935	(11)	19,690	(5)
Total	518	(100)	2,667	(100)	184	(100)	888	(100)	65,591	(100)	376,889	(100)

*Includes 620 men whose race/ethnicity is unknown.

FEMALE ADULT/ADOLESCENT AIDS CASES BY EXPOSURE CATEGORY AND RACE/ETHNICITY, REPORTED IN 1994, AND CUMULATIVE TOTALS, THROUGH DECEMBER 1994, UNITED STATES

EXPOSURE CATEGORY	White, Not Hispanic				Black, Not Hispanic				Hispanic			
	1994		CUMULATIVE TOTAL		1994		CUMULATIVE TOTAL		1994		CUMULATIVE TOTAL	
	NO.	(%)	NO.	(%)	NO.	(%)	NO.	(%)	NO.	(%)	NO.	(%)
Injecting drug use	1,259	(40)	6,141	(43)	3,360	(42)	16,069	(50)	1,099	(39)	5,519	(46)
Hemophilia/coagulation disorder	11	(0)	65	(0)	7	(0)	25	(0)	—	—	6	(0)
Heterosexual contact:	1,243	(39)	5,207	(37)	2,777	(35)	10,481	(33)	1,291	(46)	5,125	(43)
Sex with injecting drug user	503		2,408		1,018		5,498		498		3,045	
Sex with bisexual male	154		853		140		646		59		253	
Sex with person with hemophilia	36		189		11		32		7		16	
Sex with transfusion recipient with HIV infection	34		218		17		89		12		69	
Sex with HIV-infected person, risk not specified	516		1,539		1,596		4,216		715		1,742	
Receipt of blood transfusion, blood components, or tissue	129	(4)	1,551	(11)	133	(2)	776	(2)	48	(2)	413	(3)
Risk not reported or identified	506	(16)	1,202	(8)	1,739	(22)	4,470	(14)	376	(13)	846	(7)
Total	3,148	(100)	14,166	(100)	8,016	(100)	31,821	(100)	2,814	(100)	11,909	(100)

| | Asian/Pacific Islander | | | | American Indian/Alaska Native | | | | Cumulative totals* | | | |
| | 1994 | | CUMULATIVE TOTAL | | 1994 | | CUMULATIVE TOTAL | | 1994 | | CUMULATIVE TOTAL | |
EXPOSURE CATEGORY	NO.	(%)	NO.	(%)	NO.	(%)	NO.	(%)	NO.	(%)	NO.	(%)
Injecting drug use	7	(14)	48	(17)	20	(48)	79	(50)	5,749	(41)	27,092	(48)
Hemophilia/coagulation disorder	—	—	1	(0)	—	—	—	—	18	(0)	97	(0)
Heterosexual contact:	22	(45)	129	(44)	18	(43)	56	(35)	5,353	(38)	21,021	(36)
Sex with injecting drug user	7		40		11		34		2,032		11,039	
Sex with bisexual male	7		38		3		6		363		1,798	
Sex with person with hemophilia	1		3		—		2		55		242	
Sex with transfusion recipient with HIV infection	1		12		—		—		64		389	
Sex with HIV-infected person, risk not specified	6		36		4		14		2,839		7,553	
Receipt of blood transfusion, blood components, or tissue	8	(16)	68	(23)	1	(2)	10	(6)	319	(2)	2,819	(5)
Risk not reported or identified	12	(24)	44	(15)	3	(7)	14	(9)	2,642	(19)	6,589	(11)
Total	49	(100)	290	(100)	42	(100)	159	(100)	14,081	(100)	58,428	(100)

*Includes 83 women whose race/ethnicity is unknown.

DEATHS IN PERSONS WITH AIDS, BY RACE/ETHNICITY, AGE AT DEATH, AND SEX, OCCURRING IN 1992 AND 1993; AND CUMULATIVE TOTALS REPORTED THROUGH DECEMBER 1994, UNITED STATES[1]

Race/Ethnicity and Age at Death[2]	Males 1992	Males 1993	Males Cumulative Total	Females 1992	Females 1993	Females Cumulative Total	Both Sexes[3] 1992	Both Sexes[3] 1993	Both Sexes[3] Cumulative Total
White, not Hispanic									
Under 15	54	47	408	27	43	295	81	90	703
15–24	181	181	2,084	39	44	313	220	225	2,397
25–34	5,429	5,432	40,377	377	435	2,709	5,806	5,867	43,086
35–44	7,844	8,007	53,979	382	537	2,404	8,226	8,544	56,383
45–54	3,460	3,630	23,330	167	196	918	3,627	3,826	24,248
55 or older	1,372	1,304	10,298	144	121	1,191	1,516	1,425	11,489
All ages	18,340	18,602	130,679	1,136	1,376	7,846	19,476	19,978	138,525
Black, not Hispanic									
Under 15	122	136	925	105	136	923	227	272	1,848
15–24	225	202	1,782	105	133	792	330	335	2,574
25–34	2,913	3,129	21,699	912	1,027	6,524	3,825	4,157	28,224
35–44	4,342	4,902	27,671	1,208	1,367	6,835	5,550	6,269	34,506
45–54	1,627	1,960	10,131	282	403	1,863	1,909	2,363	11,994
55 or older	730	785	4,330	157	184	942	887	969	5,272
All ages	9,960	11,114	66,637	2,769	3,250	17,911	12,729	14,365	84,549
Hispanic									
Under 15	57	61	430	37	54	381	94	115	811
15–24	102	100	1,005	42	54	324	144	154	1,329
25–34	1,907	1,896	13,576	395	392	2,592	2,302	2,288	16,168
35–44	2,333	2,502	15,321	376	490	2,316	2,709	2,992	17,637
45–54	923	935	5,659	121	164	719	1,044	1,099	6,378
55 or older	352	390	2,308	60	74	349	412	464	2,657
All ages	5,675	5,885	28,366	1,031	1,228	6,698	6,706	7,113	45,064
Asian/Pacific Islander									
Under 15	1	2	16	—	3	6	1	5	22
15–24	1	6	26	—	1	5	1	7	31
25–34	56	70	462	3	6	41	59	76	503
35–44	102	109	653	9	13	56	111	122	709
45–54	54	52	333	6	6	35	60	58	368
55 or older	12	16	124	4	4	28	16	20	152
All ages	226	255	1,614	22	33	172	248	288	1,786
American Indian/Alaska Native									
Under 15	—	2	10	—	1	4	—	3	14
15–24	1	3	20	—	—	2	1	3	22
25–34	36	42	206	4	4	27	40	46	233
35–44	19	42	167	4	4	22	23	46	189
45–54	5	14	59	—	1	6	5	15	65
55 or older	4	6	25	—	1	3	4	7	28
All ages	65	109	492	8	11	64	73	120	556
All racial/ethnic groups									
Under 15	234	248	1,790	172	237	1,615	406	485	3,405
15–24	510	493	4,921	186	232	1,437	696	725	6,358
25–34	10,358	10,580	76,407	1,694	1,864	11,904	12,052	12,445	88,312
35–44	14,667	15,581	97,941	1,985	2,417	11,657	16,652	17,998	109,598
45–54	6,080	6,604	39,569	577	770	3,548	6,657	7,374	43,117
55 or older	2,477	2,507	17,119	365	384	2,516	2,842	2,891	19,635
All ages	34,328	36,015	238,125	4,979	5,904	32,744	39,307	41,920	270,870

Data tabulations for 1992 and 1993 are based on date of death occurrence. Data for deaths occurring in 1994 are incomplete and not tabulated separately, but are included in the cumulative totals. Tabulations for 1992 and 1993 may increase as additional deaths are reported to CDC.

Data tabulated under "all ages" include 445 persons whose age at death is unknown. Data tabulated under "all racial/ethnic groups" include 390 persons whose race/ethnicity is unknown.

Includes 1 person whose sex is unknown.

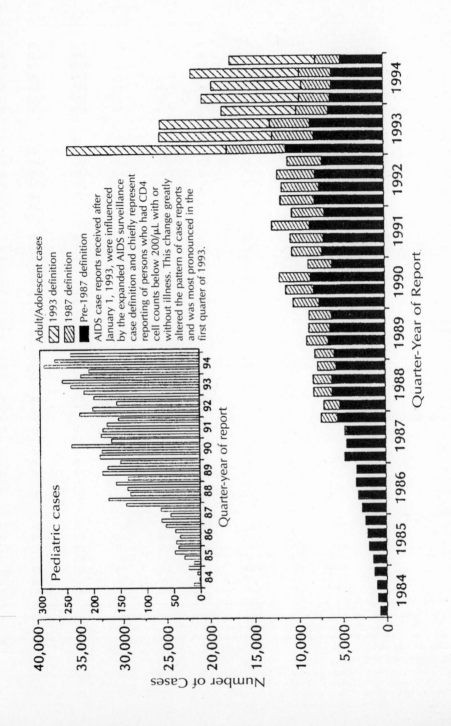

Adult/Adolescent cases

1993 definition

1987 definition

Pre-1987 definition

AIDS case reports received after January 1, 1993, were influenced by the expanded AIDS surveillance case definition and chiefly represent reporting of persons who had CD4 cell counts below 200/μL with or without illness. This change greatly altered the pattern of case reports and was most pronounced in the first quarter of 1993.

Pediatric cases

Quarter-year of report

Number of Cases

Quarter-Year of Report.

Persons Reported to Be Living with HIV Infection (Not AIDS) and with AIDS, by State and Age Group, Reported through December 1994[1]

State of Residence (Date HIV Reporting Initiated)	Living with HIV (Not AIDS)[2]			Living with AIDS[3]			Cumulative Totals		
	Adults/ Adolescents	Children <13 Years Old	Total	Adults/ Adolescents	Children <13 Years Old	Total	Adults/ Adolescents	Children <13 Years Old	Total
Alabama (Jan. 1988)	3,544	31	3,575	1,318	16	1,334	4,862	47	4,909
Alaska	—	—	—	101	1	102	101	1	102
Arizona (Jan. 1987)	2,713	22	2,735	1,298	7	1,305	4,011	29	4,040
Arkansas (July 1989)	1,170	12	1,182	811	14	825	1,981	26	2,007
California	—	—	—	27,454	150	27,604	27,454	150	27,604
Colorado (Nov. 1985)	4,955	28	4,983	1,880	11	1,891	6,835	39	6,874
Connecticut (July 1992)[4]	—	85	85	2,677	75	2,752	2,677	160	2,837
Delaware	—	—	—	520	3	523	520	3	523
District of Columbia	—	—	—	2,926	55	2,981	2,929	55	2,981
Florida	—	—	—	17,890	467	18,357	17,890	467	18,357
Georgia	—	—	—	5,176	63	5,239	5,176	63	5,239
Hawaii	—	—	—	556	6	562	556	6	562
Idaho (June 1986)	264	2	266	116	—	116	380	2	382
Illinois	—	—	—	5,430	84	5,514	5,430	84	5,514
Indiana (July 1988)	2,382	17	2,399	1,456	14	1,470	3,838	31	3,869
Iowa	—	—	—	331	4	335	331	4	335
Kansas	—	—	—	485	2	487	485	2	487
Kentucky	—	—	—	519	8	527	519	8	527
Louisiana (Feb. 1993)	3,223	29	3,252	2,675	39	2,714	5,898	68	5,966
Maine	—	—	—	274	4	278	274	4	278
Maryland	—	—	—	4,400	119	4,519	4,400	119	4,519
Massachussets	—	—	—	3,651	64	3,715	3,651	64	3,715
Michigan (April 1992)	2,004	56	2,060	2,527	31	2,558	4,531	87	4,618
Minnesota (Oct. 1985)	1,944	20	1,964	974	10	984	2,918	30	2,948
Mississippi (Aug. 1988)	2,669	37	2,706	794	13	807	3,463	50	3,513
Missouri (Oct. 1987)	3,035	32	3,067	2,525	16	2,541	5,560	48	5,608
Montana	—	—	—	64	1	65	64	1	65
Nebraska	—	—	—	230	3	233	230	3	233
Nevada (Feb. 1992)	1,761	20	1,781	909	10	919	2,670	30	2,700
New Hampshire	—	—	—	248	3	251	248	3	251
New Jersey (Jan. 1992)	8,590	272	8,862	8,251	230	8,481	16,841	502	17,343
New Mexico	—	—	—	447	2	449	447	2	449
New York	—	—	—	25,417	642	26,059	25,417	642	26,059
North Carolina (Feb. 1990)	4,675	45	4,720	2,099	42	2,141	6,774	87	6,861
North Dakota (Jan. 1988)	50	—	50	23	—	23	73	—	73
Ohio (June 1990)	1,750	13	1,763	2,321	27	2,348	4,071	40	4,111
Oklahoma (June 1988)	1,493	9	1,502	893	5	898	2,386	14	2,400
Oregon	—	—	—	1,233	3	1,236	1,233	3	1,236
Pennsylvania	—	—	—	5,176	113	5,289	5,176	113	5,289
Rhode Island	—	—	—	509	6	515	509	6	515
South Carolina (Feb. 1986)	5,048	65	5,113	2,114	23	2,137	7,162	88	7,250
South Dakota (Jan. 1988)	123	4	127	32	2	34	155	6	161
Tennessee (Jan. 1992)	2,595	31	2,626	1,839	13	1,852	4,434	44	4,478
Texas (Feb. 1994)[4]	—	162	162	12,128	119	12,247	12,128	281	12,409
Utah (April 1989)	766	5	771	432	7	439	1,198	12	1,210
Vermont	—	—	—	98	1	99	98	1	99
Virginia (July 1989)	5,267	52	5,319	2,490	64	2,554	7,757	116	7,873
Washington	—	—	—	2,395	11	2,406	2,395	11	2,406
West Virginia (Jan. 1989)	341	2	343	202	2	204	543	4	547
Wisconsin (Nov. 1985)	1,727	19	1,746	959	12	971	2,686	31	2,717
Wyoming (June 1989)	60	—	60	46	—	46	106	—	106
Subtotal	**62,149**	**1,070**	**63,219**	**159,319**	**2,617**	**161,936**	**221,468**	**3,687**	**225,155**
Guam	—	—	—	4	—	4	4	—	4
Pacific Islands, U.S.	—	—	—	—	—	—	—	—	—
Puerto Rico	—	—	—	5,586	158	5,744	5,586	158	5,744
Virgin Islands, U.S.	—	—	—	129	5	134	129	5	134
Total	**62,149**	**1,070**	**63,219**	**165,038**	**2,780**	**167,818**	**227,187**	**3,850**	**231,037**

[1] Persons reported with vital status "alive" as of the last update.

[2] Includes only persons reported from states with confidential HIV reporting. Excludes 1,505 adults/adolescents and 18 children reported from states with confidential HIV infection reporting whose state of residence is unknown or are residents of other states.

[3] Excludes 244 adults/adolescents and 4 children whose state of residence is unknown.

[4] Connecticut and Texas have confidential HIV infection reporting for pediatric cases only.

GLOSSARY OF AIDS AND HIV-RELATED TERMS

Adjunct therapies: Interventions such as acupuncture and chiropractic used to supplement traditional medical treatments.

AIDS (Aquired Immunodeficiency Syndrome): A viral suppression of the immune system that weakens the body's ability to withstand a variety of opportunistic infections, viruses, and malignancies.

Anonymous testing for HIV: Testing using anonymous identification numbers to insure that results are not publicly released but given only to the tested person. See also *Confidential testing for HIV.*

Antibodies: Cells manufactured by the immune system to target and protect against toxins and infectious agents.

Antibody test: A blood test that reveals the presence of antibodies to HIV, indicating that viral infection has occurred. The ELISA and Western blot tests are antibody tests.

Antigen: A virus, bacteria, or other foreign substance in the blood that stimulates the production of antibodies.

Antigen test: Blood test used to double-check positive results of the ELISA or Western blot antibody tests; checks for the presence of HIV itself, not antibodies to the virus.

Antiviral: A treatment that suppresses viral activity. AZT and ddI are antivirals.

ARC (AIDS-related complex): A variety of AIDS-related symptoms (such as swollen glands, fever, and diarrhea) that precede AIDS but are not severe enough to be included in the CDC definition of AIDS. This term is rarely used now and has been replaced by "HIV symptomatic."

Asymptomatic: Being without the symptoms of HIV infection, even though one may test positive for HIV.

AZT (zidovudine): FDA-approved antiviral that slows down the replication of HIV within healthy cells and helps prevent the onset of opportunistic infections. AZT often has side effects, ranging from nausea to serious liver problems.

Bactrim: Drug used to treat PCP.

B-cells: White blood cells that participate in the body's immune response to infection.

Bodily fluids: Any fluid produced by the human body, for example, blood, sweat, urine, breast milk, vaginal fluids, semen, pre-cum, and saliva. Those bodily fluids known to transmit HIV are blood, semen, vaginal fluids, and breast milk.

Candidiasis: A chronic infection with the normally harmless yeast organism, Candida albicans. In the mouth, this yeast infection is called thrush.

CD4-cells (or lymphocytes): See *T-4 (helper) cells.*

CD8-cells (or lymphocytes): See *T-8 (suppressor) cells.*

CDC (U.S. Centers for Disease Control): Federal agency of the Public Health Service that tracks the incidence and trends of communicable diseases, conducts research, and licenses clinical laboratories.

Chronic: Persistent or of long duration.

Clinical trials: Drug trials using human subjects to prove drug safety and to determine dose levels.

CMV (cytomegalovirus): A virus related to herpes that can produce retinitis (inflammation of the retina that can lead to blindness), pneumonia, hepatitis, and colitis (inflammation of the colon).

Confidential testing for HIV: Often given by private doctors and public and private hospitals, testing whose results will be recorded in the tested person's medical charts and may be disclosed without his or her permission. See also *Anonymous testing for HIV.*

ddC (dideoxycytidine): FDA-approved antiviral used in the treatment of HIV/AIDS, particularly for patients who are intolerant of or ineligible for AZT, fail AZT, or are intolerant of or ineligible for ddI. ddC often has side effects, including peripheral neuropathy, pancreatitis, diarrhea, and dehydration.

ddI (dideoxyinosine): FDA-approved antiviral that slows down the replication of HIV within healthy cells and helps prevent the onset of opportunistic infections. ddI is used particularly for people who either do not respond well to AZT or who are in advanced stages of HIV infection with severe immunosuppression. ddI often has side effects, including peripheral neuropathy, pancreatitis, diarrhea, and dehydration.

Dementia: Loss of normal brain function, evidenced as loss of memory, learning ability, and motor control.

ELISA (enzyme-linked immunosorbent assay): A blood test that reveals the presence of antibodies to HIV, indicating that viral infection has occurred. Often called the HIV or AIDS test, it is the most common test for HIV.

Epidemic: A disease that spreads rapidly and affects a large number of people.

False positive: A positive test result, when the condition is in fact negative.

Food and Drug Administration (FDA): Federal government agency that tests and licenses drugs.

Full-blown AIDS: The state of a formerly asymptomatic HIV-positive person developing one or more diseases that are symptoms of immunosuppression.

Herpes: A family of viruses including herpes simplex (cold sores), herpes genitalia (affecting the genitals), CMV, chicken pox, and shingles.

High-risk behavior: Any activity that increases the risk of HIV transmission by allowing the exchange of body fluids. This may include, for example, unsafe sex and sharing IV needles.

HIV (human immunodeficiency virus): The virus thought to be the cause of AIDS.

HIV negative: The state of having no antibodies to HIV present in the bloodstream. The person who tests negative is presumed to be uninfected with HIV. Also called seronegative.

HIV positive: The state of having antibodies to HIV present in the bloodstream.

The person who tests positive is presumed to be infected with HIV. Also called seropositive.

Host cell: Infected cell.

HPV (human pappilomavirus): Virus associated with genital warts and cervical cancer, which is common for women with HIV/AIDS.

Immune system: The body's system of defense mechanisms, through which cells and proteins in the blood and other body fluids work together to attack infection and disease-producing agents.

Immunosuppression: Weakening of the immune system that occurs as a result of HIV infection.

Incubation period: Length of time between actual HIV infection and the appearance of the first signs and symptoms of that infection.

Indicator diseases: Opportunistic infections designated by the U.S. Centers for Disease Control as indicators of "full-blown AIDS." PCP, KS, MAC, and CMV are among those indicator diseases.

Intravenous drugs: Drugs injected directly into the bloodstream through a hypodermic needle.

KS (Kaposi's sarcoma): A rare skin cancer which appears as purplish lesions.

Latency period: see Incubation period.

MAC (mycobacterium avium complex): Fungal infection normally seen in birds that attacks PWAs and is often misdiagnosed as the flu; the most common opportunistic infection in PWAs; also called MAI.

Macrophages: White blood cells that participate in the body's immune response to infection.

MAI (mycobacterium avium intracellulare): see MAC.

Nonoxynol-9: A spermicide found in some lubricants and condoms, which may help prevent HIV transmission.

Opportunistic infection (OI): An infection that takes advantage of immunosuppression to attack a person's immune system. The most commonly known opportunistic infections for PWAs are PCP, CMV, MAC, and toxoplasmosis. Some common opportunistic infections for female PWAs are PID, HPV, and chronic vaginitis.

Pandemic: A worldwide epidemic.

PCP (Pneumocystis carinii pneumonia): A common parasitic infection that attacks the lungs, leading to the most common cause of death for people with AIDS.

Pentamadine: A drug used to treat PCP.

PID (pelvic inflammatory disease): Infection that attacks a woman's fallopian tubes, ovaries, and/or uterus.

Pre-cum: Clear fluid produced by a man's penis before ejaculation.

Prophylaxis: Preventive treatment.

Protease Inhibitors: A promising new class of antivirals in clinical trials that may prevent production of new virus in cells infected with HIV. Therapy opens up a different line of defense against HIV.

PWA: Person with AIDS.

Retrovirus: A virus that contains RNA rather than DNA as its genetic material. HIV is a retrovirus.

Safer sex: An array of sexual practices that may decrease the risk of HIV infection by preventing the transmission of bodily fluids during sex. The standard "tools" of gay male safer sex are condoms and latex gloves; some forms of safer sex are kissing, jerking off, phone sex, and rubbing.

Seroconversion: Development of antibodies to HIV.

Spermicide: A chemical that kills sperm.

STD (sexually transmitted disease): Any disease that can be contracted through sexual behavior and practices. Besides HIV/AIDS, STDs include syphillis, gonorrhea, hepatitis B, herpes, chlamydia, and others.

T-cell count: A reading of the number of T-4 cells per millimeter of blood, used to determine how far a person's HIV infection has progressed.

T-cells (or lymphocytes): White blood cells that direct the rest of the immune system and are the targets of HIV; include both T-4 and T-8 cells.

T-4 (helper) cells (or lymphocytes): Antibody-triggered cells that attack invading organisms and infections; also called CD4 cells.

T-8 (suppressor) cells (or lymphocytes): Cells that shut down the immune response when the infection or invading organisms have been destroyed; also called CD-8 cells.

Thrush: See Candidiasis.

Toxoplasmosis: Infection affecting the brain.

Unsafe sex: High-risk sexual behavior, including sex without a condom or dental dam, that may lead to the exchange of bodily fluids and thus increase the odds of HIV transmission.

Vaginitis: Infection and inflammation of the vagina. When it is chronic, this can be a sympton of HIV infection in women.

Venereal disease: Another name for an STD.

Western blot test: A test believed to be even more specific than ELISA, which identifies specific antibodies to HIV. Used to double-check the results of ELISA.

White blood cells: All the cells of the immune system.

Window period: Period of time, usually six weeks to six months, between actual HIV infection and seroconversion, or the moment when the body has produced enough antibodies to the virus to be detected by a blood test. During the window period, HIV may be transmitted unknowingly.

Yeast infection: Vaginal infection that creates a white discharge.

Sources

ACT UP/NY Women and AIDS Book Group. *Women, AIDS and Activism.* South End Press, 1990.

Ford, Michael Thomas. *100 Questions and Answers about AIDS: A Guide for Young People.* New Discovery Books, 1992.

Hitchen, Neal. *Fifty Things You Can Do about AIDS.* Lowell House, 1992.

Root-Bernstein, Robert. *Rethinking AIDS: The Tragic Cost of Premature Consensus.* Free Press, 1993.

Siano, Nick. *No Time to Wait: A Complete Guide to Treating, Managing, and Living with HIV Infection.* Bantam Books, 1993.

SOME TOOLS OF SAFER SEX FOR GAY MEN

Condom: Latex shield placed over penis or sex toy during penetration. Lambskin condoms are not recommended for protection against HIV transmission.

Dental dam: A square sheet of thin latex (approximately 6" x 6") used to cover a woman's clitoris and vulva during oral sex or over the anus during rimming to prevent the transmission of bodily fluids. Its name comes from its original use by dentists to keep teeth dry during root canal, fillings, or other dental work.

Finger cot: A small latex "condom" that fits over individual fingers and prevents the transmission of bodily fluids through cuts on the hands.

Lube: Lubricant for added moisture in anal or vaginal sex.

Rubber: A condom.

Safer sex: An array of sexual practices that can decrease the risk of HIV infection by preventing the transmission of bodily fluids during sex.

For definitions of specific sexual practices, see pp. 81–97 of this book.

A GAY MAN'S GUIDE TO SAFER SEX

SAFER ACTIVITIES

Body to body rubbing
Dry kissing
French kissing (as long as there are no open sores in the mouth)
Massage
Hugging
Masturbation
Fantasy and costumes
Anal sex with a condom
Finger penetration of anus using latex gloves or finger cots
Hand penetration of anus using latex gloves
Individual sex toys

Protected oral sex with a condom
Spanking
S/M without drawing blood or exchange of bodily fluids
Any sex that doesn't exchange bodily fluids

Unsafe activities

Unprotected oral sex (without a condom)
Unprotected rimming (mouth-anus contact)
Unprotected anal sex (without a condom)
Unprotected finger or hand penetration of anus (especially if you have cuts on your hands)
Any activity that could draw blood
Sharing unprotected or unwashed sex toys
Sharing needles for IV drug use or any other skin piercing activity

Note: For sex with women, always use condoms for vaginal and anal penetration or for oral sex.

Centers for Disease Control's List of Twenty-Seven AIDS Indicator Diseases (in alphabetical order)

Candidiasis, bronchi, trachea, lungs (thrush)
Candidiasis, esophageal (thrush)
Coccidiomycosis, disseminated or extrapulmonary
Cryptococcosis, extrapulmonary (crypto)
Cryptosporidiosis, chronic intestinal
Cytomegalovirus disease (CMV)
Cytomegalovirus retinitis (CMV/eyes)
HIV encephalopathy (dementia)
Herpes simplex, chronic ulcers (HSV)
Histoplasmosis (histo)
Invasive cervical cancer
Isoporiasis, chronic intestinal
Kaposi's sarcoma (KS)
Lymphoma, Burkitt's
Lymphoma, immunoblastic
Lymphoma, primary in brain
Mycobacterium avium complex (MAC/MAI)
M. tuberculosis, disseminated or extrapulmonary (TB)
M. tuberculosis, pulmonary (TB)
Mycobacterium of other species

Pneumocystis carinii pneumonia (PCP)
Progressive multifocial leukoencephalopathy (PML)
Recurrent pneumonias within a twelve-month period
Salmonella septicemia, recurrent
T-4 cells under 200m or less than 14 percent
Toxoplasmosis of brain (toxo)
Wasting syndrome

SOURCE: Centers for Disease Control

NATIONAL AIDS ORGANIZATIONS

So many of us have felt helpless in the face of the AIDS crisis—losing friends, family, and lovers, dealing with our own illness. Our powerlessness to stop the pandemic and its shattering effects on our lives often leads to despondency. One way many of us have coped with the AIDS crisis is to get actively involved in groups and organizations that work on AIDS- and HIV-related issues, either donating time or money or both. The following is a partial list of national AIDS organizations that need your support or that can direct you to services and programs in your area.

In the United States

AIDS Action Council
1875 Connecticut Avenue NW #700
Washington, DC 20009
202-986-1300
Lobbies Congress and watchdogs national AIDS policy.

AIDS Coalition to Unleash Power (ACT UP)
496-A Hudson St. #G4
New York, NY 10014
212-564-2437
Sponsors direct actions at the national and local level to bring attention to the
   AIDS pandemic; also has chapters in Canada.

AIDS National Interfaith Network
110 Maryland Ave. NE, Suite 504
Washington, DC 20002
202-546-0807
Umbrella group of AIDS ministries that mobilizes for education and advocacy.

AIDS Project/Lambda Legal Defense and Education Fund
666 Broadway, 12th floor
New York, NY 10012
212-995-8585
Litigates test cases involving AIDS-related discrimination.

AIDS Research Alliance
621-A North San Vicente Blvd.
West Hollywood, CA 90069
310-358-2423
Conducts research on promising anti-HIV therapies.

American Foundation for AIDS Research (AmFAR)
733 Third Ave.
New York, NY 10017
212-682-7440
Research and lobbying group.

American Institute for Teen AIDS Prevention
P.O. Box 136116
Fort Worth, TX 76136
817-237-0230
AIDS education to teens, both in the U.S. and internationally.

Broadway Cares/Equity Fights AIDS
165 West 46th St., Suite 1300
New York, NY 10036
212-840-0770
Fund-raises for PWAs in the entertainment business.

Community Research Initiative on AIDS (CRIA)
275 Seventh Ave., 20th floor
New York, NY 10001
212-924-3934
Conducts clinical trials on promising therapies ignored by major drug companies

Design Industries Foundation Fighting AIDS (DIFFA)
150 West 26th St., Suite 602
New York, NY 10001
212-727-3100
Fund-raises for organizations involved in direct care, public policy, and
    prevention programs.

Gay Men's Health Crisis (GMHC)
129 West 20th St.
New York, NY 10011
212-337-3519
Plays leadership role in AIDS prevention and information dissemination.

Mobilization Against AIDS
584-B Castro St.
San Francisco, CA 94114
415-863-4676
Lobbies for increased Congressional funding for AIDS.

Irving Cooperberg *(on right)* and the late Steven J. Powsner, Esq., Presidents Emeriti, The Lesbian and Gay Community Services Center–New York *(Photo by Josh Yu)*

National Leadership Coalition on AIDS
1730 M St. NW, Suite 905
Washington, DC 20036
202-429-0930
Conducts workplace initiatives to educate employees about safer sex and to
    protect the rights of employees with AIDS.

National Minority AIDS Council (NMAC)
300 I St. NE, Suite 400
Washington, DC 20002
202-544-1076
Develops new leaders in people of color communities to address issues of HIV
    and AIDS.

People of Color Against AIDS Network
1200 S. Jackson St. #25
Seattle, WA 98144-2065
206-322-7061
Education and advocacy group for people of color communities.

Project Inform
1965 Market St., Suite 220
San Francisco, CA 94103
415-558-8669
Operates treatment information hotline, promotes immune-based research, and
    influences research regulations.

Ryan White Foundation
101 West Washington St., Suite 1135 East
Indianapolis, IN 46204
800-444-RYAN
Focuses on support to teens and hemophiliacs with AIDS and their families.

Test Positive Aware Network
1258 West Belmont Ave.
Chicago, IL 60657
312-404-8726
Peer-led support services.

Treatment Action Group
200 East 10th St. #601
New York, NY 10003
212-260-0300
Watchdogs AIDS research establishment and influences treatment policy and
    regulations.

For a listing of local AIDS/HIV services, contact the U.S. Conference of Mayors, 1620 I St. NW, Washington, DC 20006, 202-293-7330. Many local AIDS
groups and organizations are also listed by state in the Gayellow Pages (Renaissance House, Box 292, Village Station, New York, NY 10014-0292).

In Canada:

Canadian AIDS Society
170 Laurier Ave. West #1101
Ottawa, Ontario K1P 5V5
613-563-4998
Provides support services, education, and advocacy; also information about local
    AIDS organizations.

AIDS- AND HIV-RELATED NEWLETTERS AND MAGAZINES

AIDS Treatment News, 800-873-2812. One of the first newsletters; easy to read and informative.

Art & Understanding, 800-841-8707. Glossy magazine of literary and visual AIDS.

Being Alive/Los Angeles, 213-667-3262. Clear and factual.

BETA (San Francisco AIDS Foundation), 415-863-2437. Western and alternative therapies.

Body Positive, 212-721-1346. Treatment information plus personality profiles.

Community Prescription Service InfoPack, 800-842-0502. In-depth and easy-to-read articles.

Critical Path AIDS Project, 215-545-2212. For those who can't get information otherwise, such as prisoners.

Diseased Pariah News, 510-891-0455. An angry 'zine.

GMHC Treatment Issues (Gay Men's Health Crisis), 212-337-3695. From the first organization to deal with the epidemic; lots of information on clinical trials.

Journal of the Physicians Association for AIDS Care, 312-222-1326. For doctors and other health care workers.

Notes from the Underground, 212-255-0520. From the PWA Health Group, a buyers club; an important source on alternative treatments.

Positively Aware (Test Positive Aware Network), 312-472-6397. Easy to read and informative.

POZ, 800-883-2163. Slick, polished, easy to read; news, interviews, information.

PWA Newsline (PWA Coalition/New York), 800-828-3280. News, activism, politics, treatment.

SIDAahora (PWA Coalition/New York), 800-828-3280. PWA Newsline in Spanish.

STEP Perspectives, 800-869-7837. Intensive treatment coverage, not easy reading.

Women Being Alive (Being Alive/Los Angeles), 213-667-2735. Support and information for women living with AIDS or HIV.

WORLD (Women Organized to Respond to Life-Threatening Diseases), 510-658-6930. Personal stories, news, and information for women living with AIDS or HIV.

Reprinted with permission from *POZ* magazine, 1995.

NATIONAL AIDS HOTLINES

AIDS Clinical Trials Information Services   800-TRIALSA
   TTY/TDD 800-243-7012

AIDS Project Los Angeles	800-922-2437
CDC (Centers for Disease Control) AIDS Hotline	800-342-AIDS
in Spanish 800-344-SIDA	
National AIDS Hotline for Hearing Impaired	800-243-7889
National Hospicelink	800-331-1620
National Native American AIDS Hotline	800-283-2437
National Sexually Transmitted Diseases Hotline	800-227-8922
Project Inform National Hotline (AIDS treatment)	800-822-7422
Toll-Free Directory Assistance (call for your state's own	
toll-free AIDS hotline)	800-555-1212

SOURCE: *POZ* magazine, Number 5, December 1994/January 1995

The Centers for Disease Control operates an automated information line, through which you can get the latest statistics and facts about AIDS in the United States and internationally, either by listening to a series of recordings or following the steps to get the information via fax. The telephone number is 404-639-3524 and operates continuously.

ONLINE: AIDS-SPECIFIC BULLETIN BOARDS

You can access information about AIDS treatment from the following computer bulletin boards, or join in an AIDS community discussion—right in your own home.

HIV/AIDS Information BBS (CA)	Modem #: 714-248-2836
Fog City BBS (CA)	415-863-9697
Black Bag Medical BBS (DE)	302-994-3772
AIDS Info BBS (OH)	614-279-7709
Midwest AIDS/HIV Information Exchange (IL)	312-772-5958
Critical Path AIDS Project (PA)	215-463-7160
AIDSNet (NY)	607-777-2158

SOURCE: *POZ* magazine, Number 5, December 1994/January 1995

BUYERS CLUBS

Buyers clubs purchase experimental AIDS and HIV medications, as well as FDA-approved drugs, vitamins, and supplements, and offer them for sale to the general public.

Atlanta Buyers Club	404-874-4845
PWA Coalition Boston	617-266-6422
DBC Alternatives (Dallas)	214-528-4460
Colorado Health Action Project (Denver)	303-837-8214

Health Link (Ft. Lauderdale)	305-565-8284
DAAIR (New York City)	212-689-8140
PWA Health Group (New York City)	212-255-0520
PACT for Life Buyers Club (Tucson)	602-770-1710
Healing Alternatives (San Francisco)	415-626-4053
AIDS Manasota (Sarasota, Fla.)	813-954-6011
Carl Vogel Center (Washington, D.C.)	202-289-4898

SOURCE: *POZ* magazine, Number 5, December 1994/January 1995

FIFTEEN MAJOR AIDS TREATMENT CENTERS IN THE UNITED STATES

This ranking is based on overall quality of care, determined by such factors as reputation, mortality rate, technology, number of residents to beds, number of nurses to beds, and number of M.D.s to beds.

*San Francisco General Hospital
*Johns Hopkins Hospital (Baltimore)
*Massachusetts General Hospital (Boston)
*University of California San Francisco Medical Center
*UCLA Medical Center (Los Angeles)
*Memorial Sloan-Kettering Cancer Center (New York City)
*New York University Medical Center (New York City)
*University of Miami Hospital and Clinics
*Mayo Clinic (Rochester, Minnesota)
*New York Hospital—Cornell Medical Center (New York City)
*Mount Sinai Medical Center (New York City)
*Columbia-Presbyterian Medical Center (New York City)
*University of Washington Medical Center (Seattle)
*Deaconess Hospital (Boston)
*Beth Israel Hospital (Boston)
*Duke University Medical Center (Durham, North Carolina)
*Barnes Hospital (St. Louis)
*Rush-Presbyterian-St. Luke's Medical Center (Chicago)
*Stanford University Medical Center (Stanford, California)
*Indiana University Medical Center (Indianapolis)

SOURCE: *U.S. News and World Report,* July 18, 1994

TEN THINGS YOU CAN DO ABOUT AIDS

Here is a list of ten things you can do to make a very personal difference in the fight against AIDS.

1. Donate blood to a local AIDS clinic or service organization. (There is no risk of HIV transmission in donating blood.)
2. Give a person with AIDS a ride to and from the doctor's office.
3. Volunteer an afternoon helping a person with AIDS with routine chores: go grocery shopping, walk the dog, make a bank deposit, clean, do the laundry, or make dinner.
4. Read to a friend with AIDS who has lost his or her eyesight to CMV retinitis.
5. Have a garage or apartment sale and donate the proceeds to a local AIDS organization.
6. If you're having a birthday party for yourself or your partner, ask guests to bring a check made out to the AIDS service organization of your choice in lieu of gifts.
7. AIDS caregivers often forget to take time for themselves or feel they aren't entitled to it. Offer to substitute as caregiver for an evening so the caregiver can go out with friends or have time to himself or herself.
8. Write a letter to your congressperson or senator about the need for a national health care plan that addresses the concerns of people with AIDS.

Senator _____	Representative _____
United States Senate	U.S. House of Representatives
Washington, DC 20510	Washington, DC 20515

9. Organize a canned food drive at work or at school and give the donations to a local AIDS service organization that provides meals to people with AIDS.
10. Contact the national television networks when they broadcast either noteworthy or inaccurate reports and programs about HIV and AIDS. Let the network presidents know you support or are displeased with their programming.

ABC	NBC
77 West 66th Street	30 Rockefeller Plaza
New York, NY 10023	New York, NY 10112

CBS	FOX
7800 Beverly Boulevard	P.O. Box 900
Los Angeles, CA 90036	Beverly Hills, CA 90213

BOOKS AND PAMPHLETS ON AIDS EDUCATION, TREATMENT, AND PREVENTION

AIDS Project Los Angeles. *AIDS: A Self-Care Manual.* (1987)

Baker, Ronald, Jeffrey Moulton, and John Tighe. *Early Care for HIV Disease.* (1994)

Bartlett, John G., and Ann K. Finkbeiner. *The Guide to Living with HIV Infection.* (1991)

Callaway, C. Wayne. *Surviving with AIDS: A Comprehensive Program of Nutritional Co-Therapy.* (1991)

Dalton, Harlon L., Scott Burris, and the Yale AIDS Law Project. *AIDS and the Law: A Guide for the Public.* (1987)

Dansky, Stephen. *Now Dare Everything: Tales of HIV Related Psychotherapy.* (1994)

Delaney, Martin, and Peter Goldblum. *Strategies for Survival: A Gay Men's Health Manual for the Age of AIDS.* (1987)

Eidson, Ted, ed. *The AIDS Caregiver's Handbook.* (1993)

Ford, Michael Thomas. *100 Questions and Answers about AIDS: A Guide for Young People.* (1992)

Gray, John, Phillip Lyons, and Gary Melton. *Ethical and Legal Issues in AIDS Research.* (1994)

Harding, Paul. *The Essential AIDS Fact Book.* Revised ed. (1994)

Hitchens, Neal. *Fifty Things You Can Do About AIDS.* (1992)

Kaiser, Jon D. *Immune Power: A Comprehensive Healing Program for HIV.* (1993)

Kittredge, Mary. *Teens with AIDS Speak Out.* (1991)

Kloser, Patricia, Craig Kloser, and Jane MacLean. *A Woman's HIV Sourcebook: A Guide to Better Health and Well-Being.* (1994)

McCormack, Thomas P. *The AIDS Benefit Handbook.* (1990)

Madansky, Cynthia, and Julie Tolentino Wood. *Safer Sex Handbook for Lesbians.* Lesbian AIDS Project/Gay Men's Health Crisis, Inc. (1993)

Martelli, Leonard J., et al. *When Someone You Know Has AIDS.* Rev. edition. (1993)

Mikluscak, Cindy, and Emmett E. Miller. *Living in Hope: A Twelve-Step Approach for Persons at Risk or Infected with HIV.* (1991)

Morales, Julio, and Marcia Bok. *Multicultural Services for AIDS Treatment and Prevention.* (1994)

O'Connor, Tom. *Living with AIDS: Reaching Out.* (1987)

O'Sullivan, Sue and Pratibha Parmar. *Lesbians Talk Safer Sex.* (1992)

Patton, Cindy, and Janis Kelly. *Making It: A Woman's Guide to Sex in the Age of AIDS.* (1987)

Pinsky, Laura, and Paul Harding Douglas. *The Essential HIV Treatment Fact Book.* (1992)

Pohl, Mel, Densiton Kay, and Doug Toft. *The Caregiver's Journey: When Someone You Love Has AIDS.* (1990)

Richardson, Diane. *Women and AIDS.* (1988)

Shealy, C. Norman, and Caroline Myss. *AIDS: Passageway to Transformation.* (1994)

Siano, Nick. *No Time to Wait: A Complete Guide to Treating, Managing, and Living with HIV Infection.* (1993)

Tatchell, Peter. *Safer Sexy: The Guide to Gay Sex Safely.* (1994)

Walker, Mitch. *Men Loving Men: A Gay Guide and Consciousness Book.* (1994)

AIDS IN LITERATURE: A READING LIST

Novels (N), Short Story Collections (S), Young Adult Novels (YA), Anthologies (A), and Poetry Collections (P)

Avena, Thomas, ed. *Life Sentences.* (1994) (A)

Baker, James Robert. *Tim and Pete.* (1993) (N)

Barnett Allen. *The Body and Its Dangers.* (1990) (S)

Boucheron, Robert. *Epitaphs for the Plague Dead.* (1985) (P)

Bram, Christopher. *In Memory of Angel Clare.* (1988) (N)

Brown, Rebecca. *The Gifts of the Body.* (1994) (N)

Calhoun, Jackie. *Lifestyles.* (1990) (N)

Cameron, Lindsley. *The Prospect of Detachment.* (1990) (S)

Cameron, Peter. *The Weekend.* (1994) (N)

Chappell, Helen. *Acts of Love.* (1989) (N)

Claiborne, Sybil. *In the Garden of Dead Cars.* (1993) (N)

Coe, Christopher. *Such Times.* (1993) (N)

Cuadros, Gil. *City of God.* (1995) (N)

Daniels, Peter, and Steve Anthony, eds. *Jugular Defenses.* (1995) (P)

Davis, Christopher. *Valley of the Shadow.* (1988) (N)

_____. *The Boys in the Bars.* (1989) (S)

de la Pena, Terri. *Latin Satins.* (1994) (N)

Dent, Tory. *What Silence Equals.* (1993) (P)

Donnelly, Nisa. *The Love Songs of Phoenix Bay.* (1995) (N)

Duplechan, Larry. *Tangled Up in Blue.* (1989) (N)

Feinberg, David B. *Eighty-Sixed.* (1989) (N)

_____. *Spontaneous Combustion.* (1991) (N)

Ferro, Robert. *Second Son.* (1988) (N)

Hadas, Rachel. *Unending Dialogue: Voices from an AIDS Poetry Workshop.* (1991) (P)

Hansen, Joseph. *Early Graves.* (1987) (N)

Hite, Molly. *Breach of Immunity.* (1993) (N)

Hoffman, Alice. *At Risk.* (1988) (N)

Hunter, B. Michael, ed. *Sojourner: Black Gay Voices in the Age of AIDS.* (1993) (A)

Indiana, Gary. *Horse Crazy.* (1989) (N)

Johnson, Fenton. *Scissors, Paper, Rock.* (1993) (S)

Johnson, Toby. *Plague: A Novel About Healing.* (1987) (N)

Kerr, M. E. *Night Kites.* (1986) (YA)

Klass, Perri. *Other Women's Children.* (1990) (N)

Klein, Michael, ed. *Poets for Life: 76 Poets Respond to AIDS.* (1990) (A)

Leavitt, David. *A Place I've Never Been.* (1990) (S)

Lynch, Michael. *These Waves of Dying Friends.* (1989) (P)

McGehee, Peter. *Boys Like Us.* (1991) (N)

Mars-Jones, Adam. *Monopolies of Loss.* (1993) (S)

Martinac, Paula. *Home Movies.* (1993) (N)

Maso, Carole. *The Art Lover.* (1990) (N)

Maupin, Armistead. *Sure of You.* (1989) (N)

Mayes, Sharon. *Immune.* (1987) (N)

Micklowitz, Gloria D. *Good-bye, Tomorrow.* (1987) (YA)

Monette, Paul. *Love Alone: Eighteen Elegies for Rog.* (1988) (P)

_____. *Halfway Home.* (1991) (N)

_____. *Afterlife.* (1989) (N)

Mordden, Ethan. *Everyone Loves You: Further Adventures in Gay Manhattan.* (1988) (S)

Musto, Michael. *Manhattan on the Rocks.* (1989) (N)

Obejas, Achy. *We Came All the Way from Cuba So You Could Dress Like That?* (1994) (S)

Peck, Dale. *Martin and John.* (1993) (N)

Preston, John, ed. *Hot Living: Erotic Stories about Safer Sex.* (1985) (A)

Quinlan, Patricia. *Tiger Flowers.* (1994) (YA)

Rees, David. *The Wrong Apple.* (1988) (N)

_____. *Letters to Dorothy.* (1991) (S)

Rule, Jane. *Memory Board.* (1987) (N)

Ryman, Geoff. *Was.* (1992) (N)

Saint, Assotto. *Saints.* (1989) (P)

Schreiber, Ron. *John.* (1988) (P)

Schulman, Sarah. *People in Trouble.* (1990) (N)

Uyemoto, Holly. *Rebel Without a Clue.* (1989) (N)

Weir, John. *The Irreversible Decline of Eddie Socket.* (1989) (N)

White, Edmund, and Adam Mars-Jones. *The Darker Proof: Stories from a Crisis.* (1988) (S)

Wolverton, Terry, ed. *Blood Whispers: L.A. Writers on AIDS.* 2 vols. (Vol. 1, 1991; Vol. 2, 1994) (A)

BIOGRAPHIES, AUTOBIOGRAPHIES, MEMOIRS, AND PERSONAL NARRATIVE

Ascher, Barbara Lazear. *Landscape Without Gravity: A Memoir of Grief.* (1992)

Callen, Michael. *Surviving AIDS.* (1990)

Chase, Clifford. *The Hurry-Up Song: A Memoir of Losing My Brother.* (1995)

Cox, Elizabeth. *Thanksgiving: An AIDS Journal.* (1990)

Fisher, Mary. *Sleep with the Angels.* (1992)

Fried, Stephen. *Thing of Beauty: The Tragedy of Supermodel Gia.* (1993)

Glaser, Elizabeth, and Laura Palmer. *In the Absence of Angels: A Hollywood Family's Courageous Story.* (1991)

Guibert, Herve. *To the Friend Who Did Not Save My Life.* (1991)

Hudson, Rock, and Sara Davison. *Rock Hudson: His Story.* (1986)

Jarman, Derek. *Modern Nature.* (1994)

Kramer, Larry. *Reports from the Holocaust.* (1989)

Mass, Lawrence D. *Confessions of a Jewish Wagnerite: Being Gay and Jewish in America.* (1994)

Monette, Paul. *Borrowed Time.* (1988)

_____. *Last Watch of the Night: Essays Too Personal and Otherwise.* (1994)

Money, J. W. *To All the Girls I've Loved Before: An AIDS Diary.* (1987)

Petrow, Stephen. *Dancing in the Darkness.* (1990)

Preston, John. *Personal Dispatches.* (1989)

Reed, Paul. *The Savage Garden: A Journal.* (1994)

Rieder, Ines, and Patricia Ruppelt, eds. *AIDS: The Women.* (1988)

Rist, Darryl Yates. *Heartlands.* (1993)

Rudd, Andrea and Darien Taylor, eds. *Positive Women: Voices of Women Living with AIDS.* (1992)

Solway, Diane. *A Dance Against Time: The Brief, Brilliant Life of a Joffrey Dancer.* (1994)

Valdiserri, Ronald. *Gardening in Clay: Reflections on AIDS.* (1994)

Whitmore, George. *Someone Was Here: Profiles in the AIDS Epidemic.* (1988)

Wiltshire, Susan Ford. *Seasons of Grief and Grace: A Sister's Story of AIDS.* (1994)

Wojnarowicz, David. *Close to the Knives: A Memoir of Disintegration.* (1991)

ESSAYS, THEORY, AND CRITICISM

ACT UP New York Women and AIDS Book Group. *Women, AIDS, and Activism.* (1990)

Altman, Dennis. *AIDS in the Mind of America: The Social, Political, and Psychological Impact of a New Epidemic.* (1986)

Baker, Rob. *The Art of AIDS.* (1994)

Bateson, Catherine, and Richard Goldsby. *Thinking AIDS.* (1988)

Boffin, Tessa and Sunil Gupta, eds. *Ecstatic Antibodies: Resisting the AIDS Mythology.* (1990)

Browning, Frank. *The Culture of Desire: Paradox and Perversity in Gay Lives Today.* (1993)

Carter, Erica, and Simon Watney, eds. *Taking Liberties: AIDS and Cultural Politics.* (1989)

Corea, Gena. *The Invisible Epidemic.* (1992)

Crimp, Douglas. *AIDS: Cultural Analysis, Cultural Activism.* (1988)

_____. and Adam Rolston. *AIDS DemoGraphics.* (1990)

Doyal, Lesley, Jennie Naidoo, and Tamsia Wilton, eds. *AIDS: Setting a Feminist Agenda.* (1995)

Fee, Elizabeth, and Daniel M. Fox, eds. *AIDS: The Burdens of History.* (1988)

Feinberg, David B. *Queer and Loathing: Rants and Raves of an Aging AIDS Queen* (1994)

Fitzgerald, Frances. *Cities on a Hill.* (1986)

Kinsella, James. *Covering the Plague.* (1989)

McKenzie, Nancy F., ed. *The AIDS Reader: Social, Political, and Ethical Issues.* (1991)

Miller, James, ed. *Fluid Exchanges: Artists and Critics in the AIDS Crisis.* (1992)

Murphy, Timothy. *Ethics in an Epidemic: AIDS, Morality, and Culture.* (1994)

Murphy, Timothy F. and Suzanne Poirier, eds. *Writing AIDS: Gay Literature, Language, and Analysis.* (1993)

Nelson, Emmanuel S. *AIDS: The Literary Response.* (1992)

Pastore, Judith. *Confronting AIDS Through Literature.* (1993)

Patton, Cindy. *Sex and Germs.* (1985)

_____. *Inventing AIDS.* (1990)

_____. *Last Served? Gendering the HIV Pandemic.* (1994)

Root-Bernstein, Robert. *Rethinking AIDS: The Tragic Cost of Premature Consensus.* (1993)

Schecter, Stephen. *The AIDS Notebooks.* (1990)

Schneider, Beth E., and Nancy E. Stoller. *Women Resisting AIDS: Feminist Strategies of Empowerment.* (1995)

Shilts, Randy. *And the Band Played On.* (1987)

Sontag, Susan. *AIDS and Its Metaphors.* (1989)

Watney, Simon. *Policing Desire: Pornography, AIDS, and the Media.* (1987)

_____. *Practices of Freedom: Selected Writings on HIV/AIDS.* (1994)

AIDS ON THE STAGE AND SCREEN

The following are some of the depictions of AIDS on the stage and screen since the mid-1980s. For further reading, see *The Art of AIDS* by Rob Baker (Continuum Publishing Company, 1994).

Plays

Night Sweat, by Robert Chesley (1984)
The Normal Heart, by Larry Kramer (1985)
As Is, by William M. Hoffman (1985)
Jerker, by Robert Chesley (1986)
Beirut, by Alan Bowne (1987)
Safe Sex, by Harvey Fierstein (1987)
Dog Plays, by Robert Chesley (1989)
The Baltimore Waltz, by Paula Vogel (1992)
Falsettos, by William Finn and James Lapine (1992)
The Night Larry Kramer Kissed Me, by David Drake (1992)
Roy Cohn/Jack Smith, by Ron Vawter (1992)
Angels in America, by Tony Kushner (1993)
Jeffrey, by Paul Rudnick (1993)
The Destiny of Me, by Larry Kramer (1993)

Feature-length Films

Buddies (1985)
Parting Glances (1986)
Longtime Companion (1990)

Philadelphia (1993)
Blue (1993)
Zero Patience (1993)

Peter's Friends (1992)
Under Heat (1992)
The Living End (1993)

Savage Nights (1994)
Boys on the Side (1995)
The Cure (1995)

Made-for-TV Movies

An Early Frost (1985)
Tidy Endings (1988)
Andre's Mother (1990)
Our Sons (1991)
Citizen Cohn (1992)

And the Band Played On (1993)
Roommates (1994)
A Place for Annie (1994)
My Brother's Keeper (1995)

Independent Documentaries

Chuck Solomon: Coming of Age (1986)
Dying for Love (1987)
Common Threads: Stories from the Quilt (1989)
Tongues Untied (1989)
Absolutely Positive (1991)
Non, Je Ne Regrette Rien (No Regrets) (1992)
One Foot on the Banana Peel, the Other Foot in the Grave (1992)
Sex Is . . . (1992)
Silverlake Life: The View from Here (1992)
The Heart of the Matter (1993)
Fighting in Southwest Louisiana (1994)
Living Proof: HIV and the Pursuit of Happiness (1994)

VIII

National Directory
of Lesbian and Gay Community
Centers

Compiled and edited by Richard D. Burns, Executive Director,
and Rhett Wickham, Executive Assistant
Lesbian and Gay Community Services Center, New York
(© LESBIAN AND GAY COMMUNITY SERVICES CENTER–NEW YORK)

The Lesbian and Gay Community Services Center of New York is delighted to offer you a comprehensive guide to the gay and lesbian community centers serving our communities across the country. The National Directory is now in its ninth edition and still growing!

Each year since 1987, lesbian and gay community centers from across the United States have gathered together in a session at the annual conference of the National Lesbian and Gay Health Foundation. In June of 1994, representatives from more than thirty centers gathered for an all-day meeting at the New York Center and began the formation of a National Association of Lesbian and Gay community centers.

Convened by the centers in Dallas, Los Angeles, Minneapolis, New York, and Colorado, the association will work to foster the growth of gay and lesbian community centers around the country and share ideas and program models. Meetings of the association in 1995 took place in June in Minneapolis at the National Lesbian and Gay Health Conference, and in November in Detroit at the annual National Gay and Lesbian Task Force Creating Change Conference.

Arizona

Valley of the Sun Gay and Lesbian Community Center
3136 N. 3rd Ave.
Phoenix, AZ 85103

Hours of Operation: 10 A.M. - 10 P.M. seven days a week
Tel. 602-265-7283 Fax 602-234-0873

Major Programs and Services offered include: Lesbian and Gay Community Switchboard; Arizona AIDS information Line; Valley One in Ten youth group; and VOIT—anti-violence program

Publish a quarterly newsletter

Barb Jones, Co-Chair
Tom Kinkel, Co-Chair

Founded in 1993, Annual Budget for 1994—$100,000
1 full time staff member

Wingspan
422 North Fourth Avenue
Tucson, AZ 85705

Hours of Operation: Monday through Saturday, 1 P.M. to 7 P.M.
Tel. 602-624-1779 Fax 602-620-6341

Major Programs and Services offered include a youth group, meeting spaces, information phone line, lending library, and an art gallery.

Ernie Slaight, Volunteer Coordinator
Marcia Paris, president
David Dyde, vice president

Founded in 1988. Annual Budget in 1995—$21,000
No paid staff.

Publish a newsletter called *The Center*, six times per year.

California

The Billy DeFrank Lesbian & Gay Community Center
175 Stockton Ave.
San Jose, CA 95126

Hours of Operation: 6 P.M. - 9 P.M. M-F, Noon - 6 P.M. Sat. & Sun.
Te. 408-293-3040 Information and Referral #408-293-2429
Fax 408-298-8986 E-Mail address: BDFCPRES@AOL.COM
America On-Line Address:BDFCPRES SERPER

Major Programs and Services offered include information and referral; peer counseling; youth services; social/recreational services/ mental health program; addiction outreach program; volunteer resources; community drop-in; and meeting space.

Publish a monthly newsletter

Ralph M. Serpe, Program Director
Lisa Yamonaco, President
John Linder, Executive Vice President

Founded in 1981, Annual Budget for 1994—$340,000
2 full-time staff, 2 part-time staff

Gay & Lesbian Community Center
Building located at:
1995 East Main Street
Ventura, CA 93001

Mailing address at:
PO Box 2206
Ventura, CA 93002

Hours of Operation: 10 A.M. - 4 P.M. & 6 - 9 P.M. M-F
Tel. 805/653-1979; no Fax

Major Programs and Services offered include 12-step meetings, rap groups, anti-violence project, counseling, youth program, arts program, library, resource and referrals, and meeting space. Publish a monthly newletter—*Out'n'About*

Ron Cayou, Co-Chair
Edie Brown, Co-Chair
Neil Demers-Gray, Founder/Financial Officer

Founded in 1991, Annual Operating Budget for fiscal 1995—$28,000
No paid staff.
Rent their space.

Pride Center Sonoma County
205 Fifth Street
Santa Rosa, CA 95401

Hours of Operation: Not yet established as of this edition
Tel. 707/573-9463

Patrick Lancaster, Co-Chair
Mary Toth, Co-Chair

Founded in 1995. Newly established
Rent their space

The Edge
   39160 State Street
   Fremont, CA

   Hours of Operation: Varied depending on staffing.
   Tel. 510/790-2887 Fax 510/713-6679

   Major Programs and Services offered include meeting space, drop-in space, community announcement bulletin boards, housing referral boards, gay men's support group, gay men of color support group, women's support group, men's social group, lesbian social group, and HIV education and prevention services.

   Mike Kemmerrer, Coordinator

   Founded in 1995. Operation Budget for 1995 not provided.
   One full-time staff member.
   Rent their space.

Stonewall Alliance Center
   PO Box 8855
   Chico, CA 95927

   Building located at:
   341 Broadway
   Chico, CA 95928

   Hours of Operation: 3 - 6 P.M. T-F
   Tel. 916/892-3336 No Fax

   Major Programs and Services offered include Crisis Intervention phone line (916/893-3338), youth program, counseling, AIDS/HIV support and recreation services, library, community resources, and a memorial quilt project.

   Publish a monthly newsletter, *Centerstone*

   Greg Williams, Executive Director
   Dr. Robert Zadra, Co-Chair
   Rae Morrison, Co-Chair

   Founded in 1990. Annual Operation Budget for 1995—$160,000
   One full-time staff, 3 part-time staff.
   Rent their space.

The Gay and Lesbian Community Services Center of Orange County
   12832 Garden Grove Blvd., Suite A
   Garden Grove, CA 92643

   Hours of Operation: 9 A.M. - 10 P.M. M-F
   Tel. 714-534-0862 Fax 914-534-5491

   Major Programs and Services offered include gay and lesbian support groups; special interest groups; youth services; referral; counseling; AIDS education; and HIV support services.

M. Dan Wooldridge, Executive Director
Kathy Yhip, Board Chair

Founded in 1972, Annual Budget for 1995—$800,000
7 full-time staff, 4 part-time staff

Gay and Lesbian Resource Center
126 E. Haley St., Ste. A17
Santa Barbara, CA 93101

Tel. 805-963-3636 Fax 805-963-9086

2255 So. Broadway, No. 4
Santa Maria, CA 19345

Tel 805-349-9947 Fax 805-349-8638

Derek Gordon, Executive Director
Kathy Hoxie, Santa Maria Office Manager
Marian Bankins—Board President
Marsha Trott—Board Secretary

Founded 1976, Annual Budget for 1994—$1.25 Million
20 full-time staff, 6 part-time staff

Gay and Lesbian Resource Center of Ventura County
363 Mobil Ave.
Camarillo, CA 93010

Hours of Operation: 10 A.M. - 10 P.M. seven days a week.
Tel 805-389-1530 or 646-5884 No Fax

Major Programs and Services offered include counseling; support groups; speakers bureau; classes and workshops; telephone information and referral; HIV/AIDS assistance programs; and various classes.

Publish a newsletter four times per year

Ed Noel, Executive Director
Claire Connelly, President
Mary Long, Treasurer

Founded in 1983, Annual Budget in 1994—$12,000
1 full-time staff member

Lambda Community Center
PO Box 163654
Sacramento, CA 95816

Building located at:
1931 L Street
Sacramento, CA 95814

Hours of Operation: 10 A.M. - 9 P.M. Mon-Fri; 12 P.M. - 9 P.M. Sat. & Sun.
Tel. 916-442-0185 Fax 916-447-5755

Major Programs and Services offered include: AIDS Education and Prevention; Youth Program; Health Education for Lesbian; Lambda Players Theatre Group; and Lambda Letters letter writing campaigns.

Publish a Monthly Newsletter

Joanna L. Cassese, Executive Director
Larry Hoover—Board President
Kathleen Finnerty, Board Vice-President

Founded in 1978; Annual Operating Budget for 1995—$250,000
4 full-time staff, 2 part-time staff

The Lesbian and Gay Men's Community Center
PO Box 3357
San Diego, CA 92163

Building located at:
3916 Normal St.
San Diego, CA 92103

Tel. 619-692-2077 Fax 619-260-3092

Hours of Operation: 9 A.M. - 9 P.M. Mon.-Sat.; 10 A.M. - 7 P.M. Sunday.

Major Programs and Services offered include a Mental Health Services for Lesbian, Gay and HIV related issues; Lesbian Health Project; Youth Program; and Crisis Line.

Publishes a Quarterly Newsletter

Karen Marshall, Executive Director
Ann Wilson—Board President

Founded in 1973, Annual Budget for 1995—$820,000

7 full-time staff, 12 part-time staff

Gay and Lesbian Community Services Center of Long Beach
(previously listed as Long Beach Lesbian-Gay Community Center)
2017 E. 4th St.
Long Beach, CA 90814

Hours of Operation: 9 A.M. - 10 P.M. M-F, 9 A.M. - 6 P.M. Sat.
Tel. 310-434-4455 Fax 310-987-5202

The Center's Major Programs and Services offered include support and rap groups; legal, psychological & unemployment counseling; community activities program; information referral services; and twelve step programs.

Publishes a monthly newsletter

Jack M. Newby, Executive Director
Mary Martinez, Board Chair
Ernie Villa, Board Vice-Chair

Founded in 1978, Annual Budget for 1995—$500,000
9 full-time staff, 3 part-time staff

Housed in the building owned by ONE in Long Beach, a consortium of six organizations, including the Center.

Los Angeles Gay and Lesbian Community Services Center
1625 N. Schrader Blvd.
Los Angeles, CA 90028

Hours of Operation: 9 A.M. - 10 P.M. M-Sat, 9 A.M. - 6 P.M. Sun.
Tel 213-993-7600 Fax 213-993-7699
E-mail addess: GAYLESBLA@aol.com

Major Programs and Services offered include employment training and placement; Mental Health Services; Addiction Recovery Services; Youth Services; Homeless Youth Shelter; legal services; AIDS/HIV Medical Clinic; Audre Lorde Lesbian Health Clinic; Anonymous HIV test site; HIV Prevention Education, cultural programming; and computerized AIDS information network.

Publish a quarterly newsletter

Lorri L. Jean, Executive Director
Gwen Baba, Board Co-Chair
Loren Ostrow, Board Co-Chair

Founded in 1971, Annual Budget for 1995—$13.8 million
200 full-time staff

Pacific Center for Human Growth
2712 Telegraph Ave.
Berkeley, CA 94705

Hours of Operation: 10 A.M. - 10 P.M. M-F, 6 P.M. - 10 P.M. Sat. & Sun.
Tel. 510-548-8283 Fax 510-548-2938

Major Programs and Services offered include lesbian, gay, bi, trans speakers bureau; community space; peer support groups; HIV services; individual, couple and family counseling; info and referral switchboard; and Building Bridges—an anti-homophobia training program for other organizations.

Robert Fuentes, Board Chair

Founded in 1976, Annual Budget in 1995—$310,000
10 part-time staff

Deaf Gay and Lesbian Center
150 Eureka St., Suite 108
San Francisco, CA 94114

Hours of Operation: Call for operating hours.
Tel. 415/255-0700TTY; Fax 415/255-9797

Major Programs and Services offered include counseling, advocacy and refer-rals, peer counseling, community education, workshops, and support groups.

Publish *DGLC Update* newsletter.

Founded in 1992. Annual Operating Budget for 1995—$48,000
1 full-time staff, 1 part-time staff
Rent their space

San Francisco Community Center Project
3543 18th St., Box 21
San Francisco, CA 94110

Tel. 415-255-4545 no Fax

Currently a volunteer run planning project

Planning began in 1994; Annual Operation Budget for 1995—$40,000

"We are still in the planning phases of center development. We have yet to lo-cate a suitable site for the Center."

Lavender Youth Recreation & Information Center (LYRIC)
127 Collingwood St.
San Francisco, CA 94114

Tel. 415-703-6150 Fax 415-703-6153

Hours of Operation: 10 A.M. - 6 P.M.

Major Programs and Services offered include: Youth Talkline—24 hour infor-mation and referral phone line that is staffed by peer listeners in the evening; After School Program—provides after school activities for youth under 18 five days a week; Pro Active Youth—provides job readiness training to youth under 18; Young Women's Program (Young Tongues)—does a weekly rap group and ongoing workshops and special events for women under 24; Young Men's HIV Prevention & Education Program—does a weekly rap group and ongoing work-shops and special events for men under 24.

Publishes a Quarterly Newsletter

Ken Bukowski—Interim Executive Director
Vanessa Vishit-Vadakan—Board Co-Chair

Founded in 1989; Annual Operating Budget for 1995—$375,000

6 full-time staff; 2 part-time staff

Spectrum Center for Gay, Lesbian and BiSexual Concerns
100 Sir Frances Drake Blvd.
San Anselmo, CA 94960

Tel. 415-457-1115 Fax. 415-457-2838
Hours of Operation 9 A.M. to 9 P.M. M-Th, or by special arrangement.

Major Programs and Services offered include Rainbow's End, Teen Program, Youth Adult Program, Seniors' Program, Parenting Program, Support Groups, and Special Recreation Program.

Pat Tibbs—Executive Director
Tom Matteoli—President
Janice Azebu—Treasurer

Founded in 1982; Annual Operating Budget for 1995—$321,000

2 full-time staff; 6 part-time staff

Publish *Spectrum*, a newsletter, four times a year.

The Santa Cruz Lesbian Gay Bisexual and Transgendered Community Center
PO Box 8280
Santa Cruz, CA 95061

Building Located at
1328 Commerce Lane
Santa Cruz, CA

Hours of Operation, daily 12 noon to 10 P.M., call ahead as schedule varies.

Major Programs and Services offered include Pride Celebration, lending library, resource directory, information and referral, events sponsorship, meeting space, and drop-in space.

Mark Krikava, Co-Chair
Merrie Schaller, Co-Chair

Founded in 1980; Annual Operation Budget for 1995—$20,000

No Paid Staff

Publish *New and View of Santa Cruz*—a monthly newsletter.

COLORADO

Gay, Lesbian & Bisexual Community Services Center of Colorado
P.O. Drawer 18E
Denver, CO 80218-0140

Cheryl Schwartz—Executive Director
Jill Olliver, MSW—Board President
John Bloechl—Board Vice-President

Founded in 1976, Annual Budget for 1994—$194,000
5 full-time staff, 1 part-time staff member

The Lambda Community Center, Inc.
1437 East Mullberry, Suite #1
Fort Collins, Colorado 80524

Hours of Operation: 12 P.M. - 9 P.M.
Tel. 303-221-3247 Fax 303-482-5815 (note: update did not list a fax #)

Major Programs and Services offered include: Youth Group; Anti-Violence Project; Support Groups, Resource Library; Business Referrals; Educational Workshops; and Recreational-Groups.

Publish a Bi-monthly Newsletter

Stacey Shelp—Executive Director
Ken Hoole—President
Gary Schluter—Secretary

Founded in 1994, Annual Budget for 1995—$12,000
1 part-time staff

CONNECTICUT

Gay and Lesbian Community Center
(Previously listed as Project 100)
1841 Broad St.
Hartford, CT 06114

Hours of Operation: 2 P.M. - 10 P.M. M-F, Sat. "per event," 12 P.M. - 5 P.M. Sun.
Tel. 203-724-5542 Fax 203-724-3443

Major Programs and Services offered include AA recovery programs; health services; recreational programs; educational forums; and a theatre company.

Publish a monthly newsletter

Michael G. Louzier, Executive Director
Roy Moeckel, Board President
Thomas Bowie, Jr., Board Vice-President

Founded in 1988, Annual Budget for 1995—$131,000
One full-time staff member, 1 part-time staff

Tri-Angle Community Center, Inc.
Building located at:
25 Van Zant St., Suite 7-C
East Norwalk, CT 06855

Mailing address
Tri-Angle Community Center, Inc.
P.O. Box 4062
East Norwalk, CT 06855

Hours of Operation: 7:00 P.M. to 10:00 P.M. M-Th, Occasional weekend hours.
Tel. 203-853-0600 Fax 203-853-0600
America On-Line Address: tccenter@aol.com

Major Programs and Services offered include discussion groups for day, lesbian
and bi as well as minority and youth; resource room of books and periodicals;
meeting space; and a Community Directory of businesses and services.

Publish a monthly newsletter, *News and Views,* available on America Online at
NewsViews@aol.com

Len Horey, President
David Carroll, Treasurer

Founded in 1989. Annual Budget for 1995—$50,000
No Paid Staff

FLORIDA

The Lesbian Gay and Bisexual Community Center, Inc.
1335 Alton Rd.
Miami Beach, FL 33119

Hours of operation: 6 P.M. - 9 P.M. seven days a week
Tel. 305-531-3666

Major Programs and Services offered includes meeting space; information resource and referral; Miami Beach HIV/AIDS Project providing education and
sponsoring support groups and services; anti-crime project with Miami Beach
Police Department; youth outreach; and Community Organization Round-
table.

Publish a bi-monthly newsletter

Patricia Perreir-Pujol, Co-President
Mitchell Haymes, Co-President

Founded in 1992, Annual budget for 1995—$42,000
No full-time staff, 2 part-time staff

Compass, Inc.
2677 Forest Hill Boulevard #106
West Palm Beach, Fl 33406

Tel 407-966-3050 Fax 407-966-0039

Lisa McWorter, M.S.—Executive Director
Andy Amoroso, Board President
Sheldon Hartman, Board Treasurer
Kathryn Jakabein, Board Clerk

Founded in 1988, Annual Budget for 1994—$165,000
4 full time staff

Gay and Lesbian Community Center of Greater Fort Lauderdale
Building Located at:
1164 East Oakland Park Boulevard
Fort Lauderdale, FL

Mailing Address:
PO Box 4567
Fort Lauderdale, FL 33338

Hours of Operation: to be determined
Tel 305-563-9500 Fax 305-779-2680

Major Programs and Services offered include meeting space; telephone information and referral services; and various other programs in development.

Publish a monthly newsletter

Delia Loe, Executive Director
Alan E. Schubert, President
Leon J. Van Dyke, Vice President

Founded in 1993, Annual Budget for 1995—$132,801

The Gay and Lesbian Community Center of Tampa
1222 S. Dale Mabry, #350
Tampa, FL 33629
Tel. 813-273-8919

Major Programs and Services offered include a phone tree; social, recreational and fundraising events listed on the message of the above listed number, including locations, times and dates.
Dr. Craig Linden, Board Co-Chair
Linda Hallgren, Board Co-Chair
Trey Clark, Community Outreach Director

Founded in 1994, Annual Budget not established at time of writing
No paid staff.
Raising funds for a space at time of publication

Gay and Lesbian Community Services of Central Florida, Inc.
Mailing address
PO Box 533446
Orlando, FL 32853-3446
Building located at:
714 E. Colonial Drive
Orlando, FL 32803

Hours of Operation: 11 A.M. - 10 P.M. Mon-Fri; 12 P.M. - 5 P.M. Sat.
Tel 407-425-4527 Fax 407-423-9904

Major Programs and Services offered include: Social and Support Groups; Professional Counseling Referral Information; Crisis Intervention; The Triangle Newspaper; Media and Library; Advocacy; Hate Crime Reporting; Meeting Space; and numerous social activities and events.

Publish a Monthly Newspaper—*The Triangle*

Lyle C. Miller—Center Coordinator
Julie Whitley—Board President
Francis Ferguson—Board Treasurer

Founded in 1978; Annual Budget for 1995—$120,000
One full-time staff member, no part-time staff

Gay Switchboard of Gainesville
Box 12002
Gainesville, Fl 32604

Tel. 904-332-0700

Doug Dankel, Coordinator

Founded in 1981, Annual Budget for 1994—$1,300
10 part-time Paid staff

GEORGIA

The Atlanta Gay Center
63 Twelfth Street
Atlanta, GA 30309

Tel. 404-876-5372

Joseph Lillich, Administrator
Donald W. Smith, Ph.D., Chairperson

Founded in 1976, Annual Budget for 1994—$100,000
One full-time paid staff.

Atlanta Lambda Center
  Building located at:
  1518 Monroe Drive
  Atlanta, GA 30324

  Mailing Address:
  PO Box 15180
  Atlanta, GA 30333

  No regular hours of operation.
  Tel. 404/662-9010; no Fax

  Publish an occasional newsletter, *Atlanta Lambda Center Newsletter*

  Major Programs and Services currently under development

  David Herman, Board Co-Chair
  Sandye Lark, Board Co-Chair

  Founded in 1992. Annual Operating Budget for 1995—$12,000
  No paid staff.
  Rent their space.

ILLINOIS

The Frank M. Rodde Fund; operating as
  The Les-Bi-Gay Community Center of Chicago
  3023 N. Clark #747
  Chicago, IL 60657

  Tel 312-334-2174 Fax SAME
  E-mail MJH 123 @aol.com

  Dale Muehler, Executive Director
  Michael J. Harrington, President
  Kenneth Allen, Vice President

  Additional information not available at this of this printing

INDIANA

Up The Stairs Community Center
  3426 Broadway
  Fort Wayne, IN 46807

  Hours of Operation: 7 P.M. - 10 P.M. Mon. - Thurs., 7 P.M. - Midnight Fri. & Sat.,
  7 P.M. - 9 P.M. Sunday
  Tel 219-744-1199 Fax - none

  Major Programs and Services offered include: Fundraising Dances for New
  Years and Gay/Lesbian Pride; G/L Resource Center & Archives; Open Door

Chapel; G/L Helpline; Friday night drop-in; and space rental to various groups including AA, HIV Testing Site, FAIR Civil Rights Group, and Ladies After Dark (L.A.D.)

Fred Hefter, spokesperson, treasurer and board member

Founded in 1983; Annual Operation Budget for 1995—$4,800
No paid staff

IOWA

GLRC—Gay and Lesbian Resource Center
Box 7008
522 11th St.
Des Moines, IA 50309

Tel. 515-281-0634 Fax 515-284-8909

Bill Crews, President
Todd Ruopp, Vice President

Founded in mid 80's, Annual Budget for 1994 $30,000
No paid staff

KANSAS

The Center - Wichita
Mailing address:
P.O. Box 1357
Wichita, KS 67201
Building located at:
111 N. Spruce
Wichita, KS

Tel. 316-262-3991 No Fax

Major Programs and Services offered include: Lesbian, Gay, Bi AA Meetings; the Kansas Gay and Lesbian Archives; Weekly Coffee House; Weekly Lesbian Coming Out Support Group; Wichita Gay and Lesbian Alliance; HIV/AIDS Clothes Closet; Community Information Center.

Publish a Monthly Newsletter

Phil Griffin—Center Co-Chair
Steve Aaron—Center Co-Chair

Founded in 1993; Annual Operation Budget for 1995—$20,000
No paid staff

LOUISIANA

Lesbian and Gay Community Center of New Orleans
816 N. Rampart St.
New Orleans, LA 70116

Hours of Operation: Noon - 6 P.M. seven days a week
Tel. 504-529-2367 Fax 504-527-5334

Major Programs and Services offered include information and referral service, weekly youth program, lending library, weekly movies, meeting space for groups, monthly art shows, seminars and forums and a twenty-something group.

Publishes a quarterly newsletter

Renee Parks, Co-Chair
Clarke Broel, Co-Chair

Founded in 1992, Annual Budget for 1995—$12,000
No paid staff

MAINE

Northern Lambda Nord, Inc.
Community Services Center
POB 990
Caribou, ME 04736

Tel. 207-498-2088

Founded in 1994
No other information is available at time of this printing.

MARYLAND

Gay and Lesbian Community Center of Baltimore
241 W. Chase St.
Baltimore, MD 21201

Tel. 410-837-5445 Fax 410-837-8512

Michael B. Linnemann, Center Coordinator
Karen Jordan, President

Founded in 1977, Annual Budget for 1995—$320,000
Five full-time staff, 2 part-time

Michigan

Affirmations Lesbian Gay Community Center
195 West Nine Mile Road
Ferndale, MI 48220

Hours of Operation: 9 A.M. - 11 P.M. M-F, Noon - 7 P.M. Sat., Noon - 11 P.M. Sun.
Tel. 810-398-7105 Fax 810-541-1943

Major Programs and Services provided include a switchboard; peer support groups for men, women, couples, singles, and a mixed group; and community outreach.

Publishes a monthly newsletter

Jan Stevenson, Executive Director
Tom Wilezak, President
Shea Howell, Board Member

Founded in 1989, Annual Budget for 1995—$376,396
5 full-time staff, 3 part-time staff.

Minnesota

Gay & Lesbian Community Action Council
310 E. 38th St., Room 204
Minneapolis, MN 55409

Tel 612-822-0127 or 1-800-800-0350 Fax 822-8786

Ann DeGroot, Executive Director
Tom Hoch, Board Chair

Founded in 1986—Annual budget for 1994—$800,000
10 full-time staff, 2 part-time staff

Missouri

Metropolitan St. Louis Lesbian, Gay, Bisexual and Transgendered Community Center
Mailing address
Box 4589
St. Louis, MO 63108
Office located at:
438 N. Skinner Blvd.
St. Louis, MO 63130

Hours of Operation: 10 A.M. - 5 P.M. Mon, Wed, Fri & 4 P.M. - 10 P.M. Thurs.;
Sat & Sun by arrangement
Tel 314-997-9897 Fax 314-862-8155

Major Programs and Services provided include: 25 Organization Community Voice Mail System; Education Forums; Candidates; Forum for Aldermanic President; and a Lending Library for books and videos.

Publishes a monthly Calendar of Events

Mark Maloney, Office Manager
Robert Hollander, Board member
Sharon Cohen, Board member

Founded in 1993, Annual Operating Budget for 1995—$8,000
No paid staff

NEBRASKA

Panhandle Gay and Lesbian Support Services
 PO Box 1046
 Scottsbluff, NE 69363-1046

 Tel. 308-635-8488 Fax - none

 Diane Crystal, Director
 Rae Ann Schmitz, Core Group Member
 Roni Reid, Core Group Member

 Founded in 1993, Annual Budget for 1994—$600
 One part-time staff member.

NEW JERSEY

Gay and Lesbian Community Center of New Jersey, Inc.
 Mailing address:
 PO Box 1316
 Asbury Park, NJ 07712
 Building located at:
 515 Cookman Ave.
 Asbury Park, NJ 07712-1316

 Tel. 908-775-4429, 774-1809 Fax 908-774-5513
 Hours of Operation: Seven days a week 12:00 P.M. - 8:00 P.M.

 Major Programs or Services offered include: Meeting Place of gay, lesbian, bi and trans groups; referral services; monthly socials; and a lecture series.

 Publishes a Quarterly Newsletter

 Steve Russo, Board President
 Kathy Taggart, Board Vice-President

 Founded in 1994, Annual Operating Budget for 1995—$65,000
 No Paid Staff

Pride Center of New Jersey
Building Located at
211 Livingston Ave.
New Brunswick, NJ 08901
Mailing address
PO Box 1431
New Brunswick, NJ 08903

Hours of Operation: 11 A.M. - 1 P.M. and 7 P.M. - 10 P.M. Mon. & Tues., 7 P.M. - 10 P.M. Wed. & Thurs., call for other times.
Tel 908-846-2232 Fax - none

Major Programs and Services offered include a hotline; library; men's rap group; women's group; P-Flag; Log Cabin Club; Teachers Caucus; Lesbian Mothers; ACOA; SAGE; Bisexual Network of NJ; OA; lesbian health services; monthly rollerskating; and winter and fall NJ Gay Lesbian Street Fairs.

Ray Johnson, Co-Chair
Gina Pastino, Co-Chair

Founded in 1991, Annual Budget for 1995—$18,000
No paid staff

Rainbow Place of South Jersey
Building located at
1103 North Broad Street
Woodbury, NJ 08096
Mailing Address
PO Box 682
Bellmawr, NJ 08099-0682

Hours of Operation: call for specific hours
Tel 609-848-2455 Fax: 215-951-0342
E-Mail address: ALLEN219@AOL.COM America On-Line address: ALLEN219

Major Programs and Services offered include social and cultural events; referral information; and peer support services.

Publish a bi-monthly newsletter

Laurin Stahl, Co-Chair
Preston Brooks, Co-Chair

Founded in 1993, Annual Budget for 1995—$15,000
No paid staff

NEW YORK

Capital District Gay and Lesbian Community Council
Building located at
332 Hudson Ave.
Albany, NY 12210
Mailing address
PO Box 131
Albany, NY 12201

Hours of Operation: 7 P.M. - 10 P.M. M-Th, 7 P.M. - 11 P.M. F-St. 2 P.M. - 10 p.m
Sun.
Tel. 518-462-6138 No Fax

Major Programs and Services offered include support groups; programming
throughout the Albany area; and a 24 hour information line.

Publish a monthly newsletter called "Community"

Bill Pape, President
Mark Daigneault, Vice President

Founded in 1970, Annual Budget for 1995—$100,000
No paid staff

Gay Alliance of the Genesee Valley
179 Atlantic Avenue
Rochester, NY 14607.

Tel. 716-244-8640 Fax 716-244-8246

Tanya Smolinsky, Center Director
William Pritchard, Acting Board President

Founded in 1973, Annual Budget for 1994—$125,000
1 full-time staff, 2 part-time staff

The Lesbian and Gay Community Services Center
208 West 13th Street
New York, NY 10011

Hours of Operation: 9 A.M. - 11 P.M. seven days a week
Tel. 212-620-7310 Fax 212-924-2657
E-Mail address: lgcsc_nyc@aol.com

Major Programs and Services offered include meeting space for over 400
groups; Project Connect alcoholism and substance abuse recovery counseling;
Center Bridge AIDS bereavement program; Youth Enrichment Services crea-
 tive arts programming for youth people ages 21 and under; Gender Identity
Program; in-house and on-the-road community orientation; Voter Registration;
Global Action Project for human rights; Center Kids lesbian/gay family project;

Pat Parker/Vito Russo Library; National Museum of Lesbian and Gay History; dances twice a month; Lesbian Softball Tournament; Mediation Services; information and referral; Lesbian Health Fair; In Our Own Write creative writing classes and readers series; Lesbian Movie Night; Center Stage theatre parties; Annual Garden Party kicks off NYC's G/L Pride Week.

Publishes a newsletter every other month—*Center Voice*—& monthly calendar of events Center Happenings.

Richard D. Burns, Executive Director
Judith E. Turkel, Esq., Board President
Janet Weinberg, Board Co-Chair
Michael Seltzer, Board Co-Chair

Founded in 1983, Annual Budget for 1995—$3.3 Million
36 full-time staff, 9 part-time staff

The LOFT
PO Box 1513
White Plains, NY 10602

Tel. 914-948-4922 Fax - none

Dr. Zelle W. Andrews, Co-President
Lester Goldstein, Co-President

Founded in 1990, Annual Budget of $50,000 for 1994
No paid staff

Pride Community Center
PO Box 6608
Syracuse, NY 13217-6608
Tel. 315/446-4436

Projected opening date: Spring 1996, providing educational programs, support groups, and an information line

Publish a monthly newsletter, *Pride News*

John Brown, Founding Committee Chair

Founded in 1995; projected operating budget for fiscal 1996—$15,000
No paid staff
Currently seeking physical plant

NORTH CAROLINA

Gay and Lesbian Helpline of Wake Co.
PO Box 36207
Raleigh, NC 27606-6207

Tel. 919-821-0055

Noah Ranells, Co-Director
No additional information as of this writing

OHIO

The Gay and Lesbian Community Center of Greater Cincinnati
Building located at:
700 West Pete Rose Way
Cincinnati, OH 45203

Mailing Address:
PO Box 141061
Cincinnati, OH 45250-1061

Hours of Operation: 6 - 9 P.M. M-F, 12 - 4 P.M. Sat. & Sun.
Tel. 513/651-0040; no fax

Major Programs and Services offered include information and referral switch-board, library and archives meeting space, community calendar of events, community resource area for copying, faxing and work on personal computer.

Publish a quarterly newsletter—*Outlooks*

Jill Benavides, General Director

Founded in 1991. Annual Operating Budget for fiscal 1995—$25,000
No paid staff
Rent their space

Dayton Lesbian & Gay Center
PO Box 1203
Dayton, OH 45401

Tel. 513-274-1776

Leon Bey, Chair
Debbie Ranard, Board Member
Bob Daley, Board Member

Founded in 1976, Annual Budget for 1994—$25,000; No staff information provided

Lesbian/Gay Community Service Center
Mailing Address
PO Box 6177
Cleveland, OH 44101

Building located at:
1418 W. 29th St.
Cleveland, OH 44113

Tel. 216-522-0199 Fax 216-522-0026
America OnLine address: CLEVLGCSC or RAINBROOK
E-Mail address: CLEVLGCSC@AOL.COM

Hours of operation: 9 A.M. - 5 P.M. M-F
Hotline open 7 days a week 3 P.M. - 10 P.M.
Computer Hotline open 24 hours a day, 7 days a week

Major Programs and Services provided include: Hotline; Youth Program (PRYSM); HIV Positive Program; meeting space; Drop-In/Information Bulletin Board; anti-discrimination work; and a Speakers Bureau.

Publishes a Quarterly Newsletter

Judith Rainbrook, Executive Director
Frank Lowery, Jr., Board President

Founded in 1975, Annual budget for 1995—$230,000
4 full-time staff, 1 part-time staff

Stonewall Union Community Center
(previously listed as Stonewall Community Center)
47 W. 5th Avenue
Columbus, OH 43201

Hours of Operation: 9 P.M. - 5 P.M. M-F and evenings as scheduled.
Tel 614-299-7764 Fax/TTY 614-299-4408

Major Programs and Services provided include Anti-Violence Project; Fight and Right project; Annual Pride March (10,000 people last year); a twice weekly Television Program; and a booth at the Ohio State Fair.

Publish a monthly newsletter

Gloria McCauley, Interim Executive Director
Susan Bader, President
Jeff Jones, Vice-President

Founded in 1981, Annual Budget for 1995—$150,000
1 full-time staff, 3 part-time staff

OKLAHOMA

The Oasis Gay, Lesbian and Bisexual Community Resource Center
2135 NW 39th St.
Oklahoma City, OK 73112

Tel. 405-525-2437

Christopher Bruce DeVault, Executive Director

Founded in 1982, Annual Budget for 1994—$50,000
1 part-time staff member

OREGON

Lesbian Community Project
800 NW 6th, Room 333
Portland, OR 97209

Hours of Operation: 9 A.M. - 4 P.M. Monday - Thursday; 9 A.M. - Midnight
Friday
Tel. 503-223-0071; fax 503-242-1967

Anti-Violence Hotline 503-796-1703

Major Programs and Services offered include: Anti-Violence Project and Hotline; Lesbian Health Project; The Oregon Lesbian Conference; Voter Registration; For Love and Justice—A Walk Against Hate; Lesbian Film Festival; Over
35 Group; Safer Sex Workshops; Coming Out Series; Presentations to High
School and College Classes and business and social service organizations,
churches and other groups; and some thirty other programs and services.

Publish a monthly newsletter

Laverne Lewis, Executive Director
Susan Bryer, President

Founded in 1986, Annual Budget for 1995—$100,000
2 part-time staff

Lesbian Gay Bisexual Community Resource Center
PO Box 6596
Portland, OR 97208

Tel. 503-295-9732 Fax - none
Darci Chapman, Co-President
Kim Grittner, Co-President

Founded in 1993, Annual Budget for 1994—$1,000
No paid staff

PENNSYLVANIA

Penguin Place: Gay & Lesbian Community Center of Philadelphia, Inc.
Mailing address
P.O. Box 12814
Philadelphia, PA 19108
Building located at:
201 S. Camac St.
Philadelphia, PA 19107

Hours of Operation: 6 P.M. - 10 P.M. Mon-Fri; 10 A.M. - 6 P.M. Sat., 3 P.M. - 9 P.M.
Sun.

Tel. 215-732-2220 Fax - none

Major Programs and Services provided include: Library and Archives; Counseling Services; Youth Group; Out Music; Team Philadelphia Sports; and an Art Gallery.

Publish a quarterly newsletter

Michael J. LoFurno, Board Co-Chair
Pamila Florea, Board Co-Chair

Founded in 1974, Annual Budget for 1994—$50,000
No paid staff

The Gay & Lesbian Community Services Center of Philadelphia
Mailing Address
537 N. 3rd Street
Philadelphia, PA 19123

Tel. 215-238-9792; Fax 215-238-9263

A recently formed organization currently seeking information from other Centers on programs, annual reports, start-up experience, and advice and structuring.

Jonathan Cabiria, Board Member

Mission statement is ". . . to support the well being of Philadelphia Gay, Lesbian, Bisexual and Transgendered persons by providing essential human services to the community; by organizing and sponsoring the community activities"

SOUTH CAROLINA

South Carolina Gay and Lesbian Community Center
Building located at:
1108 Woodrow St.
Columbia, SC 29205

Mailing Address:
South Carolina Gay and Lesbian Community Center
PO Box 12648
Columbia, SC 29211

Hours of Operation: 1 P.M. - 6 P.M. Wed., 7 P.M. - 11 P.M. Fri., 1 P.M. - 8 P.M. Sat. & Sun.
Tel./Fax 803-771-7713

Major Programs and Services offered include a library; youth groups; lesbian coming out group; info and referral line; and gay men's HIV & social group

Publish a bi-monthly newsletter

Matt Tischler, Co-Chair
Kristen Gregory

Founded in 1989, Annual Budget for 1995—$35,000
No paid staff

TENNESSEE

Memphis Gay and Lesbian Community Center
PO Box 41074
Memphis, TN 38174

Tel. 901-728-4297 Fax - none

Michael Ricks, President
Vincent Astor, Vice President

Founded in 1989, Annual Budget for 1994—$12,000
No paid staff

TEXAS

HAPPY Foundation
411 Bonham
San Antonio, TX 78205

Hours of Operation: varies—best to call
Tel. 210-227-6541 No Fax

Major Programs and Services offered include a gay and lesbian archive collecting all kinds of history for research projects.

Gene Elder, Executive Director

Founded in 1988. Budget not provided.
No paid staff

Community Outreach Center
P.O. Box 64746
Lubbock, TX 79464-4746

Tel. 806-762-1019

Natalie Phillips, President
Bill Sommers, Vice President
Kara Carthel, Board Member

Founded in 1989, Annual Budget for 1994—$14,000
No paid staff

Cornerstone
Building located at:
425 Woodward
Austin, TX 78704

Mailing address:
PO Box 3164
Austin, TX 78764

Hours of Operation: not provided for this edition
Tel. 512/416-1616; fax 512/445-5518

Currently seeking physical plant to house numerous non-profit gay, lesbian and bisexual service organizations. Working in cooperation with Metropolitan Community Church of Austin.

Publish a semi-annual newsletter, *The Cornerstone*

Kenneth Martin, Moderator of the Board
Glen S. Baum, Board Member

Founded in 1995; no projected budget as of this edition
9 part-time staff

Gay & Lesbian Community Center
Building located at
2701 Reagan Street
Dallas, TX 75219

Mailing address
PO Box 190869
Dallas, TX 75219-0869

Hours of Operation: 9 A.M. - 9 A.M. M-F, 10 A.M. - 6 P.M. Sat., Noon - 6 P.M. Sun. & Holidays.
Tel. 214-528-9254 Fax 214-522-4604
E-Mail address: foundgay@onramp.net

Major Programs and Services offered include Community Hotline (214-528-0022); g/l helpline; gay/lesbian speakers bureau; adult education; meeting spaces; Welcome Wagon; gay 101 workshops; Community Switchboard; Community Calendar; g/l archives; and a research library.

Publish a monthly newsletter

John Thomas, Executive Director
Steve Hawkins, Board President
Jan Mock, Board Vice President

Founded in 1984, Annual Budget for 1995—$500,000
4 full-time staff, 4 part-time staff
(Center is part of a larger multiorganizational program)

LAMBDA Services
Mailing address:
PO Box 31321
El Paso, TX 79931-0321
Offices located at:
910 N. Mesa
El Paso, TX 79902

Hours of Operation: 7 P.M. - 11 P.M. Mon., Wed., Fri. & Sat.; Office open 8 A.M. - 5 P.M. Mon. - Fri.
Tel 915-562-4297; fax 915-532-6919
E-Mail Address: LAMBDAelp@aol.com America OnLine: LAMBDA ELP or LAMBDAtx

Major Programs and Services include: HIV Testing; 24 Hour switchboard, Helpline and Teen Helpline; Anti-Violence Project; Youth OUTreach Services; Women's Services; and Public Information Speakers Bureau.

Publish a monthly newsletter

Rob Knight, President
Katherine Kelly, Vice President
Alejandro Herrera, Secretary

Founded in 1991; Annual Operating Budget for 1995—$10,000
5 full-time staff, 15 part-time staff

WISCONSIN

The United
14 W. Mifflin St., Suite 103
Madison, WI 53703

Tel. 608-255-8582

Jane Vaneerbosch, Director
Sande Janagold, Board Treasurer
Greg Hines, Interim Board President

Founded in 1978, Annual Budget for 1994—$51,000
1 full-time staff member, 1 part-time staff member

IX

National Directory of Lesbian and Gay Organizations and Resources

---

GENERAL/ACTIVIST

African-American Lesbian and Gay Alliance, P.O. Box 50374, Atlanta, GA 30302

Black Lesbian and Gay Leadership Forum, 1219 South La Brea Ave., Los Angeles, CA 90019, 213- 964-7820

Gay, Lesbian, and Bisexual Speakers Bureau, Public Education Services, Inc., P.O. Box 2232, Boston, MA 02117, 617-354-0133

Irish Lesbian and Gay Organization (ILGO), 208 West 13th St., New York, NY 10011, 212-967-7711 x3078

National Coalition of Black Lesbians and Gays, P.O. Box 19248, Washington, DC 20036

National Gay and Lesbian Task Force, 1734 14th St., NW, Washington, DC 20009, 202-332-6483

National Latino/a Lesbian and Gay Organization, P.O. Box 44483, Washington, DC 20026

Overlooked Opinions, Inc., 3712 North Broadway, #277, Chicago, IL 60613-9941, 312-929-9600.

Queer Nation, c/o Lesbian and Gay Community Services Center, 208 West 13th St., New York, NY 10011, 212-260-6156

Trikone, P.O. Box 21354, San Jose, CA 95151. 408-270-8776—gay and lesbian South Asians

AIDS/HIV

AIDS Action Council, 1875 Connecticut Avenue NW #700, Washington, DC 20009, 202-986-1300

AIDS Coalition to Unleash Power (ACT UP), 496-A Hudson Street #G4, New York, NY 10014, 212-564-2437

AIDS National Interfaith Network, 110 Maryland Avenue NE, Suite 504,Washington, DC 20002, 202-546-0807

AIDS Project/Lambda Legal Defense and Education Fund, 666 Broadway, 12th floor, New York, NY 10012, 212-995-8585

AIDS Research Alliance, 621-A North San Vicente Blvd., West Hollywood, CA 90069, 310-358-2423

American Foundation for AIDS Research (AmFAR), 733 Third Ave., New York, NY 10017, 212-682-7440

American Institute for Teen AIDS Prevention, P.O. Box 136116, Fort Worth, TX 76136, 817-237-0230

Broadway Cares/Equity Fights AIDS, 165 West 46th St., Suite 1300, New York, NY 10036, 212-840-0770

Canadian AIDS Society, 170 Laurier Avenue West #1101, Ottawa, Ontario K1P 5V5, fax: 613-563-4998

Community Research Initiative on AIDS (CRIA), 275 Seventh Ave., 20th floor, New York, NY 10001, 212-924-3934

Design Industries Foundation Fighting AIDS (DIFFA), 150 West 26th St., Suite 602, New York, NY 10001, 212-727-3100

Gay Men's Health Crisis (GMHC), 129 West 20th St., New York, NY 10011, 212-807-6664, hotline: 212-807-6655.

Mobilization Against AIDS, 584-B Castro St., San Francisco, CA 94114, 415-863-4676

National Leadership Coalition on AIDS, 1730 M Street NW, Suite 905, Washington, DC 20036, 202-429-0930

National Minority AIDS Council (NMAC), 300 I Street NE, Suite 400, Washington, DC 20002, 202-544-1076

Project Inform, 1965 Market St., Suite 220, San Francisco, CA 94103, 415-558-8669

Ryan White Foundation, 101 West Washington St., Suite 1135 East, Indianapolis, IN 46204, 800-444-RYAN

Test Positive Aware Network, 1258 West Belmont Ave., Chicago, IL 60657, 312-404-8726

Treatment Action Group, 200 East 10th Street #601, New York, NY 10003, 212-260-0300

For a listing of local AIDS/HIV services, contact the U.S. Conference of Mayors, 1620 I St. NW, Washington, DC 20006, 202-293-7330. Many local AIDS groups and organizations are also listed by state in the *Gayellow Pages* (Renaissance House, Box 292, Village Station, New York, NY 10014-0292).

AIDS HOTLINES

AIDS Clinical Trials Information Services, 800-TRIALSA, TTY/TDD: 800-243-7012

CDC (Centers for Disease Control) AIDS Hotline, 800-342-AIDS; in Spanish: 800-344-SIDA—popularly known as the National AIDS Hotline.

National AIDS Hotline for Hearing Impaired, 800-243-7889

National Hospicelink, 800-331-1620

National Native American AIDS Hotline, 800-283-2437

National Sexually Transmitted Diseases Hotline, 800-227-8922

Project Inform National Hotline (AIDS treatment), 800-822-7422

Toll-free Directory Assistance, 800-555-1212 (call for your state's own toll-free AIDS hotline)

ARCHIVES/LIBRARIES

Archives Gaies du Quebec, 4067 St-Laurent, Suite 202, Montreal, QC H2W 1Y7C, 514-287-9987

Blanche Baker Memorial Library and Archives/ONE, Inc., 3340 Country Club Drive, Los Angeles, CA 90019, 213-735-5252

Canadian Gay Archives, P. O. Box 639, Station A, Toronto, Ontario M5W 1G2.

Dallas Gay and Lesbian Historic Archives, 2701 Reagan, Dallas, TX 75219, 214-528-4233

Douglas County Gay Archives, P.O. Box 942, Dillard, OR 97432-0942, 503-679-9913

Gay and Lesbian Archives of Washington, DC, P.O. Box 4218, Falls Church, VA 22044, 703-671-3930

Gay and Lesbian Historical Society of Northern California, P.O. Box 424280, San Francisco, CA 94142, 415-626-0980

Henry Gerber/Pearl M. Hart Library and Archives, Midwest Lesbian/Gay Resource Center, 3352 N. Paulina St., Chicago, IL 60657, 312-883-3003

Homosexual Information Center, 115 Monroe St., Bossier City, LA 71111.

International Gay and Lesbian Archives, P. O. Box 38100, Los Angeles, CA 90038-0100.

Lesbian and Gay Historical Society of San Diego, P.O. Box 40389, San Diego, CA 92164, 619-260-1522

National Museum and Archive of Lesbian and Gay History, Lesbian and Gay Community Services Center, 208 West 13th St., New York, NY 10011, 212-620-7310

New York Public Library, Division of Humanities, Social Sciences, and Special Collections, Fifth Avenue and 42nd St., New York, NY 10018, 212-930-0584

Pat Parker/Vito Russo Center Library, Lesbian and Gay Community Services Center, 208 West 13th St., New York, NY 10011, 212-620-7310

Stonewall Library and Archives, 330 SW 27th St., Fort Lauderdale, FL 33315

ART AND DESIGN

The NAMES Project (AIDS quilt), 310 Townsend St., Suite 310, San Francisco, CA 94107, 415-882-5500, fax: 415-882-6200

Organization of Lesbian and Gay Architects and Designers (OLGAD), P.O. Box 927, Old Chelsea Station, New York, NY 10113, 212-475-7652

ATHLETICS/SPORTS

Federation of Gay Games, 584 Castro St., Suite 343, San Francisco, CA 94114

International Gay Bowling Association, 1730 Pendrell Street #402, Vancouver, BC, 604-689-5146

International Gay Figure Skating Union, P.O. Box 1101, New York, NY 10113, 212-691-1690 or 212-255-0559

International Gay Rodeo Association, 900 East Colfax, Denver, CO 80218, 415-861-0779.

Stonewall Climbers, P.O. Box 445, Boston, MA 02124—rock and ice climbers worldwide

EDUCATION—TEACHERS/STUDENTS

American Federation of Teachers, National Gay and Lesbian Caucus, P.O. Box 19856, Cincinnati, OH 45219

Center for Lesbian and Gay Studies (CLAGS), Graduate Center of the City University of New York, 33 West 42nd St., Room 404N, New York, NY 10036, 212-642-2924

Coalition for Lesbian and Gay Student Groups, Box 190712, Dallas, TX 75219, 214-621-6705, fax: 214-528-8436

Gay Teachers Caucus of the National Education Association, 32 Bridge St., Hackensack, NJ 07606, 201-489-2458

National Gay and Lesbian Task Force Campus Project, 1734 14th St., NW, Washington, DC 20009, 202-332-6483

Network of Gay and Lesbian Alumni/ae, P.O. Box 53188, Washington, DC 20009

FILM/TELEVISION

Alliance for Gay and Lesbian Artists in the Entertainment Industry, P.O. Box 69A18, West Hollywood, CA 90069

Frameline, 346 Ninth St., San Francisco, CA 94103, 415-703-8650

Gay and Lesbian Alliance Against Defamation (GLAAD), 150 West 26th St., New York, NY 10001, 212-807-1700

In the Life, 39 West 14th Street, Suite 402, New York, NY 10011, 212-255-6012—monthly public TV program

Professionals in Film/Video, 336 Canal St., 8th floor, New York, NY 10013-2022, 212-387-2022

FOUNDATIONS/FUNDING SOURCES

Colin Higgins Fund of Tides Foundation, 1388 Sutter St., San Francisco, CA 94109, 415-771-4308

Funding Exchange/OUT Fund, 666 Broadway, Suite 500, New York, NY 10012, 212-529-5300

North Star Fund, 666 Broadway, New York, NY 10012, 212-460-5511

Out of the Closet Foundation, 20084 Cherokee Station, New York, NY 10021, 212-472-3573

Paul Rapoport Foundation, 220 East 60th St., New York, NY 10022, 212-888-6578

Stonewall Community Foundation, 825 Third Ave., Suite 3315, New York, NY 10022

HEALTH AND MEDICINE

Association for Gay, Lesbian, and Bisexual Issues in Counseling, Box 216, Jenkintown, PA 19046

Association of Lesbian and Gay Psychiatrists, 1439 Pineville Road, New Hope, PA 18938

Committee on Gay and Lesbian Concerns, American Psychological Association, 1200 17th Street NW, Washington, DC 20036, 202-336-5500

Education in a Disabled Gay Environment (EDGE), P.O. Box 305, Village Station, New York, NY 10014

Gay and Lesbian Medical Association, 273 Church St., San Francisco, CA 94114, 415-255-4547

International Advisory Counsel for Homosexual Men and Women in AA, P.O. Box 90, Washington, DC 20044-0090

Lesbian, Gay, and Bisexual People in Medicine, 1890 Preston White Drive, Reston, VA 22091, 703-620-6600

National Association of Lesbian and Gay Alcoholism Professionals, 204 West 20th St., New York, NY 10011

National Gay and Lesbian Domestic Violence Victims' Network, P.O. Box 140131, Denver, CO 80214

National Lesbian and Gay Health Association, 1407 S. Street NW, Washington, DC 20009, 202-939-7880, fax: 202-797-3504

Pride Institute, 14400 Martin Drive, Eden Prairie, MN 55344, 800-54-PRIDE

Project Connect, Lesbian and Gay Community Services Center, 208 West 13 St., New York, NY 10011, 212-620-7310

Society for the Psychological Study of Lesbian and Gay Issues, American Psychological Association, 1200 17th Street NW, Washington, DC 20036, 202-336-5500

HOME AND FAMILY

Center Kids: The Family Project, Lesbian and Gay Community Services Center, 208 West 13 St., New York, NY 10011, phone: 212-620-7310, fax: 212-924-265

Children of Lesbians and Gays Everywhere (COLAGE), 2300 Market St., #165, San Francisco, CA 94114, 415-206-1930, also Box 187, Station F, Toronto, ON M4Y 2L5

Gay and Lesbian Parents Coalition International (GLPCI), P.O. Box 50360, Washington, DC 20091, 202-583-8029

Gay Parents Coalition, P.O. Box 19891, Washington, DC 20036, 202-583-8029

Hetrick Martin Institute for Lesbian and Gay Youth, 2 Astor Place, New York, NY 10003, phone: 212-674-2400, fax: 212-674-8650

Lavender Families (formerly Lesbian Mothers National Defense Fund), P.O. Box 21567, Seattle, WA 98111, 206-325-2643

National Coalition for Gay and Lesbian Youth, P.O. Box 24589, San Jose, CA 95154-4589, 408-269-6125

National Federation of Parents and Friends of Gays, 8020 Eastern Ave., N.W., Washington, DC 20012, 202-726-3223

National Register of Lesbian and Gay Unions, 125 Cedar Place Penthouse, New York, NY 10006

Parents of Lesbians and Gays (P-FLAG), 1012 14th St., N.W., #700, Washington, DC 20005, or Box 27605, Washington, DC 20038, phone: 202-638-4200, fax: 202-638-0243

Partners, P.O. Box 8685, Seattle, WA 98109

Senior Action in a Gay Environment (SAGE), 305 Seventh Ave., New York, NY 10001, 212-741-2247

LEGAL ISSUES

American Civil Liberties Union Lesbian and Gay Rights/AIDS Project, 132 West 43rd St., New York, NY 10036, 212-944-9800

Lesbian and Gay Law Association of Greater New York (LEGALE), P.O. Box 1899 Grand Central Station, New York, NY 10163, 212-305-5100, 212-459-4873 (lawyer referral; 24-hour answering service with next-day call-back)

Gay and Lesbian Advocates and Defenders (GLAD), P.O. Box 218, Boston, MA 02112, 617-426-1350

Lambda Legal Defense and Education Fund, 666 Broadway, 12th floor, New York, NY 10012, 212-995-8585

National Lesbian and Gay Law Association, Box 77130, National Capital Station, Washington, DC 20014, 202-389-0161

LITERATURE/PUBLISHING

Gay and Lesbian Task Force, American Library Association, 50 East Huron St., Chicago, IL 60611

Gay Writers Caucus, National Writers Union, 13 Astor Place, New York, NY 10003, 212-580-2206

Lambda Literary Awards, c/o *Lambda Book Report*, 1625 Connecticut Ave. NW, Washington, DC 20009, 202-462-7924

Gay and Lesbian Committee, PEN American Center, 568 Broadway, New York, NY 10012, 212-334-1660

The Gaylactic Network, P.O. Box 127, Brookline, MA 02146-0001—science fiction

The Publishing Triangle, P.O. Box 114, Prince Street Station, New York, NY 10012

MEDIA

Gay and Lesbian Alliance Against Defamation (GLAAD), 150 West 26th St., New York, NY 10001, 212-807-1700

Gay and Lesbian Press Association, P.O. Box 8185, Universal City, CA 91608-0185

GayNet, P.O. Box 25524, Albuquerque, NM 87125-0524, 505-243-2540—news wire service for gay publications

In the Life, 39 West 14th St., Suite 402, New York, NY 10011, 212-255-6012—monthly public TV program

Lesbian and Gay Public Awareness Project, Box 65603, Los Angeles, CA 90065

National Gay and Lesbian Journalists Association, 874 Gravenstein Highway South, Suite 4, Sebastopol, CA 95472, 707-823-2193, fax: 707-823-4176

This Way Out, P.O. Box 38327, Los Angeles, CA 90038—internationally distributed weekly radio program

MISCELLANEOUS

Digital Queers, 584 Castro St., # 150, San Francisco, CA 94114, 415-252-6282—computers

Gay Officers Action League (GOAL), P.O. Box 2038, Canal Street Station, New York, NY 10012, 212-996-8808

Gay Pilots Association, P.O. Box 1291, Alexandria, VA 22313, 703-660-3852

Lesbian and Gay Labor Network: Coalition of Labor Union Activists, P.O. Box 1159, Peter Stuyvesant Station, New York, NY 10009, 212-923-8690—not a job finding service

Lesbians and Gays in Telecommunications (LEGIT), P.O. Box 8143, Red Bank, NJ 07701

Liatris International, P.O. Box 1336, Davis, CA 95617-1336—gay and lesbian horticulturists

National Organization of Gay and Lesbian Scientists and Technical Professionals, P.O. Box 91803, Pasadena, CA 91109, 818-791-7689

MILITARY

American Federation of Veterans, Suite 811, Veterans Hall, 346 Broadway, New York, NY 10013, 212-349-3455

Gay and Lesbian Military Freedom Project/National Gay and Lesbian Task Force, 1734 14th St., Washington, DC 20009, 202-332-6483

Gay, Lesbian, and Bisexual Veterans Association of America, 1350 North 37th Place, Milwaukee, WI 53208, fax: 414-933-6233

PERFORMANCE

Gay and Lesbian Association of Choruses, P.O. Box 65084, Washington, DC 20035-5084, 202-467-5830

The Glines, 240 West 44th St., New York, NY 10036, 212-354-8899

Lambda Performing Arts Guild of America, P.O. Box 140131, Denver, CO 80214

Lesbian and Gay Bands of America, P.O. Box 57099, Washington, DC 20037-0099

Music Industry Network of Gays and Lesbians (MINGL), P.O. Box 20357, Columbus Circle Station, New York, NY 10023, 718-858-8647

OUTMUSIC: Gay/Lesbian Musicians, Composers, and Lyricists, P.O. Box 1575, New York, NY 10013, 212-330-9197

The Purple Circuit, Artists Confronting AIDS, 684 1/2 Echo Park Ave., Los Angeles, CA 90026

The Ridiculous Theatrical Company, 1 Sheridan Square, New York, NY 10014, 212-691-2271

Theater Rhinoceros, 2926 16th St., 16th floor, San Francisco, CA 94103, 415-552-4100—produces lesbian and gay theater

WOW (Women's One World) Cafe, 212-460-8067—lesbian theater company

POLITICS/GOVERNMENT

Egale, P.O. Box 2891, Station D, Ottawa, ON K1P 5W9, 613-230-4391

Gay and Lesbian Victory Fund, 1012 14th St. NW, #707, Washington, DC 20005, 202-842-8679—supports openly gay/lesbians political candidates

Human Rights Campaign Fund, 1012 14th St. NW, #607, Washington, DC 20005, 202-628-4160—lobbies Congress, undertakes political action and grassroots organizing

International Gay and Lesbian Human Rights Commission, 540 Castro St., San Francisco, CA 94114, 415-255-8680

International Network of Lesbian and Gay Officials, 3801 26th St. East, Minneapolis, MN 55406-1857

Log Cabin Federation, 212-886-1893—gay Republicans

National Gay and Lesbian Task Force, 1734 14th Street NW, Washington, DC 20009, 202-332-6483—lobbying, political action, grassroots activism

RELIGION

Affimation/Gay & Lesbian Mormons, P.O. Box 46022 Los Angeles, CA 90046, 213-255-7251

Affirmation: United Methodists for Lesbian, Gay, & Bisexual Concerns, P.O. Box 1021, Evanston, IL 60204, 708-475-0499

American Baptists Concerned, 872 Erie St., Oakland, CA 94610-2268, 510-530-6562

American Gay & Lesbian Atheists, P.O. Box 66711, Houston, TX 77266, 713-862-3283

Axios: Eastern & Orthodox Christians, 328 West 17th St. #4-F, New York, NY 10011, 212-989-6211; 718-805-1952, ask for Nick

Brethren/Mennonite Council for Lesbian & Gay Concerns, P.O. Box 65724, Washington, DC 20035-5724, 202-462-2595.

A Common Bond, P.O. Box 405, Ellwood City, PA 16117, 412-285-7334—ex-Jehovah's Witnesses

Dignity USA, 1500 Massachussetts Ave. NW #11, Washington, DC 20005, phone: 202-861-0017, fax: 202-429-9898—Catholic

Emergence International: Christian Scientists Supporting Lesbians, Gay Men & Bisexuals, P.O. Box 6061-423, Sherman Oaks, CA 91413, 800-280-6653

The Evangelical Network, P.O. Box 16104, Phoenix, AZ 85011-1610

Evangelicals Concerned, 311 E. 72nd St. #1-G, c/o Dr. Ralph Blair, New York, NY 10021, 212-517-3171

Friends for Lesbian & Gay Concerns, P.O. Box 222, Sumneytown, PA 18084, 215-234-8424 (ask for Bruce)

GLAD (Gay, Lesbian & Affirming Disciple) Alliance, P.O. Box 19223, Indianapolis, IN 46219-0223

Honesty: Southern Baptists Advocating Equal Rights for Gays & Lesbians, P.O. Box 2543, Louisville. KY 40201, 502-637-7609

Integrity, Inc, P.O. Box 19561, Washington, DC 20036-0561—Episcopal

Interweave (Unitarian Universalists for Lesbian, Gay & Bisexual Concerns), 25 Beacon St., Boston, MA 02108-2800, 617-742-2100

Lifeline Baptist, 1635 Forest Hill Ct., c/o Rev J. T. Williams, Crofton, MD 21114-1813

Lutherans Concerned/North America, P.O. Box 10461, Chicago, IL 60610-0461

Maitri Dorje: Gay & Lesbian Buddhists, 212-619-4099, ask for Bill or Peter

National Congress for Lesbian Christians, P.O. Box 814, Capitola CA 95010

National Council of Churches, Commission on Family Ministries & Human Sexuality Office, Rev. Joe H. Leonard, 243 Lenoir Ave, Wayne PA 19087-3908

National Ecumenical Coalition, Inc, 1953 Columbia Pike #24, Arlington, VA 22204-4569

National Gay Pentecostal Alliance, P.O. Box 1391, Schenectady, NY 12301-1391, 518-372-6001

New Ways Ministry (Catholic), 4012 29th St., Mount Rainier, MD 20712, 301-277-5674, fax: 301-864-6948

Phoenix Evangelical Bible Institute, 1035 E. Tyrney, Phoenix AZ 85014, 602-265-2831

Presbyterians for Lesbian/Gay Concerns, P.O. Box 38, c/o James Anderson, New Brunswick, NJ 08903-0038, 908-249-1016; 932-7501

Radical Faeries, P.O. Box 1251, New York, NY 10013, 212-625-4505

Reformed Church in America Gay Caucus, P.O. Box 8174, Philadelphia, PA 19101-8174

Seventh Day Adventist Kinship International, P.O. Box 3840, Los Angeles, CA 90078-3840

Silent Harvest Ministries, P. O. Box 190511, Dallas, TX 75219-0511, 214-520-6655

Supportive Congregations Network/ Mennonite & Brethren, P.O. Box 479241, Chicago, IL 60647-9241

Unitarian Universalist Association, Office of Lesbian, Bisexual & Gay Concerns, 25 Beacon St., Boston, MA 02108-2800, 617-742-2100

Unitarian Universalist Bisexual Network (UUBN), P.O. Box 10818, Portland, ME 04104

United Church of Christ Coalition for Lesbian/Gay Concerns: Ohio, 18 N. College St., Athens OH 45701, 614-593-7301

United Community Church of America, Office of the General Superintendant, P.O. Box 7654, Jackson, MS 39284-7654, 601-924-3333

United Lesbian/Gay Christian Scientists, P.O. Box 2171, Beverly Hills, CA 90212-2171, 310-850-8258

Unity Fellowship Church, 230 Classon Avenue (at Willoughby Ave.), Brooklyn, NY, 718-636-5646

Universal Fellowship of Metropolitan Community Churches, 5300 Santa Monica Blvd. #304, Los Angeles, CA 90029, 213-464-5100

Witches/Pagans for Gay Rights, P.O. Box 4538, Sunnyside, NY 11104-4538

World Congress of Gay and Lesbian Jewish Organizations, P.O. Box 3345, New York, NY 10008-3345

TRAVEL

Gay Hospitality Exchange International, P.O. Box 612, Station C, Montreal, QC H2L 4K5

Gayroute: Tour Gay Canada, Box 314-G, Station deLorimier, Montreal, QC H2H 2N7

International Gay Travel Association, P.O. Box 4974, Key West, FL 33041, 800-448-8550

Index

Page references to illustration are cited in italics.